LIVES IN EDUCATION

SKETCH OF A YOUNG GIRL SUPPOSEDLY SAPPHO, BASED ON FRESCO
AT POMPEII

LIVES IN EDUCATION

*People and Ideas
in the Development of Teaching*

L. GLENN SMITH
Iowa State University

JOAN K. SMITH
Loyola University of Chicago

F. MICHAEL PERKO
Loyola University of Chicago

ELIZABETH L. IHLE
James Madison University

DALTON B. CURTIS, JR.
Southeast Missouri State University

JACK K. CAMPBELL
Texas A & M University

MICHAEL V. BELOK
Arizona State University

GERALD L. GUTEK
Loyola University of Chicago

MARTHA TEVIS
Pan American University

WILLIAM BURT LAUDERDALE
Auburn University

CLAUDIA STRAUSS
College of Staten Island, CUNY

PAUL TRAVERS
University of Missouri — St. Louis

Educational Studies Press

Library of Congress Cataloging in Publication Data

Smith, L. Glenn, 1939-
  Lives in Education.

  Bibliographical references and index.
  1. Education—Philosophy—History. I. Smith, L. Glenn
(Leonard Glenn), 1939- .
LB17.L58   1984   370'.92'2   84-13796

Educational Studies Press wishes to acknowledge
the assistance of the Iowa State University
Research Foundation, Inc.

Illustrations by Jeffrey R. Smith
Cover design by Bob Zimmerman

Educational Studies Press
The Quadrangle
Iowa State University
Ames, Iowa 50011

ISBN: 0-934328-01-3

Parts of chapter 7 appeared in a slightly different
version in *Vitae Scholasticae* 2 (1983): 243-66.
© 1983 by the Research Institute for Studies in
Education, Iowa State University.

To all people who have tried — or who yet will try — to make teaching better

"Historical labels like last week's slogans serve their term and are replaced by others equally mortal; it is the living individual who captures the imagination. Queen Mary did not burn Protestantism at the stake, she burnt Hugh Latimer. If history becomes anonymous it becomes inevitable, and the individual is cast out with yesterday's refuse."

CHARLES F. MULLETT, *Biography as History*

CONTENTS

INTRODUCTION

Education is an old activity, but teaching is a new profession. Since humans have been on earth—between two and four million years according to recent estimates—people have been showing each other how to do things. On the other hand schools, a term derived from a Greek word implying leisured study by groups of people, are much more recent. From available evidence schools are probably no more than five thousand years old, dating back at most to about 3,000 B.C. in Sumeria and a little less than that in Egypt.[1] The idea that those who teach need special training for what they do has been accepted for only a few hundred years. The practice of instructing people about teaching dates from the seventeenth century when Roman Catholics and Protestants began competing for better methods of instruction and developed what would later be called "normal" training. In the nineteenth century, teacher training began to be common. Late in the twentieth century, many people still question its effectiveness. Teaching as a profession is in most respects less than two centuries old.

Because the process of teaching a society's young involves many questions that are political, social, and philosophical, educators must have more than technical skill. It is essential that teachers know how to operate a classroom, organize and present material, keep records and report progress, and determine how much learning is taking place in particular subjects. But there are much larger questions at issue. For example, should all people be required to have some schooling? If so, how much? Should some areas of knowledge/skill be taught to everyone? Should the wealthy or well-placed be entitled to more or better education than the poor? Should women and men be prepared for different roles? And there are many more.

To help place these and related issues into perspective, teachers need to know something about how we got the schools and educational practices we have. To put it another way, it is often easier to make choices about where you want to go if you know where you have already been.

There are several ways of approaching this task. One is to organize the information around topics such as "curriculum," "racism," "teachers," and so forth. Another is to look at the established disciplines (such as history, philosophy, anthropology, and sociology) to see what writers from these areas think about schools and education. Still another is to examine the ideas of great men in the educational past (that's not a Freudian slip—up to now it has been almost exclusively *men* whose ideas have been presented). Yet another is to trace educational theories and school practices from some time in the past to the present day.

We have combined elements of several of these traditions in organizing our presentation around the lives of some people whose ideas/activities illuminate the development of schools and teaching. Of course, this is an artificial device. Half a hundred individuals have not contributed all that is important or controversial in educational theory or practice. And we do not mean to suggest that biography is all that matters in educational history. We do believe that many of the issues and concepts with which teachers, children, and other citizens must grapple can best be understood in a developmental context. One way to make this material less abstract than usual is to show it in the lives, thoughts, and careers of particular people. In the chapters that follow, we examine a variety of educationally important individuals since the times of the ancient Greeks. Differing in so many ways, all of these people—the great and ordinary alike—have contributed to that transmission of culture which we call education.

WHY BIOGRAPHY?

At this point, we might well ask ourselves, "Why use a biographical approach to the study of educational history?" The answer has been provided, in part, by the noted historian Barbara Tuchman, who says biography is the prism through which history is best viewed.[2] Because biography allows us to see the universal exemplified in the story of a particular person, it serves as a microcasm for any particular era. Sappho and Aristotle, for example, help us to understand Greek culture and society during the times in which they lived. Christine de Pisan's life adds another dimension to Renaissance humanism. The experiences of Melanchthon and Loyola provide insight into the meaning of Reformation Europe. Emma Willard and Horace Mann serve as windows on the culture of mid-nineteenth century America.

Biography also caputres the imagination. We hope you will be fascinated, inspired, or captivated by at least one of the personalities whose biographical sketch you will read. People after all are interested in other people. We are more likely to be engaged by the story of someone like ourselves than by a chronicle of some diplomatic maneuver or intellectual event. Even the story of someone quite ordinary like Johannes Butzbach helps us to place ourselves at a particular place in time. Our interest, too, is caught not only by the sterling qualities of some of figures, but by their flaws as well. If Martin Luther was neurotic and Booker T. Washington a petty tyrant, neither of them is trivialized by these weaknesses. Rather they appear to us as lifelike, and in so doing help us to understand their experiences. The dictim of newspaper editors that people are intrinsically interesting applies to history as well.

What themes emerge from the biographies in this collection? Each of us would probably answer this in a slightly different fashion, but there are some elements which seem to appear throughout the individual accounts. These tell us a good deal about both the commonalities in schooling over the ages, and about the evolution of the educational process. The capsule biographies remind us again and again that education has a human face. The processes of teaching and learning, in the long run, depend on the personal impact of one human being on another. While the educational theories of individuals from da Feltre to Montessori have had their impact on education, even these have been useful only to the degree that a particular teacher takes them, assimilates them into her or his own style, and uses them in an educational setting.

A good illustration of the impact of an individual teacher is found in ancient Greece. Socrates inspired students by his use of penetrating questions to draw understanding from them. During the last years of his life, and especially during his trial, he so inspired one student that this young man, nicknamed Plato, himself became a major philosopher and educator. Plato in turn served as a model for his student, Aristotle, whose philosophical system has endured to our own time. Thus each gifted teacher produced another in a kind of chain reaction. Such contact between teacher and student is the critical event in the educational process: biography brings us face to face with the human experience—in history and in our contemporary world.

At the same time that we recognize the human dimension of education, these biographies also show how organized reflection on the educational process brings about growth and development. Since the earliest days of formal schooling, thoughtful individuals have analyzed education, though from different perspectives. Socrates, Locke, and Dewey, among others, have looked at education in a philosophical way. Aquinas, Luther, and Loyola viewed it from a religious perspective. Building on the primitive psychology of Aristotle and others, twentieth century scholars such as Watson and Montessori have expanded our knowledge of the cognitive process. Still other thinkers—for example, Christine de Pisan, Webster, Mann, Neill, Counts, and Naumburg—chose to concentrate on education as a social activity with broader purposes than cognitive development. There are probably an infinite number of ways in which such reflection can be organized. Each shows a particular facet of the experience of teaching and learning. Taken together they help those engaged in the educational enterprise to move forward and provide still better learning experiences for future generations of students.

An optimistic theme which emerges from this book is the gradual broadening of education, both in scope and level of sophistication. The process of schooling itself has become more complex as the developing social sciences have helped to create new curricula and schools. This is, however, only part of the story. For a long time education was a luxury available mostly to a small elite. There were many efforts to extend educational opportunities to more people, and schooling gradually has become more accessible. But accident of birth still affects the process.

Another aspect of this broadening scope of schooling has been the opening of education to previously excluded groups of people. The education of women, advanced by courageous individuals like Mary Wollstonecraft and Emma Willard, was continued in a later era by Ella Flagg Young and Margaret Haley in their crusade for the rights of women educators. Sarah Winnemucca and women like her helped to open American schooling to neglected native Americans while blacks were provided with hope and opportunities by individuals of the stamp of Fanny Jackson Coppin, Booker T. Washington, and W. E. B. DuBois. The story of schooling is one of struggle to extend learning to a wider range of people, providing more years of formal education to a greater percentage of each successive generation. The sagas of many of our subjects bear witness to these developments. They also illustrate that equality is not yet fully achieved.

Throughout this biographical collection, too, are examples of the ways in which education is linked to the popular culture of the times. From the Homeric Age to our own, formal schooling has been used not only for the development of intellectual and practical skills but also for the assimilation of individuals into the society. Whether the goal was to produce the civic virtue of *pietas* (a Roman concept), to aid in the process of religious conversion, or to celebrate the ideal of a republican America, schools have served as vehicles for social development and control. It is not surprising that they have been at the center of political controversy. We will see, for example, how John Hughes battled the New York Public School Society in his efforts to make public schools less Protestant. Because education is such an important means for the transmission of culture, the society at large has a great interest in exactly what values are taught. One result of all this is the growing awareness that educational history is not quite the neat and tidy process we have sometimes thought. Our biographical subjects remind us that schools exist within a social context and are subject to a variety of political forces. Human institutions that they are, schools are subject to all the messiness of any human activity. Biography helps us to see this less antiseptic but more accurate picture of education.

BACKGROUND AND CAUTION

Before describing the life of our first subject, that of Sappho of Lesbos, a few cautions are in order. First, because our vocabulary is so thoroughly in the

Greek tradition, there has long been a strong tendency to assume that the Greeks were just like us, especially that they thought as we do. This is a mistake. One of the concepts which we hope to illustrate is that "mind" or "thinking" are socially and culturally dependent. To put this differently, the ways in which we conceptualize have evolved over the past three thousand years. Space does not permit development of this argument. The point was advanced several years ago by historian James Harvey Robinson in *The Mind in the Making.* More recently (and from a strong technical base), psychologist Julian Jaynes has made a similar claim in *The Origin of Consciousness in the Breakdown of the Bicameral Mind.*[3]

Jaynes argues convincingly that our ancestors for several thousand years prior to about 1200-800 B.C. were "bicameral." That is, they literally heard voices, much as contemporary schizophrenics do. These voices directed their behavior. People were not "conscious" in our sense. The right half of the brain (for right-handed people) spoke to the left half and told people how to behave in new or uncertain situations. Jaynes' physiological and psychological explanation of how this worked are too involved to be detailed here.* Perhaps it is enough to say that we have become gradually more introspective and more aware of our thoughts and feelings.

One result of increasing consciousness has been the growth of uncertainty. In a bicameral state, behavior was directed by the voices. Disagreement with instructions from one's voice was not possible. But then neither was doubt present. As people no longer heard voices, they had to find other sources of authority for their actions. Some turned to prophecy or mysticism. Others put their main faith in the traditions of their group. Out of the search for suitable guides to life came a substantial interest in the thoughts and experiences of human beings—and in the consequences of various kinds of actions. You will see a variety of responses in the lives which follow of what Jaynes portrays as the dilemma of human awareness. The Greeks, whom we are about to describe, were just at the stage of emerging consciousness.

Another piece of background information to keep in mind is that there are two essentially different types of education coming out of all the early cultures. One of these was for the preparation of a warrior; the other was more "bookish" and resulted in the training of a civil servant or literary person. Both were elite oriented—that is, they aim at educating a minority of the population, usually male. The two kinds of education were not mutually exclusive. Greek schooling began in the Homeric period (somewhere around 1000-800 B.C.) as chivalric

---

*Jaynes defines consciousness not as being awake versus asleep or thinking as opposed to not thinking or learning versus not learning. Rather, he defines it in terms of six elements: (1) *spatialization*—the "mind space" or imaginary area where the other five elements take place and where we play back and project our life's experiences; (2) *excerption*—the way in which we selectively think of a few things to stand for the whole (for example clowns or cotton candy may be what we excerpt when we are asked to think of circus); (3) *analog "I"*—the ability to imagine ourselves in various situations; (4) *"metaphor me"*—the ability to sit back and objectively evaluate ourselves (in our mind spaces) in particular situations; (5) *narratization*—our practice of structuring selected events in our experiences into a "life story" or narrative; and (6) *conciliation*—the way we automatically incorporate unrelated elements together; for example, think of a mountain, then a valley, then a tower, then a lake; we add each element to our mental picture, but we don't all have the same picture.

training for warriors. It gradually became more oriented to written information. By about the fourth century B.C. it was primarily literary. The early nearly exclusive emphasis on sport and games (physical education) and on an aristocratic code of (military) conduct had steadily diminished—at least everywhere except in Sparta.

1

THE GREEKS

The earliest Greek educator about whom we have any information is also one of the controversial figures of Western history. Her name was Sappho. She was head of a women's finishing school. The island of Lesbos from which she came and on which she spent much of her life has inspired the word *lesbian*. Her poetry and some stories about her life have given the word its meaning of homosexual love between women. So, no sooner are we launched on this discussion than we have need of the caution that we must understand the Greeks in terms of how they themselves thought and not merely assume that they must have shared our own attitudes.

Sappho of Lesbos (c. 630-past 572 B.C.)

Actually, we know little with certainty about Sappho herself and, as a recent book about her puts it, "about that little there is doubt."[1] Even of her poetry we have only fragments. She wrote more than twelve thousand lines, but just a few hundred survived—and those by accident. These few make us wish for more. For example:

> Experience shows us
> Wealth unchaperoned
> by Virtue is never
> an innocuous neighbor[2]

In 1073 authorities in Rome and Constantinople publicly burned all the known poems of Sappho and of her male contemporary, Alcaeus. Most of the lines that we now have were accidentally discovered by archaeologists in 1898 at Oxyrhynchus, Egypt. Some papier-mâché coffins that they excavated had been made from scraps of old books. These contained fragments of Sappho's poems.[3] Sappho was born sometime in the last half of the seventh century B.C. in the town of Eresus on Lesbos, a prosperous Aeolian Island colony a few miles off the coast of present-day Turkey. She was almost certainly from an aristocratic family; her father may have been a wealthy wine merchant. Lesbos was famous for its wine. Alcaeus, another famous poet from Lesbos during Sappho's time, summed it up this way:

> Let us drink deeply;
> in summer to cool our thirst,
> in autumn to put a bright color upon death,
> in winter to warm our blood,
> in spring to celebrate nature's
> resurrection.[4]

When Sappho was still young, the family apparently moved to Mytilene, the chief city of the island. Not much else is known about her family except that she had three brothers, the eldest of whom married an Egyptian. Sappho strenuously opposed the marriage because she thought the woman did not care about her brother and was merely going to take all the money she could get from him. Sappho married once—very likely at about the age of twenty, as that was when aristocratic women were supposed to get married. The legend is that her husband was a wealthy merchant from the island of Andros. This may well be true because her father would have almost certainly arranged the match. She had at least one child, a daughter whom she named Cleis (probably after her own mother of the same name). She was widowed at some unknown point, perhaps in her thirties, and she spent several years in exile. A dictator named Pittacus, who represented the interests of merchant and poorer classes, banished several people including Sappho because of an unsuccessful revolt by the aristocracy. We have no way of knowing whether Sappho was actively involved or merely identified with the wrong crowd.

Before and after this period of exile, she spent most of her time in Mytilene. While there she taught several young women useful and decorative arts, including how to dance, sing, and play instruments. Whether this was a *thiasos* (girls' school) or a tutorial situation is not clear. One historian puts it this way:

> In Lesbos and probably at other places in Greece there were several such boarding schools, in which the young girls of well-to-do families lived together under the supervision of well-educated, experienced women. They spent their days performing cult rituals in the service of the love-goddess, Aphrodite. But they also received instruction in singing, dancing and poetry, learned the rules of social etiquette, good taste, knowledge and sensitivity in the arts of love, practiced an instrument, bound garlands of flowers and did handwork; but they were deliberately kept at a distance from political events of their time.[5]

In keeping with the standards and practices of her male counterparts, Sappho fell in love with some of her pupils. Her feelings about these attachments formed the basis for some of her poems and for scandalized attitudes about her which have persisted to the present, although they did not start until centuries after her own time. The following lines, weakened by translation, will give some idea of Sappho's style and of her feelings for Brachea, a former pupil who was taken away by marriage—an event which was expected of all respectable girls and arranged by parents.

> Ah, in my mind he shares the high gods' fortune,
> And is their equal, who may come beside you,
> And sit with you, and to your voice so lovely
>   Attend and listen!
>
> And he may hear your laughter, love-awaking,
> Which makes my heart beat swiftly in my bosom.
> But when I see you, Brachea, O my voice
>   Fails me and falters!
>
> And my tongue stumbles even when I glimpse you;
> Through all my flesh the fire goes swiftly running;
> My eyes see nothing, and my ears hear only
>   My own pulse beating!
>
> O then the sweat streams down me and I tremble,
> In all my body. Pale as the grass I grow!
> And death itself, my strength and powers fading,
>   Seems to approach me.
>
> So like a poor man I must be contented
> *To worship from afar your golden beauty,*
> *To hear you laugh and speak of all your loving*
>   *Only to others.*[6]

Nothing is known about when or how Sappho died. A legend which dates from several centuries after her time held that she committed suicide by jumping off a cliff. According to the story—which must have appealed to male vanity—she did this because she was rejected by a handsome young sailor who thought she was too old. There is no evidence for either of these traditions, and her poetry suggests she would not have approved of suicide:

> To die is evil,
> The Gods think so,
> Else they would die[7]

GREEK SEXUAL ATTITUDES

The unflattering story that Sappho was an ugly dwarf also circulated well after her lifetime, but there is no evidence to support it. According to the Greek ideal, people should be tall, fair skinned, and blond. We have no contemporary description of Sappho, though there is a suggestion that she was a small woman. No record exists of her ever having been accused of being unattractive during her own time. Indeed, her contemporary Alcaeus made advances to her. "Violet-crowned, pure, sweet-smiling Sappho, I want to say something to you, but shame prevents me." Her reply? "If your wishes were fair and noble, and your tongue designed not to utter what is base, shame would not cloud your eyes, but you would speak your just desires."[8]

Sappho's life is important in several ways. For one thing, as Verna Zinserling says, it is "the first time we hear the voice of a woman speaking about her sex. She stands upon a lonely peak in the ancient world, but by the fifth century successors had appeared in Boeotia."[9] For another, it illustrates an aspect of Greek life and education which must be understood in its own terms, not of ours. This is the matter of love and sexuality in the Greek context.

There has long been a tendency to regard Sappho's relationship with her pupils as some sort of startling aberration or inversion rather than as typical of the classical Greek approach to aristocratic education. The truth of the matter is that neither Sappho's behavior nor her poetry raised an eyebrow among her peers. Her attitudes were thoroughly typical of the aristocratic class in her society. "Greek culture differed from ours in its readiness to recognize the alternation of homosexual and heterosexual preferences in the same individual," says the author of a recent scholarly study of Greek sexual attitudes. The culture also differed from ours in "its implicit denial that such alternation or coexistence created peculiar problems for the individual or society." The Greeks gave a "sympathetic response to the open expression of homosexual desire in words and behavior," and showed a decided "taste for the uninhibited treatment of homosexual subjects in literature and the visual arts."[10] It was not the sex of one's love object but the strength of attraction which counted most.[11]

As we shall see in a moment, these attitudes toward friendship, love, and sexuality had a bearing on educational practice and attitudes. But before explaining this connection, a brief description of educational practice is in order.

In all of the Greek city-states of Sappho's time, aristocratic boys received a chivalric education starting at the age of six or seven and continuing to about puberty or a little beyond. They went to an open air school, called a *palaestra.* This name originally designated a place for gymnastic activities, but grammar and music teachers made arrangements with the owners of the palestra to add their instruction and this completed the school's structure. The curriculum was music, gymnastics, reading, writing, and poetry—especially Homer's *Iliad* and *Odyssey.* These were long epic poems written in praise of *areté* or honor resulting from a personally heroic deed. The aim of this kind of schooling was to produce a well rounded, courageous, warrior/citizen. While boys were young, their father's assigned a family slave, called a *paedagogos,* to accompany them to and from school and to protect them from harm, including unwelcome sexual attention from older men.

In the century after Sappho lived, some city-states became wealthy enough to build large gymnasiums. These became the social center of Greek society. In these surroundings the boy's advanced education—consisting of the fine points of military tactics, athletic skill, male social etiquette, and philosophy— came during his teens from older men.

Mature men watched the teenaged boys, formed attachments, and courted those whom they found most appealing—an attraction especially measured in terms of physical beauty. "It must be emphasized that the Greeks did not call a person 'beautiful' by virtue of that person's morals, intelligence, ability, or temperament," says K. T. Dover, "but solely by virtue of shape, color, texture, and movement."[12] The emphasis was on love, affection, deep friendship, and devotion—not on the physical/sexual part of the relationship (pederasty is the term most often used for this). The latter, however, was neither ignored nor discouraged.

What this means is that in aristocratic Greek society, teaching beyond the rudiments of the palaestra was ideally an extension of a romantic relationship. Any adult male might aspire to become the lover and mentor/teacher of a beautiful teenaged boy. But he would not do this for money, because to do so would prostitute a highly esteemed relationship. (Prostitution was legal and existed in several grades, but to be caught acting as a prostitute or pimp would call the good standing of a citizen into serious question.)

It should be emphasized that the attitudes and practices described so far grew out of a two class society in which citizens had most of the rights and slaves did most of the work. As cities grew, what we would now call a middle class emerged. The members of this group were people who owned little or no land, but who were not slaves. They found themselves at odds with the aristocrats over power and respectability. By the fourth century B.C. many people in this group disapproved of homosexuality, no doubt partly because it seemed too aristocratic.

THE GOLDEN AGE

When Sappho died in the sixth century, no Greek city was large. Some people were quite well off, but most wealth was still based in land. Sparta, with its powerful army, large slave base, and conservative society, was widely re- garded as the leading city-state. But within a few decades, several others grew rapidly. Notable among these were Syracuse, Corinth, and Athens. Improve- ments in naval skills brought an expanded trade and accompanying wealth.

The Athenians were particularly well placed to profit from these developments because they had an excellent harbor and had developed advanced designs for their ships and effective fighting tactics at sea. In 480 B.C. Athens defeated Persia in a decisive military encounter. The fact that the Athenian navy was prominent in this victory gave Athens a particular psychological and trade boost, launching that city on what later historians would call a "golden age."

There are several consequences for our story of this increasing wealth. One is that while the number of aristocrats stayed about the same as in the past, the number of slaves, artisans, and merchants greatly increased. As the group of people below the level of the aristocracy and above that of the slaves grew and made money in the expanding economy, they pressed to be included as citizens with full access to the schools, gymnasiums, political life, and legal machinery. Aristocrats were generally put off by this competitive push from people whom they considered inferior to themselves. But everywhere except in Sparta they reluctantly conceded much of what the rising group of "free men" wanted. This general atmosphere of upward mobility, to borrow a term from sociology, disturbed many aristocrats and led to threats, intrigues, charges, plots, trials, assassinations, occasional battles, and frequent exiles.

Another result of the increased wealth and aspirations was a demand for education. Teachers of grammar (reading and writing), music (including poetry), and gymnastics offered to provide the same kind of teaching for the sons and perhaps the daughters of the merchant and artisan class as the aristocracy had long enjoyed. And for those who wished to further pursue what we would perhaps call higher studies—geometry, astronomy, political science, rhetoric, philosophy—there grew up a class of professional teachers called *sophists.*

Many of the sophists, being on the cutting edge of thought in their society, were caught up in an emerging mood of partial skepticism about religious beliefs. The life of Homeric Greece had been rich in gods. Practically every occurence from birth to death was accounted for in terms of the pleasure of anger of one or more of these many deities. If a needed rain fell, farmers said that Zeus had taken pity on them because of the previous drought which had in turn been caused by the ill will of some other god. Every family had its own gods; each city enjoyed a special protector (Athena for Athens, for example); and every phenomenon of nature or special activity engaged the interest of some particular divine being. Each had his or her own temple, cult, legends, rituals, and these were totally bound up with every aspect of life. By the fifth century, however, some people were growing increasingly skeptical about some of the religious traditions. In Julian Jaynes' terms, they were becoming conscious, and this included an awareness that the traditional religious explanations did not fit well in many cases with their own experiences.

Protagoras (c. 490-c. 420 B.C.)

The increased demand for education provided a market for people skilled in teaching the most desired skills. The first person known to us to have publicly declared himself to be a professional teacher was born in the town of Abdera, an Ionian colony on the coast of Thrace. He was not from a wealthy family.

Indeed, his father was so unimportant that there is even confusion about his name. Whoever he was, his son had to begin adult life as a humble porter. A doubtful source has it that Protagoras was educated by Democritus—famous for atomic theory and materialism—after the latter happened to see a device that the young porter had invented for carring loads. Presumably he was so favorably impressed with Protagoras' intelligence and disposition that he offered to educate him. The same source holds that Protagoras served as secretary to Democritus for a time; he certainly might have repaid his master with this service while learning even more.

Having acquired an education through hard work and good fortune, Protagoras began a teaching career in the country towns around Abdera. He lived on whatever small fees his pupils' parents were willing or could afford to pay. He was kind to people, and they liked him. He became good at teaching, so his reputation began to spread.

PROTAGORAS' PHILOSOPHY

Protagoras is most famous for asserting that accurate knowledge of being or existence is not attainable by humans. Avoiding speculation about the cosmos, he concentrated on human beings, their knowledge and society. "Concerning the Gods, I am not able to know to a certainty whether they exist or whether they do not," he is reported to have said. "Man is the measure of all things—of those that are, that they are, and of those that are not, that they are not," is his most famous saying.[13] Philosophers and historians have debated whether Protagoras meant that each individual person's experiences and perceptions are the ultimate measure of reality or whether it is collective human experience that determines this. The disagreement continues over which, if either, of these two ways of viewing reality is better. Pragmatists prefer the collective interpretation and existentialists the individual one.

Whatever Protagoras' exact meaning, he thought human beings capable of learning enough about their world to solve their problems, and he believed that everyone could acquire excellence. All citizens *if properly taught* possess enough virtue and intelligence to participate in the governing process. "We benefit, I believe, from one another's fair dealing and good character, which is why everyone is eager to teach the next man and tell him what is right and lawful," he said. "Even the wickedest man who has been brought up in a society governed by laws is a just man . . . if you were to compare him with men without education, or courts, or laws, or any coercion at all to force them to be good."[14]

A PRACTICAL COURSE OF STUDY

When questioned about what curriculum he offered, Protagoras replied: "What I teach is the proper management of one's own affairs, how best to run one's own household, and the management of public affairs of the city both by word and action."[15]

These were useful skills indeed. The ability to think clearly, speak persuasively, manage one's personal life satisfactorily, and enter prudently into public discourse was certainly a solid basis for success. To do all this within a context of high moral integrity and good citizenship, as Protagoras said he could teach people to do, certainly would be of benefit. Beyond improving the civic life of the *polis* (city), these skills would be of extraordinary practical value to individuals. This was particularly true in a society where *all* legal questions were ultimately decided by mass juries—and where each individual was prosecutor or defender as the situation demanded. The ability to reason clearly and speak persuasively could have profound importance for a family's property or a person's life or liberty.

The practical value of what we would today identify as lawyers' skills were not lost on Protagoras or his contemporaries. His successful practice of analyzing the constituent elements of an effective speech—and then teaching these to people who wanted to learn to be good orators—set the primary focus of much Greek education. It would become the central preoccupation of higher schooling in the Roman Empire.

Protagoras was shrewd enough to see the value of his instruction and charge accordingly. Responding to the suggestion that his fees were exorbitant, he announced that any pupil who felt the tuition unreasonable could state (at a sacred shrine) what he thought fair and pay that amount. One writer has wryly noted that this may have been a risky suggestion from a person who doubted the gods, but there is no extant account of any student following this procedure.

Protagoras' critics admitted that he was a perfect gentleman in personal conduct. Some, however, disliked his claim that humans can never have exact knowledge. Others were fundamentally opposed to his democratic leanings. Most opponents feared his analytic skills, referring to him as a "slippery arguer in disputatious contests fully skilled."[16]

PROTAGORAS IN ATHENS

After traveling extensively and establishing a large reputation, Protagoras finally arrived in Athens, which was by then (433) becoming known as the most exciting city in the Greek world. He moved in the highest circles. Pericles, Athens' head of state, befriended him and many people sought to make his acquaintence. But after a public lecture, conservative elements in the city agitated to have him banished. They based their official objections on his comments about the gods, but their deepest fears were probably activated by his encouraging remarks about democratic government. Not content with banning him from the city, the Athenians also voted to burn all copies of Protagoras' books. "Calling them in by the public crier, and compelling all who possessed them to surrender them," they burned them in the town market.[17]

There is no record of what happened to Protagoras after he left Athens. One tradition has him living to ninety. Another asserts that he died in a shipwreck while on his way to Sicily. However he met his end, he left a philosophic legacy that would not be popular until the nineteenth century in America. As we shall have occasion to notice later in this volume, people like Francis Wayland Parker, John Dewey, Margaret Haley, and Ella Flagg Young agreed with his assumptions about democratic government, the educability of all people, the dignity of teaching as a vocation, the tentativeness of human knowledge, and the desirability of solving individual and social problems on the basis of experience rather than inherited absolutes.

Socrates (c. 470-399 B.C.)

One of Protagoras' most fundamental critics was a younger contemporary named Socrates who came from equally humble origins. Socrates is a much more widely recognized figure, however, due partly to the dramatic circumstances surrounding his death. The fact that more people agreed with the main tenets of Socrates' philosophy than with those of Protagoras, at least until about a century and a half ago, may be a contributing factor as well. Socrates' life has been so dramatically presented by his pupil and friend Plato that his name has become for many people a symbol of all that is best, most humane, and right in teaching and in personal integrity.

SOCRATES AS HERO

Given these facts, a brief caution is again in order—the same one that we raised in discussing Sappho. People must be understood in the context of their own times and not of our own. If Julian Jaynes is correct, this reminder is particularly in order for Greek history from about the third century B.C. and earlier. The persistent tendency to "read" immediate preoccupations back into the past—historians like to call this "presentism"—is nowhere more evident than in the way people have treated Socrates. The "Socratic method," which was invented by Protagoras or someone even earlier, has been widely heralded as a good model to follow in teaching. Moreover, his life has become for many, as noted above, the personification of virtue. The idea that its author had love affairs with boys is so unappealing to many that even twentieth century authors have felt compelled to explain away the evidence. A. E. Taylor, for example, in an otherwise excellent book, completely buckles when he encounters the homosexual episodes in Socrates' life. These are merely jokes, he concludes. They couldn't have really happened. The truth of the matter is rather simple. They did happen, just as with Sappho, but people at the time thought them normal.[18]

EARLY LIFE

Socrates was born in Athens around 470 or 469 B.C. His father was an artisan, a stone cutter/sculptor, and his mother a midwife. Later Socrates would joke that he himself was an intellectual midwife, helping to bring other people's ideas into the world. There is no mention of his having any brothers or sisters. Nothing is known about his childhood. He may have learned his father's trade, but it is not clear that he ever practiced it. Other facts demonstrate his desire to climb to a higher rung on the social ladder in the boisterous, growing Athens of his day. No doubt his family supported, and probably originated, this ambition. He studied with and may have become the lover of Archelaus, a teacher noted for his sophistic skills and interest in natural science. Also, he married the granddaughter of an aristocratic and famous Athenian general.

When Protagoras visited Athens, Socrates was in his middle thirties. He was already launched on a career as a teacher, but was certainly not yet as famous as the visitor from Abdera. Apparently the whole city was abuzz with the news of the great teacher's presence and Socrates wanted to meet him. To do so, he went with a wealthy young aristocrat—probably one of his own pupils—who wanted to study with Protagoras. This gave Socrates the opportunity to engage his competitor in a discussion/debate. Our only account of this meeting comes from Plato, who was born several years after the event but who probably got his information from Socrates. He portrays the outcome as a draw, but Socrates' description reveals something of the relative status of the two.

Socrates and his pupil called at the house where Protagoras was staying and found him walking in the colonnade. On either side of him were young men from prominent local families and a number of foreigners (that is, non-Athenians). "Protagoras collects them from every city he passes through, charming them with his voice like Orpheus, and they follow the sound of his voice quite spellbound," said Socrates. "I was absolutely delighted by this procession to see how careful they were that nobody ever got in Protagoras' way, but whenever he and his companions turned round, those followers of his turned smartly outwards in formation to left and right, wheeled round and so every time formed up in perfect order behind him."[19]

Socrates had already begun developing a local reputation as a teacher when he encountered Protagoras. In the next few years his fame increased. His marriage into the aristocracy probably helped. He was part of Pericles' social circle. He dressed well and had enough money to invest. Whether he made this money from tuition fees, got it through marriage, or came by it in some other way is not apparent. When he was older, Socrates was a severe critic of the sophists' practice of taking pay for teaching. It is not clear whether he felt that way when he was in his thirties.

The only account of Socrates written while he was still living is in Aristophanes' The Clouds. The play, first produced in 423, caricatures the Athenian philosopher as a naturalistically inclined sophist who will teach paying students how to make wrong arguments seem stronger than correct ones so they can avoid paying just debts. It is difficult to know how much of the attitude is exaggerated for comic effect, but it is probably based partly in fact. As a young man he had flirted with the naturalistic opinions of his teacher Archelaus, but somewhere along the way he discarded these in favor of more aristocratic beliefs. By the end of his life, and perhaps considerably earlier, his attitudes were extremely elitist.

None of this should be taken to suggest that Socrates was not honest, intelligent, or hardworking. He was surely not the first and certainly not the last person to have his views altered as his social, political, and psychological circumstances changed. It does further illustrate the fact that he was fully part of the atmosphere in which he lived. This participation included a record of valor in the Peloponnesian Wars. Because these conflicts had an important part in his eventual death, a brief explanation is in order.

ATHENS AT WAR

Beginning about 435 and lasting for more than thirty years were a series of armed encounters between various city-states. Sparta, Corinth, and other members of the "Spartan League" feared that Athens was growing too powerful. A series of battles took place, interspliced with months and years of noncombat. In the early phase, Pericles tried to win by having all Athenians come into the walled city while the navy raided Spartan positions. Living conditions in the embattled city were not sanitary. Plague broke out killing many people, including Pericles.

Socrates fought bravely in the early part of the war. Several years later (424), he was in battle along side his lover and pupil, a beautiful young man named Alcibiades. Socrates even gave up his claim to a prize for valor in favor of his friend.

Athens was unable to conclude the hostilities satisfactorily partly because of internal dissension over policy. One group of extreme democrats wanted to prosecute the war aggressively. They were attracted, among other things, to the possibility of making money by capturing slaves and territory. Another faction of extreme aristocrats grew increasingly disaffected with the war because they had little to gain from victory and because they had a greater sense of identity with their Spartan fellow aristocrats than with their democratic competitors at home. Between the two groups were moderates trying to reconcile the two camps. As the war dragged on, members of both groups became increasingly suspicious of one another.

Socrates' personal views are not recorded, but he was linked with the extreme aristocrats in several ways. One was the fact that Alcibiades went over to the Spartan side after bungling a campaign as general for the Athenians. The aristocrats did not particularly mind, but the democrats were outraged—in fact they had Alcibades assassinated—and Socrates' love affair with him had been common knowledge. In 406 ten aristocratic generals were indicted for allowing many sailors to drown in a storm with no rescue attempt. Socrates found a legal dodge to block the intended mass trial.

More devastating was an episode in 405. The Spartans caught the Athenian navy off guard and demolished it. Without supplies from the sea, the city was soon forced to surrender to the Spartan army which had it under siege. The Spartans killed fifteen hundred democrats and created a new government under the control of thirty of the most extreme aristocrats. Seizing a chance to rid themselves of political opponents, and make a tidy profit by confiscating their property in the process, the so-called Thirty Tyrants instituted a savage reign of terror. Within four months they executed so many hardline democrats, moderate democrats, and even moderate aristocrats that almost everyone in the city except the members of their own small but powerful faction was up in arms against them. The leader of the notorious Thirty was Critias, an aristocrat who began his young adulthood as a democrat, but who had changed his views under a brief tutelage of Socrates. In fact, Socrates had a number of close friends among the Thirty, though he refused to obey some directives from them.

SOCRATES' VIEWS

Socrates had taught a generation of young Athenians the ideals, metaphysics (views of ultimate reality), and values which were entirely friendly to aristocracy and "profoundly anti-democratic, striking at the very theoretical roots on which the democratic way of life (even in a slave-owning democracy) was founded."[20] The basic tenet of Socrates' teaching was that knowledge comes not through the senses as Protagoras had claimed but through logic and contemplation. He agreed with the Pythagoreans who taught that: (1) ideas and not physical things were the basis of ultimate reality; (2) that mathematics was the avenue to truth; and (3) that the virtuous few should rule the many who were incapable of knowing much about mathematics or virtue. The Pythagorean theorem was their symbol of justice. In a right angled triangle, $a^2 + b^2 = c^2$ without regard to the length of a or b. Therefore it followed that talent, virtue, insight, and power could be distributed in vastly different proportions to different parts of society—as they obviously were—but the society would still be "just" or in geometric balance. It was a theory that fit nicely with aristocracy.

Socrates embodied some of his teaching in stories or allegories. One of the most famous of these is related by Plato with Socrates speaking (in the first person) to Plato's brother Glaucon:

> And now, I said, let me show in a figure how far our nature is enlightened or unenlightened:—Behold! human beings living in an underground den, which has a mouth open toward the light and reaching all along the den; here they have been from their childhood, and have their legs and necks chained so that they cannot move, and can only see before them, being prevented by the chains from turning round their heads. Above and behind them a fire is blazing at a distance, and between the fire and the prisoners there is a raised way; and you will see, if you look, a low wall built along the way, like a screen which marionette players have in front of them, over which they show the puppets.
>
> I see.
>
> And do you see, I said, men passing along the wall carrying all sorts of vessels, and statues and figures of animals made of wood and stone and various materials, which appear over the wall? Some of them are talking, others silent.
>
> You have shown me a strange image, and they are like strange prisoners.
>
> Like ourselves, I replied; and they see only their own shadows, or the shadows of one another, which the fire throws on the opposite wall of the cave?
>
> True he said; how could they see anything but the shadows if they were never allowed to move their heads?
>
> And of the objects which are being carried in like manner they would only see the shadows?
>
> Yes, he said.
>
> And if they were able to converse with one another, would they not suppose that they were naming what was actually before them?
>
> Very true.

And suppose further that the prison had an echo which came from the other side, would they not be sure to fancy when one of the passers-by spoke that the voice which they heard came from the passing shadow?

No question, he replied.

To them, I said, the truth would be literally nothing but the shadows of the images.

That is certain.

And now look again, and see what will naturally follow if the prisoners are released and disabused of their error. At first, when any of them is liberated and compelled suddenly to stand up and turn his neck round and walk and look towards the light, he will suffer sharp pains; the glare will distress him, and he will be unable to see the realities of which in his former state he had seen the shadows; and then conceive some one saying to him, that what he saw before was an illusion, but that now, when he is approaching nearer to being and his eye is turned towards more real existence, he has a clearer vision—what will be his reply? And you may further imagine that his instructor is pointing to the objects as they pass and requiring him to name them—will he not be perplexed? Will he not fancy that the shadows which he formerly saw are truer than the objects which are now shown to him?

Far truer.

And if he is compelled to look straight at the light, will he not have a pain in his eyes which will make him turn away to take refuge in the objects of vision which he can see, and which he will conceive to be in reality clearer than the things which are now being shown to him?

True, he said.

And suppose one more, that he is reluctantly dragged up a steep and rugged ascent, and held fast until he is forced into the presence of the sun himself, is he not likely to be pained and irritated? When he approaches the light his eyes will be dazzled, and he will not be able to see anything at all of what are now called realities.

Not all in a moment, he said.

He will require to grow accustomed to the sight of the upper world. And first he will see the shadows best, next the reflections of men and other objects in the water, and then the objects themselves; then he will gaze upon the light of the moon and the stars and the spangled heaven; and he will see the sky and the stars by night better than the sun or the light of the sun by day?

Certainly.

Last of all he will be able to see the sun, and not mere reflections of him in the water, but he will see him own proper place, and not in another; and he will contemplate him as he is. . . . And when he remembered his old habitation, and the wisdom of the den and his fellow-prisoners, do you suppose that he would felicitate himself on the change, and pity them?

Certainly, he would.

. . .Imagine once more, I said, such an one coming suddenly out of the sun to be replaced in his old situation; would he not be certain to have his eyes full of darkness?

To be sure, he said.

And if there were a contest, and he had to compete in measuring the shadows with the prisoners who had never moved out of the den, while his sight was still weak, and before his eyes had become steady (and the time which would be needed to acquire this new habit of sight might be very considerable), would he not be ridiculous? Men would say of him that up he went and down he came without his eyes; . . . and if any one tried to loose another and lead him up to the light, let them only catch the offender, and they would put him to death.[21]

SOCRATES' DEATH

With the Spartans preoccupied by their own internal politics (slave revolts were a constant worry for them), the exiled democrats staged a successful though somewhat shaky comeback in Athens. The leader of the returned democrats was Anytus, a moderate whose property had been confiscated when he went into exile and whose son had stayed behind to study with Socrates. The son became a drunk. Anytus did not try to recover his property and he did not attempt to punish the remaining members of the aristocracy. But he blamed Socrates for his son's alcoholism, and he was determined to have him indicted.

Anytus and two others brought a charge of impiety against Socrates. It alleged that he did not believe in the normal gods, but rather in "demoniacal beings," and that he had corrupted youth with these beliefs. (A charge of impiety was the same kind of catch-all for Athenians as income tax evasion or misuse of the mail to contemporary Americans.) Aristophanes' dramatic picture of him as a cynical word merchant was still widely known. In his later years, Socrates dressed carelessly, perhaps because he had lost his invested money, and said that he was surprised at how many things there were that he did not want. But he did enjoy all-night dinner parties, at which he had the reputation for being able to drink everyone else under the table. Combine this with the general knowledge that Socrates was stringently anti-democratic, and one cannot be surprised that many on the jury must have been unsure just what to make of the old man whom his peers had wanted to decorate for bravery twenty years earlier. Socrates denied the charges, but a narrow majority of the five hundred man jury found him guilty. He was given the opportunity of suggesting a suitable penalty. His friends begged him to name a reasonably stiff fine which they would have paid for him. Instead, he specified a token amount. When a ripple of disapproval ran through the jury, Socrates clinched the matter by stating that even the smallest sum was too much. Actually, he said, the city should give him a life pension. That did it. The Greeks despised *hubris* (unwarranted pride). The jury voted the death penalty.

Even this could have been easily avoided. Friends arranged Socrates' escape by bribes and begged him to go away with them to some pleasant spot. Many people on the jury would have been satisfied to see the matter end with exile. Socrates, however, refused to go and spent his last days calmly discoursing with friends. One of his wives brought his youngest child and was crying over the injustice of the sentence. He dismissed them with the comment, "Would you rather I were dying justly?" But the young blond lad Phaedo got lots of hugs and affection. "Tomorrow, Phaedo, I suppose that these fair locks of yours will be severed [cut in mourning]," he said while fondling his friend's head and hair.[22]

Plato (428-347 B.C.)

On the appointed day, Socrates calmly drank hemlock and died. One of his aristocratic young students, profoundly affected by Socrates' final years and dramatic death, immortalized him in a series of accounts that have become classics of Western literature—"the man we hold best, wisest, most upright of his age."[23] The young man's name was Plato.

PLATO'S FAMILY BACKGROUND

Both sides of Plato's family were among the oldest, most aristocratic families of Athens. His mother's cousin was Critias, leader of the Thirty Tyrants, and another of the Thirty was her uncle. This was Charmides, a general who was killed in 403 in a battle between aristocrats and democrats. Plato's father traced his ancestry back to Poseidon, god of the sea. Conservative politics was almost in the family's genes. When Plato was born in 428, his family named him Aristocles—best, most renowned.[24] He later acquired the nickname Plato because of his robust, broad shouldered build.

Plato had two brothers, Glaucon and Adimantus, and one sister, Petone. His sister's son, Speusippus, was later affiliated with Plato in his educational work. Plato's father seems to have died when Plato was still young. His mother married her uncle, a man named Pyrilampes, who was implicated in a political murder when he was younger. He was acquitted of the charge and seems to have spent the time after marrying his niece in the politically inoffensive pastime of breeding peacocks. There is no information about how he treated Plato or how they got along or, for that matter, what Plato thought about his mother, father, or childhood.

About all that is definitely known about Plato's youth is that he received the kind of education in grammar, music, gymnastics, and poetry that were appropriate for a lad in his circumstances. He certainly mastered grammar, as evidenced by his later power as a writer, and he probably also did well in the other parts of his schooling. Much later a story circulated that he had wrestled in the Isthmian games, but there is no proof either way. His physical appearance must have been quite adequate, yet there is no indication that people gave him much attention for his looks. On the other hand, his stepbrother—Pyrilampes' son—was so goodlooking that practically every fashionable Athenian male fell in love with him. However, he was regarded as being too stupid to be fit for anything but horsemanship.

EFFECTS OF SOCRATES' DEATH

Plato thought he was headed for a career in Athenian politics. His whole family must have been preoccupied with the brawling conflicts through which he was growing up. As it turned out, his voice was thin and unimpressive, and he just didn't seem terribly motivated to a military career. What he found really engaging was Socrates and his dialetical (arguing various sides of issues) teaching. The energetic program of political terror pursued by cousin Critias repelled Plato (and Socrates possibly), but there is no evidence that he ever disavowed the theory behind it.

When Socrates came to trial, Plato was present. An account written much after the time claims that Plato, apologizing for his youth, stood to speak for Socrates and was shouted down. It certainly could have happened. On the day that Socrates drank the hemlock, Plato was too ill to be present.

After Socrates' death several of his close associates, including Plato, thought going abroad a safer course of action than staying in Athens. A group of them traveled to Megara, where they stayed with some Pythagoreans. Plato went on eventually to Cyrene, where he visited a noted mathematician named Theodorus. From there he traveled to southern Italy and Sicily and finally to Egypt. He especially admired the Egyptian priests and their profound sense of ancient culture.

While Plato was in Sicily, he went to Syracuse where he met Dion, son-in-law of the city's ruler, Dionysius I. Plato and Dion became lovers and lifelong friends. Plato wrote a poem to him. In fact, many of Plato's poetic efforts show a strong preoccupation with the theme of love between man and boy. Dionysius I was the strong-handed leader of democratic factions in Syracuse, and he understood well and disapproved thoroughly of the implications of Plato's Socratic/ Pythagorean messages to Dion. He had Plato arrested and sold into slavery. Friends ransomed the young aristocrat and he returned to Athens.

PLATO'S ACADEMY

Back in his home town after more than a decade of travel, Plato bought land and a building near a public gymnasium and grove of trees—we would probably call it a public park—not far out of town. The park was named for an early hero, Academus, who had been turned into a minor god. Plato's building fronted on the grove of trees, so that he and his associates could also use the public buildings of the gymnasium if they wished. The Academy was the oldest of three state-sponsored gymnasia in Athens. The other two were the Lyceum, which was established by Pericles and supposed to be patronized by the wealthiest citizenry, and the Cynosarges which was patronized by foreigners.[25]

Just how Plato's "academy" functioned is not completely clear. Later commentators have referred to it as a school and as the first university. The concepts are related, but they are misleading. The establishment combined the functions of a social club with strong religious underpinnings, a political interest group, and a modern unaffiliated research institute or "think tank." There were no fees, but people needed to be wealthy enough to support themselves in good style or they would be out of place. Young men of about sixteen could join the

Academy's fraternity, but it is not at all certain that there was a series of sequenced or formal courses.

Plato's group observed religious rituals, held frequent *symposia* (dinner parties at which the participants entertained each other with poems, songs, stories, and conversation—all aided by adequate portions of wine), and some members gave public lectures. Plato, himself, seems to have rarely given either public or private lectures. One reason for this was probably that he was not good at it. Another may have been a reluctance to expose his ideas to the kind of public scrutiny that he thought had played a part in Socrates' conviction by a democratic jury. Plato described himself as "first among equals" in the establishment. There were no examinations, no graduation or certification, but the members shared their work with each other.

Outside of Athens, Plato entered indirectly into political activity. At the request of his close friend, Dion, he made two more trips to Syracuse. When Dionysius I died, Dion had Plato tutor young Dionysius II into correct thinking and away from democratic ideas. Dion's opponents were not pleased, however, and convinced the youth to throw the pair out. Dion lived lavishly in exile on an estate near the Academy. An attempt late in Plato's life to reconcile Dion and Dionysius met with no success. Plato barely escaped with his hide after some Pythagorean friends interceded on his behalf. Several members of the Academic fraternity wrote constitutions and laws for various areas, but Plato and his group avoided mingling in Athenian political life. In Plato's view, discretion probably was the better part of valor in view of what had happened to Socrates.

For the most part, Plato appears to have lived in quiet comfort with his friends. He had money—probably from his family, in any case he left two farms and a fair amount of gold and silver to his brother Ademantus when he died—and he indulged poetically and otherwise in the physical pleasures. He is said to have had several male lovers and at least one mistress, but he never married. It is interesting to contrast the communistic ideal that Plato set forth in *The Republic* for his aristocratic class (they could own no property) with the reality of his own inherited wealth. Also, some of what Plato wrote sounds like he was opposed to slavery, but he had five slaves of his own. Four of these he willed to Ademantus; the fifth, Diana, he set free in his will.

IDEALISM

Throughout his life Plato remained committed to the main tenets of Pythagoreanism. He is usually credited with developing a "theory of ideas," but much of the theory was already explicit or implicit in the doctrines of Pythagoras and his followers. Stated briefly it runs something like this: For every sensible "thing" or item which we can perceive, there exists an underlying "idea" or universal organizing principle. For example, it is not enough to recognize beautiful statues, buildings, people, etc. It is beauty itself which is the organizing universal. Moreover, there is a dichotomy (split) between the world of sensation and the ideal (idea-l) world. The ultimate task of learning is to discover the organizing principles or ideas. One does this by thinking, and partly by remembering the lessons learned in earlier lives by one's transmigrating soul. As with the Pythagoreans, mathematics is the key for unlocking the secrets of the ideal world and Plato also believed in a mystical numerology.

The arresting feature of Plato's theory is that what is ultimately "real" is permanent, changeless. The senses give us information that is a shadow or distorted reflection of what is real and true. We can get opinion through the sensible world, but never accurate information. Truth can be ascertained only by the mind (or soul) through contemplation. But only a few are capable of knowing this truth. Here Plato's disillusionment with democracy shows strongly.

In *The Republic,* Plato has Socrates propose a utopian educational system which strongly resembled Spartan practice. All children were to belong to the state. They would be products of group marriages and would be examined at birth for defects. Those who survived this inspection were to be reared in public nurseries. All would receive a traditional gymnastic, grammar, music, and patriotic training to age eighteen. After military training and ten years of service on active duty, a small number of the "best" would be allowed at age thirty to spend five years of further contemplation and study getting to know rationality and the good. Then a few of the best of these would spend fifteen years apprenticed to good rulers who knew how to balance wisdom and power. At fifty these few best people could become philosopher-kings. All this fit well with Plato's view that the irrational and chaotic impulses within the individual must be given order by the soul, and the chaotic and irrational individuals in society must be given order by the dictates of the philosopher-king.

EDUCATION OF WOMEN

Plato argued in *The Republic,* and again at the end of his life in *The Laws,* that women should receive exactly the same education as men, including military training. This may have had no more relationship to Plato's real life than his theories of slavery and property, but the tradition is that among Academic circles were two women—Lastheneia of Mantinea and Axiothea of Philus—"who used even to wear men's clothes," says one ancient source.[26]

Whether this marks Plato as an original feminist well ahead of his time or as simply part of his fantasized desire for old Spartan ways (at one time, Spartan women could exercise naked—gymnos—in public just as men could), it did not have very much practical impact on the lives of ordinary women in his time. Whatever Plato's views, they were probably less negative toward women than those of most of his male contemporaries who agreed that women were inferior to men in all important respects. Women were rarely spoken of as if they had much intelligence, so Plato's practice looks enlightened on this score. He did explain that one main reason for educating women was that if they were not educated, they did so much more harm than did men. This argument, in various forms, would pass as an *enlightened* justification for women's education for more than two thousand years after Plato's time.

PLATO'S CONSERVATISM

There has been a strong tendency, and one that has rarely been resisted, for educational philosophers to see Plato as a unique genius, delivering a system of objective thought, rather than as a person who typifies a great deal of the best and the worst of his own time and place. To read Plato for his literary and historical value is instructive. To implement his ideas for either education or politics in the twentieth century would place one on the far right politically.

We have already illustrated Plato's espousal of the political view of his family and class. He ignored experimental science in favor of religious and political interests. The theories he propounded he mostly borrowed from other people, but he was certainly original in the way he wrote them up. He shared the views of many other members of his social class on politics, economics, social theory, education, sexuality, and infanticide. (Infanticide was the practice, delegated to fathers, of examining infants for "defects" and if any were found of "exposing" the children until they died. It was a widespread practice and constituted one approach to family planning.)

Plato put most of his ideas into written dialogues, and these were preserved by his followers. They are so engagingly written that people still enjoy reading them whether they agree with the profoundly aristocratic implications or not. If Alfred Nobel had lived in fourth century Greece, he would have given Plato a prize for literature, but not for political theory.

In his old age, Plato restated some of his earlier ideas, added a few more, and cast them all in a spirit of intolerance and rigidity. He wanted a totalitarian state with censorship of everything. A state religion with taboos against all forms of sexuality except between people married to each other and then only for the purpose of producing children. People who refused to accept the religion would be killed. A psychoanalyst looking at the Academy's founder would certainly wonder where all this hostility came from. In addition, he thought the body was evil and the soul pure. He was evidently afraid of his anger. For example, a historian writing five centuries later said that on two occasions Plato was in such a "passion" that he wanted to beat a slave but feared to do it himself, apparently because he might kill or damage the property.[27]

Plato lived to be about eighty-one and tradition has it that he died contentedly at a wedding reception. The story has the earmarks of invented legend. However he died, members of the Academy attended the funeral. He was buried at the Academy and friends put up several inscriptions commemorating him. One is supposed to have read:

> Here, first of all men for pure justice famed,
> And moral virtue, Aristocles lies;
> And if there e'er has lived one truly wise,
> This man was wiser still; too great for envy.[28]

At least this indicates how his associates thought he wanted to be remembered.

One of his younger colleagues built an altar to him. This was Aristotle, certainly one of the most dedicated members of the Academic group, who would continue some of the ideas and traditions learned in Plato's circle and develop others of which the dedicated Platonists would not approve. The Academy itself lasted almost nine hundred years. Both it and Plato's writings would be important parts of the Western intellectual and educational traditions.

Aristotle (384-322 B.C.)

One of Plato's brightest pupils/colleagues was Aristotle. He came to the Academy in his seventeenth year from a northern Greek city-state, Stagira. He remained in this Academic brotherhood for the next twenty years, first as pupil and then as teacher.[29] Evidence from the past does not allow us a complete picture of their relationship, but we do know that Plato and Aristotle shared a mutual friendship and respect for each other. Plato referred to Aristotle as the *Nous* (mind) or "intellect of the school," while Aristotle paid tribute to his master years later when he said that Plato "clearly revealed, by his own life and by the methods of his words [that] to be happy is to be good."[30]

Even though Aristotle was to become much more scientific and empirical than Plato, he remained reluctant to criticize the theory of ideas because of his affection for the Academy's founders. Only truth was more valuable to Aristotle than his love for his Academic colleagues.[31]

ARISTOTLE'S BACKGROUND

By looking at Aristotle's early background—he was the son of Nichomachus, a physician—we can see why he eventually incorporated empirical observations into his Platonic views of universal truth. In fact, some historians think that if he had not remained with Plato all those years, he would have developed a better scientific mind.

Aristotle probably learned his scientific inclinations at his father's knee. The latter was a court physician to a Macedonian king, and it was the custom for such medical men to train their sons into their profession at early ages. Their training included dissection and surgical observations.[32]

Orphaned as a teenager, the young Aristotle was left a substantial inheritance, including his mother's property in yet another northern city, Chalcis. Shortly after the death of his parents, he traveled from Stagira to Athens, leaving behind a brother, Arimriestus, and sister, Arisneste. Why he went to Athens to study under the sixty-one year-old Academy head is not clear. Probably it was a natural step for one interested in learning, because Plato and Athens were famous for philosophy.

A FOREIGNER IN ATHENS

For the next forty-five years (from age seventeen to sixty-two) he pursued what he later called ultimate happiness in the form of a contemplative life, even though such a lifestyle brought him a good deal of hardship and often loneliness. While studying in Athens, his biggest problems stemmed from the fact that he was not an Athenian citizen. Instead, he was a metic—a resident alien—with connections to a region (Macedonia) that aroused great hostility in certain political circles. These strong negative feelings were the result of a collapsing Greek confederacy and a rising Macedonian dictatorship.

His first encounter with this hostile sentiment probably came during the year 347 when, shortly before Plato's death, one of the Greek cities was destroyed. Along with Xenocrates, another Academic, Aristotle probably traveled to the court of Greek born Hermias. He was Aristotle's former pupil and lover at the Academy, and had risen from slavery to the status of dictator in upper Asia Minor.

Here, Aristotle spent about three years studying with a small Platonic group. During his stay, he began categorizing some of his biological observations. It was also here that he married Hermias' niece and adopted daughter, Phythias. But shortly thereafter political turmoil forced the group's departure. Hermias was eventually assassinated by the Persians. This loss no doubt left its mark on Aristotle, who wrote a poem eulogizing Hermias.[33]

They next retreated to Sappho's city of Mytilene on the island of Lesbos, where his good friend and fellow Academic, Theophrastus, lived. Along with his host, Aristotle spent the next years studying marine life and natural history. It was during this period that he became the father of a daughter, Pythias. Then the account gets fuzzy. We know that Aristotle's wife died and that he also had a son, Nicomachus. Some sources say that after the death of his wife, he took up with her freed slave, Herpyllis, who was his son's mother. Other sources doubt that Nichomachus was illegitimate, because Aristotle's will did not treat him as such.[34]

LIFE AS A TEACHER

Whatever is the case, we next encounter Aristotle (c. 342) back in Mieza at the Macedonian court where his father had been physician. Aristotle was called there by Philip of Macedon to tutor Alexander, his flamboyant thirteen-year-old son who was destined to become Alexander the Great. Having studied politics and government under Platonic tutelage, Aristotle was eager to take on the education and training of this future ruler. Tradition has it that the philosopher prepared a special edition of Homer for the future king and taught him politics and rhetoric.

Aristotle was able to induce his pupil to rebuild Stagira which had been destroyed in battle. As regent director, while his father was away in battle, Alexander not only had the authority to launch such a building program, but he also commanded Aristotle to draw up a constitution and set of laws for the master's old home town. This caused citizens of Stagira to eulogize Aristotle after his death as "The Lawgiver."

In 334, when Alexander acceded to power, Aristotle returned to a more accepting Athens. Athenian aristocracy was pro-Macedonian, but the populist factions continued to resent the long-arm dictatorial rule of Alexander. The resentment remained mostly buried for the next ten years, although Aristotle felt the sting of many negative remarks. These ranged anywhere from attacks on his physical appearance (they exaggerated his thin legs, balding head, and vocal lisp) to his lavish overindulgence in the sensual pleasures of life. He seems to have managed to ignore these slanders and to enmesh himself in the pursuit of a scientific based wisdom.

THE LYCEUM

Aristotle began teaching with Theophrastus in one of the prominent Athenian gymnasia—the Lyceum around 334. Located just outside the city wall, the Lyceum was known for its beautiful orchard groves and covered walkways or peripatos. It was in the peripatos that the metic began his school of thought. Like the Academy, the school operated as a close, intimate brotherhood devoted to the pursuit of truth. Also, its leader did not charge fees, although gifts were accepted—especially from Alexander. But unlike the Academy, the school had no building, because as a foreigner Aristotle could own no property. He was then forced to conduct his school in the public peripatos of the gym—a situation which led to his school being called the Peripatetic School.

Another difference between the Academy and the Lyceum lay in teaching styles. Plato distrusted the written word and lecturing. This feeling was probably reinforced for Plato when, on the occasion of his only public lecture, everyone but Aristotle got up and left. Aristotle later explained that when Plato's title "On the Good" was announced, people assumed that they would hear a practical pleasure-oriented lecture and not an analysis of the transcendental soul. Aristotle, on the other hand, valued both lectures and the written word. In regard to the former, he thought that masters had to be sure to let their audiences know what to expect before embarking on the diatribe (discourse). As for written work, the Lyceum became known for its voluminous library.

Aristotle lectured to his fellow scholars in the morning and they copied the lectures. He used charts, tables, and diagrams when helpful. In the afternoon he would deliver a more popular lecture to the public at large. Dialectics (the dialogue favored by Protagoras, Socrates, and Plato) was not a method that he approved. Aristotle encouraged his band of scholars to pursue all forms of knowledge which interested them. Hence, their work included such activities as collecting the records of Athenian dramatic performances, compiling a list of Olympic Game victors, recording various state constitutions, and categorizing zoological and botanical data. In the Lyceum, biology—not mathematics—had the place of honor.[35]

ARISTOTLE'S VIEWS

While some of Aristotle's scientific observations led to useful conclusions, others did not. He concluded, for example that women had fewer teeth than men. Today, we would say that his sample was not representative of the population, but the findings reinforced his belief that the female was an undeveloped male with no potential for full development. More generally, Aristotle thought that the female sex was an inferior form of humankind—maimed males— but a "necessary anomaly." He accepted their inferior status in society, as he accepted slavery, as a part of natural law.

If all women were emotionally and physiologically inferior, certain men were intellectually and morally inferior. Thus, slavery was the most appropriate and productive state for such men. He also suspected that the heart was the seat of the senses (and the mind or soul) and was convinced that it was the center of all emotion. He thought the brain's function was to cool the blood.[36]

With respect to the moral and social natures of humans, Aristotle may have been more accurate. He thought people were social animals, living best in a small city-state (polis). The supreme good, he concluded, was happiness, but he knew that people disagreed over what constituted happiness. For the illogical masses who had less rational control over their emotions, happiness was centered in sensual pleasures and material wealth. While Aristotle assumed that a certain level of wealth and self sufficiency was necessary to happiness, it was not the ultimate good. For more superior people honor was happiness; but, said he, neither honor nor a political life of power could lead to true happiness. Such prizes were not in the control of their recipients. They could be taken away by their bestowers, leaving an unhappy individual. Hence, a life which enhanced people's uniqueness (their rationality) was for Aristotle the ultimate good. Most people, however were not morally and intellectually *trained* for such a virtuous life. So he concluded that few would or could pursue it. (Here, Aristotle was acknowledging the importance of environmental factors.)

Ideally, education (*paideia*) should cultivate those right habits which would in turn, develop moral and rational virtues—for example, train the child to exercise his rational will over his baser and lustier appetites. This ethical and intellectual training or character development of correct habits Aristotle thought could best be achieved by daily practice (for moral virtue) and a liberal education (for intellectual virtue).

For the peripatetic philosopher, a liberal education was one which enhanced and developed the intellectual side of man—his essence. No specific list of subjects would guarantee a liberal education, but it would typically come through such studies as logic, rhetoric, math, music, and the sciences. Aristotle did not believe that practical training for some particular function was liberating. This was the purpose for which men trained slaves and animals. Vocational subjects were not liberating, because they treated man as a means to some other end product. Consequently, learning which was geared to some other goal, such as producing wealth or gaining fame, was servile or illiberating.

Politically speaking, then, by taking a person's nature and the effect of environment into account, all varieties of people—from the servile to the wealthy and morally/intellectually virtuous—could live cooperatively and productively in the polis. For proper social functioning, education should be in the hands of the city-state. This in turn should be run by members of a large middle class, because they were the least likely to suffer from the extremes of poverty or wealth. Temperance and moderation were watchwords for this social scientist.

It can thus be seen that Aristotle differed from his master at the Academy in one monumental way: he trusted his natural observations. He also placed man's essence within man instead of in some transcendental (idea) soul. And he heralded human differences brought about through the interaction of nature and nurture. Likewise Aristotle placed all other essences in their physical/biological containers or bodies so that one could understand the world and arrive at truth and generalizations through careful study of these elements.

However, he did not exclude logical deductions based on unobservable intuitions. These he called his first principles or self-evident truths. Consequently his science became a refined Platonic idealism, "employing both induction from experience and deduction from universal self-evident truths."[37]

As for the latter, Aristotle became a master logician in deductive, syllogistic reasoning.

ARISTOTLE'S LAST DAYS

In 323 Alexander the Great died and the old anti-Macedonian sentiment reared its head and lashed out, once again, at Aristotle. The peripatetic was formally accused of impiety. The charge was based on the poem he had written to Hermias. Recalling the fate of Socrates, Aristotle said, "I will not let Athenians offend twice against philosophy."[38] He withdrew to his mother's estate in Chalcis. The sixty-two year old master left the Lyceum school in the hands of Theophrastus.

Aristotle lived at Chalcis only a few months, for he was already suffering from some type of stomach disorder. Living a lonely, exiled life, he wrote to a friend: "The more I am by myself, and alone, the fonder I have become of myths"[39] He died a few months later and his remains were removed to Stagira. His will specified that they be those of his wife's as she had requested. Sources conflict as to what actually happened. Stagira seems to have claimed to have his ashes in an urn.

The Lyceum continued to flourish under Theophrastus who served as head master from 322-286. Then, in the hands of other less equiped peripatetics, it started a gradual decline as a learning center. Beyond 86 B.C. it ceased to be an instrument of Greek (or Roman) education.[40]

Despite the Lyceum's demise, Aristotle's influence, remained. He did not really found biology, constitutional history, or social science, but he did more for them than perhaps any other ancient. Obviously, he and his colleagues produced some conclusions based on bad reasoning, yet his work in ethics and politics are unrivalled in fame and influence. One writer has called him "the first of Schoolmen" and "the master of those who know."[41] Seven centuries later he was still influential among Neoplatonists, and in the thirteenth century he was at the center of the intellectual debate that accompanied the rise of modern science (Chapter 4).

In the second century before Christ, the Romans took over the Greeks. They left the various philosophical schools in operation—there were quite a number of them in several Greek cities by then—because they felt culturally inferior to the Greeks and wanted to study in the famous centers of learning. The Romans did, however, assume control over the selection of the head masters of the schools. One exception to this general rule took place in the second century A.D. when Trajan's widow, Plotina, convinced her adopted son Hadrian to grant a perpetual exemption to the Epicureans. The school of Epicurus, which stressed temperance as a means of maximizing pleasure and minimizing pain, could always be headed by a Greek. Heads of all the other philosophical schools still had to be Roman citizens.[42]

2

THE ROMANS

If Greek culture can be remembered for its intellectual and ethical sophistication and emancipation, then Roman civilization is best characterized by its moral virtue or intense patriotism toward the city-state. While some historians have found the provincial zeal of the Romans refreshing after the degeneracy of Greece, others describe them as morally rigid, rural, barbarians—slaves to the state—compared to an emancipated, enfranchised Greece.[1]

BACKGROUND

For our educational purposes we need to drop in on Roman society about the time of Sappho—the sixth century B.C. Here we would find a small, religious,

25

landed aristocracy who worked the land themselves. The Latin language reveals just how agrarian they were. Deriving their alphabet from the Etruscans, an Asian people who tried to rule and urbanize the Roman tribes, many of their words came from the soil. For example, joy (*laetus*) described a well-manured ground; happiness (*felix*) referred to a fertile soil; truthfulness or sincerity (*sincerus*) was pure honey without beeswax; fruitfulness (*frux*) was profit; and fame (*egreguis*) referred to a beast separated from the rest of the herd. The later grand Roman villas can be traced back to rudimentary farmhouses. The kitchen gardens behind the old one room houses were partially enclosed to include a dining room and separate kitchen (*peristyle*). The one room hut became the den, office, library. The farmyard was enclosed to be a receiving living room (*atrium*), and a hallway (*vestibule*) leading to the atrium was added.

LEARNING IN THE EARLY REPUBLIC

Education was adapted to this rural aristocracy. The child born into one of the aristocratic clans learned the importance of the family unit as the backbone of society. The father (*pater*) held sovereign authority in all matters connected to his family. The mother—a well respected member of the family—was responsible for educating her children in the rudiments of learning and the lifestyle befitting a Roman aristocrat. From about the ages of seven to sixteen a son left the care of his mother and came under the tutelage of his father. Daughters stayed home to learn domestic skills; however, sons were supposed to learn how to emulate their fathers.

By following his pater around, the young aristocrat saw all sides of the life which was ahead of him. At sixteen this home instruction (*educatio*) came to an end as the son put on the adult cloak (*toga virilis*) and became a citizen. However, he still had not finished his education. Ahead of him lay a year of preparation for public life and at least ten years of military service.

Nothing was so important to Roman citizens as military and public service, under divine guidance of their gods. For Romans, all three of these elements were inseparable. With respect to his religion each family head (*pater*) was also the priest in his family, and many later Roman villas contained sacrificial alters. His code for living was a mixture of old tribal customs and priestly commands. Public worship was conducted by several associations (*collegia*) of priests, each under the direction of a *pontifex maximus.* These were chosen by the aristocracy from their own group for a term of service. The most influential of the colleges was that of the *augures* who interpreted the will of the gods by watching birds in flight. (Using Jaynes' terms, we would assume that fifth century Roman aristocrats were generally free of hearing the voices of the gods since they were looking for signs or omens from them). These colleges would later perform additional duties such as keeping historical annals and recording laws—tasks for which Roman Catholic monasteries would be known still later.

ROMAN SOCIAL STRUCTURE

The legacy of public/military life for the Romans was an outgrowth of earlier tribal customs, and can best be seen through a description of the social structure. At the top of the ladder were the previously described landed gentry, originally consisting of about three-hundred patres, or clan heads. Most of these upper class patres had clients—that is, freemen, who were dependent upon the patres' patronage for land and protection and who in turn helped the patre, served under him in war, and voted as the pater suggested. These powerful family heads comprised the senate. This latter group was the governing body and furnished the generals of Roman society. Its chambers (*curia*) were in the Forum (town center, market place). Next came a group of wealthy bankers and businessmen called *conscripti* or *equites*—the former term denoting their obligation for military service and the latter their military horsemanship. Then came other businessmen, artisans, traders, and farmers—the peasants or plebians—who were foot soldiers. All these were freemen. There was one final class of slaves.[2]

As the conscripti grew in wealth and military power, they demanded a voice in the senate. Their discontent spread to the plebian classes who finally (494 B.C.) refused to fight or work for Rome until they got some of the conquered lands and more voice in governing affairs of the republic. Long standing abuse of the plebs eventually contributed to the fall of the republic. But in their earlier years, their revolts produced rewards: the conscripti were admitted to the senate; and the senators were forced to write down the secret tribal and religious codes into a usable set of laws. The Twelve Tables (450 B.C.) were the result.

Down to the second century B.C., Roman citizens memorized these laws in their youth. The senate and later emperors would modify, elaborate, and redefine them. They remained the basic core of Rome's famous jurisprudence for the next nine hundred years. The Twelve Tables were placed in the Forum for all to view, and thus the hodgepodge of tribal ritual and priestly command was transformed from the divine law into civil laws. This separation of religion and state took a final step when, in 280 B.C., a man named Corincanius began teaching the Roman laws. Soon after, the lawyer became more dominant than the priest in Roman life.

GREEK INFLUENCE

One other major element made up a large part of third and second century Roman education. This stemmed from the fact that Rome became Hellenized (strongly influenced by the Greeks) as Greek colonies and cities could not withstand the power of the Roman legions. It was not difficult for the Romans to adapt much of the Greek culture to their own lifestyle. Geographically as early as the fourth century Greek ways were as close as Naples, Salerno, Pompeii, Tarentum, and Herculaneum—all in the southern part of the Italian peninsula. Then, too, as Romans began conquering the Mediterranean (300-100 B.C.) they found that Greek culture and language were everywhere.

Greek literature was introduced. Andronicus was from Tarentum and taught and wrote in both Greek and Latin. In fact, he translated Homer into Latin, thus producing the first Latin literary piece. The final act came with the conquest of Greece itself in 146 B.C. Of course, one of the most important elements to permeate Rome was the Greek intellectual way of looking at the world. The Romans were attracted to the Greek schools of philosophy—especially those which enhanced a civil course of life. Aristotelian logic and rhetoric became indispensible to the Roman senator-turned-lawyer, for these studies allowed him to persuade, argue, and plead a case more effectively. In fact, for a time, such a Roman was commonly called an orator, a pleader, or an advocate. The ethical branches of philosophy even fit the old Roman morality so that orators were admonished to study ethics in order to be good, moral men. In fact, "philosophy" meant logic under the republic and a prescriptive or normative ethics under the early empire.[3] At this point rhetoric, logic, and philosophy completed their evolution toward preeminence in the education of Romans. They studied the other Greek subjects, but to a lesser degree. Music was somewhat important because it lent grace and rhythm to the oration, but singing and dancing were usually considered either immoral or almost frivolously silly. Astronomy was useful to the Roman military because it helped with geographical locations in battle. Arithmetic was used in business (counting) and geometry helped the surveyor and architect—two important professions in Rome.

Rome also adopted Greek as its cultured language, so that the educated citizenry was truly bilingual. This was due in part to the fact that Greek had the writings of Homer and others. Latin had no written literature until after the third century B.C. Thus, we have those seven subjects that became known to the Romans and their descendants as the Liberal Arts (*Artes Liberales*): literature (grammar), rhetoric, logic (philosophy), and less important, astronomy, music, geometry and arithmetic. (The first three of these were sometimes called the *trivium* and the other four, the *quadrivium*.) Physical education was used in so far as it aided hygiene, but most Romans did not care for nude exercise. Elaborate public bathhouses were the places that they preferred for recreation—not the gymnasium.

BILINGUAL EDUCATION

We now have all of the necessary ingredients for a Roman (Graeco-Roman) education. From the second century B.C. on, the Romans had three levels of schooling—all bilingual. The first level was the primary school (*ludus*). More and more, as the republic declined, aristocratic boys (and some girls) of age seven or so were sent to a *ludus magister* (elementary school master) where they were taught the alphabet, then reading and writing together, and finally counting. The ludus was usually conducted in a shop in one of the forums. The following is an account taken from a schoolboy's book (200-210 A.D.):

> When day breaks I wake up, call the slave [*pedagogue*], and get him to open the window—which he does at once. I sit up, sit on the edge of the bed, and ask for my shoes and stockings because it is cold [otherwise, he would have put on his sandals without bothering about stockings].

As soon as I have put my shoes on I take a towel—I have been brought a clean one. Water is brought me in a jug so that I can wash. I pour some of it over my hands and face and into my mouth; I rub my teeth and gums; I spit out, blow my nose and wipe it, as any well brought-up child should.

I take off my nightshirt and put on a tunic and girdle; I perfume my head and comb my hair; I put a scarf round my neck; I get into my white cloak. I leave my room with my pedagogue and nurse and go and say good morning to my father and mother. I say good morning to them both and kiss them.

I go and find my inkstand and exercise book and give them to the slave. Then everything is ready, and, followed by my pedagogue, I set off through the portico that leads to the school.

[He may buy a pastry and eat it on the way.]

My schoolfellows come and meet me; I say hello to them and they say hello back. I come to the staircase. I go up the stairs quietly, as I should. In the hall I take off my cloak, run through my hair with my comb, and go in, saying, "Good morning, master." The master embraces me and returns my greeting. The slave hands me my writing-boards, my ink-stand and my ruler.

"Good morning, everybody. Let me have my place [seat, stool]. Squeeze up a bit." "Come here." "This is my place!" "I got it first!" I sit down and get to work.

I have finished my lesson. I ask the master to let me go home for lunch; he lets me go; I say goodbye to him, and he returns my farewell. I go home and change. I have white bread, olives, cheese, dry figs and nuts; I drink some fresh water. Having finished my lunch, I go off to school again. I find the master reading; he says to us, "Now to work again!"

I do my copying. When I have finished, I show it to the master, who corrects it and copies it out properly. . . . "I can't copy: copy it out for me, you can do it so well." I rub it out; the wax is hard, it should be soft.

"Do the up-strokes and the down-strokes properly! Put a drop of water in your ink! You see, it is all right now." "Let me see your pen, your knife for sharpening the reed pen." "Let me see it! How have you done it? It's not bad. . . ." Or he may easily say: "You deserve to be whipped! All right, I'll let you off this time. . . ."

I must go and have a bath. Yes, it's time. I go off; I get myself some towels and I follow my servant. I run and catch up with the others who are going to the baths and I say to them one and all, "How are you? Have a good bath! Have a good supper!"[4]

As the preceding quotation shows, the Roman boy was accompanied to the ludus by his slave who, if the boy was lucky, knew Greek. If the boy missed a lesson or gave a wrong answer the master flogged his hand with a cane. Whipping as an incentive to learn was the norm. "The youth has a back and attends when he is beaten," said an ancient Egyptian proverb. "The ears of the young are placed on the back." This was the dominant attitude throughout most of the world down to rather recent times.

Around the age of twelve, the boy went on to a school of the *grammaticus* or grammar school. Here he learned Latin grammar—first from Andronicus' translation of Homer and later from the Latin poetry of Virgil (*The Aeneid, King Midas, Pyramus & Thisbe*—from which Shakespeare later borrowed the story of Romeo and Juliet), Horace, and Ovid. He also studied the Greek classics and, therefore, learned Greek here if he had not already done so in the ludus or from his slave.

Some people, particularly the wealthy, did not use either the ludus or the grammar school. The cost of attending the ludus was the equivalent of approximately half a bushel of wheat per month. This meant that the ludus magister did not occupy a high status position and also that most masters wanted as many boys as they could get so their incomes would improve. Grammar schools charged about four times the ludus rate. Those who could afford it often preferred to employ tutors rather than send their children to a public school. Also, at age sixteen boys from the most aristocratic families traditionally spent a year in the company of a distinguished man—in some cases their own fathers—learning the duties, manners, and attitudes of senators. This was called the *tirocinium fori.*[5]

The final level of education was that of the *rhetor* who taught the skills of oratory. Not all upper class boys readily succumbed to the education of a rhetor. Only those who were destined for public prominence went to him, for normally his instruction led to law and the bar (pleading, oratory). Such was the life of Marcus Tullius Cicero.

Cicero (106-43 B.C.)

The Roman historian Plutarch tells us a legendary story that the orator's last name meant twisted vine (*cicer*) and stood for an ugly wart that inhabited an ancestor's nose. What is probably closer to the truth and more in the Latin tradition, however, is that his ancestors raised the common crop, chick-peas— also *cicer.* Cicero says in his *Laws* that he came from a modest villa in the mountain town of Arpinum between Rome and Naples.

A TRADITIONAL EDUCATION

Cicero's father was probably from the equites class and rich enough to afford a Greek poet as his son's tutor. In any case, we know that early on Marcus learned both Greek and Latin. At the age of sixteen, the youth then prepared for public life—tirocinium fori—under Q. Mucius Scaevola, one of the greatest lawyers of his time. Marcus went everywhere with him and extended his tirocinium beyond the traditional year as he began to study law. He seems to have feigned a weak constitution, thus avoiding his military duties.

Scaevola died about 88 B.C. and soon after Cicero began practicing law. The first case to bring him some fame was one where he succeeded in pleading against a client of the most powerful man in the senate—the dictator Sulla. Perhaps fearing Sulla's revenge, but also feeling the need to learn more, Cicero traveled to Greece (80-76 B.C.) to study philosophy and rhetoric. From Athens he went to the island of Rhodes where there was a famous lecturer on rhetoric—Apollonius—and another on philosophy—Poseidonius. It was at Rhodes that he perfected the flowery, eloquent style of oratory for which he became famous.

POLITICAL CAREER

The year 72 B.C. found Cicero back in Rome and married to Terentia. Her handsome dowry gave him the financial backing necessary to enter politics. By 70 B.C. he was accepting another politically explosive case as pleader for the Sicilian town of Syracuse. It had charged a wealthy senator named Verres with bribery, extortion, and unjust tax assessments. Again, Cicero won. Verres fled into exile. This victory, and the courage it showed, won him enough support to successfully run for one of the two headships (consulships) of the senate. In 63 B.C. he was elected, but he was coming into the political arena at a time when the republic was waning. Rome was in its seventieth year of civil war and strife.

The prime cause for this turmoil was the aristocracy's treatment of the plebs. It will be recalled that members of this class had been unhappy prior to the writing of the Twelve Tables. Exploitation of them had grown until the republic was being overthrown. The plebian (*populares*) cause was the liberal one in that it called for more equal distribution of conquered lands and more rights for the peasants. The conservative *optimates* (patricians and conscripti) were desperately clinging to the republican senate by giving dictatorial powers to strong consuls—for example, Sulla with his ten year term.

No doubt, Cicero's courage appealed to the conservatives when they elected him consul. But the discontent and resentment against him and the optimates were deep-seated enough for him to fail reelection. Cicero, however, thought he had done a remarkable job, adding: "My own applause has the greatest weight with me." His written works reveal his incredible vanity, his preoccupation with wealth, and his claims of modesty: "If ever a man was stranger to vainglory [vanity] it is myself." He had opinions of his contemporaries and, although he did not say it himself, he probably enjoyed the gossip circulating about his rival, Julius Caesar—that Caesar "was the husband of every woman and the wife of every man."[6]

On the other hand, we see the pride Cicero had in his children through the care he took to provide exceptional tutors for his two sons and in the mania that swept him when his beloved daughter Tullia died. His patience with the chronically ill and grouchy Terentia wore out in his final years. He divorced her for a younger woman named Publilia. But her jealousy over his daughter ended that marriage, too.[7]

EDUCATIONAL IDEAS

Cicero wrote his most important educational treatise, *On Oratory (de Oratore)*, around 55 B.C. after his return from a two-year exile imposed while the populares were powerful. In this dialogue he appeals to younger generations to aim at a wider and broader education than the narrow pursuit of rhetoric so common to his day. Thus, his target is what we would call higher education and not the familial *educatio* or the bilingual liberal arts grammar school—other than the fact that he admonishes parents to teach a thorough Latin before embarking on Greek.[8] In the schools of rhetoric and philosophy, on the other hand, a Roman citizen needed a broader instruction—one that would produce wisdom, patriotism, courage, Aristotelian temperance, moral goodness, and oratorical eloquence. Hence, the orator became for Cicero what the philosopher-king was to Plato. Studies were to include law and rhetoric, philosophy, psychology, politics, ethics, military and naval science, medicine, geography, astronomy, and history. With regard to the latter Cicero wrote: "To be ignorant of what happened before you were born, is to live the life of a child forever."[9] The Romans, however, did not heed such advice readily, and education remained narrow in its oratorical pursuit.

LAST DAYS

By 44 B.C. Cicero's political and personal life was coming to a tragic end. On the Ides of March (that is, the 15th), the newly appointed dictator and aristocrat-turned-populare Julius Caesar, was stabbed to death in the senate forum—a victim of a well-organized assassination plot which included his friend and probable illegitimate son Brutus. Caesar's friends suspected Cicero of participating in the plot (though he was later vindicted), and offered a reward for his assassination. His servants persuaded him to leave one of his villas for a safer place, but before his litter was out of the garden, soldiers overtook him. Cicero "commanded his servants to let down the litter; and stroking his chin, as he used to do, with his left hand, he looked steadfastly upon his murderers, his person covered with dust, his beard and hair untrimmed, and his face worn with his troubles," says Plutarch's account. Most bystanders looked away as he calmly exposed his neck to his decapitators. His head, along with his right (and writing) hand, was displayed in the Forum where his eloquent voice had so often been heard.[10] Story has it that the wife of one of his enemies disliked him so much that upon passing the rostra where his head was hung, she vehemently stuck his inanimate tongue with her hatpin.[11]

Cicero's influence on education, however, has enjoyed longevity. From the thirteenth century through the sixteenth it became the basis for the Renaissance ideal of education. Any study of the humanities owes its existence in some measure to him.

Quintilian (A.D. 35-95)

It did not take Rome twelve hundred years (to the Renaissance) in order to rediscover Cicero, for a century after his death a Spanish-born Roman named Marcus Fabius Quintilianus was already popularizing the best in Ciceronian scholarship.

We know little of Quintilian's early life. He was born in Calagurris in northern Spain to the son of a rhetor called to Rome. It was in Rome that Quintilian received his education under some of the city's best grammarians and rhetors.

By now Rome had settled into dictatorial rule, but not easily. Octavius Augustus Caesar—Julius' nephew—had restored harmony to the war torn populace. In A.D. 14 he was succeeded by his weak stepson Tiberius (A.D. 14-37). Quintilian probably witnessed the despotic rule of Caligula (A.D. 37-41) and the weak reign of Claudius (A.D. 41-54). It was towards the end of Claudius' rule that Quintilian returned to Spain as a rhetoric teacher and advocate. He became a client of the Spanish governor, Galba, and upon the death of the infamous Nero (A.D. 54-68), the governor was called back to Rome to reign. By then Galba was old and stingy. So many factions resented him that the soldiers beheaded, "be-armed," and "be-lipped" him a few months later.

It is likely that Galba called Quintilian to Rome to teach. But it was not until Vespasian ascended to the throne (A.D. 69-79) that Quintilian was imperially financed in his profession. Vespasian reduced tax burdens for teachers and endowed the first chair (professorship) in rhetoric in the empire. It was to this first endowed (salaried) chair of rhetoric that Quintilian came. In the next ten years others were endowed by the empire, but the Roman or upper chair was the first.

Sometime during the rule of Domitian (A.D. 81-96), and probably around A.D. 88, Quintilian left the chair to become tutor to Domitan's two grandsons. He also started writing his famous *Institutes of Oratory* (*Instituto Oratoria*) as a prescription for his own sons. But tragedy befell his personal life. Both his sons and his wife died, leaving him to outlive all of the people who meant the most to him.

EDUCATIONAL THEORY

The *Institutes of Oratory* are in the tradition of Cicero's *On Oratory,* for which Quintilian had great respect. Like his predecessor, Quintilian believed in a broad, well-rounded study centered on oratory. Good literature took the place of Cicero's history as the medium from which to embark. But unlike Cicero, Quintilian felt that Greek should be learned early. Children would learn Latin in any case, but they needed special instruction for Greek.

Quintilian's description of the ideal teacher is both sensible and modern sounding:

> Let him therefore adopt a parental attitude to his pupils, and regard himself as the representative of those who have committed their children to his charge. Let him be free from vice himself and refuse to tolerate it in others. Let him be strict but not austere, genial but not too familiar; for austerity will make him unpopular, while familiarity breeds contempt. Let his discourse continually turn on what is good and honourable; the more he admonishes, the less he will have to punish. He must control his temper without however shutting his eyes to faults requiring correction: his instruction must be free from affectation, his industry great, his demands on his class continuous, but not extravagant. He must be ready to answer questions and to put them unasked to those who sit silent. In praising the recitations of his pupils he must be neither grudging nor overgenerous: the former quality will give them a distaste for work, while

the latter will produce a complacent self-satisfaction. In correcting faults he must avoid sarcasm and above all abuse: for teachers whose rebukes seem to imply positive dislike discourage industry.[12]

The student, on the other hand, must become a good person through his studies—excellent in knowledge, speech, and character. Finally, talent is essential. Without natural gifts, technical rules will be useless.

In regard to childhood education, Quintilian was ahead of his time. Above all, he warned that the child must not learn to hate those studies that he is too young to love. Therefore, amusement and play should be used along with rewards. Flogging "is a disgraceful form of punishment fit only for slaves," and should be abolished. It leads to fear which restrains some and unmans others. There is no substitute, admonishes the orator, for "knowing" the child, and understanding his uniqueness. All children, moreover, deserve equal attention and class sizes should be small enough to allow for this. Finally, Quintilian thought that schools were better than tutors, because they promoted competition—a natural part of society.[13]

Quintilian died (c. A.D. 96) during the reign of Trajan—a period of relative tranquility in Roman society. In stressing humane practices, individuality, and play, he was advocating practices that Western society would take sixteen-hundred years to accept. His concept of the proper *content* of education were influential in the Middle Ages and in the Renaissance. Cassiodorus (Chapter 3), da Feltre and Erasmus (Chapter 4) all read him with approval.

By the time Quintilian died, one of the Empire's major problems was evident. This was the process by which emperors were chosen and "unchosen." The chief element in the process was the Praetorian Guard, a special army unit created by Octavius (Julius Caesar's successor). Originally, it was to have been a bodyguard for the emperor. Before long there were nine "cohorts" of these guards, with 600 men in each. From being the protectors of the emperors, they became powerful masters. Candidates for the emperor's chair found it necessary to give a sizable "donation" (bribe) to each of the 5,400 guards before they could be selected. The office almost always went to the highest bidder who, in turn, levied enough taxes to get back the money spent in being elected. If the Praetorians became dissatisfied with the performance of an emperor, they usually assassinated him. This would give rise to a new round of "donation" bids. It was not a particularly effective way of getting competent executives, but it was a quick means of dispensing with unwanted ones. This and other problems led to a gradual decline in the government's vitality, resulting finally in the "fall" of the empire. At the same time, another force was emerging that would replace the fading military legions. This was the Christian development that had its origins only a few years after the empire began.

Both the problems of the empire and the emergence of the Christian movement were evident during the reign of Nero, born in A.D. 37. Nero's mother, Agrippina, put him on the throne at the age of seventeen by feeding poison mushrooms to Claudius, her third husband (Nero's adopted father). Mother and son gave a generous donation to the Praetorians and ruled together for a time. But Nero had learned his mother's tactics. When she opposed his divorcing his wife, Octavia, to marry someone else, he had guards kill his mother. He was twenty-two at the time. His second wife, Poppaea, convinced him to have his first wife killed. Three years later, Poppaea died in an advanced stage of pregnancy from, according to stories, being kicked in the stomach by Nero when she scolded him for coming home late from the races. Nero then saw a young boy who looked like Poppaea and had him castrated after which they were married in public ceremony. Nero "used him in every way like a woman." Someone remarked that it was too bad Nero's father hadn't had the same kind of wife.[14]

THE CHRISTIAN TRANSFORMATION

In the summer of 64, a fire started in Rome that burned for nine days and destroyed two-thirds of the city. Thousands died and hundreds of thousands were homeless. Nero had wanted to rebuild Rome and rename it Neropolis. Rumor spread that he had caused the fire to be set. There was never any proof one way or the other, but to take the heat off himself Nero needed to blame someone. He chose the Christians, a group that was not approved of by most Romans but that had been tolerated up to then. Tacitus, who disliked the Christians, put it this way:

> To scotch the rumour, Nero substituted as culprits, and punished with the utmost refinements of cruelty, a class of men . . . whom the crowd styled Christians. . . . First, then, the confessed members of the sect were arrested; next, on their disclosures, vast numbers were convicted, not so much on the count of arson as for hatred of the human race. And decision accompanied their end: they were covered with wild beasts' skins and torn to death by dogs; or they were fastened on crosses and when daylight failed were burned to serve as lamps by night.[15]

Four years later, the Praetorian Guard forced Nero to kill himself.

This was not the end of persecuting the Christians, however. In the short run, savage treatment slowed the spread of the new faith. But soon, as Tacitus noted, people began to pity the Christians. More than pity, the striking faith of some condemned members of the Christian group provided the public with the impression that there must be something to beliefs for which some died so readily. Around 108, the bishop of Antioch, a man named Ignatus, was on his way to Rome to be executed because he would not give up the faith. He wrote letters to friends begging them not to interfere:

> I am dying willingly for God's sake. . . . Entice the wild beasts that they may become my tomb, and leave no trace of my body, that when I fall asleep I be not burdensome to any. . . . I long for the beasts that are prepared for me. . . . Let there come upon me fire, and cross, and struggles with wild beasts, cutting, and tearing asunder, rackings of bones, mangling of limbs, crushing of my whole body, cruel tortures of the devil, may I but attain to Jesus Christ.[16]

The example of martyred Christians gave a rigorous, almost revolutionary, stamina to the movement. A century after Ignatus, a young man named Origen (Origenes Adamantius) saw his father beheaded for the faith. He became so ascetic that he finally castrated himself to improve his faith. His extensive writings became quite influential in the movement. By 300 Rome contained an estimated 100,000 Christians, and the movement was spreading rapidly in other parts of the empire.

Many different interpretations and beliefs developed within the Christian tradition. By the end of the fourth century, eighty different groups claimed to have the one true way. The Roman members of the church exerted particular authority because of the city's prominence. In 313 Emperor Constantine legalized Christianity and converted himself, though he waited till he was dying to be baptized. He also moved the seat of the empire to Constantinople (today Istanbul, Turkey) and this accelerated the decay of political power in Rome. At the same time, the office of bishop of Rome became increasingly important. It would be several generations before the Christian church was triumphant, but the process was well underway. Aristocratic families began abandoning the old Roman religion for the new one. Families that had once contested for the emperorship now vied for the bishop's throne (cathedra, chair, see) in Rome. By 400 there were magnificent churches. One visitor was surprised to discover that the bishop of Rome lived like a prince and acted as if he were an emperor. An increasingly elegant Christian society emerged, featuring aristocratic prelates to whom power and influence flowed as wealthy followers turned to them for guidance.

In almost every area of the empire, the office of bishop became the chief administrative, judicial, even military, unit as Roman jurisdiction broke down in the fifth century. The same education and training that had prepared one for the office of prefect (governor) was a useful background for bishops. The church gradually assimilated Roman educational provisions. As the empire's military and governmental effectiveness faded, its language, legal code, educational approach, and organizational structures were adopted and handed on by the Roman church.

At the heart of the new religion was a potential increase in consciousness. It stressed not merely legal rituals and proper overt conduct, but correct thinking and self-analysis. What one thought was as important as what one did. To be saved, a person should try to be free of both sinful thoughts and base actions. The approach to perfection called for a rigorous program of self-awareness and control. Perhaps all would fall short; many would give up; but the thread would remain part of the tradition. The ideal of perfection was not invented by the Christians, but they combined it with a powerful faith and added the notion that anyone—free or slave, poor or rich, woman or man—could potentially achieve it.

A short time after Constantine declared Christianity the favored religion, serious levels of disunity became apparent. His announcement of a new official religion was an important step. It did not force everyone to convert, but it did strongly encourage such changes. Important government officials were increasingly becoming Christians; churches grew in size and wealth. At the same time, differences of interpretation—reflecting in many cases competition for leadership—came forcefully into view.

In the early days of the Christian movement, the chief emphasis was on accepting the teachings attributed to Jesus and on the second coming of Christ. Many converts expected the return of the Messiah in a matter of days, weeks, or at most a few years. The longer this event of enormous significance waited to occur, the further it was projected into the indefinite future. At the same time, immediate problems of organizing, governing, and explaining the new faith loomed bigger.

As noted earlier, by the fourth century there were so many explanations of the right interpretation of oral and written traditions that even to list them would be laborious. These were not merely abstract differences either. Advocates of conflicting persuasions not only argued with each other; sometimes they resorted to open violence in trying to get their candidates named to significant offices. Moreover, people from various provinces of the empire tended to espouse the interpretations best accepted in their own regions so that nationalistic (anti-Roman) sentiments were mixed into the disputes. By 300 it was not unusual to find Christian factions agreeing more with some non-Christian groups than they did with each other. This situation is illustrated in the remarkable careers of Hypatia of Alexandria and Augustine of Hippo.

Hypatia (c. 360-415)

The subject of this sketch was unusual, though not because she was well educated. Many Roman women were cultured and educated, and quite a few were politically powerful. They were not expected, as were respectable Greek women, to stay out of public view, but Roman society was by no means free of the double standard. Hypatia was unique in holding a public chair of philosophy in Alexandria, one of the prominent cities of the empire. So far as our incomplete records show, she was the only woman to hold such a post.

FAMILY AND EDUCATION

We do not know when or where Hypatia was born or anything about her mother. She was famous by the late fourth century, however, so she could not have been born much later than our estimated date of 360. Her father was Theon, director of the Museum at Alexandria. The city was nearly seven hundred years old by Hypatia's time, having been founded by Aristotle's pupil. It was one of the leading cities of the empire. It was famous for astronomy, having been the home of Ptolemy, and for medicine, because Galen had practiced there. It was large, with an estimated population of 800,000, and the Museum was known all over the Roman world as a center of study. Hypatia's father was the last person to be recorded as director at the Museum. By the late fourth century the empire was no longer in good condition. One result was that peace and order were not always maintained even in Rome itself, much less in other cities.

Hypatia's own education is not described in any remaining records, but because of her father's position she would have had access to lectures from the leading mathematicians, astronomers, and philosophers of her day. The most influential philosopher in Alexandria during the century preceding Theon's directorship was a Greek educated Egyptian named Plotinus. He lived like a Christian saint, ate no meat, avoided all sexual relations (but did not condemn sex for others), and taught a version of Platonic idealism. He was a friendly contemporary of the Christian ascetic Origen, mentioned earlier.

HER WORK AND VIEWS

Hypatia knew the work of Plato, Aristotle, Plotinus, Origen, and others, and was part of what was called the Neoplatonic movement. She coauthored with Theon a commentary on Claudius Ptolemy's *Syntaxius,* an influential book which rejected Aristarchus' theory that the earth revolves around the sun. (Arab scholars regarded Ptolemy's work so well that they called it *Al-megiste* ["the greatest"]. Medieval Europe corrupted this into *Almagest.* The book and its views dominated European astronomy until Copernicus, Galileo, and Newton replaced it.) Hypatia wrote other works on astronomy and mathematics, but none of these has survived.

As holder of the Chair of Philosophy at the Museum, Hypatia "profited so much in profound learning that she excelled all philosophers of that time"—at least according to a Christian historian named Socrates. She lectured on Plato, Plotinus, and "the precepts and doctrines of all sorts of philosophers" to "as many as came to hear her." She also took pleasure in explaining difficult philosophical points to interested listeners anywhere she found them, including on the streets of Alexandria. People "flocked unto her lessons from every country," and were impressed by her "courage of mind." She was not afraid to "present herself before princes and magistrates. Neither was she abashed to come into the open face of the assembly." All men added Socrates, admired her and held her in reverence "for the singular modesty of her mind."[17]

Perhaps historian Socrates overstated the case a little. *All* men did not like Hypatia. But many did regard her highly. Some of her pupils fell in love with her. In true Platonic form, however, she reminded them that they were only in love with a physical appearance and not the true essence or soul. There is no record that she married; probably she agreed with Plotinus in thinking that marriage would hinder her quest for philosophic perfection, a preoccupation of the Neoplatonists. She did maintain friendships and correspondence with both Christian and non-Christian colleagues.

CAUGHT BETWEEN FACTIONS

One of Hypatia's friends was Orestes, prefect (governor) of Alexandria. Orestes was not a Christian and he did not approve of efforts by a local Christian faction to run all Jews out of the city. The Jews were a numerous minority and Cyril, bishop of the Christian church in Alexandria, had encouraged monks under his control to force them to leave. Angered that Orestes would not support this action, some monks stoned him. When Orestes recovered he had the leader of this group arrested and executed.

Some of the Christians circulated the rumor that Hypatia was to blame. It was she, they claimed, who stopped Orestes from coming over to their side. One day in March 415 a group of frenzied monks, under the lead of one of Bishop Cyril's minor staff members, followed Hypatia. Finally, they stopped her carriage, dragged her into a nearby church, ripped her clothes off, and "rent the flesh of her body with sharp shells until the breath departed out of her body."[18] Then they ripped her body apart and burned the remains. Cyril was powerful enough to prevent Orestes from having them punished for the act.

The whole episode illustrates the emerging power of the bishops in major cities as the imperial government could no longer enforce order. It also illustrates the extent to which some bishops and monks were willing to use the "ways of the world"—assassination, intrigue, power politics—to get what they wanted.

Augustine (354-430)

Another African was born at about the same time as Hypatia, only farther to the west. He lived through the same turbulent conditions. In the end he became a major force for the Roman church in its battle to subdue not only nonbelievers but competing factions within the Christian community. His name was Augustine. He and Hypatia never knew each other. Perhaps it's just as well. They would have had many common interests, but Augustine's mother, Monica, would not have approved. She did not intend to let anything or anyone take her son away from her. He resented her strong influence and tried to escape, but finally gave in to her wishes.

EDUCATION FOR MOBILITY

Augustine was born on the outskirts of the Roman Empire in Thagaste, Africa (today Souk Ahras, Algeria). His father, named Patricius, was educated to some extent and was a citizen, but the family did not have much money. Augustine's parents understood, as did many other African families in similar circumstances, how valuable an education could be. Without a good grammar schooling the African citizen would have to stay in his small town and scrape out the best meager living he could. If he could secure a rhetorical education, however, much was possible: money, perhaps a lucky marriage into more money and influence, and possibly a climb through the civil service into respectability.

Patricius and Monica struggled to educate their son. Patricius worked hard to come up with his son's tuition. But Augustine had to come home from school for one year because there was not enough money. Finally, a local wealthy land owner became Augustine's patron. Why he did this is not clear. He may have been one of Patricius' relatives.[19]

For Augustine, school was not pleasant—at least not in the beginning. Like other children he liked to play, but he had to spend his time memorizing spelling, grammar, vocabulary, and arithmetic facts. Augustine hated Greek and arithmetic and did not learn them well. The standard remedy for any school failure despite Quintilan's admonitions, was a good beating. Augustine got his share of these. Later he would remark on the injustice of adults beating children for playing while the adults defined their own playing as part of "business." It was no great consolation to Augustine that the treatment he received was standard. He developed an excellent memory and a love for Latin (but not Greek) literature.[20]

Augustine started a rhetorical education at Madaura, a larger town some miles away, but a shortage of money again brought him home. By the time he was seventeen, he was off to Carthage to further his education. It was an exciting time. He discovered the theater, and especially liked sad love stories that made him cry. He entered rather fully into the rowdy antics of student life. He particularly enjoyed discovering why Monica had so often warned him against the wiles of attractive women. The fling did not last long. Patricius died about a year after Augustine got to Carthage. He had not been a Christian until near the end of his life. Monica, who had put up with some indiscretions from her husband, seems not to have been broken up over his death. She redoubled her efforts to get her son straightened out. She had always intended that he both be a Christian and that he do well socially.

Under pressure from his mother, Augustine gave up his playboy ways, took a concubine (mistress), and began to settle down. Taking a mistress was a kind of second class marriage, tacitly sanctioned when the woman was from a lower social background than was the man. Augustine said later that he loved his spouse, but he never mentioned her by name in any of his writings. One child, a boy named Adeodatus, resulted from this respectable arrangement. Augustine did not welcome the new responsibility at the time, but later decided that it was a good thing and that he loved his son.

At nineteen, still in Carthage, Augustine underwent what he described as a profound religious conversion. He was already a Christian of sorts, having grown up under Monica's influence. When he had fallen ill as a boy, he had asked to be baptized. This second conversion, however, was something different. It happened when Augustine read a book by Cicero called *The Hortensius.* The book said that the highest good was to seek "wisdom." Augustine confessed that he was "left with an unbelievable fire in my heart, desiring the deathless qualities of Wisdom." He thought it was the way to approach God.

Augustine turned to the Bible to find his wisdom and came away with many questions. For example, how should one account for injustice, death, cruelty, and sin if God was all knowing and all powerful? Why does a believer pray earnestly to God for help in doing right—and then do wrong anyway?

THE WISDOM OF MANI

Augustine found his answers in the teachings of a brotherhood of missionaries who called themselves Manichees or Manichaeans, followers of a third century mystic named Mani. They had elaborate secret rituals and prayers, an "elect" of men and women pale with fasting, and gorgeous parchment scrolls of Mani's teachings. They taught that there is a dual nature of reality, one of God and one of the devil. God is not all powerful. Part of the time He prevails, some of the time the devil wins. Humans have both natures. If we intend well but sin anyhow, that is a matter of the devil getting the upper hand over God at that moment. It is not really our fault. This comforting philosophy had an obvious appeal. But the Roman church bishops in Africa regarded its adherents as dangerous subversives.

Shortly after his conversion to Mani's ideas, Augustine moved back to his hometown to teach grammar and literature. Monica was appalled to learn that her twenty-one year-old son was a Manichee. She locked him out of her house, but he soon converted many other young men—and some not so young—to his point of view. Within a year of his return to Thagaste, however, a close but unnamed friend of Augustine's died. Tired of his mother's nagging, his pupils' rusticity, and his town's isolation, he returned to Carthage to continue teaching there.

CONTINUING THE SEARCH

For the next few years, Augustine lived in Carthage. Although he had some difficulties with his wealthy pupils, he did make money. He made friends in the governing group. He could see himself becoming a landed gentleman not too far off in the future. Yet, he was not happy. He had tired of Manichaeism, but had not overtly rejected it. Monica wanted him to return to Thagaste. Some of his associates encouraged him to go to Rome, where they had promising connections to whom they would introduce him. So in 382 he decided to try his luck there.

When Monica heard of his plan, she put strong pressure on him to return to Thagaste—or, alternatively, to take her to Rome with him. He didn't like either choice and lied to her in order to slip away. As the wind caught the sail of his ship, he could see Monica—she had now figured out his deception—standing on the shore weeping bitterly over being left. In Rome Augustine fell dangerously ill. He, himself, associated the illness with guilt over trying to break with his mother.

The year Augustine spent in Rome was not especially comfortable, but it was profitable. He met important people and as a result was offered the Chair of Rhetoric in Milan. Because Milan was something of an imperial resort away from Rome, it had become a second capital and was an important post. He accepted, and Monica soon showed up to join him.

The Milan experience was a turning point. The bishop there was Ambrose, already celebrated as a courageous and eloquent figure in the emerging Church. Monica pursued Ambrose in promoting her idea of her son's best interest. She also arranged a marriage for Augustine into a socially superior family. The only hitch was that before the family would agree to the betrothal, Augustine would have to rid himself of his common law wife of fifteen years. He seems not to have hesitated long. He said he was sorry to see her go, but she was soon on her way to an African monastery. Adeodlatus stayed with him. The projected marriage was postponed for two years—presumably because the future bride was too young. While Augustine waited, he took up with another woman.[21] The wedding never happened. Whether it was called off by Augustine or his prospective in-laws is not clear. Augustine, who had been toying with the idea of a public conversion to the Roman Church under Ambrose, saw a vision and had another profound experience of conversion. He was baptised by Ambrose, and decided to give up his pursuit of wealth and fame.

FROM RHETORICIAN TO BISHOP

Not long after Augustine's conversion, Monica died. Augustine, who was socially beyond his element in Milan anyway, decided to return to Africa. He made sidetrips to Rome and Carthage, but by 388 he was back in Thagaste. Within a short time his best friend and his son both died. A couple of years later, Augustine traveled down to Hippo on the coast not far from his hometown. He intended to establish a monastery there, and did so, but the local bishop recognized a good opportunity and engineered Augustine's election by the congregation as his assistant and likely successor.

Augustine proved as good as his Hippo sponsor hoped he'd be. He publicly debated the best Manichaean advocate and defeated him so roundly the man would not show his face in town again. He tried to do the same with the Donatist group, but they would not take the bait. (The Donatists were a rival Christian group who did not recognize the Roman bishops. They had their own bishops and the two groups resorted to physical combat in some areas.)

Augustine was a powerful speaker and writer. His classical education—even if it did lack Greek—stood him in good stead in the battle of the Roman church against competing groups. He spent the rest of his life as bishop of Hippo. He settled disputes and generally tended to the many religious, legal, personal, and community needs of his district. By the time he died, the Roman church had defeated its rivals in Africa, but the empire had virtually come to an end.

In 429-430 invading tribes called Vandals (hence, our term "vandalism") laid siege to North Africa. Some of the bishops resisted and were killed. Many of the people did not resist. Augustine lived long enough to watch Roman society collapse in his part of the world and in the summer of 430 died after contracting some sort of fever. For men like Augustine, Christianity outside of Roman civilization did not seem possible.

Augustine remained a powerful influence because his many writings survived. He would come to be regarded as one of the "fathers" of the Western (Roman) church. His autobiographical *Confessions* are a major source of knowledge about education, culture, and life in his time. They became a model for some later people, among them Guibert of Nogent and Peter Abelard, whose lives are described in the next chapter.

The world of Augustine was clearly one of changing conditions. Invaders replaced Romans on the imperial throne. First one and then another "barbarian" (that is, non-Romanized) group captured territory that had been part of the empire—for example, England fell to Germanic tribes (Angles, Saxons, Jutes) and Spain to Vandals in the fifth century. At the time, most people with a classical education viewed the breakup of Roman political authority as a calamity for civilization. Many Christians, like Augustine, had their faith rooted so strongly in a Roman context that they could hardly imagine any other possibility.

THE MEDIEVAL TRANSITION

Historians must rely on metaphor and analogy, but sometimes wrong impressions result. They used the term *medieval* (middle) in the first place because they thought of the period from about 500 to 1200 as an interlude between the "brilliant" cultures of Greece and Rome and the "rebirth" or renaissance of interest in them during the thirteenth to sixteenth centuries. The negative impression created by the use of images such as "dark ages," "a cloud of ignorance descending on Europe," and "the lamp of learning growing dim" has left the impression that nothing of educational importance occurred during these "Middle Ages."[22]

This mistaken conclusion is reinforced by the seeming remoteness of medieval life from our own, and by the violence, superstition, and intensely religious orientation of so many people. But the medieval people did not invent superstition, violence, or supernatural explanations for everyday events. Rather, they inherited them. "Jesus was born into a world pervaded by the supernatural," writes Roland Bainton. "Belief in demons, exorcism, and magic was virtually universal."[23] It is true that guilt, fear, shame, and threats of damnation were significant controling elements in medieval society and that some religious leaders stressed the terrors of hell because they were convinced that nothing could move people like "the terrific." It is also true that the medieval period witnessed a fusion of Christian values with many Greek and Roman educational and cultural practices. From this long evolution came much of the educational structure of the contemporary world.

In the turbulent period following Augustine's death, the Roman aristocracy struggled to retain the cultured features of civilization as they had known it. This was not an easy task. By the mid fifth century, Attila the Hun, operating out of his capital in present-day Hungary, stopped just short of sacking Rome. In a few years (476), Odoacer became the first non-Roman to occupy the imperial throne. Much later a historian named Gibbon would cite this as the "fall" of the empire. Diseases and plagues hit the population of Rome, reducing the city to a fifth of its original 1.5 million people, as aqueducts and other public facilities were no longer well maintained.

MAINTAINING ROMAN TRADITIONS

Despite the political and economic changes, some families were able to continue life pretty much as usual. This included educating their children in the classical Greek and Roman traditions. To do this, they made whatever kind of peace with the new ruling groups they thought manageable. Sometimes they were successful and sometimes not. The transition shows plainly in the lives and careers of the sons of two wealthy families. Both boys were well educated, both rose to high rank under the Gothic (German) emperor Theodoric, and both influenced education and thought for a thousand years. They did not, however, fare equally well.

Boethius (c.480-c.524)

Anicius Manlius Severinus Boethius was slightly the older of the two, having been born into an aristocratic Roman family about 480. Boethius' father was a high government official. He provided his son with a solid liberal arts education before sending him to Athens for years of further study. This experience gave the young Roman a love of the classics. He translated a number of Greek texts into Latin. As a member of a family which was "one of the richest and most illustrious in the Empire and long distinguished by public service," Boethius himself entered political life at age thirty. He said that he only left his study for public office because of Plato's belief that philosophers should be leaders. He would find need for the comforts of philosophy before he finished with politics.[24]

For thirteen years, Boethius was one of Theodoric's trusted officials. He rose ultimately to the position of master of offices—roughly equivalent to prime minister today—and was noted for his generosity and eloquence. There was a gulf between the Goths and the Romans, however, which the latter's feelings of superiority did little to narrow. The Goths were Christians, but they were of the Arian persuasion. This meant that they denied the Trinity. Roman Christians believed in the Trinity, and Boethius had written in defense of the Roman interpretation. There were rumors of a senatorial plot to depose Theodoric. Boethius was implicated in what were probably trumped up charges, though we can't be sure now.

Against this background Justin, who was emperor of the eastern part of the Empire, issued an edict in 523 against Arianism. Theodoric suspected that his Roman officials were waiting for an opportunity to depose him and that Justin's new law would be their excuse. Boethius and one other official were arrested, charged with treason. Theodoric may have doubted Boethius' guilt. At least he kept him in prison for a year before having him executed. During that time, Boethius wrote his most famous book which he titled *On the Consolation of Philosophy*. The only true happiness lies in union with God, Boethius concluded, and Theodoric shortly dispatched him to join his creator. "A cord was twisted around his forehead until his eyeballs sprang from their sockets, and then, in the midst of his torture, he was clubbed to death."[25]

Cassiodorus (c.483-c.575)

One of Boethius' contemporaries fared better. Either he was luckier than his colleague or more careful not to offend the king—or perhaps a little of both. Flavius Magnus Aurelius Cassiodorus was from Calabria rather than Rome, but he too came from a wealthy family and he received an excellent classical education. He served Theodoric just as Boethius had done, but without being suspected in the alleged conspiracy. His *History of the Goths*, which aimed to show skeptical Romans that the invaders also had noble ancestors and a record of great deeds, may have helped his cause.

After Theodoric lost power, Cassiodorus retired to his family estate in Calabria and founded a monastery whose monks specialized in copying texts, both religious and secular. Cassidorus set aside a special room called a *scriptorium* for this purpose. He also supervised translations and copy work, setting a high standard for both.

Cassiodorus did not become a monk himself, but he influenced the scholarly part of monastic development. He agreed with Boethius that the seven liberal arts (grammar, rhetoric, logic [or dialectic], arithmetic, music, geometry, and astronomy) were the elements of a good education—whether one intended a secular or religious vocation. He died on his estate at the age of ninety-two. As a cultured Roman Christian, he epitomized for many the best of both worlds.[26]

INFLUENCE OF BOETHIUS AND CASSIODORUS

Of the two, perhaps Boethius had a more specific impact on the history of thought. His translation of Aristotle's *Organon* (logical treatises) and Porphyry's *Introduction to the Categories of Aristotle* were the leading texts in logic for the next seven centuries. These kept alive the ideas that would become the basis for the dispute over "universals" and "particulars"—or "realism" and "nominalism" (treated in the next chapter)—which would flower in Paris and elsewhere as universities were beginning to develop. His writings on the syllogism inspired several centuries of scholarly struggle for greater rationality and more logical expression of thought. He did a great deal to make the field of philosophy more systematic than it might otherwise have been in his time. His writings on theology and music were also much read for several centuries.

Both Cassiodorus and Boethius typified the kind of liberal education that Aristotle had advocated and that Roman wealth had made possible. It had been pursued as an ideal for a thousand years before they lived and would remain the ultimate standard for many centuries after their time. It was most accessible to aristocrats, because it required leisure. But as Augustine's life had shown, a "liberal" education was useful in both church and state, and could transport anyone lucky enough to acquire one into aristocratic company. The Roman empire was dead. But Greek and Roman cultural ideals flourished in Christian schools fastened securely on Roman underpinnings.

SKETCH OF CICERO, BASED ON A BUST

3

THE MONASTICS

Boethius and Cassidorus represent something of a bridge between the Roman world and that of medieval Europe. They stood at the beginning of important developments in education. As Roman political and economic structures broke down in first one area and then another, a new organizational force appeared. It was destined to have major educational significance. This was the monastic establishment whose houses dotted the European landscape for many centuries.

BEGINNINGS OF MONASTERIES

We have already noted the existence of monasteries by the early fifth century. Augustine sent his common-law wife to one and founded a monastery himself in Hippo. Hypatia was killed by a group of Coptic (Egyptian) monks from around Alexandria. Actually, the beginning of monastic life in the West is dated with unusual precision. Despite the early existence of religious communities around the time of Christ, the first famous person identified as a Christian hermit was an Egyptian named Anthony. He was from a wealthy background. In A.D. 271, when he was a little more than twenty and shortly after his parents had died, he heard the following words of Jesus read: "If you will be perfect go, sell all you have, and give to the poor, and come follow me." He gave away his property, except for enough to support a younger sister. Then he sent her to live in a community of religious women—an indication that such Christian nunneries already existed. He had been a loner as a child. After his conversion, he withdrew to the desert where he undertook a solitary life of prayer, self-assessment, manual labor, and contemplation. He lived to a grand old age— well over one hundred—and became quite famous. As people sought his advice and assistance, he retired further and further from civilization.[1]

By the early fourth century, many people were retreating into the Egyptian desert. Inspiration from examples like Anthony's was one reason; the fact that authorities did not usually pursue accused criminals into the wastelands no doubt added some converts. Monks were also soon exempt from taxes, military service, and some forms of required labor. The physical climate, which permitted a year-round existence on a sparse diet in caves on uninhabited land, was an additional factor encouraging solitary life in Egypt. But the main impetus came from civil unrest resulting from the Roman legions' inability to keep out invading tribes on the African frontier, and from a growing reform sentiment within some parts of the Christian community.

It was at about this time (313) that Constantine declared Christianity the empire's favored religion. While no one was forced to convert, many aristocratic and middle class citizens saw advantages in adopting the emperor's faith. Churches grew in size and wealth. At the same time, differences of interpretation—reflecting, as we have noted in chapter 2, regional disputes and leadership competition—came forcefully into view. As one religious historian has put it, this brought about "the swift transformation of the Christian church from a persecuted and fervent sect into a ruling and rapidly increasing body, favored and directed by the emperor, membership of which was a material advantage." The resulting relaxation of standards and diminished emphasis on austerity caused the Christian church to become what, in the words of David Knowles, it remains:

> a large body in which a few are exceptionally observant and devout, while many are sincere believers without any pretension to fervour, and a sizeable number, perhaps even a majority, are either on their way to losing the faith, or retain it in spite of a life which neither obeys in all respects the commands of Christ nor shares in the devotional and sacramental life of the church with regularity. Under such conditions there has always

occurred a revolt of some or many against what seems to them prevailing laxity.[2]

Each revolt has inevitably contained a strong educational element.

SYSTEMATIZING A MOVEMENT

At the onset monasticism consisted of individualistic hermits, like Anthony, but growing numbers brought the need for organization. From living alone or in pairs or threes, people began to associate regularly for spiritual assistance. Soon they were forming groups. A man named Pachomius (286-346) is credited with originating a "rule" or set of written procedures for monastic life. He was an Egyptian who converted to Christianity as a young man and tried life as a hermit for a time. He became increasingly convinced that living with others made Christian perfection more attainable. He was a superb administrator, with a less ascetic approach to life than some of his contemporary desert dwellers. He forbade meat and wine, but allowed cheese and fish. His most important contribution was the rule by which he governed several thousand monks. This ultimately formed part of the basis for the procedures that European monastic houses would follow.

Pachomius retained for himself and his monks vows not to engage in sexual activity or to acquire personal wealth. He added the obligation of obedience. Giving up one's personal will to the best interests of the whole group as specified by one's superior became part of spiritual growth. Pachomius as governor general organized his followers according to economic skills into "houses" of about fifteen to thirty people—in other words, bakers in one, tailors in another and so on. Excess produce was floated down the Nile to Alexandria and sold, thus providing money for the group's needs and for charity.

A number of seekers after Christian perfection found Pachomius' rule not stringent enough, and continued their individual pursuit of salvation. Some chained themselves to rocks, others boxed themselves into the ground from the waist down, and a few followed the example of a Syrian named Symeon who spent more than three decades on a thirty foot high column near Antioch, with bare essentials of life being sent on a rope. People sometimes came from long distances to seek advice or to invoke the blessings and prayers of such obviously tough-willed saints.

In the Italian and Western European areas, this olympic style of individual asceticism did not win many converts. A moderate form of group monasticism did catch on, however, and by the time Germans were on the imperial throne there were thousands of monks scattered about much of Italy, Spain, and France. They would soon establish themselves in England and Ireland. Most of these groups were quite small at first, but by the sixth century some were growing larger. They followed whatever regulations (rules) their founders preferred and their members accepted. Some, like the one started by Cassiodorus, stressed copy work; many were largely agrarian, and all were preoccupied with prayer and contemplation.

Benedict (480-c. 543)

In 480, one of monasticism's most famous people was born. This was Benedict of Norcia, author of the most celebrated and widely used set of European monastic regulations. Despite Benedict's later fame, not much is known about his life. He was from a distinguished family in central Italy and was educated in Rome. At a site near an artificial lake where Nero had once had a villa, he tried life as a hermit. He had great difficulty overcoming his sexual fantasies—at least according to Gregory I who lived just after Benedict's time. The "wicked spirit," says Gregory, would not let him forget a woman, the memory of whom "so mightily inflamed . . . the soul of God's servant . . . that, almost overcome with pleasure, he was of a mind to forsake the wilderness." He found the cure in a nearby brier patch: "He cast [off] his apparel, and threw himself into the midst of them, and there wallowed so long that when he rose up all his flesh was pitifully torn."[3]

MONTE CASSINO AND THE RULE

Finding solitary life difficult, Benedict decided to found a grand monastery. He was familiar with Cassiodorus' establishment and two or three other noted centers. After several faltering attempts in which his fellow monks found his requirements too severe—to the point that some attempted to poison him according to one story—Benedict succeeded. He took a group of followers to Monte Cassino, a fortified hill on the Apian Way (military road from Rome to the south coast).

Monte Cassino has been destroyed or seriously damaged on several occasions, but it has been restored each time and remains a symbolically important establishment. Of most significance for the development of education, however, was Benedict's rule. Based on several earlier documents, including that of Pachomius, it laid down a moderate approach to government that ultimately came to be followed by most European monastic establishments.

Benedict's rule assumed poverty, chastity, and obedience. It laid out a system of government based upon the Roman family. The abbot (or father) was to rule his children, the monks, with love and understanding. He could prescribe punishment, including flogging or ultimately dismissal from the order, for those who did not fulfill their obligations. Vacant abbacies were to be filled after consultation with members of the order and there were provisions for removing seriously incompetent abbots. But once installed they were practically immune from impeachment. Red meat was excluded, except for the sick, while fish, cheese, foul, wine, and vegetables in season were allowed for all. The spirit of monasticism suggested restraint in the consumption of food and wine, but the abbot was to recognize differences resulting from physical labor, personal need, and climate.

Benedict thought it essential that monks be literate. This was partly because he was impressed with the copy work of Cassiodorus' group. ("Every word you write is a blow that smites the devil," Saint Bernard of Clairvaux later said.)[4] It was also because people needed to be able to read scripture. Hence, if new members of the house (*novices*) were not already literate, they would receive "abc" instruction from the master of novices. But monastic education went beyond elementary (*internal*) instruction for novitiates. Nearly all Benedictine houses also maintained *external* schools for children who did not intend to join the order. Sometimes these were taught by a monk or nun from the monastery. In other cases, the house paid a salary to an outsider. Either way, monastic establishments provided instruction in Latin (and sometimes Greek) grammar, rhetoric, logic and religion to youth in rural areas and in cities.

Benedict died at Monte Cassino some time after 546. He had a sister named Scholastica who lived as a nun. Tradition holds that she was an abbess, or head of a female monastic order, but this is not certain. Women's monastic houses did follow Benedict's rule in many instances.

Between the sixth and ninth centuries, monasteries were started in many parts of Europe. Even though most of them were small at first, they often grew to be the most important economic and educational units in their particular localities. "Undistracted by desire for visible success and fear of failure, the monk was able to concentrate all his [or her] energies upon the task at hand. . . . Refusing to be the slave of the material universe, [she or] he became its master."⁵

"HAPPY CHRISTIAN FACTORIES"

The following description of St. Gall (or St. Gallen) in the mountains of Switzerland, while a bit romanticized by the nineteenth century abbess who wrote it, reminds us of how influential monasteries became. The house was started by Irish travelers in the sixth century. By 800 it was a primary center of learning:

It lay in the midst of savage Helvetian wilderness, an oasis of piety and civilization. Looking down from the craggy mountains, the passes of which open upon the southern extremity of the lake of Constance, the traveler would have stood amazed at the sudden apparition of that vast range of stately buildings which almost filled up the valley at his feet. Churches and cloisters, the offices of a great abbey, buildings set apart for students and guests, workshops of every description, the forge, the bakehouse, and the mills, for there were ten of them, all in such active operation that they every year required ten new millstones; and then the house occupied by the vast numbers of artisans and workmen attached to the monastery; gardens too, and vineyards creeping up the mountain slopes, and beyond them fields of waving corn, and sheep speckling the green meadows, and far away boats busily plying on the lake and carrying goods and passengers—what a world it was of life and activity; yet how unlike the activity of a town! It was, in fact, not a town but a house—a family presided over by a father. . . . Descend into the valley, and visit all these nurseries of useful toil, see the crowds of rude peasants transformed into intelligent artisans, and you will carry away the impression that the monks of St. Gall had found out the secret of creating a world of happy Christian factories. . . . Visit their scriptorium, their library, and their school, or the workshop where monk Tutilo is putting the finishing touch to his wonderful copper images, and his fine altar frontals of gold and jewels, and you will think yourself in some intellectual and artistic academy.[6]

Tutillo was one of several noted teachers associated with St. Gall. He was powerfully built, had a fine voice, could preach eloquently in Latin or Greek, but was noted for humility. He was especially famous for carving, painting, musical composition, and singing. He was also knowledgeable in mathematics and constructed an astrolabe for astronomical work.

MONASTIC LIFE

Monastic life was not easy, either physically or psychologically. Schedules varied by region and by time of year, but the usual hour for getting up was from 2:00 to 4:00 A.M. Reading, meditation, singing/chanting, prayer, and religious ceremony occupied about eight hours in the day, as did various forms of work, but these were interspliced with each other. Meals, rest, conversation, and sleep took up the remaining eight hours. Bedtime was around dark, as indeed it was for many other people in a time when candles furnished the only artificial light. In northern climates, monks sometimes suffered frostbite while copying texts in winter.

On the psychological side, the monastic ideal demanded a great deal of introspection and self-awareness. It was not enough to refrain from making angry or jealous remarks; one had to learn how not to think them. It was not sufficient to abstain from sexual activity. In modern psychological terms, simply repressing or ignoring one's feelings would not do. It was essential to be fully aware and to try to come to grips with how one felt.

Monastic life may have been difficult, but it offered some quite tangible advantages. It made possible an educated and cultured existence lived in a context of service to others. It provided an environment for faith in a power and set of values that transcended the often violent and sordid conditions of life. This was as true for women as for men. If anyone escaped the ravages of military action—a frequently recurring situation—monastics did. Medical attention was always available, food was usually adequate and healthful, living conditions were simple but aesthetically pleasing, and sexual abstinence provided a break from a succession of pregnancies and children that typified much family life.

MONASTERIES' CONTRIBUTIONS

Monasteries had many functions, and in the long run "became a politically potent, intellectually vibrant, and artistically rich force which transformed Western Civilization."[7] They were politically significant because they were so economically powerful. Since monks consigned to the order the extra wealth their labor had created, monasteries were able to buy additional land, build mills and barns, purchase breeding animals, or construct churches—an activity which furnished jobs for many skilled artisans. They also reclaimed mountain, swamp, or forest land that would otherwise have been unproductive. They furnished schooling to boys and girls in their own geographic areas and sometimes beyond. They often took in orphaned children. They possessed the most reliable medical knowledge then extant, and had people experienced in its application. They preserved and improved engineering skills, especially in architecture and surveying. They provided the only important source of agricultural experimentation for many centuries.

Far from being merely static repositories of ancient knowledge, monastic houses furnished the conditions for the creation of new information. Musical notation, for example, was invented at Pomposa in the eleventh century by a monk named Guy of Arezzo. Until then, there was no effective way of writing down how a song should be rendered. Learning songs and chants was a matter of hearing someone else sing them and then memorizing the patterns.

> After seeking for a long time for some easy and precise system, Guy one day recognized in the chant to which the hymn of St. John the Baptist was ordinarily sung an ascending diatonic scale in which the first syllable of each line occupied one note. . . . He applied himself to teach this chant to his pupils, and to render them familiar with the diatonic succession of the syllables, *ut, re, mi, fa, sol, la.* Next he arranged the notes on lines and intervals, and thus produced the musical staff with its proper clefs. By means of these improvements he found himself able, in a few months, to teach a child as many as a man. However, such a storm of jealousy arose against him on the score of his discovery, that he found himself obliged to leave the monastery; and accordingly, in 1024, he travelled to Rome, where Pope John XIX warmly received both him and his newly invented gamut."[8]

Monasteries not only saved earlier treasures, but created new art and trained artists. Entertainers—actors, jugglers, clowns, singers, dancers, and others—were needed to help provide hospitality to travelers, many of whom were important people. Hence, the monastic house hired a variety of local and regional talent, thus supporting the performing arts.

Monasteries were also rehabilitation vehicles for some criminals. About 986, for example, a woman named Elfrida was directed to establish a monastic house at Wherwell in England. She spent six years there (until she died) reflecting on why it had not been a good idea to murder her husband and son-in-law. They also sometimes provided a retirement setting for some people who preferred to live their last days in contemplation with support from good company rather than alone. Christine de Pisan, for example, spent the last fifteen years of her life at the aristocratic Abbey of Poissy (Chapter 4). They could even be a substitute for divorce for people who had finished rearing their families. Peter Abelard's parents, about whom you will read in this chapter, apparently took this route.

THE CAROLINGIAN RENAISSANCE

The western European medieval world was largely rural. Population centers rarely had more than a few thousand people, although towns did grow in size and number from about the ninth century on. A major factor in the growth of city life and the spread of Christianity to northern Europe was the stability brought about by the political/military success of a Germanic family from about 600 to 800. The first member of the Carolingian family to become prominent was Pepin I (the Elder), a nobleman whom the Merovingian King Clothaire II named his "mayor of the palace" or business manager.

Because most of the kings in the Merovingian family neglected administration in favor of palace intrigues and sexual exploits, the Carolingian mayors of the palace gradually gained control over the army, courts, and finances. One of these, Charles Martel (the Hammer), illegitimate grandson of Pope Zacharias, sent the last "do nothing" Merovingian King, Childeric III, to a monastery. In 754 Pope Stephen II declared Pepin III *rex Dei gratia*—king by the grace of God. Pepin gave the papacy a large "donation" of land and set the stage for Christianity to become the official religion of the German part of Europe. When he died in 768 his two sons Acrolom II and Charles succeeded.

Most of the area of the Roman Empire was Christian by the seventh century, as was Ireland. But some non-Latinized, northern Germanic and Scandinavian tribes continued to raid British and continental areas. After the mid-seventh century Arabic converts to Mohammed's Islam made rapid conquest of the territory from Jerusalem around the Mediteranian to southern Spain. In fact Charles Martel stopped the Moslem advance into Europe in 732 at the battle of Tours in France. Charles Martel and Pepin the Short encouraged Christian missionaries in the German area, but it was Charles who made Christianity the official religion of all the territory that he controlled.

Charlemagne (742-814)

Charles the Great (Charlemagne) was called Karl by his Germanic youthful peers. His place of birth is not recorded, but he no doubt had a traditional aristocratic—that is, military—education. He spent more time hunting than with books. At six-feet four inches, he was taller than most of his contemporaries. Energetic, intelligent, honest, and fair-minded, he was an effective king when at twenty-six he began to share power with his brother. The two of them might have been in civil war if Carloman II had not died of natural causes three years later.

Some historians continue to repeat the claim that Charlemagne could not write. This comes from a story told by Eginhard, his secretary and biographer, to the effect that "he tried to write and constantly carried little tablets about him, that in his leisure moments he might accustom his hand to the drawing of letters, but he succeeded badly, having applied himself to the art too late." Probably this refers to his attempt to learn calligraphy—the art of decorative manuscript writing. He obviously could write; a copy of the gospels, corrected in his hand, has been preserved.[9] Princes often signed documents with an "X" even though most knew how to write. Aristocrats did not need to write with careful legibility, because they could dictate to secretaries who specialized in the art of writing clearly.

Charlemagne was frequently involved in military actions during the four decades of his rule. He made himself king of Lombardy (northern Italy) early in his reign and reconfirmed "Pepin's donation" to the papacy. With the exception of a campaign against the Moslems in Spain, most of his military engagements were successful. He soon controlled the territory that would later become France, Belgium, Holland, the Netherlands, Germany, Switzerland, Austria, northern Italy and Yugoslavia, and western Hungary and Czechoslovakia.

Charlemagne could be ruthless: he gave defeated Saxons a choice of baptism or death—and had 4,500 of them executed one afternoon when they waited too long to decide. On Christmas day, A.D. 800, King Charles, wearing the robes and sandals of a Roman patrician, knelt in prayer before the altar in St. Peter's Basilica in Rome. Pope Leo III suddenly produced a jeweled crown. Placing it on Charles' head, he proclaimed him Emperor and Augustus.

This "Holy Roman Empire" is Charlemagne's main claim to historical significance. It united Europe as it had not been since the height of the Roman Empire and as it would not be again until Napoleon. But this accomplishment in itself is not as interesting to the student of education as is the so-called Carolingian renaissance which reached its peak under Charlemagne. His father and grandfather had welcomed monastic establishments and renowned scholars; King Charles cultivated intellectual developments in his realm at least as energetically as he fought battles. His chief lieutenant in this campaign to civilize and Romanize Europe was an Englishman named Alcuin.

Alcuin (735-804)

Born in Northumbria about seven years before Charlemagne, Alcuin was christened Ealh-wine. He was from a good family, and received a classical education at the cathedral school of York near his birthplace. (Cathedral schools were much like external monastic schools.) Archbishop Egbert of York kept Alcuin on as a teacher. About 770 Alcuin became a deacon—a rank in the lay clergy just below that of priest, carrying a salary but not requiring all of the responsibilities of a priest. Eight years later he became head of the cathedral school. He extolled the virtues of monastic life, but never became a monk himself.

Alcuin and Charlemagne met at Parma (Italy) in 781 while Alcuin was on a continental trip to secure books for his school. Charlemagne had already imported several noted scholars, partly by offers of generous pay and partly by his own enthusiasm for each master's skills. He convinced Alcuin to take charge of the palace school at the capital in Aachen (Aix-la-Chapelle). The fact that Danes were burning monasteries in northwest England, and that Charlemagne guaranteed a high salary made the offer particularly attractive.

The Carolingian renaissance required the efforts of many people and involved five elements: (1) encouraging all monasteries and cathedrals to furnish schooling, including to children of serfs as well as to those of free parents; (2) correcting existing religious books and making accurate copies of Greek and Roman texts; (3) improving knowledge of Latin and Greek grammar in Germanic areas, and Romanizing pronunciation—people in southern Europe caricatured German accents as barbarian and unsophisticated ("the barbarous harshness of their cracked throats when . . . they endeavored to emit a gentle psalmody,"

said John the Deacon, "out of a certain natural hoarseness sent forth grating
sounds like that of carts on a high road");[10] (4) giving the vernacular (German)
language and literature a more systematic written form; and (5) standardizing
and reforming religious doctrine and practice by supressing heretical movements. The curricular framework in which all this was cast was basically that
of the seven liberal arts as advocated two centures earlier by Boethius.

The first element found expression in letters from Charlemagne to all bishops
and abbots in 787 and 789. It is not clear how well the directive on not making
social class distinctions was carried out; it may have been more a well inten-
tioned wish than a reality. The copying of texts was widely done and included
the careful decoration of manuscripts by miniature drawings for which the
Carolingian renaissance has become noted. In the matter of pronunciation,
Roman cantors gave instruction for singing and Alcuin instituted accent and
punctuation marks "as might enable even the unlearned to read without any
gross error."[11] German language and literature especially interested Charlemagne. He wrote down popular folk songs and he started a German grammar
which was finished after his death. Both Alcuin and Charlemagne wrote against
religious doctrines that they considered heretical, and Charlemagne did his best
to uphold orthodoxy.

All of this activity had a strongly religious orientation, but no one should
suppose that it was joyless. Charlemagne was a lively, practical man with a zest
for life. He had eight legitimate and ten illegitimate children by four successive
wives and five mistresses. He loved his family, preferring that his daughters
stay home and have affairs rather than marry and leave. Charlemagne entertained himself at meals by listening to Augustine's *City of God*—not through
excessive piety, but because he was busy and intellectually voracious. Alcuin,
too, enjoyed life. He liked Virgil and other classical writers. He sustained his
work with "large goblets of Greek wine," and steaming dishes of savory
food.[12]

After fourteen years at Aachen, Alcuin accepted Charlemagne's offer to become head of the Abbey of St. Martin of Tours. This was a noted and wealthy
establishment, controlling some twenty thousand serfs. The fact that Alcuin,
who had never been a monk, could become abbot of a wealthy and prestigious
monastery illustrates something of the complex interrelationship between social origins and leadership positions in church and state. It was not unusual for
people of humble birth to join monasteries or hold minor lay clerical offices.
Indeed, the church offered considerable avenues for social mobility to the bright,
hardworking, and lucky. But abbots, abbesses, and lay clergy in the rank of
bishop or higher were usually of noble birth. Given the power and wealth
involved in these offices, it is no surprise that ambitious families usually wanted
as much control as they could get over the most prestigious abbacies and
bishoprics.

Alcuin died eight years after going to Tours, but in that time he made the
monastery one of the most noted centers of learning of the time. Charlemagne
lived ten years longer. His descendents ruled whatever they could hold together
of the Holy Roman Empire for 173 years. None was as effective as he had been,
but many of the educational improvements remained.

THE MEDIEVAL MIND

By the eleventh century most of Europe was at least nominally Christian, and the monastic ideal was widely admired if not universally practiced. Many people mixed in their own localities' inherited folk beliefs and superstitions with Christian doctrines. People hoped that they would go to heaven, but feared it would be hell instead. Theologians taught and believed that "many are called but few are chosen." Consequently, most of the human race would be resting down under in the lower part of the earth, a location later affirmed by Thomas Aquinas. Infants were no exception. Remorsefully, St. Augustine had concluded that infants who died before they were baptized went to hell due to their vicarious connection with original sin. Later the doctrine was changed to an eternity in limbo for the unbaptized infant, and a life in purgatory (popular by 1070) for sinners who had not fully redeemed themselves.

Guilt and terror are brutal feelings for the human psyche and, no doubt, some medieval people had their bouts with madness and insanity. One historian concludes that "the flight of thousands of men and women from the world, the flesh and the Devil into monasteries and nunneries suggests not so much their cowardice as the extreme disorder, insecurity, and violence of medieval life."[13]

Some people reported dreams and visions of hell in detail. For example, in the twelfth century Monk Tundale vividly described a constantly agonizing and screaming Satan, bound to a burning gridiron by red hot chains. This devil seized the damned and crushed them like grapes with his teeth, swallowing them down his burning throat. Assistant demons helped devour sinners by beating them to a pulp, boiling them, or slicing them up with saws.

To the medieval imagination, the devil was real and could—with the help of his demons—be found prowling around everywhere. Common opinion had it that Satan was a great admirer of women, so that he often used their smiles and feminine wiles to lure poor innocent men. Some lonely women even helped the belief out: one Frenchwoman admitted that she frequently slept with satan and through his efforts had given birth to a monster with a wolf's head and serpent's tail. This pervading demonology included a less serious side as well. People saw some demons as light-hearted mischiefmakers—tearing clothes, producing holes in garments, spoiling food, or throwing up dirt on people who were walking.

Charlemagne and Alcuin—as did many other well-educated people—discouraged superstition, and regarded as heretical too strong an emphasis on images, icons, and relics. Nevertheless, by the eleventh century some churches and monasteries were participating in a craze for locating saints' remnants. They were supported in this by popular enthusiasm. A church which could boast of having saintly bits and pieces could bring lavish gifts and insure a prosperous future for itself. For instance, St. Peter's Basilica claimed to have the bodies of Peter and Paul. Another said it had pieces of the real cross of Jesus along with his cradle. Still another had the original stone tablets used for the Ten Commandments. And yet another enshrined the head of John the Baptist in a silver cup.

Some relics were authentic, but the craze continued to grow to ridiculous proportions: three different churches claimed to have the corpse of Mary Magdalen and five churches in France said they held the one true relic of Christ's circumcision. Bodies of saints were exhumed and dismembered so several churches or abbeys might house their remains and become more famous and powerful. By the thirteenth century church officials were able to put a stop to the more excessive of these practices. The ideal of Christian perfection remained one of the driving forces in life, as the lives of Guibert, Abelard, and Heloise illustrate. In the remainder of this chapter, we will see some of the basic strengths and fundamental problems of medieval life.

Guibert of Nogent (c. 1064-c. 1128)

By studying Guibert, we can get insight into the education, training, and formation of a medieval personality. Patterned after Augustine's *Confessions,* Guibert wrote his life story in three short books: his early years, his life as a monk, and his years as an abbot. His critical self-analysis reveals the usual type and level of consciousness existing in the twelfth century—so much so that French historian LeFranc has called him "practically a modern man."[14]

Guibert was so preoccupied with introspection and self-analysis that he failed to regard certain pieces of information readily available in the usual autobiography such as place and date of birth and parental lineage. It is likely, however, that he came from minor nobility—vassals—in the village of Clermont about thirty-five miles north of Paris. His parents were betrothed to each other while they were still young teenagers. They had difficulty in consummating their marriage due to what they considered to be a hex (bewitchment) placed by a jealous old woman.

Guibert's mother had learned to be "terrified of sin, not from experience, but from the dread of some sort of blow from on high, and . . . this dread had possessed her mind with the terror of sudden death."[15] The young and inexperienced husband was not able to break this spell of fear until he had conceived a child with another woman. In the meantime neighbors tried to seduce the bride, but to no avail. Guibert may have been his parents' third child, at any rate he was their last. The labor was so long and difficult that, according to our pious author, his father dedicated the life of his unborn child to God. The infant, though premature and unusually small, finally arrived and his mother's life was spared. However, the boy was made to feel that his life almost caused his mother's death.

Guibert's father died, probably in battle, when his young son was eight months old. Guibert's mother hired nurses to care for his physical needs while she molded his character. Guibert saw himself as his mother's favorite child, while a brother "earned his punishment in hell."[16] He thought of his mother as beautiful, proud, kind, intelligent, pure, virtuous, chaste, and strong-willed. But he also remembered her as self-centered, cruel, and hard. These ambivalent feelings can best be understood through the next series of events in his life.

Since Guibert was destined for the life of a cleric, chivalry and knighthood were not areas for him to learn. Consequently, when he was four or five his mother hired a tutor for him. This tutor seems to have been a surrogate father who, in turn, played the part with a "harsh love." Longer on anger than knowledge, he often subjected Guibert to brutal beatings for not knowing the things he as tutor could not teach. From the ages of six to twelve Guibert—at least according to his adult memory—never played, had no friends, never left the company of this tutor, or had a holiday. "In everything," he wrote, "I had to show self-control in word, look, and deed."[17]

After one particularly severe beating from the tutor, Guibert's mother removed his shirt to see the welts and bruises. Intensely distressed at the sight, she gave him the chance to renounce the life of a cleric for knighthood, but he refused. During this period he developed a repressive guilt over all bodily habits. Such treatment shows itself in his later writings when he goes out of his way to tell stories pertaining to loss of bodily and sensual control.

When Guibert was about twelve or thirteen, his mother withdrew into a nearby nunnery at St. Germer. Catching himself up in a similar elation, the tutor also entered a monastery. Having no sense of direction and feeling totally rejected, Guibert became "rowdy." However, upon hearing of the boy's debauchery, his mother paid the abbot at St. Germer to take him in. This done, Guibert settled into a life of an oblate—a stage that did not presuppose he would join for life. (An oblate was one who lived in a monastery but took no irrevocable vows until he or she was mature enough to make a choice for or against a cloistered life.) Shortly after, however, he decided to enter the novitiate against his mother's wishes. Apparently she had decided he was too young to take such a permanent step.

Guibert remained at the abbey under his mother's watchful eye for the next twenty-five years. During this period he wrote of his bouts with insanity: the vivid nightmares he experienced only to awaken and see the devil standing over him; his screaming fits over these hallucinations, which ended only when someone would come in and keep him from going crazy; his confessions to his mother of the difficulty he was having in repressing evil (sex-related) thoughts. Since uncontrolled visions and terror are common in contemporary personality disorders, we may well wonder how frequently the medieval mind suffered from such hallucinations.

In 1103-1104, fearing that he was amounting to nothing, various family members tried (unsuccessfully) to buy Guibert an abbacy (such bribery known as simony). At about the same time, members of the new and small abbey of Nogent heard of his good works. They offered the position of abbot to him. He accepted and, for the first time in his life, Guibert left the control of his mother who died two years later.

Guibert has been remembered for his piety and for his written works. Besides his memoirs, he wrote accounts of the first crusade and the bourgeois rebellions in twelfth century France. But his memoirs are illuminating from our standpoint, because they reveal an often tormented personality suffering from guilt over the inability to control and deny sensual fantasies, and in keeping with Jaynes' notion, Guibert's account may also suggest an evolutionary step in the making of the psyche.

A NEW KIND OF MASTER

Neither monastic nor cathedral schools made the clear distinction that the Romans had done between the kind of instruction given in the ludus and that of the grammar school—what we differentiate as elementary and secondary. Children typically learned to read in a psalter (a collection of all or some of the psalms). In aristocratic families, mothers often taught their offspring the alphabet and how to read before sending them to school. At school children expanded their vocabularies through glossaries, which could be either vernacular/Latin or Greek/Latin. They also practiced religious chant, finger computation, and writing skills. Nearly all schools also taught spelling, grammar, poetry, and prose writing. Logic (dialectics), rhetoric, arithmetic, geometry, and astronomy (mixed with astrology) were offered too, but not all teachers were competent in these subjects. After the ninth century music also became much more specialized.[18]

The example of Guibert's tutor offers some insight into teaching methods, though it is difficult to know how typical he was. Certainly masters resorted to the rod to get their pupils to penetrate the "thickets of the grammatical wilderness." One of Alcuin's contemporaries counseled teachers, probably with no more effect than Quintilian had done six centuries earlier, to: "Act with moderation and do not birch them, or they will return to their beastliness after correction. A master who, in his anger, reprimands a child beyond measure should be pacified and corrected. Strong-arm methods may render a child naughtier than ever."[19]

The general atmosphere encouraged docility. One did not challenge the teacher's knowledge or interpretation: "Be on guard against giving credence to your own discoveries rather than to the examples of your master," was the advice of one monk. "The more one defends his own curiosity, the more he finds himself in error."[20]

The monastic ideal stressed teaching as a Christian duty, rather than to gain money or notoriety. The lure of fame and fortune, however, was too much for some people to resist. The example of men like Gerbert of Aurillac must have spurred the imagination of the ambitious. Born to a poor family in south central France at the end of the ninth century, he attended the local monastic school. He became a noted teacher of music, mathematics, and logic at Rheims. Scholars flocked to him from France, Italy, Germany, and Britain. Ultimately he became archbishop of Ravenna and indeed closed his remarkable career as Pope Sylvester II.[21] Every poor lad in France must have been heartened by Gerbert's success. Certainly the life of Peter Abelard illustrates the emergence of ambitious professional teachers—a prerequisite to the development of universities.

Peter Abelard (1079-1142)

Most of what we know about Peter Abelard's life and his love affair with the attractive and intelligent Heloise (or Eloise) comes from Abelard himself. In 1132 he wrote a long essay/letter entitled *The Story of My Misfortunes*. Addressed to "a friend," this essay is really an autobiography. Characterized by a rather bitter, egotistical, and arrogant tone, it gives an account of his turbulent life to that point. Some historians have dismissed him as well as his academic and religious accomplishments. According to the Danish historian Leif Grane, however, there is evidence to corroborate much of what Abelard claimed. And, if we remember that: (1) the last decade of his life to that time had been sheer misery from any standpoint; and (2) his letter had been only intended for the eyes of a friend who could comfort him in his despair, we can perhaps forgive some of his egotism.[22]

EARLY LIFE

Abelard said that he became interested in pursuing an academic life as a young teenager. His family lived in northeast France (Brittany) and was of such a social stature that, being the eldest of several boys, he was supposed to inherit his chivalrous father's estate and become a knight himself. But instead, he gave this up at about age fifteen, and headed for the Paris area where there were several masters known for their intellectual talents.

One of his first teachers was Roscelin, a notorious dialectician in the eyes of some church authorities. Upon leaving Roscelin, he apparently stopped in other towns. His journey to Paris, which was about 150 miles from his home, took him nearly six years. Upon his arrival in Paris around 1100, he no doubt went directly to the school at Notre Dame Cathedral. William of Champeaux, master of the school and archdeacon of the cathedral, had a reputation as an outstanding dialectician.

No sooner had William noticed his new pupil's keen mind than he fell victim to it. It was customary for young scholars to show deference—almost reverence—to their masters. They were even supposed to respect scholars who were older and had studied longer than themselves. But our young clerk pursued his love for logic so passionately that he had no time for such rituals. He soon demonstrated his intellectual prowess by successfully refuting some of William's statements. In defeating the teacher, however, he also crushed the disciples, consequently incurring their wrath. "Out of this," says Abelard, "sprang the beginning of my misfortunes, which have followed me even to the present day [1132]; the more widely my fame was spread abroad, the more bitter was the envy that kindled against me."[23]

The dialectical or logical discrepancy which led to William's downfall stemmed from a difference in perspective between master and scholar. William's lectures were concerned with the nature of life and its relationship to after-life or life beyond our awareness. Based on Platonic assumptions, William argued that words such as "man," "tree," "animal," had a "universal" or "real" meaning beyond our sensory awareness and understanding of them. Believers in universal or other world "things" would be called "idealists" today, but then they were called "naive realists." They hoped to logically demonstrate that universals were more real than particular men, trees, or animals. Of course, if one could logically and semantically prove the existence of the universal "God," then one's scholarly reputation was greatly enhanced. And if one could demonstrate the logical connection between worldly things and their universal equivalents—say, for example, men and God—it was all the better. This latter connection was, in essence, what William was trying to do when Abelard mercilessly showed him the error in his logic.

Abelard did not see the linguistic validity of his master's defense of universals. Aristotelian thinking was just coming into vogue, and Abelard advanced the notion that dialectics was confined to linguistic logic or the science of words and word meanings, whereas study involving "things"—worldly or otherworldly—was physics or metaphysics, not dialectics. William did not make this distinction. He admitted defeat and ceased to teach dialectics. Peter could not understand why. Probably the fact that Abelard had embarrassed William in front of a large crowd may have affected William's decision as well. In any case, the brash young scholar gained a following and decided to open his own school. William, as archdeacon, prevented it from happening in Paris, so Peter was forced to move to a town close to the city.

BEGINNING A TEACHING CAREER

To Abelard, the archdeacon's behavior was the result of his envy and jealousy, but there may have been more to it than that. A custom reinforced by canon law encouraged masters to receive permissions (licenses) to teach. These came from bishops, but in larger towns they often delegated this authority to a chancellor or scholasticus. Sometimes this official licensed masters to handle the various arts, reserving theology for himself. In theory anyone who taught in the diocese—whether at the cathedral or in a rented room—needed the chancellor's approval.[24] And it was not uncommon for these "permissions" to be purchased from the official, hence giving the chancellor or scholasticus power and profit.

It had also become the unwritten custom, and an essential piece of scholarly etiquette, for established masters to approvingly receive new teachers into the fold through a ceremony known as *inception.* This only occurred after an adequate period of study and an initial lecture given under the watchful eye of the master. The headstrong Abelard followed neither of these rituals when he opened his school. But for the time being it did not matter: Shortly after he began his teaching, Abelard "was smitten with a grievous illness, brought upon me by my immediate zeal for study." He returned home to Brittany to convalesce for several years.

By the time Peter Abelard returned to Paris (1108), William had left Notre Dame for the Abbey of St. Victor and the life of a monk. He continued giving public lectures, but in rhetoric, not dialectics. Abelard tells us, "To him did I return, for I was eager to learn more of rhetoric from his lips; and in the course of our many arguments on various matters, I compelled him by most potent reasoning first to alter his former opinion on the subject of universals and finally abandon it altogether."

We may well suspect Abelard's reason for returning to harangue his former master. In all probability the thought of another victory, and hence more fame, had something to do with his motives. In any event, William abandoned lecturing as a career and Abelard's fame increased. In fact, William's replacement at Notre Dame gave up his position to Abelard and voluntarily became his student. Peter's victory was shortlived, though. William successfully plotted the removal of this new teacher and replaced with him a professor who did not feel compelled to turn over the teaching to Abelard.[25] According to Abelard, William could not long, in truth, bear the anguish of what he felt to be his wrongs, and shrewdly he attacked me that he might drive me forth. And because there was nought in my conduct whereby he could come at me openly, he tried to steal away the school by launching the vilest calumnies against him who had yielded his post to me, and by putting in his place a certain rival of mine. So then I returned to Melun, and set up my school there as before; and the more openly his envy pursued me, the greater was the authority it conferred upon me.

Not long after, William took his monastic brotherhood away from the city to live a more perfect ascetic life. This signaled Abelard's return, and he quickly set about to ruin his new rival's school at Notre Dame. Upon hearing this, William returned to St. Victor to help defend his protégé, but to no avail. In fact, says Peter, "After our master returned . . . [the new master] lost nearly all of his followers and thus was compelled to give up the direction of the school."

FURTHER STUDY

Left with no significant rival, Abelard was probably ready to reap the fruits of victory when a family incident called him home. All of the children were now grown, so Abelard's parents had decided to dissolve their home and enter monastic life. His father had already done so, and his mother wished to say farewell to her eldest son before following her husband. What influence the mother, Lucca [Lucia] had on Peter, we do not know; but instead of returning to Paris, he left for Bec in Laon to study the higher subject of theology with Bec's famous abbot, Anselm. Abelard tells us that his decision was affected by the news that William—who had been Anselm's student—had become bishop of Chalôns. Many other prominent people had also studied under Anselm who was noted as a theologian. Danish historian Leif Grane thinks that his mother's influence may have been a factor. She probably hoped that the study of theology under a famous master like Anselm might take her son to a bishop's chair.

Philosophically, Anselm agreed with the naive realists in preferring universals over particulars. He was a good speaker, but he was not a particularly adept logician. Therefore, it is not surprising that our aggressive scholar found him boring and easy to conquer. According to Peter, Anselm's lectures consisted of superficial interpretations of the Bible—in other words, according to Abelard, empty rhetoric based on faulty assumptions. "When he kindled a fire," says our author, "he filled his room with smoke, but did not light it up."[26] Consequently, Abelard quit attending the lectures. This riled Anselm's disciples who sarcastically asked Abelard if he thought that he could interpret the Holy Writ. He said he could, and invited the challengers to his lecture on Ezekiel the following day. Ezekiel was considered to be the most difficult of all books in the Bible, and even Anselm's followers thought he needed more time, but Peter replied, "it was not my custom to advance through practice but through talent."[27] He was so entertaining that the students asked for more. Once again he was collecting pupils. Anselm (supported by his two devout followers, Alberic of Rheims and Lotulf of Novara) forbade Abelard to give any more lectures, so he left Laon and returned to Paris. A dejected Anselm died shortly thereafter.

Alberic and Lotulf preferred charges against Abelard for delivering these lectures, not because he had no license, but because he had begun teaching "without a master." Apparently, the theology lectures were viewed as his inception into the guild (association) of masters, an act which presupposed his own master's approval.[28]

This breach of etiquette did not hinder Abelard's appointment as *magister scholarum* or head master at Notre Dame—the position he had long desired. Such an appointment brought him security, because it meant that he became an irregular cannon subject to church authority. (An irregular canon was a member of the brotherhood but took no vows and wore no clerical garb with its respective hair style or tonsure. Such rights were reserved for the regular clergy.) For the next couple of years Notre Dame gathered an unprecedented number of scholars who came to study under the renowned Abelard. During this period the Isle of Notre Dame became known as the Latin quarter, because all of the students spoke and studied in Latin. Peter Abelard had no effective rivals, a condition that was probably boring for him. He turned his attentions elsewhere.

Heloise [Eloise] (c. 1100-1164)

Looking back on his life, Abelard admitted that all this fame and fortune had left him arrogant, and he searched for new conquests. Such a personal victory he found in the niece of one of his canonical brothers, Fulbert. Here is how Abelard tells it:

Now there dwelt in that same city of Paris a certain young girl named Heloise, the niece of a canon who was called Fulbert. Her uncle's love for her was equalled only by his desire that she should have the best education which he could possibly procure for her. Of no mean beauty, she stood out above all by reason of her abundant knowledge of letters. Now this virtue is rare among women, and for that very reason it doubly graced the maiden, and made her the most worthy of renown in the entire kingdom. It was this young girl whom I, after carefully considering all those qualities which are wont to attract lovers, determined to unite with myself in the bonds of love, and indeed the thing seemed to me very easy to be done. So distinguished was my name, and I possessed such advantages of youth and comeliness, that no matter what woman I might favour with my love, I dreaded rejection of none. . . .

Thus, utterly aflame with my passion for this maiden, I sought to discover means whereby I might have daily and familiar speech with her, thereby the more easily to win her consent. For this purpose I persuaded the girl's uncle, with the aid of some of his friends, to take me into his household—for he dwelt hard [close] by my school—in return for the payment of a small sum. My pretext for this was that the care of my own household was a serious handicap to my studies, and likewise burdened me with an expense far greater than I could afford. Now, he was a man keen in avarice, and likewise he was most desirous for his niece that her study of letters should ever go forward, so, for these two reasons, I easily won his consent to the fulfillment of my wish, for he was fairly agape for my money, and at the same time believed that his niece would vastly benefit by my teaching. More even than this, by his own earnest entreaties he fell in with my desires beyond anything I had dared to hope, opening the way for my love; for he entrusted her wholly to my guidance, begging me to give her instruction whensoever I might be free from the duties of my school, no matter whether by day or by night, and to punish her sternly if ever I should find her negligent of her tasks. In all this the man's simplicity was nothing short of astounding to me; I should not have been more smitten with wonder if he had entrusted a tender lamb to the care of a ravenous wolf. . . . There were, however, two things which particularly served to allay any foul suspicion: his own love for his niece, and my former reputation for continence.

Why should I say more? We were united first in the dwelling that sheltered our love, and then in the hearts that burned with it. Under the pretext of study we spent our hours in the happiness of love. . . . What followed? No degree in love's progress was left untried by our passion, and if love itself could imagine any wonder as yet unknown, we discovered it. And our inexperience of such delights made us all the more ardent in our pursuit of them, so that our thirst for one another was still unquenched.

In measure as this passionate rapture absorbed me more and more, I devoted ever less time to philosophy and to the work of the school. Indeed it became loathsome to me to go to the school or to linger there; the labour, moreover, was very burdensome, since my nights were vigils of love and my days of study. My lecturing became utterly careless and lukewarm; I did nothing because of inspiration, but everything merely as a matter of habit. I had become nothing more than a reciter of my former discoveries, and though I still wrote poems, they dealt with love, not with the secrets of philosophy. Of these songs you yourself well know how some have become widely known and have been sung in many lands, chiefly, methinks by those who delighted in the things of this world. As for the sorrow, the groans, the lamentations of my students when they perceived the preoccupation, nay, rather the chaos, of my mind, it is hard even to imagine them.

But finally Fulbert discovered the lovers:

Oh, how great was the uncle's grief when he learned the truth, and how bitter was the sorrow of the lovers when we were forced to part! With what shame was I overwhelmed, with what contrition smitten because of the blow which had fallen on her I loved, and what a tempest of misery burst over her by reason of my disgrace! Each grieved most, not for himself, but for the other. Each sought to allay, not his own sufferings, but those of the one he loved. The very sundering of our bodies served but to link our souls closer together; the plentitude of the love which was denied to us inflamed us more than ever. Once the first wildness of shame had passed, it left us more shameless than before, and as shame died within us the cause of it seemed to us ever more desirable. . . . According-ly, on a night when her uncle was absent, we carried out the plan we had determined on, and I stole her secretly away from her uncle's house, sending her without delay to my own country. She remained there with my sister until she gave birth to a son, whom she named Astrolabe. Meanwhile her uncle, after his return, was almost mad with grief; only one who had then seen him could rightly guess the burning agony of his sorrow and the bitterness of his shame. What steps to take against me, or what snares to set for me, he did not know. If he should kill me or do me some bodily hurt, he feared greatly lest his dear-loved niece should be made to suffer for it among my kinsfolk. He had no power to seize me and imprison me somewhere against my will, though I make no doubt he would have done so quickly enough had he been able or dared, for I had taken measures to guard against any such attempt.

At length, however, in pity for his boundless grief, and bitterly blaming myself for the suffering which my love had brought upon him through the baseness of the deception I had practiced, I went to him to entreat his forgiveness, promising to make any amends that he himself might decree. I pointed out that what had happened could not seem incredible to any one who had ever felt the power of love, or who remembered how, from the very beginning of the human race, women had cast down even the noblest men to utter ruin. And in order to make amends even beyond his extremest hope, I offered to marry her whom I had seduced, provided only the thing could be kept secret, so that I might suffer no loss of reputation thereby. To this he gladly assented, pledging his own faith and that of his kindred, and sealing with kisses the pact which I had sought of him—and all this that he might the more easily betray me.

Abelard then left for his sister's house to bring Heloise back in order to marry her. But, according to Abelard, his mistress wanted no part of marriage. First of all, she said that she did not believe that her uncle would be appeased; and second, that it would bring disgrace upon him in his clerical career. She quoted passages from the Bible which scorned marriage. She reminded him of the warnings against marriage given by various church fathers. And finally, she offered Cicero who said that he "could not devote himself to a wife and to philosophy at the same time." Her arguments were to no avail; Abelard could not be swayed. Tearfully she consented, but only on the condition that the marriage be kept a secret among her uncle and a few close relatives.

MARRIAGE

After the marriage, Heloise returned to her uncle's house, and Abelard re-sumed teaching as if nothing had transpired. Doubtless his students were still singing his love songs, for Heloise tells us that "all streets, every house, echoed with my name."[29] But all of this was just too much disgrace for Fulbert who told everyone around that his niece was married to Abelard. His tattling only added to his indignity, however, because Heloise vehemently denied her uncle's assertions. Fulbert was furious. Abelard continues the story:

> Her uncle visited her repeatedly with punishments. No sooner had I learned this than I sent her to a convent of nuns at Argenteuil, not far from Paris, where she herself had been brought up and educated as a young girl. I had them make ready for her all the garments of a nun, suitable for the life of a convent excepting only the veil, and these I bade her put on.
>
> When her uncle and his kinsmen heard of this, they were convinced that now I had completely played them false and had rid myself forever of Heloise by forcing her to become a nun. Violently incensed, they laid a plot against me, and one night, while I, all unsuspecting, was asleep in a secret room in my lodgings, they broke in with the help of one of my servants, whom they had bribed. There they had vengeance on me with a most cruel and most shameful punishment, such as astounded the whole world, for they cut off those parts of my body with which I had done that which was the cause of their sorrow. This done, straightway they fled, but two of them were captured, and suffered the loss of their eyes and the genital organs. One of these two was the aforesaid servant, who, even while he was still in my service, had been led by his avarice to betray me.

Abelard was convinced that his physical disablement was deserved punishment for his lusty sins. He felt utterly disgraced, however, and decided to seek refuge in the monastery of St. Denis in Paris. He also told Heloise to take the vows of the Argenteuil sisterhood. The young bride grieved much at this situation, feeling that if she had remained his mistress, none of this would have been necessary. She said that she was not smitten with convent life and weepingly took her vows only because Abelard commanded her to do so.

The situation was a tragedy of errors, but if we remember the time period in which it took place, we can view it more clearly. First of all, for a *magister scholarum* to be married would have been unusual, but for him to have a mistress would have been a more common practice. Moreover, while having a mistress would not help his ambitions to become a bishop, it would not be an automatic bar to high clerical office as marriage would be. Heloise's desire to remain his mistress was motivated by the same wish to keep the marriage secret. Elizabeth Hamilton agrees, on the other hand, that Abelard kept control over his possessive love for her by marrying her and committing her to a nunnery after his physical disability. In this way she could never remarry. And Heloise freely and shamelessly admitted that she would have done whatever Abelard asked, since she regarded him as more her master than God.

On the other hand, Leif Grane gives another vantage point from which to view their circumstances. He thinks that Abelard was caught between two passions—his love of teaching and his love for Heloise. Yet he made her "so much the central figure of his life that apparently without hesitation he discarded everything he had won in the world of learning."[30] Also, while Heloise's love seems much more altruistic and selfless than Peter's we should remember that she did not need to fear losing him to someone else (after his incapacity) as he did her.

ABELARD AS MONK

At St. Denis, Abelard felt no hesitation in judging his companions against the highest standards. With his own sexual passions unexpectedly removed, he commenced to make his life truly devoted to God. Unfortunately, he saw decadence and impiety among his monastic brothers who cared little for his sermonizing. They did, however, like the attention his students brought (it did not take them long to track down their teacher). They pestered him to resume his lecturing, and St. Denis complied by providing rooms and less than adequate quarters for his disciples.

During this time Abelard completed a book on theology, only to have it condemned by officials who had been successfully persuaded by Anselm's heirs, Alberic and Lotulf. Not only was Abelard forced to burn his own book—a fate which he said hurt him more than his previous physical wounds because it was the only copy—but he was also briefly imprisoned. Upon his return to St. Denis (c. 1122), he asked if he could take leave of the abbey so long as he never took other monastic vows. Eventually, permission was granted.

Tired of people and conflict, Abelard's plan was to seek solace in nature. He erected a small reed and straw chapel on a piece of ground presented to him by the nearby bishop. This chapel was 75-100 miles southeast of Paris. Abelard called it the Paraclete (Comforter). Again, it did not take long (1123) for his students to catch up with him, and soon his chapel was surrounded by hut type domiciles. Abelard found himself teaching and writing again. From 1124 to 1126 the students cultivated fields and built a large complex of stone and wood buildings. Their devotion gave Peter Abelard renewed vigor, while it only supplied his enemies with the desire to defeat him once and for all. He said that he lived in constant fear of being dragged up before some council and branded a heretic.

ABELARD AS ABBOT

A desire to escape his enemies led Abelard to accept the offer from St. Gildas in Brittany to be their abbot. His ambition for high office probably entered into the decision as well. But this was tantamount to going from the frying pan into the fire. Abelard tells us:

> The land was barbarous and its speech was unknown to me; as for the monks, their vile and untameable way of life was notorious almost everywhere. The people of the region, too, were uncivilized and lawless. Thus, like one who in terror of the sword that threatens him dashes headlong over a precipice, and to shun one death for a moment rushes to another, I knowingly sought this new danger in order to escape from the former one. I held it for certain that if I should try to force them to live according to the principles they had themselves professed, I should not survive. And yet, if I did not do this to the utmost of my ability, I saw that my damnation was assured. Moreover, a certain lord who was exceedingly powerful in that region had some time previously brought the abbey under his control, taking advantage of the state of disorder within the monastery to seize

all the lands adjacent thereto for his own use, and he ground down the monks with taxes heavier than those which were extorted from the Jews themselves.

The monks pressed me to supply them with their daily necessities, but they held no property in common which I might administer in their behalf, and each one, with such resources as he possessed, supported himself and his concubines, as well as his sons and daughters. They took delight in harassing me on this matter, and they stole and carried off whatsoever they sould lay their hands on, to give up trying to enforce discipline or else abandon my post altogether. Since the entire region was equally savage, lawless and disorganized, there was not a single man to whom I could turn for aid, for the habits of all alike were foreign to me. Outside the monastery the lord and his henchmen ceaselessly hounded me, and within its walls the brethren were forever plotting against me. . . .

Oh, how often have they tried to kill me with poison, even as the monks sought to slay St. Benedict! . . . When I had safeguarded myself to the best of my ability, so far as my food and drink were concerned, . . . they sought to destroy me in the very ceremony of the altar by putting poison in the chalice. One day, when I had gone to Nantes to visit the count, who was then sick, and while I was sojourning awhile in the house of one of my brothers in the flesh, they arranged to poison me, with the connivance of one of my attendants, believing that I would take no precautions to escape such a plot. But divine providence so ordered matters that I had no desire for the food which was set before me; one of the monks whom I had brought with me ate thereof, not knowing that which had been done, and straightway fell dead. As for the attendant who had dared to undertake this crime, he fled in terror alike of his own conscience and of the clear evidence of his guilt.

After this, as their wickedness was manifest to every one, I began openly in every way I could to avoid the danger with which their plots threatened me, even to the extent of leaving the abbey and dwelling with a few others apart in little cells. If the monks knew beforehand that I was going anywhere on a journey, they bribed bandits to waylay me on the road and kill me. And while I was struggling in the midst of these dangers, it chanced one day that the hand of the Lord smote me a heavy blow, for I fell from my horse, breaking a bone in my neck, the injury causing me greater pain and weakness than my former wound.

HELOISE AS ABBESS

In the meantime, Heloise, who had become abbess at Argenteuil, was threatened with eviction for herself and her sisters. The abbot at St. Denis found that he could lay claim to the convent and requested the nuns to leave. Upon hearing of this plight, Abelard offered the Paraclete to the sisters who eagerly accepted and asked for his assistance. For a brief time Abelard preached to and helped the nuns. He even envisioned ending his life there near his wife, serving them as their spiritual advisor and preacher. But all too soon the rumors concerning his earlier love affair with Heloise started up again. Unable to quiet these suspicions, he returned to his unruly monastery at St. Gildas. It was during this return that he wrote the autobiographical essay/letter quoted above. He said that he hoped death would soon end his misery.

We know from Heloise's correspondence that his letter eventually found its way to her. It may in fact have been intended for her. She then resumed communication with him, lamenting that after thirteen years she had not changed her feelings at all and that her life was still devoted to and dependent upon Abelard: "For you are the only one capable of bringing me sorrow and joy, or of rendering me consolation."[31] She called herself a hypocrite, because her vows had meant little to her. Instead of lamenting their shameful affair, she confessed that she could only sigh at what she had lost. Finally she begged him to at least respond to her letter and provide his Paraclete with guidance. He did return her letter. He said that life was undoubtedly harder for her now because she was not free of her passion as he was. But he admonished her to see him as a brother, more than a lover, and in this way they could renew their love in Christ who had "shown them His mercy."

They continued to correspond. Heloise asked him to complete a set of rules for her sisters to follow. She also wanted him to compose some new poems, because many of the current ones were impossible to put to music. These requests, once again, renewed Abelard's energies, and he involved himself totally in their fulfillment.

ABELARD'S LAST DAYS

By 1141 circumstances took another turn for the worse as he again came under judicial condemnation for his theological works. One of his enemies, a conservative monk named Bernard of Clairvaux, had launched a vendetta against Abelard and, being close to the pope, was quite successful in his attack. Convinced of his innocence, Abelard set out for Rome to redeem himself. Fortunately for Abeland, Peter the Venerable, abbot of Cluny, intervened on his behalf. He could have had no better or more powerful ally. Cluny was the largest and wealthiest monastery in Europe, and its abbot at that time enjoyed power equal to that of papacy. The final result was that Abelard was vindicated and allowed to spend his last years in the reverent peace and quiet of Cluny's main establishment.

He died while studying. His last notes revealed that he was hardly a broken man. He considered himself to be "the greatest master of his time whose legitimate reputation neither envy nor persecution has been able to assail." Peter the Venerable wrote to Heloise after Abelard's death and arranged to have his body removed to her convent in order to fulfill a request which Abelard had made to Heloise earlier. An interesting part of his letter pointed to a totally different Abelard during his Cluny stay: "I remember having seen no person to compare with him in humility, both as to habit and behaviour. . . . And although, because I wished it, he occupied a high rank among the great host of our brothers, one would be forced, upon seeing his miserable clothing, to believe him the most inferior of all."[32] The abbot continued by telling how Abelard was content with the least possible of all things; he spent his time reading and praying, and only spoke when he was asked to preach to the brothers or to instruct them in their reading.

Heloise died twenty years later and at her request was buried with Abelard. Unfortunately, we have no way of knowing if she ever found peace and comfort in her last years. (In the letter that Peter the Venerable wrote to Heloise, he commented that he had long heard her praises sung as abbess. So perhaps she did find the inner peace and piety that Abelard wanted for her.) As for Abelard, his reputation and writing lingered on through his students and theirs. He singularly influenced the intellectual climate that led to the birth of the universities and a more enlightened study of theology. Though his immodesties overshadowed his intellectual accomplishments in future historical accounts, it seems safe to say that many of his self-evaluations were more accurate than arrogant.

Euphemia of Wherwell (before 1200-1257)

Before leaving this chapter, which has stressed the monastic contributions to Western learning, a brief discussion of medieval women's education is in order. We know that there were women's monasteries at least as early as the fifth century, but no comprehensive history of female religious orders exists. We have enough isolated accounts to know that they were widespread and numerous. ("In what is called the modern world their numbers and the variety of their rules and occupations have exceeded those of all the monks and orders of men put together.")[33] They provide the only academic instruction available to women on a systematic basis, other than tutors, for over a thousand years.

Not only did women's monastic houses provide internal and external schools just as did those for males, they also furnished opportunities for women to become agriculturists, business managers, teachers, physicians, scholars, and administrators. The career of Euphemia, abbess of the monastery of Wherwell near the south central coast of England, serves as an example of monastic education for women.

We know little of Euphemia's life before she became abbess of Wherwell in 1226. She was a member of the convent and may have been a friend of the preceeding abbess, a woman named Maud who had been in charge for forty years. The abbey owned five villages and other property. Euphemia spent thirty-one years effectively administering the monastery. Under her care, the number of the "Lord's handmaidens" increased from forty to eighty women.

Euphemia affected numerous repairs and additions to the physical plant. They included a new and large infirmary "away from the main buildings." Under the infirmary dormitory, she had constructed "a watercourse, through which a stream flowed with sufficient force to carry off all refuse that corrupt the air." She also had a chapel built for the infirmary along with a large enclosed garden. She tore down and rebuilt the presbytery of the church, and replaced the bell tower over the dormitory when the old one fell down one night. She moved and enlarged the barnyard area because the "amount of animal refuse was a cause of offense to both the feet and nostrils of those who had occasion to pass through." She also built a wall around the court area and "round it she made gardens and vineyards and shrubberies in places that were formerly useless and which now became both serviceable and pleasant."

Not only did Mother Euphemia renovate the monastery itself, she also rebuilt manor houses and farm houses in two of the five villages. She increased the mill capacity of the monastery. As her biographer said of her, she "so conducted herself with regard to exterior business affairs, that she seemed to have the spirit of a man rather a woman."[34] The lessons of practical administration acquired by thousands of abesses in the medieval period cannot have been lost on the cumulative experience of women's education.

By the eleventh century western Europe was quite different from the way it had been when Benedict started his monastery at Monte Cassino. Villages dotted the landscape where none had existed before. Some of these had already developed into cities. Before 1100 it would have been difficult to find more than 3,000 people in any town north of the Alps. By 1200 Paris had grown to 100,000 and the villages of Douai, Lille, Ypres, Ghent, and Bruges each had increased to 50,000 souls. Forests were cleared, swamps drained, and prairie put into cultivation. What had been a barbarian, tribal frontier was populated by folk who were at least partially Romanized and nominally Christian. The success of the monks had laid the foundation for the next stage of European development.

FROM MONASTERY TO UNIVERSITY

In the dynamic period from the tenth century to the Black Death (1379), much of the organizational structure of the modern world began to emerge. Educationally this included the development of universities. The increasingly urban and complex nature of the social order determined much of what happened. The growth of cities either produced or acted as a catalyst for several changes: (1) a growing bourgeoisie (merchant class) vying with older power groups for access to political privilege and education; (2) the revival of guilds to represent the interests of merchants and artisans; (3) the emergence of monastic orders rooted in the urban poor rather than in the agricultural wealth of rural areas; (4) an increasing need for legal knowledge to settle conflicts; (5) the application of logic to religious tradition as a way of reconciling inherited traditions with changing conditions; and (6) a renewed interest in Greek and Roman traditions as a tool for legitimizing a variety of interests. Each of these points requires a brief explanation.

We have already seen that cities declined as the Roman Empire was overrun by Germanic invaders. Rome in fact became a shadow of its former self. The area north and west of the Alps was a frontier yielding slowly to the civilizing force of the monastic establishments. Villages developed along rivers, well-traveled roads, and especially in association with monasteries and castles. As these grew, shops became larger, trade increased, and merchants prospered. Some cities began to issue money and other negotiable instruments to make transactions easier.

In most cases villages were under the jurisdiction of either a monastery or a local noble on whose land they were located. Sometimes both a baron or duke and an abbot or abbess claimed authority and disputed rents and other control privileges. Of course bishops and archbishops tended to locate their headquarters in the more important cities, thus introducing another claim to authority and source of conflict. Some of these officials were ambitious and struggled for authority with abbots, dukes, kings, and sometimes with the papacy itself. Political and military power traditionally rested on land ownership and was, therefore, ultimately rural. The growth of urban centers, and a monied economy, offered an increasingly significant counterbalance to this tradition. From the tenth to thirteenth centuries many towns and cities tried to become independent of traditional control.

One of the most successful devices for gaining autonomy came in the form of charters or other grants of privilege from nobles or church officials who needed money. Merchants lent the money in return for assurances of independence. In other cases citizens resorted to armed revolt. Sometimes this was successful and sometimes not. Guibert of Nogent, whose life we noted in this chapter, has left a graphic account of what happened at Laon (France) when the bishop tried to suppress the newly formed "commune" (citizens' organization). This was in 1115:

> On the fifth day of Easter week ... there arose a disorderly noise throughout the city, men shouting "Commune!" ... Citizens now entered the bishop's court with swords, battle-axes, bows, hatchets, clubs, and spears. ... The nobles rallied from all sides to the bishop. ... He hid himself in a cask ... and piteously implored them, promising that he would cease to be their bishop, would give them unlimited riches, and would leave the country. And as they with hardened hearts jeered at him, one named Bernard, lifting his battle-ax, brutally dashed out the brains of that sacred, though sinner's, head.[35]

The villagers burned the cathedral and went on a rampage of several days before a royal army crushed their revolt.

In their up and down struggles for independence and political power, the city dwellers found Roman legal and organizational patterns useful. Of particular value was the guild, an ancient Roman form of corporate association with a recognized history of legitimacy. These went under various names—*collegia, scholae, sodalitates, artes, universitae.* The leading merchants were the first to employ this approach, but crafts practioners quickly followed suit. Bankers, notaries, clothiers, wool merchants, physicians and druggists, silk dealers, furriers, tanners, innkeepers, armorers, and others formed themselves into collegia—the classical Roman term for religious associations. The primary intent of these organizations was to gain a monopoly on the trade with which they dealt, but they provided many incidental services: life insurance, schools for youth, burial. In the long run, political enfranchisement came through guild membership and even nobility found it necessary to be nominal members in order to participate in town politics.

Most guilds favored the children of existing members in their recruitment and admission procedures. Members joined through an apprenticeship system which culminated in an examination. Only those who satisfied existing masters of their skill could be admitted to mastership themselves. This process gave each guild a great deal of power. People who had not reached the final level could work only as day laborers for other masters.

We have noted extensive educational activity, beginning with the Summerians and continuing through the Greek, Roman, and Christian monastic traditions. But until about the eleventh century practitioners of the teacher's art had not associated with each other in any sort of legal corporation. In the twelfth century however, this issue became a matter of lively contest. The growth of cities and of guilds dealing with mercantile and craft interests encouraged liberal arts masters to form their own collegia. Paris, Oxford, and Bologna led the way.

PARISIAN DEVELOPMENTS

The rapid growth of Paris, its central location, and the reputations of people like William of Champeaux attracted young men from all over western Europe. Abelard is a good example of this phenomenon. His own notoriety, in turn, helped increase the flow of students.

The whole enterprise was informal and somewhat chaotic. Hundreds, eventually thousands, of teenagers—fourteen or fifteen was the average age—flocked to a booming city where many of them did not speak the native language. Latin was the medium of study and would do for most shopkeepers, but food and lodging were expensive and the possibilities for losing one's money and innocence were everywhere at hand. Wealthy families sent servants to aid their children and a number of religious orders bought or built monastic houses near the study centers to protect their young student members. Boys who did not belong to either of these groups had to get along as best they could. Girls did not go.

In general, landlords and merchants had the upper hand. Students had to have food, housing, and supplies. The guide for setting prices tended to be whatever the traffic would bear. But students were not ultimately helpless, because most sizeable towns wanted both the renown and the profit that came from being a center of study. So the threat of walking out to another location— if carried out en masse—acted as a partial counterbalance to the merchants' greed.

A Paris tavern riot in 1200 illustrates the point. Some German students were having a drink when the servant of one of them—the bishop-elect of Liège—got into a dispute with the bartender/owner who struck the servant. The students in turn beat up the inn-keeper and left. He called the provost of Paris (roughly superintendent of police) who led a band of armed citizens in an assault on a German student hostel. Several students were killed, including the bishop-elect. An appeal to the king for redress brought quick results, apparently because he feared the students might otherwise leave Paris. The citizens who had attacked the students were sentenced to life in prison. The provost broke his neck trying to escape from jail, but some of the townsmen got away. Their houses were burned. The king granted a charter to the students and their masters which: (1) guaranteed ecclesiastical rather than civil trial for any scholastics arrested for any cause; (2) required citizens to volunteer information against anyone they saw mistreating a student; and (3) mandated that future provosts upon taking office should appear at an assembly of scholars in a Paris church and swear to respect and protect scholastic privileges.

Student concerns were only one part of a complex picture. Another important factor was the rapidly increasing number of masters of arts who were competing with each other for pupils. Many of the young men who crowded into Paris preferred to stay upon completing their studies. For most, teaching was a natural way to earn a living. This led to an oversupply of masters, forcing down income and threatening established teachers. Common sense suggested two potential remedies. One was to slow down the rate at which new masters were being created. The other was to increase the supply of students by ensuring that no one could pursue the "higher" faculties of theology, law, or medicine without first spending several years studying the arts under an approved master. Both these solutions could best be carried out if masters incorporated themselves into guilds.

THE CORPORATION

The process of masters forming a corporation (*universitas*) happened in stages, starting in the closing decades of the twelfth century. By 1230 guilds of masters were firmly established at Paris, Oxford, Bologna, and some other places.

In Paris, the recently formed masters' corporation tried to limit the number of new masters by having the chancellor of the cathedral issue licenses to only those people whom they as a group approved. In 1210 they brought a suit in a papal court against the chancellor to this effect. Pope Innocent III sided with the masters. But the chancellor, in keeping with a long tradition of granting licenses to any applicant not guilty of heresy, paid no attention. Perhaps encouraged by the fees and gifts he received from each successful applicant, he saw no need to change custom.

This dispute dragged on for several years. Finally, in 1229 the masters were able to take advantage of an unrelated grievance. Some students had 'found sweet and good wine' in a suburban tavern, but when the bill arrived they said it was too high. Words led to blows. The bartender called in neighbors who helped him beat up the students and throw them out. They returned with reinforcements the next day, thrashed the inn keeper and set his taps running. He called on the provost, who brought an armed band of mercenary body guards—"the savage police of a savage city" as one historian refers to them. They killed several students. The masters called a cessation, and demanded reparations for the students. They also said they would not return until the chancellor started consulting them before licensing people.[36]

The strike lasted two years. It ended with a papal court limiting the powers of both bishop and chancellor in favor of the masters' universitas. This included recognition of the legality of cessation as a means of redressing grievances—an important concession in the guild's long range attempts to gain a monopoly over the control of all teaching.

MENDICANT COMPETITION

When the masters began to return to Paris in 1231, they discovered some people had not stopped teaching. Masters at several monasteries, especially of the recently formed Dominicans and Franciscans, were not concerned about fees. These groups had formed partly in protest to the Benedictine establishments like Cluny, which they viewed as too aristocratic and worldly. Dedicated to serving the poor and preaching the gospel, the mendicant (wandering) friars had early begun to acquire corporate property around the study centers like Paris and Oxford. They discouraged young members of their orders from studying with most masters, thinking them too worldly. Moreover, the friar doctors (from *docere,* to teach) were willing to offer theological instruction to people without regard to whether they had studied with or been approved by members of the masters' universitas.

Given these conditions, it is not surprising that the secular masters' guild regarded the "black friar" teachers as strike breakers and scabs—much as contemporary union members think of people who cross picket lines to work. Ultimately, the masters' corporation was able to compel the friar doctors to join the guild and honor the group's rules. This process, however, required several decades, and numerous legal suits and strikes in Paris, before it was accomplished. Oxford and other study centers witnessed similar conflicts with the same ultimate results.

Tensions between university masters and independent teachers continued in some cities for centuries. But a revolutionary change had occurred, as a four thousand year tradition gradually ended. From 3000 B.C. in Sumeria to the formation of masters' corporations, education had generally taken place in a free market atmosphere. Anyone could teach who had pupils, and students could leave one master or school for another, or study any subjects in any order according to their preferences. But as masters in the great study centers of Europe gained control over the licensing monopoly—today we call this graduation—the length, order, and level or mastery required in the curriculum were slowly standardized. In the nineteenth century, this kind of control was assumed by national governments and extended to pre university levels of schooling. By the 1960s some critics of educational arrangements were arguing for the laissez faire approach of earlier times.[37]

Thomas Aquinas (c. 1225-1274)

The most famous of the friar doctors to study or teach in Paris was a gentle monk named Thomas Aquinas. He was born about 1225 to a noble Italian clan in the family castle of Rocca Secca near Naples.

In that era parents frequently dedicated the youngest son to the church. So when Thomas was only five, his parents brought him to the Benedictine order of monks at the Abbey of Monte Cassino where he was to be an oblate. However, the young age at which parents surrendered their child to the influence of the members of a religious order would tend to facilitate his choice of a religious vocation.

Because of the position of the family, his parents hoped that their son would grow up to become abbot of Monte Cassino, an important political and religious post. Also, the Benedictine order was especially favorable to this aristocratic family because it was a respected, well established order which was devoted to scholarly, literary, and artistic pursuits.

AQUINAS THE STUDENT

Thomas' education at the abbey was primarily religious but also included reading, writing, mathematics, grammar, harmony, and Latin. There is no evidence that he was dissatisfied with his life or training, and so he probably would have remained there and taken his final vows as a Benedictine monk if times had remained peaceful. However, the abbey was "a frontier fortress" between the Papal States and Frederick II's Kingdom of Sicily which included Naples, the abbey, and Aquinas' birth place. A succession of popes feared Frederick's ambitions, specifically that he would isolate and encircle the Papal States. In 1239 (about nine years after Aquinas had entered the abbey) Frederick was excommunicated for the second and last time by a distrustful pope. This signaled the beginning of a long period of strife, and Monte Cassino was affected immediately because of its strategic location. Frederick's troops occupied the abbey and expelled most of the monks. Obviously it was no longer a safe place for the young Aquinas.[38]

After returning home for a visit, Aquinas enrolled at the *studium* in Naples to study liberal arts and the natural philosophy of Aristotle, the latter an area of study which was forbidden in some places because of controversies concerning the interpretation of Aristotle's thought. Naples had only recently been established as a study center by Frederick, who was eager for its success. The course of study, therefore, was more varied than at studia influenced more directly by church officials.

The method of instruction was Scholasticism, or the kind of dialectical reasoning typical of Abelard's study and teaching. Aquinas would have been assigned to one master who would have been responsible for his student's moral and intellectual development. In pursuing his studies he would have read the text, engaged in disputations, and participated in refutations of the master's lectures.

As a student Aquinas was an avid reader and a serious scholar. However, his handwriting was illegible and never improved in later life with the result that many of his writings were referred to as *littera inintelligibilis* and "can only be read by palaeographers who have made a special study of them."[39] He was tall, overweight, absentminded, and quiet—characteristics which made him seem dull and plodding to those who did not look beneath the outer man.

A well known story illustrates the difference between Aquinas as he appeared and as he really was. After completing his studies at Naples he went to Paris where he studied with Albert the Great, a respected theologian. He was so quiet during Albert's lectures that the other students nicknamed him the "Dumb Ox." A fellow student, taking pity on the "Dumb Ox," offered to help him review the lecture, and Aquinas accepted with humble thanks. During the review he so astonished the "tutor" with his brilliance that the "tutor" asked Aquinas to tutor him in the future. Eventually Albert learned of his silent, retiring student's talents and brought forth Aquinas' abilities in class by assigning him a difficult question. When Aquinas' turn came to answer his question, he evoked this response from his famous teacher: "We call this man the Dumb Ox but he will eventually bellow so loudly in his teaching that he will resound throughout the whole world!"[40]

Aquinas' attitude about study was summarized in a letter to a young friar:

Since you have asked me, my very dear John in Christ, how you should apply yourself in order to gain something from the treasure-house of knowledge, let this be the advice handed down to you by me on this subject.

Make up your mind to start on small streams rather than to plunge into the sea; for one should progress from easier matters to those that are more difficult. This is, then, my advice and instruction for you. I counsel you to be slow to speak and slow to take the speaker's stand. Embrace purity of mind; do not neglect prayer; cherish your cell most of the time, if you wish to be admitted to the vintage-room [of knowledge]. Be friendly to all men; do not be curious about the private activities of other people; do not try to be overfamiliar with anyone, for too much familiarity breeds contempt and provides an opportunity for neglecting one's studies.

Do not get interested in any way in worldly talk or deeds. Avoid idle talk on all matters; do not fail to imitate the example of holy and good men; do not be concerned about what speaker you are listening to; instead, when something good is said, commit it to memory. Be sure that you understand whatever you read. Make certain that you know the difficulties and store up whatever you can in the treasure-house of the mind; keep as busy as a person who seeks to fill a vessel.

Do not seek higher positions. Follow in the footsteps of Blessed Dominic who brought forth and increased the buds, the flowers and the fruits that were useful and wonderful in the vineyard of the Lord of Hosts, as long as he lived.

If you follow these words of advice, you will be able to attain your every desire.[41]

AQUINAS THE DOMINICAN

While Aquinas was pursuing his studies at Naples, he became acquainted with members of the Order of St. Dominic and decided to become a Dominican friar rather than a Benedictine monk. This greatly distressed his aristocratic family. The Benedictines were respectable and they were the choice of his family. The Dominicans were members of a new order which explicitly criticized the Benedictines and devoted themselves to preaching among the poor and to earning their living by begging. Aquinas' family considered the group and its practices to be beneath his social station. In later years he wrote, "On this decision [to enter the religious life], blood relatives are not friendly but unfriendly. . . . So, in such a case, the advice of relatives is especially to be avoided."[42]

His family so strongly opposed his decision that his brothers kidnapped him when he was on a journey with several fellow monks. The brothers returned him to a family castle where he was detained for about a year while all of his family attempted to persuade him to change his mind. His brothers resorted to methods other than verbal persuasion. One evening they sent an attractive young woman to his room to seduce him. Upon seeing her Aquinas snatched a burning stick from the fire and chased her from the room. He then fell into a deep sleep and dreamed that his loins were bound tightly with a girdle of virginity. He is reported to have never felt lust after that. He remained a virgin all of his life.

" 'From that time onwards,' says his earliest biographer, 'it was his custom always to avoid the sight and company of women—except in the case of necessity or utility—as a man avoids snakes!' "[43] He would find Aristotle's view of females naturally attractive. His opinion of women can be seen in the *Summa Theologica.* When he discusses the question "whether outward pain is greater than interior sorrow," he quotes Ecclesiastes 25.17: "The sadness of the heart is every wound, and the wickedness of a woman surpasses all other wickedness, as the text implies, so sadness of the heart surpasses every outward wound."[44]

After Aquinas' release, the Dominicans, recognizing his exceptional intellect, sent him to Paris to study, to teach, and to earn a master of theology license (an eight year program). During this time he began his very considerable writings on theology. At the age of thirty-four Aquinas left Paris and spent ten years in Italy preaching, teaching, and writing. Then he returned to Paris to occupy one of the Dominican chairs of theology where he continued producing works of extraordinary length and quality.

Aquinas has been said to have perfected Scholasticism. He is credited with applying Aristotelian logic to Christian theology. He justified both faith and reason, long considered incompatible: "Since revelation is a 'fact'—true philosophy and theology can never be in opposition when they deal with the same questions; and revealed truths, incomprehensible to the intellect, must be accepted on faith. The finite reason can never comprehend the infinite, but it can prove the validity of the preambles of faith and show that faith is not unreasonable."[45] Of all of his works the *Summa Theologica,* which employs Aristotelian logic to prove church doctrine, is the best known.

LAST YEARS

In 1272 Aquinas was named Regent of Studies for the Dominicans at Naples, where he taught and continued to write until 6 December 1273. "While saying mass that morning a great change came over him, and afterwards he ceased to write or dictate. Urged by his companions to complete the *Suma,* he replied: "I can do no more; such things have been revealed to me that all I have written seems as straw, and I now await the end of my life."[46]

Early in 1274 Aquinas, who was in poor health, set out for a general council of the church to be held in Lyons. On the way he injured his head on a tree branch and stopped to rest at the Cistercian monastery in Fossanova. There he weakened and died. The Cistercian monks refused to give up the body, and later they "seem to have boiled the flesh off the corpse, so that they could keep the bones 'in a small place.' " Only in 1369, forty-six years after the canonization of St. Thomas Aquinas, were his remains returned to the Order of St. Dominic by a directive from Pope Urban V. Today "the relics of Friar Thomas are still preserved in the parish church of St. Sernin."[47]

Aquinas was the quintessential medieval monk. Yet his work, which was not widely appreciated in his own day, has modern significance. As we shall note in the final chapter of this book, twentieth century thinkers (Jacques Maritain, for example) still draw significant inspiration from it.

SKETCH OF DESIDERIUS ERASMUS

4

THE HUMANISTS

Life in thirteenth century Europe was varied and exciting for many people. The dynamic thrust of monasticism had reached its high point. It had transformed vast sparsely settled regions into productive farms and towns. But as the economies of several regions boomed, and towns like Paris grew large, monastic approaches to life and learning seemed insufficient to many people. We have already noted the beginnings of university development. Even this evolution continued, and the scholastic approaches to learning so typical of Paris—linguistic analysis based on syllogistic logical forms—ceased to appeal as widely as they had in Abelard's time. What emerged was something that has been variously labeled "the new learning," "humanism," and the "Renaissance." All these are potentially misleading terms, but we have retained them because they are usual and because they do offer a convenient shorthand way of referring to certain aspects of this time period. Central to the discussion are language and political developments associated with the growth of nationalism.

THE RENAISSANCE

Historians see the Renaissance in very different ways. Some would narrow it to a short period of time, while others would extend it from 1300 to 1700. For those who follow a strict definition of "humanism" include not only in literary activity of the period, but also the interest in the church and civil government which many intellectuals had. For our purposes, the Renaissance runs from about 1300 to 1600 and *humanism* includes the intellectual activity concerned with classical texts *and* with their application to daily life.[1]

If we look at the politics of the times, it is easy to see why the early Renaissance occurred in Italy. In much of Europe, regions had begun to come together in the great nations we know today (for example, England and France). During the thirteenth and fourteenth centuries, most of these were at war. England and France fought over the French throne from 1337 to 1415 in what is called the Hundred Years War. The Holy Roman Empire under the German Hapsburgs extended its power into what is now Austria and Czechoslovakia in a series of bloody battles with local kings. Add to these wars the beginnings of religious conflict, as well as a great plague called the Black Death (1348-49), and we have a picture of Europe staggering under continual turmoil.

Italy was an island of relative peace in this sea of trouble. The southern part of the peninsula was ruled by a fairly stable monarchy, while the pope governed much of its central region. Northern Italy, the cradle of the Renaissance, was composed of a number of independent cities as well as a kind of miniature kingdom under the domination of the city-state of Milan. While the Milanese Visconti family gradually took over many of northern Italy's independent cities between 1350 and 1400, there was still relative peace. Led by the still free cities of Venice, and especially Florence, northern Italy concentrated its resources on business, literature, and the arts, instead of expensive wars.

The results were intellectually exciting. As cities had become more important, and business had flourished, a new middle class of merchants had grown up, anxious to demonstrate its importance and sophistication. Like the "robber barons" of nineteenth century America who would make their money in shady business deals, and spend it on art museums and opera, these fourteenth century businessmen commissioned artists to produce statues and paintings, and hired tutors to instruct them and their children. Thus, scholars were able to support their writing by teaching for a living, and, in a few cases, were paid simply to think and write. The flourishing economy encouraged such artistic and intellectual pursuits.

Along with this, there was a shift away from the scholastic emphases of the Middle Ages. In the early fourteenth century, the Florentine author Petrarch had urged his countrymen to close their Aristotle and open their Cicero. Now, dialectics and theology were seen as less important than the writings of classical Greek and Roman authors. To these ancient writers, Renaissance thinkers turned to discover both the style in which people ought to write and speak, and the eternal truths which ought to govern society.[2]

In order to use the wisdom of these ancient authors, their writings had to be carefully studied. This created problems. Because books were still copied by hand, there were few of them around. Since many of the classical works had been written over a thousand years previously, the odds were small that copies would have survived at all, much less in one piece. Many Greek and Latin works had been lost, either because all of the copies had been destroyed—we only know about these through other contemporary authors who refer to them—or because they sat undiscovered on the back shelves of some monastery library. Card catalogs had not been invented. Parts of some works survived, as did whole works which had been copied with so many mistakes that they were nearly useless. Another major problem was that almost no one in western Europe could read Greek. While scholars knew about Homer and other classical Greek authors and, in a few cases, even had copies of their works, few people were able to read them in the original language.

Renaissance scholars worked hard to solve these problems. Many inaccurate texts were edited, and attempts were made to reconstruct entire works from the fragments which remained. Searches of libraries sometimes yielded copies of works which people thought no longer existed. The discovery in 1418 of Quintilian's works in the library of St. Gall is an example of this. Books were copied and recopied, so that a number of scholars and wealthy people were able to amass extensive libraries.

The problem of learning Greek was solved, in part, by historical events in the East. During the early Renaissance period, the Greek city of Constantinople was under increased pressure from the Turks who had taken over much of Asia Minor. People began to flee to western Europe, among them scholars and teachers. They taught both the Italian humanists and their pupils to read Greek, and opened up a whole new world of literature in the process. A typical example was Manuel Chrysoloras (c. 1355-1415) who began the teaching of Greek classics at the University of Florence.

THE HUMANITIES

The Medici's, a powerful Florentine family from 1389 to 1534, encouraged new literature and art (such as that of Leonardo da Vinci and Michelangelo Buonorroti), and they also sponsored activity designed to find and preserve copies of Greek and Roman masterpieces. (In 1445 the family borrowed a Greek name, academy, for an institute it founded in Florence. The purpose of this academy was to further the study of art and literature, including history. They coined the term "humanities" to represent this kind of study.) The Renaissance focused on understanding the human condition through studying history, and expressing this understanding in elegant written style, epecially that of Cicero. Of major importance was the stress on writing—not just in Latin but also in the vernaculars (mother tongues, such as English, Italian, Czech, German). In the hands of various religious reformers, this would be the beginning of mass elementary instruction in vernacular languages.

The first thrust of what would come to be called the "new learning" was not religious. It began with the poetry of people like Dante Alighieri (1265-1321) and his fellow Florentine, Francesco Petrarch (1304-74). It was furthered by the work of Parisian born Giovanni Boccaccio (1313-75) who wrote poetry and stories like *The Decameron* in Italian (and lectured at the University of Florence on Dante's work). This Italian activity had an early counterpart in England, Walter Map (1103-1175), an Oxford archdeacon, wrote in English of England's heritage—including the first full written account of King Arthur and his sixth century knights—and Geoffrey Chaucer (1340-1400) wrote his *Canterbury Tales*, patterned strongly after Boccaccio's *Decameron*.

All of these happenings helped to create the intellectual excitement of the Renaissance. Western Europe was exposed to long forgotten classical literature. Scholarship was no longer unconcerned with the events of daily life; rather, the humanists used the writings of orators such as Cicero and the histories of Herodotus and Xenephon to inspire a return to the ancient virtues of personal integrity and civic responsibility.

The Renaissance thus served as a bridge. On the one side lay medieval education with its emphasis on scholastic philosophy and theology. On the other was modern schooling which would stress vernacular (modern) languages and natural science. It is in the context of this shift in Western society, with its accompanying excitement and anxiety, that we view the accomplishments of Vittorino da Feltre.

Vittorino da Feltre (c. 1378-1446)

Given da Feltre's stature as a Renaissance humanist, it is somewhat strange that we know little about him. Like many other teachers, he was devoted to his work, and wrote little himself. Perhaps he was so impressed with Roman and Greek literature that he felt unable to match its excellence. At any rate, before his death he destroyed the only writing he had done, some poems composed in his youth. What we know of da Feltre we know from the accounts of others, and these are uniform in their praise.

EARLY LIFE AND EDUCATION

Vittorino was born at Feltre, in the eastern Alps, in 1378 or 1379, the son of a minor official. The first record we have of him comes in 1396, when he entered the University of Padua.[3] This was the same year in which the University of Florence, also in northern Italy, had hired Manuel Chrysoloras as the first professor of Greek in the West. Padua, like Florence, was very much under the influence of the "new learning," with its emphasis on the classics. Petrarch's library had been given to the university, providing it with many new texts. A great number of the students were from nearby Venice, which was a center of contact between Greece and western Europe. Da Feltre's education began with members of the arts faculty, with whom he studied Latin grammar and literature, philosophy and rhetoric, and canon (church) law. This was a fairly typical course of study for the time, since Padua's curriculum was still medieval. The only unusual feature was the study of canon law, suggesting that da Feltre was considering a career in the church.

Although we cannot be sure exactly when Vittorino completed all these studies, it is definite that they were finished by 1411. While he had received his Laurea (doctor's degree), he never wore the academic robes and ring to which he was entitled. Such an action was typical, as we shall see, of the quiet and simple lifestyle which he would maintain until his death.[4]

All during his university time, he was both a student and a teacher. Like many talented but poor students, he put himself through the university by teaching younger boys. Even after completing his degree, he remained around the university for a total of almost twenty years, teaching and studying. Vittorino became interested in mathematics, which at that time was not usually a part of the curriculum. To satisfy his curiosity, he contracted with a private teacher to give lessons to his children in return for mathematics classes for himself. By the end of his stay at Padua, he himself was teaching both Latin grammar and mathematics as a private tutor.

A major influence on da Feltre during this period was Gasparino Barzizza, who came to the university as a teacher in 1407. Barzizza was devoted to the study of the Roman author Cicero, whom he believed to be a model of literary style, as well as personal virtue and citizenship. We know that Vittorino was one of Barzizza's students, and it is probably from him that he picked up his conviction that classical literature could be reconciled with Christian life.

Another important influence on Vittorino was Guarino da Verona, a fellow student at Padua who was to become almost as famous a teacher as da Feltre. In 1415, Vittorino left Padua for Venice, and spent eighteen months studying Greek with Guarino who had established a school there. Guarino was one of the few people in western Europe who could speak and write Greek, having been a student under Manuel Chrysoloras.[5]

VITTORINO AS TEACHER

Armed with this new knowledge, Vittorino returned to Padua to begin his own school. Because schools of this period were individual operations, and there was no compulsory education, each teacher had to attract his own students. De Feltre seems to have had no problem in this regard. Besides his extensive knowledge of Latin, his skills in mathematics and even more sought after abilities in Greek guaranteed him students. He had no shortage of paying customers, so he was able to take poor children along with the wealthy. In effect, he set up his own scholarship program, using the high fee charged to wealthy youngsters to subsidize the education of the poor. This concern with providing schooling for any talented boy was not unique to Vittorino, but it was one of his lifelong activities.

In 1422, Barzizza resigned his professorship at the University of Padua to take up another one at Milan. Vittorino, age forty-four, moved into Barzizza's recently vacated position. Something seems to have gone wrong, for da Feltre resigned his new position the same year, and left Padua. Whether he was unhappy with the students or the university itself is not known, but this brief interval was his only brush with university teaching.

In 1423, da Feltre began a school at Venice for the children of wealthy merchants. The situation was close to ideal. Because of Venice's ties with

Greece, he would have opportunity to purchase scarce Greek books. He was near old friends such as Guarino and other scholars. His reputation guaranteed him all the students he could handle. However, he had no sooner gotten settled than he picked up all of his belongings and moved again.

Why did Vittorino leave such an ideal situation? Put simply, it was because he received an offer he couldn't refuse. Marquis (roughly, duke) Gianfrancesco Gonzaga of Mantua was looking for a prominent teacher for his household. Because his title was a little shakey, he wanted to compensate by proving to everyone that he was sophisticated and intelligent (not to mention wealthy) enough to hire a well-known teacher and thinker. He had first approached Guarino, who refused. Vittorino, too, declined the offer, but Gonzaga wouldn't take no for an answer. He offered to let da Feltre set his own salary, and told him he could use his time as he saw fit. While da Feltre realized that accepting this offer would end any possibility of a career in the church, the opportunity was too good to pass up. In 1423 he moved to Mantua, where he was to spend the rest of his life.

At the court of the Marquis, Vittorino was responsible for the education of five children. In addition, he accepted students from other prominent Mantuan families, as well as the children of some of his own friends (for example, those of Guarino), and as many as seventy poor students. The marquis was true to his promise of support, even providing an elaborate villa which da Feltre christened "La Giocosa" (the pleasant house) as a site for the school. This property gave Vittorino a perfect setting, since he believed that the environment for a school should be pleasant, and that there should be room for the pupils to engage in physical activity.

Several years earlier, Vittorino had been influenced by the writings of Greek Petrarch on education, as well as the discovery of a previously lost manuscript by the Roman author Quintilian on schooling. At Mantua, he set about putting the ancient ideals of these authors into practice. In the Middle Ages, Latin had been studied only as a tool for further work in philosophy and theology with little attention paid to style, and Greek had been studied only by a few monks. Vittorino set about reversing all of this. Beginning with basic grammar, he went on to teach Roman and Greek literature. Textbooks of the period were difficult to understand, with the hardest material frequently presented first and with no explanation.[6] Da Feltre went through the texts line by line, talking about literary style, explaining difficult terms, and lecturing on the theme and characters.

Vittorino's school placed great emphasis on public speaking and memory training. Students also were required to speak Latin and to learn to write it. In order to learn Greek and improve their Latin, they would take a passage from some Greek author, and translate it into Latin, using the style of some particular Roman writer. While Greek was less emphasized than Latin, the major Greek poets and historians were studied. The goal was to make the students as fluent in Latin as they were in Italian, and to teach them enough Greek to read the classics. All of these efforts were aimed at producing the Renaissance ideal, individuals who would live out the virtues of personal honesty and civic responsibility which were to be learned from the study of the classics.

Though da Feltre never married, his students were his family. In the classroom, he spent extra time with those who needed help, or were especially talented. Outside of school, he listened to their problems and helped them smooth over difficulties with parents. In warm weather, he took them on field trips. Since the students lived with him, he knew them well and they, in turn, regarded him as a sort of extra parent.

Vittorino was deeply convinced that education was not simply a matter of intellectual activity. The same personal austerity which caused him to buy rough wool clothing and to wear sandals even in the winter made him insist that even his wealthiest pupils live simple lives. Unlike Guarino, he believed that physical activity was an important part of education, and encouraged students to play games and engage in athletic competition. Along with this, he communicated his own deep religious faith. In his school, religion was part of the normal classroom study. Outside of class, he took the students to mass several times a week, and required that they follow his example of confessing their sins to a priest at least once a month. By involving himself in the extracurricular life of the students, da Feltre hoped to show them that education was concerned with establishing moral values and not just communicating facts.

Vittorino's conviction that classical learning should lead to personal morality and public service was exemplified in his own life. Though occupied with his students, he found time to take part in the life of the city, continually helping the poor with financial gifts and educating many of their sons free of charge. Churches and clergy were the recipients of continual gifts, many of which he provided anonymously. While he was well paid by the marquis, he spent almost everything on his students, the poor, and the church. At his death, his entire estate consisted of a small piece of land, his books, and his clothing.

Worn out by years of constant work, Vittorino's health, which had never been all that good, broke down in 1444. The following year, he was continually ill with attacks of fever. On 2 February 1446, he died at Mantua. True to his principles, his will specified that the funeral be as simple as possible.

CONTRIBUTIONS

How should we evaluate da Feltre's contribution to Western education? Intellectually, he was highly competent but not outstanding. His mastery of Greek was never great, and he left no important writings (nor, for that matter, any unimportant ones). Unlike some other humanists, he wielded little direct political power. Because his activities were confined to Padua, Venice, and Mantua, he had only a small circle of friends. While we have six hundred of Guarino's letters to friends, only six of Vittorino's have survived. Clearly, da Feltre's importance must lie in other areas.

Vittorino is remembered because of his unique ability to translate the values of an era into a specific educational program. His school was steeped in the Renaissance pursuit of virtue and love of learning. Vittorino's own life proved that the ideal could be achieved. Destined never to achieve personal intellectual greatness, he was the teacher of humanists such as Lorenzo Valla who would shape their age. One scholar puts it this way: "Vittorino's school at Mantua . . . lasted from 1423 to his death in 1446, and its extraordinary qualities—the social mixture of princes and poor men, the humanity with which the humanities were inculcated, the psychological finesse and moral fervour of the master—have made it the most famous school of all times."[7] While this appraisal is probably a bit exaggerated, Vittorino's survival in the writings of students and friends, despite his own lack of literary productivity, is the best possible testimony to the effect he had on the lives of those around him and through them, on the development of Western civilization.

WOMEN AND THE NEW LEARNING

Historians have generally portrayed the Renaissance as a movement which embodied an enlightened attitude toward education for women. It is true that some famous humanists—Erasmus, for example—advocated education for women, but most males did not favor sexual equality in any sphere, including schooling. Several female humanists, however, did. In the fourteenth century, a public debate began over the place of women in society. It was just the beginning of a series of controversies not yet entirely resolved. It did not begin with the work of the subject of this sketch, but it is through her that we see it come into sharp focus.

Christine de Pisan (c. 1364-after 1429)

Christine de Pisan was born in Venice in late 1363 or early 1364. Her father, Tommaso di Benvenuto da Pizzano, was a well-paid official of the city of Venice. He had been born in Pizzano, a village near Bologna. He studied at Bologna and was elected to a position as lecturer there in 1342. His specialties were medicine and astronomy, including a lot of astrology, but like other scholars of his time he had studied all the common branches of knowledge. His wife was the daughter of a friend and was probably a number of years younger than he. Christine was their first child.[8]

Tommaso was ambitious. He was buying property around Bologna with his Venetian salary when the king of France sent an invitation for him to visit Paris. The king, Charles V, was the most famous crown head in Europe and Paris was the most celebrated city. It was a good opportunity for Tommaso and he took it. Charles was interested in astrology and Thomas of Pisan was noted for his knowledge in this field. The family stayed in Bologna while Thomas checked out the situation in Paris. Four years later they came to join him. He had by then become one of the king's close advisors.

Life in Paris was good for Christine, and probably for her two youngers brothers as well. King Charles paid Thomas well. The family lived comfortably. Christine had nice clothes and, although she was not aristocracy, some of her friends were from the most powerful families in France. Her education was typical of what liberal humanists approved for aristocratic and wealthy middle class girls at the time: manners, morals, etiquette, reading, and writing. Christine overheard many conversations between her father and his intellectual friends, but did not pay much attention to them. She was around the king and other significant political figures, but did not think much about politics. She behaved herself and developed the skills and attitudes that a good girl should. She did not think of herself as beautiful—though she did say that she had a pleasant and sound body—but she attracted a lot of male attention as a young teenager. Her mother and father arranged a marriage for her when she was fifteen. This seems young to us, but it was normal, in fact may have been a little older than usual, for her time. The general operating theory had long been and would long remain that women bloom early, mature fast, and fade quickly. So parents commonly arranged marriages for twelve to fifteen year-old girls. Men did not usually marry until their mid-twenties or later.

MARRIAGE

Christine's father apparently had numerous offers for his daughter's hand, some from wealthy and aristocratic men. He rejected these in favor of a young man of twenty-four, Etienne of Castel, a student/scholar from a well-established but not rich family in Picardy. Etienne and Christine had known each other all of her life. She thought him "beautiful both in face and in body." He seems to have returned her high regard. They were a happy couple. The king helped by giving Etienne a very good position as secretary and notary.

One year after Christine and Etienne married, the king died. His successor, Charles VI, was a twelve year old boy whose advisors did not like Thomas de Pisan. Christine's father lost his position and quickly became a sick, helpless old man. Etienne did well, however, and soon was a well-paid councillor to the king. Christine's family, including two younger brothers, depended on her and Etienne for support. This seems to have been no problem financially since she and Etienne made enough to buy a large house and to have seven servants.

In 1381, two years after she was married, Christine had a daughter. Following that came a son, who apparently did not live. Then in 1385 she had another boy whom she named Jean. She said the births were difficult and painful, but she seems to have loved her children and to have been a good mother. Her father died, and her mother (whom she regarded as a kind and good person) moved in with her family. So did her two younger brothers. It was a busy life and Christine was happy. Not, however, for long.

Christine and Etienne had been married ten years when, one day in 1389, a message arrived that Etienne was dead. It was totally unexpected news. He had gone with the king on some routine business to Beauvais about forty miles north of Paris. He had become suddenly ill. There was no doctor and before anyone could figure out what was wrong he died. "I was so confused with grief that I became a recluse, dull, sad, alone and weary," she later wrote. She hoped she would die herself, and it would be many years before she stopped thinking almost constantly of her misfortune. The pressing demands of a four year old son, an eight year old daughter, as well as the need to support her mother and two younger brothers, soon forced Christine to involve herself again with life.

A WIDOW'S EDUCATION

The standard behavior expected of any young widow was that she mourn briefly and quickly remarry. This was particularly true for someone like Christine. She was attractive and well situated to make a socially and financially advantageous marriage. She was accustomed to a style of life that required money and now she had little. Her husband's salary stopped immediately upon his death. He had bought some property that he intended to go to her, but it was tied up in the courts. Despite these problems, she refused to get married again.

Still emotionally upset, Christine hired lawyers to help her get the back salary and the property that were her husband's. The lawyers were not honest—in any case they did not produce any positive results—so she began watching them to see what they were doing. She went to court herself to try to get matters resolved, but the justices delayed, played tricks, shifted her case to other courts, and generally made themselves obnoxious. It was such an unheard of thing for a woman to try to represent herself in court (she fired her lawyers), that men whistled, did cat calls, and made sexually loaded remarks when she went out in public. She pawned her furniture, borrowed money, and continued her fight. It took her seven years to get her husband's back salary paid and seven more to win part of the property that should have gone to her in the first place. "Leeches of fortune" was the term she used for the officials involved in this long dispute.

To understand the preceding situation and what followed, it is necessary to remember something about the status of women at the time. We have already noticed the double standard prevalent in Greek and Roman societies. The Christian movement accorded some status and importance to women. The women's monasteries offered an alternative to the dependence of marriage, but most of the church fathers were suspicious of sexuality and regarded women as Satan's agents to tempt men to sin. Moreover, power rested on military strength and this in turn was an exclusively male enterprise. With rare exceptions, women were excluded from practical military knowledge. Both civil and canon law gave husbands the right to beat their wives. Civil law excluded women's testimony in court because of "frailty," and it imposed only half the fine for an offense against a woman as for the same offense against a man. Thomas Aquinas' justification of Aristotle did some useful things for human thought, but one of them was not to advance the cause of equality between the sexes. Aquinas argued (following Aristotle) that nature always wants to produce a male. Woman, therefore, is something defective—perhaps a result of the father's failure to have enough generative power or of some outside interference, maybe a damp south wind. Woman is weak in body, mind, and will. She needs man for everything; he needs her only to have children. She should regard man as her natural master and be happy to submit to his corrections and discipline. Children should love their fathers more than their mothers. Not all men agreed with Aquinas, but his attitude was shared widely. There were probably many women who did not agree, but it was a difficult fight as Christine was about to learn.[9]

In the middle of her grief and her frustration, Christine wrote a poem (a *ballade*) to give vent to her feelings. Friends said she should write more, and she did. These were mostly love poems and were written in the vernacular (French in this case), just as Dante's and Boccaccio's had been. (Dante, by the way, was Christine's favorite poet.) To help pass the time and to increase her knowledge of the world that she was writing about, the young widow began to read. She started with history, and read several Roman and a number of medieval authors. Finally she came to the standard item of French courtly education in her time. This was the *Roman de la rose,* a poem of twenty-one thousand lines written about a century earlier by two different men. The chief author was Jean de Meun, a French cultural hero. He had woven into his allegorical poem current beliefs and knowledge on every subject under the sun.

THE "WOMEN'S QUARREL"

One of de Meun's subjects was the nature of woman. According to him she was selfish, disloyal, couldn't keep secrets, deceived men viciously, and was an easy victim of flattery. Men suffered continuously from woman's nature and this had been known since ancient times, said de Meun. Christine was not favorably impressed. She did not think this description fit her or many of the women she knew. On the other hand, she had spent years trying to get elementary economic justice out of the courts. She had put up with taunts, pressure, and deceit. She had heard men brag about their sexual conquests of women who thought they were serious when they were not. It didn't make sense to her. As one historian puts it, "This may be the first recorded instance of a woman's feminist consciousness being raised by her life experiences."[10] She decided to write a reply. Actually she wrote several at various points during the remainder of her life.

Christine criticized de Meun for devoting so much space to techniques for seducing virgins. It shouldn't take much planning anyway, she said, if women were all as simpleminded as de Meun thought. One of the religious arguments, favored by Aquinas, de Meun, and others, was that God had made man first and had then made woman from a small part of man. Woman, therefore, was to man about as significant as one small rib is to the whole organism. Christine turned this around by arguing that woman may even be superior to man, because God created her not out of ordinary clay but from the body of man— "the most noble of earthly things."[11] Finally, she indicted de Meun for his contention that marriage was an unnatural state. He had said that it was better not to marry since people are obviously not monogamous by nature and will violate their vows. Christine pointed out that this attitude was clearly against Christian doctrine.

No one had criticized the number one poet of France. And now he was being attacked by a woman! Many people thought this preposterous. One of the king's secretaries, a man named Gontier Col, tried to silence Christine through intimidation and insults. Being a woman, she had not likely thought of the criticisms herself, wrote Col. Probably she was being used by others. This was the only way he could account for the fact that she had written anything against that "true catholic, solemn master, doctor in theology and excellent philosopher who knew all that the human understanding can know."[12] Christine did not scare and she would not be bluffed. She defended her position effectively and courteously. She won some powerful supporters, notably Jean Gerson, chancellor of the University of Paris. This *querelle des femmes,* as it came to be called, certainly did not end in Christine's time, but her work was an important beginning of the public debate about women's rights that continues to the present.

Part of the whole debate involved the question of the extent to which women should be educated and what the curriculum should be. Most of the humanist educational theorists approved of educating aristocratic women, but thought careful censorship needed to keep out any material that might excite women sexually. The argument that women were constitutionally too frail and weak to stand up to schooling or that they would suffer nervous breakdowns if they studied "difficult" subjects like mathematics did not come up during Christine's time. Both theories were circulating two centuries later, however, and were held by many educated men as commonplace knowledge by 1800.

Her own experiences and observations convinced Christine that women could learn as well as men if they were taught the same things. She thought learning the "greatest of all riches" and that it would be good if all children could come to know "what a splendid thing it is to have a liking for knowledge, and how wretched it is to be ignorant!"[13] She wrote, among many other things, a book of practical advice to women on how to get along in the world and solve their problems. When a man expressed his disapproval of her own desire to learn by saying "it does not become a woman to be learned, as few of them are," she replied quickly "that it less becomes a man to be ignorant, as so many of them are." In one of her later works, she posed the question of why so many male writers expressed bad opinions of woman's nature. She had one of her characters give two possible explanations: (1) that it all began with Eve, and men have not gotten over their grudge; (2) that men secretly realize that women are superior to them, both in capacity and in "nobility of natures," but don't want to acknowledge this fact.

If all this makes Christine sound anti-male generally, it is misleading. She held both her father and her husband in the highest esteem, and she also respected and liked a number of other men during her own time. She was a strong advocate of marriage, and felt that hers had been good even if it was too short. As one of her biographers sums it up, she had simply come to think that "women must have their own definite place in the scheme of things, not a place in opposition to the world of men, but of equal importance to theirs. . . ." Five hundred years later, women (and some men) would advocate the same idea, but it would still meet with opposition.

A PROFESSIONAL AUTHOR

As for the rest of the facts of Christine's life, not too many are known. She earned a living for about fifteen years starting around 1400 as a writer. She was one of the first people to do this—since the printing press did not yet exist and there were no royalties for authors. As her fame as a poet spread, aristocratic people wanted copies of her work. She made these as requested, including having some of them nicely illustrated, and presented them accompanied by an appropriate dedication. The new owner almost always supplied a gift of money in return.

Christine did not confine herself to poetry. In 1404 Philip, Duke of Burgundy, asked her to write a history of the reign of Charles V—his brother and the man who had brought Christine's family from Bologna to Paris. She was glad to comply, because she had respected the king. She read the official chronicles, interviewed people who had been around Charles, wrote down her own recollections and the stories her father had told her, and then organized her account around her perception of the kind of person he was. She had really developed for herself many of the techniques of modern historians, and her account contained stories and information that would otherwise not have been preserved. Later historians used it heavily, but often did not cite it. Her work was not widely known after she died so they may have thought no one would be the wiser.

Beginning in 1410, and lasting off and on for years, France was involved in civil war. Christine had become an astute political observer and predicted what would happen if reforms were not made. She turned out to be correct. She also foresaw that England would take the opportunity of unrest to try to seize land in France. She was no democrat, but she believed the common people had grievances that should be corrected. She wrote letters, appealing to those who might have been able to change things, but they ignored her advice. As she saw war coming inevitably, she read everything available on all aspects of fighting and chivalry. As a result she wrote a long manuscript on military tactics—when to fight and when not to, how to supply troops, what to do about morale, how to treat civilians, a complete treatment of heraldry, and many other related topics. It is possible that she wrote this for her son, Jean, for whom she had secured a knightly (military) education in two different aristocratic households. She did not mention him, and we do not know what happened to him. It is possible that he was killed in some of the fighting. Many of the men she knew were, and she did say that she had had great "anxieties and troubles" in 1416-1418.

FINAL YEARS

In 1418 she went to the Abbey of Poissy just a few miles northwest of Paris, near Arguentile where Eloise had been. Her daughter had chosen, at about the age of fifteen, to join the abbey. This had been strongly against Christine's wish, but she did not forbid it. She and her daughter had remained on good terms, and the daughter had repeatedly urged her mother to give up all the struggle and come to the monastery. For ten years Christine wrote nothing and then, in 1429, she wrote one last poem. The occasion for that was the act of another woman famous in French history.

By the late 1420s England was winning the battle against France. The French king, Charles VII, had never been crowned. Paris was occupied by the English. A sixteen year old girl in the eastern French town of Domremy heard voices and had visions of religious figures telling her to save France and take the king to Rheim to be crowned. Her father, a prosperous farmer named Jacques d'Arc, swore he would drown her before he would let her go, but she got a horse and rode 450 miles in eleven days to reach the king. He did go with her to Rheim and was crowned. The city of Orléans had been under seige by the English for some time. They were out of supplies. Joan d'Arc and some soldiers rode to the city. She had a white military outfit and rode a black horse. Her presence so aroused the city that they followed her and other military leaders into a battle against the English and won. She was twice wounded in battle, but fought bravely and effectively.

Christine was delighted at the news of Joan's triumph. She wrote in celebration of the event. "What an honor for the feminine sex, which it seems that God loves!" she wrote. Nothing else was heard from her. "The year of her death is not known," says one biographer, "but one cannot help hoping that she died soon after that swansong, and did not live long enough to hear of the terrible end . . . of the maid who had crowned her long belief in women and defeated the enemies of the country she loved so well."[14]

The "terrible end" for Joan of Arc came in 1431. Not long after Christine's poem, she was captured by French forces not loyal to the king. Charles, who owed her a great deal, did nothing to help, and the English got her through a large bribe. Under English supervision she was put on trial for heresy. She was told to disavow the voices she heard, but she would not. Actually, the result was predictable. The English king, having paid heavily for her, wasn't about to let her go. She was burned at the stake and, choking on the smoke, she said her voices had not led her astray. A rare outbreak of bicameral thinking gave France a hero and proved Christine correct in thinking women could do anything men could.

Joan of Arc's courage and Christine de Pisan's clear logic and forceful style would not win for women anything like equality for a long time to come. Although some of Christine's work was among the first to be published by Caxton on his printing press toward the end of the fifteenth century, most of it would remain unpublished. Soon after her time, the work was practically unknown in Europe. It is only now beginning to be resurrected in any kind of popular way.

By the late fifteenth century, the new learning was spreading to many important centers of learning in northern Europe. The next three biographies illustrate this fact and also show how humanism became linked with religious reform.

Johannes Butzbach (1478-1526)

Johannes ("Hans") Butzbach was born in Miltenberg (West Germany today). When he was less than a year old he went to live with his father's sister because his mother was pregnant. (Knowledge of how to prevent conception consisted of advice like "let the woman suspend the tooth of a child over her anus." The notion that a married woman should enjoy any right over her own body, including the right to refuse sexual intercourse to her husband, was foreign to both law and practice so it was usual for women to be pregnant again soon after giving birth.) The practice of farming children out was common practice throughout the medieval period and beyond. In this case little Hans was probably lucky because his aunt was childless and, according to his later recollection, cared for him "most lovingly and tenderly."[15]

At six years of age young Hans' aunt sent him to school. He said she enticed him to go with cakes, figs, raisins, and almonds. According to him, this was customary. He apparently did not do well in school, although it was probably not a good school. In any case he disliked the experience and soon encountered another custom—one that had not changed in the thousand years since Augustine's day. "When I did not want to go, she saw to it that I was driven by sharp switches."

When Hans was about ten, his foster mother was, in his words, "visited by a sickness, and it pleased God to let her depart this life." At this turn of events, he returned to his original home and renewed his efforts to play hooky. After a brief period of success, he was caught. "My mother took me by the collar and dragged me to school." This was evidently toward the end of the day. The master, who was just leaving, gave his assistant permission to "'beat him severely as he deserves." Two decades later, Hans described what happened in the following words:

> Wrathfully the heirling, as we called him, seized me, stripped my clothes from me and bound me to a post; and then the harsh man exerted all his strength to beat me without mercy. My mother had hardly left the school, when she heard me screaming and wailing so terribly that she turned quickly, came to the door, and when my torturer lessened his blows a little, shouted at him to stop. But he as though deaf to her cries, did not stop, but struck all the harder; meanwhile the whole school had to sing a song. When he stopped attacking me so savagely, my mother forcefully opened the door, and rushed in. But when she saw me bound to a post and so horribly cut up by the heavy blows and covered with blood, she fell swooning to the floor.

When his mother revived, she "attacked the schoolmaster with harsh imprecautions" and swore that her son would not go to the school again. (Whipping children was accepted as a common and necessary control device, but the severity and relish with which this man administered his thrashings must have caused many people in Miltenberg to hate him. The town council made him a bailiff in charge of prisoners to get him out of the school.) Hans then undertook a different educational venture: "While this was happening to me, our neighbor's son, a grown student, returned from a foreign school. He ingratiated himself with my father and requested that I be put to study with him." The young man assured Hans' father (Conrad) that "elsewhere, with him, I would, in a short time, make greater progress in learning than I would here in years."

A WANDERING SCHOLAR

Even though Hans was only eleven or twelve, Conrad agreed to send him away with this "scholar." The parents bought their son clothes, books, and supplies, and they gave their young neighbor money and the promise of more if it was needed. In return the neighbor promised to take good care of their son and to send word often of his well-being and progress. Conrad made the sign of the cross over a jug of wine and each person in the family, and the neighbor, drank in turn a solemn toast to seal the bargain. Then, accompanied by sobbing goodbyes from both parents, the neighbor and his young charge set off for nearby Nuremberg.

It seems harsh for parents to send a twelve year old away to wander for years in the company of a lad only a few years older himself. It was not unusual under the circumstances, however. For one thing, Conrad felt that he was dying from an unnamed "protracted illness." There was no insurance or social security. When people like Conrad died, the family's income stopped. Women with young children to raise almost always remarried quickly if they could. In that event, the children by the earlier marriage were often treated badly by their stepfather, and were usually put to work or apprenticed as early as possible. Conrad was in a hurry to get his son educated before it was too late. His premonition was right. He died within a year and his wife remarried. It was to his younger half-brother, Philipp, that Johannes Butzbach later addressed the autobiographical account from which our data about his life are drawn.

There is another reason that young Hans' educational journey was not unusual: he was participating in a custom of long standing. It had been standard practice for hundreds of years for scholars as young as thirteen or fourteen to wander from place to place in search of instruction by noted teachers. (Abelard took several years to reach Paris because of studying with people along the way.) It was also commonly agreed that wandering students, being churchmen, could beg for their food if they were in need. Of course, those who were not needy were more likely to succeed at their studies. In the German speaking area, the wandering scholars came to be called "bacchants." The precise history of the term is not clear. It may have been derived from the term *vagantes* (wanderers) or from Bacchus, the god of wine. Many of the wandering bacchants did seem to have a keen preference for alcoholic beverages. As a group, they were not generally noted for high morals or good manners. But by Butzbach's time, the practice was well established. Conrad Butzbach had himself been a young wandering scholar. Perhaps that was why he cried so much at seeing Hans leave. He knew what hardships likely awaited him.

Hans embarked on his new life anticipating high adventure; by the end of the first day he got a good indication of how things would go. The bacchant stopped at an inn a few miles from Miltenberg. He threw a party with some of the money given him by the Butzbachs, but Hans went to bed with no supper. Succeeding days were worse. The farther away from Miltenberg the pair wandered the more cavalier the bacchant became. After two months the money ran out and Hans had to start begging. He hated this but if he resisted, the bacchant beat him "with his fists and staff." This, too, was customary. Many of the bacchants had younger boys as pupils. These were called "abc-shooters"—"abc" because the pupils were supposedly learning their abc's; "shooter" from *Schutzen* which can also mean protector or defender. Shooters were expected to beg for their bacchants. Many others could have given a similar description to one that Butzbach recounted:

He forced me to beg in villages that were so filthy and muddy, that I often waded in mire to my ankles, sometimes even to my calves; and at times, like one walking in dough, I could move neither forward nor backward. Sometimes I was attacked so viciously by watchdogs that, I believe, if the owners had not come to my assistance, I should have been torn to pieces. The scholar himself had a dislike for begging, and did not do it, whereby he escaped being mocked by the country people as a great, dirty lazybones who would not work, and also escaped getting covered with mud, which, as he well knew, was very deep in the villages during wet weather. Moreover, to avoid being molested by dogs, he betook himself across fields and meadows, in order to get around the villages.

Ultimately the pair ended up in Kaden, Bohemia (50 miles west of Prague, Czechoslovakia. The rector there gave them a student lodging, but after a time they moved 250 miles southeast to Eger (in Hungary today), because they feared an outbreak of plague. There both bacchant and shooter got positions as tutors in well-to-do families, but the "scholar" beat Hans severely when Hans refused to beg for two other bacchants. The family offered their young tutor protection, but he ran away out of fear of the bacchant. He worked briefly in an inn, from which he was more or less kidnapped by a Bohemian aristocrat. He spent the next few years in and around Prague working for several different nobles. On the whole, he was treated well. He learned to ride and swim. He liked the food, but later his feelings of German nationalism and his monastic training led him to write of "the barbarous speech of the super-barbarous Bohemians." Butzbach described the Bohemians as "wild," "superstitious," and "heretical."

At about age eighteen Butzbach made his way back to his hometown. His father had died; his mother was remarried and pregnant. His stepfather cut Hans' hair "upon which I had bestowed a great deal of care while in Bohemia," had him "fitted out with other clothes," and apprenticed him to a tailor. The two years he spent there, Butzbach remembered with regret: long hours, hard work, "harsh words from my master and the household, and sometimes hard blows, cold and heat, hunger and thirst in the extreme; what I had to suffer in these and many other kinds of distress, could hardly be written in a large book."

HUMANISM AT DEVENTER

With his apprenticeship ended, Butzbach found a position as tailor to a monastery—St. John the Baptist in the mountains of Rheingau. His experiences as a "lay brother" and his recollections of his father's desire that he become a priest turned his thoughts to a religious vocation. Most monasteries would not take adults unless they had a needed skill or were educated already. His mother offered him money so he could return to school. Butzbach went to Deventer in the Netherlands, a school founded in 1380 by the Brotherhood of the Common Life. The school at Deventer, and some others run by the brotherhood, had become famous for teaching "humanism" or the "new learning." Many monasteries, partly in response to the criticisms of reformers, recruited heavily in these schools. To successfully complete the course at Deventer meant automatic offers from desirable establishments.

Butzbach's first attempt ended in failure. His background was poor. He was much older than most of the other pupils in his class. His own sense of inadequacy—and the resulting discomfort—was large. He had little money. So he quit, but a little later his mother obtained more money for him (at considerable cost to herself). Butzbach's stepfather gave him five florins. "He knew also that my mother had a treasured florin which she had received from Hillig [Butzbach's father], with which he had betrothed himself to her. With all authority, he demanded it for me. But my mother did not wish to give it up, and had intended to give me another florin instead, behind my stepfather's back. As a result, a terrible quarrel arose between them, which ended in my mother being severely beaten and having her hair torn. When I saw this, I threw aside my luggage and money, and with my bothers and sisters, offered resistance to my stepfather in order to protect mother. I succeeded in dragging her from under his feet.'' The stepfather later apologized to Butzbach, passing the whole incident off as having been created only by his great interest in seeing his stepson get an education.

Butzbach returned to school. This time he did better. In two years, he moved from the eighth class (the eleventh was the lowest) to the third. He almost quit several times. He suffered a variety of physical ailments that may have been partly induced by psychological stress: boils, fevers, scabs all over his body, swollen limbs, and ulcers. When a representative of the monastery of Laach (near Koblenz, West Germany) made a recruiting speech, Butzbach decided to join. He was then twenty-two. He and one other Deventer student made the trek to Koblenz, but only Butzbach took the final vows. He became master of novices. At twenty-nine he was chosen the house's prior, an office he filled until his death thirteen years later. He seems also to have been ordained a priest, thus fulfilling his parent's chief ambition for him.

BUTZBACH IN RETROSPECT

Johannes Butzbach was a sensitive person who felt keenly the wrongs and injuries that he experienced. He was not exceptionally intelligent or singularly courageous. He did not invent any new pedagogical theory, and he did not comment perceptively on his own educational experiences. In terms of the ideal monastic model under which he operated, he did cope successfully with his life experiences. His account contains a pervasive mood of subdued self-pity, but he describes himself as having achieved a measure of calm victory over his turbulent feelings.

Butzbach's account is useful for two reasons. One is that he supplies details of educational life in the fifteenth and sixteenth centuries that help fill in our knowledge. More important, Butzbach experienced similar circumstances to Thomas Platter (described in Chapter 5). Their responses were somewhat different.

Like Guibert of Nogent five centuries earlier, Butzbach saw nearly everything in terms of God's will, the tug between good and evil, and the supernatural forces implied or described in the teachings of the church. His schooling at Deventer was superior in its time, and as we shall see, produced men like Desiderius Erasmus and others who favored reform. Butzbach's monastery was part of the internal church reform tradition, but his own thinking remained conventional.

Butzbach described the Bohemians as superstitious. After telling the story of a particularly obnoxious count in Bohemia, he noted with satisfaction that ''as a just punishment from God, evil spirits at night shattered his castle and destroyed its walls.'' He expressed no skepticism at Bamberg's claim of having two of the six pitchers in which Christ turned water to wine at a wedding feast and also that the town owned the sword with which Peter struck off the ear of Malachi in the Garden of Gethsemane. Of his self-doubts and anxieties at Deventer, he had a simple explanation: "More than anyone can imagine, the devil tempted me, and pursued me with his deceitful promptings, and dazzling promises." Although he was beaten by numerous men and treated kindly by many women during his wandering boyhood years, he had a powerful distrust of women: "Whom have the women not worsted and deceived!" He did not say whether he had enjoyed any of the worsting or deceiving. Finally, although he had hated his own days as a shooter, Butzbach recommended that his younger half-brother undergo the same process. He could see no way of breaking the cycle in which both he and his father had been trapped. Perhaps, realistically, there was none.

Another person whose birth appeared inauspicious attended Deventer a few years before Butzbach was there. His name was destined to become virtually synonymous with the new learning. This was Desiderius Erasmus, "Prince of Humanists," and a man whose name is associated with an entire era.

Desiderius Erasmus (c. 1466-1536)

Born the illegitimate son of a priest and a physician's daughter, Erasmus intentionally obscured the details of his birth. Poverty and a weak physical constitution led him to be sensitive all his life. His early education was with the Brothers of the Common Life and at about age thirteen he was left an orphan. His guardian, Erasmus maintained, pressured him into entering an Augustinian monastery at the age of eighteen. He was ordained a priest at twenty-two, left the monastery, and came under the patronage of the Bishop of Cambray who gave him financial aid and permission to study at the Sorbonne.

Erasmus, as an adult, classified himself as a citizen of the world with Holland his fatherland and Latin his mother tongue. He traveled from country to country enjoying the friendship of many people. Invited to England, he was a confidant of Thomas More, John Colet, and other English humanists. His connection with them was so close that he was considered by some to be an English humanist. He lived for a time in all the major countries of Europe but made only one trip to Rome.[16]

ERASMUS AS AUTHOR

Erasmus was a prolific writer all his life, producing literary works from schoolbooks to theological treatises. His major work is *In Praise of Folly*. In it he satirized the excesses of the society of his day. His *Enchiridion, or Handbook of the Christian Soldier* has been called "the book that made the Reformation" because in it Erasmus spoke out against the abuses in the church and the need for reform.[17] He also translated the New Testament from Greek into Latin. This work was replete with errors and was condemned at the Council of Trent. His criticism of Luther in *On the Discussion of Free Will* was the first public attack on the teachings of that reformer.

Erasmus is known as one of the great writers of Renaissance humanism. His stature in church history is lessened for some because he was a moderate unwilling to leave the church. In the present ecumenical age, his reputation is once more being restored to its former high place. Erasmus believed in reform of the church and directed his efforts to that end until death stilled his pen.

Some have questioned whether he was primarily a Christian or a scholar. Erasmus considered himself first and foremost a Christian. He made no distinction between scholar and Christian. He was a Christian scholar. To be a true follower of Christ, for Erasmus, was to do away with ignorance. His first rule was "to understand as clearly as possible [about Christ] and about the Holy Scriptures handed down by his spirit, . . . not to entertain belief only by lip service—coldly, listlessly, hesitantly, as most Christians do—but let it permeate your whole being, let it be deeply and immovably fixed until there is not even an iota contained in Scripture that does not pertain to your spiritual well-being."[18]

Though written nearly twenty years before Luther put forth his doctrine that faith, alone, was necessary for salvation, and not meant as a refutation to Luther's doctrine, Erasmus' second rule for the Christian soldier is "to enter upon the way of spiritual health, not slowly or timorously, but resolutely, whole-heartedly, with a confident—if I may use the expression—pugnacious spirit, ready to expend either your goods or your life for Christ."[19] He went on to lay down twenty more rules and an epilogue for many of the vices.

As a Christian moralist, Erasmus reconciled the study of the ancient philosophers with a Christian outlook by stressing the lessons one could learn by reading them as history.

> They err, therefore, who affirm that virtue is won by handling affairs and by contact with life, without aid from the teaching of philosophy. . . . A long and manifold experience is, beyond doubt, of great profit, but only to such as by the wisdom of learning have acquired an intelligent and informed judgement. Besides, philosophy teaches us more in one year than our own individual experience can teach us in thirty, and its teaching carries none of the risks which the method of learning by experience of necessity brings with it.[20]

Philosophy, in this instance, means the theory, knowledge, and the social and historical lessons learned from the past.

Erasmus was a pacifist. He did not think the world could be Christian unless it was a peaceful, well-ordered place. He opposed rulers and rich people who promoted war—the former for the purposes of territorial gain and the latter for money. He objected to rulers who exposed young men "to so many dangers, and often in a single hour . . . make so many and many an orphan, widow, and childless old man."[21]

EDUCATIONAL VIEWS

The aim of education for Erasmus was social. He addressed a nobleman with the fact that "your children are begotten not to yourself alone, but to your country: not to your country alone, but to God"[22] He stressed faith and good works more than dogma. The good deeds of individuals would result in a well ordered social structure. This could only be accomplished through a liberal education.

The best education for Erasmus was a return to the ancient Greeks and Romans. Since astrology and geography at this time was not sound knowledge, Erasmus would use them only to make the writings of the ancients intelligible. To those who would condemn the study of classics Erasmus argued that: (1) it was through these cultures that Christianity was first spread; (2) this study was a necessity to anyone who wanted to search out the truths of religion and scripture; and (3) their study was approved by the early fathers of the Church—Basil, Jerome, and Augustine.

Erasmus referred to public schools in more than one of his writings. By this he meant what the Greeks and Romans had—a school in public rather than tutors at home. He did stress a philanthropic obligation for nobles and statesmen to help the poor but deserving student. Along with Thomas More, whose practice of educating his daughters Erasmus greatly admired, he wanted women to be educated in a carefully censored curriculum. He would have parents exercise a great deal of caution in finding good teachers for their children.

Erasmus wanted parents to realize that learning begins at birth. He even hinted at the idea of prenatal learning. He pleaded for early learning of Latin, saying "it is as instinctive with children to imitate as it is easy for them to remember." He did not think that the study of Latin would appeal to the child, but counted on the teacher to inspire the young. He thought teachers should be sensitive to the talents of individuals so that each child would be able to pursue the right course of study for his or her particular bent. He disapproved of harsh discipline, but recommended that the unmotivated be "turned out to the plough or the pack saddle." Erasmus favored reaching the young with games. He cited an instance where the letters of the alphabet were made into cookie form and as they were learned could be eaten.

TEXTS

Erasmus' greatest practical contributions came in the texts he wrote and in his efforts to develop a curriculum and method of instruction for St. Paul's grammar school, run by John Colet in London. His schoolbooks were so widely used during the sixteenth and seventeenth centuries that it is difficult to exaggerate their influence.

Erasmus was one of the cast of characters involved in the development of the famous textbook known as Lily's Grammar which became the authorized Latin grammar by proclamation of Henry VIII in 1540. Others involved were William Lily, Thomas Linacre, John Colet, and Cardinal Woolsey. This grammar was used in English schools for several hundred years.[23]

Many of Erasmus' schoolbooks were put together for other purposes and then adapted for the use of schools. One of his most famous works was *The Colloquies,* printed originally without his knowledge in 1518 as the *Familiarium colloquiorum formulae.* It had a long and checkered career. The first edition was a collection of single sentences, conversations, questions and answers, useful to a beginning student of Latin. Some of the material is the sort found in courtesy manuals. A great deal of the remainder is dialogue which beginning students would memorize. Starting with a section "On the First Meeting," it moves through various forms of greetings. Many of the dialogues are amusing. A case in point is "George/Livinius":

George.   Just what coop or cave do you come from?

Livinius.   Why ask such a question?

George.   Because you're ill fed. Because you're so thin you're transparent; you creak from dryness. Where've you been?

Livinius.   Montague College.

George.   Then you come to us full of learning.

Livinius.   Oh, no—full of lice.

George.   Fine company you bring with you!

Livinius.   Yes indeed; it's not safe nowadays to travel without company.

George.   I recognize the academic set.[24]

As the original *Colloquies* began to have a great acceptance, Erasmus turned his attention to them and began revising and expanding many of the formulae into longer pieces. The result was "a book of unusual variety: debates on moral and religious questions; lively arguments on war, government, and other social problems; advice on how to train husbands, wives and children; discourses on innkeepers, beggars, pets, horse thieves, methods of study—all this and much more."[25] This remarkable book was soon being used not only in schools but was also read by adults for pleasure and information.

Erasmus also put together another book which served to introduce boys to the elements of oratory or rhetoric. Its title is instructive: *De Utraque Verboram ac Rerum Copia* or *On Copia of Words and Ideas.* The translators of this book point out the unavailability of a suitable English word. A sixteenth century student defined *copia* as the "faculty of varying the same expression or thought in many ways by means of different forms of speech and a variety of figures and arguments."[26] Briefly what it all amounted to was an effort to vary writing and speech in as many ways as possible. Students who have been told to enrich their style by using a variety of different words to express similar ideas have some idea what it is all about. Students during the sixteenth century spent a great portion of their time in taking Latin texts and sentences and trying to express them in different ways. For this purpose, Erasmus' book and others were of great use. The usefulness of these books is attested by their numerous editions—85 of *De Copia* during Erasmus' lifetime and more than 150 printings during the sixteenth century.

An examination of *De Copia* will remind the present-day students of the modernity of much of the work. For example, the topics covered are synonymia, low words, metaphors, allegory, hyperbole, and practice. "This training in varying speech," said Erasmus, "will be useful in every way for attaining good style, which is a matter of no little moment. In particular, however, it will be useful in avoiding tautology, that is, repetition of the same word or expression, a vice not only unseemly but also offensive."[27]

Elegance is something also sought by many in writing and Erasmus made this an important part of his approach. What he wrote about this made sense, just as did most of what he had to say. It was not his fault if some were imbued with his ideas without having his ability to make subtle distinctions. Too many probably borrowed his methods, leaned heavily upon them but never really grasped their spirit. "What clothing is to our body, diction is to the expression of our thoughts," said Erasmus. The *Copia* is a storehouse of wonderful phrases, figures of speech, and pithy sentences. Erasmus made several distinctions in the forms. "Some are universal in application," he wrote, "as: Envy is its own punishment. Others are not suitable unless related to a subject, as: Nothing is so popular as kindness. There are others which refer to a person, as: The prince who wishes to know all things must ignore many." He continued in this vein with example after example. His favorite source was Cicero. But there were many others: Aristophanes, Euripides, Homer, Horace, Livy, Quintilian, and Vergil.

Erasmus wrote many more schoolbooks, but we will content ourselves with discussing one more—his famous *Adagia*. This was a collection of several hundred Latin proverbs with comments. This book printed in 1500 was also used as a schoolbook or a reference book by many students. Erasmus' technique was to present a proverb and then to make extensive comment upon it. An example is the proverb "Festina Lenta," or "make haste slowly." Erasmus commented that this proverb has within it a riddle since it has contradictory terms. How can one make haste slowly? The answer is that sometimes it is better to proceed slowly in deciding to take a course of action but once a decision has been made then one can move quickly. He pointed out that this proverb was a favorite of two great Roman emperors, Octavius Augustus and Titus Vespasianus.

In the process of discussing the proverb, Erasmus also unraveled a host of symbols. For in discussing an ancient Roman silver coin, he wrote that on one side was an effigy of Titus Vespasianus and on the other an anchor with a dolphin wound around the middle. According to Erasmus this meant the same as saying of Augustus Caesar, "hasten slowly." He based this interpretation upon a book of symbols. He then followed with a long discussion of symbols and also of the nature of the dolphin, which the ancients seemed to have held in high esteem just as many scientists do today. After the digressions, Erasmus returned to a discussion of three meanings of the proverb: First to "wait a little before tackling a matter"; second, "that the passions of the mind should be refined by reason"; and third, it "points out that precipitate action should be avoided in everything."[28]

A great number of proverbs discussed by Erasmus are still part of common speech. Some examples:

A necessary evil.
There's many a slip twixt the cup and the lip.
To leave no stone unturned.
Let the cobbler stick to his last.
Dog in the manger.
A rare bird.
One swallow doesn't make a summer.
I'll sleep on it.
Up to the ears.

The success of Erasmus' work was a little more phenomenal. Consider that the last work, the *Adagia,* was translated into English, French, Italian, German, Dutch and other languages. The work went through 120 editions before 1570 and is still used. The 1970 edition of *Books in Print* lists the *Adages of Erasmus* published by the Cambridge University Press. We have given the figures on the *Copia,* one of the "best sellers" of its time. The *Colloquies* was another matter. It was one of the most widely used textbooks in the sixteenth and seventeenth centuries. Moreover, it was condemned by the Council of Trent in 1564. The University of Paris had earlier banned its use. Charles V invoked the death penalty for its use in schools. The book made strange allies—Luther joined Charles V in condemning it. Only the Bible outsold it up to 1550.[29]

Erasmus and many reformers did not separate humanism from religion, but we must be careful not to confuse *humanism* with *humaneness.* Some Renaissance people were the very essence of charity and, like Erasmus, thought kindness inseparable from learning and living. The central thrust of humanism, however, was the study of humans through classics. It did not necessarily imply a particular assumption about morality, as the next biography reveals.

Niccolò Machiavelli (1469-1527)

The inclusion of Niccolò Machiavelli in a collection of educational biographies seems at first glance to be a bit strange. Machiavelli was never a teacher like da Feltre, nor was he directly involved in educational policy formation. He had a good education, but was not a scholar of the caliber of someone like Erasmus. In another sense, however, Machiavelli had a profound though indirect influence on the development of education in the West. In order to understand that influence, it is first necessary to see what political and social events shaped his thought.

FLORENTINE POLITICS

The city in which Machiavelli lived, Florence, was the political and military capital of northwestern Italy, and a major commercial city of Europe. Italy, at that time, was more a collection of independent cities than a nation with a central government. Some of these had been republics for a long time (in

Florence's case, since at least A.D. 1000), and the more powerful of them ruled a good deal of territory. For example, the city of Pisa was controlled by Florence.

During the fourteenth and fifteenth centuries, the republican governments of several of these cities were gradually replaced by strong rulers who came to control their political lives. During most of the fifteenth century, Florence had been ruled by the Medici family, which held power by a combination of force and promoting prosperity. Probably the greatest of these was Lorenzo da'Medici (1449-1492), called the Magnificent. Under the leadership of Lorenzo, a great patron of the arts and a shrewd politician, the city prospered, though at the price of personal freedoms.

Machiavelli was born in 1469, during the height of the Medici rule, to an upper middle class family. His father, Bernardo, was a lawyer and collector of books. At the age of seven, young Niccolò began to learn Latin, and later also studied mathematics. Although some authors paint Machiavelli as a great classical scholar, there is no evidence to support this. He knew Latin, but no Greek. His father probably had no intention of schooling him as a humanist; his career was to be that of a lawyer or public official, not a teacher or scholar.[30]

During Machiavelli's youth, Lorenzo da'Medici had taken over the Florentine government almost completely. Gradually, the city became more and more corrupt morally, as politics, an honorable profession in the days of the republic, became less and less respectable. In 1478, the city had revolted against the Medici, an uprising which was swiftly suppressed when the city's hired soldiers proved to be cowards in battle.[31] In observing all of this, Niccolò was learning lessons which he would later formulate into political theories of how a state should be run.

One bad feature of this kind of government was that the success or failure of a city depended heavily on the ability of the prince. Piero da'Medici, who succeeded his father Lorenzo, was incompetent and, in 1494, he and his supporters were forced into exile. Florence once again took on a republican form of government, with a system of elected officials. Most of these held office for short periods of time (two years at the most), because the people feared that any long-term official would become entrenched in power, and be a threat to liberty. The result was a city in which there was constant political activity, since someone was always being elected to office.

While many citizens of Florence could theoretically hold office, wealth and family reputation were the most important criteria. This caused a split between the common people, who were taxed but would never be elected to office, and those who were almost guaranteed power by their wealth and pedigrees. Within the Great Council and other government bodies, there were also numerous factions which constantly fought with each other.

The major governing bodies of Florence were quite large during this period. Members were chosen by lot or automatically entitled to membership on the basis of family background. The Great Council, for example, had about three thousand members.[32] Obviously, such large organizations could not carry on the day-to-day work of government. This was handled by smaller groups of semi-professional civil servants who functioned as the executive branch of government.

Another major factor in the Florentine political equation from 1494 to 1498 was a Dominican priest, Savonarola, who exerted a great deal of indirect pressure on the councils. Initially preaching against moral and political corruption, Savonarola went on to attack the pope and his court for abandoning gospel values in favor of worldly ones. He insisted upon rigorous public morality, and tried to create a Florentine state run on religious principles—a government dedicated to God. In advocating such radical change, however, Savonarola made a great many enemies including, not surprisingly, Pope Alexander VI. Finally, in 1498, the Dominican was condemned as a heretic and burned at the stake. Florence's brief flirtation with religious rule was over.

A DIPLOMATIC CAREER

Five days after Savonarola's execution, Machiavelli entered the Florentine civil service as second chancellor. Basically, this meant that he was a secretary in the state government. His appointment was somewhat unusual, since posts of this kind usually went to lawyers. While he was fairly well educated in literature, he hadn't yet written anything that would have made him famous. What he lacked in background, however, Niccolò made up in eagerness and native ability.

Machiavelli's first diplomatic mission in 1500 sent him to France. During this period, Italian politics had gotten even more complicated (though it hardly seems possible!). Italy was ruled by five major power blocks; the cities of Florence, Venice and Milan in the north, Naples in the south, and the semi-independent Papal States in the center of the country. These were roughly balanced in terms of power.

While Italy was fragmented, large states which were the beginning of modern nations were gradually forming across the Alps. Spain had been united under Ferdinand and Isabella, Germany was being drawn together by the Holy Roman Emperor, and France was coalescing into a single nation. All of these possessed more power than the isolated Italian cities, and all of them had their eyes on Italian territories.

An opening came when Ludovico Sforza, the prince who ruled Milan, invited the French in 1494 (the year of the reinstatement of the Florentine republic) to make a claim to Naples. When the French invaded, they were driven back by a coalition of states which included Milan (such political double-dealing was routine during the period), but their rapid advance into Italy showed the rest of Europe how ripe Italy was for the picking.

In 1499, the French returned, seized Milan, and reasserted their claim to Naples, with the help of Venice and the pope. The Spanish, meanwhile, moved in to counter the French presence, and ended up getting a piece of Naples for themselves. Florence, like the other city-states, had to pay "protection" to friends and enemies alike. Frequently, it was hard to tell exactly which were which.

As a result of these invasions, Florence, which had become allied with France, had lost the city of Pisa. Machiavelli's mission in 1500 was to try to get French support for a Florentine effort to retake Pisa. Initially, the French offered sympathy but no cash. Finally, Machiavelli and his colleagues were able to get an agreement and return to Florence. All in all, the mission was a diplomatic failure, but a personal success for Niccolò. For the first time, he saw how government and commerce were conducted in another country. This helped to give him a perspective on Florence's situation. Again, his working knowledge of politics was growing.

In 1502, two key people came into Machiavelli's life. Piero Soderini, a highly respected but anti-aristocratic citizen, was elected chief magistrate of Florence for life. Soderini took to Machiavelli, because of Niccolò's talent and middle-class background, and helped to promote his career. As his first mission, Machiavelli was sent to negotiate with Cesare Borgia, the duke of Valentenois, who was becoming a major political force in Italy.

An illegitimate son of Pope Alexander VI, Borgia was conspiring with his father's help to unite all of Italy. Allied with the French, Cesare had proven himself to be a formidable leader. Machiavelli's task was to stall Borgia on the Florentine alliance which he wanted. In the process, Niccolò got a first-hand look at a shrewd, powerful man who seemed on the verge of completing the impossible task of uniting Italy. Borgia's exercise of power, which we might describe as an "iron fist in a kid glove," would become Machiavelli's model for statesmanship in his major work, *The Prince.*

Soon, however, Borgia's luck ran out. In 1503, his father the pope died while Cesare himself was seriously ill. The new pope, Pius III, died after twenty-six days, and elected in his place was Julius II, a lifelong enemy of the entire Borgia family, who had forced him to spend ten years in exile. Until his death in 1513, Julius would wage a relentless crusade to drive the French from Italy, making war on Venice and pressuring Florence in his attempt to build an anti-French alliance. He would eventually ruin Cesare Borgia, and bring down the Florentine republic in the process.

While all of this was going on, Machiavelli was engaged in a constant series of diplomatic missions. In 1503, he went to Rome to try and persuade the pope to give aid against the Venetians who had just attacked Florence. The year 1506 found him trying to raise a Florentine militia, a pet project throughout his entire life, as well as on a second mission to the pope. In 1507 he was named secretary of the Council of Nine, a new group set up to oversee the city's military affairs, a job which paid no salary but increased his prestige. He even traveled to Germany in 1507 to negotiate a treaty with Emperor Maximillian (and to spy on the emperor's war plans). In the next several years, he traveled again to France, as well as various parts of Italy on state business. During all this time, his wife and several children remained at home, though we may wonder what they thought of his continued absences, not to mention his "jet set" lifestyle.

Despite the efforts of Machiavelli and his colleagues, however, there were far too many diplomatic fires to be put out. Florence had stubbornly insisted on keeping its alliance with France, despite an obvious decrease in French influence. The pope, meanwhile, became stronger and stronger, taking vengeance on those Italians who had sided with France. When the French withdrew complete-ly in 1512, the pope reclaimed a number of northern Italian cities, and demanded that the Florentines enter the anti-French alliance.

Machiavelli now became as much a soldier as a statesman. Always on the move, he recruited and trained a militia, knowing that an army was Florence's only chance for survival. His efforts, however, came too late. The pope attacked

Florence with a professional Spanish army, which cut through the untrained militia like a hot knife through butter. Florence had no choice but to surrender.

LOSS OF POWER

The Florentine defeat spelled the end of the republic. The pope, heavily in debt to the Medici, removed Soderini as head of the council and encouraged the Medici to return. Within a few months, they had once again assumed control. Their return also had an immediate personal result for Machiavelli: it brought his career as a civil servant to its end.

Niccolò had hoped that, like most of the Florentine diplomats, he would be able to keep his job under the new administration, since he regarded himself as a servant of the state rather than of any particular individual. Unfortunately for him, the Medici rulers did not agree. In fact, he was virtually the only major civil servant dismissed by the new government. He had been identified too closely with the old regime; now, he would have to pay the price.

Things went from bad to worse for Machiavelli. He was first of all ordered to pay a large fine, and told not to leave Florentine territory for a year. Then, he was implicated in a plot to overthrow the new government, and arrested, imprisoned, and tortured in an effort to extract a confession. Only with the election of Pope Leo X in 1513 (ironically, Leo was a Medici, too) was there a general amnesty which freed Niccolò from prison.

Paradoxically, what appeared to be an unrelieved disaster in Machiavelli's life was probably the best thing that ever happened to him. The Medici return freed him from the day-to-day tasks of a diplomat, and gave him the quiet time to think and write. One scholar has compared his life during this period to a meadow beginning to bloom after a long winter, a poetic evaluation which makes some sense. Given the leisure he had never previously had, Machiavelli began to reflect on his own experiences and the political situation of Florence, and to ask himself what it all meant.[33]

WRITING CAREER

The first important writings to come out of this reflection were the *Discourses,* essays written on the themes of the Roman historian Livy. His goal was to study the qualities of an ideal republic. Familiar with the works of Livy from his school days—his father had written an index to some of them—Niccolò used Livy's writings as a springboard to propose some of his own political ideas. Good laws, he argued, are absolutely necessary in a free society. There is also a need to balance the different interest groups in the society, and especially to avoid the kind of tension between nobility and people which had created so many problems in cities like Florence.[34] Moreover, he continued to insist that the voice of the people is to be taken seriously since "the people are more prudent and stable, and have better judgment than a prince; and it is not without good reason that it is said, 'The voice of the people is the voice of God.' "[35] Finally, he argued that nothing is absolute: laws must be made with a view to supporting the customs which are already present, and political decisions must be made in light of the specific times in which individuals live.

In the midst of these reflections on the nature of republics, Machiavelli made an abrupt shift to a study of the qualities of an absolute ruler. This work, *The Prince,* was written in 1513 and is easily the most famous of his writings. The *Prince* is, simultaneously, representative of the humanistic tradition and different from much of it. Throughout the Middle Ages and Renaissance, there had been many works written as handbooks for rulers. This style of writing, called the "mirror of princes," sought to challenge leaders to greatness by laying before them the virtues of classical rulers like Augustus Caesar. The humanists generally used such classical models as absolute patterns for contemporary life. Machiavelli, however, combined Latin authors with his own experience, and arrived at a synthesis which looks more like political science than classical rhetoric. Machiavelli is not really trying in the *Prince* to present an accurate account of the qualities of various ancient rulers; rather, he picks specific examples (and, at times, distorts them) to illustrate principles derived primarily from his own experience.

Several themes dominate the *Prince.* The absolute unreliability of using hired armies was a conviction proven time and time again in Machiavelli's experience. Mercenary troops have no real loyalty to the state, but only to the highest bidder, and cannot be relied upon in a tough fight,. The quality which Machiavelli thought most desirable in a ruler, and which he spoke of again and again, is *virtù,* which might be translated as personal force or charisma. A successful prince, according to Machiavelli, ought to be feared, but not hated. His only study should be war, with all of its rules and disciplines. In the final analysis, however, only *virtù* counts. Other qualities are only virtues or vices depending on whether they help or hinder the political functioning of the state. Ends always justify means.

For Machiavelli, the other important forces in life are *Fortuna* (fortune) and *Necessità* (necessity). The latter, however, can be used by the shrewd ruler to create opportunities, provided that he has *virtù. Fortuna* can also be counterbalanced, but only by swiftness of thought and decisiveness of action. In what is probably his most famous image (not to mention his most chauvinistic), Machiavelli compares fortune to a woman who must be held down and beaten in order to be controlled. The last chapter of the *Prince,* however, departs from the rational tone of the rest of the work. Whatever else motivated Machiavelli, patriotism was an important value, and he closes the work with an impassioned plea for a strong ruler to unite Italy and heal the wounds caused by the invading barbarians (otherwise known as northern Europeans).

During this period of reflection and writing, Machiavelli continued to live in constant hope that he would be accepted by the Medici family and allowed to resume his diplomatic career. The *Prince* was first dedicated to Guiliano da'Medici, then in 1516 rededicated to Lorenzo da'Medici (the grandson of Lorenzo the Magnificent) when Guilano died. In spite of all his attempts, Machiavelli was unable to repair the damage to his career. Needing some sort of activity, he began to take minor commissions from merchants in the city to handle their business in other parts of Italy. While bankruptcy proceedings were hardly special missions to the emperor, they at least made Niccolò feel that he was doing something valuable. He also continued with his writing, producing the *Art of War* (1519), as well as several comic and dramatic works, and finishing the *Discourses.*

By the early 1520s, Machiavelli had begun to make his way back into government circles. He was still more involved in business matters than in those of
state, but now he went armed with letters of recommendation from Cardinal
Gulio da'Medici. In 1520 he was offered a diplomatic post with the small republic
of Ragusa, but refused because it would have meant leaving Florence to serve
foreigners. Finally, in 1521, the Medici gave him a small commission to negotiate with a group of Franciscans, and asked him to recruit a famous preacher
for Florence while he was about it. Although this was hardly the sort of thing
Niccolò had been used to, he jumped at the chance to ingratiate himself with
the Medici.

MORE POLITICAL TURMOIL

Just as things had begun to improve, however, the wheel of Machiavelli's
fortune turned once again. In 1521, the Medici Pope Leo X died, and was
replaced by a stiff and pious Flemish cardinal, Adrian VI. Cardinal da'Medici,
who had hoped to be elected, returned to Florence and took up the reins of
government. In June of 1522, there was a move to assassinate the Cardinal,
and Machiavelli's friends were again among the plotters. In the same year,
Niccolò's brother Totto, a good and pious priest, died. Again, Niccolò returned
to the country to write and think.

In 1523, Pope Adrian died, and this time, Cardinal da'Medici was elected. The
new pope, who took the name Clement VII, allied himself with the Germans
when his French allies were defeated. The emperor agreed to support the
Medici rule in Florence, and the Florentines were made to pay the bill. Machiavelli went to Rome to present Clement with a copy of his Florentine *Histories,*
which Niccolò had dedicated to him. In return, he received a minor commission
from the pope, the first of several which were to come in the next few years.
It seemed that Machiavelli's career was back on track.

Historical events, however, once again intervened. The pope's enemies (and
there were many of them) prepared to challenge his rule. Machiavelli found
himself once again preparing Florence for war, and traveling to attempt a
peace. In April 1527, rumors swept through Florence that the Medici were
abandoning the city. Only at the last moment was a revolt averted. In May,
however, Rome itself fell to an army of Spanish and German mercenaries who
pillaged the city, and forced the pope to take refuge in the fortress of Castel
San'Angelo and pay a ransom for his own release. Italy was now firmly under
the control of foreigners. Florence returned to the constitution formulated by
Savonarola, and ordered the young Medici ruler to leave the city.

Now, Machiavelli was again in the position of having supported the wrong
people, this time the Medici. His fears that having served the Medici would once
again end his career just as it was getting off the ground were justified. Another
diplomat was promoted in his place and Niccolò, who had first suffered because
he had served a republican government, now was passed over by another
republican government. Perhaps, fortunately, he died shortly afterwards, on 21
June 1527.

MACHIAVELLI'S SIGNIFICANCE

How should we evaluate Machiavelli? Certainly, he was hardly the model of the successful humanist engaged in education and the pursuit of learning. He was too much the man of action for that. Neither did he embody traditional humanist values. As a diplomat, he practiced the deception he had advocated in the *Prince*. His personal life included the virtual abandonment of his wife and five children (the first of whom, at least, was a complete disappointment to him) in favor of a lifestyle which included a series of affairs and at least one mistress.[36] Even his political analysis was flawed. While he believed that it was impossible to build a state on the basis of a mercenary army, such armies were a major factor in the rise of modern states like France and Germany. What Machiavelli had advocated was more a federation of states in Italy under a strong prince than a modern nation. In the final analysis, it probably would not have worked.[37]

At the same time, Machiavelli's press has been much worse than he probably deserves. People tend to remember the *Prince,* with its emphasis on a despot, and forget about the *Discourses,* a series of studies of republican values. Even in the *Prince,* it almost seems as if Machiavelli takes certain positions for shock effect. It is not entirely clear what he believed. In spite of his insistence that all ethics depend on the immediate situation, he seemed attached to the medieval Christian attitude that to seek after monetary gain is evil. It is important to remember, too, that, as the English essayist Macaulay pointed out, Machiavelli must be seen in the light of his times. The complicated politics of Renaissance Italy (believe it or not, we have simplified them!) probably encouraged a more devious way of looking at life.[38]

Machiavelli stands at the doorway of the modern era. He might well be considered the first political scientist, seeking to provide a reasoned explanation for human activity in the political sphere. As a result, he insisted that politics had its own set of rules which differed from those that govern other institutions. Brutal as this sounds, Machiavelli "tells it like it is," without the hypocrisy which is frequently a part of political rhetoric.[39]

The emphasis which Niccolò placed on experience also marks him as a modern man. Classical examples abound in his works, but his own experience was the most important source. The disastrous use of foreign mercenaries led him to condemn them in any form. His first-hand experience of the danger of indecisive rulers in Florence resulted in his glorification of decisive action. He used the classics rather than worshiping them, and builds them into the future.

Machiavelli's influence on the development of Western education was indirect. Not a teacher himself, his political theory has nonetheless been studied by generations of students. The modern state which lies just beyond the horizon of his writings ultimately produced the systems of education which all of us have experienced. If people are to be citizens of a nation like the United States rather than of Chicago or Boston or Cheyenne, they must be taught common ways of seeing themselves and the world around them. Thus, Machiavelli's theories found their logical expression in the state supported educational systems which came to predominate.

Along with this, Machivelli's distrust of the church and its political influence caused him to see religion as important in the state because of its role in uniting a people, rather than for any transcendent value. Increasingly, schooling would be taken from the hands of the church, and done in secular settings which usually have reflected the general religious values of the population. The education of children in the United States, for example, has been largely in secular institutions with a Protestant religious flavor. State rather than church involvement in education represents a marked change from earlier times. While such a shift would not be accomplished in Machiavelli's own age, his ideas paved the way for it.[40]

Machiavelli's importance to education lies principally in his role as a spokesperson for the modern world. A tough-minded political theorist who was shaped as much by his experience as his reading, he represents the beginnings of the world of nations which we know today rather than of small regions, a world which has produced the education that has shaped all of our lives. As the ambiguous epitaph on his tomb indicates, "Words fail to describe such a man."

5

THE REFORMERS

From Abelard's day to the late 1400s more than seventy-five universities were started. By 1490, seventy of these were still functioning.[1] The Roman church had passed its high water mark and was in many respects in a slow decline. There were still many pious believers, but every level of the church had dark corners needing reform. The papacy had always had its highs and lows. There were more downs than ups in the fourteenth and fifteenth centuries. Discipline was lax in many monasteries. The functions of priests were often performed by substitutes (*vicars*) who had to charge fees for baptism, marriages, and other church functions because the titular priest kept most of the salary for himself. That the church had become for some an avenue to privilege and a way of avoiding grinding toil was evident in Abelard's time. Special *canon* courts in which professional church people were tried for civil offenses gave them a decided edge over the remainder of the population in obtaining justice. The only crime usually punishable by death for a member of the religious establishment was open treason to the church (heresy). Murder or lesser crimes against a non-church person usually provoked only a fine.

The taxation of peasants, merchants, and small farmers helped support the relatively luxurious lives of professional church people. Many ordinary folks resented the mockery of students and other clerics who had the protection of canon law but felt little need to observe the church's obligations. When economic and social resentment combined with feelings of thwarted nationalism, the stage was set for what historians would call the Reformation.

John Wyclif (1320-1384)

There had been recurring reforms of abuses since the early days of the Christian movement. In late fourteenth century England, an Oxford lecturer voiced almost all the criticisms that Luther, Calvin, Zwingli and others would level at the political/religious establishment more than a century later. This was John Wyclif, the mouthpiece of a strong anticlerical group in the English court.[2]

BACKGROUND

John was from Hipswell, Yorkshire in north England—near the village of Wyclif. He became a lecturer in theology at Oxford after having studied there, and spent one year (1360) as Master of Balliol College. He received several benefices (salaries) from the pope after being ordained as a priest. These were from parish churches (with vicars acting in his stead), while John continued to teach at Oxford. He wrote a great deal on many subjects, and some of what he wrote pleased the anticlerical elements in the government.

A lot of money was going annually from the English treasury to Rome. The English king, Edward III, refused to pay the "tribute" in 1366 and assigned John the task of writing a justification.[3] He complied, arguing that charity begins at home and that England needed the money more than Rome did. In any case, he said, the pope was only entitled to any money as an act of charity—a free offering. When a leading member of the anticlerical party, John of Gaunt, proposed confiscating some of the church's property, John Wyclif preached several sermons in justification of the idea. He even suggested that the English church should be independent of Rome. Many people were not willing to go that far, but the idea of taking away the church's property was attractive—especially to Edward III. With it, he could maintain 15 earls, 1,500 knights, 6,200 squires, and have quite a lot of cash left over for himself.[4] The king rewarded Wyclif with the rectory of Lutterworth for his service.[5]

WYCLIF'S IDEAS

Wyclif went much further than his economic justifications for the English crown. He anticipated almost every major criticism and argument of the later Reformation. He said that "good works" did not save, only God—who had always known who was predestined for salvation or the reverse—could provide salvation through His grace. Good works might indicate that one was among the elect, but did not affect the outcome. He said that Christians answer directly to God and need no priests or intermediaries. He thought that no priest or church should have any property. Ideally believers should own everything in common. Despite this position, he said the "powers that be" are also ordained of God, and he apparently did not give up his own incomes. He attacked church professionals for favoring the rich while not caring for the poor. He called them "robbers," "ravishing wolves," "gluttons," "devils," and "apes."[6]

There were numerous—really continuing—efforts by various church officials to silence Wyclif. Because papal leadership was not strong and because Wyclif had a good deal of popular as well as aristocratic support, none of these was successful. In 1381, however, there was a revolt in England. One of the leaders, a preacher named John Ball, quoted Wyclif to justify the insurrection. Wyclif denied favoring armed rebellion against authority, but the king had him barred from Oxford anyway. He retired to Lutterworth. There he organized a band of "Poor Preaching Priests" called Lollards. They continued expounding his ideas. He and two others translated the Bible into English. He believed that every person should be taught to read it.

Wyclif's ideas traveled quickly through the university circuit to other countries. In 1384 the pope summoned him to Rome, but instead of going he suffered a stroke and died. Thirty-one years later his ideas had become so influential in the thinking of reformers that the Council of Constance, as part of trying to silence one of his advocates, had his bones dug up from Lutterworth and thrown into a nearby creek.

John Huss (1369-1415)

The same council meeting that had Wyclif's bones thrown in the stream condemned the rector of the University of Prague to be burned at the stake for advocating similar ideas. This was John of Husinetz, the most popular preacher in Prague at the time. He had come to Prague at the age of twenty-one.

The university, as a full-fledged operation, was less than fifty years old and was divided between Bohemian (mostly Czechoslovakian) and German students and masters. The Germans did not yet have any universities of their own, so they had flocked to nearby Prague when it opened. Now they outnumbered and outvoted their Czech colleagues. Huss, selected as rector in 1402, was a strong adherent of Wyclif's ideas and was the recognized leader of the Bohemian reformist party. Almost every issue split along nationalistic lines. The Bohemians wanted reform; the Germans championed the papacy. Huss and his party believed in (naive) realism; the Germans advocated nominalism (see Chapter 3).

To complicate the picture, there was a three way struggle underway over who was really the pope. The two groups took differing positions, and the Czech king, Wenceslaus IV, was trying to stay neutral because he was barely hanging on to his throne. The Bohemians supported Wenceslaus. The Germans did not. When Wenceslaus altered the voting balance in the university to give the Czech's more clout, the Germans called a cessation and left town.[7]

This rhubarb was in 1409. By 1411 Huss was hiding out in the country and the local archbishop was in hot pursuit of him for preaching heresies. In 1414 a general council met at Constance to attempt a resolution of the three rival popes. It seemed a good time to iron out some of the difficulties over Huss's opposition. Emperor Sigismund (King of Hungary [1387-1437] and Holy Roman Emperor after 1411) promised a safe conduct for Huss to go to Constance on the northern Swiss border. The council, alarmed at Huss's teachings, had him imprisoned. Deliberations dragged on for months. Finally, Huss was condemned. Sigismund and others urged the reformist professor to take back the beliefs that offended the council. He refused to recant. In July 1415—one thousand years after the mob killed Hypatia—Huss walked under guard to a pile of wood outside the city. He was given one final chance to retract and refused. Huss said he was sure that Wyclif was in heaven and that he was confident of being with him; however, if Wyclif was in hell, he would also be glad to join him there.[8] The archbishop of Milan committed his soul to the devil, and as noon approached the fire consumed John Huss as he sang hymns.

Huss's executioners threw his ashes into the Rhine. Civil war broke out in Bohemia, with almost all Czechoslovaks taking the view that Huss was a martyr. (Five hundred years later they would take the day of Huss's death as the date of the chief national holiday.)

Europe's turbulent political climate continued through the fifteenth century. By the 1480s the Ottoman Turks controlled the Balkans and would soon stand at the gates of Vienna. United resistance to this possible invasion was hardly possible in a Europe that was more and more divided politically. In Germany, internal problems had encouraged a power shift from the emperor to individual towns and, especially, to regional princes. The Renaissance had contributed to the problem by encouraging nationalism. It was into this world of conflict and change that the Reformation's most famous character was born.

Martin Luther (1483-1546)

Martin Luther was born on 10 November 1483 into a society far more medieval than Renaissance in tone. He was the second son of a prosperous Saxon miner. His world was one in which there was a strong belief in the constant presence of evil spiritual powers, and one which tended to view religious observance in a highly mechanical way (I do something for God, and He does something for me).

YOUTH AND SCHOOLING

Luther's own education was along medieval lines. After early studies at local schools, he went to the University of Erfurt at seventeen, completing his bachelor's degree in 1502 and his master's in 1505. Since we hear little about him during this period, it seems safe to assume that he was a normal student. About this time, Luther began to show the tendencies toward depression and religious self-examination which would continue for the rest of his life.

In July 1505, Luther was caught in the open during a thunderstorm. Fearing that he would be killed by lightning, he vowed to enter a religious order if he were spared. While Luther was not obliged to keep a vow made under fear, he nevertheless did, and fifteen days later, entered the monastery of the Augustinian hermits at Erfurt. The fact that Luther made his decision so quickly may well be an indication that he was ready for some kind of life change. The community which he joined was the most prestigious in town, and serious in observing monastic rules. For someone who had already been plagued with doubts about his own salvation, entry into such an order would have been a logical step.

Historians interested in understanding Luther's personality have psychoanalyzed him with varying degrees of success.[9] It does seem clear that Luther's relationship with his father was a key factor in his own development. Hans Luther was a man given to acting on impulse. When Martin entered the monastery, Hans immediately disinherited him only to reinherit him a few weeks later. At the dinner following Luther's first mass, Hans publicly rebuked his son for not having been as obedient as he should have been. While it is over simple to lay the Lutheran Reformation solely at the doorstep of a son's unresolved conflicts with a domineering father, Luther's difficulty in dealing with church authority probably had some root in this paternal relationship.

The religious training Luther received was quite brief. Less than two years after his entry into the monastery, he was ordained a priest. It tells a lot about the times to say that Luther's training was better than that of most priests. After ordination, he continued his study and in 1508 was appointed a lecturer in philosophy at the University of Wittenberg. After several years, he was recalled to Erfurt, and became involved in the study of theology which would have such a great influence on his life.

SPIRITUAL CONVERSION

During these years, Luther's early peace in the monastery gave way to despair. He had become gripped by *Anfechtung,* a human struggle with temptation, which involved a deep religious conflict.[10] Luther had been exposed to the nominalist theology of William of Occam which insisted that God could never be known by human reason or pleased by human activity.[11] The young priest, already guilt ridden, began to despair of his own salvation. He could see no possibility of ever pleasing God no matter what he did. Counselors encouraged him to remember that repentance begins with the love of God, and pointed out that "God is not angry with you, you are angry with Him.[12] Luther sank more and more deeply into his depression.

The period from 1513 to 1518 was the beginning of Luther's spiritual conversion. Out of his despair, he began to realize that, through Scripture, individuals can come to faith by God's grace, and be made just by Him despite their own sinfulness. The answer to Luther's problem of how to achieve his salvation was that he had been asking the wrong question. He could do nothing to merit salvation by himself. Instead, by receiving the grace of God in faith, Martin was to find peace by throwing himself on God's mercy, and letting God do the work.

Luther continued his theological education during this crisis, receiving his doctorate in 1512, and went back to Wittenberg to teach. University education during this time was different than today. Instead of individual courses, a lecturer would begin a kind of running commentary on some work, and continue until the book was finished (however long it took). Then, he would take up another book, and begin the process again. Starting with the Psalms, Luther taught on the Bible, continuing on to Paul's letters to the Romans, the Galatians, and the Hebrews. (The fact that Luther chose to comment on Galatians and Romans is in itself significant because these letters of Paul explicitly deal with the question of how people are made just.)

Luther's movement away from the church of Rome was not something which happened suddenly. Only over time did his theology take shape, and his questions about the authority of the pope develop. One of the principal events in this process was the controversy on indulgences which began in 1516. Traditionally, the Roman church taught that even after sins were forgiven in confession, some temporal punishment still remained. The church, however, could commute this punishment on the condition that the penitent perform certain actions or say certain prayers. By Luther's time, these indulgences had become so associated with financial offerings that it appeared a person could buy his or her way out of purgatory with the purchase of indulgences.

BREAK FROM ROME

In 1510 the pope was in the process of rebuilding St. Peter's. He offered an indulgence to those who confessed their sins and made a financial contribution to the building fund. John Tetzel, a Dominican priest, was given the task of preaching the indulgence in Luther's part of Germany. Tetzel, whom no one ever accused of being subtle, went from town to town preaching and gathering funds, claiming that "when a coin into the coffers rings, a soul from purgatory springs."[13] Luther was offended by Tetzel's preaching on several accounts. First of all, the indulgence was put into a more prominent place than the sacrament of confession which was a prerequisite for it, a perversion in his eyes. Secondly, he was aware that half of the money collected was going to the German banking family of Fugger to pay for the transportation of the funds to Rome and to repay the family for helping the local bishop buy his office. If we add in the amount paid to Tetzel and his servant, less than half of the money collected ever reached Rome.

Luther preached against indulgences in 1516, arguing that they were opposed to true repentance. A year later indulgences became the central theme of his famous Ninety-Five Theses, which he posted on the door of the castle church at Wittenberg. This action was not particularly radical: the door was used as a kind of bulletin board to post the propositions of a professor who wished to debate an issue, though no one took up the offer in this case. The theses (propositions) were circulated throughout Europe in printed form, however, and began to be treated as a manifesto, enlisting the support of other reform minded individuals.

Opposition to Luther began to mount, but no immediate action was taken against him for political reasons. The Holy Roman Emperor, Maximillian, was dying and one of the leading candidates for his job was Charles of Ghent, the king of Spain. If Charles were elected emperor, much of Europe, including large sections of Italy, would be united under a single strong ruler. The papal court (*curia*) feared that they would be squeezed out of power if this occurred. One of the keys to the imperial election was Frederick of Saxony, one of the electors. He ruled Luther's section of Germany. While an unknown Augustinian priest who had strange ideas inspired no fear in the curia, Frederick did. Papal authorities, therefore, proceeded against Luther cautiously.

Papal representatives tried to get Luther to retract his ideas. Their efforts, however, only caused him to raise ever more serious questions about the Roman church. What had been a relatively simple questioning of indulgences now extended to the authority of the pope and the value of certain sacraments. Luther had come to believe that "where the word of God is preached and believed, there is the Church," independent of pope or bishop.[14]

In 1519 Charles of Ghent became emperor. There was no longer any need for the papal court to humor Frederick. In 1520 Luther was formally excommunicated, although the decree could not be promulgated in much of Germany because of support for him. The pace of the Reformation now began to accelerate. Luther wrote extensively for an ever widening audience. In 1521, he was declared an outlaw at the Diet of Worms, and went into hiding under Frederick's protection at Wartburg Castle, where he continued to write. Eventually, he returned to Wittenberg in triumph. In 1525, the last important event of Luther's life occurred. This was his marriage to Katie von Bora, a former nun.

Luther was also engaged during this later period of his life in continual attempts to temper the ideas of more radical reformers. While Luther had raised questions about the scriptural bases for several of the sacraments, he had never challenged the mass. Now, Zwingli and others proposed doctrines more anti-Roman than Luther's. Luther's criticism of learning that was not biblically oriented was amplified by Carlstadt and others into the contention that all education was anti-religious and dangerous. They concluded that most schooling, and especially university education, ought to be abolished.

LUTHER ON EDUCATION

It was against the background of these controversies that Luther's ideas on education began to emerge. For him, education was necessary to Christian life, because a person's eternal salvation depended upon his or her ability to read and understand Scripture. Thus, Luther provided a strong religious reason for basic literacy. He also saw human life as divided into three interrelated spheres: the family, the state, and the church. Each of these was important, since each contributed to salvation. And, Luther argued, all these were benefited by an educated population. In a "Letter to the Christian Nobility of the German

Nation" (1520), he insisted on this, but he argued for a reform of the arts and theology faculties in all German universities.

Luther's first major educational work, the "Letter to the Mayors and Aldermen of Germany on Behalf of Christian Schools" (1524), took up these themes in some detail. In it, he argued that schooling had deteriorated as a result of political turmoil. Because some parents neglect schooling out of a lack of piety or their own inability to teach, the welfare of the state demands that mayor and aldermen support schooling—even to the extent of providing funding. More is demanded, however, than mere literacy training. The study of languages and the liberal arts are necessary. Because Scripture had been tainted by inaccurate translations, any educated man (university education was not usually available to women) must know the classical languages for these are "the scabbard in which the word of God is sheathed."[15] The needs of civil government also demanded liberal education in order to provide competent officials for the state.

The theme of an educated leadership is expanded in the "Sermon on the Duty of Sending Children to School" (1530). In this sermon, prepared as a model for evangelical preachers, Luther argued for schools to furnish ministers for the spiritual sphere of human activity and to provide civil authorities for the political sphere. For parents to provide a son for the ministry is a service to both the spiritual and temporal realms, because civil peace is one of the fruits of the ministerial office. While the temporal ministry is not as important as the spiritual, it is still ordained by God. Without it people would not be able to live together in society. Lawyers and scribes are important because they formulate the laws, and help people to learn them. Especially important are schoolmasters, whose role is almost as important as that of ministers. In fact, said Luther, "If I had to give up preaching and my other duties, there is no office I would rather have than that of school teacher. For I know that next to the ministry, it is the most useful, greatest and best; and I am not sure which of the two is to be preferred."[16] If a country cannot provide people for such key roles, he argued, it deserves to perish.

Less idealistically, Luther pointed out that education for the ministry virtually guaranteed employment, because a great number of parishes had no pastor. Similarly, he thought competent civil servants, also in short supply, likely to be rewarded with wealth, importance, and prestige.

These religious and secular reasons for why the state should support education were among Luther's favorite points. The state also, according to him, should compel attendance at school so that individuals would be available to fill the spiritual and secular offices, for the same reason that the state can draft individuals into the military to insure national defense.

Luther's involvement in the practical side of education was also extensive. His translation of the Bible into German was one of the great educational achievements of the time. A measure of its success is that between 1522 and 1534, twenty thousand copies of the New Testament section were printed, a staggering number if we take the low level of literacy into account. Also of educational value were the more than thirty popular hymns he composed. In an era in which many could not read and more could not write, an efficient way of communicating religious ideas was in hymns which could be sung and remembered. That some of these have survived to our own day ("A Mighty Fortress is Our God," for example) testifies to their appeal.

Organizationally, Luther was involved in the foundation of a Latin school at Wittenberg which provided, to use our labels, elementary, secondary, and higher education for boys as well as a primary school for girls. He also helped sponsor a reform of the University of Wittenberg along evangelical lines, with biblical theology taking the role of primacy from scholastic philosophy.

SIGNIFICANCE

It was as a teacher and preacher that Luther made his greatest educational contributions. His role was that of the charismatic leader, rather than the speculative thinker or organizational administrator. Even before his split with the Roman church, Luther was a popular lecturer at Wittenberg. After a decline in university enrollment to a low of fifty in 1525, the student population of Wittenberg rose to seven hundred by 1543, largely as a result of Luther's lectures. Contemporary accounts paint a portrait of a teacher deeply concerned about the material and spiritual welfare of his students, as well as one good-humored enough to join in their initiation rites and games. After his marriage to Katie von Bora, his house became a center of student activity. Many of the students lived and ate with his family. Concerned with the intellectual and religious development of those he taught, he found them scholarships and occasionally, wives as well.

The last years of Luther's life were given to teaching, preaching, and his continual efforts to spread the Reformation. His lecturing continued, as did his constant discussions, many of which have been preserved in *Table Talks,* transcripts of his mealtime conversations. Frequently, he was obliged to travel in order to help some local community in its reforming effort or to settle disputes. It was in this latter role that he undertook a winter journey in 1546 to help settle a family dispute between two princes in Mansfield. On the return trip, he grew increasingly weak and died on February 18 before reaching home.

Luther's contributions to education came mainly from the theological underpinnings which he provided for schooling. As each person became more directly responsible for his or her salvation, the need to be able to read Scripture provided a religious basis for schooling. The insistence that the state had an obligation to support such education set the stage for public support of education and for compulsory attendance laws. Luther's disenchantment with speculative scholastic philosophy moved schooling more in the direction of practical learning. Martin Luther had helped to bring about a change in the religious fabric of Europe and, in the process, had also helped to recast the direction of European education.

If Martin Luther was the heart of the German Reformation, his younger colleague and friend, Phillip Melanchthon, was its right arm. A brilliant teacher and superb organizer, Melanchthon put many of Luther's reforms into operation.

Phillip Melanchthon (1497-1560)

In many ways, Luther and Melanchthon are a study in contrasts. Like Luther, Melanchthon came from a relatively prosperous family: his father was a metal worker, probably an armor maker. Phillip, who was born in 1497 (fourteen years after Luther), had a different youth than did Martin. Where Luther's world had been medieval, Melanchthon was a child of the Renaissance. After his father's death in 1507, he came under the influence of his granduncle, John Reuchlin, one of the most distinguished humanists of the age. Reuchlin guided Phillip's early education. By the youth's fifteenth birthday, he could read and write Latin and Greek and was acquainted with grammar, arithmetic, rhetoric, history, and geography.[17]

At the age of twelve, which was only slightly younger than usual for the time, Phillip began life as a student at the University of Heidelberg. He was more gifted than most of his professors, so he studied largely on his own. He received his bachelor's degree in 1511, and his master's in 1514. The emphasis of his study was not theology, but classical languages. Early in his education, he became convinced like Luther that scholastic philosophy was wrong, but unlike Luther, laid the blame not on Aristotle's ideas, but on poor translations which distorted the meaning of the text. This concern for accuracy in translation was to become one of the major themes of Melanchthon's life.

In 1518, Melanchthon went to Wittenberg University as professor of Greek. There he fell under Luther's influence. Already, he had become convinced of the need to return to a study of the Bible to understand Christian life. He had begun to raise questions about the Catholic church even before he met Luther, whose presence at the university acted as a catalyst for the development of Melanchthon's own theology.

In many ways, Melanchthon fits the stereotype of the eccentric genius. He was thin, walked with a limp, and had a speech impediment. Luther described him with a word we would probably translate as "wimp." Phillip was so completely absorbed in his study, in fact, that Luther had to convince him that marriage would be more than a perpetual inconvenience to his life of scholarship. In intellectual matters, however, Melanchthon was neither absent minded nor clumsy. Theologically, he probably exerted a stronger influence on Luther than Luther did on him, and the older man stood in continual awe of his intellectual abilities. In a variety of senses, he possessed talents which Luther lacked. Where Luther's thoughts were frequently unpolished, Phillip's were clear and specific. In situations in which Luther's short temper was likely to get the best of him, Melanchthon was contained and reasonable. His role as the official representative of Lutheran Protestantism at every major discussion between Protestants and Catholics from 1529 to 1560 is testimony to his ability to think quickly and speak diplomatically.

UTILITY OF THE CLASSICS

Melanchthon's ideas also differed from those of Luther in several ways. While he disliked the intricacies of scholastic philosophy, he was a fan of Aristotle and believed that a true understanding of his works would be useful in promoting

Christian faith. Like the Renaissance humanists, he saw a positive value in the study of classical languages. These could open religious books not available in translation. His goal was *Beredsamkeit,* "learned piety," which was the cultivation of *all* the powers of the human spirit. The use of humanism as an educational tool to promote evangelical principles was one of the great convictions of his life.

To Luther's educational thought, motivated by medieval values and Reformation theology, Melanchthon added the humanistic values of eloquence and usefulness. Knowledge was good only to the degree that it had a purpose, but traditional studies like grammar, rhetoric, and logic could help an individual to think and express ideas clearly. In addition to these subjects and the study of language, history was important because it encouraged German patriotism and it showed how God had worked in human life.

The curriculum which Melanchthon proposed gave expression to all of these values. Learning was divided into three major areas, each with its particular subjects. The teaching of thinking and reading demanded a knowledge of classical languages (Latin, Greek, and Hebrew), as well as logic and rhetoric. The teaching of natural reality was accomplished through physics, cosmology (the philosophy of the universe), physiology and psychology (more the philosophy of how we know than the experimental psychology of today). Finally, the study of ethics and politics would help people to grow in the third necessary area, that of practical life.

Melanchthon's educational theory is most clearly seen in the *Visitation Papers* of 1528. Reform minded professors from the University of Wittenberg had been asked to make a survey of religious and educational life in Saxony. Their reports painted a dismal picture of religious observance and educational opportunity. Melanchthon responded by constructing a plan for improving these local situations. In the first part, he detailed the major principles of Christian faith to be taught and carried out. In the second, he proposed a model for schooling. The *Visitation Papers* exhorted people to send their children to school and set down qualifications for teachers. Each school, according to the scheme, was to be divided into three classes. In the first belonged those who were beginning the study of Latin. To this, in the second, was added the study of grammar and a bit of religion. Finally, in the most advanced class, grammar, meter (in order to compose poetry), reading, writing, singing, logic, rhetoric, and religion were taught. Eventually, Melanchthon added a lower class to serve as a bridge between the ordinary schools which taught vernacular reading and writing, and the classical school designed to prepare male students for university study. While these reforms were never put into practice during Melanchthon's lifetime, they later served as a model for German school development.

EDUCATIONAL ACTIVITIES

Melanchthon was a consultant in the foundation or reform of a wide variety of schools. At least fifty-six German cities sought his advice when beginning schools. Throughout his life, he fought against the low quality of teachers and the haphazard support of cities for schooling, continually urging state support of schools and the payment of decent salaries to end teacher "moonlighting."

Like Luther, he considered the role of teachers to be like that of ministers since they, too, were concerned "with godly things."[18]

It was in the universities that his ideas were most clearly put into practice. His reorganization of the University of Wittenberg resulted in a more humanistic approach to the teaching of philosophy, and the hiring of humanists to teach mathematics and medicine. Melanchthon also helped reform the Universities of Rostock and Frankfurt-on-the-Oder, revised the curriculum at Colgne, Tübingen, Leipzig and Heidelberg, and founded the Universities of Königsberg, Jena, and Marburg. His abilities as an organizer as well as theoretician made him an important figure in the development of a whole network of evangelical schools.

Engaged in all these activities, Melanchthon still found time to continue his scholarly pursuits. Unhappy with the quality of available texts, he wrote books on rhetoric and logic, ethics, physics, Aristotelian philosophy, as well as on Greek and Latin grammar. Dissatisfied with the available editions of the classical authors, he turned out new ones and wrote summaries to accompany them. He advised Luther in such projects as the translation of the German Bible and the formulation of theological position papers. Phillip was gifted with both scholarly and organizational ability, as well as a formidable talent for hard work.

Though never formally ordained, Melanchthon took his ministry to students seriously. Like Luther, he was a popular teacher, attracting fifteen hundred listeners to some of his lectures. A fatherly man, he loaned students money on the slightest pretext, counseled them, and helped them find jobs. Perhaps this special interest in the welfare of his pupils was a result, in part, of a need to compensate for the disappointingly average abilities of his own children.

Melanchthon's death in 1560, three years after that of his wife and fourteen years after Luther's, marked the end of the first phase of the Reformation. Melanchthon had been unsuccessful in taking on the mantle of leadership after Luther's death. However gifted, he did not have the charismatic quality needed to fill Luther's shoes.

Melanchthon had systematized and put into practice what Luther had believed and preached. These efforts had resulted in a strong call for popular education, motivated by gospel values. German schooling, like its counterpart in other European countries, remained divided along class lines, with the ordinary people learning to read and write in German and the privileged few studying the classics and going on to the university. It may have been more extensive than it had been during the Middle Ages, though evidence on this point is scanty. Vernacular schooling for non-aristocratic girls probably became more widespread, but the Reformation tended to diminish classical schooling opportunities for females. Wherever politics made possible confiscation of Roman church property—in England, for example—governments tended to seize monastic land and buildings. In the process most external schools necessarily suspended operations. Those for males were often "refounded," but most of those for females remained closed. The result was a net loss of classical schooling opportunities for women in Protestant areas. Most Protestant (and Roman Catholic) males agreed with Luther's basic conclusion about male and female roles, though they might not have expressed the reasons as curiously as he did: "Men have broad shoulders and narrow hips, and accordingly they possess intelligence," said Luther. "Women have narrow shoulders and broad hips." The conclusion? Women "ought to stay home; the way they were created indicates this, for they have broad hips and a wide fundament to sit upon." They should "keep house and bear and raise children."[19]

If the Reformation did not bring the surge of opportunities for women that historians have thought, it did have far-reaching effects on education. Universities were becoming more broadly oriented toward the humanities rather than simply to the study of philosophy and theology. The theory had been formulated that schooling was a duty of the state, which shared responsibility for the salvation of souls with the church, and the link had been made between political stability and popular education. These ideas, forged in the furnace of the German Reformation, would be carried across the Atlantic by reform minded Puritans, and find expression in the early growth of American schooling.

The effect of Reformation thinking and politics on the life and education of a common European can be seen in the biography of Thomas Platter, a man of extraordinary persistence. A younger contemporary of Johannes Butzbach and Desiderius Erasmus (Chapter 4), Platter had an equally difficult start in life and had many similar experiences to theirs. In the long run, they would remain loyal to the reformed medieval Roman church. Living in a hotbed of Protestant revolt, Platter reached a different conclusion.

Thomas Platter (1499-1582)

While Butzbach was struggling through his studies at Deventer, his Swiss counterpart entered the world on Shrove Tuesday (the day before Lent) 1499. Thomas Platter was born in the high mountain village of Grenchen, canton of Valais, Switzerland. The bells were just ringing for mass. This "omen" and other considerations led his father to hope that he would be a priest. Both sides of the family had been in the area for a long time. His mother was the daughter of "Old Hans" Summermatter who lived to be 126 and had many children, including a son when he was past 100. (Thomas later had a son when he was 75.) Neither side of the family was well off financially.

A HARD CHILDHOOD

Plague had been common in Europe since the eighth century. There were two forms, bubonic and pneumonic, which tended to break out every nine to twelve years. Both forms were transmitted initially by fleas on black rats and then from person to person during epidemics. The bubonic form killed 60 to 80 percent of those infected. Pneumonic was always fatal. (There were periodic recurrences until the eighteenth century when grey rats killed off the black ones and when cholera and pseudotuberculosis gave immunity.)[20] Thomas' father was "taken by a plague" and died when Thomas was still an infant. The family was already in debt. His mother quickly remarried. In fact, she survived two more husbands after that and had children by all of them. She worked hard to take care of her offspring, burying two of them with her own hands. They, too, had died of plague and grave diggers were expensive. Thomas called his mother "a brave and courageous woman, though somewhat rough. . . . Toward us, the first children, she was very rough, so that we seldom came into the house."[21]

Thomas had two sisters and three brothers that he knew. He thought that there may have been more. These were all older than he and were quickly put to work when the father died. Thomas was passed around among some of his father's sisters. From the first, he saw almost nothing of his mother. "When my mother was recovered [from childbirth], she had sore breasts, so that she could not nurse me, and I never once had any mother's milk. . . . That was the beginning of my misery. I was therefore obliged to drink cow's milk through a little horn." When he was in his teens, Thomas saw his mother for the first time in many years. He did not think that she was happy to see him.

At age six Thomas went to live on a farm with one of his mother's sisters. He was immediately assigned the task of herding goats. He could not manage all eighty of them very well and was often knocked down by them and trampled. His uncle frequently beat him for letting them get in the wrong place. After two or three years, one of his aunts on his father's side tried to improve his situation by placing him in another family. They beat him less, but he had other mishaps. Once he fell into a vat of scalding milk, the result of which was permanent scars. He still had to herd goats. He narrowly escaped falling several thousand feet in the mountains one night. His frightened aunt sent him to herd cows for a different uncle, a "fiery and passionate man" who gave the boy many thrashings. Again one of his father's sisters tried to rescue him. She decided to send him to school.

Thomas was about nine when he went to learn his Latin abc's with a paternal cousin who was a priest. The treatment there made his earlier situations seem attractive by comparison. "Things really went evilly with me," is the way Thomas put it. The priest did not teach much; rather, he had his pupils in town begging for eggs. "He beat me very severely, often took me by the ears and dragged me on the ground, so that I screamed like a goat that had been stuck with a knife." This happened so frequently that "neighbors cried to him, asking whether he would kill me." At this point a teenaged nephew, Paul Summermatter, rescued young Thomas by taking him on as an abc shooter.

Platter was even younger than Butzbach had been when he began his life as an abc shooter. His experiences were similar. The pair wandered from Stalden to Zurich to Meissen to Naumburg to Halle before settling in Breslau.

> The city of Breslau had seven parishes, and each had a separate school. . . . Once there were in the city, so it was said, several thousand bacchants and shooters, who supported themselves wholly by alms. It was also said that some had been there twenty or thirty years, or longer with their shooters, who had to wait on them. I have carried home to . . . my bacchant, often in one evening five or six loads [of food]. People gave to me very willingly, because I was so small and was Swiss—for the Swiss were much liked.

Thomas was ill three times in Breslau. The town provided a hospital where the students "had good attention (and) good beds, but there was great vermin therein, as large as ripe hempseed, so that I, as others also, preferred to lie on the ground." On the whole life was pretty good in Breslau, and the little shooter and his bacchant remained there for some time: "Occasionally in summer we went after supper to the beer hall to beg for beer. Then the drunken Polish peasants gave us so much, that I have often unawares become so drunk that I could not return to school again, though I was only a stone's-throw away." Thomas summed up the Breslau situation as follows: "There was enough to eat, but we did not study much."

From Breslau "little Tommy" and Paul wandered to Dresden, Nuremberg, and finally to Munich. Thomas studied little, begged a lot, suffered beatings and threats from his bacchant, and after about six years ran away. Paul pursued his shooter, because he was so good at begging, but after wandering from Munich to Zurich to Strasbourg to Schlettstadt (and many smaller towns in between) Thomas made his escape permanent.

FURTHER EDUCATION

After a visit to his hometown, Platter returned to Schlettstadt where he studied in what he considered to be the first real school of his career. He supported himself and a friend by begging. He was about eighteen at this time. Then he traveled to Zurich where he studied with the schoolmaster of Our Lady's Cathedral, a Father Oswald Myconius. Myconius was noted as a good teacher, though "cruelly whimsical." He was tough on Platter, but liked him and made him *custos* (custodian) of the school. The protest ideas of Ulrich Zwingli were already circulating by this time. Platter still intended to become a priest, though he must have been affected by the Protestant arguments. As custos it was his duty to build a fire every morning. One day he was late and had no wood, so he hastily took a wooden statue of St. John from the cathedral church and made a fire with it. Instead of remorse, he felt a sense of exhilaration. But he was wise enough not to mention the incident to anyone until many years later. Had the wrong people found out, he thought he would likely have been killed.

These were turbulent days in Zurich. Martin Luther's German revolt was fresh news. Huldreich (Ulrich) Zwingli was preaching Protestant theology and Swiss self-rule politics. (Zwingli, born in a mountain village south of Zurich, was humanistically educated and was an admirer of Erasmus. He was a popular priest who gradually became convinced to the views of Huss. His sermons were political as well as religious, and he had become Zurich's major political figure.) The French king wanted Zurich to become part of France, and some of the large French minority in the city agreed. Rome was trying to salvage Zurich and as many other places as it could. Zwingli opposed both factions. The air was thick with intrigue, assassination plots, civil war, and double-dealing. Zwingli's preaching was convincing to Platter, so he decided not to become a priest. He acted as messenger for the Protestants and was therefore in danger many times. All the while he continued his studies.

When he was about thirty, Platter married a woman named Anna. She was an orphan who had been a servant in the Myconius family for seventeen years. Platter's account does not say very much about her, although it was written to their son Felix who may have already known most of what his father could tell. From what little is said, it appears that the two of them got on well together. They both worked hard. Thomas had a tutoring job that helped some. He had also spent a year as apprentice to a ropemaker and some time in Basel learning more of that trade. He had secretly copied Myconius' notes on Homer and Euripides, and taught school in his home canton of Valais briefly after getting married. They went to Basel from Valais, where Thomas got a position as "dispenser." This was a minor town office, but it paid enough to support his wife and daughter. He had already learned Greek fairly well and knew some Hebrew. He wanted to know more: "I studied industriously, arose early, and went to bed late. So that I have often had a headache, and had such a terrible dizziness that I often have had to hold myself up by the benches. The physician would gladly have helped me with blood-letting and mixed drugs for the stomach, but all was in vain."

Because of his dizziness, Platter and Anna took their little daughter away from Basel. They worked as servants for a physician. The doctor cured Platter of his dizzy condition by having him sleep more and eat better, but the Platters' daughter, Margaret, died of the plague and so did the doctor. Thomas copied the doctor's book of remedies and medicines before he left to live again in Zurich.

Back in Zurich, the situation was drifting quickly towards confrontation between Zwingli's forces and those of the Roman Catholic League. On 11 October 1531 Zwingli led fifteen hundred troups against eight thousand Catholic opponents at Kappel. Zwingli's forces lost. Platter was not part of the group that engaged in battle, but he was in a party of reinforcements leaving Zurich to help as the survivors came straggling back. "Some came who had only one hand, some held their head[s] between their hands, mournfully wounded and bloody," Platter remembered. "One met us also whose intestines were hanging out, so he carried them in his hands; and people went with them who lighted the way, for it was dark."

Zwingli had died in the fight. His body was drawn and quartered and ceremonially burned at the stake on a dung heap. Martin Luther, who one would have thought an ally of Zwingli's, was not upset at his death. Because he and Zwingli did not agree on some minor doctrinal matters, Luther saw his death as God's just punishment. The Zurich protest group was demoralized. Platter went back to Basel where he arranged for Myconius to come as pastor and leader of the Protestant faction in the city.

PLATTER AS TEACHER

For four years Platter worked as "reader" (assistant) in the pedagogium (university) of Basel. He and three others formed a partnership to go into the printing business, but one of the partners did not work and they made no money. Two more daughters, Margaret (probably named for the first child who had died) and Ursula, were born here, as was a son named Felix. Platter became a burgher, a citizen of the town, by being elected into the guild "Of the Bears." This was a printers' guild. Platter bought out his printing partners and worked on his own. He also purchased three houses on credit, took in boarders, and gradually made enough money to pay for the property.

When he was forty-two Platter sold his printing interests and accepted an offer from the city council of Basel to become master of the city's "gymnasium." (The term "gymnasium" was part of the Renaissance/humanistic resurrection of Greek labels. It was already in use before 1500 in Germanic areas. It designated what we would now call a secondary school, and it specialized in humanistic studies—especially Latin and Greek classics.) Platter organized the curriculum along the lines of the gymnasium at Strasbourg where his brother was a teacher. Platter had only three assistants, so he made four classes instead of the ten at Strasbourg. From the beginning he had difficulty with the Faculty of Arts at the University of Basel. He was teaching dialectics (logic) and having his students study classical authors. The arts masters wanted to reserve these for themselves. There were too many masters for the number of available students, and they were hardly enthusiastic about having Platter teach material that was too difficult for some of them. The feud lasted for years, with Platter generally winning more than the arts masters. His gymnasium was much more famous than the university in the same town.

When Platter was seventy-three he wrote for his son Felix a rather lengthy autobiographical account of his life to that point. He had acquired property. He was respected in the city and in the region. Felix had been a successful medical student at Montpellier in southern France, the most prestigious medical school of the time. Felix had also married well and was the most noted physician in Basel. But all had not been smooth. Margaret, Ursula, and Anna perished in separate "pestilences" (plagues).

After Anna died, Thomas remarried. His young wife had six children—two boys and four girls—before Platter's death at the age of eighty-three. Felix had no children but helped rear his much younger half brothers and sisters. One of the boys, named Thomas, noted Felix's success, studied at Montpellier, and became a distinguished physician. Following their father's example, both Felix and young Thomas wrote accounts of their travels and student days at Montpellier.[22]

Both Platter's and Butzbach's accounts reveal many details of life and schooling in the fifteenth and sixteenth centuries. There is an interesting difference in tone in the two autobiographies. Both men were religious and attributed much to God. But Platter did not conceptualize reality in terms of evil spirits or demons. Platter knew that his wandering days had not been best for him. Instead of subjecting his own sons to the same life, he saw to it that they received good schooling. Butzbach could only recommend to his young half brother the same course he had followed. The anti-feminist moralisms of Butzbach ("drunkeness and tipling are horrible things in women") are absent in Platter's account. Both men had strong feelings about their early lives. Butzbach, however, did not know that he had had them. If someone had suggested to him that he still felt hurt or injury over the things that had happened to him, he would not have understood what they meant. Platter's account makes the reader feel that he would have comprehended such a statement.

As we have seen, the Reformation in Germany resulted in a call for new and more universal forms of schooling. While all of this was going on, however, the Catholic church was not standing idle. Beginning even before Luther's attempt to recast Christianity, various individuals had begun to reform the church's religious observance from within. (Huss and many of his followers considered themselves good Catholics.) Historians have frequently called this Catholic internal effort at reform the Counter-Reformation. More accurately, it might be called the Catholic Reformation, since it did not arise in opposition to Protestantism, but out of a realization that the Catholic church was in need of change.[23] While efforts to check the spread of Protestantism were part of its activities, it was also deeply concerned with restoring religious faith and observance.

Ignatius Loyola (c. 1492-1556)

A major figure in this Catholic Reformation was a Spanish knight, Ignatius of Loyola. Ignatius was born in 1492 or 1493 to a family of minor nobility. He was baptized "Inigo" and later changed his name to Ignatius. After the death of his parents (he was about fourteen at the time), he was raised by his older brothers and trained to be a military officer. Ignatius became a typical swashbuckling soldier, more interested in chivalry, wine, women, and song than in religion. We know, for example, that in 1515 court proceedings were instituted against him for some unnamed but extremely serious crime.

The path of advancement for someone like Ignatius usually involved entering the military service of some prominent noble. The more powerful the lord, the greater the likelihood that the soldier would make a name for himself. With this in mind, Ignatius became a junior officer in the service of the Duke of Navarre, a distant relative. This decision was to prove fateful for the direction of his later life.

Under the strong rule of Isabella the Catholic, Spain had prospered. In 1504, however, she had died, leaving a disputed throne. One major candidate for the throne, her son-in-law Philip the Fair of France, also died in 1506, leaving Isabella's husband, Ferdinand, as the logical successor. The country remained peaceful until his death in 1516; then, things began to come apart. Ferdinand had designated his principal advisor, Cardinal Cisneros, as temporary ruler after his death. However, Crown Prince Charles had designated his tutor, Adrian of Utrecht, to govern until he took control. The arrival of Charles himself in 1517 to claim his throne settled that problem. Initially successful, Charles left the country to be crowned Holy Roman Emperor, a title to which he had just been elected, and the country rose in revolt. While the revolution was caused largely by Spanish resentment over foreign rule (Charles had lived his entire life in Belgium), some nobles used the opportunity provided by the civil unrest to claim independence from their lords and the monarchy. Ignatius was involved in the military campaigns of the Duke of Navarre's army against the rebels.

With Spain weakened by civil conflict, the French saw an opportunity to bring the disputed territory of Navarre, which had once belonged to them, back under their control. As part of a plan to accomplish this, a French army laid seige to the regional capital, Pamplona. Among the city's Spanish defenders was Ignatius Loyola. During a fierce battle, Ignatius was struck by a canon ball which passed between his legs, slightly wounding one and shattering the other. After the leg had been set by French doctors, he was sent home to Loyola to recover.

This was an era in which even bloody wars were conducted according to elaborate rules of gentlemanly conduct.

Ignatius' recovery was long and painful. It was discovered that the French surgeons had either botched the job of setting the fracture or else the leg had been moved on the trip home. As a result, the leg had to be operated on and reset. Ignatius saw that the leg was healing in such a way that it would be slightly deformed. Fearing that he wouldn't be able to wear the tight boots then in fashion in Spain, he ordered the doctors to saw off a piece of bone which protruded, along with the flesh around it. After doing this, they put the leg in traction and waited for it to heal. The end result was a long and painful recovery, during which Ignatius nearly died.

CONVERSION

For someone as active as Ignatius, being forced to lie still in bed was as bad as the pain. To distract himself, he had the castle at Loyola searched for interesting reading material, preferably novels which dealt with military exploits and romance. Unfortunately, the only two books which could be found were a life of Christ, and a copy of *The Lives of the Saints*. Figuring that any reading material was better than none, Ignatius started through these books. As he read, his view of life began to change. Instead of dreaming about the noble deeds he could do for some lord, he began to think about the great things he could accomplish for God. Romantic as always, he decided to make a pilgrimage to the Holy Land, and then to enter some monastery in which he could give his life to prayer and penance.[24]

After his recovery in 1522, he set out on what was to become a far longer pilgrimage than he had expected. In an all-night vigil at the shrine of Our Lady of Montserrat (he was inclined to make dramatic gestures), he left his sword and elegant clothing, and departed for the town of Manresa where he would live as a beggar for the rest of the year.[25] In the winter of 1523, he began his pilgrimage to the Holy Land, traveling by way of Venice and Rome. Such a pilgrimage in the sixteenth century was an involved affair. Even if one were wealthy, almost anything (for example, capture by pirates, shipwreck) could happen on the ocean voyage and, for someone like Ignatius who begged the money he needed as he went, the trip could be a real adventure. Despite numerous difficulties, he arrived in the Holy Land and visited the Christian shrines, returning to Europe in 1524.

IGNATIUS AS A STUDENT

During the pilgrimage, Ignatius had decided to become a priest. However, his early education had given him basic literacy in Spanish, but no command of Latin and no formal training in philosophy and theology. He had no choice but to begin school all over again. At the age of thirty-one, this proud soldier could be found sitting alongside boys less than half his age in a Barcelona school, studying basic Latin. Like many older students, he found that learning was difficult. In spite of his age, he made progress and in 1526 went to the University of Alcalá to begin higher studies. Again, like many students then and now, he attacked college studies without any definite plan, spending a year and a half attending whatever lectures he wanted to, in the hope that this would somehow prepare him to study theology. This lack of organization in his own early studies would be corrected in the more definite model he would propose for Catholic higher education.

Spain during this period had become deeply suspicious of any unusual religious movements, fearing they would give Protestantism a foot in the door. The Inquisition, a powerful church court, examined every person suspected of heresy. If found guilty, the person could be burned at the stake. Even if innocent, a suspect might spend a long time in prison before being cleared. During his time at Alcalá, Ignatius was investigated by the Inquisition and ordered to stop preaching and change his rough style of dress. He transferred to the University of Salamanca in 1528 and was imprisoned for twenty-one days, after which the Inquisition found him innocent and released him. On several other occasions, this staunch defender of Roman Catholicism would come under suspicion for his unusual lifestyle and preaching. It was a measure of the fear during this time that any religious difference was immediately suspect, whether the person under suspicion professed to be Protestant or not.

In 1528, Ignatius left Spain for France to become a student at the famous University of Paris. On arriving there, he discovered how little his self-selected university training had prepared him for serious study. Once again, he had to start at the beginning, learning the basics of Latin grammar and literary style with young boys.

The still medieval course of studies at Paris was divided according to subject matter. First of all, a student would begin with the Latin and Greek classics, and then move on to philosophy. After this program had culminated in the master of arts or doctor's degree (the latter was a master's degree with a fee added), an ambitious student would proceed to the study of theology, culminating in the doctor of theology degree. There was a clear hierarchy of study: first humanities, then philosophy, and finally theology were the curriculum of anyone who wanted to be considered really well educated.

Ignatius began this structured program in 1529, receiving the master's degree in 1533 and the doctorate in 1534. In that same year, he began the study of theology with the Dominican priests at the university. His formal study ended in 1535, however, when persistent stomach troubles forced him to quit without receiving the theological doctorate.

While Ignatius was studying, he engaged in a variety of other activities. His greatest gifts were not those of the literary expert or philosopher or theologian, but of a leader. In Spain, people had gravitated toward him, which was one of the reasons the Inquisition investigated him. His charismatic personality was also in evidence at Paris. Beginning with two friends with whom he roomed, Francis Xavier and Peter Faber, he gathered a group of young men around him, all of whom were university students or faculty, and deeply religious. After Ignatius led them individually through a thirty day period of prayer based on his own religious experiences, several changed the direction of their lives. Ignatius thus became the leader of this group of highly talented young men.[26]

Gradually, these friends began to believe that God wanted them to work together. In August of 1534, Ignatius and six of his associates made promises of poverty and celibacy, and vowed to go to the Holy Land to convert the Muslims. If they were unable to get to Palestine, they promised that they would go to Rome and ask the pope what they should do. Even though they had banded together, they were not entirely sure of what direction their lives should take. For the next year or so, the companions were separated, with Ignatius back in Spain recovering his health and later preaching and giving the "Spiritual Exercises" in Venice. In 1537, he sent the others to Rome to ask the pope to allow them all to be ordained. The permission was obtained and Ignatius and his friends became priests in June of 1537.

The whole group now went to Rome, where two of them began to teach theology at the pope's request. It became obvious that the political situation in Palestine would not allow them to go there as they had wished. At the pope's urging, they remained in Italy to help revitalize the church there.

THE JESUITS

The group began to take a definite shape. Initially, they had been drawn together by their friendship, and had become a band of "reformed priests." Now, they decided to ask for recognition as a religious order, with a definite structure and purpose in the church. In 1540, this group which now called itself the Society of Jesus was formally recognized as a religious order in the Catholic church.

This new order was different from those which had previously been founded. Benedictine groups had insisted that members build their activities around permanent monasteries in which they would live for their entire lives. The Franciscans, Dominicans and other mendicants had allowed their members to be transferred from place to place, but they were still bound by long periods of prayer in which the entire group was expected to participate. Going against this tradition, Ignatius insisted that the members of his Society be mobile, with no institutions which they were obligated to serve on a permanent basis. Less emphasis was placed on prayer in common, and more on personal private prayer. Ignatius' goal was to have a group of highly trained priests able to go anywhere their services were needed. This organizational vision which seems rather ordinary today was considered radical in those times, and Ignatius frequently found himself combatting the efforts of outsiders to turn the new Society into a more traditional order.

The Society initially saw its mission as evangelization rather than education. Various Jesuits (as they came to be called) began to preach throughout Italy, while others tried to check the spread of the Protestant Reformation in Germany. Several early Jesuits were theological advisors at the Council of Trent, which met in 1542 to correct Roman church abuses and attempt to stem the Protestant tide sweeping Europe. Others were active in spreading Christianity to Africa and the Far East, working in India, Morocco, and Ethiopia.

The Society itself was growing phenomenally. From its small beginnings with Ignatius and his friends in 1540, it had grown to fifteen hundred members by 1554.[27] Such rapid growth necessitated formal training for the new members. While Ignatius and his friends had all received excellent educations at Paris, many of the new recruits were not well educated. Because Ignatius believed strongly in the need for educated priests, he sent candidates for the order to Paris and other universities for training of the sort he and his companions had received. The first Jesuit connection with schools was in these residences for Jesuit students at universities such as Paris, Louvain in Belgium, Padua in Italy, and Alcalá in Spain.

From these residences, it was a short step to found separate Jesuit colleges to train recruits in humanities, philosophy, and theology. Such an institution, for example, was the college of Gandia in Spain, founded in 1545. Eventually, some of these started to accept a few non-Jesuit students along with the Jesuits, beginning the Jesuit tradition of secular education.

It was 1548 before the first Jesuit school designed specifically for lay students was founded at Messina in Italy.[28] After this, a variety of institutions developed including the German College at Rome, founded in 1552 for non-Jesuit priesthood students, and a boarding school at Vienna in 1553. By the time of Ignatius' death in 1556, he had approved the foundation of thirty-nine colleges or universities (the latter offered advanced degrees), thirty-three of which had actually been opened.[29]

During the last years of his life, Ignatius took a direct hand in supervising a variety of other religious activities. Besides the colleges and universities, Jesuits were involved in activities as different as preaching and founding homes for reformed prostitutes. During this time, Ignatius' health was getting worse. The old stomach troubles had returned and become severe. After a painful illness, he died on 31 July 1556.

EDUCATIONAL SIGNIFICANCE

Ignatius' importance to the history of Western education lies in his religious vision and organizational genius, rather than his scholarship. He had begun his education too late in life to be a great scholar, but his native shrewdness had made him a sharp observer of the way in which universities were run, and he put the knowledge to good use in founding the Society's colleges.

For him, all education, no matter how nonreligious the subject might be, had a religious purpose. Study was undertaken to aid in knowledge and love of God.[30] For members of his order, study was a preparation for helping others. For lay students, it was a way of discovering God's working in the world. Like many Renaissance educators, Ignatius believed that God lay at the basis of all serious study.

At the same time, he saw education as involving more than the individual and God. Its goal was to make each person a more useful member of the church, citizen of the state, and participant in the local community. Education was not simply aimed at personal conversion: it ought to bring about the transformation of the whole society. Study in a Catholic college or university should inspire the student with love of church and country, along with concern for others.[31] Only if a person uses all the resources available, Ignatius believed, can God be given the greatest glory, and human needs be best served.

This philosophy of education resulted in a highly practical approach to the curriculum. Whatever was viewed by the community as important subject matter could be brought into the Jesuit schools, as long as it was directed toward love of God and service of others. Subjects like law and medicine were not to be taught, however, as religion courses. They *were* to be taught, in Ignatius' view, in such a way that his twin goals be achieved. Ignatius took the best educational elements of his day, organized them from a Catholic perspective, and taught them in a way that fit the needs of the particular time and place.

This is not to say that the Jesuit curriculum depended solely on what was fashionable educationally. Ignatius had a definite hierarchy of values. Because religion was so important to him, the study of theology was supreme. After this ranked the study of philosophy and of arts and sciences, since these "dispose the intellectual powers for theology and are useful for the perfect understanding and use of it."[32] The study of Latin and Greek classics was also emphasized for two major reasons. First of all, as Melanchthon also had pointed out, the classics help students to learn the languages necessary to study Scripture and the early Christian writers. Also, since the study of the classics was an important ingredient in education of this time, it would enable Jesuit graduates to compete with students trained in other universities. In one of his letters, Ignatius commended: "For ourselves, theology would do well enough with less of Cicero and Demosthenes. But as St. Paul became all things to all men in order to save them, so the Society [of Jesus] in its desire to give spiritual assistance seizes upon the spoils of Egypt to turn their use to God's honor and glory."[33] While all education is important, that which relates most directly to God is most valuable.

The early Jesuit universities embodied these values.[34] Typically, the student would begin the study of Latin and Greek at about age ten, and proceed to classical poetry, oratory, and history. At the age of fourteen, he (there were no women in the universities) would start the course of study, lasting about three years, which led to the degree of bachelor of arts. Six months later, he would receive the master of arts. Now about seventeen years old, the student would either begin the study of law or medicine, or go on to the Faculty of Theology. The theology course would take about four years, followed by another three years for those who wished to obtain the doctorate. Our student would be about twenty-three years old when he finished the whole program. This educational framework is adapted from that of the University of Paris during Ignatius's time there. Subjects were studied in reverse order of importance with theology reserved until the student was more mature and had a good general preparation.

Ignatius' writings give careful attention to educational structures. In *The Constitutions of the Society of Jesus,* which provided the basic legislation for his new religious order, he devoted an entire section to the running of colleges and universities. His legislation drew on his own educational experience, setting out the order in which various subjects were to be taught, the types of books to be used, and the cycle on which courses would be taught, in an attempt to avoid the problems caused in his own education by the lack of a definite program of study. His experience of finding it difficult to scrape up the money necessary to pay for the elaborate ceremonies associated with awarding degrees caused him to insist that no fees were to be charged students for granting degrees. The *Constitutions* describe in detail the various officials the colleges and universities ought to have, and give their job descriptions. Though pious, Ignatius was no dreamer. Behind his religious vision was a practical mind which created structures to achieve his educational goals.[35]

What Ignatius Loyola contributed most of all was a new direction for Catholic education. The Renaissance emphasis on classical languages and literature was transforming the medieval curriculum. Ignatius saw value in both the new and the old. To the Renaissance emphasis on literature and eloquence, he added the medieval value of theological study. In a Catholic society rocked by the Protestant Reformation, he provided a new educational model.

Ignatius' view would later be codified in minute detail in the *Ratio Studiorum* (1599), a periodically revised handbook which guided Jesuit education until our own day. This document, however, is simply an extension of Ignatius' original educational ideal. By founding the Jesuits, an order which is still influential in Catholic education, he provided personnel to accomplish his vision. By legislating for Jesuit colleges and universities, he set down the structures to make it possible. Most of all, he combined medieval and Renaissance learning in a pragmatic educational system directed toward love of God and service of others. That he was successful is attested to by Protestant reactions. As the next biographical sketch illustrates, Protestants turned their attention to questions of educational method, curriculum, and organization partly out of fear that if they did not improve their own schools the Jesuits would attract their children to Catholic study centers.

The career of one of the notable figures in the history of education is a product of the religious competition and wars associated with the Reformation. Like Erasmus, he is sometimes referred to as a citizen of the world—in his case because he spent so little of his life on his own native soil. He was born Jan Kominský on 28 March 1592 in Moravia (Czechoslovakia today) near the Hungarian border. Later he Latinized his name, and we know him as Comenius.

John Amos Comenius (1592-1670)

Details of Comenius' early life are sketchy. He was the youngest of five children and the only boy. His parents were peasants, but were moderately well off financially. Like most of their neighbors, they were members of the Unity of Brethren, a Protestant group in the Huss tradition. John's father, Martin, was a prominent man in the church in Uherský Brod, a sizeable town near John's birthplace. In 1604, however, both parents and the two youngest sisters died. The orphaned boy spent a short, unhappy time with an aunt. By age sixteen he was in a grammar school maintained by the Brethren in the town of Prerov.[36]

Of Comenius' early education we know only a little. Leaders of his denomination shared Luther's and Melanchthon's general views on the importance of teaching, and every church provided a school. Comenius had attended this kind of schooling since childhood and quite possibly had learned Latin grammer before he arrived at Prerov. In any case, he certainly studied it there. He boarded in the home of Bishop John Lánecký, the school's rector (note that the Unity of Brethren retained an episcopal form of government). Lánecký treated Comenius almost as a son, calling him favorably to the attention of a nobleman who was sympathetic to the Brethren's cause. This man sponsored his attendance at the Calvinist Gymansium of Herborn (near Marburg in central West Germany today).

Comenius finished the course of study at Herborn in about two years, and then traveled a hundred miles south to spend a year at the University of Heidelberg. This, too, was a noted center of Protestant reformist theology, as one might suppose in view of Melanchthon's having helped set the curriculum. In 1614 the twenty-two year old Comenius left Heidelberg, perhaps because he had run out of money. He walked more than two hundred miles to Prague and then to Prerov, where he began teaching at his alma mater. Two years later, he was ordained a priest of the Unity of Brethren. About the same time, he married a young woman of good family who brought to the union a sizeable dowry.

Shortly after his marriage, Comenius accepted a pastorate. The rest of his life would be primarily devoted to serving his church—first as priest, then secretary, and finally as the chief bishop. His educational activities were integral to but not the main preoccupation of his existence. The basic thrust of Comenius' work was theological and political, but his most lasting contribution was pedagogical.

AT WAR AGAINST DARKNESS

It is impossible to fully understand Comenius' career without reference to the chaotic religious, military, and political developments of Europe during his lifetime. Perhaps the most direct way to illustrate this fact is to point out that the Thirty Year's War and its aftermath was coterminous with most of Comenius' adult life. "Thirty Years War" is a label applied by historians to a series of battles from 1618 to 1648 involving Sweden, Denmark, France, Spain, and several German states. There were a number of causes and ramifications— dynastic, territorial, economic, nationalistic—but religious differences provided the package in which it was all wrapped. A year without war was rare in seventeenth century Europe as various factions fought for control. Sometimes entire towns were eradicated in devastating battles.

Comenius was a fullblown partisan in this fighting—not as a soldier, but as propagandist and political organizer. What he wanted was to unite Protestants against Roman Catholics in a final drive to defeat, as he saw it, the forces of darkness. Comenius is usually depicted as an ecumenical man of peace. This was true to a point: He deplored war and frequently called for unity, but by this he meant Protestant unity. Like many zealous people, Comenius believed firmly that the road to amity lay in convincing those who differed from him of their fundamental errors.

In 1622—four years after the Thirty Year's War started—Comenius' first wife died. She had been living with her parents while her husband was in hiding. Their two infant sons were victims of the same "pestilence." Two years later the young priest remarried Dorothy Cyrill, the daughter of a Unity of Brethren bishop. Soon thereafter the Moravian Brethren moved to Leszno, Poland, a Unity stronghold. In addition to living in Poland, Comenius spent time in Sweden, England, Hungary, and Holland. He never returned to his homeland.

Comenius lived another forty-three years after leaving Moravia. He outlasted his second wife and married a third (Jane Gajus), who also died before he did. During all this time Comenius wrote more than two hundred books and pamphlets in an effort to bring about the defeat of his political and religious foes. His political judgment was colored by prophetic statements from mystics who repeatedly said what Comenius wanted to hear—that the second coming of Christ was eminent and that it would initiate a thousand year reign of peace. To help speed this event, in 1651 Comenius asked Prince Sigismund of Hungary to wage a holy war against the Hapsburgs and the papacy.

When Comenius died at the age of seventy-eight, his memory was failing, almost all of his friends and colleagues were alread dead, most of his books had been burned, his flock was scattered, and his church was in disarray. Despite this pessimistic finish, his last years had been lived in relative physical comfort in Amsterdam. But his reputation as theologian and political leader had been tarnished by his repeated trust in discredited mystical prophecies and wrong bets on which armies would triumph.

COMENIUS AS EDUCATOR

Comenius began teaching Latin when he was twenty-two. For the next two decades he would spend part of his time as schoolmaster. Educational improvement was in the air. Reformers in both Protestant and Roman Catholic countries were experimenting with and talking about expanding curriculum, making learning easier and more pleasant, and extending schooling opportunities more widely. The best organized and most generally successful group of educational innovators were members of the Society of Jesus. Finding themselves extensively involved with teaching, as noted earlier, they devoted a substantial amount of attention to curricular and methodological issues. They discouraged corporal punishment, advocated play and physical education, and encouraged teachers taking a personal interest in each pupil.[37] In 1615 an Irish Jesuit named William Bataeus teaching at Salamanca published a Latin/Spanish text (in parallel columns) titled *Gateway to Languages*. It was quickly translated into several European languages. Comenius, in 1631 at Leszno, published a Latin text patterned after Bataeus' work, including a parody on the title: *Gateway to Languages Unlocked.* This book quickly caught on because Protestants were eager to compete with the Jesuits, whose educational successes they viewed with combined feelings of admiration and fear.

With his pedagogical reputation established in northern Europe, Comenius received offers from English and continental Puritans. During 1641-1642 he was in England, but the outbreak of civil war there caused him to leave. After some traveling and negotiating he eventually settled in Elbing, a town on the coast of the northeastern German state of Prussia. He selected the location at the suggestion of Axel Oxenstierna, chancellor of Sweden, with whom he had signed a contract to revamp Swedish textbooks. He spent the better part of six years in this task, while devoting his first attention to a futile effort at uniting Protestants.

In 1648 Comenius returned to Leszno, the town that he thought of as his home. There he buried his second wife, married the third, and became senior bishop of the Bohemian branch of the Unity of Brethren. From 1650-1655 he worked on school reform in various Hungarian towns in which the Unity move-ment was strong. Then he returned to Leszno where he publicly supported the Swedish Protestant king, Charles X, in a war against the Roman Catholic Polish king, John Casimir. The Swedes lost the war—at least they failed to win it—and in the process Polish troops destroyed Leszno. Comenius went to Amsterdam where he spent the remaining fourteen years of his life.

COMENIUS' REPUTATION

Since the middle of the nineteenth century, Comenius has been depicted in German, English, American, and some French histories of education as the founder of modern, secular, government controlled, tax supported, mass school systems. This started with the work of Karl von Raumer in 1842 who wrote one of the first biographically oriented accounts of educational development.[38] (From his death in 1670 to 1842 neither Comenius' name nor his work was well known.) In the twentieth century, Americans called him "the pioneer of modern educational science."[39] Unesco made him a patron saint; Soviet, Polish, East German and other socialists have depicted him as a great social reformer and Czechoslovakian hero.

It will do Comenius' reputation no harm to correct some of these extravagant claims. The depiction of him as a modern person out of step with his own times is thoroughly misleading. He is interesting to students of education precisely because he is so typical of seventeenth century reformist Christians. Far from being unique, almost everything he advocated was being discussed and advo-cated by a number of reformers. A few examples will illustrate: first, in reference to teaching methods and learning theory; second, in the matter of structure and administration of schools.

TEACHING METHODS

We have already seen in Butzbach's and Platter's youthful experiences that pupils often suffered from poor instruction. By Comenius' day many people were criticizing these bad practices, and he joined their number. Schools he called "slaughterhouses of the mind," saying that he wanted "to free the school and young people from very difficult labyrinths."[40] He thought this could be done by having pupils study *things* before *words*, by waiting till children were ready to study, by carefully organizing material and experiences in "natural" order, by encouraging much practice, and by stimulating interest through exam-ples and classroom dramatization ("tempt the student to plunge willingly into work," as he put it). This meant having teachers who were thoughtful, patient, well-trained—much after the pattern of Jesuits. Protestant reformers feared that if they did not develop competing schools of high quality parents would turn to the Jesuits with the ultimate result of more souls gained by Rome. When Comenius encountered in Hungary opposition to his suggestions, he explained himself as follows:

My whole method aims at changing the school drudgery into play and enjoyment. That [fact] nobody here wishes to understand. The youth, including the well-born, are treated altogether as if they were slaves; the teachers rest their esteem upon stern faces, rough words, and even in beating, and wish to be feared rather than loved. How many times have I pointed out—privately and publicly—that this is not the proper way, but always in vain! I have also advised from the very beginning that some theatrical plays be introduced, for I have learned from experience that there is no more effective means for the expulsion of mental flabbiness and the arousing of alertness. But I was told that such playthings (as the producing of comedies in schools) should be left to the Jesuits; that I had been called for serious work. I used to reply: "But these playthings lead to serious goals; the Jesuits are truly the sons of the world, ingenious in their affairs, while we are truly the sons of light, unforeseeing in our affairs. They entice to themselves the most gifted heads of the whole world by their pleasant method, and make them fit, by the exercise of that kind, for their life tasks; while we remain backward with ours." Then I added: "If we had not introduced into our schools in Poland that kind of exercise, all would have been at a standstill; with it we succeed not only that our people do not send their sons to the Jesuits, but that some come to us from theirs."[41]

Comenius thought, as did many others at the time, that ideas come rather directly from sense perceptions. Hence, he believed that a pleasant physical environment was important and that pictures were desirable in classrooms. Indeed, Comenius was among the first people to use pictures as an integral part of a language text.

STRUCTURE OF SCHOOLS

Comenius agreed with Luther and Melanchthon (and reformed Christians generally) that everyone needed to be able to read the vernacular, that writing and computation skills were desirable, and that knowledge of classical languages and literature should be more widely diffused among the male population. Comenius believed that women were as intelligent as men, but that their primary household role made classical studies less essential than for males.

The necessity for universal literacy meant that every village should have a teacher (for six to twelve year olds) and that all larger towns should have classical schools (for twelve to eighteen year olds). Classes graded by age were preferable, with one teacher in charge of each class. These, however, could each have eighty or more pupils. Comenius thought a skilled teacher should have no difficulty with this number. He believed that children could help teach each other. Teachers, he said, should be reasonably compensated, perhaps on a par with the lesser clergy. Comenius thought a basic salary could be guaranteed from the town treasury or through some other source, but he saw nothing wrong in charging fees to those parents or guardians who could afford them. He hoped wealthy citizens would consider it a duty to give some of their surplus funds to pay tuition for poor children.

Comenius believed that civil and ecclesiastical authorities should cooperate in seeing that schooling was available and in supervising its quality. The contemporary American or French concept of separating church and state was unthinkable for him. The notion that schools should be without religious orientation certainly would have been as blasphemous to him and his Protestant conferees as to their Roman Catholic competitors. The purpose of education was for Comenius "that every single individual shall rise out of darkness and barbarism."[42] A Christian context was essential for this.

It is difficult to assess Comenius' educational significance. He was part of a network of Puritan oriented reformers that included among others John Drury, Samuel Hartlib, John Milton, and George Snell in England; Joachim Junge and Wolfgang Ratke in Germany; Axel Oxenstierna in Sweden; and Comenius's teacher and friend Johann Heinrich Alstead. They in turn shared many of the ideas advocated a little earlier by Francis Bacon (1561-1626) in England and earlier still by Peter Ramus (1515-1572) in France and Erasmus in Holland.[43] This seventeenth century Protestant reformist network extended into the American colonies. Comenius was reportedly offered the presidency of Harvard (at least informally) in the 1650s, but turned it down.[44] The Unity of Brethren were active missionaries in North Carolina and Pennsylvania, but beyond this the general attitudes of Comenius and his circle were shared by colonial leaders in New England from the 1630s to the 1670s.

SKETCH OF IGNATIUS LOYOLA

6

THE NEW EDUCATORS

To make periods of time more manageable, historians coin phrases which bring certain aspects of an era into sharper focus. We have been subjected to this *Zeitgeist* or "spirit of the times" approach with such labels as "the Golden Age of Greece," "the Medieval Period," "the Renaissance," and "the Reformation." Similarly, in discussing the seventeenth and eighteenth centuries, historians have used several related labels: "the Age of Absolutism," "the Age of Enlightenment," "the Age of Reason" and "the Scientific Revolution" (with its concommitant industrial transformation). Those stressing the monarchical nature of European politics with its beliefs in the divine right of kings have favored the image of absolutism. Others have emphasized the various intellectual developments which replaced a priori deduction with inductive experimentation—a substitution that led to major economic and industrial changes.

143

These two centuries can usefully be understood through the words of German philosopher Immanuel Kant (1724-1804) who, in 1784, defined the term "Enlightenment" as "man's emergence from his nonage." By nonage or immaturity Kant did not mean a lack of intelligence but rather a "lack of determination and courage to use that intelligence without another's guidance. *Sapere aude*! Dare to know. Have the courage to use your own intelligence!"[1] It is from this perspective that we will describe a backdrop to the lives that follow.

POLITICS AND ECONOMY

We have already alluded above to the fact that European society during this age was a society ruled by monarchies. The growth of commune (self governing) towns had been stifled by a shift in power from city guilds to regional kingdoms. Local nobility warred over European turf until a victor could claim supreme dominance through military power and lineage. The most famous of these monarchies was probably that of the French Bourbons with its "Sun King," Louis XIV (1638-1715; reigned 1643-1715). Others included: the English monarchs beginning with James I (1603-1625) and ending with George III (1760-1820); the German Hapsburg line, commencing under Ferdinand I (1556-1564) and ending (in a Hapsburg-Lorraine union) with Francis II (1792-1835); and the Hohenzollern House, continuing from the time of Frederick I (1415-1440) to the time of Frederick William III (1797-1840).

With the discovery of the new world came the growth of wealth and the expansion of trade. Economic power in the hands of bourgeois businessmen shifted from Italy and southern Europe to northern Europe and finally to England where the Industrial Revolution was beginning. Mercantilism, with its emphasis on state wealth rather than individual wealth or happiness, was the basis for economic policies until the middle part of the eighteenth century when this notion was challenged by Mirabeau and other French thinkers. They called for laissez-faire policies leading to more economic freedom. Consequently, by the time Adam Smith's *Wealth of Nations* appeared in 1776, the stage had already been set for some of the ideas that were to become embodied in capitalism.

Even with colonial expansion, increased wealth, and growth of trade, the quality of European life did not generally improve. Instead, the continued warfare under absolute monarchs had increased tax burdens and exploited the masses. Mercantile policies had left most European states in varying degrees of social and economic decay. At the other end was England, where the seeds for the industrial and intellectual revolutions had taken root. In the battleground of monarchical and middle class struggles, it is little wonder that Lockian ideas of a propertied citizenry under democratic rule appealed to the middle classes of eighteenth century Europe.

PEOPLE AND CUSTOMS

Socially, Europe was steeped in deep and long standing class distinctions. Many governments discouraged marriages between social classes. Spain made it illegal. In the upper classes marriages were arranged so that any type of romantic attachments tended to occur outside the marital union for both men and women. In eighteenth century France, the mistress was turned into a courtesan who was supposed to possess many skills, including the art of intellectual conversation. These skills reached perfection in the *salonieres* who ran the famous French salons.

Society was still basically agrarian, and the possession of large landed estates promoted the legality of primogeniture and entail so that property would not be carved into pieces for the many heirs. Serfdom still existed in parts of eastern and central Europe. In other rural parts, peasants owned land or rented a considerable amount of it from some noble who often allowed them to pass renting privileges on to their sons. Next came peasants owning or renting enough land to barely maintain their families. Finally, at the bottom were the farm-servants and hired laborers who could scarcely manage a level of subsistence, but who continued to grow in numbers. For all of these lower classes of peasants mass education—despite Reformation theory—was only a dream.

Certain urban areas grew rapidly during this era. By the 1780s London boasted 850,000 inhabitants. Paris claimed 650,000, and Amsterdam and Vienna each had around 20,000. This was part of a European population estimated at 160,000,000.[2] The late eighteenth century growth of cities (with its accompanying rural decline), especially in England and Wales, was a direct result of industrial and technological advances. But the merchant classes were hardly on equal footing with the landed gentry unless they could acquire enough money to become propertied. Even on the continent the day laboring proletariat were soon wandering into the cities in search of work created by industrialization. However, in countries like France most people stayed out of the cities believing that "the nation's true prosperity lay in the treasures of the earth."[3] Here again, education was connected to property and wealth; and universal schooling was generally frowned upon. Even De LaSalle and his Brothers of the Christian Schools had political problems maintaining schools for the poor.

To think of a European consciousness would be stretching a point and to describe a national consciousness would be stretching it further, even for the educated upper classes. Nevertheless, the term "cosmopolitan" seemed to have had universal meaning in literate circles. It meant "European." There were even a few faint voices who cried for a unified Europe under one rule and mistakenly thought it had arrived with Napoleon. But even before Napoleon—and despite England's intellectual influence and economic power—France managed to stamp its seal on this "enlightened age." French was the cosmopolitan language of conversation and diplomacy. Paris was the center of culture and art. It would take a disillusioned post-Napoleonic era to produce widespread national self-identification such as is implied by the terms Englishman, German, and Spaniard. As for women, any extensive consciousness raising was still many years away—even though, as we shall see in this chapter, Mary Woltenscraft set the stage in 1792 with her *Vindication of the Rights of Woman*.

ENGLISH INTELLECTUAL HERITAGE

English philosophers prepared the canvas for much of the work that was crafted by the French philosophers—Voltaire, Diderot, and Rousseau—and ultimately expanded upon by philosophers of every country. Therefore, let us briefly note three Englishmen whose ideas influenced Voltaire enough (after his 1726 trip to England) to put the French Enlightenment in motion.

First came Sir Francis Bacon (1561-1626). Born the younger son of nobility, Bacon was well educated. He spent three years at Cambridge followed by diplomatic service in France and the study of law at Gray's Inn—one of England's prestigious Inns of Court. Although he lost in his ambitions for political office, he did successfully practice law and managed to acquire wealth, property, and a secretary—Thomas Hobbes (1588-1679)—who would carry on his philosophical empiricism. Bacon wrote a great deal. In the last twenty years of life he rose from attorney general to become the king's chancellor.

In his *Advancement of Learning,* Bacon proposed a new system of thought— the inductive study of nature through the avenues of experience and experiment. In order to embark on such a study, however, the student had to clear his mind of all a priori deductions learned at the syllogistic hand of the Scholastics. But the purge did not stop with Scholasticism. It also included most ideas left from the thoughts of Plato and Aristotle. With this new scientific system of knowledge would come power, but the only trustworthy knowledge was to be found through observing nature. Beyond this human beings could know nothing, but by observing and obeying nature human knowledge and power could meet. Bacon thought that this scientific knowledge would transform society and possibly human nature itself.

Secondly, there was Sir Isaac Newton (1642-1727). Born of landed but humble country stock, Newton was educated in a local grammar school, beginning at the age of twelve. But his teachers regarded him as idle and inattentive, neglecting important subjects for others that appealed to him. Consequently, after two years he was taken out of school to help his widowed mother (of fourteen years) with farm chores. Fortunately, an uncle, who recognized the youth's mathematical genius, made arrangements for him to enter Trinity College, Cambridge. He earned his baccalaureate in four years and became a fellow of the college, lecturing and writing throughout the next thirty-five years of his life. He has been credited with systematically describing the scientific method in research and developing an approach to calculus that helped him to prove and disprove some of the astronomical theories of Copernicus, Galileo, Brahe, and Kepler. He contributed to our knowledge of growth, light, and optics. He also maintained a strong interest in astrology throughout his life.

Finally, there was the Englishman who tried to do for psychology what Newton had done for physics. That man was John Locke and his story follows.

John Locke (1632-1704)

John Locke was one of the most influential philosophers of the eighteenth century and America's debt to him has been enormous. Merle Curti called him "America's Philosopher."[4] Although he was not as prolific as some, he made up in quality what he lacked in quantity. His influence on political theory and epistemology was much greater than on educational theory, but his pedagogical thought was typical of the governing class of early American colonists.

LIFE

John Locke was the eldest son of a country lawyer. Apparently his father tutored him during his early years. At fifteen, John attended Westminster, a classical boarding school of good social reputation. There he was bored by the curriculum, but flirted with royalist political philosophy. His family orientation was toward Puritanism, however, and he later returned to that tradition. At twenty he enrolled at Christ Church, an Oxford college of venerable reputation. For the next fourteen years, Locke was student and then tutor and lecturer at Oxford.[5]

Locke studied medicine and experimental science. He was a member of the British Royal Society—the chief scientific body in England—though his fame did not rest on his own research. His philosophic justification of experimental methods was important. His knowledge of medicine did contribute, at least indirectly, to his later career. He performed liver surgery on Anthony Ashley Cooper, a man who shortly thereafter became the first Earl of Shaftesbury. Cooper thought Locke had saved his life and became a patron and friend, opening several doors to employment. Locke also imbibed a practical liberalism from Shaftesbury which he incorporated into his justification of popular government.

Locke spent several of the middle years of his life in Holland. Shaftesbury's opposition to Charles II and James II coupled with Locke's justifications for revolution against them made England a dangerous place until the late 1680s when Parliament brought in William and Mary. Locke spent his last years partly in London and partly at the Essex country estate of Lady Damaris Masham. She was married to a member of Parliament, but in earlier years Locke and Lady Masham had exchanged love letters. Locke never married. He died at her house in the fall of 1704 at the age of seventy-two.

THOUGHTS ON EDUCATION

Locke's *Some Thoughts Concerning Education* was not written as a definitive statement upon education. While Locke was in exile, a friend asked him for advice on the upbringing of his eight year old son. The letters which Locke wrote to his friend became the basis of the first draft published in 1693. Later the book was revised and enlarged. Locke was not favorable to the schools of his time. He complained of their heavy reliance upon corporal punishment. In Cicero's tradition, he recommended tutors rather than schools. He admitted schools might make a boy bolder, "and better able to bustle and shift among boys of his own age," but "that boldness and spirit which lads get amongst their play fellows at school . . . has ordinarily such a mixture of rudeness and ill-turned confidence that those misbecoming and disingenious ways of shifting in the world must be unlearnt." Locke added, "He that considers how diametrically opposite the skill of living well, and managing, as a man should do, his affairs in the world, is to that mal-pertness, tricking, or violence learnt amongst schoolboys, will think the faults of a private education infinitely to be preferred to such improvements, and will take care to preserve his child's innocence and modesty at home."[6]

Locke looked to fathers as well as tutors for the education of young gentlemen. They were the ones who would lay the foundation of virtue. "And 'tis not the waggeries or cheats practiced amongst schoolboys, 'tis not their roughness one to another, not their well-laid plots of robbing an orchard together, that make an able man," he said, "but the principles of justice, generosity, and sobriety, . . . qualities which I judge schoolboys do not learn much of one another." Locke advised getting the best possible tutor—a far better investment than a large estate or toys and other trifles, for said he, " 'tis not good husbandry to make his fortune rich, and his mind poor."[7]

Locke also cited the necessity of understanding the child's needs. He thought that schools and parents both failed in this due to excessive emphasis upon Latin grammar and the memorization of rules. Rote learning took the place of thought and understanding. Locke also believed that children should not be wearied with lectures. And tutors had to be honest, because children would easily perceive when they were slighted or deceived. Locke also wrote in some detail about the need for a proper balance between freedom and authority—the true secret of education, he said.

Locke advocated four outcomes to be kept in mind in educating the young gentlemen: virtue, wisdom, good breeding, and learning. Virtue's foundation was the result of good religious training or as Locke wrote "a true notion of God." This was best implanted in the young by having them engage in simple acts of devotion such as morning and evening prayer. Wisdom was a result of natural temper, the use of mind, and experience. Locke placed great emphasis on good breeding and distinguished two types of ill-breeding. One was extreme bashfulness. The other was a "misbecoming negligence and disrespect in our carriage." One rule would help in avoiding both, "*not to think meanly of ourselves, and not to think meanly of others.*" Locke's comment on "learning" was that many were ill-schooled by devoting too much time to Latin and Greek. He did not find Latin unnecessary but argued for a more natural way of learning Latin with time devoted to the rules of grammar.

Locke thought that a child should learn Latin and French because they were useful subjects. Usefulness was the main criterion for selecting anything to be learned. On that basis, he also recommended arithmetic, geography, chronology, history, geometry, and astronomy. Later the young gentlemen should learn civil law and the use of the English language with grace. He also advocated study of the sciences, citing the writings of Robert Boyle and Sir Isaac Newton. Dancing, fencing, and riding were appropriate, but not music or painting. A young gentleman should learn husbandry and the skills of a carpenter, joiner, or turner. Locke considered these fit and healthy recreations for a man of study or business. He was much in favor of young men learning a variety of trades, and he wanted them to know some bookkeeping.

VIEWS ON GOVERNMENT

In *Two Treatises on Government,* Locke developed a popular theory of constitutional law and government. In the second *Treatise,* "An Essay Concerning the True Original, Extent and End of Civil Government," he discussed the processes of constitutional law and government. Locke opposed absolute monarchy, basing his position on a state of nature in which all men were equal in their life, liberty, and possessions. In this state, individuals could and should punish those who harm them or break the laws of nature. This state of nature was not a state of constant warfare but, because there was no common law enforced by impartial judges, men united into a community. They did this by their own consent:

> Men being, as has been said by nature all free, equal, and independent, no one can be put out of this estate and subjected to the political power of another without his own consent, which is done by agreeing with other men, to join and unite into a community for their comfortable, safe, and peaceable living, one amongst another, in a secure enjoyment of their properties, and in a greater security against any that are not of it. . . . When any number of men have so consented to make one community or government, they are thereby presently incorporated, and make one body politic, wherein the majority have a right to act and conclude the rest.[8]

Here was the heart of the constitutional republican theory.

Locke established as the first and fundamental law of commonwealths the creation of legislative power. This was positive or social law as opposed to natural law. Locke also provided for federative and executive power. These two were united for all practical purposes. The executive executed the laws, but in final analysis power remained in the hands of the people through the legislature. The legislature was able to take the power from the executive if there was any wrongdoing. But the power entrusted to legislators could be changed or taken from them by the people if they acted contrary to the people's trust.

EPISTEMOLOGY

Locke's most influential educational ideas dealt with the theory of knowledge. He was an empiricist. His main work, *An Essay Concerning Knowledge,* dealt with the nature, origin, and validity of knowledge. He first addressed the problem of innate ideas. Plato, Descartes, and others had held that certain principles were inborn truths. Locke wanted to demolish this theory. He did so to his satisfaction by showing that innate ideas did not meet certain tests that he felt were necessary. For example, if ideas were innate they should be found in infants everywhere and also in children, savages, and the uneducated. He could find no proof for these innate ideas.

Locke went on to formulate his *tabula rasa* theory of mind. It held that in the beginning one's mind was blank. There were no innate ideas. In Book II of *An Essay Conerning Human Understanding*, Locke said:

> All ideas come from sensation or reflection and are recorded in the mind which acts like a blank piece of "white paper," that fills up, from *experience.* In that all our knowledge is founded; and from that it ultimately derives itself. That is, we either experience external sensible objects, or we witness the internal operations of our minds as we employ our thought processes.[9]

Locke called for religious toleration, but like Comenius he meant mainstream Protestant toleration. He was suspicious of all mysticism, religious visions, and miracles. His advocacy of the maximum liberty consistent with keeping an ordered society did not extend to atheists or Roman Catholics who were, in his opinion, too dangerous to be trusted. His writing appealed to many American colonists who wanted to justify greater liberty for themselves, but who did not wish to encourage people at the bottom of the social scale to expect fundamental change. His emphasis on utility rather than the inherited tradition of the liberal arts fit with the practical needs of America's frontier society, while his preoccupation with the education of middle class and aristocratic males was comforting to traditionalists. In stressing that all knowledge was relative and experiential, Locke offered a philosophical justification for rethinking the basis of curriculum. Two centures later "progressive" educators would cite Locke with approval. They would also point to the writings of a Frenchman born four years after Locke died. His name was Jean-Jacques Rousseau.

Rousseau differed in three ways from Locke, Comenius, the Jesuits, and most other Enlightenment educational theorists: (1) their search for more effective and pleasant teaching methods grew largely out of competition with various religious groups, while Rousseau was secular; (2) their ideas were cast in religious and philosophic prose, while Rousseau's were in novelistic and autobiographic form; and (3) other theorists laid the foundations for more humane methods and a more practical curriculum, but did not question the school structures of their time. Rousseau wanted to sweep these aside and start afresh with a radically different approach to teaching. For all of these reasons, his work has continued to appeal to some reform minded educators down to the present.

Jean-Jacques Rousseau (1712-1778)

French Huguenots (Protestants) suffered persecution in their Catholic dominated country. Consequently, many refugees crossed the border into the Swiss cantons of Berne, Zurich, and Geneva. It was to the latter Reformation town that Jean-Jacques' great-great-grandfather, Didier Rousseau, made his way in 1549. He was one of the early Huguenots who took refuge in the Swiss city. His craft was clockmaking. In these early years, Didier and his sons and grandsons settled into a respectable, but quiet life of hard work and some profit. It took Jean's father, Isaac, to crack the traditional mold.

Isaac had an incurable wanderlust and his passionate nature gave into his desires more often than not. Even after he married his childhood sweetheart, against her affluent father's wishes, he found himself yearning to see Constantinople. How long he left his wife, Suzanne, and their son, Francois, is not clear, but Suzanne "conjured him to return" so that advances made to her by other men in the town would stop. "He sacrificed all and did so," Jean-Jacques later said. "I was the unfortunate fruit of this return, being born ten months after, in a very weakly and infirm state. My birth cost my mother her life, and was the first of my misfortunes."[10]

EARLY LIFE

Isaac solicited the help of his unmarried sister, Susan, and a nursemaid by the name of Jacqueline. Together the three of them seem to have provided all the tender loving care necessary to so fragile a beginning. If all was not rosy, Rousseau did not seem to have been aware of it. He had only happy memories of his childhood. He thought he was the favorite of the family (to the neglect of his older brother who turned out to be the "bad seed" of the clan). Isaac would often embrace his youngest son with convulsive sighs and tears as he recalled how much he missed his wife and how much Jean-Jacques reminded him of her.

Rousseau had nothing but praise and affection for the motherly warmth and attention his Aunt Susan gave him. He particularly remembered how her singing filled his home with sweetness and gaiety. At the age of fifty-three he recalled that "the charms of her voice had such an effect on me that . . . [I] sometimes surprise [myself] weeping like a child . . . muttering out one of those airs which were the favorites of my infancy." Under his father's care, the young boy was not allowed to play with children of his own age, although Isaac did make certain that his son learned to read. The manner in which Jean-Jacques acquired this latter skill was unique. Coming from a higher social class than her husband, Jean-Jacques' mother had left a modest library of romance and adventure. Isaac felt that these would be entertaining books from which his son would develop a love for reading. Father and son found themselves so engrossed in these adventures, however, that they would alternately read to each other all night until the volume was finished and the sun was up. Ashamed of such overindulgence, the father often confided to the son that he was himself more of a child than was Jean-Jacques. Rousseau later said that this "dangerous custom" allowed him to acquire too intimate a familiarity with adult passions which he was too young to understand. (He recalled reading these as early as five or six years old.) By the time he was seven, his mother's library had been exhausted, and he got access to his maternal grandfather's collection of Christian, Roman, and Greek histories. "I had conceived nothing—I had felt the whole. This confused succession of emotions . . . added an extravagant, romantic notion of human life, which," he wrote in his *Confessions,* "experience and reflection have never been able wholly to eradicate."[11]

Rousseau continually expected the most ideal treatment and care from his friends, but consistently received less. Such circumstances invariably left him outraged or defensive and melancholy. On these occasions his vagabond spirit could only find comfort in the solitude of a natural setting away from the bondage of city life, which he felt to be cold, manipulative, and affluent.

By the time young Rousseau was ten, his father fled Geneva. Isaac's volatile temper had gotten him into a minor brawl with a French army captain. The Geneva council sided with the captain, who was higher up on the social ladder than was Jean-Jacques' father. Mr. Rousseau chose banishment over imprisonment, and asked his brother to look after Jean-Jacques. This brother (Uncle Gabriel Bernard to Jean-Jacques) had a son—also called Cousin Bernard—who was about ten years old. Together the two boys were sent to a family named Lambercier for tutoring. They boarded for the next three years with Pastor Lambercier and his unmarried sister. They were happy until both were accused of theft. Rousseau said that neither was guilty, but both were punished. They could never again feel the same affection and respect for their teachers-turned-accusers as they had before the incident. Rousseau also learned, under the paddle of Mademoiselle Lambercier, to mistake beating for erotic pleasure.

Shortly after this incident, the boys returned briefly to the uncle's house. It was now time for them both to enter into some sort of professional training. Being the son of a military general, Cousin Bernard was destined for engineering and the life of the well-bred suburbanite. Jean-Jacques, not having much income from his mother's estate, was committed to apprentice under an engraver. At fifty-three Rousseau remembered Mr. Ducammon, master engraver, as a most abhorrent fellow: mean, suspicious, and brutal with the harshest methods of discipline. Under his stern eye, the young teenager turned from a tender, affectionate boy into a liar, cheat, and petty thief. Jean-Jacques learned to spend his free hours—especially Sundays—away from the city and engulfed in the pleasures of the countryside. Often he would barely make it back before the city's gates were closed for the night.

A WANDERING LIFE

One evening in 1728, upon seeing the bridge draw up and the gates begin to close, Rousseau resolved to run away from the city and Ducammon. In so doing he had made the momentous decision of his life—to embark upon a vagabond career that would bring his volatile nature too little to the heights of ecstasy and too often to the depths of despair.

He headed south towards the Catholic town of Confignon in Savoy. Although Confignon was not more than ten miles from Geneva, it took young Rousseau several days to reach his destination as he blissfully pursued the joys of nature. Upon arriving, he went to the vicar's house. Rousseau had heard that the vicar and his family wanted to destroy the Protestant republic of Geneva. The sixteen year old boy was surprised to find the vicar friendly and amiable. Reassured by good wine and the promise of protection, Jean-Jacques agreed to place himself in the hands of a Mrs. Warren (Madame de Warens), a recent convert who received a yearly pension to care for such waywards. Her house in Annecy was fifteen miles south of Confignon. Thinking that he had just put himself in the hands of some shrivelled up old shrew, Jean-Jacques was overwhelmed to find his captor young (around twenty-eight), plumpish (but not offensively so), pretty, and friendly. Not knowing whether to romanticize or matronize her, it would take him several years to settle into a comfortable mother/son relationship. In the meantime, he began to idolize her.

Jean-Jacques was totally smitten with Mrs. Warren and wished only to stay by her side. She decided, however, that he should make another journey across the Alps to Turin (in northern Italy) where he was to take instruction in the Catholic religion. Shortly after he had left, Isaac and Uncle Gabriel rode on horseback into Confignon. Upon hearing from the vicar that the boy had gone to Annecy, the uncle returned home. Isaac went on to Mrs. Warren's. Here, he learned that his son had but left for Turin the day before. " 'Ah! the unhappy boy!' cried Isaac, with tears running, as they did so readily, from his weak eyes; 'now indeed have I lost him for ever!' "[12]

In his *Confessions* Rousseau assessed his father's paternal behavior this way:

> My father arrived at Annecy, accompanied by his friend. . . . Having traced me to the house of Madame de Warens, they contented themselves with lamenting . . . my fate instead of overtaking me, which, (as they were on horseback and I on foot) they might have accomplished with the greatest ease. . . . By a similar negligence, my brother was so entirely lost that it was never known what had become of him. . . . [Isaac] was a good father, particularly to me, whom he tenderly loved; but he likewise loved his pleasures, and since we had been separated other connections had weakened his paternal affection. He had married again at Nyon, and, though his second wife was too old to expect children, she had relations. My father was united to another family, surrounded by other objects, and a variety of cares prevented my returning often to his remembrance. He was in the decline of life, and had nothing to support the inconveniences of old age; my mother's property devolved to me and my brother, but during our absence the interest of it was enjoyed by my father. This consideration had no immediate effect on his conduct, nor did it blind his sense of duty; but it had an imperceptible effect, and prevented him making use of that exertion to regain me which he would otherwise have employed; and this I think was the reason that, having traced me as far as Annecy, he stopped short, without proceeding to . . . where he might have almost certainly found me; and likewise explains why, on visiting him several times since my flight, he always received me with great kindness, but never made great efforts to retain me.[13]

Rousseau entered the monastery at Turin on 12 April 1728. He was baptized and formally turned out on his own eleven days later. For the remainder of 1728 and part of 1729, this new convert found work as a footman (uniformed manager of horses) in two different aristocratic households. He was employed in the first until the lady of the house died. He left the second when he embarrassed himself and the attractive but somewhat arrogant daughter of the family. In this latter situation he was also supposed to wait tables. During a meal, young Rousseau found himself employing his superior knowledge of the French language and correcting a wrong usage by his employer. The girl gazed admiringly upon the new waiter. Rousseau became so nervous under her gaze that when she asked him for water, his trembling hands spilled it all over the table and his young mistress.

This bungling on his part no doubt surprised him, but certainly not as much as an earlier bit of behavior must have. While he was employed by the woman who died, he says that he found himself in a constant state of emotional turmoil "incessantly occupied with girls and women, but in a manner peculiar to myself." He continued: "My uneasiness grew to such a pitch that, unable to find satisfaction, I humored my longings by extravagant devices. I sought out shaded walks and hidden corners where I might show myself to persons of the other sex. . . . There was no obscenity in this, but much that was ridiculous," he wrote. "I offered to the eyes of the girls who came to draw water a spectacle more ludicrous than seductive. The more prudent pretended not to see me;

others began to laugh; others felt insulted, and raised a clamor." The ridiculousness of his actions stemmed from the fact that it was the exposure of his backside that produced his pleasure—perhaps a residual of Miss Lambercier's paddling days. The screams of the ladies secured the attentions of a man who then demanded to know what the lad was doing. Rousseau quickly replied that he was a foreign prince whose wits were deranged and who, if returned to his homeland, would be institutionalized. The passerby decided to accept the tale and let Jean-Jacques off with a scolding. Rousseau evidently did not repeat the behavior.[14]

He took to the road again, this time with an old friend from Geneva, but soon grew weary of his companion. Longing to see his "Mama Warren," he set out for Annecy. Not knowing what kind of reception to expect, he was pleasantly surprised when she consoled him and said that he was probably too young to be out trying to survive on his own. For the next little while—it is hard to know how long—the seventeen year old basked in the attention which his new mother figure gave him. But Mrs. Warren was acutely aware that he still had no profession, so she sent him off to a seminary to get the rudiments of Latin for the life of a priest. Rousseau hated Latin and was a hopeless failure. Next he tried music, which he dearly loved even though he had no talent for it. Under the tutelage of a friendly but alcoholic music master, Rousseau learned what he could until the man became victim to his habit.

Upon his return to Annecy, he discovered that Mama Warren had gone off to Paris with her lover/business manager, Claude Anet. Jean-Jacques innocently frolicked around with a few of the maidens in a nearby villa. Then, after several days of waiting for a mama who did not return, he decided to accompany Warren's maid to her home in Switzerland. He stopped to see his father, but Isaac could only cry over the lonely life his abandoned son led instead of offering to make a home for him.

Jean-Jacques traveled on to Lausanne where he decided that he would set himself up as a professor of music. His training was far from complete. He hardly knew how to read or write music, but that did not deter him. Living off the credit of his kindly landlord, he began to write a musical score which he planned to conduct at a local concert run solely for promising amateurs. The day for his concert finally arrived, and a nervous Jean-Jacques distributed his score to the musicians and stepped up to the podium to conduct it. It is impossible to say just how bad the noise was. The musicians were the first to laugh. Then the audience began to murmur and chuckle. Rousseau, sweating profusely, continued to the agonizing end. Humor was not the reaction he had intended, but the audience was put into such a good mood that some managed to compliment him when it was over. This increased Rousseau's humiliation and despair, and he ended up in a great fit of depression over his inability to compose music. After trying to teach a few "nasty pupils," who made fun of how little he knew, the neophyte musician gave up his self-imposed professorship and accepted an offer from a military acquaintance: attendant to an officer in Paris.

Rousseau set out for the capital city dreaming of a successful career as a military leader. When he learned that his services were to be those of a valet and not an officer, a proud but dejected Jean-Jacques left for mother Warren's house and the comfort that a long journey through the French countryside could bring. The year was 1731. For the next six years Rousseau was to live with Warren in a somewhat unusual liaison.

What we know of Mrs. Warren comes from Rousseau's *Confessions*. According to him, Francoise Louise married Mr. Warren when she was only fourteen. He was much older. Shortly afterwards she took her first lover who taught her that there was nothing wrong with sexual unions so long as couples were discreet and no one was hurt. This argument appealed to her. She refused to believe that something so natural could be wrong. Fancying herself as having a head for business, she chalked up healthy debts for her husband. Then she became a Catholic and negotiated a yearly stipend from the King of Sardinia for the care of future converts. She enjoyed a prominent social standing in Savoy as the close friend of the bishop. Rousseau said that she refused to believe that God would make her pay for her occasional love affairs. Rousseau did not say what happened to Mr. Warren, but he seemed not to have been present when Rousseau knew her.

It was probably in 1734 that Warren turned her sexual attentions to her "little one," as she had called him on occasion. Rousseau noticed a change in her— she had become withdrawn and quiet. When he asked her why, she engaged him in a walk and explained that a certain older neighbor was about to take advantage of him. To save him from this exploitation, she felt it her duty to show him the ways of love herself. She gave him eight days to come to a decision—a period which he said was one of the longest in his life. The confusion into which her proposition threw him was severe. Feeling towards her as he did, the proposed affair smacked of incest, but he was afraid to reject her. The dreaded day arrived. After his consent, she gave herself to the twenty-two year old in a cold, unpassionate, and impersonal way. With mixed feelings of fear, impatience, dread, and desire, he managed to consummate the relationship. But he was thoroughly confused. (He knew of her longstanding affair with her business manager, Claude Anet.) Anticipating the bewilderment of readers of his *Confessions* he offered this defense of Warren:

> The reader, already disgusted, supposes that, being already possessed by another, she degraded herself in my opinion by this participation, and that a sentiment of disesteem weakened those she had before inspired me with; but he is mistaken. True, this participation gave me a cruel uneasiness, as well from a very natural sentiment of delicacy, as because it appeared unworthy both of her and myself; but, as to my sentiments for her, they were still the same, and I can solemnly aver that I never loved her more tenderly than when I felt so little desire to possess her. I was too well acquainted with the chastity of her heart and the iciness of her constitution to suppose for a moment that the gratification of the senses had any influence in this abandonment of herself. I was perfectly sure that her careful attention to tearing me from dangers otherwise inevitable, and keeping me entirely to myself and my duties, made her infringe one which she did not regard from the same point of view as other women, of which more will be said hereafter. I pitied her, and pitied myself. I had an inclination to tell her "No, Mamma, it is not necessary; I can answer for myself without it." But I dared not—first, because it was a thing not to be said, and that I inwardly knew in my heart was not true;

that, in fact, a woman was necessary to keep me from other women, and secure me from temptation. Without longing to possess her, I was glad that she prevented me from wishing to possess others; so much did I look on everything which could divert me from her as a misfortune.[15]

Rousseau said that he and Anet remained friends through these rather awkward years, and that it was to the credit of Mrs. Warren that this was accomplished. Sometime around 1736, however, Anet succumbed to pleurisy and died. This left Jean-Jacques next in line as business manager. It is difficult to tell how well he played this role, for it was during this time that he developed a burning passion to be a writer of the caliber of Voltaire. He had also not given up his desire to be a musical composer. These out of reach goals left him often in states of despair and depression, although he remembered these years with Mama as some of his happiest. In 1737 his health suffered. He said that he had the vapors, a hypochondriacal ailment. Nevertheless, Mrs. Warren insisted that he make a trek to the medically famous town of Montpellier in southern France. Some biographers have suspected that she may have been growing tired of him, and there is some evidence for this notion. Upon his return a year later, he found his place occupied by a man several years younger than himself.

For a time, Rousseau pretended that nothing had changed. He, too, had had a rather sordid affair with a woman with ten children in Montpellier. After a couple of stays with Warren and a brief tutoring job, however, Jean-Jacques took leave of his dear Mama for good. He headed for Paris, the center of the French Enlightment.

Rousseau settled into a sleazy hotel near the Sorbonne. Soon he was introduced to David Diderot, one of the future leading intellectuals of the Enlightenment. Rousseau and the twenty-nine year old Diderot became friendly. He was further introduced into the fashionable set of young men and women who—having nothing better to do—flirted with the ideas of the Enlightenment philosophers. Several young married women took an interest in Rousseau and secured for him a job as the personal secretary to the French ambassador to Venice. Rousseau eagerly anticipated his new role, but once again reality fell short of his expectations. Ambassador Montaigu was stupid and arrogant—at least in Rousseau's eyes—and soon the latter was quarreling with his boss. This characterization of Montaigu was probably accurate. Rousseau's blunder was in not putting up with inferior traits in one of superior social station. He was fired from his position but not before he indulged in a few amorous adventures. Following the lead of his social superiors, he visited a couple of brothels. He escaped his first encounter without consequence, but his second trip to a different lady of the evening ended disastrously. When she disrobed Rousseau found to his dismay that one of her breasts was deformed. The sight reduced him to tears, while the embarrassed woman advised him to "leave the ladies alone, my young sir, and study mathematics."[16]

Back in Paris in 1745, Jean-Jacques resumed his residence in the same hotel and copied music for a livelihood. The owner had hired a new seamstress, a young girl by the name of Therese Lavasseur. Rousseau began defending the poor girl who was the brunt of jokes from the residents. The rather pathetic Therese came to depend on his friendship. He found himself living with her and her dominating mother, promising never to leave her or marry her. He said that he tried teaching her but she lacked the facility for learning. She never read well. She couldn't name the months of the year in order. She could not spell. After twenty years of instruction, she had difficulty in telling time. And numbers gave her trouble, especially when it came to counting money. She also tended to use the exact opposite of the word she meant. Nevertheless, Rousseau thought that she had a pure and innocent heart, devoid of all forms of deviousness, and that she was a superb cook and housekeeper. She was about twenty-two and Rousseau ten years older when he met her. She confessed to him that through lack of knowledge she had lost her virginity while still a young girl. To this ignorant companion, who was to live with him for the rest of his life, Rousseau attributed the ability to see the sometimes negative motives of his various friends and associates. This assessment is questionable. What is more probable is that when he was to become involved in one of his heated quarrels with a friend, her own fears and insecurities over losing his financial support ended up feeding his suspicions. In other words, fewer friends meant less competition.

Rousseau continued to be introduced to and patronized by the wealthy young women of Paris. His next mentor became the Marquise d'Epinay. She wanted him to act as her secretary while she wrote a book about her views on education. He had already met the very stiff but "Frenchy-German" military hero, Melchoir Grimm. The latter became part of the French Enlightenment and Epinay's lover.

In the meantime, Rousseau had become a famous author and the father of Therese's five children—all of which, by his own account, he gave to foundling homes. His motivation in abandoning his children is hard to understand. He said that he just was not cut out to be a father; and that they would get a good upbringing in this home, learn a trade, and lead the uncomplicated life of a peasant instead of fighting fame in the world of high society as he did. He must have wondered if Therese was up to motherhood, too. Also, in view of the fact that she was to later have an affair with Rousseau's friend, James Boswell (the biographer of Samuel Johnson) while still living with Rousseau, one wonders if all five were actually his.

In 1749 Jean-Jacques learned that the Dijon Academy was sponsoring an essay contest on the topic, "Has the restoration of the arts and sciences corrupted or purified morals?" He contemplated entering, and shared his ideas with Diderot who was in prison for some offensive passages in his *Letters on the Blind*. Diderot encouraged Rousseau, whose essay argued that man is by nature good and that it is society's institutions that have made him bad. To Rousseau's surprise he won the contest and became an overnight sensation. He began being invited to the most fashionable dinner parties. But in order to be true to his views, he dressed the part of a simpler man. He wore a peasant's fur hat and an old purple robe. His upper-class acquaintances also knew that he had scant training in either arts or sciences. So, between his silly looking costume and his lack of formal knowlege, the high-strung, bewildered, famous, and miserable Rousseau became the newest toy and form of entertainment for the idle rich. The higher his fame soared, the more frightened, suspicious, and reclusive he became. His volatile and angry outbursts at being abused and misunderstood began to alienate his upper class friends. In a society that still prized a strong silent and masculine reserve, his angry defensiveness was soon labelled as insanity. Rousseau was branded a madman.

The first serious charge of lunacy came over his *grande passion,* the Comtesse d'Houdetot. Rousseau was not particularly attracted to the Marquise d'Epinay, but when she introduced him to her sister-in-law, the Comtesse d'Houdetot, all passion broke loose in him. At the age of forty-five he seemed unable to control himself. The countess was friendly to him, but she did not return his passion. She was already involved with a lover, Saint Lambert, another military hero and figure of the French Enlightenment. Rousseau wrote the most romantic and emotional letters to her, while she modestly returned her appreciation. Although she remined loyal to her lover, in action at least, Saint Lambert accused his mistress of sexual involvement and reduced her to tears. The countess pleaded with Rousseau to clear her name. Diderot advised him to tell Saint Lambert that he had the utmost regard and affection for the countess, and that nothing unfaithful had occurred. Jean-Jacques did this in a letter, but added that since Lambert had accused the countess of wrong doing, she would no longer speak to Rousseau. He had lost her friendship due to Lambert's suspicions.

Rousseau also decided that the Marquise D'Epinay was responsible for Lambert's finding out about his feelings for Houdetot. He lashed out at Epinay, saying that he was tired of being chained to her. Grimm came to his mistress's rescue and broke with Rousseau, declaring that he never wanted to see him again. Diderot was appalled at Rousseau's outburst and questioned his sanity. The marquise, on the other hand, seemed hurt but somewhat contrite, and Rousseau tearfully apologized, as did she. She had been planning a trip to a famous doctor in Geneva and asked Rousseau to accompany her. He refused, giving ill health as his reason. Grimm and Diderot saw this as still another betrayal, and his alienation from them was permanent. (He later confessed that Therese had told him that the marquise was going to Geneva to end an unwanted pregnancy. Actually she was suffering from tuberculosis.)

There were others who were still friendly to him. In 1758 the Duke and Duchess of Luxemburg offered to lend him a house on their estate. Rousseau accepted and moved in with Therese. For the next four years he lived there and produced three of his most famous works: *The New Heloise* (a love story based on the romance of Abelard and Heloise that sealed his fame in the hearts of women all over Europe); *Emile* (an idealized treatise on the proper education of a boy); and *The Social Contract* (a political essay that opened with the assertion that man is born free but everywhere is in chains).

Even though *Emile* had passed the Catholic censor in France, another church official found it heretical and called for Rousseau's imprisonment or exile. In *Emile*, Rousseau not only rejected the notion of original sin, but ended up attacking all but the fundamentals of Christianity. It is a surprise that it passed the censor. Most authors published their books outside of France to avoid the tight censorship codes. *Emile* came out in May 1762. By June the author was bannished to Switzerland, as his book was burned in France. Hoping to return to his native Geneva, he was surprise when they, too, denounced him and took away his citizenship. He ended up in Berne.

It was at this time that Voltaire, an old friend-turned-enemy, decided to take pity on the outcast. In 1758 Voltaire had jealously denounced Rousseau as a monkey and a madman. Such enmity came from the fact that Rousseau was successful (apparently Voltaire had trouble accepting this) and from the fact that Rousseau encouraged Geneva not to build a theater in the town, because such an institution led to corruption. Voltaire was a playwright living in Geneva at the time. But now in 1762, he offered his home to the fugitive. Unfortunately, Rousseau never responded to the offer and Voltaire vowed to get even with his colleague. He issued one of the most scathing and disgraceful pamphlets of his career. Anonymously, he disclosed a sordid and inaccurate picture of Rousseau's shortcomings as a father, concluding that he exposed all five children on the door of an orphanage. Voltaire continued to his death to resent the popularity Rousseau maintained in Europe.

In 1765 Rousseau started his *Confessions* and decided to accept Scottish philosopher David Hume's offer to bring him to England. But he had to return to Paris to get his passport. Upon his reentry into the city throngs of people greeted him; however, he only wished to be left alone. In England it was the same way. Hume found the wandering philosopher charming and easy to get along with. He could hardly imagine quarreling with him. Shortly after Therese's arrival Rousseau requested that he, his dog Sultan, and Therese be allowed to live in the country away from the social gatherings which he had learned to detest. Hume consented, although he did not think that it was a good idea. He feared that Rousseau would get too melancholy with so little to do. Perhaps he was right. At any rate, the English papers got wind of some scandalous gossip on Rousseau, and their tone changed from praise to criticism. At a loss to understand this change, the excitable philosopher accused Hume of treachery or at least disloyalty. Hume was shocked as were the few remaining friends Rousseau had in Paris.

In 1767 Rousseau returned to Paris under a false name. He finished his *Confessions* and started the *Dialogues* and *Reveries*. In 1768 he acted as his own minister and married Therese in a mock ceremony. Finally, in 1778, he accepted the hospitality of the Marquis de Giradin at Ermenville. He reached there in spring and was taken with the natural beauty of the setting. He became a frequent companion to the marquis' young son and even played the harpsicord in a makeshift concert. Giradin said Rousseau was content.

On 2 July 1778, Rousseau rose at his usual hour of 5:00 A.M. and walked to the park. At 7:00 he drank his coffee but complained of feeling weak and cold. Then, agonizing over a severe pain in his head, he fell forward and died. An autopsy showed that the cause of death was a hemorrage. But his former friends—Grimm and others—spread the tale that he had committed suicide. On 4 July 1778 he was buried on the Giradin estate as he had requested. During the French Revolution the people elevated Rousseau to the level of secular saint and his remains were moved to the Pantheon in Paris and laid near those of Voltaire. The cliquish Paris group continued their derogation by asserting that insanity drove him to suicide. His old Enlightenment friends never forgave him for his emotional nature in an age when men were supposed to be tough, stoical, reserved, and heroic. A year after Rousseau's death, Therese married the gardener of the Giradin estate.

EDUCATIONAL VIEWS

How shall we rate *Emile*? The book bothered many people, but not reformers with an interest in providing an education for the masses or "the people," as European aristocrats were fond of saying. The work is divided into five books. The first three deal with the rearing of a boy, Emile, in a natural surrounding. The last two take Emile as a young man and place him into society.[17] Rousseau wanted a state system of public education but, because instruction was still in clerical hands, he gave Emile an unmarried secular tutor.

Rousseau thought removing the child as much as possible from parental control would make nature become the tutor's guide. Emile was to have as much freedom to explore his surroundings as safety allowed. There would be no swaddling, so the child could move freely. The baby Emile was to be breast-fed by his mother—not a wetnurse as was the custom—because the mother would have a natural love for her son. Once he developed muscular control, Emile was to begin moral training. Moral education, however, was not to come in the form of adult preaching. The tutor and parents were to teach it by setting a good example. If they were kind, understanding, and not superficial or affected, Emile would be the same way. Punishment was not necessary, said Rousseau, if children learned to suffer the consequences of their actions. Self-love was universal and necessary to preserve mankind. Out of it could grow both compassion and pity for significant others (parents) who had nourished and cared for the soul. These two feelings were a healthy basis for morality, but to distort them into dying for one's honor would be unnatural and false.

Emile's intellectual education was to begin after his moral training was well established. This would occur somewhere around the age of twelve. Emile was to acquire academic knowledge selectively. He could read *Robinson Crusoe* and study natural science. Practical application of natural subjects would enhance Emile's adequacies. Hence, working with the hands and learning skilled trades were to be part of instruction. Writing, acting, and music were not. All subjects having to do with man in society—history, philosophy, religion, politics—were to wait. By fifteen Emile would be healthy, alert, agile, and self-sufficient. At eighteen Emile could encounter religion and eventually learn about the corruptness of society through field trips to the city and study of the humanities.

In his twenties, Emile would concern himself with love and marriage. Up to then, Emile had not experienced sexual passion. But once he did, the tutor had to find him a companion—a *suitable* female companion. The tutor had already told Emile the truth about sex when he asked. Part of the truth was that it is best to marry. Together they looked for Sophie, a name they chose together because it "augurs well." (The last book is entitled "Sophie"—Countess d'Houdetot's first name.)

Her education, while also important, was to be very different. Sophie's function would be to please Emile. She was to subjugate herself to him and make herself useful and agreeable. These duties she would have learned from childhood. She should also be gay, musical, and possessed of an alert mind. This would make her fit company for a thinking Emile. The proper study for women was men. "A woman's education must . . . be planned in relation to man." To please him, "to win his respect and love, to train him in childhood, tend him in manhood, to counsel and console, to make his life pleasant and happy, these are the duties of woman for all time, and this is what she should be taught when young." Sophie's religious faith would be up to Emile, and she would have already learned to be ashamed of her sexuality so that she would be modest. Apparently women were not naturally as good as men.

Rousseau had the tutor and Emile search everywhere, including in the city, for the ideal mate. They finally discovered Sophie in the country. She was fifteen and had all of the necessary qualities, so they fell in love. They entered into a three year courtship, in which Emile sought the tutor's guidance, before they were finally married. When Sophie became pregnant, Emile asked the tutor to remain to train their child. Rousseau had already indicated that Emile's tutor must be young. Now we know why.

This romanticized view of education is certainly understandable in view of Rousseau's life. Its impact on other educational thinkers was strong. From Pestalozzi through Dewey, Rousseau would be consulted: a span of over 150 years! Unfortunately, his prescriptions were not always clear and each of his followers would have their difficulties making the doctrines work. The tension between individual freedom and social necessity is long standing in political theory and history as well as in education. It would become a perplexing dilemma for progressive educators as demonstrated by their varied explanations of what Rousseau meant by the enigmatic statement, "No doubt Emile ought to do what he wants to do, but he should do nothing but what you [the tutor] want him to do."

Rousseau's proposals for educating young men were immediately controversial, but his thoughts on women's education caused no stir. They were conventional for the time. Within a few years of his death, however, a young British woman declared war on the long-standing attitudes that confined women to separate and inferior educational, social, and political spheres. By raising the issue in fiction, she fueled a debate that grew to large proportions by the end of the nineteenth century and that remains a significant area of controversy today. Her name was Mary Wollstonecraft.

Mary Wollstonecraft (1759-1797)

Mary Wollstonecraft has established herself in the historical record as an eighteenth century feminist theorist and as a writer of pedagogic stories.[18] She set forth an interpretation of the relations between the sexes to explain, first, how women learned submissiveness, and second, how women and men could live equally in relation to each other. Her best known book and the work which gained her international recognition, the *Vindication of the Rights of Woman* (1792), contained her analysis of women's subservience. It proposed an egalitarian alternative to the sex based inequities she observed in British society. She did her writing between 1786 and 1797 against the background of revolution in France and working class agitation in England.

Mary was born on 27 April 1759 near London. She had one older and two younger brothers plus two younger sisters. Her father inherited enough money for the family to have lived comfortably, but he overspent on his own pleasures and managed badly. The result was that the family had to move often. Another was that the daughters had to work if they did not marry.

Mary experienced most of the occupations available to middle class, literate, and single young women—and found them denigrating. She left home in 1778 at the age of nineteen to become a companion for a wealthy elderly woman at the health resort town of Bath. This employment lasted for two years. In 1783, Wollstonecraft, her friend Fanny Blood, and one of Wollstonecraft's sisters opened a day school at Newington Green in north London. Wollstonecraft's other sister eventually joined the three women. Various personal difficulties, problems in raising enough money to pay the bills, and Fanny Blood's unexpected death in 1785, led Wollstonecraft to close the school in 1786. During the next year she worked as a governess for an aristocratic family in Ireland.

Between the closing of the school and Wollstonecraft's move to Ireland, she wrote her first pedagogic book, *Thoughts on the Education of Daughters*. It was published in 1786 by Joseph Johnson, a London bookseller and printer sympathetic to the English radicals of the nineties. She again turned to writing after her unhappy and short-lived employment as governess, and by 1788 decided to carve out a literary career for herself. In that year, Wollstonecraft moved to London from Ireland with the help of Johnson who provided her with regular work as a reviewer for his newly created magazine, the *Analytical Review*. Through her association with Johnson, Wollstonecraft joined company with London's leading political radicals. These included Thomas Paine, Thomas Christie, William Godwin and the artists William Blake and Henry Fuseli. In 1790 she publicly became one of them when she wrote *Vindication of the Rights of Men*. This was an angry response to Edmund Burke's conservative *Reflections on the Revolution in France*. She was one of the first to take Burke on in writing. Two years later she wrote her major book, *Vindication of the Rights of Woman*.

POWER OF EDUCATION

Wollstonecraft's ideas about women's rights were grounded in her understanding of the functions of education, both in school and in the home. At the root of her explanation for women's subjugation lay the premise that pedagogy served to empower or disenfranchise particular social groups. Wollstonecraft categorized people by sex first, then by class. She focused her analysis on women of the middle class, the group to which she belonged. Wollstonecraft argued that through their education men learned to think rationally, the skill she believed to be vital for doing everything from running the government to justly disciplining a child. This asset was intentionally missing from the education girls received. Wollstonecraft claimed that the omission of training in *reason* supported women's servitude. She believed that female education in eighteenth century Britain denied women both their reason and their liberty, rights to which they were entitled. She wanted to give women an intellectual training that would enable them to reason. The power to think rationally would lead to their liberty.

In 1792 Wollstonecraft wanted a rational education for women on two counts:

(1) it would produce independent women, and (2) it would lead to a society in which men and women were equals. By 1796, when she began the novel *Maria, Or the Wrongs of Woman*, the second of these goals did not seem viable to her. She no longer wrote about egalitarianism between the sexes. *Maria* dramatized the impossibility of Wollstonecraft's earlier dream, and concluded that rational education should teach women to live on their own—that is, without male companionship. Independent women should live either with other women or alone.

In both the *Vindication* and *Maria*, Wollstonecraft examined girls' instruction in political terms, exploring the ways by which the different education of the sexes produced subservient women and dominating men. In each book she offered different solutions for women to gain control of their lives. The originality and power of her ideas lay in her investigation two hundred years ago of the connections between girls' education, women's subjugation, and the denial of rights to women.

Wollstonecraft worked against the backdrop of "reform" movement in girls' education that aimed at ennobling female domesticity through curriculum. The reformers, who included Maria Edgeworth, Thomas Day, and Dr. Erasmus Darwin, hoped to produce women beneficial to the progress of British society. They wanted to provide girls with a practical education to improve them as wives and mothers. Notions of improvement and practicality reflected the inventive spirit of an industrializing age and domestic work was the way women could best contribute to the growth of British culture. The reformers objected to the popular mode of instructing girls in only the "accomplishments": drawing, dancing, sewing, playing a musical instrument, learning a modern foreign language. They regarded these achievements as superfluous and inhibiting to the development of English civilization.

At the heart of this movement lay the ideal of the middle-class woman: that she not earn a living; that she be economically dependent on her husband; that she not while away her leisure time on frivolous (self-indulgent) activity; that instead she use her extra hours to improve herself and her family; that she manage her household skillfully and raise her children competently; and above all, that she know her place as subservient to her husband. This ideal reflected broader changes in women's relationship to production and to the socialization of children. The responsibilities of non-aristocratic British women in contributing to a family wage diminished over the course of the eighteenth century. Consequently their symbolic significance as wives changed from partner to object of wealth and from child bearer to child rearer.[19] As children gained recognition and importance, their well-being became associated with motherly care. A new condition of "motherhood" developed as a socially desirable position by 1800, and marriage carried with it the added status of motherhood by that time. New occupations for women, that of teacher and writer, developed over the same period. Except in rare cases, however, these vocations did not provide women with the prestige that a husband and child afforded. For the most part, a stigma was attached both to a woman who worked and to the work itself. If a married woman sought employment because she needed money, both she and her husband were considered failures. If she had no husband, that condition itself signified an even greater failure.

While Wollstonecraft accepted female domesticity and shared the general

belief that formal education could "improve" a person, she also liked Enlightenment ideas of equality and had imbibed the spirit of utopian optimism characteristic of English liberalism. These ideas underlay her vision of an independent
woman, most likely married, who could earn her own living respectably if she
needed or wanted to do so. She held firm faith in the overall power of reason
to uncover truth, and indeed, based her pedagogy on the supremacy of reason.
She affirmed that rational thinking led to rational actions which could produce
republican government. She fully accepted the premise that all people, regardless of property holdings or sex, were endowed with rights that no government
could deny. A free nation based on laws established by representative government could exist where individuals would be economically independent and
politically equivalent. Education was the means to achieve the new society, and
schools were to be the agents of change.

CURING INEQUALITY

Throughout the *Vindication* Wollstonecraft used the term "oppression" to
indicate a lack of choice in all spheres of life: social, economic, political, intellectual, physical. Women, as oppressed individuals, did not have a "civil existence
in the state." They were unrepresented citizens similar to the "class of hardworking mechanics" whom despotic government oppressed. Women, however, regardless of their economic status, endured oppression by men.[20] Wealthy
women, Wollstonecraft believed, had nothing significant to do with their time
and consequently focused their unused minds on their looks and on domestic
inanities. She argued that because they could not engage in enterprise useful
for the improvement of British society, aristocratic ladies were restricted to a
narrow, domestic world of servants, children, guests, and lap dogs. She recognized that working-class women sustained a different kind of subjugation because marriage for them did not provide economic security as it did—if it
worked right—for middle-class women. Not only did working-class women
have to take menial, underpaid jobs, but they were also subject to sexual
abuse. Wollstonecraft indicated the existence of oppression for working-class
women in the *Vindication* and presented the issue dramatically in *Maria*. The
earlier work focused primarily on the conditions of oppression suffered by
middle-class women.

The *Vindication* contained Wollstonecraft's proposal for a national system of
coeducation which would produce independent women capable of making rational judgments. An elementary school would house children from all social
classes between the ages of five and nine. To reinforce her belief that the ability
to learn did not depend on sex, she advocated dressing girls and boys alike so
the instructor and the students themselves would have difficulty distinguishing
male from female. Moreover, one would be unable to identify a rich from a poor
child.

All [would be] obliged to submit to the same discipline, or leave school.
The schoolroom ought to be surrounded by a large piece of ground in
which the children might be usefully exercised, for at this age they should
not be confined to any sedentary employment for more than an hour at

a time. But these relaxations might all be rendered a part of elementary education, for many things improve and amuse the senses, when introduced as a kind of show, to the principles of which dryly laid down, children would turn a deaf ear. For instance, botany, mechanics, and astronomy, reading, writing, arithmetic, natural history, and some simple experiments in these pursuits should never encroach on gymnastic plays in the open air. The elements of religion, history, the history of man, and politics, might also be taught by conversations in the Socratic form.[21]

In an elementary school, no distinctions would be made on the basis of either sex or class. Past the age of nine, however, working-class boys and girls would be separated from each other in the afternoons so that they each could learn skills particular to their sex. These children were also to be trained in a different place from the wealthier pupils. Wollstonecraft offered training in skills that would enable working-class people, especially the women, to earn a wage respectably and to maintain their economic independence. Her pedagogy attempted to prevent the working classes from suffering the degradation of poverty by providing individuals—again mainly the women—with a trade. Wollstonecraft suggested that class divisions, at least between the working and middle classes, be maintained in schools for older children as well as in society but that conditions within each sector be improved.

Wealthier boys and girls would continue to be instructed together in the standard curriculum of a good middle-class boys' school—that is, a liberal arts education, aimed at preparing for university study, and therefore, professional careers. By suggesting that girls be provided with this sort of preparatory schooling, Wollstonecraft proposed the radical notion that the ancient professions be open to women. Even though this revolutionary idea clearly appeared in the Vindication, she did not emphasize it. Rather, she stressed the equal relationships women and men should form once women achieved independence.

Wollstonecraft assumed that equality between the sexes would be the inevitable result of coeducation, but she did not insist that it be classless. In other words, women of the middle and upper classes would not be the equals of women of the working classes but would certainly be equal to men of their own station. Neither man nor woman would control the other. Each would be free to govern his or her own life. Women would no longer be male playthings or objects of admiration and lust. Rather, women would be colleagues or companions—which is the word Wollstonecraft used—of men. This society of equals would be characterized by women acting as rational mothers within marriages based on companionship.

Wollstronecraft saw the marriage relationship as a microcosm of her society of equals. Women and men would marry for friendship instead of for reasons of property or passion. She had identified love as the condition which so clouded the rational faculties that it inhibited sound judgment in choosing a mate and perverted the feelings of parental affection. Men and women had to check their passions with reason. This continuous response would pave the way for sexual friendship. As members of rational families, children would be raised in reason and justice, because they had to pass on to their children the same values that they had received.[22] Women had the primary responsibility for making their daughters rational and their sons respectful of women. Wollstonecraft advocated that women and men have equal obligations towards maintaining the family and keeping the friendship viable, but neither would control the other in any respect. She insisted that only two equal beings could form egalitarian relationships; two unequal ones could not. By attempting to rearrange the political balance between the sexes through pedagogy, Wollstonecraft advocated a radical change in British society.

DISILLUSIONMENT

The *Vindication* expressed a utopian wish for a future where neither woman nor man would dominate the other. By 1796, when Wollstonecraft began to write *Maria, Or the Wrongs of Woman*, much of her optimism had disappeared. This was partly because of her own romantic experiences between 1792 and 1796. She had been attracted to the painter Henry Fuseli in an emotionally ambiguous way, desiring to live with him and his wife but apparently not wishing to become his lover. To her naive surprise he rejected her and retreated from their friendship by cancelling a trip to Paris that the Fuselis and Wollstonecraft had planned together to witness the events of the French Revolution. Wollstonecraft went to Paris, nevertheless, and there began an ill-fated liaison with Gilbert Imlay, an American businessman.

She and Imlay decided to live together for almost a year between 1793 and 1794. During this time she took the name Imlay, ostensibly because Americans were safer in Paris than were British citizens. In May 1794, she gave birth to a daughter whom she named Fanny Imlay in memory of her closest childhood friend, Fanny Blood. That year was the steadiest period of their relationship. Then Imlay saw her infrequently for brief intervals, always promising to return for good. The intensity of her feelings made their periods of separation unendurable for her. At one point, when she believed he was never going to return, she tried suicide. She made a second attempt by jumping in the Thames when she learned that he was involved with an actress. It was not a question of desiring marriage, but rather of holding on to a loved one tenaciously.

Wollstonecraft's need to be economically independent finally enabled her to get back on her feet and to start writing again. At about this time she entered into the most comfortable and satisfying attachment of her life, a relationship with the philosopher William Godwin. Their intellectual attraction soon broadened into an intimate romance.[23]

The marriage which resulted is generally described as a happy one, although Wollstonecraft could not bring herself to believe that it would last. She wanted emotional security in her relationships with both Imlay and Godwin. Yet when Godwin offered this to her she was unable to trust his love. Their correspondence, largely in the form of brief notes sometimes written daily, revealed her expectation that Godwin, like Imlay, would leave her. The intensity of her need for emotional certainty and her inability to trust someone's love probably stemmed from her marginal position in her original family. Her unhappily married parents denied her their attention and affection and in turn Wollstonecraft became possessive in her attachments—including her female friendships—and suspicious of love shown to her. Yet she was emotionally dependent on the loved one for self definition as evidenced most severely in her affair with Imlay.

Throughout her life, Wollstonescraft felt an overriding tension from the twin needs for dependence and independence. This conflict formed the contours of her history and gave direction to her ideas. Her polemical and pedagogical writing developed around the issue of independence, while her autobiographical fiction illustrated the impediments to that end. Although the *Vindication* has enjoyed the greater renown, Wollstonecraft's gloomy final novel, *Maria*, offers a closer look at her personal struggle for independence. As a writer Wollstonecraft turned to the novel form almost as a vehicle for self-analysis, as a way of confronting the profound feelings of abandonment and despair she had experienced between 1792 and 1796. Although *Maria* revealed Wollstonecraft's emotional past, it also contained new attitudes about the purposes of female independence.

The story of *Maria* revolved around the plights of two women: Maria Venables, a middle-class woman who had been imprisoned in an insane asylum by her husband, and Jemima, her improverished female guard. Mutual biographical recountings of these two women to each other served as the literary device through which Wollstonecraft portrayed the primary result of male domination as the victimization of women.[24] Female dependence took a turn toward the macabre in *Maria*. Not only were the minds and opportunities of Maria and Jemima restricted due to gender, but men threatened their very existence. By acquiring rational education, both women understood their oppression, fought against it, and survived.

THE WRONGS OF WOMAN

Jemima had been beleaguered by the inevitable hardships due to her sex and class. Her mother, a maid, had been seduced by a fellow servant with promises of marriage. The woman became pregnant; the man turned away. The father virtually disowned his daughter, Jemima. He sent her off to serve with another family. The master of her new household raped her and forced her to submit to him thereafter.

His wife eventually caught the pair, blamed Jemima for seducing her master, and turned her out of the house with no money. In order not to starve, Jemima resorted to prostitution. She eventually met a wealthy old man who took her on as his mistress and forced her to acquiesce to sexual demands which disgusted her. Upon his sudden death, his family put her out on the streets penniless. Several other episodes occurred before Jemima wound up in the workhouse. All of them revealed the degradation that a poor and "ruined" woman would meet.

Wollstonecraft contrived situations in which Jemima learned to reflect upon and interpret her experiences. She realized that her troubles had come only because she was a woman, and she understood that her fate had been shaped by men who had forced her into poverty, prostitution, and social ostracism. "A man with half my industry, and, I may say abilities," she exclaimed, "would have procured a decent livelihood, and discharged some of the duties which knit mankind together; whilst I, who had acquired a taste for the rational, nay, in honest pride let me assert it, the virtuous enjoyments of life, was cast aside as the filth of society."[25]

Jemima related her story to her prisoner Maria who wholeheartedly concurred with Jemima's insights. Maria agreed with her guard because she too had been victimized by male greed and self-indulgence. Maria's story included the details of her husband's deceptions. He pretended to love her when he really only wanted her rich uncle's money. Within a few years his charade had become evident. Maria had expected to find companionship based on mutual respect. Instead, she realized that marriage had meant the end of her happiness and the legal transfer of her inherited money to her spouse. She could alter her situation in one of three ways—by choosing to live apart from her husband if he agreed, by commiting suicide, or by killing him. Divorce action initiated by a woman could succeed only if the husband constantly and severely beat his wife. George Veneables did not hurt Maria physically, although he tortured her psychologically. Maria left him, actually escaped from his house, only to be recaptured and incarcerated in a private madhouse. He claimed that his wife's running away indicated her dementia, because sane married women remained with their husbands. The owners of the asylum accepted his story and imprisoned his innocent wife.

The last two chapters of the novel resolved the dilemmas Maria and Jemima faced. They escaped from the asylum and formed a domestic partnership. Jemima, however, agreed to live with Maria only if she could be Maria's housekeeper. Maria approved. Both women acknowledged social class boundaries but saw each other as women first who could provide sanctuary for each other's broken lives, thereby preventing further misfortune at the hands of men. Trust and empathy formed the basis of their shared lives. Their friendship lasted, while their relationships with men had been transitory, painful, and disappointing.

SIGNIFICANCE

Eighteenth century women generally married out of necessity to accomplish other ends, usually security and stability. Wollstonecraft suggested that if women did not marry, they could at least retain some freedom in their daily lives. This dismal portrayal of matrimony signaled an about-face from the optimistic discussion of companionship marriage in the *Vindication*. She gently proposed in *Maria* that women live unmarried with each other as protectors, helpers, confidants and that they shield each other from the dangers of men. She hinted that women should form exclusive communities.

Wollstonecraft had come to see women as victims of a male world regardless of class or education. Men legally possessed more authority than women, a fact which Wollstonecraft illustrated through the marriage between Maria and her husband. Marriage functioned as the symbol and reality of female oppression for the middle class because through matrimony a woman lost whatever civil identity she had as well as control over her material possessions. Jemima's service as mistress to wealthy men and as prostitute underscored women's sexual exploitation and its particularly harsh effect upon poor women, whom Wollstonecraft recognized as the sexual servants of higher class men. The sexual exploitation suffered by Jemima may also have served as a symbol for Wollstonecraft's perception of exploited womanhood regardless of class. Maria and Jemima turned their backs on oppressive male society to live a reasonably free existence with each other.

In *Maria*, as in the *Vindication*, children continued to be part of woman's sphere. Wollstonecraft retained her earlier view that a middle-class woman should be a mother. Maria had a daughter whom she believed had died, but Jemima located the child. The female household that Maria and Jemima established included the little girl. The importance of motherhood, however, did not seem to apply as directly to working-class women. Wollstonecraft pictured Jemima in maternal activity as Maria's caretaker in the asylum and later as her servant caring for Maria's child, but Jemima herself never became a mother. Wollstonecraft accepted the procreative link between the sexes, but tried to eliminate the responsibilities and burdens of being a wife. By recounting many incidents of male domination, Maria taught her child about the conditions necessary for women to live in freedom.

Wollstonecraft was not able to eliminate all the difficulties of being female from her own life. Not only did her childhood experiences color her adult relationships, but her love affair with Godwin resulted in her becoming pregnant. She gave birth to a daughter (who kept the habit of writing in the family by authoring *Frankenstein* and by marrying the poet Percy Bysshe Shelley). But complications after delivery (puerperal or childbed fever) brought death to Mary Wollstonecraft at the age of thirty-seven.

Wollstonecraft has been called the "first feminist philosopher worthy of the name." Perhaps this is an extravagant claim in view of Christine de Pisan's work, but Wollstonecraft did present the earliest powerful argument in English for extending to both sexes the human rights heralded by the French Revolution and by English liberals. "The *Vindication* was the first effective challenge to the entire system of male supremacy, to the traditional concepts of masculinity and femininity, and the presumption of female inferiority," says Mary Anne Warren. "It created an international sensation, made Wollstonecraft the most infamous woman in Europe, and inspired Horace Walpole to refer to her as a "hyena in petticoats."

Wollstonecraft's arguments were ignored by many people who did not want to deal with their content and were portrayed as a hysterical outburst from a scandalous person. She did nothing to diminish the assumption that working-class people should receive a less academic education than their social betters, but virtually all of the elements in the continuing debate over male/female relationships were well-developed in her writing. Her contention that independence, rationality, and strength of character were no more male than female characteristics has a particularly modern ring. Indeed, one of the major rationalizations for why most contemporary school administrators are men has been that males are more likely to possess the "right" psychological characteristics for leadership. This claim is now under serious indictment. Wollstonecraft challenged it nearly three centuries ago. Finally, her explicit disagreement with Rousseau seems right in a modern context. To justify his different education for Sophie, he postulated that little girls are naturally quieter than boys, having a genetic predisposition toward dolls and dresses instead of active play. "I have, probably, had an opportunity of observing more girls in their infancy than J. J. Rousseau," wrote Wollstonecraft. "I will venture to affirm that a girl whose spirits have not been dampened by inactivity, or innocence tainted by false shame, will always be a romp, and the doll will never excite attention unless confinement allows her no alternatives."[26]

Victor of Aveyron (c. 1788-1828)

In the year that Mary Wollstonecraft died, peasants in southern France sighted a naked boy running through some woods. Over the next two years, he was seen several more times. During the winter of 1799-1800, gossip circulated that Rousseau's noble savage had been found wandering in the southern French province at Aveyron. However, he was hardly the picture of Emile. Authorities guessed his age at around twelve to fourteen. He was four and a half feet tall and ran on all fours, swaying from side to side. He was very dirty and could make only wild gutteral type sounds. Paris newspapers dubbed him the "enfant sauvage de l'Aveyron"—the Wild Boy of Aveyron.[27]

He was quickly given to the care of a young physician who had become interested in the scientific study of retardation and sensory impairment. His name was Dr. Jean-Marc-Gaspard Itard (1774-1838). He and others hoped that this savage would shed light on the basic issue of the Enlightenment—that is, the nature of human beings. Itard named the boy Victor and eventually brought him to the Institute for Deaf Mutes in Paris. There Itard made provisions for his own housekeeper to care for Victor and embarked on a program designed to develop the boy's social, sensory, emotional, and speech skills.

Itard worked with Victor for four years, keeping a diary of observations made throughout this time. He thought that Victor progressed in all areas except the emotional. Finally the doctor abandoned the work because he felt that he could go no further with Victor. As the boy passed through adolescence, he seemed to become more violent toward the other children in the hospital. Consequently, he was finally set to live with Itard's housekeeper on a permanent basis. He died in 1828 at about the age of forty.

Itard's work with Victor elevated to a new level the emerging discussion of who could be educated and to what extent. We have already noted that the Jesuits and their Protestant competitors have begun a systematic search for more effective teaching strategies. The conditions under which they initially worked, however, precluded much thought about whether everyone could, much less should, benefit from their methods. The fact that relatively few people went beyond elementary vernacular skills was so much a reflection of inherited political, economic, and social structures that few people questioned whether it was possible to teach advanced material to most youth. The speculations of people like Locke and Rousseau suggested the potentially dramatic likelihood that environment and method were much more important than had been generally thought. Emerging sentiment favoring mass systems of public instruction lent impetus to the discussion. Itard pushed the issue further in two ways: (1) by supposing that even idiots—both a professional and popular term at the time—could learn more than anyone had supposed; and (2) by testing the matter experimentally, rather than just speculatively.

The fact that Itard was disappointed in not having gotten Victor to a verbal language phase—the boy remained mute, although he could recognize some words and phrases—did not mar the significance of the undertaking. Almost everyone thought Itard had failed. But the debates over *why* he had failed brought to light conflicting assumptions about what produces success or failure in teaching/learning situations. For example: Was Victor a congenital idiot beyond help? Had early emotional isolation made him retarded? Were Itard's methods wrong or inadequate? The assumptions anyone makes to account for learning failure remain the most revealing window to conflicting educational philosophies.

One other significant aspect of Itard's work was the large variety of teaching materials that he developed in his quest to instruct Victor. The following list will illustrate:

> a plank painted black on which everyday objects were placed and their outlines chalked; the same objects suspended underneath their designs; letter cutouts to form names; a vertical board displaying a red disk, blue triangle, and black square, and the corresponding cardboard cutouts hung from nails; similar boards with the same forms in one color, or circles of contrasting colors, or kindred geometric forms, or circles or similar hues, or irregular patches of color; a board with twenty-four slots containing two-inch letters printed on cardboard; the corresponding letters in metal; a board with two equal circles, each having six points on the circumference for placing letter cutouts; drum, bells, shovel, drumstick; various sweets, drinks, snuff; a narrow-neck vase containing hot and cold nuts, acorns, stones, a penny and a die, metal letters; a blindfold; goblets, books, nails, a skewer, chalk, various household objects.

Those who visited Victor toward the end of his life felt that he had lost whatever ground he had gained with Itard. Nevertheless, the debate continued. The chains binding the insane, the retarded, and other deviants were gradually broken. (Chaining the insane in asylums had been outlawed in France in the 1790s.) Now new ground was being broken in the education of the retarded and handicapped. Itard was an early pilgrim on this road and his student, Edward Séguin (1812-1880), traveled even farther. Their efforts contributed much to the field of anthropology, to the theories of Montessori (see Chapter 10), and to the birth of special education.

Enlightenment ideas of expanding political liberty, improving the most extreme economic conditions of the poor, and extending schooling opportunities to all youth followed many trails in Europe and America. We have noted a few of these in the thoughts of Locke, Rousseau, and Wollstonecraft. Another significant figure in these developments was a German speaking Swiss citizen named Pestalozzi. He was particularly important because several of the German states, in the shadow of Napoleon's domination, started tax funded school systems early in the nineteenth century. They did not want educational ideas from anyone who looked too French, much less the wild sounding Rousseau. They turned instead to the town of Yverdon in Switzerland where interesting sounding things were happening. The person said to be responsible was a badly dressed, absentminded man whose story follows.

Johann Heinrich Pestalozzi (1746-1827)

Although the name Pestalozzi is Italian, the family had been citizens of Zurich for two hundred years when Heinrich was born in 1746. Some members of the family had done well in the years after Heinrich's forebearers had migrated from Chiavenna because they were Protestants. By the eighteenth century, however, "early deaths" and "ill fortune" had taken a toll. Heinrich's father, Johann Baptist Pestalozzi, was a surgeon. This was not the high status position that it is today. Only physicians had university training. Surgeons merely apprenticed and usually lacked the knowledge, equipment, or facilities for operations more complicated than bloodletting. Heinrich's grandfather was pastor of a poor suburban parish near Zurich. The family was officially entitled to election to the city council—one of the small number with that privilege. This fact lent an aura of respectability, but none of the Pestalozzis had run for the council for a long time. This was another indication that they were not doing well. Heinrich's mother, Sussana Holtz, was from the country town of Wadenswil, which was part of the city-state of Zurich. No resident of the area outside of Zurich proper could be a citizen, but her family was on the rise. A number of the men were noted as physicians. Perhaps Sussana married Johann Baptist for the family's respectability. If so, she must have been disappointed because her husband did not make much money, and they were apparently not part of the "in" social set in Zurich.

The Pestalozzis had three children: Johann Baptist, the oldest; Anna Barbara, the youngest; and Heinrich in between. At thirty-three the senior Johann Baptist died. A young servant girl named Barbara Schmid ("Babeli") made the father a deathbed promise not to leave the family as long as she was needed. Sussana did not remarry, but hung on tenaciously to her would-be respectability. She "was a shy woman who lived quietly because of her small means and her country origins," was the way one biographer put it. Babeli, who was probably much like the character "Gertrude" in Pestalozzi's later writing, seemed to have been the glue that held the family together. She stayed with Sussana for over forty years, turning down better offers and a "suitable marriage," to keep her promise.[28]

EARLY LIFE

Details about how Heinrich got on in the family are scant. Pestalozzi later made several autobiographical references in which he blamed his upbringing for a variety of failures. By inference, it seemed likely that Sussana and Babeli tried to compensate for Heinrich's loss of his father by protecting him from the harsher aspects of the world. He evidently was not forced to do things he did not like, though he was almost certainly punished for relatively minor transgressions. He did not play with neighborhood children. They made fun of him with nicknames such as "Harry Queer of Foolstown." The family's socially superior attitude—without the money to support it—no doubt increased peer resentment of the children. Heinrich and his brother went to the best schools in Zurich. There is no published evidence about how his brother got on in school, but Heinrich was described as inattentive, spending much of his time daydreaming.

As a young man he learned to plan on a grand scale, to plunge into projects without adequate preparation but with unlimited enthusiasm, and to lose interest quickly when difficulties arose.

In accounting to himself and others for the succession of failures that made up his life, Pestalozzi would go through brief periods of self-doubt and blame followed by depression and self-pity, because the means of success were permanently beyond his grasp. It was almost as if a cruel fate allowed him to get his hopes high, and then without warning it swooped in to wreck everything—just as it had done when he was five by taking his father away. In looking for explanations of the failure that seemed to follow him like a personal black cloud, Pestalozzi inevitably blamed those with whom he associated. It was an unhappy psychological track around which he went many times without ever finding an escape. At the same time there was something likeable, perhaps even a little pathetic, about him that would lead many people to try to help him. In the long run he would alienate everyone who had been close to him, but his public image—and his historical reputation—was much different. In his youth, the periods of frenetic activity followed by depression were less severe than they would gradually become.

As a teenager, Heinrich joined the Society of Patriots, a reputedly offbeat group whose members advocated stoic ethics, Spartan self discipline, and a variety of reforms based on the writings of Rousseau. They aspired to perfection and virtue. Heinrich wrote for their publication, called *The Monitor*, and got himself jailed for three days. About this time he read *Emile*. He pretty much took it for gospel at the time, though later he would call it an ''impractical dreambook.'' Meanwhile, Pestalozzi considered himself a Rousseaun naturalist. He and a fellow Patriot, nicknamed Menalk, discussed their plans for the future. As usual, Heinrich Pestalozzi dreamed large things. He had already tried the ministry (under the tutelage of his grandfather), but rejected it: he forgot his sermon and stumbled over the Lord's Prayer. He dabbled at law, but found the work difficult and uninteresting. Now, he thought, perhaps he would lead a ''natural'' life on the land—farming was the thing.

Menalk, the group's informal leader, died. Heinrich made a play for his girlfriend. This was Anna Schulthess, sister of a fellow Patriot and from a respected Zurich family. She was eight years older than Pestalozzi. Nanette, as her friends called her, did not love Heinrich, and her parents objected that the young man had no profession. However, she held a deep resentment for her mother whom she regarded as domineering. She consented, therefore, to a secret engagement.

LIFE AS A FARMER

Now that he was about to become a family man, Pestalozzi embarked on the exciting adventure of learning how to be a farmer. He had no experience with agriculture, but he was confident of his ability to easily pick up the needed skills. He left for the canton of Berne to spend eighteen months on the farm of Johann Rudolf Tschiffeli, a wealthy man who had established a model farm to show the best methods of growing clover, potatoes, and madder (from which a dye was made for the newly emerging cotton industry). Nine months later Pestalozzi was back in Zurich. The family was surprised, but he reassured them that he had mastered the farming business well enough to undertake crop production on his own land—if only someone would lend him money to buy a farm. He was ready for some of the "great and important undertakings" with which he had promised Nanette his life would be filled.

Pestalozzi got some money from his family, borrowed from a Zurich banker, and bought about sixty acres near the village of Birr in the Berne canton. It took fifty separate transactions to put the final package together because most land was owned in small plots. He rented a house, and started his plowing with enthusiasm and the sure knowledge of repaying his loans quickly. He also alienated all his neighbors by refusing to let anyone walk on his land. He thought they would ruin his crops. But the right to walk from wherever one was to wherever one was going by the shortest route was a tradition honored by centuries of common practice. An outsider breaking this custom was not welcome.

Now that he was established as a farmer, Pestalozzi wrote Anna that they could get married. Her parents had consented to a public announcement of the engagement when Heinrich bought his farm, but they did this on the understanding that the couple would wait a year or two until the farm was actually going successfully. Anna wavered between the enthusiasm of her fiancé and the know-it-all sounding cautions from her mother. She agreed to marry her confident suitor. Her parents refused their blessings, a dowry, and a church wedding. But Anna was thirty-four and sick of her mother's advice—so she went ahead with a quiet wedding. The couple moved into their rented farmhouse to lead the idyllic life described by Rousseau.

To Anna's regret it quickly became evident that Frau Schulthess had not been wrong about how things would turn out. It was one thing to talk of seeking perfection in the natural surroundings of simple country life. Over a glass of wine in the company of fellow Patriots dreaming about the way things ought to be the simple life sounded ideal. Reality was much different: a grim old farmhouse, an ill-tempered husband who came home filthy demanding supper, hateful neighbors, boredom and isolation—that was Anna's life in the country. The couple quarreled. Pestalozzi sometimes criticized himself at great length: everything was his fault; he had ruined her life; there was no hope for anyone around him. On other occasions he reminded Anna that he had told her what he was like before they were married—it was her own fault if she had not believed it. Mostly he did neither of these things. He simply ignored it all as he had learned to do as a child and went on to dream of grand future schemes.

Three months after exchanging their vows, the couple conceived the only child they were to have. The boy, whom they named Jean-Jacques (after Rousseau, of course), was born in 1770. Pestalozzi was delighted. He intended to raise the boy entirely naturally. He also was building a grand new house. Anna's family had relented and given her a dowry after all. Within a short time, that money was all spent. The house was unfinished. They put a roof over the part that was done (the first floor) and let it go at that. After about four years, the Zurich bank asked Pestalozzi to repay his loan, but he could not. Again Anna's family came through with enough money to save the house and some of the land. As always, Pestalozzi had ready explanations to account for the failure of his farming business. People cheated him, he said, and Tschiffeli had not taught him the right things. Besides his neighbors were jealous and spread bad stories about him. That was why the bankers asked him to repay the loan. His plan had been a good one. It was not his fault that it failed.

PARENT AND TEACHER

Actually, during the time that the farming venture was reaching crisis conditions, Pestalozzi was busy giving his little son, Jacqueli, a "natural" education. When the boy was less than four years old, his father began what he considered to be an Emile-like education, and he kept a diary describing what he did. He was intrigued at Jacqueli's delight in discovering that water runs down hill; however, when the little boy did not answer questions correctly Pestalozzi felt it was a sign that the child was trying to get his own way. The whole matter of the child's will bothered Pestalozzi. In a curious departure from *Emile,* he required Jacqueli to read every day. If he refused—which he often did at first, partly because he could not read—the punishment was solitary confinement. It did not take the boy long to stop refusing. On one occasion little Jacqueli had a bout with what Pestalozzi called rheumatic fever. When Jacqueli resisted taking medication, the doctor recommended to Pestalozzi "that, when he was quite well, we should now and then give him harmless but unpleasant drinks and powders, so that, in case of need, he would not mind so much." Pestalozzi "saw the soundness of the idea at once."[29]

Pestalozzi's efforts to instruct his son convinced him that one should never "teach by words anything which you can teach by actual experience of things as they are. Let him see, and hear, and find out, and fall, and get up again, and make mistakes—never let words take the place of actions. . . . Let him always be busy and active and, most of the time, free. You will find that Nature is a better teacher than man." When Jacqueli's curiosity led him to investigate more things around the house than Pestalozzi wanted him to, a perfect occasion for an object lesson arose. Here is Pestalozzi's explanation:

> If, for example, I wish to forbid his annoying practice of touching all sorts of things, I go about it in this way. I put two bowls on the table, one cold, one extremely hot, and wash my hands in the cold one and place the hot one in such a position that the little one is certain to touch it and so burn his hand. "People should not touch things which they know nothing about" is my only remark as I soothe the pain of the burn with some oil. A few days later I put some hot eggs in the same place; he immediately takes hold of them and burns himself again. Then I say, "I don't like you to be always burning yourself; leave things alone till you know something about them; you should have asked what it was that stood on the table and whether you might touch it."[30]

It seemed never to have occurred to Pestalozzi that the curiosity that prompted Jacques to touch "all sorts of things" was more natural than his own elaborate schemes to burn his son's fingers.

After a few months of tutoring Jacqueli, Pestalozzi shifted his interest to a new project, one he was absolutely sure would be a rousing success. He decided to turn his Neuhof ("new farm") into a "poor school." It was common practice for farmers to take in young "apprentices" and work them hard for meager pay. Pestalozzi proposed to do this on his farm. He would teach orphans and poor children how to grow, spin, and weave cotton, and how to garden, cook, and sew. He would sell the products of their industry at fairs, and his farm would thereby become profitable. He explained that it was not only good for the children to work long hours at hard tasks, but it was also desirable for them to have rather grim accommodations and sparse food. After all, they were from poor families and would live in poverty. The sooner they grew accustomed to what was in store for them, the happier they would be in their necessary condition. He was so sure this method would do well that he predicted branch sites of other "schools" once this one was under way.

The poor school experiment at Neuhof lasted about four years. Most parents took their children away after a few months because they thought Pestalozzi was merely using them to try to make money for himself. By the end of the time, the farm was not even producing enough vegetables to feed the Pestalozzi family. The whole failed enterprise was something of a local disgrace. Anna had a nervous breakdown. Someone (probably Anna's parents) sent a family servant, an eighteen year old woman named Lisabeth Näff, to help out. She raised enough garden to feed the family, but Pestalozzi did not help her. He had tired of farming.

Pestalozzi spent his time roaming the countryside. His behavior was erratic and he dressed terribly. People called him "pestilence" and "scarecrow." He was a short man with wild, bushy hair which he did nothing to control. He must have looked frightful, often covered with mud from having fallen down. He was in such a distraught mood that he did not watch where he was going on his walks. Even as a young man a friend had said that Heinrich could not "address anyone or do anything without making an unfavorable impression through his hasty, uncouth, and thoughtless behavior." When he became excited while talking with someone, he tended to unconsciously draw himself closer and closer to his conversant's face while his own voice became shrill and loud. Neither his personal appearance nor his business acumen improved with age: on one occasion he managed to borrow some badly needed money to buy provisions for his nearly destitute family, but gave it to a stranger who told him a hard luck story on his way home.

Throughout this period some people remained friendly to the Pestalozzis— one suspects primarily out of loyalty to Anna's family and out of pity for her. The Countess of Hallwil, a widowed neighbor, befriended Anna. In fact, Anna lived at the countess' castle during much of the time after 1780. She and Heinrich were together infrequently during the remaining thirty-six years of her life.

LITERARY CAREER

A Schulthess family friend and editor named Isaac Iselin gave Pestalozzi an opportunity to write for his journal, the *Ephemerides*. With his help, Pestalozzi wrote a series of moralistic stories, entitled *The Evening Hour of a Hermit*, and a short story expanded into a novel called *Leonard and Gertrude*. This latter item was an account of a good woman (Gertrude) who kept her family together despite odds and gave a moral uplift to a sagging town. The book included touching scenes of Gertrude teaching her children by the hearth. The story did not make much money, but it did receive some favorable reviews and established Pestalozzi's name as a beginning novelist with promise.

Flushed with a little praise and success, Pestalozzi turned to writing with characteristic enthusiasm. He entered writing contests, submitting hymns, moral tales, more novels, political tracts, and philosophical treatises. He dreamed of becoming a playright. He hoped some of his writing would "prove that I am suited for a government post." He sent copies and wrote letters to anyone he thought might help him get an appointment, but none came. Most of what he wrote was dull, rambling, repetitive. He rarely finished any of the projects he tackled. His handwriting was terrible and he spelled badly. Anna recopied and cleaned up much of what he wrote. In general, he tended to reflect the point of view of whatever government was in power. Until 1798 none of this worked, and he later admitted in a letter to the Countess of Hallwil that during this period he would have liked to "spit in every man's face."[31]

In 1798 Napoleon's troops invaded the Swiss area and set up a government called the Helvetian Republic. Pestalozzi wrote favorably about these developments and encouraged people to accept the new government. The fighting had left a number of orphaned children. The new government decided to establish a "poor school" at a town called Stans where there was a Capuchin monastery with available buildings. Pestalozzi was offered the job of operating this rescue mission. After two decades of trying to secure a government job, he finally had one. "I am undertaking one of the greatest tasks of our time," he said in leaving for his new assignment.[32]

RETURN TO TEACHING

In the beginning, Pestalozzi had charge of about fifty children. Except for a housekeeper, he was alone with the responsibility of organizing a school, developing a plan for teaching the children some skills with which they could make a living, and also giving them "abc" instruction. According to Pestalozzi all went well despite hardship. "I am wiping out the disgrace of my life," he wrote to the Countess Hallwil. "The virtue of my youth is being restored." Just what really went on is difficult to know. The only account we have is one left by Pestalozzi himself. "When children were persistently obstinate and rude severity was necessary, and I had to use corporal punishment," he later wrote. The children welcomed his ear pulling and blows, Pestalozzi assured his readers but (he added) "others misunderstood me." The government inspected the school, but could not make heads or tails out of what Pestalozzi was doing or what he planned. At the end of five months they closed it. Orphans stayed with the Capuchins. Other children returned to their homes. Pestalozzi was out of a job.[33]

After a period of depression, nervous fits, and throwing up blood, Pestalozzi managed to secure a position as assistant in the poorest school in Burgdorf, a small town in the Emme River valley. The school consisted of seventy-three boys and girls from noncitizen families. Its chief aim was to teach the pupils to read and spell. However, his success with girls might be questioned since he never called on them. This attitude was reflected in *Leonard and Gertrude* when the latter said "Books should be to a woman like a Sunday gown, and work like her everyday clothes."[34] The parents felt that Pestalozzi did not perform well and asked for his dismissal in a short time. He then taught for a few months in a small "dame school."

Details of what happened next are confusing because most writers have depended on Pestalozzi's memory and explanations. An account based on diaries of another man who was a central figure in what transpired suggests the following sequence of events.[35]

During the time that Pestalozzi was teaching in the dame school, the newly established Helvetian government in Berne appropriated the castle at Burgdorf for the purpose of establishing an *école normale*—that is, a normal (ordinary) teacher training school. By turning out skilled teachers with correct political views, the government hoped to extend its base of support. J. R. Fisher, a twenty-seven year old Berne inspector of schools, was assigned the job of organizing the normal school. The plan was to locate children whose parents were too poor because of the war's disruptions to adequately support and educate them. They would be moved to Burgdorf, housed with local families, and educated at the castle. When they reached an appropriate level of age and skill, they would go out to be village teachers. The other crucial element in this plan was to hire one or more good teachers to be in charge of the children's development.

Fisher found the pupils he needed and their main teacher in the eastern Swiss canton of Appenzell. The teacher's name was Hermann Krüsi. At twenty-five he already had an excellent reputation based on six years of dedicated work in village schools. He brought twenty-six children across 120 miles of mountains to begin the work. When he arrived he met Pestalozzi whom Fisher had allowed to occupy a room in the castle. Fisher had also secured for Pestalozzi a position in a boys' school in Burgdorf. (Evidently Pestalozzi had felt under so much tension in the dame school that he thought he had suffered a heart attack.) Thus Pestalozzi was teaching in a school for the sons of poor citizens—there was also a school for sons of wealthier citizens—and living in the castle where Krüsi ran a school and also lived.

The order of the next series of events, which apparently happened in a short period of time, is also unclear. Krüsi's school prospered and added local paying pupils to those he had brought. Fisher caught typhus and died after an illness of a few days. Pestalozzi suggested to Krüsi that he (Pestalozzi) was about to open a school of his own but that it would perhaps be better if they combined forces. Krüsi agreed and wrote to a friend he had known in Appenzell, inviting him to join him. This was J. G. Tobler, a forty-year-old man who had studied theology at Basel, who had spent a number of years as a tutor and teacher, and who had developed a keen interest in child psychology. The Helvetian government continued its support. It granted the castle rent free, provided gardening land and a supply of wood for heat, and furnished a subsidy for printing curricular materials. There was a salary arrangement, but apparently only for Krüsi and Tobler. They shared with Pestalozzi and other co-workers who later joined them. One of Tobler's friends soon arrived to help. This was Johannes C. Buss, a twenty-four-year-old bookbinder whose father had been a servant in a famous theological school in Tübingen. Buss had done well in preparatory school and had intended to enter the theological seminary, but a rule was passed preventing working-class boys from attending. He was bitterly disappointed at having to learn a trade and welcomed Krüsi's invitation to teach art and math in the Burgdorf castle.

The relationship between the four men was cordial. There was no leader although Pestalozzi in his middle fifties was considerably older than the other three. Krüsi, Tobler, and Buss were unassuming men from lower-class backgrounds. Each was dissatisfied with his own knowledge and teaching performance and wanted to improve. They knew Pestalozzi's general reputation—many people said he was crazy and recounted stories of his erratic behavior—but they were willing to look beyond the surface. There was something about him that drew them to him. Each felt a little sorry for him, but at the same time they accorded him respect. He was, after all, the author of *Leonard and Gertrude* and had some standing as a literary figure. None of the three could make much sense of what Pestalozzi tried in the classroom; he yelled in a high-pitched voice, made pupils repeat complicated sentences they did not understand, and insisted that all learners do two things at once—for example, shout the sounds of the alphabet while having a drawing lesson. The fact that Pestalozzi obviously did not know what he was doing was encouraging in one sense, however. It meant that none of them needed to fear failure. The search for better methods could involve extensive experimentation. There was one other aspect of Pestalozzi that helped initially. That was his grand dream of a better world if only they could unlock the secret of effective teaching. The group felt confident that their quest was important enough to be worth personal sacrifice.

The Burgdorf castle experiment prospered from the first. At the same time that Itard was teaching the Wild Boy, Krüsi, Tobler, and Buss worked out new teaching materials and tried them: moveable letters for reading and spelling, pebbles and beans for arithmetic, drawing exercises as preparation for writing, slates and slate pencils instead of pens and paper. The three of them did most of the teaching as well. Pestalozzi said prayers in the evening and worked up endless lists of consonant/vowel combinations that the children were to practice orally in order to help them spell and read. Pestalozzi also continued revisions on his unfinished writing projects.

After eighteen months some officials from Berne inspected the school. They were generally impressed with what they saw and one of their group, J. S. Ith, wrote a report praising the school and describing the approach. Pestalozzi had explained to the visiting delegation that what they saw were his ideas in practice. Ith's report circulated widely and was picked up by many German language periodicals. It credited Pestalozzi with having invented a new method and approach to elementary teaching.

A steady stream of visitors from many parts of Europe came to Burgdorf to see the school. If "Father" Pestalozzi's "assistants," as he now insisted his co-workers refer to him and to themselves, were surprised that what they had thought of cooperatively as "the method" had been transformed into "Pestalozzi's method," they did not say anything to the outside world. They continued to believe in the value of what they were doing. Krüsi recruited other friends whose skills were invaluable in the school's development. Visitors continued to publish to the world the image that Pestalozzi liked best for himself—that he was the essence of self-sacrifice, a kind of pedagogical Jesus Christ whose only strong feeling was one of love for the downtrodden of the world.

In 1801 Jacques Pestalozzi died at Neuhof. His life had not been a happy one. After his father's short-lived "natural" instruction, his mother tried to teach him reading and religion. At twelve he still could not read. Heinrich sent him to Basel to apprentice in a friend's shop. There the lad developed symptoms of "falling sickness" (epilepsy) and returned without learning a trade. Pestalozzi blamed himself briefly, then decided it was his friend who had "ruined" his son. Jacques was described as "a grumbler and hard to please," and as dull and irritable. He had convulsions accompanied by delusions. Pestalozzi liked other young men much better than his own son. To one he said, "Oh, if only you were my son! Then I should not be going out of the world so lonely."[36] (This was while Jacques was still living.) The parents had managed to arrange a marriage for their son in the 1790s to Anna Magdalena Frölich. She was three years older than Jacques and brought a dowry which Pestalozzi immediately spent. Jacques and his wife—mostly his wife—ran the Neuhof (and a cotton works on it) until he died. The parents met at their son's graveside—probably the first time they had seen each other since Pestalozzi had left for Stans. Anna went back to the Hallwil castle. The daughter-in-law returned to Burgdorf with Pestalozzi, where she worked as a housekeeper for several years and finally remarried. (She died in Yverdon at the age of forty-seven from a "pestilence" brought in by troops who camped nearby.)

Back at the Burgdorf castle, Father Pestalozzi was managing, mostly with Krüsi's help, to add several new assistants to his staff. The most notable of these were Johannes Niederer (1779-1843), a young Protestant minister from Appenzell. Among the new staff were also Johannes von Muralt (1780-1850), a young man, from an old Zurich family, whom the children liked very much, and Joseph Schmid (1787-1850), a fifteen-year-old strong willed lad from Austria, who quickly learned how to manipulate Pestalozzi.

In 1804 the Helvetian central government of Switzerland fell and individual cantons resumed their governmental powers. Napoleon decided that a divided Switzerland might serve his interests better than a united one anyway. There was a backlash of resentment against French interference in German speaking cantons like Berne (in which Burgdorf was located). The Berne city council sent an inspection team to reexamine what was now known as Pestalozzi's school. This time the report was not favorable. The Berne officials issued an eviction notice, though they did offer on a yearly basis a house left vacant by a religious order in Münchenbuchsee. All salaries stopped.

YVERDON

One contingent from Burgdorf accompanied Buss and another assistant to an abandoned castle near the town of Yverdon in the newly created canton of Vaud. This was a French-speaking area and Pestalozzi was identified as a supporter of the earlier French-inspired central government. Pestalozzi and the main group of pupils and assistants went to Buchsee. They soon joined the others at Yverdon, however, because the Buchsee area already had a school on the estate of Phillip Emanuel von Fellenberg (1771-1844). His father had been governor of the area in which the Neuhof was located and had been kind to Pestalozzi. The younger Fellenberg bought the estate (called Hofwyl) in 1799 and had opened two different schools—an expensive one for the sons of aristocrats and an industrial training school for poor boys. The difference between Fellenberg's "poor school" and the one Pestalozzi had tried at Neuhof was that Fellenberg's worked. The boys learned real farming and technical/engineering skills with which they could make a living. (They also had better food than Pestalozzi's school up the road.) Father Pestalozzi, perhaps realizing that his own efforts would likely be overshadowed by young Fellenberg's success, left for Yverdon.

The institute at Yverdon lasted in some form for twenty years. But the internal workings were never tranquil, and by 1810 the most able assistants began to leave. By 1817 all but Schmid were gone and the operation was pretty much in shambles. The reasons were not hard to understand when one examined Pestalozzi's operating procedures. Everyone was up and going at 5:30 A.M. In the early days assistants were expected to teach ten hours per day and live and eat with the boys. Three nights a week after dinner, all assistants had to meet to discuss pupil progress, thrash out problems, and make suggestions about "the method." These sessions, which lasted far into the night, were filled with conflict. Pestalozzi did not attend. He merely received individual reports from each assistant afterwards. Besides this, Pestalozzi expected everyone to work for no individual outside credit. What anyone wrote or did belonged to Pestalozzi for public credit. He would praise people individually and within the "family" group. He also popped into classes at unexpected times to make suggestions. He liked to wake up at two or three o'clock in the morning and start dictating to his secretary (or to one of the assistants). He expected people to get out of bed at any hour his own irregular schedule suggested to correct and recopy his scribbled notes. His own mood swung between elation and dejection. In his frequent depressions, he exploded with negative remarks to and about people. He would usually apologize later, but a growing residual of hurt feelings ran through the ranks of assistants.

By 1808 the undercurrent of unrest in the school was so strong that Pestalozzi tried desperately to regain their support through pity. At the New Year's day address, which he always gave and which was a major occasion, Father Pestalozzi brought in a coffin, complete with a skull and crossbones decoration. He stood with the death box beside him during the address. He knew he had not done well, he said, but he would shortly be dead and out of the way. After his death he hoped that all would pull together for the common good. He loved all of his assistants like true sons.

About this time, Tobler left. In 1810 Johann Elias Mieg, a Heidelberg man who had spent four years as business manager, left. The institute was soon in grave financial trouble. Mieg returned briefly two years later to help get the establishment back on its feet, but found Pestalozzi so hard to work with that he gave up. By 1812 it was time for another death scene from Pestalozzi. This time he dictated his dying thoughts to Krüsi. He was in bed from having accidentally jammed a knitting needle into his ear. Fortunately, Anna inherited some money and once more salvaged her husband's sinking ship. Instead of feeling gratitude, Pestalozzi was irritated because she held back some of the money for their only grandson, Gottlieb. (Anna also gave the Neuhof to Gottlieb under terms that made it impossible for Pestalozzi to ever sell it.)

A large bone of contention with all of the older staff had been that Pestalozzi treated Schmid as his favorite while blaming others for his own failures. They had worked hard and sacrificed much before Schmid arrived, but somehow it was Schmid who constantly got the master's approval. Schmid knew Pestalozzi's needs and fed them. For example, in 1809 on Pestalozzi's birthday, Schmid presented a manuscript entitled *The Elements of Form and Number*. Pestalozzi regarded this as a major theoretical breakthrough, and published it under his own name. (In point of fact, it seems to have made no lasting contribution to educational theory.) Niederer especially resented Schmid because he himself had been Pestalozzi's chief ghostwriter up to that time. The competition finally came to a head over a woman for whose attention both were vying. She chose Niederer, and Schmid left in a rage. He started a school of his own in Austria and wrote a scathing attack on Pestalozzi and Yverdon.

STUDENT LIFE

An Englishman who had been a student at Yverdon about 1814 wrote an account of his recollections. He was from the right social class to have attended Westminster School in England before going to Switzerland. He remembered Pestalozzi as a kindly but eccentric old gentleman. He thought the treatment generally much better than at Westminster—it and other "public schools" in England were notorious for floggings—but he did not remember the teaching or the food with any great nostalgia. He described the lessons as hour-long rote memory sessions which everyone repeated in unison. He remembered the Latin/Greek tutor as competent and kind. Besides learning those two subjects, he said what the pupils mostly got was a "love for natural history and a very unambitious turn of mind." He recalled the classrooms as consisting

of a number of detached chambers, each of which issued upon a corridor. They were airy—there was plenty of air at Yverdon—and lofty as became so venerable a building; but they were upswept, unscrubbed, peeled of their paint, and, owing to the little light that could find its way through two very small windows punched out of the fortress walls, presented, save at mid-day, or as the declining sun illumined momentarily the dark recess, as comfortless a set of interiors as you could well see. It required, indeed, all the elasticity of youth to bear many hours' daily incarceration in such black-holes, without participating in the pervading gloom. Such dismal domiciles were only fit resorts for the myopic bat, who would occasionally visit them from the old tower; for the twilight horde of cockroaches, which swarmed along the floor, or the eight eyed spiders who colonized the ceiling. . . . If these apartments looked gloomy in their dilapidations and want of sun, the somber effect was much heightened by the absence of the ordinary tables and chairs, and whatever else is necessary to give a room a habitable appearance.[37]

In 1815, Anna came to Yverdon to live for a little time before she died. She was buried on the grounds, and Pestalozzi took the occasion of her funeral to rally support from his assistants in the name of his dead wife. By this time, however, Schmid was back. Pestalozzi had decided he could not live without him. The institute was again in serious financial trouble, so Pestalozzi gave Schmid a free hand in running the place. Schmid increased the workload and cut salaries. That was the last straw for the few remaining old hands. Hermann Krüsi started his own boy's school in the town of Yverdon in 1816. The following year Niederer quit to join his wife in running a school. He had not married the woman over whom he and Schmid had quarreled. Instead he married Rosette Kasthofer, the owner of a girls' school in Yverdon. Niederer explained his reasons in a public statement that left Pestalozzi "seized with such a rage, even frenzy, that he was in danger of losing his reason."

With everyone but Schmid gone, the teaching was left to the older boys who were quite young themselves. Finally, even they organized and rebelled against Schmid. The institute was in such monetary difficulties that Fellenberg offered to help. Pestalozzi agreed to merge what was left of his failing school with the ones at Hofwyl. But when the newspapers carried the story that he needed assistance, he became so enraged that he tore up the agreements. Schmid raised some money by taking up a subscription for Pestalozzi's "collected writings." These were so slow in appearing that many of the contributors backed out.[38]

YVERDON'S DEMISE

As financial and other difficulties mounted Pestalozzi became increasingly preoccupied with blaming his early associates for his troubles. He launched an attack on Krüsi and Niederer, accusing them of his institute's troubles and calling them false friends. At about the same time Schmid got Pestalozzi to request a major extension of the rent free agreement on the castle (so Schmid could continue using the facility long after Pestalozzi died). Krüsi and Niederer brought a suit against Schmid that ultimately resulted in his being declared an undesirable alien by the Vaud government. Pestalozzi desperately tried every emotional trick in his repertoire to get his old assistants to back off, but they refused. Schmid was expelled. This meant the end of the Yverdon operation. In 1825 Pestalozzi, Schmid, and four pupils left for the Neuhof. All of the teachers refused to go. "They did not think they owed it to Pestalozzi to sacrifice their careers," as one writer put it.

Since Pestalozzi had intended to run a "poor school" at Neuhof, he was having a new building erected with money from an appeal. However, no teachers and few pupils came, and the school did not open. Finally, he decided to devote his time to writing, and renewed his attack on his old assistants, especially Niederer and Krüsi. In *The Story of My Life as Head of the Institutes in Burgdorf and Yverdon*, he again accused his associates of being untrue. Niederer went to his files and retrieved personal letters, legal documents, financial accounts, and initiated a reply which indicted Pestalozzi's motives and personality. He felt that Pestalozzi had betrayed the idea and power of "the method" which he and others had worked hard to build up. Fellenberg, too, refuted Pestalozzi's claims in articles in the Zurich newspapers. When Pestalozzi read the replies to his comments, he became thoroughly agitated, contracted a fever, dictated a vindication of Schmid as his true friend and savior, and died. None of the old associates attended the funeral. Schmid spent the rest of his life in Paris. Nothing more was heard from him on the educational front. His younger sister, Katarina, had married Gottlieb. They had one son, Karl, who never married. He was a teacher at the Technical University of Zurich.

The experiment that started in Burgdorf in 1800 had a profound effect on the development of educational thought and practice. It happened at a time when people all over Europe were looking for ways to implement mass schooling. This was particularly true in some of the German states. In 1809 a philosopher named Johann Gottlieb Fichte made a series of addresses following Prussia's defeat by Napoleon. He called for a government sponsored school system in Prussia and specifically cited Pestalozzi's efforts. Over the next few years the Prussian government paid for a number of men to spend time at Yverdon studying "Pestalozzi's method." They were often shocked at discovering a different reality than they had expected before arrival. Nevertheless, Pestalozzi was cordial to visitors, and they felt sorry for him. Based on observing Krüsi and other assistants, they took away various notions of what "the method" was and of what "object teaching" meant. However there was general agree-ment on several items: (1) all people, including the poor, could and should learn; (2) learning began at birth and therefore required parental attention; (3) instruc-tion should involve dialog between teacher and learner and should be centered around objects more than books; (4) drawing, music, and physical activity were essential parts of learning; (5) teachers could improve by discovering how to properly structure their presentations and finding out how children learned. The latter included the notion of beginning with simple and concrete rather than complex or abstract material and of relating new information to what the child already knew.

"Pestalozzianism" and object teaching found its way to several countries, but especially Prussia, England, and the United States. There were many routes. Most of the people who had worked at Burgdorf or Yverdon started their own schools in Europe and North America. Many visitors—there was a steady stream of them from Ith's report in 1802 until Yverdon closed—wrote their own accounts of what object teaching meant, so that a growing literature emerged. Much of this found its way to American educationists through Henry Barnard's *American Journal of Education* (Chapter 7). After 1862 another source for Americans was the normal school at Oswego, New York where Hermann Krüsi, Jr., after a thorough training by his father, joined others in showing a generation of American teachers what object teaching meant. The English version of Pestalozzianism reached Americans through Robert Owen (Chap-ter 7). Owen's son studied at Yverdon. Finally, a major part of the German tradition continued in the kindergarten movement which began through the work of one of the young men who made the trek to Yverdon to learn how to teach better. His name was Froebel. He is the subject of the next biographical sketch.

Friedrich Froebel (1782-1852)

In his autobiography Froebel tells us, "I was early initiated into the conflict of life amidst painful and narrowing circumstances; and ignorance of child-nature and insufficient education wrought their influence on me."[39] He was referring to the unfortunate circumstances surrounding his birth and early years. He was born on 21 April 1782 at Oberweissbach in the Thuringian Forest, part of a small principality in the state of Schwartzburg-Rudolstadt, Germany. He was the last of five sons born to a mother who died when he was nine months old. His four brothers were: August, the eldest who went into business and died young; Christoph, a clergyman in Griesheim who was the father of Julius, Karl, and Theodor; Christian, who was associated with Friedrich after 1820; and Traugott, who studied medicine at Jena, became a doctor and was appointed burgomaster at Stadt-Ilm. The father, Johann Jacob, was a Lutheran minister belonging to the old or more conservative school of Protestantism. His parish consisted of about five thousand people spread over half a dozen villages.

FAMILY LIFE

When young Friedrich was four years old his father remarried. Prior to this time his care was entrusted to servants and his four older brothers to whom he had become devoted. Then, with the arrival of a new mother, the four year old turned much of his love to her. However, he was soon to feel her rejection when she became pregnant and gave birth to her own biological son. (His stepbrother, Karl Poppo, was born in 1786 and died 25 March 1824. He was first a teacher, then publisher.)[40] From this point on, he became introspective and self-analytical. His natural curiosity and energy was labeled as mischievous and bad, by his parents; yet he was acutely aware that these negative motivations for his behavior were inaccurate by his feelings. His home environment was as physically confining as it was psychologically constricting, for he was not allowed to wander outside the fences and hedges surrounding his house.

After the difficult time he had teaching Friedrich to read, his father often lost patience while instructing the youth in other areas. Consequently, the boy went to school for the rest of his education. However, his father did not send him to the village boys' school but rather to the one for girls. Froebel later described the school as "exactly suitable for a child such as I was."[41] He was placed in close proximity to the teacher which meant that he was with the older girls instead of female pupils closer to his own age. At some point in all of his youthful experiences, he realized that he was not going to hell and began to identify with Jesus—discoveries that he later regarded as his introduction into higher spiritual life.

By the time he was ten a maternal uncle, Superintendent Hoffman of Stadt-Ilm, requested that Friedrich live with him. His life with his uncle was antithetical to that with his father. He was trusted; he was free to roam the nearby forest and countryside exploring nature. He joined the upper class of the town school and slowly entered into the sports and games of the schoolboys, thereby strengthening his underdeveloped physical self.

He returned to his father's house in 1797. After much deliberation it was decided with his approval that he should become an apprentice to an agriculturist in order to become a forester and learn valuing, geometry, and land surveying. Although his older brothers (Christoph and Traugott) were studying at the University of Jena, Froebel did not join them, because his stepmother was afraid the finances would be depleted for her own son's university education. His father wanted him to seek a post in the treasury, but that would have meant starting as a personal servant to a higher treasury official—something young Froebel regarded as against his nature. So forestry was the answer, and at the age of fifteen and a half he started his apprenticeship at Neuhaus also in the Thuringian Forest.

EDUCATION AND EARLY CAREER

It turned out that the forester was not expert in many of the areas in which he was supposed to instruct the young apprentice, and he blamed the youth for his own shortcomings. In typical fashion young Froebel withdrew inwardly while managing to teach himself some of the necessities of geometry. However, the forester wrote a letter of complaint to the father. Friedrich was able to effectively defend himself to his father and his brother, Christoph, but not to his stepmother. So once again, he found himself confined to his father's house.

Then, his father needed to send money to his brother Traugott who was studying medicine at Jena. Friedrich had little to do, so he was made messenger. The intellectual atmosphere of this university town in 1799 was exhilarating, and with the help of his brother and a small inheritance from his mother, he persuaded his father to let him stay and matriculate. In the one summer and three semesters that he was there, he found he liked geometry best and experimental physics least.

A financial problem arose for his brother Traugott, and Friedrich made him a loan. By the end of his first year the elder Froebel had not repaid the money, and the younger Froebel was going in debt. Father Froebel decided that Friedrich had been irresponsible and refused to pay his debts. He later changed his mind when Friedrich agreed to leave Jena and to relinquish his claim to any paternal inheritance. In the meantime, however, the young Froebel spent some time in the university prison where he passed the time studying geometry, Latin, art, and Scripture. When he was released he returned home and continued to voraciously read from his father's library until he went to Hildburghausen to study agriculture in 1801. However, father and son remained estranged until 1802 when, prior to the latter's death, he forgave Friedrich.

For the next fifteen years Froebel held various positions: actuary in a forestry department; land surveyor, secretary and accountant at a large country estate; student of architecture at Frankfurt; teacher; tutor; visitor twice to Yverdon; student at the universities of Göttingen and Berlin; and a Prussian Volunteer Corps soldier fighting Napoleon. During this time Froebel blossomed into a Christian mystic searching for his own calling and Christlike life on earth. Through all of his single-minded searching, lack of finances never deterred him. Indeed, luck came in the form of loans from his brother and an inheritance from Uncle Hoffman. With regard to Yverdon Froebel later said that languages were not taught well and there was much strife and conflict among the faculty.[42]

Finally, in 1816, realizing that instructing the young held a special attraction for him, he opened the Universal German Educational Institution at Griesheim in Rudolstadt. The establishment of this school had special family meaning. Froebel's favorite brother Christoph had died of typhus while tending to the wounded. He left a wife and three children. Friedrich vowed to become a father to these orphaned children and decided to open a school in Christoph's home in Griesheim. Christoph's widow later bought a farm in Keilhau, and Froebel moved the school there. It is unclear whether the widow expected him to be a husband to her. At any rate in September 1818, he married Henrietta Hoffmeister, a friend from Berlin "with a like love of nature and of childhood as my own, and a like high and earnest conception of education." Shortly thereafter, Frau Froebel deeded her farm to her brother-in-law and went to live in Volkstadt.[43]

THE CHILDREN'S EDUCATOR

In Keilhau prior to his marriage, Froebel had been joined by his army soul mates Heinrich Langethal and William Middendorff. But the next decade was another unsettling one. In 1826 he published *The Education of Man*—a full-scale account of his educational theories and principles. By 1828 Middendorff's nephew, Johannes Barop joined the Keilhau school staff, and together the group planned for a National Educational Institute in Helba. However, they abandoned the plan two years later for lack of financial support. From 1831 to 1837 Froebel was involved with four other schooling ventures in Wartensee and Willisau (in Lucerne), Burgdorf (in Berne) and then back to Rudolstadt. Finally in 1837 he settled upon Blakenburg and opened the Institute for the Occupations of Little Children.

In this setting Froebel began developing a series of didactic materials which he called *gifts* and *occupations*. The gifts were six sets of concrete geometric shapes which the children could manipulate and thereby discover the ideas of nature and the quality of things in the universe. They were arranged in order from the simple concepts and operations to the more complex. The first gift, "the gift of potential," consisted of six soft balls of various colors—the primary ones of red, yellow, and blue, and secondary colors of green, violet, and orange. This gift revealed unity of size, shape, and texture while demonstrating individuality or diversity of color. For Froebel this gift was analogous to the child's soul which also had potential.

The second gift, "the gift of origination," included three geometric wooden forms, all demonstrating either explicitly or implicitly the elements of plane, line, and point: (1) a sphere; (2) a cube (regarded by Froebel as a sphere turned inside out); and (3) a cylinder (the evolution of both spheres and cubes). This evolution related to the soul's free movement as it developed.

Gifts three through six, "the building gifts," were cubes, divided and subdivided various numbers of times and in various ways to expose smaller cubes, oblong blocks, bricks, and triangular prisms. Through these the child learned number, geometry, arithmetic, parts of a whole, separation, production, and evolution. Froebel also related these gifts to the genealogy of family and the production of successive generations. (Froebel also developed gifts seven and eight, but there is disagreement as to what they were and how they were to be used.)[44]

The occupations developed out of using the gifts and were supposed to put into practice what the child had learned from the gifts. Also, the occupations utilized materials that could be transformed: paper constructing, cardboard cutting, sand molding, clay modeling, and wood building. There were also the occupations of sewing, weaving, and drawing—all of which involved a lot of self-activity. The latter was one of the most important principles in the Froebelian method. To round out his program Froebel also included games, plays, singing, and dancing—more self-activity.

Although he was never really known as a philosopher or writer, Froebel did try to popularize his theories and practices through journal articles, lectures, and a book of songs, games, and stories called *Mutter und Kose-lieder* (*Mother and Nursery Songs*).

The name *kindergarten* (children's garden) was first used in 1840 for Froebel's establishments in Blankenburg and Rudolstadt. In 1849, he started another institution in Liebenstein for the training of teachers, but there were personal as well as professional setbacks. In 1839 his first wife died. He remarried in 1851 against the wishes of his Keilhau associates. They thought his second wife, Louise Leven—thirty years his junior—was socially inferior. In 1850 he met a woman who was to become instrumental in making the kindergarten an international movement. Her name was Baroness Bertha von Marenholtz-Bülow.

A year after Froebel's first meeting with Bülow, the Prussian government banned all kindergartens. The government said they were unchristian. (Froebel was also too democratic sounding for the conservative regime then in power.) After that Froebel's health started to fail, and he died on 21 June 1852. Eight years later the ban was removed through Bülow's efforts, and Froebel's widow began to train kindergarten teachers again.

It was under Frau Froebel that Bülow's American counterpart to the movement, Elizabeth Palmer Peabody, studied in 1867-1868. In America the first German speaking kindergarten was opened in 1855 in Watertown, Wisconsin under Margarethe Schurz—Froebel's student. Peabody opened her first with instruction in English in Boston in 1860. Finally, in 1873 Susan Blow financed the first public one in St. Louis. By the twentieth century, kindergartens were an important element in American education.

7

THE AMERICANS

Europeans theorists like Rousseau, Pestalozzi, and Froebel wrote about changing education to make it more flexible, practical, and child centered—better
suited to common people. Their work circulated widely and was influential. But
another force was at work which would alter the form and content of teaching
more profoundly than would any European theorist. This was the immigrant
experience in the North American wilderness. By the time Froebel died in 1852,
the development was well advanced. For more than two and half centuries
Europeans had been pressing into the vast regions between Mexico City and
Montreal. In the process, education was transformed.

The driving energy was religious. The Jesuit motto, "for the greater glory of
God," expressed the Roman Catholic ideal of the movement. Mission schools
up the West coast and down the Mississippi River reflected their dedication. For

Protestants, Comenius' ambition to compel savages to civilization was more to the point. Indeed, in 1622 John Brinsley set the tone for the Puritan approach in the earliest known book in English about educational methods. He addressed it to "all the ruder places"—Ireland, Wales, and Virginia. His aim was "to reduce a barbarous people to civilitie."

EARLY SCHOOLING EFFORTS

From the first, English settlers in Virginia and Massachusetts feared the debilitating effects of the endless frontier. No sooner were the colonies well planted than efforts began for establishing schools. By the 1640s officials in Virginia, Massachusetts, and Connecticut feared that colonists were too careless of school arrangements. One result was legislation requiring parents and masters to see that all children could read and had a trade and also that larger towns should have classical schools and smaller ones some kind of vernacular instruction. This was not in itself different from English practice at home, although fining areas that did not comply, and sending the money to the next closest school, may have been an innovation prompted by the fears noted above.

There were two unique aspects of the American colonial situation—or three if one counts the fines mentioned above. The first was the fact that early on settlements deviated from the intended European pattern of houses clustered together in a village with settlers traveling out to their plots to farm them. The colonial land distribution system was based on this assumption, with each person receiving small strips in several locations rather than one larger one. But colonists did not keep this pattern long. Instead they quickly began trading, buying, and selling to consolidate their property. They also built houses based on their farming interests rather than around the village common as they were supposed to do. Their leaders, steeped in European tradition, worried about this and tried to discourage it. Connecticut officials pointed out to settlers after a devastating Indian raid that obviously God intended people to live in towns. But neither the original plan, later warnings, nor fear of attack halted the practice.[1]

As a direct result of the settlement pattern, the natural assumption about schooling changed. Originally, schools had been in cities, or at least villages. But when villages ceased to be the characteristic mode of living, schools had to move to the country too.

The second new element was the environment. This is multifaceted, but overriding all was survival. Just as the school's location had to accommodate to new living patterns, its calendar had to fit with agricultural necessity. School had to be held in the winter so it would not interfere with farming operations, but this meant that attendance would vary with weather conditions. Children who lived on the wrong side of a stream, for example, could not go to school when the water was too high. It was not realistic for teachers to assume that students would arrive at precisely the same time every day or that everybody would be present on a given day.

There were other effects that followed from the two or three aspects mentioned above and the story is much more complex than it appears, but this brief preface will set the stage for the remaining discussion. These developments were certainly evident before 1700 and were general shortly after that. Preliminary investigation suggests that it was true of northern and southern colonies and those in between. It appears that a school developed as soon as enough families with children lived within two or three miles of each other. In the Midwest, this was usually five to ten families. In ranching areas distances were greater.

The schooling was paid for either through a tax levied by the families on themselves (usually in proportion to the amount of land owned or improved) or by tuition. Often a combination of the two methods was employed. Taxation provided a base salary and the teacher was free to charge a specified fee per child, including a larger amount from those who had not paid any tax. There was nothing to stop an enterprising teacher from getting up a school entirely based on fees subscribed by parents. In any case the teacher usually had to collect any tuition due either monthly or at the end of term. There was a decided economic advantage in keeping pupils and parents satisfied.

COLONIAL AND EARLY NATIONAL SCHOOLING

The contemporary image of the one-room school is that it was a piece of ephemeral Americana, like cattle drives and Miss Kitty's saloon, though less colorful. But the reality behind those two facets of popular culture was short-lived. The one-room school on the other hand was still going strong after more than two centuries. As late as 1928 (less than two generations ago) the U.S. Office of Education noted that 63 percent (153,306) of all the elementary school buildings (244,128) in the country were still of the one-room variety.[2] A recently issued (1979) and well regarded text, Robert Church's and Michael Sedlak's *Education in the United States*, dismisses these schools with the comment that parents expected little from them; that there was no pressure to teach anything useful; and that they were "backward" and characterized by "intellectual inefficiency" and "drab and claustrophobic" environments. Their interpretation, though stated more forcefully than some others, is the standard.

Actually, this interpretation is based on the assessments of several nineteenth century people, including some that you will read about in this chapter. Until a generation after the end of the American Revolution, people seem to have taken these schools for granted, though even before the break with England some of the wealthier class began endowing "academies" which offered commercial and college preparatory courses not usually found in the "common" or district schools. After the Revolution, people began to pay more attention to education and to ask what kinds of schools Americans should want and expect. In the early years, people like Noah Webster were typical. He was especially interested in making the curriculum reflect American ideas.

By the 1820s to 1840s people like Horace Mann and Henry Barnard—feeling the sting of English caricatures of Americans as crude and uncivilized—sought to make the common schools town instead of rural dominated. They wanted statewide, and eventually nationwide, systems to enforce their vision of civilization. Others, like Emma Willard and Bishop John Hughes, agreed but wanted to be sure that women and Roman Catholics were not excluded. Robert Owen had a vision of how to provide this kind of education to workers.

It was during the first half of the nineteenth century that most of the issues still agitating Americans appeared: Were the schools good enough? Were teachers properly trained? What should the curriculum be? Should it be general for everyone? How much choice should pupils and parents have? Who should pay for schools? Who should run the schools? How should they be organized? How much and what kind of religious or moral theory should be included? How much right to not participate should people have who disagreed with what was being done?

Noah Webster (1758-1843)

One of the ironies of history is that the man termed "Schoolmaster to the Republic" spent only a short period teaching school. Still the designation is an apt one, for Noah Webster spent most of his life instructing in some fashion or other. His media were many—schoolbooks, magazines, newspapers, pamphlets, essays, and letters. It seems almost as if Noah Webster was fated to the task. Practically his first writings were on educational topics. Writing on the state of American education in 1790, Webster pointed out the many inadequacies of education of the time. His argument was that economy applied to education of the young is false economy, a theme he was to return to time and again in later years. The schoolhouses were in disrepair, books appeared to be unavailable or parents failed to provide them, the worst possible provisions for education were made. But despite these facts, schools generally were provided throughout the country, a fact that allowed Webster to conclude that parents were convinced "of their utility and importance."[3]

EARLY LIFE AND CAREER

Noah Webster was born 16 October 1758 in Calvinist Connecticut. His early education was in his own eyes inadequate. The common books used were Thomas Dilworth's spelling book, a primer, a Psalter and the Bible. But just as many other individuals, Webster may not have been completely accurate in the appraisal of his own early schooling, since he became a highly proficient reader and writer—a master of the journalistic style. He may have done this mainly on his own, but the seed and desire had to be planted. It is probable that the schools had a little more to do with this than he may have thought.

His father was a staunch member of the church, and his mother was descended from William Bradford, Governor of Plymouth. While Noah had imbibed many of the heady ideas of the Enlightenment, having read Rousseau and others, his religious enthusiasm was not pronounced in his earlier years. He entered Yale College in 1774 and came out still convinced that religion and morality were the foundations of social and political stability and of virtue. But by 1808 he had become a firm Calvinist. Thus, in his schoolbooks and essays his sentiments as to the necessity of religion and morality being tied in with education was more than just a bow to the conventional ideas of his time. They were part and parcel of his very being. Religion, morality and virtue were fundamental truths for him. Small wonder that he caught the spirit of the times and became an ardent nationalist. Thus was formed the second basic attitude that permeated all of Webster's thinking and writing. He was an American through and through.

Webster's financial condition at the end of his college education may also have been a contributing factor to his feeling about schools. His father's financial position was at its lowest point. Webster had little in the way of career prospects—there was no family business to enter, no profession other than teaching that his education had prepared him for unless it was the ministry. He took the route of schoolteaching but not for long. His nature was such that he would have been restive to say the least had he continued teaching for any length of time, even though he valued schooling: "The education of youth [is] an employment of more consequence than making laws and preaching the gospel, because it lays the foundation on which both law and gospel rest for success.[4]

Faced with the difficulty of making his own way, his basic attitude was in many ways formed by the fact that he had prevailed against great odds. Joel Barlow, a Yale student with Webster, expressed their common circumstances in a letter to him: "You and I are not the first in the world to have broken loose from college without friends and without fortune to push into public notice. Let us show the world a few more examples of men standing upon their own merit and rising in spite of obstacles."[5] Webster proposed to do just that and, as his later writings show, he believed others could do the same with a little help. Anyone could rise in the world if only they formed the proper virtues and secured the necessary knowledge. Indeed, Webster was a product of his same times, coming to maturity during the American Revolution.

EDUCATIONAL VIEWS

Noah Webster was an amazingly versatile man. He was at one time or another a successful newspaper editor, magazine editor, pamphleteer, compiler of schoolbooks, lawyer, politician, and scholar. The latter was in all likelihood his greatest achievement. He labored the longest part of his adult life in the making of the monumental *An American Dictionary of the English Language*, (1828). This was the culminating work of his plan for the education of American youth begun in 1783 with the publication of his first schoolbook, *A Grammatical Institute of the English Lanauge, Part I.* This was the famous speller which was to exercise an influence upon Americans beyond what anyone, including Noah Webster, anticipated. The original speller occupied 119 pages. Gradually, however, it evolved into a much longer book, containing fables, woodcuts, lessons on domestic relations, and a moral catechism. Webster originally intended to call the speller "The American Instructor," but was persuaded by Ezra Stiles to give it the longer and more pretentious title. As the speller evolved in 1788, he changed the title to *The American Spelling Book,* and to the public it became the "blue-backed speller."

Webster's purposes were clear. He intended to promote American literature and uniformity of speech, patriotism and nationalism, morality and virtue, and religious truths. He also intended to develop a system of national education.

The speller as indicated did evolve, and as it evolved new functions were added. In fact, it became part one of his system of national education. Parts two and three were still to come, along with a number of other important additions. In a preface to *The American Spelling Book,* he said the speller might facilitate the education of youth and enable teachers "to instill into their minds with the first rudiments of language, some just ideas of religion, morals and domestic economy." What Webster proposed to do was to provide a vehicle of self-advancement, as well as an "engine of nationalism."[6] In fact, all of Webster's schoolbooks were designed to prepare young Americans for "getting ahead," the sort of self-improvement of which Americans were to become so fond. They would teach the young American how to speak and write correctly, how to behave, while providing him with a body of useful knowledge and making him more moral.

The original "courtesy" books had been plans of education for the gentleman. Their utility for the man hoping to rise in the world was obvious. The key ideal of the courtesy tradition was virtue. As the courtesy books became more and more sought after by middle-class citizens and as England became more Puritan, the connection between virtue and religion became more and more emphasized. For example, the speller was heavily laden with religious material. Although it did not contain morning or evening prayers, it did have many references to religion or religious ideas. Later Webster would incorporate a "moral Catechism" at the end of *The American Spelling Book.* The virtuous man would be religious, and the religious man would be virtuous. Religion would serve as the basis of good character, and manners would be conceived of as "character in action."

This leads to but one conclusion—that Noah Webster was particularly sanguine about the prospects of improving the morals and manners of men under the proper conditions and believed the United States was the ideal place to try this experiment. Here was an opportunity to build a new society, free of the corruptions of previous societies. Webster maintained that the type of society desired depended to a great extent on the education practiced in the society.

The idea of national character utilized by so many writers of this period was the basis for Webster's arguments. National character was firmly established in despotic states and the vast empires of Asia because education was made subservient to the government. Laws, manners, and language were uniform in these areas because of despotic control of both education and religion. But it is these very factors that created national character and the sense of a cohesive society. Education of young American republicans, then, was of primary importance. The forming of nationality and national character needed to be a deliberate act. It could only be accomplished by the formation of a general system of education for all Americans including the poor. But it would be much later before he would reiterate his conviction that education was the most efficacious means of eliminating poverty:

> To form plans for diffusing literary and moral improvement among the poorer classes of citizens, in connection with religious instruction, will be no less our pleasure than it is our duty. To draw from the obscure retreats of poverty the miserable victims of ignorance and vice, to enlighten their minds and correct their evil habits, to raise them to the ranks of intelligent,

industrious, and useful members of society will never cease to be the object of deep solicitude with a wise legislature.[7]

These were the aims of education as Webster understood them. Maxims, adages, and select sentences were useful, but moral truths were also effectively presented in fables. However, there was still the basic criterion by which Webster measured all educational activity. Fundamentally, the criterion was usefulness. Only that which was useful should determine the curriculum selected. In examining the modes of European education and their applicability to America, two criteria were basic: usefulness and whether they were conducive to republicanism. He proposed to examine European practices in respect to arts and sciences and in respect to their connection with morals and government. However, he presented strong objections to sending boys to Europe for an education or for securing teachers from there. A foreign education, he thought, was detrimental to the political interests of Americans. Boys educated in Europe during their impressionable years may return Englishmen, Scotsmen or Frenchmen. If someone argued that European schools and universities were better than those of America, the remedy Webster gave was not in sending boys to Europe but in improving American educational institutions. Finally, he was opposed to the Grand Tour of Europe which was often a finishing touch of a young gentleman's education. He proposed that a tour through the United States ought to be substituted and considered an essential part of an American youth's liberal education.

As for the curriculum Webster believed that the first error was too much attention to dead languages. The study of Latin and Greek was especially valuable at one time and still was valuable for scholars and members of the learned professions since they were the repositories of knowledge of Europe. But this was no longer the case. English was now the repository of as much learning as the languages of Europe once were. Furthermore, it had many advantages other languages did not possess. What gain would a merchant, a mechanic, a farmer, derive from an acquaintance with the Greek and Roman tongues? Even if there were some advantage for the above studying Latin and Greek, would the advantages compensate for the loss of valuable time employed in studying them to achieve competence? "Life is short, and every hour should be employed to good purposes," he affirmed. Again he wanted to know how any parent could justify their sons spending years studying rules of syntax when they might be studying their own language and its writers of ethics, geography, history, commerce, and government. On the other hand, Webster was willing to concede that Latin should be used for epitaphs, inscriptions on monuments and medals, and writing designed for perpetuity.[8]

Webster was also not against the study of English grammar, even though some thought it to be a dry study. He agreed that learning definition, rules, and names of parts of speech without understanding what one learned was surely irksome, but he also thought that if grammar could be "taught by the help of visible objects, [so that] children [could] perceive that differences of words arise from differences in things, . . . the study [could become] entertaining as well as improving." Again, he made the point that if language was taught by rote, it mattered little whether the rules were in English, Latin or Greek, but if ideas were what the children should acquire then it was easier for them to do this in their own language. Still later in the same essay he stressed that the senses were the "inlets of our knowledge." Abstract definitions could be repeated time after time without being understood, "but that a table is the name of an article and hard or square is its property is a distinction obvious to the senses and consequently within a child's capacity."

EDUCATIONAL CRITICISMS

Although Webster is never given credit for the idea, he seems to have been one of the first individuals to advocate the elective system in education. He wrote, "Perhaps it may also be numbered among the errors in our system of education that in our universities and colleges the students are all restricted to the same course of study, and, by being classed, limited to the same progress." He had some strong doubts about the efficacy of this system. Classing may be necessary but why could not students be advanced from lower to higher classes as a reward for industry and achievements? He advocated specialization instead of a broad education. He did not believe that a planter should have to study conic sections or a merchant the rules of Greek: "Life is too short to acquire, and the mind of man too feeble to contain, the whole circle of sciences." Even the greatest genius could not master all subjects. If a person were going to qualify for a profession, it was "necessary that they should attend closely to those branches of learning which lead to it."[9]

Webster then turned to arts and sciences which every male should learn. He believed that everyone should write and speak their native language correctly. Mathematics is useful, and "the rules of arithmetic are indispensably requisite." Depending on what occupation a boy would enter, his education should be adjusted accordingly. The farming areas should provide the country schools with "some easy system of practical husbandry." If a boy read books of this type he would store in mind facts which might not be understood in youth but which later would be recalled into practice. Writing with an almost Herbartian touch, Webster justified this storing of the mind because, "This would lead the mind to the subject of agriculture and pave the way for improvements." These young men destined for the mercantile line, after they had mastered their own language might then study a living language or two that would be useful in their business. He then advocated the study of chronology, geography, mathematics, history, laws of commercial nations, business principles and general principles of government. By sixteen the boy would have completed his education. Webster concluded, "Such a system of English education is also preferable to a university education. . . ." In fact Webster went so far as to state, "Indeed it appears to me that what is now called a *liberal education* disqualifies a man for business."[10]

Webster was convinced that the principal defect in American education was the lack of good teachers in academies and common schools. Schools should be staffed with men of "unblemished reputations" and possessed of the necessary abilities. He would prefer children to have no education rather than to have a bad one. The vices and habits that they would pick up from incompetent and immoral schoolmasters were much more difficult to eradicate than "to impress new ideas." If the pupils had esteem and respect for the master, he would have authority. This in turn would lessen the likelihood of dependence upon the rod because pupils would fear the displeasure of the teacher more than the rod.

Again Webster saw as a defect in the schools the lack of proper books, because they were filled with respect for foreign and ancient nations. However, Webster countered this with the following: "Every child in America should be acquainted with his own country. He should read books that furnish him with ideas that will be useful to him in life and practice. As soon as he opens his lips, he should rehearse the history of his own country, he should lisp the praise of liberty and of those illustrious heroes and statesmen who have wrought a revolution in her favor."[11]

Webster was also convinced of the importance of education for American women, since they formed the disposition of youth and controlled the manners of the nation. Their education should form their manners, and it should be a useful education. Women should be taught to speak and write English in addition to arithmetic, geography, and literature. He did not feel he could prescribe a course of reading for all women but he did think that they should be acquainted with the writers on human life and manners.

Webster knew what had to be done. The American states were by no means a nation. They possessed for the most part a common language, one criterion of a nation, but the number of non-English peoples was substantial. Irish, Scots, French, and others flocked to the United States. There were the old Dutch and German groups. Marcus Lee Hansen comments, "Tradition reckons the number of immigrants during the quarter-century from 1790 to 1815 at [about] . . . two hundred and fifty thousand."[12] It is to Webster's credit that he understood the problem so well. It is also to his credit that he bent his efforts to forge the American nationality and sense of identity, and that he did it with all the energy he possessed and all the resources and means he could command. Surely no one could fault him for wanting to develop a sense of nationality, patriotism, and a prosperous body of individuals and nation. These were also goals of Benjamin Franklin and Horace Mann, the subject of our next life.

Horace Mann (1796-1859)

Horace Mann's place of importance in American history is secure, and his influence on educational thought and practice enduring. While his achievements suggest—and rightly so—a man of great vision, energy, and ambition, the certainty reflected in his essays and speeches wrongly suggests a man self-assured and intellectually satisfied. His driving passion for altruistic causes came from a troubled childhood and a life marked by deep personal tragedy. His contributions to important and lasting public policy, which set in motion the public school movement in America, were shaped as a result of private agonies and as a clear response to serious psychological needs. To those committed to and appreciative of the idea of public education, the debt to Horace Mann is not lessened by that circumstance.

EARLY FORMATIVE YEARS

Horace Mann was born in 1796, the fourth of five children, to Thomas and Rebecca Mann. The three boys and two girls in that family represented the third generation brought up on the same farmland near Franklin, Massachusetts. The Mann homestead was essentially a self-sufficient operation, with crops, livestock, and human labor providing food, clothing, and shelter. There was by necessity unceasing attention given to chores, and the absence of distractions from the daily grind wore thin the respect of Horace for farming as a way of life. Though a strong work ethic was to remain a lasting value, farming was never to be a serious contender as a vocational choice for Horace Mann.[13]

Typical of prosperous nineteenth century New Englanders, attention was given in the Mann household to the formal learning of youngsters. The rudiments of becoming a literate and moral being were made available to Horace both in the home and at a primitive one-room schoolhouse. He benefited a great deal from his older sister Rebecca's efforts to hear his lessons—even when "winter school" was not in session.

In Mann's young and formative years, a profound and lasting influence was provided by the person who attended to the religious affairs in the Franklin community: the Reverend Nathaniel Emmons. Emmons was well educated, steeped in and totally committed to the tenets of his faith, and thoroughly persuasive as an orator. In Mann, he found himself preaching to a serious child who deeply felt the messages advanced. The Emmons message focused on the need to fear God. God was pictured as a force of retribution who intervened in the lives of men to punish wrong-doing, watched the deviants in need of punishment, and sustained a capacity and willingness to make that punishment awful and eternal. As a young man, Horace wrestled against such a view in search of a benevolent deity who would be worthy of his esteem and especially his affection. The yoke of Emmons had taken such a hold, however, that for the rest of his life Mann could remember the instant of his conversion away from a religion of gloom and dread and toward the acceptance of a God of charity and love.

Even in later years Mann would not be free of Emmons. A tragic incident regarding his brother would haunt him throughout his life. Steven, his older brother by two years, committed an act frequently targeted by Emmons as a most infamous offense against the Almighty—the violation of the Sabbath. At age sixteen Steven missed a church service to go fishing and was the unfortunate victim of drowning. For Emmons the event underscored the wisdom of an abiding fear for righteous punishment. Though Mann could never admit to such a lesson, the tragedy was for him so overwhelming that he would never be released emotionally from the horror of such a conviction. At that most impressionable adolescent stage, there was solidified a sense of fatalism and a dark dimension to his character.

Steven's drowning had followed by only one year the death of his father, Thomas. The absence of those two men on a working farm made Horace's decision to leave home especially difficult. He was, however, steadfast in his commitment to pursue a professional career, and his initial goal was a degree in higher education.

THE YEARS IN PREPARATION

Brown University in Providence, Rhode Island, was the school he selected to attend, and at eighteen years of age he began his preparation to meet the entrance requirements. With characteristic zeal and no small measure of grit, he dedicated his first year of work to self-directed study. Then, he hired a classicist as a tutor for the study of standard works in Latin and Greek and a minister with notable previous success in such efforts, to work with him in mathematics. The rather rigorous oral examination conducted by a three-man board at Brown was passed by a twenty-year-old Mann with such aplomb that he was not only admitted to the university but also granted sophomore status.

Contrary to the conventional wisdom of present-day arch conservatives in education (who tend to equate nineteenth century university study with the lofty pursuit of truth) even the prestigious Brown could be a bore. Whether studying the ancient classics or contemporary geography, logic or public speaking, the pedagogy typically differed little from what was found in the most uninspired lower schools, with recitation dominating as the favorite mode of instruction. But tedium never acted as a deterrent to Mann. No assignment was too trivial to warrant anything but a serious effort from the young scholar whose only intention was to excel. His dedication to college work and his involvement in extracurricular activities and important debating societies increasingly brought him recognition and respect from faculty and peers. In 1819, Brown University awarded Horace Mann the bachelor of arts degree and conferred upon him its highest honor as valedictorian of the graduating class.

Mann settled near his home of Franklin to work as an apprentice in an established law firm, a job which consisted of tending to clerical duties of the most menial sort. Less than a year later, he willingly accepted an offer by the president of Brown to join the university staff in a tutorial position. Only one year previously, Mann had been a dutiful student, polite to his teachers, and prompt in the exercise of his assignments. In his students, he found a total absence of those same qualities, and—though still a young man himself—he came to feel very distant from his new charges. Tension grew, and hostility increasingly surfaced. After only two years, Horace Mann voluntarily ended his tenure at Brown to once again become a student. He was much more comfortable with the notion of accepting rather than providing instruction, and so it was with enthusiasm that he enrolled in the highly touted Tapping Reeve's law school in Litchfield, Connecticut.

Litchfield was a magnificent and demanding law school, attracting many young men whose careers were to be notable and whose contributions were to be distinguished. Once again, Horace Mann was equal to the challenge. He was rigorous in the attendance of lectures, prepared and skillful in moot court presentations, and highly respected by colleagues at the customary informal debates of law. Better still, the intellectual excitement and friendly atmosphere seemed to take the somber edge off his compulsiveness, and he eased into a gentler lifestyle, where parties and social gatherings were enjoyed with grace and good humor.

At the completion of law school, Mann began to practice in Dedham, Massachusetts. Actually, the legal field was saturated with lawyers of every possible stripe in terms of commitment, training, and moral standards. As a group they were held, and often for good reason, in no great esteem by the community at large. Once again, an enormous capacity for work, a need to succeed, and a trust in virtue set Mann above the crowd.

Dedham was a bustling and expanding commercial center, and it provided the perfect environment for a man of professional ambition to thrive. A set of fortuitous circumstances worked to honor Mann as a major speaker at important and well-attended public celebrations. His immediate public popularity initiated important private business contacts, and his legal concerns thereby expanded beyond minor problems of individual litigation into the complex and profitable arena of corporate law. He invested his personal finances wisely and became a respected member of the business community. Crucial political and social contacts were maintained by a rigorous schedule of correspondence with fellow lawyers and friends across the state. He performed effective yeoman duty for the Republican party. On his second attempt, and after only five years a resident of Dedham, his fellow citizens elected Horace Mann representative to the Massachusetts General Court. The base of operation for the very promising political career of legislator Horace Mann was thereby shifted to Boston in 1827.

THE LEGISLATIVE YEARS

The decade that Horace Mann faced in elective office would represent for him years of political triumph and personal tragedy. In the political arena, his colleagues came to understand early on that no situation would arise in which Horace Mann would knowingly violate his admittedly loftly moral standards. His political star rose quickly because his word could be trusted, he was thorough in the preparation of his legislative homework, and he was an inordinately able speaker.

Work habits that had become so publicly evident at Brown and Litchfield once again served Mann in the General Court. Committee assignments which put him in a leadership role assured the assembly a resident expert on the issues involved by the time legislative bills were submitted for review. He fought hard for any number of causes, ranging from religious freedom to railroad expansion, from temperance to the proper care of the insane. He was undeniably his most eloquent as a speaker and tenacious as a champion for those causes that were overtly moral and that directly affected society's disenfranchised. There is no better illustration of this compassion for the downtrodden than in his work on behalf of those committed as insane to jails and poorhouses.

The typical practice in the early nineteenth century was to treat in a barbaric fashion anyone labeled as insane. Those so diagnosed were literally discarded to the most wretched physical conditions of primitive jails and poorhouses, where they were left, poorly nourished, to suffer the extremes of the natural elements and to live in their own filth. The plight of these unfortunates was brought to the attention of Mann in his official capacity as legislator, but his campaign on their behalf clearly reflected a private horror at the inhumanity expressed by their circumstance.

Mann launched a statewide survey to document the exact treatment and support given to the cause of the insane. He made visitations to see firsthand the conditions of their care. He studied the literature of his day to become well versed in more enlightened treatment procedures and their effects on the inflicted. He presented before the General Court the first case promoting state assistance for the insane—an impassioned plea that paved the way for the acceptance of his bill to finance a hospital for their care. He chaired a governor's commission to carry out the mandates of that legislation. He personally, and in detail, directed the efforts of that commission in the establishment of the first state hospital for the insane in Massachusetts, breaking new ground in everything from architecture to operational procedures. His effort was momentous, revealing much about the person Mann and portending future decisions that would as much affect his own life as that of his constituency.

While Mann was taking charge of his political life, his personal life seemed at the mercy of forces both capricious and beyond his control. To remark that Horace Mann was an austere person represents something of an understatement, and that characteristic was reflected no more starkly than in his relationships with women. He enjoyed and benefited from the company of intelligent and well-read women. Though he was quite comfortable in their presence, it was a comfort sustained by motives so puritanical as to do justice to the standards of Nathaniel Emmons. Such motives inspired in Mann a certain emotional aloofness concerning women, a state of affairs which dissolved completely in the presence of Charlotte Messer.

The president of Brown University (who chaired the committee that examined and accepted Horace Mann as a student and later hired him as a tutor) was Asa Messer, and Charlotte was his third daughter. Though junior to Mann by thirteen years, she willingly accepted his formal proposal of a courtship. The wooing was carried out in a way consistent with Mann's history, that is, all correspondence and visitations met the rigorous requirements of good taste. But even the ritualistic demands of propriety could not disguise the fact that Horace Mann had fallen overwhelmingly in love. At the very height of his bliss, the seeds of impending tragedy became visible to him. Sallowness developed in Charlotte's complexion; there was a loss of energy and a persistent cough. He knew the signs well; his father had died of consumption.

Horace Mann and Charlotte Messer were married on 29 September 1830. They settled in Dedham, but, because of her ill health, they had to accept lengthy separations in order for her to receive care under the supervision of her parents in Providence. In spite of the difficulties, she and Horace had a very close and loving relationship. He was keeping a vigil at her bedside when she died on 1 August 1832. She was twenty-three years old.

The impact of Charlotte's death devastated Mann, and it had long term consequences on both his private and public life. Time did not heal this wound. Instead the tragedy festered inside him as he lived out his mourning. His personality took on a morose quality, and he became something of a recluse. Formerly dapper, his hair turned white and his dress acquired a drab and even sloppy look. His interests took an anti-materialistic bent, and he showed unusual ambivalence on matters of religious conviction. He withdrew from politics and became openly disillusioned with his former colleagues in the statehouse. Yet there remained a persistent and lurking attachment to humanitarian causes and occasional acknowledgments by him that such causes could spark an active interest and a personal involvement.

Long accustomed to his vigor, close friends refused to accept his decline into a pathetic figure. Unrelenting in their encouragement and support, they especially appealed to his sense of obligation regarding morality in government. Their efforts to stir him to action were much aided by overt signs of social disintegration—notably the blatant self-interest reflected in legislative actions by elected officials, mob violence in the streets, and indifference toward the disenfranchised by the moneyed class. Convinced that such social malignancies were primarily an outgrowth of Jacksonianism and the "spoils system," the Whigs mounted an especially energetic political campaign for state offices in Massachusetts. Though equivocating until late in the campaign, a persuaded Mann finally allowed his name to be entered on the Whig slate for state senator. In tribute to his former stature as a powerful political figure, the opposition made him a special target for their counter charges against the Whigs. The Whig victory was sweeping on a statewide level, and Horace Mann was among those who took the oath of office in January 1835.

Mann was an effective and esteemed public servant, and after only one year in office was elected president of the senate, only to be reelected to that post on the first ballot in his second year. To a vast number of political observers, Mann was a natural future choice as a gubernatorial candidate of the Whig party, with obvious promise at the national level. To those who knew him well, however, there was little doubt that the fiery disposition toward political causes had been blunted, maybe irrevocably, by personal tragedy. For the time being, Mann's political future was not to be settled in the excitement of a ballot count for a state or national office, but by a legislative act so harmless as to not even arouse public notice.

Hoping to bring order to the disparate educational opportunities in Massachusetts, the legislature passed a statute which created a board of education to act in an advisory capacity to the state government. Several of Mann's close friends who had been selected to serve on the board knew of his growing pessimism about the "general good" being served by political solutions and recognized that a humanitarian cause might revitalize his activist tendencies. In this spirit, they suggested that he consider the secretaryship of the board of education. A sustained period of agonizing introspection followed as Mann faced the possibility of relinquishing tremendous political power to accept a post which granted no formal powers and for a social cause which was not part of his experiences.

It is, of course, impossible to explain fully the reasons for his decision to accept the post. However, using especially the content of Mann's personal journal, one of his finest biographers, Jonathan Messerli, captures clearly the spirit in which the secretaryship was accepted. "Upon the self-imposed asceticism of the last five years, he now hoped to superimpose a new altruistic purpose. Taking the classical stance of a martyr and envisioning himself clad in an armor of 'truth and duty,' which shielded him against the slings and arrows of his adversaries, he stood ready to face the imminent challenge."[14]

Such motives may sound overly pompous to the twentieth century ear in a culture not accustomed to martyrdom. If the vision of himself as a crusader was exaggerated, so too was the personal pain that allowed for such a political sacrifice.

THE YEARS AS EDUCATOR

Unfortunately, Massachusetts had not escaped from a smugness and complacency which is occasionally derived from pride in one's heritage. Such an attitude works hard against any social reformer and Mann was no exception. The great challenge for him was to shake Massachusetts out of its doldrums and fashion an educational movement that would serve well the people across the entire state. His was a vision of a uniquely American institution—"Mann's school was to be common, not in the traditional European sense of a school for the common people, but in a new sense of a school common to all people."[15]

The immediate task for Mann was to become informed on the literature available regarding the education of young people, garner information on the status of education in Massachusetts, and inspire statewide a commitment to that common school ideal. In 1837 he began by contacting powerful friends who set up "conventions" across the state, and Mann applied his considerable skill as an orator to personally promote his cause. His effect on audiences could be enormous as he sought, and often gained from them, a pledge to improve their local schools. On these trips Mann inspected schools and requested the advice of public officials and parents. He constantly mailed out circulars requesting information about textbooks, buildings, and financial support.

By January 1838 when he was ready to submit his first report to the board of education , he had traveled in excess of five hundred miles on horseback and collected and organized an impressive fund of information about the status of education in Massachusetts. What he found was total disorder and blatant inadequacies: defective school buildings, teachers' lack of preparation, confused and erratic local taxation policies, insufficient funds, scanty materials and books, and deficient supervision.

Mann's discoveries were not really that surprising, but the very act of documenting them and making serious institutional inadequacies public ultimately had a constructive effect on school reform. He used the annual report to the board as a clarion call for legislative action that would remove these deficiencies and as a consciousness raising instrument that would inspire broad based public support for education. The annual reports to come from Mann's pen were so timely and well written that their effect was lasting and was felt far beyond the borders of Massachusetts. As the historian Lawrence Cremin remarked: "His twelve annual reports to the Board range far and wide through the field of pedagogy, eloquently stating the case for the public school and insightfully discussing its problems. The cogency of their analysis is measured by their striking relevance today; to peruse them is to consider some of the most fundamental problems of contemporary American education."[16]

Mann was able to coalesce support for the common schools through these annual reports precisely because he crafted pertinent arguments to appeal to a variety of important constituencies. To those businessmen grown insecure about the increasing violence and vandalism plaguing the cities, Mann sold them the common school as a means of building character and promoting protection of property. The benefit to the rich was further linked to a hope for the poor in that education would prevent poverty and wipe out factitious social distinctions.

To those who would withhold support for any "Godless" institution, Mann assured them a common school system would recognize religious obligations. To reassure those frightened by the prospect of doctrines being taught alien to their own, Mann promoted nonsectarian education, in which teachers would advance those common principles of the various sectarian creeds and read, without comment, from the Bible. And finally, to that constituency committed to and concerned about the furtherance of a democratic state, Mann held that these schools would instill democratic ideals and training in self-government.

The annual reports, circulars, speeches and the *Common School Journal*—a journal founded and edited by Mann—served as vehicles for establishing a new level of discourse and interest on concerns of professional education. He spoke with insight to the issues of curriculum development, teacher qualifications, motivation, discipline, methods of teaching reading, and—with phrenology receiving his unequivocal endorsement—learning theory. He established teacher institutes and argued on behalf of circulating libraries within school districts and for local/state partnerships in support of public education. He fought for the development of standards in the selection of textbooks and for the improvement of school buildings. In a word, he tried to take a totally fragmented and under-financed hodgepodge of school efforts and fashion a fiscally sound statewide system of public education.

Even a cursory look at progress made in Massachusetts during Mann's twelve-year tenure as secretary of the board of education reveals an impressive record of accomplishments. Annual state appropriations to education doubled during that period, and local taxation increased at an even faster rate. Teacher salaries improved by more than 50 percent. An extraordinarily significant shift in funding occurred as private schools slipped badly, from 75 to 36 percent, in their share of total allocations to education in the state. There was widespread consolidation, and the length of school terms more than doubled. A fund in excess of $2 million was appropriated to school buildings and equipment.[17]

One accomplishment of Mann's was such a source of pride to him that it deserves special mention. In 1838, he was drawn aside at a social gathering by philanthropist Edmund Dwight and quietly guaranteed $10,000 to improve teaching in Massachusetts. The one condition attached to the gift was that the state legislature had to match the amount. Mann was both surprised and extremely gratified by the generous offer. Teacher training in the United States was at that moment a beleaguered affair, represented by little more than several books in general circulation on "school-keeping" and sporadic attempts by various academies to establish courses in pedagogy. Mann quickly decided to use the Dwight offer not as a subsidy for existing instituitions to attend to pedagogical concerns, but rather for the creation of a system of schooling dedicated to the singular purpose of teacher preparation: the normal school.

With the Dwight incentive, Mann successfully fashioned a legislative package that not only provided for state assistance but also required local financial support for the establishment of these normal schools. True to their heritage, descendants of the pilgrims in famous old Plymouth County wished the honor of being first to host such an institution. There was standing room only at the meeting called to formalize that commitment, and those in attendance heard the cause for teacher training given justification by men of rare eminence such as Horace Mann, John Quincy Adams, and Daniel Webster. The occasion was auspicious also by the historic fact that the school was to be the first of its kind in America. Eventually the citizens of Plymouth County equivocated, and the distinction of being first to have a tax funded normal school went to Lexington, Massachusetts in July 1839.

With an absence of precedent to guide decisions on curriculum, methods, and materials, the normal school beginnings were clumsy at best. However, by the mid-1840s, several such institutions were thriving in Massachusetts, with impressive programs of one-year duration, capped by three weeks of practice teaching. The opportunity to initiate a program of formal preparation of teachers as a companion to the common school movement was an honor felt very deeply by Horace Mann.

THE FINAL CAMPAIGNS

If the decade of the thirties were for Mann years of remorse, endless toil, and martyrdom, the forties would show a circumstance of some relief and even measured improvement. In the early spring of 1843, Mann abruptly, and to the amazement of all acquaintances, proposed marriage to a close friend of long standing, Mary T. Peabody. She was a lovely lady of great intelligence and sensitivity, and had been for years secretly in love with Mann. True to his compulsive ways, they spent their honeymoon on an international tour to study foreign social institutions, especially the Prussian schools. Mann hoped to translate into less autocratic terms some of the highly touted Prussian practices for use by Massachusetts educators. The observations of these schools recorded by him and Mary formed the content of his remarkable *Seventh Annual Report.*

By the late 1840s, Mann felt secure that the common school movement had stablized and even that fresh leadership might facilitate its growth. He left the secretaryship in 1848 to accept the seat in the United States House of Representatives vacated by the death of John Quincy Adams. In Washington, Mann distinguished himself nationally as one of the most adamant critics of slavery, and with his unbending opposition to the Compromise of 1850 (with its provision for a fugitive slave law which would compel the North to protect the work of slavehunters) he seriously jeopardized his political future. His vehement attacks on the compromise angered the more "flexible" Whigs and, under the leadership of Daniel Webster, they wrested from Mann the 1850 nomination for the Eight Congressional District seat. In an unprecedented move, he ran as a Free Soiler and came away the victor by a margin of forty-one votes.

Mann accepted his final great challenge in 1852, when he was selected the first president of Antioch College in Yellow Springs, Ohio. That Antioch should prosper was crucial because it sought to give expression on America's new frontier to what Mann considered immensely worthy causes: nonsectarianism and coeducation. Though now frail and sickly, Mann drove himself on behalf of his new moral campaign. Struggling under extremely primitive conditions, he and Mary were able to make the college operational but were not able to overcome the mismanagement of the trustees. Ironically, Antioch both went bankrupt and was made fiscally sound in April of 1859, as the school was auctioned off, only to be purchased by wealthy Eastern friends of Horace Mann. Their commitment was that Antioch as well as Mann's educational principles were to be preserved. Such a victory for Mann was substantial, though blemished by the toll it took on his health. Physically weakened and exhausted by the workload and pressures at Antioch, Mann could not stave off a bout with typhoid, and he was dead by early August of that same year.

Many of Mann's contemporaries considered him overbearing and insensitive to those whose commitments he did not share, for example, his seeming lack of concern with the exclusive use of the King James version of the Bible in what were allegedly nonsectarian schools. He was excessively thin-skinned. Friend Theodore Parker spoke to the issue of Mann's critics and noted that if "one of the little mosquitoes bit him, Mann thought he had never taken quite notice enough of the creature till he had smashed it to pieces with a 48-pound cannon-shot which rung throughout the land."[18]

Mann is held responsible by some for setting in motion a cumbersome bureaucracy that deadens rather than releases the creative force of children. He has been accused of acting as an unwitting lackey for the business community, using the schools to develop for them a skilled labor force and as an instrument to placate and control the disenfranchised.

What is for certain is the enormity of Mann's commitment to public education. His successes in Massachusetts literally set precedent for the rest of the country, and education in America as we know it today carries the very distinctive mark of his work. The spirit of his intentions was simply to make effective the obligations of a just society to educate all of its citizens. These intentions did not go without parallels. For example, his counterpart in Connecticut is the subject of our next biography.

Henry Barnard (1811-1900)

Regarded as a significant American educator of the nineteenth century, Barnard's one profound interest was *The American Journal of Education*. This journal has immortalized his name in the annals of educational history. In thirty-one volumes he brought to educators an overview of foreign and American educational philosophy, events, biographies, and administrative information at all levels. His consuming desire throughout was to advance the cause of the American common school,

EDUCATION AND CHARACTER

Barnard was born in Connecticut in 1811, attended Monson Academy (Massachusetts) and Hopkins Grammar School (Connecticut), enrolled in Yale in 1826, and graduated in 1830. While in college he developed an avid interest in classical and English literature and history. He used much of this content to good advantage as a member of the debate team. His scholarship matured in literature, Latin, and Greek, but in 1835 his career took a new turn. After returning to Yale and passing the bar examination, he accepted the position of attorney and counselor at law in Connecticut; however, he wanted to tour

Europe first. He quickly procured letters of introduction from such men as William Wordsworth and Thomas Carlyle, who expedited his journey through much of western Europe. He went on foot through large portions of Scotland and Switzerland and from his tour of Europe, he developed a deep interest in universal education. He paid particular attention to prevailing social conditions, which included an interest in homes, schools, occupations, and charity and recreational facilities.

His father's failing health in 1836 shortened his stay in Europe, and soon after returning to Connecticut he was elected as Hartford's representative in the legislature. In 1838 he was responsible for a legislative act to provide for better supervision of common schools.[19] This contribution changed his career considerably, because from this point on his efforts were directed toward the task of universalizing education in the United States.

He subsequently became the secretary of the Connecticut School Board of Commissioners (1838-1842); the founder and editor of the *Connecticut Common School Journal* (1838-1842); the secretary (sometimes called agent) of the Rhode Island School Board (1845-1849); the superintendent of the Connecticut Common Schools (1849-1855); and a delegate to the International Exposition of Educational Methods held in London, 1854. His editorship of *The American Journal of Education* (1855-1882) was an awesome job in itself, yet he served as the chancellor of the University of Wisconsin (1859-1860) and as president of St. John's College in Annapolis (1866-1867). In addition to this list of endeavors, he was appointed the first United States Commissioner of Education (1867-1870).

COMMON SCHOOL EFFORTS

Barnard's written interest in foreign education began in 1838 with accounts of European education appearing frequently in his *Connecticut Common School Journal*. One of the more significant articles of this nature appeared in July 1840. Originally the article was an appendix to Barnard's second report to the Connecticut School Board of Commissioners the preceding May. Prior to the report a special committee, with the assistance of Barnard, compiled documents relating to popular education in America and Europe. It served then as the fourth appendix to the secretary's report so "that the legislature and the people might compare our own system of common schools with those to be found elsewhere."[20]

The entire issue was devoted to a survey of education in both areas, consisting of descriptions and an abundance of data. It was believed that the value of the American common school would be enhanced by placing this storehouse of data before school committees, teachers, and parents of every school district in Connecticut. Calvin Ellis Stowe's description of elementary education in Europe, Victor Cousin's observations on the Prussian and Dutch school systems, and Alexander Dallas Bache's summary of educational progress in European primary schools are excellent examples of primary sources used in this compilation. The issue is encyclopedic and similar to much of the later work found in Barnard's *American Journal.*[21]

Barnard had hopes that this report would do more than improve the "usefulness" of the common school in his state. Writing in 1855 he told of the value of such a report. Many in Connecticut believed that their system was the best in the world and that little educational progress had been made in other states and countries. Knowing this, he felt compelled to destroy such a smug impression, for he knew that as much, if not more, progress was being made on both sides of the Atlantic. Thus, he entered into efforts that paralleled Mann's struggle in Massachusetts.

Barnard did not intend to lead his public schools to the point of emulation of other systems, but he had hoped that Victor Cousin's attitude in France could prevail in Connecticut—"that the true greatness of a state does not consist in borrowing nothing from others, but in borrowing from all whatever is good, and in perfecting what it appropriates."[22]

Barnard went to Europe again in the early 1850s to regain his health and collect material which would supplement that collected in 1835-1836. These documents and his firsthand impressions of Europe served as the basis for one of his major works entitled *National Education in Europe.* The important aspects of most of the documents on foreign education which were to be used throughout the life of the *American Journal of Education* were pulled together and put into this volume. Aspects of general education, the training of teachers, agricultural schools, and institutions for juvenile delinquents received attention. He also incorporated many parts of the reports of Stowe, Bache, and Mann. Barnard felt that this text contained more accurate statistics and information concerning the entire subject of public education in Europe than could be found anywhere in the English language.[23] The areas included in the text were primarily those of western Europe: the German states, Switzerland, France, Belgium, Holland, Denmark, Sweden, Norway, Russia, Greece, Italy, Spain, Portugal, Scotland, Ireland, and England. Whenever Barnard described foreign education, the emphasis was almost always on some aspect of European education.

Barnard wrote several books on foreign education systems designed to stimulate educational programs in America. Many of his separate publications were extracted from his *American Journal.* His first tour of Europe in 1835 and his 1854 trip to England provided the basis for nearly all his articles of this nature in addition to many of his books.

Probably the best written discussion Barnard engaged in concerning the value of examining foreign educational systems is found in his eighth report as state superintendent in Connecticut, made to the legislature in 1853. He stated that whatever one may think of the practical value of the progress made in various European countries, it could not be denied that much of the progress made in Germany, Holand, and Switzerland would be applicable in the United States, particularly in relation to professional education and the progressive improvement of elementary school teachers.[24] He saw the public schools of certain areas of Europe making excellent progress, but he also saw other areas hampered by national custom, aristocratic resistance, and oppressive governments. Still, he believed that the public school could mitigate these forces by serving as an agent of social reform. In this respect, Barnard had much in common with future progressive educators.

Despite the progress made in most of Europe, Barnard thought that the public schools there did "not turn out such practical and efficient men as our own common schools, acting in concert with our religious, social, and political institutions." He believed that in America the political factors—free press, town and school district assemblies, and close contact with those in public life—could offset the weaknesses of the public school. Combine these freedoms with the moral discipline one learns in his struggle to achieve self-reliance and the balance is in favor of the American scholar. Fixed customs and laws enervated the efforts of those European students subjected to despotic rule. But he reiterated, this superiority in America "is not due to the school, but is gained in spite of the school."[25] The educational goal should be the betterment of the school by fusing the forces of the home and society with that of superior instruction.

Barnard's interest in education abroad continued throughout most of his life. He thought that one of the values of looking at education beyond one's geographic borders was to obtain "a knowledge of the manner in which attempts have been made to solve the problem of public instruction in other countries." He added that these systems, however, should not serve as complete models for emulation. Here it is assumed that he was utilizing the principle of appropriating only the better qualities of other systems. He was specific as to those developments in some countries worthy of consideration: (1) teaching as an art; (2) professional and public aspects of teaching considered from a legal viewpoint; (3) school inspection; (4) parental obligation concerning school attendance; and (5) extension of schools beyond the elementary level.[26]

Barnard's involvement in foreign education was unmatched by any individual of the nineteenth century. His major interest was the development of the common school, and to improve this institution he looked to Europe for precedent, particularly in Prussia, Switzerland, and Holland. He made few comparisons of a cultural nature in his writing; that is, he did not discuss the problems of transplanting an institution from one society to another. However, he did believe in modifying foreign educational practices to fit American needs, although his publications dealt more with the descriptions of practices than with cross-sectional comparison of assumptions, ideals, or problems. His discussion of educational practices also dealt slightly with concomitant social forces, even though he admitted that they possibly have more influence on the student than the school itself. But Barnard's yeomanlike efforts are not diminished by these criticisms. It would also be naive to assume that he thought little about the necessary cultural assimilation of several foreign educational practices. America needed trained teachers and strong common schools. This was an immediate need which deserved his full attention. Because he supplied an abundance of source material, Americans themselves could compare their educational facilities with the more progressive systems and hence make the necessary improvements.

Henry Barnard was also the first U. S. Commissioner of Education, presiding over the newly created department from its inception in 1867 until 1869 when it was reduced to bureau status due to Barnard's mismanagement and neglect. Consequently, the following year he was forced to resign, because he had failed to execute the duties required by the law that created the department. First and foremost, Commissioner Barnard had not managed to give Congress his first annual report on the state of educational conditions in the country. (Instead, the

long overdue nine-hundred page report discussed his plans for the department.)
Also, he had not investigated the status of land grants given under the Morrill
Act of 1862. Finally, he had made no suggestions for improving schooling in the
District of Columbia. Connected to this inactivity was the fact that he disliked
the Capital's physical and social climate and was usually found at his home in
Hartford working on his *American Journal of Education*.[27]

Throughout his last thirty years, Barnard continued to remember his Washington experience as a dismal period in his life. Nevertheless, his general reputation as an educational equal to Horace Mann remained intact. This was
probably due in part to the thirty-one volumes of the *American Journal of
Education* which stand as a lasting tribute to a productive life. In this area there
is little doubt that Henry Barnard contributed immensely to educational developments in the United States. Through its pages readers were given firsthand
knowledge of the latest designs in school architecture, plus the educational
practices and experiments occurring in Yverdon, Oswego, New York, and New
Harmony, Indiana. This latter Pestalozzian utopia was the vision of Englishman, Robert Owen, who attempted to create heaven on earth through his
dream of a new commonwealth.

Robert Owen (1771-1858)

English capitalist turned utopian socialist, Robert Owen headed up a transat-
lantic movement that attracted converts in Europe and America. In developing
an educational theory combining many strands, Owen saw education as a total
process of character formation and argued that "man's character was made
for him and not by him." For him education would create a new society based
on the equality of persons inhabiting a community of common property. Dedicated to creating a new society through character formation, Owen advocated
early childhood or infant education as the first step in the process. Owen's
educational plan called for conditioning children in the correct dispositions in
the infant school and fitting men and women to live in the communal society.
The following sections will examine Owen's life, educational ideas, and contemporary relevance.

EARLY LIFE

Robert Owen was born in 1771 in Newtown, Montgomeryshire, in north
Wales.[28] Owen claims to have been a precocious child who mastered his lessons quickly and thoroughly. He judged himself to be popular with peers and
adults and agile in games and dancing. Owen wrote that Newtown's schoolmaster recognized his aptitude and relied on him to tutor slower children. From
childhood through adulthood, Owen's personality was embued with self-
confidence that gave him an optimistic but also unrealistic appraisal of his own
powers of accomplishment.

In 1781, the ten-year-old Owen left Newtown to seek fame and fortune in the
industrial city of Manchester where from 1781 to 1789, he worked as a shop

boy and assistant in a drapery shop. In 1791, Owen established his own cotton-spinning plant and gained sufficient prominence in Manchester's business community to be named a member of the Literary and Philosophical Society and the board of health.

The year 1799 was a turning point in Owen's life when he and his partners purchased David Dale's cotton mills in New Lanark, Scotland. Owen married Dale's daughter, Ann Caroline, and located in New Lanark where he planned to create a model factory community that would earn a profit for its owners but yet be a humane place for its workers. Arriving in New Lanark, Owen discovered little to give him encouragement. A typical early nineteenth century English factory town, cotton mills dominated New Lanark's bleak landscape. The mills were worked by members of entire families and also a large number of ill-clad and undernourished orphans. Owen was especially depressed by the sad condition of the six- seven- and eight-year-old child operatives who worked from six in the morning and until seven at night. New Lanark's society was plagued by disorder, poverty, and social strife. Undaunted, the ever optimistic Owen compiled a catalog of the problems to be solved at New Lanark. To be corrected were distrust, disorder, theft, drunkenness, personal quarrels, and religious contention.

Almost immediately upon arriving, Owen set out to reform life and education and inaugurated his plan for ameliorating New Lanark's social condition. In so doing, he announced his guiding operational principle: "Any general character, from the best to the worst, from the most ignorant to the most enlightened, may be given to any community, even to the world at large, by the application of proper means; which means are to a great extent at the command and under the control of those who have influence in the affairs of men."[29]

Based upon his theory of character formation, Owen developed his design of communication control. If the proper community is established and guided by the correct principles of social science, then human character could so be shaped that the good in human nature is developed to its highest potential.

Owen began his plan of community reform by winning the confidence of his employees who were also the citizens of New Lanark. He curtailed the sale of gin and worked to reduce alcoholism. He improved the homes, streets, and sanitary conditions in the town. Fuel and clothing were sold by the company stores at profitable but reasonable prices.

Owen's most striking innovations were directed to improving New Lanark's educational conditions. He discontinued employing the very young children in the mill. Although he preferred to delay the child's entry into the work force until age twelve, Owen yielded to parents who wanted their children to begin work at age ten. Owen also established an educational institute for children between the ages of five and ten who were taught without expense to their parents.

EDUCATION AT NEW LANARK

A complete account of Owen's educational program at New Lanark has been recorded by his eldest son, Robert Dale Owen, in *An Outline of the System of Education at New Lanark*.[30] Like Rousseau, Pestalozzi, and other naturalistic educators, Owen advocated the abolition of external rewards and punishments. This latter practice assumed that children were responsible for their actions. Owen, who claimed that a person's character was formed by environmental forces, denied that human beings were responsible for their behavior. External rewards and punishments of an artificial nature fixed the child's existing character and worked against changing his or her internal disposition. It also created attitudes of superiority and inferiority in the children and stimulated antagonism and egotistical competition. According to Owen educationally valuable rewards and punishments were the result of experiencing the natural consequences of actions. Owen wanted children to recognize that their actions had social consequences which were either detrimental or advantageous to the community.

An able educational theorist in his own right, Owen devised a version of the object lesson that somewhat resembled Pestalozzi's approach. Owen's basic instructional method used objects and involved simple, direct conversations about these objects. However, these lessons were but one part of a varied and often inconsistent curriculum. Like the naturalistic educators, Owen felt that reading was begun too early with materials not easily understood by children. In teaching reading, the general principle was that children should not read anything that they could not understand and explain in their own words. Owen believed that little volumes of voyage and travel, illustrated by plates, pictures, and maps, were most appropriate to children's interests. Believing that a child had a limited attention span, he also advised that lessons were never to last more than thirty-five minutes.

Writing should begin as soon as the student could copy a fair text and should cultivate a fair business hand in the learner. Owen made use of dictation in which the child copied the teacher's words. Short sentences that illustrated history or geography were most suitable for teaching children to write. To teach arithmetic, Owen recommended using Pestalozzian principles by which learners began with concrete objects, counted them, added them, and subtracted them. Only after relating quantity to objects were students to proceed to more abstract computations.

Under one heading, Owen integrated instruction in natural history, geography, ancient and modern history. He classified these subjects together since they could be taught according to the extemporaneous lecture method in which the teacher lectured to classes of forty children. He also admonished lecturers to strike a balance between necessary details and unnecessary particulars. Avoiding minor details, the teacher was to give students a clear outline of the major points of the lecture. If the students learned the important generalizations, then they could fill in the details. Natural science was of primary importance for students in that it gave them a basic understanding of their world. The divisions of nature into animal, vegetable, and mineral kingdoms were to be explained. Specimens illustrating mineralogical and botanical classifications were to be shown to students. For geography, children were taught the form of the earth, and its divisions into land and water. The four continents were identified as well as the major islands, oceans, seas, lakes, and rivers. Owen believed it important for children to develop a world or international perspective that opened their minds to other peoples and cultures. Children were to be introduced to the world's countries, their peoples, customs, and products.

Always antagonistic to organized religion, Owen believed that the various churches supported traditionalism and impeded human progress. Religious education, he argued, interjected bias, dogmatism, and contention into the schooling of children. Opposing the view that human nature is either innately evil or depraved due to the effects of Adam's original sin, Owen contended that people's inherently good characteristics needed only a correct environment to come to perfection. Although he wanted moral education based on his view of human nature and social science, Owen reluctantly compromised with New Lanark parents who wanted the catechism taught to their children.

Believing that a genuine education was a multidimensional process, Owen also sought to cultivate the aesthetic side of a child's nature. All children, above age five, were taught singing by ear and by notes. Owen enjoyed dancing and believed that it was a pleasant, healthful, natural, and social exercise that improved carriage and deportment.

OWEN'S SOCIAL THEORY

As his fame spread, Owen was no longer content to play the role of local reformer. He turned to lecturing and writing in the belief that he was destined to create a "New Moral World." In 1813, his *A New View of Society* proclaimed a new social science with a form of education that was conducive to social change.

Owen's theory of social change was derived from his economic opinions. An early nineteenth century mill owner who had amassed a fortune and reputation as a levelheaded and profit making businessman, Owen rejected the exploitative relationships associated with the English entrepreneur's economic policies. Although condemning early industrialism's exploitation, Owen accepted increased economic growth and productivity as beneficial to mankind. A modernizer who believed that much of early industrialism's hardships were unnecessary, he argued that economic growth and abundance could be achieved without human suffering. He felt that it was the working classes who paid for industrial growth with their suffering and misery. For him, the price was too high as well as unnecessary.

His views were precipitated by his own experiences at New Lanark and by his observations of nineteenth century English society. In insisting that a man's character was "formed for and not by him," he stressed the role of environment in shaping human character. If the environment were properly organized, then those who interacted with it would be shaped by its wholesome stimuli. Owen regarded the cooperative community as the ideal environment for shaping the moral inhabitants who would dwell in the new social order.

Believing that the "New Moral Order" would come about peacefully and nonviolently, Owen turned to education as the instrument to create the new society. By using tracts, polemics, books, and lectures, Owen sought to gain converts for his new society. As the prophet of the coming order, he used education to disseminate the knowledge of the social system and to nurture the desire to live in the cooperative commonwealth. His communities of cooperation were to be educative environments that would shape the new moral order by forming the new moral citizen. Schools in these egalitarian communities would raise up future communitarian generations.

Owen, who rejected revolutionary violence and class warfare, was dubbed a utopian by the Marxists. Holding that social change could be achieved without violence of any kind, Owen believed that when people were convinced of the inequalities of the old system that they would rush to replace it with his vision of the humane society. Since humans were not responsible for forming their own character and behavior, class hatred was irrational and irrelevant to achieving the new society.[31] Owen was certain that the most rational and enlightened of all classes would unite to effect social change. Owen's rejection of class conflict and revolutionary violence led Marx and Engels to condemn Owenism as utopian socialism—a soft-headed approach to class struggle that deluded the working classes and detoured them from their true revolutionary role. Engels in *Socialism, Utopian and Scientific*, commended Owen for his social analysis but condemned his failure to understand the significance of class antagonisms. Unlike Marx, who believed that the proletariat would be led by an elite vanguard, Owen held that with proper education all people could contribute to establishing the cooperative commonwealth.

Owen's design for a new society resembled that of the eighteenth century philosophers who attempted to explain physical and social reality in terms of a few fundamental laws of immense power and scope. Like these writers of the Enlightenment he believed that the order and clarity of the physical realm could be extended to the social world. He also believed that he had created a new social science that explained and conformed to the basic laws governing the universe, since he thought it possible to discover social laws in the same way that scientists discovered the laws of physical reality. For the Owenites social science became a synonymn of socialism, and the method of studying society to discover the laws that governed people and formed their characters.[32] Using the premise that the controlled environment would produce the desired personality type, Owen became a thoroughgoing social engineer. He believed that the social scientist, armed with the laws of social organization and human development, could construct a planned community whose residents would be developed according to a preferred society blueprint. Since social engineering was a way of creating the new citizen who would inhabit the new moral order, Owen saw himself as the chief engineer who would create the reconstructed social order of the "New Moral World."

Owen's educational theory rested on his central thesis that human character is made by life in society. Recognizing the formative role of enculturation, human character resulted from the basic experiences that persons had as members of a social group, living within a particular societal mode. The reconstructing of society would lead to a fundamental reshaping of human character. By living in a properly constituted community and by being educated in the laws of society, the citizens of the new social order would end the chaos of the old, irrational, disintegrative society. For Owenite social science, education was broadly construed as the total process of enculturation which included schooling. In the past, the old, immoral, and discordant society that transmitted to children by the culture and by erroneous religious and classical forms of schooling. In the new society, a new form of schooling based on social science would facilitate the creation of the new community.

Owen's theory of social science and social engineering was characterized by its originator's comprehensive goal of changing the entire society. His theory was a comprehensive plan for reconstructing society, and it branched out into economic, social, political, and educational areas. Owenite social science sought to inaugurate a comprehensive reconstruction of society and through such a reordering to restore integrity to personal and social life. Owen's community, a crucial component in his theory of social change, was related to institutional reconstruction. Since institutions worked to shape human character, social change could occur only as religious, political, economic, social, and educational institutions were altered. Owen believed that European institutions, resting on long-standing and deeply embedded traditions, were more difficult to reconstruct than those of the United State which were newer, more flexible, and more amenable to reorganization. Hence, he came to the United States in 1825 to embark on the New Harmony communitarian experiment.

OWEN IN AMERICA

From 1824 until 1828, Owen sought to implement his social and educational theories in New Harmony, a small Indiana town that he had purchased from the Rappites, a sect of German Pietists. Drawn to the United States with the belief that the American frontier was well suited to social experimentation, Owen believed that the United States was free of the prejudices and traditional encumbrances of the Old World. After two separate addresses to the United States Congress on his plan for social reconstruction, Owen came to New Harmony to create a frontier utopia. His open invitation to any and all who would be communitarians brought an unusual assortment of scholars, scientists, zealots, opportunists, farmers, and eccentrics to the southern Indiana town. Some of the Harmonists were well-known individuals such as William Maclure, Thomas Say, Gerard Troost, and Joseph Neef while others were obscure with no particular claim to fame.

Owen planned to create a community of equality at New Harmony in which the inhabitants would commonly own the town's property. Education was to be an important community undertaking, and Owen planned to develop comprehensive educational institutions, ranging from nursery schools to adult education lectures. The ever optimistic Owen predicted that New Harmony would be so successful and prosperous that other communities would organize in imitation. From the New Harmony center, Owen envisioned a network of satellite cities springing up to encompass the earth. Thus, communitarian education would create and sustain his envisioned "New Moral World": "The world will thus be governed through education alone since all other governments will then become useless and unnecessary. To train and educate the rising generation will at all times be the first object of society, to which every other will be subordinate."[33]

Owen's educational program at New Harmony was closely related to communitarian social experimentation.[34] Since social regeneration was to be done peacefully, education was Owen's primary tool of reform. He believed that life in the small, voluntary, experimental community would reform its residents. Historian Arthur Bestor has commented on the tendency of early nineteenth century educational reformers to think in communitarian terms: "There were educationists to whom the relationship between school and society appeared a reciprocal one. The school should respond to social change, they held, but it should also be an instrument for effecting desirable alterations in society. In their hands educational reform became a branch of social reform."[35]

NEW HARMONY EXPERIMENT

Schooling at New Harmony represented a shift in educational theory and practice from the classics to utilitarianism. Owen's unconventional educational experiment on the American frontier was designed to advance the progress of the agricultural and industrial working classes. He regarded the Greek and Latin language curriculum as an archaic pedagogical residue that was irrelevant to scientific and industrial progress. Owen saw communitarian education to be a means of improving the condition of working people during the dehumanizing stages of early industrialization. His educational program was directed to utilitarian ends as well as socioeconomic reconstruction.

A key provision in Owen's New Harmony plan was the abolition of private property which he identified as the source of human and social evils. Common property and common education, the "great equalizers," would erode class conflict and contention. On 1 May 1825, the "Preliminary Society of New Harmony" organized "to improve the character and conditions of its own members, and to prepare them to become associates in independent communities, having common property."[36] Ten months later, on 5 February 1826, an overly optimistic Robert Owen proclaimed the "Community of Equality." The New Harmony Constitution committed its members to "equality of rights" and "equality of duties" within a society of "cooperative union" and a "community of property." New Harmony's constitution restated the basic Owenite conceptions of character formation, cooperation, and education: "Man's character, mental, moral, and physical, is the result of his formation, his location, and . . . the circumstances within which he exists." Accordingly, the members of the community

> shall be considered as one family, and no one shall be held in higher or lower estimation on account of occupation. There shall be similar food, clothing, and education, as near as can be furnished, for all according to their ages; and, as soon as practicable, all shall live in similar houses, and in all respects be accommodated alike. Every member shall render his or her best services for the good of the whole, according to the rules and regulations that may be hereafter adopted by the community. It shall always remain a primary object of the community to give the best physical, moral, and intellectual education to all its members.[37]

Unfortunately for Owen, his plan for a new American social order did not succeed. Displaying a chronic tendency to disharmony, the inhabitants of New Harmony endlessly debated over constitutions, quarreled over property division, and disputed over social and educational theories and practices. With the community in the throes of disintegration, Owen and his chief associate, William Maclure, quarreled, conducted litigation against each other, and then divided what remained of the community of unity. In 1828, Owen left New Harmony and returned to his native England where he optimistically continued to work for communitarianism, the improvement of working conditions, and the creation of universal education until his death in 1858.

Perhaps the best assessment of Owen sees him as a visionary who believed it possible to create a better world with better inhabitants upon it. As a social critic and educational critic, his diagnosis pointed to needed reforms. His social and educational proposals revealed the sociological matrix within which schooling operates. Unfortunately, he also was a presumptuous man who felt that he could manage persons by manipulating their environment.

Owen, Mann, Barnard, Webster—indeed most theorists who considered themselves part of the reforming tradition—advocated tax funded schools for all. They thought individuals would be improved both morally and intellectually and that society would benefit. But who should decide the curriculum? Traditionally the answer had been that parents and the local community should choose. With more and more Roman Catholic immigrants arriving, the "friends of education," most of whom were descended from the Puritan Protestant tradition, began to doubt the wisdom of continuing this tradition. The conflict shows clearly in the life and activities of our next subject, John Hughes.

John Hughes (1797-1864)

At first glance, Bishop John Hughes of New York is an unlikely candidate for inclusion in a collection of educational biographies. Hughes was neither a teacher, educational theorist, nor school administrator. In spite of this, however, he was a key figure in the development of Catholic schooling in America. Ironically, he was also partly responsible for the development of American public education along secular lines.

EARLY LIFE AND CAREER

Hughes was born in northern Ireland in 1797, the third son of a poor farmer. Life was especially difficult for the Irish during this period. Much of Ireland's land was owned by absentee landlords and farmed by local tenants. The Irish were a conquered people, unable to govern themselves or practice their Catholic religion freely. Hughes later reminisced about being told as a boy that "for five days I was on a social and civil equality with the most favored subjects of the British Empire. These five days would be the interval between my birth and my baptism."[38] As soon as he formally became a Catholic, he sacrificed most of his civil rights. In the long run these early experiences of religious persecution would motivate his crusade for Catholic rights in the United States.

Due to these problems John's father went to America with his second son Patrick and in the following year sent for John. The boy arrived in Baltimore and went to work as a gardener at Emmitsburg, Maryland, the location of the most famous American Catholic seminary of the period, Mount St. Mary's. Hughes tried several times to gain admission, but the rector, the Reverend John Dubois, felt that the school was already too crowded and that Hughes was too old to be a successful student. It seems that Hughes simply rubbed Dubois the wrong way.[39] Whatever the case he refused to admit the twenty-one year old applicant.

John Hughes, however, was already showing the stubborn streak which would make him a difficult opponent in future years. He refused to give up his dream of becoming a priest and eventually gained admission to the seminary through the intervention of Elizabeth Bayley Seton, an Episcopalian widow who had converted to Catholicism and was the founder of a community of nuns. (Seton would later become the first American born saint.) At the age of twenty-three, Hughes was finally admitted to the seminary.

Given his age and background, it is hardly surprising that Hughes was not a typical student. For the most part he was a loner separated by age and personality from his much younger classmates. As a prefect (student disciplinarian), he had a reputation for being stern and humorless. Students delighted in playing pranks on him, and faculty members thought him proud and stubborn. His only source of support was the Reverend Simon Bruté, the seminary's saintly religious counselor who would one day also be a bishop as would Dubois.

Hughes was ordained in 1826 and almost immediately became involved in a religious controversy which established his style of action for later years. The unsettled character of the Catholic church in America in the early nineteenth century meant that it attracted more than a few undesirable clergy from overseas. European bishops or religious superiors who were having problems with a priest would occasionally give him the choice of going to America or leaving the priesthood. Others came because they couldn't get along with their parishes and hoped to make a new start in another country. The result was an American church in which bishops had a lot of authority on paper but very little in fact.

Previous to Hughes's ordination there had been a fight for some years in Philadelphia between the bishop and lay people over whether the bishop had the right to appoint parish priests. Through newspapers Hughes exchanged letters with Protestant clergy over this issue. Here as in later fights, Hughes' style was anything but restrained. He would meet an attack with a counterattack instead of taking a more gentlemanly approach. Nevertheless, he began to establish a reputation as a champion of Catholic rights.

Along with these flashier activities, Hughes worked hard at the more traditional aspects of his priestly ministry. He was a concerned pastor for his people, and worked to provide for their religious needs. Besides supporting his own congregants he helped to raise money for several communities of sisters and was instrumental in the founding of a Catholic orphanage in Philadelphia. Hughes gained respect from Catholics and Protestants alike by remaining in the city during a cholera epidemic in 1833 to minister to the needs of his flock. Initially an uninspiring preacher (he memorized one sermon and used it on every occasion) he improved his style to the degree that he was soon traveling as far as New York to be a guest speaker for special occasions. This oratorical ability was put to the test in 1833 in a series of public debates with a Presbyterian minister named John Brekinridge. Over the course of a hot summer the two hurled charges and counter charges at each other over the comparative merits of Catholicism and Protestantism. Hughes's arguments were theologically thin at times, but he never seemed to lack insults to hurl at his opponent. Blunt and aggressive, he was emerging from an uncertain seminary career as a confident if overly forthright spokesperson for American Catholics.

Given his leadership ability and increasing visibility it was inevitable that Hughes would become a candidate for bishop. In 1833 he was considered along with John Baptist Purcell—the new president of Mount St. Mary's—for the post of bishop of Cincinnati. Ironically, a mix-up prevented Hughes from receiving the post. An American bishop who was consulted by the officials in Rome responsible for appointing bishops recommended that Hughes be sent to Cincinnati rather than Purcell, since Hughes was a self-made man who would understand life in a frontier town better than the more cultured Purcell. However, the Roman official who made the appointment thought that Purcell was the self-made man, and appointed him instead.[40]

In spite of this confusion, and the bluntness which made many Catholic leaders nervous about Hughes, he soon became a bishop. His former seminary president, Dubois, had become bishop of New York in 1826. Now aged, it was obvious that he needed assistance. In 1837, Hughes was appointed coadjutor bishop of New York. This meant that he was a kind of co-bishop, rather than merely an assistant. Dubois had a series of strokes shortly thereafter, and Hughes took over control of the diocese in 1839. While it was logical under the circumstances for Rome to give Hughes full power a clash with Dubois came immediately. The older bishop bitterly resented being forced to hand over control and withdrew into himself for the remaining three years of his life. Never a fan of Hughes to begin with (remember that Dubois had tried to keep him out of the seminary), the older man would refer to him only by his formal title until the end of his life.

THE SCHOOLING CONTROVERSY

In 1839, Hughes went abroad to raise money and recruit personnel for his diocese. During his absence a controversy erupted that would provide the platform from which he would make a distinctive contribution to American educational history. In order to understand the conflict, however, we must first have some sense of what life and schooling were like for immigrants in nineteenth century America.

During the colonial period American society had generally been anti-Catholic. Then, during the Revolutionary War prominent American Catholics like Charles Carroll, a signer of the Declaration of Independence, had made Catholicism more acceptable. Most of these early Catholics were from Maryland and tended to be wealthy and well-educated with the same English manners and customs as their Protestant neighbors.

The great influx of European Catholic immigrants in the early nineteenth century was very different from these earlier Anglo-American Catholics. Largely German or Irish in background they had few of the manners and little of the education of the Maryland gentlemen. Their different way of speaking English (or inability to speak it), obvious poverty, and lack of culture encouraged the hostility of native born Americans. Their presence also drove down wages, since the desperate immigrants were willing to work for lower wages than those born in the United States. This encouraged even more resentment.

The Catholic faith of the immigrants became one more thing which the native citizens held against them. While American Protestants had at least tolerated the Maryland Catholics, the continuing arrival of these newcomers caused many Protestants to fear that America was being taken over by Catholics whom they had been taught to regard as agents of the devil. Throughout this era Protestant magazines continually expressed the fear that this massive immigration was a prelude to a future Catholic takeover of America, when the pope would move to the United States and take up residence in the Middle West.

While these fears seem bizarre or just plain silly to us, they didn't to many nineteenth century Americans. By 1825, 11 percent of New York's population was Irish and by 1845, this had increased to 35 percent. In fact, by 1855, more than half of the city's residents were foreign-born and more than half of the foreign-born were Irish.[41] Given this inpouring of foreigners anything seemed possible to hypersensitive native born Americans.

These great immigrations brought an ever increasing number of children, either foreign-born or with immigrant parents, to the streets of cities like New York. Early in the nineteenth century, however, public schooling was either nonexistent or in its infancy. The organized systems of schools which we know today were still many years away.

For the most part schools meant for the poor in New York (and cities like it) had been supported by a combination of meager state funding and private charity. In the first years of the nineteenth century, much of the schooling for those unable to pay was in the hands of a private organization called the New York Free School Society. This organization, founded in 1805 by wealthy Protestants, sought to provide a free education for those unable to pay in the city's other schools. Like other educational ventures, including those supported by church groups, this free school society was given a share of state tax money to accomplish its purpose. At this time separation of church and state was not yet an issue, and the lines of distinction between religious and public institutions were blurred.

The first controversy over the use of public money for religious schools in New York came in 1824. In that year it was discovered that a local Baptist church was using school money from the state of New York to build a church. In the furor that resulted, the state legislature gave the common council (city council) the right to distribute and supervise the use of state school funds in New York City. As a result denominational schools were cut off from state funding.

While all of this was going on, the New York Free School Society (which was now called the New York Public School Society) had become the major sponsor of schooling in the city. In addition to receiving the lion's share of the state school money, the public school society was also given a special real estate tax by the legislature in order to turn its semiprivate "free schools" into genuine public ones. By 1840 the society was in control of nearly one thousand schools in New York City.

Although free schools in New York were no longer under denominational control, their tone was still highly religious. For most of us who have grown up with a secular public school system, it is hard to realize that such schools were, until almost the beginning of this century, religious in a variety of ways. A sort of general Protestantism permeated the atmosphere and curriculum of the schools. The King James (Protestant) version of the Bible was used as a textbook, and students were taught to regard Protestantism as the highest form of religious belief. For America's school leaders Protestantism was *the* American religion and should be taught as part of the American school curriculum.

If this general Protestant tone weren't enough, public schools of the era also were frequently anti-Catholic. History books stressed how Catholic monarchs in Europe had burned Protestant reformers at the stake and insisted that Catholicism was really superstition rather than Christian religion. Not surprisingly, such bias discouraged Catholic attendance at public schools. Of twelve thousand Catholic children in the city in the late 1830s, only a few were in the common schools. Since there were only a few Catholic schools in the city (eight in 1839), most Catholic children simply didn't go to school.

By the time Hughes arrived on the scene New York Catholics were beginning to get angry about having to pay taxes for schools their children weren't able to attend. In 1834, Bishop Dubois had tried to have Catholic teachers hired in a school district in which most of the pupils were Irish, as well as to have Protestant religious principles removed. The public school society rejected his request, arguing that Catholics were asking for privileges granted to no other religious groups.

Catholics then began to seek political support for their position. In New York's governor William Seward they found an ally. Seward, who would later become Lincoln's secretary of state, believed strongly in the inalienable rights of people as expressed in the Declaration of Independence and in the Judeo-Christian idea of the unity of humankind. More practically he saw the possibility of improving his political position by gaining the support of New York's Irish Catholics. Thus, he encouraged Roman Catholics in 1840 to petition the common council for a share of state funds in order to support their own schools. This petition was rejected by the council, which argued that giving state money to the Catholics would amount to public support of a religious denomination.

At this point, Hughes returned from Europe and took direct charge of the Catholic efforts. Under him the fight broadened from one for public funds into a demand for tolerance of religious differences and respect for immigrant rights. Catholics rallied to Hughes, not only to gain school support, but also to express their frustrations at social and economic discrimination. In a series of debates with Hughes, the anti-Catholic sentiments of public school society officials swiftly surfaced. It was probably lucky for Hughes that they did, since only the anti-Catholic rhetoric of society leaders prevented his own superficial treatment of the school issue from becoming apparent.[42]

An attempt to reach a funding compromise was unsuccessful and in 1841 the city's aldermen voted again to deny the Catholic petition. Catholics then took the battle to the state legislature. In April 1841 New York Secretary of State John Spencer—who was also the state superintendent of schools—presented a plan to the legislature which threatened the domination of the public school society. According to this plan the religious tone of the local schools would be determined by the religion of the majority of residents in a school district. Effectively, this would give Catholics control of their own schools.

The debate now centered on which of two views of public schooling would become law. The one advocated by the Catholics was that the majority should be able to determine the shape of the local schools. The other advocated by almost everyone else was that there should be some kind of public control, but some limits should be placed on a community's power to force its views on all children. Needless to say, the public school society, now on the defensive for the first time, opposed any attempt to make the public schools in Irish neighborhoods more Catholic in tone.

While all of this was happening, New York was preparing for state elections. This caused Hughes to shift his attack to the political sector demanding that local candidates take a stand on state aid to Catholic schools. The results of the 1841 elections showed that although Catholics were not an absolute majority, they held the political balance of power. While those candidates who had only Catholic support lost the regular Democrats who had failed to receive Catholic endorsement also went down to defeat. The Catholic vote had become decisive, an important factor in the local political equation.

In 1842 the matter of restructuring New York's public schools came before the legislature again. Funding of Catholic schools seems to have faded somewhat as an issue; instead, the new bill made provision for the local election of public school commissioners. This action was calculated to break the power of the public school society. However, the society's efforts to stop the legislation were unsuccessful. In November the assembly passed the new school law, and the senate followed suit in April (by a one vote majority). The bill was signed into law by Seward three days before the spring New York City elections. In the resulting election riots, the Catholic bishop's house was nearly burned with the elderly Dubois still inside, but the domination of the public school society had been ended for good. While the Bible was still used in the city's schools within a year Jewish citizens who had sat quietly through the earlier controversies would protest the schools' Christian orientation, and other groups would later file test cases causing the eventual removal of religion completely. As one commentator has pointed out the result was that "for the first time in its history, New York City would have a school system that was directly controlled by the people and entirely financed from the public treasury."[43]

While this legislative solution represented an end for Seward, it was only a midpoint for Hughes. The bishop saw the victory in terms of the evils which it ended rather than the benefits which it conferred. As time went on, Hughes began to attack as "godless" the very schools from which he had helped to remove Protestant religious influence. Having helped to provide immigrants with the means of controlling their own children's education, New York's Catholic bishop proceeded to turn his back on the public schools.

After the "school war" of 1840-1842, Hughes concentrated more of his efforts on developing a network of parochial schools to replace the public ones. By 1854 there were 10,061 pupils studying in New York's twenty-eight parochial schools and the number of students had increased to 15,000 by 1862. In the process of crusading for Catholic rights, John Hughes had also become a leader among the American Catholic bishops in promoting a separate network of schools to meet the particular needs of immigrant Catholics.[44]

In building New York's Catholic schools Hughes relied on his usual style of leadership, demanding absolute control. Typically blunt and aggressive he quarrelled with at least one community of sisters over his right to direct their activities and fought with the Jesuits who staffed Fordham University over the ownership of part of the school's property. While Hughes was always a superb organizer, his lack of diplomacy seemed at times to create as many enemies inside his church as outside.

Hughes began to emerge as a national figure during this period. In 1847 he preached to the U.S. House of Representatives and in 1860 was voted by the heavily Protestant senior class of the University of North Carolina as their choice for graduation speaker. With the approach of the Civil War, Hughes became an ardent Union supporter ordering the American flag to be flown from New York's Catholic churches. Although he did not oppose slavery, a position which earned him further dislike from the city's Protestant abolitionists, he felt that the southern states must be considered in rebellion.

FINAL YEARS

Even though his health had been failing, Hughes undertook a government mission in 1861 at the request of his old friend Seward and President Lincoln. In order to gain foreign support for the Union position, Hughes traveled to France and spoke with the French cardinals, as well as Louis Napoleon. After a journey to England and Ireland, he returned to the United States in 1862. Both his European church superiors and American Catholics were unhappy with this sort of open political activity by a bishop. Once again, Hughes had acted on his convictions without much thought about the consequences: again, he had been left isolated and exposed.

Through the winter of 1862-1863, the bishop's health steadily worsened. Added to his physical ills was the increased racial bigotry of his flock as manifested in the *Freeman's Journal*, a New York Catholic paper. In July 1863 there were riots in New York over the recently instituted military draft. New York priests tried unsuccessfully to calm the city's Irish, and finally Hughes called their leaders together outside his home. Although he was so weak that he had to speak to them from a chair, he reasoned with them for an hour. Influenced by the bishop the crowds dispersed. The draft riots, however, had broken this elderly bishop's spirits. Over and over during the years of strife he had insisted that Catholics could be good Americans. Now, he felt betrayed by the actions of his own people.

Hughes withdrew from public view during the last months of his life, and died on 3 January 1864. Though the *Freeman's Journal* and the abolitionist press of New York gave only routine attention to his death and funeral, the common council ordered all city offices closed in his memory, and the flags on public buildings flown at half mast. Some one hundred thousand gathered in and around the unfinished St. Patrick's Cathedral to attend his funeral. This outpouring of popular sentiment was a fitting final tribute for the bishop who, as the preacher at the funeral mass remarked, had "fought the good fight."

One of the ironies of Hughes' history of educational leadership is that a principal accomplishment was in direct opposition to what he had set out to do. In taking on the public school society, his intention had been to obtain state funds for Catholic schools. Instead, he had helped to create a school system from which religion was absent. In Hughes's eyes such secularization was no improvement; he believed that religion was a necessary component in the education of young people.

To admit that Hughes was unable to accomplish his stated goals, however, is not to say that he failed as an educational leader. Indirectly, he helped to establish a principle which has come to dominate American public education, that is, that the local community should have some measure of control over the schools attended by their children. More directly, he was instrumental in the development of the extensive network of parochial schooling which has become an important part of the American educational landscape.

Hughes stands most of all as a kind of symbol of the needs and aspirations of the "new Americans" of the period, for he had also suffered oppression in Europe and had immigrated to find a new future. Like them, he knew the experience of social and economic discrimination in the new land. Hughes's popularity, in spite of his blunt and autocratic style, is testimony to his ability to articulate the basic human needs for respect and tolerance felt by so many of his flock. In both his fights with the public school society and his development of Catholic education, Hughes's forthright defense of his values and beliefs helped a whole generation of his fellow immigrants feel that they too had values worth defending, and an important place in American life.

8

THE OUTSIDERS

Although schooling became increasingly available to the American populace during the colonial (1607-1787) and national (1789-1860) periods, not everyone had an equal chance to benefit from the growing number of educational institutions. As John Hughes's biography shows, religious affiliation could affect schooling opportunities. People's access to formal education also had a lot to do with their sex, race, economic status, place of birth, and present geographical location. If a native-born white male were middle or upper class and lived in an urban area in New England, his chances of being schooled were far greater than a female slave in the rural South or a newly arrived immigrant from Europe. Although there are exceptions to any generalization, males' education generally received more attention than females; whites' more than blacks' or Native Americans'; older immigrants' more than those recently arrived. These factors were further complicated by place of residence. Urban areas often had more schools than rural ones, but access—especially for women—was often greater in the country than in town.

This chapter focuses on developments in the education of women, blacks, and Native Americans. Progress was slow and often dependent on the other factors mentioned above—economic status and geographical location. Nevertheless, by the end of the nineteenth century, women and blacks at least had increased their access to education.

WOMEN'S EDUCATION (1620-1800)

Education for girls and women in the colonial and national periods was tailored to fit their traditional future roles as wives and mothers. Although learning the three Rs was often considered important for household recordkeeping and the early education of their offspring, little thought was given to educating them for any other purposes.

Although both sexes generally received rudimentary education, learning letters and basic reading skills were all girls could generally expect. In many cases, their further training in household arts and economy was conducted by their mothers or, in some cases, by apprenticeship. Because girls were not allowed to attend colleges, they were rarely admitted to the college preparatory Latin Grammar schools. If their parents were financially able and willing, girls might receive further formal education from a tutor.[1]

Around 1700, the growth of a prospering commercial middle class triggered the establishment of a new kind of secondary school. The "English" schools were designed to teach subjects directly useful to their pupils. While these trained boys in navigation, surveying, bookkeeping, penmanship, and accounting—skills which helped them in careers—girls were trained to be ornamental as they learned dancing, singing, musical instruments, drawing, French, and fancy kinds of needlework. These schools for girls were eventually called "finishing schools" and became popular for girls whose families could afford to send them. Learning such skills was useful in that they helped facilitate marriages with middle and upper-class men; however, they did little to prepare women for any kind of life outside the home. They were an extension into the colonies of the kind of education that Wollstonecraft criticized.

During the last decades of the 1700s, special schools for girls began to be established in greater numbers. Usually they were called seminaries. Their purposes varied. Some were for polite learning. Some were for the improvement of women who were or hoped to be teachers. In the latter case the curriculum was similar to the English department of male academies with their emphasis upon the study of modern languages, science, and practical subjects. An example of a female seminary was the school of Sarah Pierce at Litchfield, Connecticut, established in 1792. The school had a long history and some distinguished students, among them Catharine and Harriet Beecher. It was located a few doors away from the Beecher house. Catharine Beecher did not speak highly of her education there, but many other people held the school of Sarah Pierce in high esteem. The curriculum basically consisted of history, grammar, arithmetic, geography, penmanship, painting, embroidery, and music.

Pierce's school produced Catharine Beecher, but another school not usually accorded the credit it should receive for furthering women's education was run by Joseph Emerson at Byfield, Massachusetts. Emerson was a staunch advocate of women's education. Emerson's school produced two famous figures in women's education—Mary Lyon and Zilpah P. (Grant) Banister. Both were greatly influenced by Emerson: Lyon called him, "My dear Teacher! Now in Heaven."[2]

Reverend Emerson's school in 1820 enrolled about fifty or sixty students who ranged in age from "gay misses of ten to sedate, grown women." Zilpah Grant was twenty-five when she attended. There was a strong religious tone to the school. Emerson held devotional services both morning and evening. His course on mental philosophy included logic, no small advance in the usual fare of female education in his day. He also taught arithmetic, reading, spelling, and vocabulary—and how best to teach these subjects. His school provided thorough drill in English grammar. Also studied were ancient history, natural philosophy, and astronomy. Students read some of the masterpieces of English literature, especially Milton and Shakespeare, but were cautioned about them. The textbook used in the second term of mental philosophy was Duguld Stewart's work popularly referred to as "Stewart on the Mind." Emerson provided the young women with a good education.

Emma Willard (1787-1870)

Due to the work of Emerson, Pierce, and others, the way was prepared for women to take up the task of conducting female seminaries or academies providing high level education. Emma Willard was one who turned all of her efforts to improving the education of women. Emma's educational interests began at an early age, and she was able to secure a good education. She was one of ten chidlren born to Samuel Hart and Lydia Hinsdale, both of early Connecticut families. There were also seven children from Hart's first marriage. Emma attended a district school, but got more benefit from her father's reading to the family every evening. She became a voracious reader, and the village library supplied her with books of history, travel, and poetry.

BECOMING A TEACHER

Emma's own account of completing her education and becoming a teacher affords insight into the drive that made her successful:

> Near the close of my fifteenth year, a new academy was opened about three-quarters of a mile from my father's house, of which Thomas Miner, a graduate and once a tutor of Yale College, was the principal, afterwards well known as an eminent physician, president of the State Medical Society, and one of the most learned men of our country. Before the opening of the academy, my mother's children had each received a small dividend from the estate of a deceased brother. My sister Nancy determined, as

our parents approved, to spend this in being taught at the new school; but having at that time a special desire to make a visit among my married brothers and sisters in Kensington (whose children were of my own age), I stood one evening, candle in hand, and made to my parents, who had retired for the night, what they considered a most sensible oration, on the folly of people's seeking to be educated above their means and prescribed duties in life. So Nancy went to school, and I to Kensington. A fortnight after, one Friday evening, I returned. Nancy showed me her books and told me of her lessons. 'Mother,' said I, 'I am going to school to-morrow.' 'Why, I thought you had made up your mind not to be educated, and besides, your clothes are not in order and it will appear odd for you to enter school Saturday.' But Saturday morning I went, and received my lessons in Webster's Grammar and Morse's Geography.

Mr. Miner was to hear me recite by myself until I overtook the class, in which were a dozen fine girls, including my elder sister. Monday, Mr. Miner called on me to recite. He began with Webster's Grammar, went on and on, and still as he questioned received from me a ready answer, until he said, 'I will hear the remainder of your lesson to-morrow.' The same thing occurred with the Georgraphy lesson. I was pleased, and thought, 'you never shall get to the end of my lesson.' That hard chapter on the planets, with their diameters, distances, and periodic revolutions, was among the first of Morse's Geography. The evening I wished to learn it, my sister Lydia had a party. The house was full of bustle, and above all rose the song-singing, which always fascinated me. The moon was at the full, and snow was on the ground. I wrapt my cloak around me, and out of doors of a cold winter evening, seated on a horseblock, I learned that lesson. Lessons so learnt are not easily forgotten. The third day Mr. Miner admitted me to my sister's class. He used to require daily compositions. I never failed, the only one of my class who did not; but I also improved the opportunities which these afforded, to pay him off for any criticism by which he had (intentionally though indirectly) hit me,—with some parody or rhyme, at which, though sometimes pointed enough, Mr. Miner would heartily laugh,—never forgetting, however, at some time or other, to retort with interest. Thus my mind was stimulated, and my progress rapid. For two successive years, 1802-3, I enjoyed the advantages of Dr. Miner's school, and I believe that no better instruction was given to girls in any school, at that time, in our country.

My life at this time was much influenced by an attachment I formed with Mrs. Peck, a lady of forty, although I was only fifteen. When we were first thrown together, it was for several days, and she treated me not as a child, but an equal—confiding to me much of that secret history which every heart sacredly cherishes; and I, on my part, opened to her my whole inner life, my secret feelings, anxieties and aspirations. Early in the spring of 1804, when I had just passed seventeen, Mrs. Peck proposed that a children's school in the village should be put into my hands. The schoolhouse was situated in Worthington street, on the great Hartford and New Haven turnpike; and was surrounded on the other three sides by a mulberry grove, towards which the windows were in summer kept open.

At nine o'clock, on that first morning, I seated myself among the children to begin a profession which I little thought was to last with slight interruption for forty years. That morning was the longest of my life. I began my work by trying to discover the several capacities and degrees of advancement of the children, so as to arrange them in classes; but they having been, under my predecessor, accustomed to the greatest license, would, at their option, go to the street door to look at a passing carriage, or stepping on to a bench in the rear, dash out of a window, and take a lively turn in the mulberry grove. Talking did no good. Reasoning and pathetic appeals were alike unavailing. Thus the morning slowly wore away. At noon I explained this first great perplexity of my teacher-life to my friend Mrs. Peck, who decidedly advised sound and summary chastisement. 'I cannot,'' I replied; 'I never struck a child in my life.' 'It is,' she said, 'the only way, and you must.' I left her for the afternoon school with a heavy heart, still hoping I might find some way of avoiding what I could not deliberately resolve to do.

I found the school a scene of uproar and confusion, which I vainly endeavored to quell. Just then, Jesse Peck, my friend's little son, entered with a bundle of five nice rods. As he laid them on the table before me, my courage rose; and, in the temporary silence which ensued, I laid down a few laws, the breaking of which would be followed with immediate chastisement. For a few moments the children were silent; but they had been used to threatening, and soon a boy rose from his seat, and, as he was stepping to the door, I took one of the sticks and gave him a moderate flogging; then with a grip upon his arm which made him feel that I was in earnest, put him into his seat. Hoping to make this chastisement answer for the whole school, I then told them in the most endearing manner I could command, that I was there to do them good—to make them such fine boys and girls that their parents and friends would be delighted with them, and they be growing up happy and useful; but in order to this I must and would have their obedience. If I had occasion to punish again it would be more and more severely, until they yielded, and were trying to be good. But the children still lacked faith in my words, and if my recollection serves me, I spent most of the afternoon in alternate whippings and exhortations, the former always increasing in intensity, until at last, finding the difference between capricious anger amd steadfast determination, they submitted. This was the first and last of corporal punishment in that school. The next morning, and ever after, I had docile and orderly scholars. I was careful duly to send them out for recreation, to make their studies pleasant and interesting, and to praise them when they did well, and mention to their parents their good behavior.[3]

For the next few years, Emma alternately taught and attended female seminaries in Hartford. In 1807 she became an assistant teacher in an academy at Westfield, Massachusetts. After a year, she accepted the headship of a female school in Middlebury, Vermont. The school was successful at first, but Emma ran into difficulty over denominational politics. She married a physician there, Dr. John Willard, who was politically well connected. Until his death several years later, he was her companion and supporter in advocating the cause of women's education. In 1814 Mrs. Willard opened the Middlebury Female Academy.

Willard was a tireless worker in the cause of women's education and was held in high esteem by other educators. At one point she traveled some eight thousand miles lecturing on women's education. A member of many educational associations, she contributed to the improvement of women's education by this means and also through her numerous publications. Some of her more important works were A *Plan for Improving Female Education* (1819), *History of The United States* (1828), *Universal History* (1837), and *Ancient History* (1847). Together with William C. Woodbridge she published a school geography.

Willard was convinced that public support was necessary for the orderly development of women's education and that it was in the interest of society to provide the needed money. She believed that the education of men and women should differ. Women, she held, needed special training because of their role as mothers and the great influence they exerted in child rearing. She recommended boarding schools as a means of protecting and guiding young women. Her position in regard to women and their relationship to men was not that of the modern feminist. She held that women must be "good wives, good mothers, or good mistresses of families: and if they are none of these, they must be bad members of society." Women must be obedient to men. Only education could save women from frivolous, wasteful pursuits. By education, girls would be guided to intellectual goals and proper values. They, in turn, would pass these on to their children, ensuring the continuance of the republican form of government and society.

THE PLAN

The New York state legislature invited Willard to present her *Plan for Improving Female Education* in 1819. Here is what she told the legislators:

Studies and employments should . . . be selected from one or both of the following considerations; either because they are peculiarly fitted to improve the faculties; or, because they are such as the pupil will most probably have occasion to practice in future life. These are the principles on which systems of male education are founded, but female education has not yet been systematized. Chance and confusion reign here.

Education should seek to bring its subjects to the perfection of their moral, intellectual and physical nature; in order that they may be of the greatest possible use to themselves and others: or, to use a different expression, that they may be the means of the greatest possible happiness of which they are capable, both as to what they enjoy and what they communicate. Those youth have the surest chance of enjoying and communicating happiness, who are best qualified, both by internal dispositions and external habits, to perform with readiness those duties which their future life will most probably give them occasion to practice.

Not only has there been a want of system concerning female education, but much of what has been done has proceeded upon mistaken principles. One of these is, that without a regard to the different periods of life proportionate to their importance, the education of females has been too exclusively directed to fit them for displaying to advantage the charms of youth and beauty. Though it may be proper to adorn this period of life, yet it is incomparably more important to prepare for the serious duties of maturer years. Though well to decorate the blossom, it is far better to prepare for the harvest. In the vegetable creation nature seems but to sport when she embellishes the flower, while all her serious cares are directed to perfect the fruit.

Another error is, that it has been made the first object in educating our sex, to prepare them to please the other. But reason and religion teach that we too are primary existences, that it is for us to move in the orbit of our duty around the Holy Center of perfection, the companions, not the satellites of men; else, instead of shedding around us an influence, that may help to keep them in their proper course, we must accompany them in their wildest deviations.

I would not be understood to insinuate that we are not in particular situations to yield obedience to the other sex. Submission and obedience belong to every being in the universe, except the great Master of the whole. Nor is it a degrading peculiarity to our sex to be under human authority. Whenever one class of human beings derive from another the benefits of support and protection, they must pay its equivalent obedience. Thus, while we receive these benefits from our parents, we are all, without distinction of sex, under their authority; when we receive them from the government of our country, we must obey our rulers; and when our sex take the obligations of marriage, and receive protection and support from the other, it is reasonable that we too should yield obedience. Yet is neither the child, nor the subject, nor the wife, under human authority, but in subservience to the divine. Our highest responsibility is to God, and our highest interest is to please him; therefore, to secure this interest, should our education be directed.

Neither would I be understood to mean, that our sex should not seek to make themselves agreeable to the other. The error complained of is, that the taste of men, whatever it might happen to be, has been made a standard for the formation of the female character. In whatever we do, it is of the utmost importance that the rule by which we work be perfect. For if otherwise, what is it but to err upon principle? A system of education which leads one class of human beings to consider the approbation of another as their highest object, teaches that the rule of their conduct should be the will of beings imperfect and erring like themselves, rather than the will of God, which is the only standard of perfection.[4]

The response was favorable, but the legislators did not offer any money.

Willard turned to the city of Troy, New York. They bought her a building and offered financial aid until the school was on a self-supporting basis. It opened in 1821. Her school at Troy added several courses that were not usual for women: algebra, geometry, history, geography, and natural philosophy (botany). Her sister, Almira Lincoln Phelps, wrote popular texts in botany, history, and geography.

Willard was principal of the Troy Female Seminary for seventeen years. The school became an important center for training teachers. Women who intended to become teachers but could not afford the tuition received loans to be repaid after they were employed. More than two hundred teachers graduated from Emma Willard's school before tax funded normal schools were established. Some believed it was "the highest recommendation for a teaching position that the country offered."[5] Willard traveled widely in Europe and America studying educational conditions. She was superintendent of schools in Kensington, Connecticut in 1840—probably the first woman to be elected to such a position. She turned over the Troy seminary to her son and his wife in 1838. She married Christopher Yates that year, but divorced him in 1843. The Troy seminary was renamed the Emma Willard School in 1910.

Emma Willard was one of a growing number of women who became active in teaching in the nineteenth century. As the country's population increased and moved west, sentiment for women's education increased. Attitudes on the frontier tended to favor useful, rather than ornamental or liberal, education. And the necessity of separating boys and girls in schools seemed less and less practical. In the East, more conventional beliefs prevailed. The development of what we would now call women's higher education followed a parallel rather than integrated track with that for men. One of the significant people in that process was Mary Lyon.

Mary Mason Lyon (1797-1849)

Mary Lyon was born in rural Massachusetts and spent much of her youth attending one-room schools and keeping house for an older brother. Her father died when she was young. At fourteen, she became a teacher. She was paid seventy-five cents a week and was "boarded round," a custom of having the teacher live short periods in each student's home. This practice was cheaper than paying a salary sufficient to allow a teacher to maintain a place of her own, and it also let the community keep tabs on the teacher's conduct. It also allowed the teacher to know her pupils well. In 1817 Lyon enrolled for the first time for advanced training at a nearby seminary. Over the next decade she alternated teaching with periods of dedicated study at various academies. These years increased her self-confidence and sophistication and helped her make friends who would play important roles in her future academy's development. One of these was Zilpah P. (Grant) Banister in whose Ipswich Female Academy Lyon worked as an assistant teacher from 1828-1834.[6]

FOUNDING A SEMINARY

The years of study and teaching gave Lyon several convictions which later made her seminary unique. She wished to ease for other women the difficulty she experienced in scrimping to accumulate tuition money. Accordingly, she decided that her students would do as much domestic work around the seminary as possible so the costs of attending would be low. Furthermore, teachers were expected to accept modest salaries as their contribution to low-cost education. She also learned that most women's schools were short-lived, usually closing because of insufficient endowment. Consequently, she resolved not to establish a seminary until it could be financed soundly. She also decided that middle-class women were the most appropriate students for her skill. "This middle class contains the main spring, and main wheel, which are to move the world," she wrote.[7] Indeed, Lyon wanted to move the world. She resolved that graduates of her school would not be parlor ornaments but servants to humanity.

In 1834 Lyon took the first steps in making her dreams of a women's school a reality. She outlined her idea in a pamphlet which circulated among the many friends she had made through her teaching. A committee, mostly composed of ministers, sought financial backing for the school. Believing that a women's school would encounter less opposition if men obtained funds, Lyon tried somewhat unsuccessfully to stay in the background. Money trickled in—from homemakers, students, businessmen, and parents who hoped to send their daughters to the school. Lyon insisted on a New England location, and eventually chose the town of South Hadley in western Massachusetts because it agreed to contribute $8,000 of the $20,000 needed to open the school. The community probably thought that having a well established school would add to the town's prestige, provide better education for local women, and improve the town's economy. The school was named Mount Holyoke Female Seminary after a nearby landmark. Ground was broken for the first building in 1836, and classes began the next year.

Student life at Mount Holyoke was a combination of rather conventional educational practices of the day and some new experiments. The result was one of the most successful women's schools in New England. Its first student body, chosen from twice as many applicants as available spaces, numbered eighty. In just a decade after additional campus construction the enrollment nearly tripled. Mary Lyon's educational philosophy shaped and permeated the institution's growth.

A student today would likely be overwhelmed by the religious emphasis of Mount Holyoke, but in this regard the seminary differed little from its contemporaries. Lyon had maintained that the school's "brightest, most decided feature will be, that it is a school for Christ."[8] This purpose was carried out not only in the mandatory religion classes for seniors that Lyon herself taught but also in revival sessions, prayer meetings, fast days, and missionary gatherings. Each student had to classify herself as to her state of religious grace, and those "without hope" were given special attention. It is not surprising that a number of Holyoke alumnae married missionaries trained at nearby Amherst College. Others became missionaries themselves, or volunteered for teaching assignments on the American frontier.

LIFE AT HOLYOKE

Another characteristic that Mount Holyoke shared with its contemporaries was the number and extent of rules regulating student life. By 1839 the rules numbered 106, and some students found them tedious. There were safety rules regarding the use of the Franklin stove and sperm oil lamps found in every room. Other rules about running, talking, hours of rising and retiring, and tardiness were designed to develop responsible and ladylike students.

The idea of *in loco parentis,* that the school should function in place of the parent, accounted for strict behavior codes, which students sometimes resented. Lyon herself believed strongly in this concept. She preferred to think of Mount Holyoke as a large family and hoped to give the school a homelike atmosphere. Lyon herself, occasionally referred to as a "mother superior," had dynamic energy and a charismatic personality that helped soften the hard edges of the behavior code.

With so many regulations it may not be surprising to learn that turnover at Mount Holyoke was high, but again this characteristic was common to most schools. Only a third of the student body returned from year to year, and only 10 percent graduated from the three-year course. Although some students were expelled and others may have left because they were unhappy, the most common reasons given were impaired health, insufficient money, matrimony, and complications at home. Because any training at a school so advanced as Mount Holyoke made a woman highly educated by contemporary standards, many women probably considered one year to be sufficient.

Despite its religious emphasis, rules, and high turnover, it would be impossible to dismiss Mount Holyoke as just another female seminary. Its attitude toward academics differed radically from most women's finishing schools. Lyon sought earnest students who had already proven themselves and who wanted to further their training. Preference was given to women who had already been teachers and who were older than sixteen. Prerequisites included knowledge of grammar, geography, American history, arithmetic, and philosophy. The "juniors," as the first year students were called, studied rhetoric, ancient geography, world history, political science, geometry, and physiology. The second year students, the "middle" class, continued grammar and added botany, algebra, natural history, and philosophy. The seniors studied chemistry (taught by Lyon herself), astronomy, geology, church history, religion, logic, and rhetoric. The curriculum of the seminary most definitely resembled contemporary college courses of study in its emphasis on religion during the senior year. Unlike most colleges, however, it did not require Greek or Latin. The former was not offered at all, and the latter was only an elective. Overall the curriculum was far more academic than that of the typical female seminary of the day. The faculty was composed almost entirely of women educated at other seminaries. Women had been excluded from degree granting colleges prior to 1836, so the absence of college educated faculty is not surprising.

Lyon's philosophy of women's education did not exclude the development of ladylike arts and behaviors, but she felt that these were secondary. Cultivating ornamental branches of knowledge like singing and drawing before mastering academics, she wrote, was "like polishing cork or sponge, instead of marble." Her desire to turn out responsible, religious women manifested itself in an emphasis on simple food and dress and the cultivation of virtues like order, punctuality, health, and economy.

Lyon fulfilled her dream of providing a quality education at low cost. One reason for her success was Mount Holyoke's domestic system in which students and teachers cared for their own needs. She felt also that the system helped develop character. Unlike Emma Willard and Catharine Beecher, both of whom thought that teaching the domestic arts was a proper function of a woman's school, Lyon maintained that household skills were a responsibility of the family, not the school. Divided into circles with a leader, students were assigned work they had learned in their own homes like cooking, baking, making fires, and setting tables. They spent about an hour a day on such tasks, except on Monday. That day, strangely titled recreation day, began at 3:00 A.M. with fires being lighted in the laundry room. The day included thorough cleaning of rooms, scrubbing floors, washing and mending clothes, and the writing of a weekly composition.

Life at Mount Holyoke was not all work. Students were required to walk at least a mile a day, and visits to nearby Amherst College were common. However, students were carefully chaperoned and were not allowed to dance. Students read for self-improvement, but Lyon discouraged novel reading as injurious. Baskets of treats often arrived from homes and provided occasions to be celebrated. Fads in the early years of Mount Holyoke included valentines, phrenology, and autograph books.

Mary Lyon and her school were the subjects of some derogatory comments. The press called it a "rib factory" and a "protestant nunnery," but Lyon had overcome great obstacles in the past and such comments did not discourage her. As one writer said, "It was called unnatural, unphilosophical, unscriptural, unpractical, and impracticable, unfeminine, and anti-Christian."[9] That last catalog of epithets is a list of all the familiar prejudices against women at that time. Critics of academic education for women said it would warp their minds and personalities, make them unfeminine, and was against religion and nature. Furthermore, it was not likely to work. Not everyone held to these views, however, and the dire predictions of failure proved unfounded. Mary Lyon, Mount Holyoke, and women's education prospered.

By the time Mary Lyon died in 1849, Mount Holyoke had gained a national reputation. Lyon had been consulted by many other educators wishing to establish schools, and Mount Holyoke itself served as a model for similar schools in Ohio and California.

WOMEN'S COLLEGES

By 1850 the idea of providing women higher education did not seem so bizarre as it had when Mary Lyon, Emma Willard, and Catharine Beecher pioneered in the 1820s and 1830s. Women were rapidly replacing men as teachers in elementary and sometimes secondary schools. The need for better educated teachers made more advanced women's schooling plausible. The idea that better educated women made more effective and morally influential wives and mothers was gaining popularity. With slavery drawing increasing attention to the idea of equal rights for everyone, some people began to think that even women might have rights—like the right to a higher education.

The effects of these new thoughts on women's education were felt first in the West and gradually drifted eastward. Oberlin College in Ohio was the first to admit women to its college program in 1837. It had admitted blacks at its founding four years earlier. Antioch College, also in Ohio, began to admit women in 1853 when Horace Mann became its president. The University of Iowa, created by the state's constitution in 1846, admitted women when it opened. With tradition and sex stereotyping less apparent on the frontier than on the

Atlantic seaboard, coeducation became the norm in the West. In the East, however, women's higher education continued its separate course.

Easterners preferred the idea of a college entirely for women. A generous endowment from Matthew Vassar in 1861 was the basis for the establishment of Vassar College in Poughkeepsie, New York. A decade later Wellesley College was established. In their earliest years standards were similar to Mount Holyoke's. Smith opened its doors with fourteen students in 1875. Harvard began an "Annex" for women in 1879; it took its own name, Radcliffe, in 1894 when it received the power to grant degrees. Bryn Mawr in Pennsylvania opened in 1885. By then it was becoming common for women's colleges to have entry requirements that were identical to those in the long established male institutions.

Although none of these schools was an immediate threat to Mount Holyoke, they stimulated the older institution to self-assessment. In many ways, the seminary had kept up with the times. The three year program had been expanded to four in 1861. With the installation of bathrooms, steam heating, and gas lighting, student living had become more comfortable. New academic buildings, several library expansions, stiffer admission and graduation requirements, and more guest lecturers had improved the academic program. Although rules were still stringent, student life now included some social activism and national issues, a student newspaper, and the establishment of a branch of the Women's Christian Temperance Union. The school drew students from other countries as well as from nearly every state. It had produced such well-known alumnae as the poet Emily Dickinson, Louisa M. Torrey (the mother of William Howard Taft), and the feminist Lucy Stone.

Despite these accomplishments, some unease persisted. As the nineteenth century had worn on, the term *seminary* had come to be applied only to women's schools, and therefore began to suggest a second-class status. Being graduated from a college seemed a lot more prestigious than being a seminary graduate. At Mount Holyoke's semicentennial in 1886 the issue of changing its name was hotly discussed. Although some wanted to rename the institution Mary Lyon College, Mount Holyoke Seminary and College was the choice. A bill making the change passed the Massachusetts legislature unanimously in 1888, and the new college was authorized to grant both bachelor of art and bachelor of science degrees. It immediately raised its entrance requirements and revamped its curriculum. The college proved so popular that the seminary was discontinued in 1893, and its name was simply shortened to Mount Holyoke College.

GRADUATE EDUCATION

Women's admission to schooling beyond the baccalaureate degree became an increasing problem as the nineteenth century progressed. As graduate and professional schools sprang up, hardly anyone thought of admitting women. The famous 1848 women's rights conference at Seneca Falls, New York, pointed out the absence of women in medicine, law, and theology in its listing of wrongs to American women, but few steps were taken to correct this injustice until late in the century.

Two contrasting trends in the century contributed to the concern over women's post-baccalaureate education and access to the professions. Restricting women was the growing popularity of the idea of women as creatures too frail and pure to be sullied by the nation's seamy problems. It was all right to be a teacher of young children and youth—a morally uplifting task—but to aspire to teach college age students, to practice law or medicine, or to preach was an outrage against female nature. Simultaneously, women's work as teachers, as activists in the abolitionist and other social reform movements, and as volunteers in various kinds of church and missionary activities had given them a keener sense of social ills and injustices. Heightened consciousness stimulated a desire for new avenues for service and careers.

As what we now call graduate education developed in the nineteenth century, the most prestigious institutions refused admission to women. Several factors accounted for this reluctance. Because attending graduate school was so far removed from what was considered women's proper role, few thought that women might seek admission and fewer still thought graduate work would be appropriate for them. Another problem was women's preparation; often the academic training offered in women's colleges or the separate curriculum designed for them in coeducational schools was defined as inadequate preparation for graduate work. Finally, many of the women who were qualified to do graduate work had little incentive for doing so. Members of the middle or upper classes did not usually train for independent careers. Poor women had difficulty in obtaining the necessary skills.

As always, of course, there were exceptions to these generalizations. Some women developed scholarly expertise at home like Maria Mitchell, astronomer and later professor at Vassar. Other women, like Martha Carey Thomas, earned their degrees in Europe. The University of Iowa offered graduate admission to women by 1860. The Iowa State Agricultural College (now Iowa State University) admitted women and men to graduate study from its opening in 1869. The University of Pennsylvania offered women graduate admission in 1882. The first female graduate students helped ease the way for others. Thomas became the dean and later the president of Bryn Mawr, a new women's college established in Baltimore by Pennsylvania Quakers. Under her influence it became the first women's college to offer graduate work and fellowships to women. Other universities followed in the 1890s. When the University of Chicago first opened its doors in 1892, it offered graduate work to both sexes. Others did the same: Columbia (1890), Brown (1891), Yale (1891), Harvard (1894), and Johns Hopkins (1907).

What could a woman do with advanced training? She was most likely to be hired by a women's college or in a smaller school. Fearing that women on a faculty would lower prestige, the nation's most outstanding male or coeducational colleges were reluctant to hire them. The problems of lower salaries and rank and fewer promotions faced women as well and have not completely disappeared today. Nevertheless, the growth of the nation's higher education was so rapid that employment in higher education was available to women who sought it.

PROFESSIONAL TRAINING·

Throughout much of the nineteenth century advanced schooling was not essential for a professional career; a person was considered competently trained for a career by assisting a practicing doctor or lawyer. There had always been theological schools, but many ministers, especially in evangelical sects, were simply ordained as ministers by their congregations.

Women who wished to practice law had two admissions hurdles to overcome: being admitted to a law school and later being admitted to the bar. The first was far easier than the second. Law schools developed somewhat more slowly than medical schools and, except for the most prestigious ones, were sometimes short of students. Being new institutions, they were not so encrusted with decades of tradition. These factors facilitated women's admission. The law school of Washington University of St. Louis admitted both sexes when it opened in 1867 and graduated its first woman four years later. By 1900 most law schools admitted women, but the holdouts included Harvard, Yale, Columbia, Washington and Lee, and the University of Virginia.

After securing a legal education either through law school or an internship, a person had to get admitted to the bar before setting up practice. Women found a sizeable amount of prejudice against such admission. It was argued that the contracts a married woman lawyer made would not be binding, that having women lawyers would conflict with common law, and that licensing women would also be to agree that they could serve as sheriffs, judges, and governors. It was even suggested that women might be an unpredictable influence on the administration of justice. Finally, there was the old saw about women being too delicate to endanger themselves with legal matters.

Because each state supreme court decided who it would license to practice law, the time of women's admission varied from state to state. Myra Bradwell of Illinois was the first to be admitted. Denied a license by the court in 1872, Bradwell was admitted the following year after the Illinois legislature passed a law that no one could be denied participation in any occupation except the military on account of sex. Women were admitted to the bar in several other states by a similar procedure. The first woman to be admitted to the bar of the United States Supreme Court was Belva Lockwood in 1879. Many early female lawyers worked within the legal industry rather than practicing law directly. Bradwell, for example, founded and edited the *Chicago Legal News*.

Establishing "firsts" in theological education and ordination is somewhat difficult because various levels of education and many denominations are involved. One name stands out, however: Antoinette Brown (Blackwell), sister-in-law of the Blackwell sisters discussed later. Brown was the first woman to complete the undergraduate theological course at Oberlin College in 1851 and was ordained two years later as a Congregational minister. She was probably not the first American woman minister if the Quakers are considered. Believing in the equality of all people and having no paid ministry, the Quakers encouraged women's participation in all spheres of religious life including public preaching.

Most denominations were not so egalitarian in their thinking as the Quakers were, and often women were barred from ordination by the Biblical injunction about women's keeping silent in the church. This prohibition also slowed women's admission to postgraduate theological seminaries; the first of these to admit women was the Hartford Theological Seminary in 1889.

As in other professions, both medical education and its practice presented difficulties to aspiring women. They had to struggle for admission to medical colleges and to clinical instruction, and often faced prejudice from male medical colleagues and the population they wished to serve.

Opinion about the suitability of medical education for women was divided. On the one hand, it was argued that medical education for women was a natural extension of their roles as moral guardians and homemakers. Who more than a mother would wish to guard a person's health? This was opposed on the other hand by the stereotype of female delicacy. Surely a physician's work was too arduous and coarse for a woman to be mixed up in it, though perhaps a woman could suitably aspire to be a nurse or other health care worker. This view prevailed throughout much of the nineteenth century.

The first medical school to admit women, Geneva College in central New York state, did so in 1847 when the faculty let the students vote whether to admit a female applicant, Elizabeth Blackwell. Thinking that her application was a joke from a rival school, they accepted it and then ostracized Blackwell when she actually registered for classes. She graduated with honors two years later. Despite her outstanding record, Geneva refused to admit her sister in 1851.

The reluctance of medical schools to admit women forced the development of medical schools solely for women. One was begun in Boston in 1848 and another in Philadelphia in 1850. Elizabeth Blackwell established another in 1868 in New York City with higher standards than the previous two. Other schools sprang up in Illinois and Ohio. Gradually major universities opened their medical schools to women. The Universities of Iowa and Michigan were early leaders. When Johns Hopkins, one of the most prestigious medical schools in the country, admitted women in 1893, others soon followed. However, many schools screened women's applications far more rigorously than men's.

A significant part of medical training involved clinical experiences and hospitals were reluctant to allow women to train. Part of this unwillingness stemmed from a fear of patients' reactions to female doctors. Another element was the hostility of the medical staff and other residents. Tension was so intense at first that several of the women's medical colleges had to open their own hospitals or dispensaries to give their students clinical experience. Some early female doctors went to Europe for further training. As major medical schools admitted women, however, access to hospital experience grew easier.

Women's success in being admitted to medical societies was similar. As late as 1859 prejudice against women was still so strong that the Philadelphia County Medical Society resolved that any member who consulted a female doctor would lose his membership. As the number of women doctors increased and no calamities resulted from their work, barriers to membership in professional societies fell.

Elizabeth Blackwell (1821-1910)
Emily Blackwell (1826-1910)

Despite the hostility of many male professionals to sharing their occupations with female colleagues, there were some men who encouraged women's achievements. Examples of those can be seen in the biographies of two extraordinary women, Elizabeth and Emily Blackwell. First within their family and later within their circle of friends and the medical establishment, men encouraged them to use their potential and develop medical careers.

Elizabeth and Emily were among the twelve children born to Samuel and Hannah Blackwell of Bristol, England. Their father, a sugar refiner, was a dissenter from the Church of England and an activist in reform movements like abolition, temperance, and women's rights. His religion barred his children from public schools, so they were all educated by private tutors who taught the same curriculum to both sexes. Their mother was supportive of her husband's reforms and her children's careers. In 1832 the family moved to New York and later to Ohio. Among their new American friends were Quakers who helped Blackwell get established in business—the abolitionist William Lloyd Garrison, minister Henry Ward Beecher, and his sister Harriet Beecher Stowe. This familial and social environment produced remarkable children. Besides Elizabeth and Emily, one sister became a newspaper correspondent and another an author and artist. Brothers Samuel and Henry, also reformers, married respectively Antoinette Brown, the first American woman minister, and Lucy Stone, a crusader for abolition and women's rights.[10]

Exposed to role models like their father and family friends, the Blackwell sisters were well educated and progressive thinkers. After their father's death in 1836, both of them taught school to help support the family and to earn money for their medical education. Elizabeth's motivations to be a physician apparently stemmed from her desire to promote moral reform and to diminish the likelihood of marriage. Emily, however, had had a natural inclination toward science and nature since childhood and found medicine an obvious outlet for her interests. She was also influenced by Elizabeth's example.

MEDICAL EDUCATION

Elizabeth first studied medicine with two physicians in the Carolinas while teaching school. She continued her studies with two Quaker physicians in Philadelphia as she began applying to medical schools. She was rejected by every medical school in Philadelphia and New York City as well as by Bowdoin, Harvard, and Yale before she was accepted by Geneva in 1847. During the summer of 1848 she was unexpectedly admitted to do clinical work at Philadelphia Hospital and gained knowledge that helped her write a dissertation on typhus among Irish immigrants. Her experience helped her realize the importance of hygiene and sanitation which remained a major part of her medical philosophy throughout her career. After graduating from Geneva in 1849, Elizabeth continued her clinical training in France and England. She returned to New York City two years later.

Emily also faced difficulty being admitted to medical school. She was finally accepted by Rush Medical College in Chicago in 1852 only to be forced out a year later when the Illinois Medical Society censored Rush for admitting a woman. She completed her medical studies at Western Reserve in Cleveland in 1854. She then studied in Scotland and later as a physician's aide was admitted to clinical work in Germany.

Elizabeth had great difficulty setting up practice when the city's physicians barred her from established clinics and hospitals. She gave a few lectures on hygiene and attracted the attention of some Quaker women who brought her patients. By 1853 she was able to open a part-time clinic in a tenement district and four years later expanded it into the New York Infirmary for Women and Children. It still exists. By the mid-1850s Elizabeth was not so terribly alone as she had been a few years earlier. She had adopted a daughter in 1854, and Emily and another woman physician joined her practice. Emily became the infirmary's chief administrator and surgeon and also helped win for it a small amount of state funding. The infirmary soon gained the support of some of the city's male physicians, and both the *New York Tribune* and the *New York Times* encouraged its growth in their columns.

Elizabeth took on new responsibilities in the 1860s. She helped select and train nurses for the Union during the Civil War. In 1868 she established a Woman's Medical College associated with the infirmary. Among its innovations were entrance examinations, a three-year course (instead of the customary one or two years), and longer academic terms. The college continued until the Cornell Medical School began to admit women in 1899.

Although she had become a naturalized American citizen in 1849, Elizabeth had remained attached to England. She returned there in 1870, setting up practice in London and serving briefly as a professor of gynecology at the London School of Medicine for Women. Although poor health forced her early retirement, Elizabeth continued to write essays and to lecture occasionally. She died in 1910.

Emily remained in the United States and continued the expansion of New York Infirmary. She began courses for nurses in 1858 and increased the program over the years. In 1866 she began a home social service, the first medical social service in the country. In 1871, fifteen years after she had begun her practice, she was invited to join the New York County Medical Society. She served as dean of the infirmary's medical school and as professor of obstetrics and gynecology for thirty years. Retiring in 1900, she died ten years later just a few months after her sister.

AMERICAN INDIAN EDUCATION

Emily and Elizabeth Blackwell were the exceptions as far as women's higher education was concerned. For women fortunate enough to be white and to have sufficient funds to attend college, schools such as Mount Holyoke provided opportunities unavailable to their predecessors. However, not everyone had those advantages. Native Americans, for example, had a far less happy and successful history of education in the nineteenth century.

Educators like to think of their profession as one that increases people's opportunities to live a better life. When nineteenth century American Indian education as administered by whites is examined, this assumption is questionable. The history of the schooling of American Indians is a sorry tale. Good intentions were skewed by cultural blindness, political machinations, and greed. When Europeans began coming to North America, there were several hundred different Indian tribes and many languages. Without formal schools Indians had obviously educated their children successfully. For generations, they had passed on the skills needed for survival and for preserving their values and their heritage. Although with so many tribes it is hard to generalize, methods commonly used for this education included the emulation of adults, public praise and recognition, oral recitation, and occasionally ridicule. Indian values included cooperation and loyalty to family and tribe; these clashed with nineteenth century American ideals of rugged individualism and competition.

Shortly after Europeans began to settle in North America, they sought to "civilize" the Indians and educate them according to their own standards. Both Spanish and French missionaries were involved in Indian education before the English King James decreed in 1617 a mission to do the same. Dartmouth, Harvard, and William and Mary all made provisions for Indian education in the colonial period.

England and later the United States considered each tribe as a sovereign nation and negotiated treaties with them as settlers moved westward. Usually such documents contained clauses about providing schooling and health services, but they also contained a clause nullifying these provisions if there were tribal opposition. This latter clause was generally cited when the government's failure to provide health and educational services was questioned.

Before the Civil War, efforts to educate the Indians in European ways were jointly made by religious groups and the government. The goal of this education was to Christianize and civilize the Indians, and few attempts were ever made to incorporate Indian culture. The Indian Civilization Act of 1819 appropriated a total of $10,000 for Indian education, and federal contracts were let with missionary societies to operate Indian schools. Despite the constitutional violation of separation of church and state, these contractual arrangements lasted until 1873.

With the increasing numbers of settlers moving West after the Civil War, the "Indian problem" became more acute. Indians were increasingly pushed onto reservations, and traditionally nomadic Indians were given barren land for farming. Supplies and equipment for reservations were scarce, and schooling available only to a few. Some federal legislators, fearful that education would allow Indians to compete more succcessfully with whites, were reluctant to appropriate more funds. In 1887 the Dawes Severalty Act stripped 41 million acres from the Indians by converting many reservations into individually owned plots of 40, 80, or 160 acres. The Indians, however, could not sell these allotments for twenty-five years. The "surplus" land on these reservations was then sold to settlers and the funds used for Indian education and civilization.

The kinds of schooling offered to the Indians were obviously diverse. Some schools were run by missionaries with a sectarian purpose. As frontier areas were designated as safe, old army forts were transformed into schools and run by the Bureau of Indian Affairs (BIA). Many Indian schools were on reservations. Often short of supplies, they were run by teachers, usually white, appointed by the BIA. A sizeable number of educators, however, believed that Indians were best educated in boarding schools. They thought that Indian children would learn best by being away from their families and tribes. Here they could be forced to speak English sometimes under the threat of corporal punishment, forbidden to practice their native religion, and boarded with white families during vacations. There were numerous instances of Indian children being forcibly removed or tricked from their homes without their parents' consent. After such an education, these children did not fit well into tribal life and were often also barred from white society by prejudice. The most famous of the boarding establishments was the Carlisle Indian School in Pennsylvania. Founded by Richard Henry Pratt in 1879, it was closed in 1918. Subjects covered in Indian schools were typical of the day; few attempts were ever made to integrate Indian culture or language into the curriculum. After the Civil War, emphasis was placed on developing Indians' occupational skills, with agriculture and homemaking being the most common.[11]

Sarah Winnemucca (1844-1891)

One Indian who bridged the gap between the Indian and white worlds was Sarah Winnemucca. A daughter of a Paiute chief and granddaughter of the Indian who accompanied Fremont into California, Winnemucca learned English by working in the home of an Army officer. At sixteen she and her sister were enrolled in a California convent school but had to withdraw after white parents objected to their presence. They returned to their home in Nevada, and Winnemucca worked as a domestic while trying to continue her education alone. Although she spent part of her small earnings on books, she never read at a level that satisfied her.[12]

Winnemucca spent a large portion of her adult life working as a translator and spokesperson between the Paiutes and whites. Her dealings with both the military and BIA agents convinced her that the former was far more dependable and trustworthy. By speaking out on numerous occasions against fraud, political appointments of unqualified agents, and misuse of Indian land and labor, she became the object of a BIA investigation that sought to discredit her. However, her experience with the military and her public speaking tours first in California and later in the East made her friends who staunchly defended her against attack. She met twice with United States President Rutherford B. Hayes to plead for better treatment for the Paiutes.

Winnemucca had worked briefly as a teacher's aide in 1875, and her 1883 speaking tour in the East renewed her early interest in education. In Boston, she became good friends with Mary Tyler Mann, the widow of the famous Horace Mann, and Elizabeth Palmer Peabody, a pioneer in American kindergarten education. She completed a book, *Life Among the Paiutes: Their Wrongs and Claims*, which Mary Mann edited. With proceeds from its sale and additional funds collected by Peabody, Winnemucca wished to start a school for Paiute children; however, at the site she originally chose the teaching position was given to the local BIA agent's wife. Her own school was finally founded in 1886 on her brother's farm. In addition to teaching academics, Winnemucca advocated Indian-controlled education and Indians' right to run their own lives. A visitor to the school wrote Peabody that the school was well run despite extraordinary obstacles that settlers had placed in Winnemucca's way. Neither Peabody nor Winnemucca was able to raise enough money to keep the school running after 1887. Winnemucca also was in poor health; she worked again as a domestic and died worn out in 1891.

It would be satisfying to end this brief survey by reporting that Indian education was transformed in the current century, but that did not happen. Although most Indian children today attend nearby schools, some are still in boarding schools. The most recent decades have witnessed greater attention given to Indian language and culture. A chronic problem, still not completely resolved, is who shall pay for the education of Indian children—the reservations, the state, or the federal government.

BLACK AMERICAN EDUCATION

As was true for white Americans, the quality of black Americans' education in the nineteenth century was heavily dependent on their geographical location and their economic status. Unlike whites, however, wherever blacks lived, even if they were free, they faced racial prejudice that limited educational opportunities. At the beginning of the nineteenth century, few white Americans believed in the equality of all races. They disagreed, however, about the extent to which blacks should be considered below white norms and over what had brought about the supposed inferiority. While the South relied on slavery, the North used disenfranchisement, job discrimination, and limited access to schooling to perpetuate a lower status for blacks.[13]

Until just a few decades before the Civil War, many Southerners argued that some education was necessary for slaves to serve their owners best. Education, whether academic or craft oriented, made slaves more versatile to serve the needs of a self-sufficient plantation, small farm, or in some cases an urban business. As abolitionst sentiment grew and slave revolts, led by literate blacks such as Nat Turner or Denmark Vesey, occurred in the 1830s, southern white opinion changed. Laws were passed prohibiting the teaching of slaves, and even schools for the region's few free blacks were closed. The only kind of education left to southern blacks had an oral tradition. White Southerners sent ministers to preach the importance of Christian submission, while many black slave communities had clandestine religious services of their own and passed on their heritage in stories and songs. Slave children learned attitudes, values, and skills from the adult slaves in their community. Occasionally they learned the rudiments of academics by playing school with white children.

The North certainly offered blacks a freer life than the South did, but racism still abounded. Horace Mann's so-called common school movement did not stimulate the North to integrate its schools. Some northern states excluded blacks by law, while others insisted on segregated schools. In the face of such white apathy and racism, blacks in many communities formed their own schools under the auspices of religious, philanthropic, or community improvement groups. The breakthrough for integration of public schools came in Massachusetts. After years of pressure from the black community in Boston and a court case that was argued unsuccessfully for the black plaintiffs by Charles Summer, the noted abolitionist and senator, the state legislature passed a law prohibiting segregation by race or religious affiliation in 1855. Although the law did not erase racial prejudice, it led the way for other states to pass similar legislation after the Civil War.

A major controversy in nineteenth century black education involved deciding what kind of curriculum was most appropriate. In many instances this topic was also related to debates over intelligence. In most of the country the kind of education usually favored was vocational training—so that its recipients could be self-sufficient in the case of free blacks, or a source of income, in the case of slaves. A major difficulty in the North with this approach was that racial prejudice sometimes kept workers from being hired. Also, the teaching facilities were sometimes so dated that the training was useless. Vocational training can be expensive, and many communities were simply unwilling to spend money for vocational training for blacks. In the South, before the Civil War, the problems of hiring, modernity of facilities, and expense were minimal because skilled slaves generally learned their trades from local craftspeople and were employed by their owners or rented out. Afterwards, however, the South had little money to spend on anyone's education. The famous black vocational schools established in the South after the war, Hampton and Tuskegee, were heavily dependent on philanthropy.

Although many black leaders were initially pleased with the emphasis on vocational training, by the turn of the twentieth century some felt that vocational education actually perpetuated a lower social and economic status for blacks rather than helping them achieve equality. (Compare the discussion in chapter 10 on W. E. B. Dubois with the information which follows.) Fanny Marion Jackson Coppin fits very nicely into this curriculum controversy. She helped change the orientation of Philadelphia's black school from totally academic to vocational.

Fanny Jackson Coppin (1837-1913)

Unlike many well-educated blacks of the nineteenth century, Coppin did not have the initial advantages of freedom or wealth. She was born a slave in 1837 in the District of Columbia, and according to her account, her Aunt Sarah, earning $6 a month, saved $125 to buy Coppin's freedom. She then lived and worked with another aunt in Massachusetts and at fourteen moved to Rhode Island. There she worked in the household of a literary and cultured family who allowed her one hour every other afternoon to study. She attended a local black public school and took private music lessons. Later she graduated from the Rhode Island State Normal School, a teacher training institution that offered an education on a level similar to today's high schools. In 1860, with help from Aunt Sarah, she entered Oberlin College in Ohio, one of the few colleges in the nation then open to blacks or women. She received her bachelor of arts degree in 1865, one of the first black women to do so.[14]

INSTITUTE FOR COLORED YOUTH

In the 1800s, there were few careers open to college educated women of any race, and like the majority of them Coppin entered teaching. She was hired by the Institute for Colored Youth in Philadelphia to teach advanced mathematics, Latin, and Greek, and to be the principal of the girls' high school division. In 1869 she became the head principal, the first woman to hold that position.

The institute had originally been established in 1837 at the behest of a Quaker, Richard Humphreys, who wanted to test blacks' capability for higher learning, and its curriculum had been academic. Coppin wished to expand its mission to include vocational preparation. In 1871 she persuaded its board of trustees to add a normal training program. The famous Philadelphia Centennial Exposition of 1876 stimulated Coppin to expand the Institute even further. Impressed by the exhibits of industrial and manual training in other nations, she sought similar training at the institute. She argued that the only place a black child could receive any industrial education in Philadelphia was in a poor house or prison. More than a decade passed before Coppin raised enough money to open a vocational center. In 1889 classes were first offered in plastering, brick-laying, carpentry, shoemaking, printing, and tutoring for boys; dressmaking and millinery for girls; and stenography, typing, and cooking for both sexes.

In the meanwhile Coppin had led the school in other educational innovations. She began sending regular reports on students' progress and conduct to parents. She introduced practice teaching into the normal program. She briefly added German to the curriculum until the board cancelled it. The board also refused to allow her to open a kindergarten.

Fanny married Levi Coppin in 1881 and, unlike most women of her day, continued her work outside the home. Levi was a minister and later a bishop in the African Methodist Episcopal Church, and gradually Fanny found new ways to utilize her educational talents through church work. She became a spokesperson for black women at conferences as far away as California and London. After resigning from the Institute for Colored Youth in 1902, she accompanied her husband to a bishopic in South Africa and did missionary work there. In 1913, a few years after the Coppins' return, she died in Philadelphia.

The institute with which most of Coppin's career was associated continues until today. After her resignation, it became even more vocationally oriented under a principal whose philosophy was similar to Booker T. Washington's. In 1904 the institution moved to Cheney, Pennsylvania. It became a state normal school in 1920 and Cheney State College in 1951.

The Civil War represented a great turning point in American history. Most obviously, the "peculiar institution" of slavery was ended in the United States. In addition, the profound economic and social changes which had begun in the years before the war became even more pronounced. While the war was the major political event of the era, it was also a symbol of differences between the ways in which both people and the nation itself saw themselves. Economically, increased industrialization was making its presence felt in North and South alike.

Booker T. Washington (c. 1856-1915)

It was into this time of political and social ferment that Booker T. Washington was born, sometime between 1856 and 1859. Washington spoke of his birth in a log cabin which measured about 14 by 16 feet.[15] His mother was the cook for both the slaves and the white owners of the plantation. His father was a white man whom he never knew. Booker's stepfather, also a slave, lived on another plantation and so saw his wife and stepchildren infrequently.

While our image of plantation society usually involves large estates and huge houses with white pillars and verandas, such was not usually the case. Although there were more than two million slaves in the early 1860s, only 2,300 owners had more than a hundred.[16] The Washington family's owner had only ten slaves, and the "white folks house" was a two story log cabin. As a result, both blacks and white were vital parts of the plantation's economy. Even as a small child, Booker was put to work holding horses for the white women when they went riding.

EARLY LIFE

As the Civil War progressed, its effects were felt on the plantation. Certain foods like sugar became scarce. Two of the white family's sons were wounded in the Confederate army, and one, much loved by the slaves, was killed. As the Union army moved further and further south, blacks began to talk more openly of freedom. One day, a Union officer appeared on the owner's porch, and read the Emancipation Proclamation. Booker T. Washington was now free—at least legally.

While many freed slaves stayed on to work for their former owners, exchanging a share of their crops (hence the term "sharecroppers") for land and seed, the Washington family moved on. Washington's stepfather, who lacked both ambition and common sense, had left his plantation during the war, and was now working in a salt mine in Malden, West Virginia. Probably because he needed more cheap labor, he sent for his wife and step children (two of her own and one whom she'd adopted).

In many respects, Malden was worse than the plantation. Free blacks replaced slaves working in the salt mines which were already outdated and dangerous. The family's living quarters were dirty and jammed in with those of other miners. Young Booker was to spend his life in this setting until 1871, working in salt and then coal mines, filthy and dangerous labor which he came to hate.

During this time, Booker's first attempts at schooling began. A bright child, he soon learned to distinguish numbers. These were used to indicate which worker had packed a particular salt barrel. In addition, his mother managed to get a copy of Webster's blue-backed speller, and he painfully tried to teach himself the alphabet. In order to get some formal schooling, he worked early in the mornings, went to school, and immediately went back to work until evening. His stepfather, however, soon insisted that he needed the boy's income, and Booker's formal education came temporarily to a halt.

EDUCATION

In order to escape the mines, Washington began to work as a kind of houseboy for the mine owner's wife. A demanding boss, Mrs. Ruffner insisted that things be cleaned to perfection. For all her sternness, however, she was kind and encouraged the former slave to learn to read. Some of the men who worked in the mine had begun to talk about a school in Hampton, Virginia which had been founded to educate black teachers. In the fall of 1872, Washington set out, determined to achieve an education for himself.

The Hampton Normal and Agricultural Institute was the product of an extraordinary man, General Samuel Chapman Armstrong. The American Missionary Association had asked Armstrong to found a black teacher training and industrial school in the Virginia area where he had been working for the Freedmen's Bureau, a relief agency for blacks. It was a wise choice. The son of parents who were missionaries in Hawaii, Armstrong had commanded black troops in the Civil War and emerged as one of the Union's youngest generals. His parents' experience with industrial schools for Hawaiians, coupled with his natural conservatism, convinced him that education in the trades was the ideal for blacks. Hampton became the theory's proving gound.

Washington arrived at the school with only the clothes on his back. His entrance exam was unique: the principal asked him to clean a room. Realizing that his future hung in the balance, Booker swept and dusted several times. Upon inspection, the principal pronounced herself satisfied. Washington's student days had begun.

Booker's career at Hampton, which was basically a high school, lasted three years. During this time. he learned a good deal about discipline and the value of hard work, serving as a janitor to pay his tuition and wearing secondhand clothing sent from the North. Nevertheless, he thrived. A summer visit to Malden with its sense of aimlessness contrasted sharply with the orderly life at Hampton. In General Armstrong, Booker had found the father he had never known. Most of all, he had absorbed Armstrong's educational philosophy of vocational education to produce black self-reliance which would direct his life.

Washington was one of the 20 percent of his entering class who graduated from Hampton in 1875. He then went back to Malden, quickly becoming involved in day, evening, and Sunday schools. Soon he was teaching more than 180 students. In 1878, he left Malden to study at Wayland Seminary, a small Baptist theological school in Washington, D. C. Wayland, unlike Hampton, emphasized the liberal arts rather than industrial subjects. It reinforced Washington's conviction that liberal education was not practical for most blacks, because it gave them no skills with which to earn a living. After an 1879 invitation to return to Hampton to give a speech on commencement day, Washington was invited by Armstrong to accept a teaching position there.

POLITICAL CLIMATE

Southern political life was in a state of flux during these years. Under the "home rule" policy of Andrew Johnson, Lincoln's successor, southern states had passed laws to "keep blacks in their place." A radical Republican Congress had retaliated, however, by passing legislation to promote civil rights and pun-ish the South. The 1867 Reconstruction Act divided the southern states into military districts policed by Union troops, and ordered new state constitutions which would allow blacks to vote. Positively, this legislation had the effect of giving the former slaves a voice in government. Negatively, it propelled many unqualified and greedy men into public office. In reaction, whites founded the Ku Klux Klan and the Knights of the White Camellia, terrorizing the black community and promoting racial hatred.

As time went on, southern whites gradually came back into the control of state governments. By the middle 1870s, all of the former states of the Confed-eracy except South Carolina, Louisiana, and Florida had "redeemer" white governments. Tennessee passed a law forbidding intermarriage in 1870, and the beginnings of laws mandating segregation in schools, on trains, and in public places had appeared by 1875. More conservative Republicans gained control of the party in 1876, spelling the end of its support for black rights. A southern senator accurately though crudely described the situation in the South after the 1876 departure of federal troops: "Whites rose in righteousness and right. We took the government; we stuffed the ballot box; we bulldozed the niggers and we shot them. And we are not ashamed of it."[17] With little political influence, blacks' hopes of real freedom began to dim.

It was in this context that Washington began the work for which he would become famous, the foundation of Tuskegee Institute. In 1881, Colonel W. F. Foster, an ambitious Alabama politician seeking the black vote, went to a former slave turned hardware store owner and struck a bargain. In return for swinging the black vote in his favor, Foster would sponsor a bill in the Alabama legislature for a state supported black teacher training school. The result was an appropriation of $2,000 a year for a school at Tuskegee.[18]

TUSKEGEE INSTITUTE

Although the citizens had wanted a white teacher, Washington was what they got. In this town of two thousand people, he began the school with thirty students in an old church and abandoned shack. Soon after his arrival, he spotted a plantation on the edge of town for sale at $500. Between money raised by local citizens and a large personal loan from the Hampton treasurer, Washington was able to purchase the property. The reason the plantation had been such a bargain was because the main house had burned down, and the fields were overgrown. The students were housed in shacks, and frostbite was common in the schoolrooms that first winter. If industrial education had not existed, Washington would have had to invent it. With so little hard cash, the Tuskegee Normal and Industrial Institute had to depend on student labor to provide its necessities.

Armed with little besides his convictions, Washington set out to realize his vision. His biggest job was persuading the students, whose educational model was that of white liberal arts schools, that manual labor was not a disgrace. By a combination of diplomacy and example, Washington got them to work. Stu-dents began to repair buildings and plant crops. In 1883, he started his most famous self-help project. Noticing that the local soil was mostly clay, he became convinced that the students could make their own bricks. The fact that no one at Tuskegee quite knew how bricks were made did not faze him. They tried twice, and failed. The third time, the kiln burned out. Having run out of funds, Washington pawned his watch to finance another try. This time the experiment worked, and Tuskegee students were in the brickmaking business. Soon their bricks were going not only into Tuskegee buildings but into new construction in the town. The brickmaking venture had become a symbol of the way in which young blacks with industrial training could achieve economic independence and, in the process, contribute to the prosperity of the local community.

Starting with those skills most necessary to the school's survival, Washington moved on to found a variety of industrial departments. Between 1883 and 1892, Tuskegee got into the business of carpentry, printing, cabinet and mattress making, wheel making and wagon building, tinsmithing, harness and shoe making, home economics, and nursing. The agricultural department which had started with a blind horse as its only livestock had branched out into scientific farming; poultry, cattle, and pig raising; and beekeeping. The original 30 students had become 169 by 1884 and had grown to 712 in 1894, with fifty-four teachers and administrators.[19] Students' days began at 5:00 A.M. and ended at 9:30 P.M. Almost all time was programmed in detail. Students were required to work, and not allowed to smoke, drink, or gamble. In many respects Tuskegee looked like a military school. Only officers were allowed to go to dances which the girls on campus sponsored.

All of the expansion required money, and Washington's role soon moved from that of principal to professional beggar. His fund raising efforts would eventually project him into the national spotlight, but it was rough going in the early days. New England church groups had dug deep into their pockets for black projects in the past, many of which never came to fruition. Yankees had become skeptical, and Washington returned from several trips depressed with the results.

Washington gradually became skilled at manipulating people. Individuals who gave small gifts initially found themselves courted, and frequently became major benefactors. The railroad magnate Huntington, steel tycoon Carnegie, and the Alabama legislature all made sizeable constributions. Endowments by the Peabody and Slater Funds provided regular help. Washington's combination of homespun eloquence and support of the status quo struck exactly the right note. By 1915, Tuskegee's endowment totalled $2 million, the largest of any black or white college in the South.[20]

EDUCATIONAL POLITICIAN

These fund raising trips gave Washington wide exposure. An articulate black who preached a gospel of self-help appealed to northern industrialists and southern whites alike. In 1893, he gave his first speech, a five minute presentation to a Christian conference in Boston. Much to his surprise, he was received enthusiastically. A variety of other opportunities came his way, until he received an invitation to speak at the opening of the Atlanta Exposition in 1895.

The Atlanta speech (also called the "Atlanta Compromise") marked Washington's entry onto the national scene. For the first time, a black was appearing in the South on the same program as white dignitaries, and Booker was determined to make the most of it. His speech stressed the solidarity of interest between southern whites and blacks, and emphasized his evolutionary (rather than revolutionary) approach to civil rights. Admitting that serious errors had been committed in the Reconstruction Era, he went on to assure his audience that "the wisest among my race understand that the agitation of questions of social equality is the extremest folly, and that progress in the enjoyment of all the privileges that will come to us must be the result of severe and constant struggle, rather than of artificial forcing." Washington ended with a plea for economic cooperation between blacks and whites, predicting that "this, coupled with our material prosperity, will bring into our beloved South a new heaven and a new earth."[21]

To say that the speech was a success would be an understatement. One observer commented, "The fairest women in Georgia stood up and cheered. It was as if the orator had bewitched them."[22] He had barely finished when the governor rushed across the stage to shake his hand. Only with difficulty did Washington get through the crowd. Well-wishers stopped him on every street corner. Newspapers across the country hailed him as spokesman for the black race. Booker T. Washington was the man of the hour. Ironically, many blacks boycotted the exposition because of its segregated facilities.

The next several years brought a flood of speaking engagements and civic honors. Harvard gave him an honorary degree in 1896, and the *Washington Post* proposed him for secretary of agriculture. In 1897, he took Boston by storm, speaking at the unveiling of a statue commemorating a white soldier who led black troops in the Civil War. In 1898, the Slater Fund sent Washington on a speaking tour of the South. Whites were both impressed with his "rags to riches" story, and relieved that the most prominent black American held little hatred for past injustices. His philosophy of gradual change in race relations was reassuring.

At the same time, Washington's political prominence grew. In 1897 the Secretary of Agriculture toured Tuskegee, to be followed by President McKinley in 1898. When Theodore Roosevelt became president after McKinley's assassination, Washington became black America's principal advocate. On most matters concerning blacks, including political appointments, Roosevelt depended heavily on him.[23] Their relationship led to a national furor in 1901 when Roosevelt invited Washington to dinner at the White House. Southern newspapers were outraged, although the controversy soon blew over. Booker T. Washington had become a major figure in American civic life.

Tuskegee was still the primary focus of Washington's attention. Even on the road, he received daily reports about the most minute happenings at the school and continued to rule it with an iron hand. Unlike Hampton, which had a largely white faculty, Tuskegee's permanent faculty (at Washington's insistence) were all black. In 1896, he hired the noted agricultural chemist, George Washington Carver, and continued to recruit talented black teachers. He also broadened Tuskegee's scope. The first Tuskegee Negro Conference was held in 1892 to provide a forum for blacks to discuss the future progress of the race. In 1900 he founded the National Negro Business League to provide the same opportunity for exchange by black businessmen. Washington's flair for showmanship asserted itself in the establishment of the Movable Farm Demonstration, a traveling exhibit which included animals, growing plots of vegetables, and modern farm machinery, aimed at introducing rural farmers to the wonders of scientific agriculture.

Another major concern for Washington was his family. His first marriage to a childhood sweetheart, Fannie Smith, had ended in her 1884 death. In the following year, he married Tuskegee's first teacher, Olivia Davidson. These marriages left him with three children when Olivia died in 1889. His marriage in 1893 to another teacher, Margaret Murray, brought the family together once again. While Washington's love for Olivia seems to have prevented a close relationship with Margaret, he remained a concerned father and educational guide for the children.

WASHINGTON UNDER FIRE

In spite of all his achievements, Washington was not universally praised. Some blacks, especially among the college educated, saw his gradualism as a sellout, and believed that industrial education condemned future generations to second-class citizenship. The Harvard and German educated social philosopher W. E. B. DuBois attacked Washington bitterly, preferring to stake the future of black America on the "talented tenth" of college educated black youth. Writers like Kelly Miller challenged Washington's right to speak for the black community: "Mr. Washington is not a leader of the people's own choosing. He does not command an enthusiasm and spontaneous following. . . . His method is rather that of a missionary seeking the material and moral betterment of an unfortunate people, than a spontaneous leader voicing their highest self-expression.[24] Articulate northern blacks like Monroe Trotter and George Forbes attacked him continuously in print.

People disenchanted with Washington's policies came together in 1905 in the Niagara Movement. By 1910, this organization had become the National Association for the Advancement of Colored People (NAACP). Washington's stubborn insistence that his was the only approach led him to rehabilitate the defunct Afro-American Council and support the more moderate Urban League (1911) in an effort to check the militants.

National events also contributed to a lessening of his political influence. The election of Taft in 1908 reduced his "clout," although he still had a voice in political appointments. The 1912 election presented him with a problem. Theodore Roosevelt, running on the Progressive ticket, had trimmed his views on race to woo southern support. Taft, the Republican, was not a black favorite, and Wilson, a southern Democrat, was seen as dangerous. Unwilling to abandon the Republican party, Washington supported Taft. When Wilson won, Washington lost his place in the corridors of power.

In spite of these problems, Tuskegee's president was still involved with a variety of projects. In 1911, at the insistence of the school's directors, he took a three month educational and social trip to Europe, which he turned into a study of social conditions, published as The Man Farthest Down (1912). His earlier The Story of My Life (1900) and the more refined Up From Slavery (1900-1901) had long since been translated into many languages, making him an international celebrity. Programs ranging from John D. Rockefeller's General

Education Board and the Julius Rosenwald Fund for black schools to National Negro Health Week occupied his attention.

Washington's school also required his presence. The benevolent dictatorship of Booker and his handpicked officials had given Tuskegee a consistent philosophy, but had also created some problems. By the twenty-fifth anniversary, 1,600 students (who had made 970,000 bricks that year) were enrolled. Tuskegee had probably grown beyond the administrative ability of any one person, especially one who spent so much time away from campus. Younger faculty were unhappy with some policies. Washington's lack of attention to detail almost cost him older teachers like Carver, who wrote in 1914 threatening to quit because he had not had a raise in salary since he arrived in 1896. In 1913, the addition of a new heating plant had pushed the school beyond its budget. Income was still not keeping pace with expenditures.

A "workaholic," Washington simply pushed himself harder to make ends meet. In spring of 1915, he took to the road again, touring Massachusetts, New York, Illinois, Iowa, Kansas, Nebraska, and Nova Scotia to raise money for the 1913 deficit. On 25 October he collapsed in New York of nervous exhaustion and advanced arteriosclerosis. Knowing that he was near death, he asked to return home. He died on 14 November 1915, the day after he arrived at Tuskegee.

CONCLUSION

The controversy surrounding Washington has continued after his death. Critics have argued that his public statements have seriously hindered the civil rights movement. Certainly the Atlanta Exposition speech helped to establish the "separate but equal" doctrine, which the U.S. Supreme Court made the law of the land in 1896.[25] While Washington himself had become less tolerant of southern white attitudes in his later years, he must still bear some of the responsibilities for having helped to form them.

Washington, however, was more involved in promoting civil rights than was known during his lifetime. Working quietly behind the scenes, he lobbied against efforts to restrict black voting rights, tapping even Catholic bishops to obtain support.[26] An expert fund raiser, he frequently supplied money for court cases involving black rights and helped plan legal strategy. While his public image was one of passive acceptance, Washington worked to undermine the very institutions he seemed to tolerate. More than most people, the sharp separation between public and personal life makes any accurate assessment of what Washington really believed difficult.[27]

Questions have also been raised about the value for blacks of the sort of industrial education Washington advocated. Were vocational schools aids to success or obstacles? Some of Washington's critics have argued that only if blacks were given the same education as whites would equality happen. For the critics, Washington's educational philosophy was as much a sellout as his political and economic stances. This judgment may be a bit harsh. Washington came onto the scene during a time in which black attempts at political and social equality were frustrated by the South's increasingly repressive laws. Economic independence seemed to offer the only realistic vehicle for black improvement.

Industrial education emerged as the most logical strategy for him. Washington's concern for agricultural education for rural blacks must be seen as part of a general concern of both black and white industrial educators to keep America's rural population on the farms.

The failure of industrial education, despite Washington's convictions, probably had more to do with economics and psychology than anything else. By 1915, his educational theory was out of date. Just as Tuskegee was turning out skilled craftspeople, the demand for unskilled labor in factories was increasing. In the long run, Tuskegee was training people for nonexistent jobs. Its model was more appropriate for the early nineteenth than the twentieth century. Washington may have been wrong in believing that economic success would produce respect for blacks—the question of racial tension involved far more than economics—but economic power was surely part of the equation.

In the final analysis, Booker T. Washington deeply influenced American educational development. Tuskegee shaped the lives of countless black schoolteachers and professionals who made significant contributions to American life. Its programs served as stepping stones for many to the kind of university education DuBois favored. Indeed, by Washington's death, Tuskegee was already beginning to look more like a college than the elementary and high school he had begun. Washington's greatest contribution, however, had more to do with personality than institution building. He helped to create a national climate which supported education for blacks, even in the face of some southern resistance. His success in fund raising generated income not only for Tuskegee but a host of other educational projects as well. Most of all, he offered in his person a success story with which black and white alike could identify. His own desire for education and a better life inspired many to sacrifice for the same ends.

Future generations would rightly insist that the doctrine of "racial merit," which based human rights on ability to perform, had no place in American society. However, Washington's larger belief that schooling could be used to improve the social, political, and economic lives of people would continue into our own day with the development of special and bilingual education, academic enrichment, and affirmative action programs to meet a wide variety of needs. While American education may never justify the high hopes Washington had for it, the challenge he offered and the bridges he built have helped schooling in the United States to become more sensitive to the great diversity of people it must serve.

9

THE PROGRESSIVES

By the end of the nineteenth century a reform movement was underway—one that cut across all segments of American life. From the 1890s to the 1920s critics examined many aspects of government and culture in the United States and found serious problems. Once again, in Zeitgeist fashion historians have applied the label "Progressive Era" to this time period, and it is usual to think of the reformers as "progressives." According to Ralph Henry Gabriel:

Progressivism was a mass movement which united diverse elements in American society. It transcended the agrarianism and the sectionalism of the Populists and the humanitarianism of such urban reformers as Jacob Riis and Jane Addams. It was a crusade in which farmers, wage earners, and small business men all marched shoulder to shoulder. . . . They put

255

their faith in science . . . [This] pragmatism and science worship of the Progressive Faith were veneers laid on ethical beliefs which in American history were as old as puritanism.[1]

By the end of the nineteenth century memories of the most destructive and divisive war in American history were beginning to recede. Slavery was legally ended, but severe racial and ethnic prejudice remained. Women's representatives had officially launched the Woman Movement at Seneca Falls, and Susan B. Anthony was at its forefront for suffrage. The economy was recovering from a severe recession; and industrialism had brought financial rewards to a comparatively small proportion of second generation immigrants, such as Chicago's Phillip Armour, George Pullman, and Cyrus McCormick. But overcrowded and unsanitary conditions in the cities were intensified by the steady flow of immigrants. In Chicago the number skyrocketed to 200,000 a year so that by 1890, 80 percent of Chicago's population was foreign born. The Haymarket Riot of 1886 signaled the tensions between the capitalist and the immigrant worker. The number of farms tripled between 1860 and 1910, but by 1900 farmers had a smaller share in the national wealth than they did in 1860.

The social issues which faced reformers on the eve of the twentieth century centered around the following problems: (1) the growth of big business and urbanization versus agrarianism and rugged individualism; (2) inequalities in the distribution of wealth resulting in distinct social class divisions; (3) political corruption and the breakdown of moral and ethical codes at all levels of society—especially the upper; and (4) the denial of political and economic rights to blacks, women, and other minority groups.[2] Exposure of these problems was basically left to journalists who came to be known as "muckrakers." Unmasking corporate malpractices and exposing political dishonesty became the most common form of muckraking.

At the same time progressive educational leaders turned to the schools as the vehicle which could cure the country's social ills. One of the most noted and eloquent advocates of this brand of progressive education was U.S. Commissioner of Education, John Eaton (1829-1906). Eaton noted several conditions for schools in an address to a group of educators known as the "friends of education." This group used the child-centered ideas of Rousseau, Froebel, and Pestalozzi and called for a system of free, tax supported, public education in the 1880s. In the thirty-eight states and ten territories, ungraded schools prevailed over graded, and the average person attended four and one half years of school. The pupil teacher ratio was sixty to one. Only 2.5 percent of the seventeen year olds graduated from any kind of secondary school—private academies being more numerous than public high schools. Corporal punishment was still the norm and reconstruction had unsuccessfully ended and schools of mixed color were "too insensitive" an issue. St. Louis had the only public kindergarten and the average annual teacher's salary was less than $400. But, cautioned Eaton, if the long road stretches ahead it is not as long as it once was. "Universal education must ultimately and completely triumph."

The "friends of public education" contended that tax supported common schools would alleviate the social evils of crime, poverty, intemperance, and industrial capitalism by equalizing opportunities for every rank in life. Slowly through the eighties and nineties the dominant *laissez faire* philosophy toward education gave way to a doctrine of social responsibility and public control. With this shift the progressive movement was born, and the son of a Vermont grocer—John Dewey—was to become its most vocal twentieth century supporter.

Dewey and the other four biographies included in this chapter typify the various aspects of this movement—from G. Stanley Hall whose type of social control would not threaten the existing social order to Margaret A. Haley whose form of progressivism would call for a return of American democracy to the common people.

G. Stanley Hall (1844-1924)

Among the several pioneers of modern psychology and education, Granville Stanley Hall stands out as one who devoted his life to establishing the means for promoting these two fields of study and activity. He founded the first psychological laboratory in America, created and edited three professional journals, led the way in refocusing American education on the child, and served for more than thirty years as president of Clark University, a center of experimental psychology and child study. He is probably best remembered for giving Sigmund Freud his first academic recognition anywhere in the world by bringing him and Carl Gustav Jung to America in 1909.

YOUTH AND EDUCATION

The son of Granville Bascom and Abigail Beal Hall, Stanley was born 1 February 1844 in the small farming village of Ashfield, Massachusetts. There his parents reared him in an atmosphere characterized by the virtues of thrift, self-help, and individuality. Abigail Hall, a pious and gentle woman, frequently read to Stanley, and his younger brother and sister, Robert and Julina, from the Bible, *Pilgrim's Progress*, *Uncle Tom's Cabin*, and the works of Shakespeare, Scott, and Dickens. She wanted Stanley to enter the ministry, but reluctantly accepted his choice of an academic career. Granville Hall was a stern man of Calvinistic leanings, a man of quick and violent temper who demanded obedience from his children. He was an advocate of practical scientific farming, yet seemed to be dissatisfied with his lot as a farmer. A respected community leader, he was sent to the state legislature on the Know-Nothing ticket in 1855. Despite his austere personality, he showed concern for his son's welfare by securing an exemption from military service for him at the time of the Civil War, a fact that Stanley later regretted.

Stanley Hall clearly reflected the influences of his Puritanical home and the rural New England environment. He felt warmly toward his mother, and seems to have absorbed her interest in literature and her tendency to avoid a confrontation. Although he desperately wanted the respect of his father, he harbored hostility toward him. As an adult, ironically, he exhibited some of his father's authoritarian characteristics. At the same time, he tried to use his positions of authority to skirt conflicts.

Living in a village nestled in the Berkshire Mountains, Hall developed a life long interest in the natural environment and the effects of nature on human life. He also learned the moral precepts of the community. Following his schooling at the Ashfield Academy, he showed his sense of duty and independence at the age of sixteen by obtaining a job as a teacher in a nearby hamlet.

In 1862, Hall left Ashfield for Easthampton, Massachusetts where he attended Williston Academy in order to complete his secondary education. The program at Williston was rigorous, having been designed to prepare young middle class boys for entry into Harvard and Yale. Hall struggled with his studies and with the difficulty of being away from home for the first time. By the end of the school year, he stood in the middle of his class.

With his departure from home, Stanley Hall continued his struggle for independence. His antagonism toward his father probably was the basis for his desire for independence from authority and for freedom of thought. And his introduction to science and philosophy at Williams College seemed to fuel the fire of separation not only from his father's authority, but from that of established religion. At the same time, Hall's love of literature and his romantic notions about nature were so deeply imbedded in his psyche as to temper his thinking throughout his life.

Hall found the classical studies of his first two years at Williams "fearfully hard," although by midwinter 1864 he ranked sixth out of forty-three, and by the end of his second year the program had become less challenging. In his junior year, he took work in history, natural science, and modern languages. The courses were exciting, but not difficult. Thus, he found time to join a scientific club, and to explore and write about the natural surroundings of Worcester. His inspiration apparently came from the romantic literature and the lectures of Ralph Waldo Emerson who had twice visited the Williams campus. It was, however, his senior year that brought the most significant studies of his undergraduate program.

In the senior philosophy course, President Mark Hopkins presented a religious hierarchy of existence and some notions from faculty psychology. As a consequence, Hall became interested in natural science and the philosophy of nature. But Hopkins' moralistic viewpoint did not appeal to him. In contrast Hall found important ideas in the suggestions of his rhetoric professor, John Bascom who systematically challenged the position of President Hopkins. Hall recalled that Bascom was chiefly interested in John Stuart Mill and in the central role of feelings in thought and conduct. He seemed to have supported Hall's romantic leanings and enhanced his independence.

Following his graduation from Williams in 1867, Hall pursued further work in philosophy at Union Theological Seminary in New York City. He followed the normal course of theological studies, but spent his free time in escapes from orthodoxy. His extracurricular reading included the works of Ernest Renan and David Friedrich Strauss, both of whom portrayed Jesus as a moral man wrapped in biblical legend. O. B. Frothingham's notion of God's immanence in all of nature also intrigued Hall. Other diversions included trips to the seedy districts of the city, attendance at the theater, and visits to various denominational groups. In addition to these activities three people seem to have been important to Hall's intellectual growth at Union. George Sylvester Morris, recently returned from Germany, became Hall's idol and guided him in philosophy. Henry

B. Smith was particularly significant in that he introduced Hall to systematic theology, and may have suggested that he go to Germany for further study. Finally, Henry Ward Beecher, pastor of the Plymouth Church of Brooklyn, admitted Hall to his prestigious theological seminar. He also secured a $500 grant that enabled Hall to go to Germany in June 1869 where he spent fifteen months enjoying the culture and studying philosophy, systematic theology, and natural science.

When he returned to Union, it became quite evident that Hall had adopted some German ideas. He had studied positivistic (natural science based) philosophy and historical criticism with Adolf Trandelenburg, Morris' teacher. And he learned of the importance of the historical process from Johann Droysen. The clearest evidence of the influence of these unorthodox ideas on Hall's thinking came from his advisor's response to his trial sermon. All Henry B. Smith could do was pray for Hall's soul. But Hall remained sufficiently orthodox to receive his degree.

EARLY CAREER

At this point Stanley Hall rejected a clerical career in order to teach academic philosophy. Unfortunately, no position was immediately available, so during the next two years he tutored the children of wealthy banker Jesse Seligman and continued his investigation of science and positivistic philosophy. He devoted a great deal of time to the study of evolutionary theory and Hegelian philosophy. For the time being Hegel enabled him to develop a system that combined religion and evolutionary science. Eventually, Hall gave up his belief in the supernatural and chose naturalism as the basis of his thinking. Finally in the late summer of 1872 Hall secured a position as professor of rhetoric and English at Antioch College in Yellow Springs, Ohio.

After four years at Antioch, Hall became dissatisfied with his job, and decided to take a leave of absence. He intended to go back to Germany, but stopped in Cambridge, Massachusetts at Harvard University to study the "new psychology" with a young assistant professor named William James. This was the only place in America where one could take work in psychology. Most of Hall's courses were with James. He also conducted experiments with James' equipment and in Henry Bowditch's physiology laboratory. In 1878 Hall passed his final oral examination and was awarded a Ph.D. degree in psychology, the first doctorate given by the Harvard philosophy department and the first in the field of psychology anywhere in the country.

The following summer he decided to return to Germany in order to sharpen his skills in physiology and its application to psychology. He began his studies in Berlin where he attended lectures on physical science given by Herman von Helmholtz, and worked with Hugo Kronecker in the new physiology institute. In 1879 he moved to Leipzig and became the first American to work in Wilhelm Wundt's experimental psychology laboratory. He continued his study of physiology with Johannes von Kries. This second foray into the natural sciences in Germany resulted in Hall's rejection of metaphysics and adoption of psychology as a natural science. Just prior to leaving for Leipzig, in September 1879, Hall had married Cornelia Fisher, an acquaintance from Yellow Springs, Ohio who had come to Germany to study art.

During the next decade, Hall was able to capitalize on the growing interest in natural science in America. His knowledge of the scientific techniques being applied in psychology and his belief in and ability to convince others of the importance of science to humanity thrust him into prominence in the fledgling community of graduate education. He first became popular as a lecturer in pedagogy at Harvard, while awaiting a permanent academic appointment. Hall brought the authority of science to the educational reform movement based on interpretations of Rousseau, Pestalozzi, Froebel, and Herbart. Although he held to traditional notions of discipline, he captivated the educational community with his theories of child development based on evolution. He believed that humans repeated the evolution of the race as they grew from childhood into adulthood, and that education should follow the natural impulses of the child under adult guidance. Hall was probably the first person to make a sustained argument for the scientific study of children. He thought such investigations would provide an empirical foundation for the romantic decree to follow the child's impulses, so popular among educators of the day.

Hall supported his argument in 1883 in an article entitled "The Contents of Children's Minds" which was based on data gathered by means of a questionnaire, one of the first of its kind in psychology. The article was an immediate success and an important tool in Hall's effort to create a child study movement. But his early work in what Lawrence Cremin called the "Copernican revolution in the classroom" was short-lived. By 1885 Hall was devoting his full attention to experimental psychology at the Johns Hopkins University in Baltimore, Maryland.

In March 1882 Hopkins President Daniel Coit Gilman appointed Stanley Hall as as part-time lecturer in psychology and pedagogy. He joined two other part-time instructors, George Sylvester Morris and Charles Saunders Peirce. Within two years both Morris and Peirce were gone, and Hall had become a professor of philosophy. Gilman would not rehire Peirce and had chosen Hall over Morris for the one full-time position. Thus by 1884 the philosophy department at Hopkins was headed in the direction of scientific psychology instead of introspective philosophy and Morris' Hegelianism.

In the meantime Hall had opened an experimental laboratory in his first term in the spring of 1883, traditionally recognized as the first of its kind in America. And he had found four graduate students who were interested in psychological observation and experimentation: James McKeen Cattell, Joseph Jastrow, Edward M. Hartwell, and John Dewey. Of the four only Cattell and Jastrow became experimental psychologists. Hartwell became a physician and Dewey a distinguished philosopher and educator, yet both retained an abiding interest in psychology. Apparently Hall was always able to attract graduate students to the experimental laboratory.

During the 1880s Hall concentrated on laboratory studies thereby ensuring that his work and the image projected by it were rigorously scientific. It was this aspect of Hopkins program, moreover, that was most influential in the growth of American psychology. One university after another opened an experimental laboratory. Hall also was critical of work in psychology that was not experimental. Despite having studied with eminent philosophical psychologist William James and having briefly delved into psychical research, he objected to the lack of scientific rigor in these two fields. Finally, when he founded the *American*

Journal of Psychology in 1887, he intended to provide a means of expression for his colleagues and for defining the field of psychology. He also was determined that this would be a periodical exclusively devoted to experimental work.

In addition to his laboratory work, Hall began a serious attempt to devise a theoretical foundation for the new psychology. He wanted to develop a theory that included the evolutionary ideas of Herbert Spencer and Ernest Haeckel as well as the experimental theories of Wundt and his German colleagues. As might be expected, this task could not be accomplished either quickly or easily. In fact, he wrestled with the problem for more than twenty years, never achieving the goal of a complete psychological theory. Two things seemed to hamper his efforts. First, he was never able to free himself of the emotional hold of German idealism. Second, he chose to give up the relative freedom of a professorial position in favor of the more demanding job of a university president.

UNIVERSITY PRESIDENT

The board of trustees of the newly founded Clark University in Worcester, Massachusetts had noted Hall's organizational ability and had offered him the presidency of that institution. Hall accepted and resigned from Johns Hopkins in April 1888. He immediately undertook the task of organizing the university and its program. The result of his work was a graduate institution with a scientific orientation. The school had five departments—psychology, biology, chemistry, physics, and mathematics—and a faculty of established and promising scholars. Like Herbert Spencer, Hall believed that scientific knowledge was the most valuable of all knowledge. As he put it, "The university . . . should represent the state of science *per se.* It should be strong in those fields where science is highly developed, and should pay less attention to other departments of knowledge which have not reached the scientific stage."[3]

Of course, Hall's own department of psychology met the standards of science by concentrating on experimental investigations and by drawing on the strength of the disciplines related to the "new psychology" such as biology and the emerging field of anthropology. Clark's distinction in psychology, moreover, encouraged the growth of the experimental program at Harvard. The competition between these two departments was in part a product of the rivalry between two of the acknowledged leaders in the field of psychology, G. Stanley Hall and William James.

It is ironic that just as he had reached the pinnacle of his career certain events should bring Hall down from that peak. Some of these were of his own doing, while others were beyond his control. The first was the sudden accidental death of his wife and daughter on 15 May 1890. Hall went into a deep depression that nearly resulted in his complete withdrawal from Clark, but he found solace in a renewed faith in God, thus marking the end of his struggle with questions of religion.

The second was a crisis over Hall's administration of Clark University precipitated by his mishandling of a growing financial problem. In 1891 Jonas Clark became disenchanted with his school, and began to reduce his monetary support. Hall tried unsuccessfully to keep the problem from the faculty. They saw this act as typical of his authoritarian measures that had included attempts to interfere with the work of junior faculty members and the arbitrary distribution of unfixed funds. The upshot was a series of confrontations between Hall and the faculty, and ultimately the departure of more than half of the faculty and nearly three-fourths of the students. It took years for Hall and Clark University to recover from the devastation.

Despite the crisis at Clark, Hall remained one of the leaders in the field of psychology. He was instrumental in the founding of the American Psychological Association in 1892, serving as its first president. He also continued to edit the *American Journal of Psychology*, which became the source of his third problem. Hall's arrogance about the importance of experimental psychology and his criticism of "unscientific" psychology was apparent in his own writings in the journal. For example, in the early 1890s he issued scathing reviews of the textbooks written by William James and George T. Ladd, the other two elders in the field. His capricious use of authority with the journal alienated some of his younger colleagues, and brought about the founding of the *Psychological Review* by James McKeen Cattell and James Mark Baldwin in 1894. The worst offense, however, was Hall's claim in an editorial in 1895 that he was the primary and most influential leader in the establishment of experimental psychology in America. The shock waves that rolled through the psychological community in reaction contributed to Hall's fall from power and to his personal break with William James.

THE CHILD STUDY MOVEMENT

Amid these professional calamities one pathway for accomplishment remained open to Hall. After an absence of six years, he returned to the child study movement in 1891. Over the next three years, he increased his involvement in education through informal meetings at National Education Association conventions, the *Pedagogical Seminary* (a journal he founded in 1891) and the summer session for educators held at Clark. By 1894 he had become a prominent spokesperson for child study, having addressed audiences throughout the nation.

In that same year, Hall enunciated the gospel of the movement before the newly founded Child Study Department of the NEA. Seeing this endeavor as a moral commitment for educators, Hall asserted, "The little child standing in our midst is, I believe again to be the regeneration of education, to moralize it, to make it religious, to bring the child (because it brings the school) home to the hearts of the men and women, where children should always find a warm place."[4] He followed this declaration with an outline of the goals for child centered education: children should learn of the joy of good health, become sensitive to nature, and recognize that "life is for service." Hall, however, was not merely concerned with preaching about such ambiguous aims. He seriously attempted to find a scientific basis for devising means to those ends.

For more than a decade Hall, some of his students, and numerous educators involved in the movement, gathered data about children through questionnaire surveys. These investigations were founded on two principal themes, physical development and psychological aspects of child development and education. Some of the results were useful or at least suggestive; but most of the data were of little value since many of the researchers were ill-trained in scientific methods. Nevertheless, Hall's own studies produced a picture of childhood whose dominant characteristic was imagination. He concluded that, moved by strong feelings and impulses, the child's world was separate from that of adults but represented a true line of development that had to be taken. Like Rousseau, however, Hall saw a need for adult guidance as education supported natural growth.

A second and perhaps more personally satisfying result of Hall's investigations into childhood was the publication of *Adolescence* in 1904. In this massive two volume study Hall described what he thought to be the most critical step toward adulthood. Adolescence was a period characterized by rapid mental, physical, and emotional growth driven by a new burst of energy. It was a time of conflicting emotions. Hall argued that adolescence was to be prolonged to enable the individual to develop fully and to learn self-control. And the heart of adolescent growth lay in the treatment of sexuality. Sublimation of sexual energy through chastity and in religious endeavor would enable the adolescent to accomplish the shift from selfishness to altruism, but adolescence was not solely to be focused on emotional stability. Proper adolescent development, according to Hall, should result in a "mental unity" of desires, beliefs, and volitions.

Adolescence was also the place where Hall most systematically described his genetic psychology. After more than a quarter of a century of intellectual struggle, he produced a synthesis whose foundation was Darwinian and that included both recapitulation and neo-Lamarckian theories. He argued that the life force was expressed in hunger, love, and the myriad of related "instinct-feelings" which guided growth, reproduction, and behavior. Despite criticisms of such notions, Hall also thought that we were influenced by "life-habits: inherited from our ancestors." Thus, normal human growth depended on the supression of primitive inpulses by more civilized faculties and the sublimation of impulses into socially acceptable behavior. In the end Hall placed greater weight on feelings and the unconscious than on consciousness and maturity. His theory was more biological than environmental.

Hall's genetic psychology also contained elements of Freudian theory. Having studied Freud's work since the mid-1890s he found his own notions about the importance of human sexuality, particularly in adolescence, reinforced by psychoanalytic theory. *Adolescence* contained several favorable citations of Freud's ideas.

In 1908, Hall saw a chance to introduce Sigmund Freud directly to the American psychological community by bringing him to the second decennial celebration of Clark University the next year. Held in September 1909, the conference was attended by a group that included the most eminent psychologists in the country. It also marked the beginning of a long period of interest in Freudian psychology among Americans. This conference was obviously of great importance to Freud, and was likely Hall's most significant professional triumph.

The years following the Clark meeting, however, brought some adjustments in his acceptance of psychoanalytic theory. Many of Hall's academic and child study colleagues strongly criticized the emphasis on sexuality in *Adolescence* and in his book, *Educational Problems*, published in 1911. As a consequence, Hall began to change his position. He became critical of the breadth of sexual symbolism in Freud's writings, and later added some of Jung's and Adler's ideas to his viewpoint. In the meantime his frank discussions of sex had become an embarrassment to the child study group, and had contributed both to its reorientation toward social development of children and to Hall's departure from the movement.

FINAL YEARS

During this period, Hall renewed his interest in social issues and religion. He remained concerned about the importance of education and science to social, cultural, and even racial progress. He also took an interest in racial minorities in America. On the subject of women's rights, however, he urged women to retain their femininity. Finally, Hall devoted much attention to religion. In 1904, he had started a third journal, *The American Journal of Religious Psychology and Education,* and in 1917 presented his religious speculations in *Jesus the Christ in the Light of Psychology.*

G. Stanley Hall retired in 1920 after thirty-one years as president of Clark University. In the remaining years of his life, he continued to engage in intellectual activities, producing a description of a utopian society called *The Fall of Atlantis* in 1920 and his memoirs, *The Life and Confessions of a Psychologist*, in 1923. On 24 April 1924, Hall died following a series of illnesses.

Hall was one of the most significant figures in the founding of the "new psychology" in America. He was largely responsible for setting the course of psychology in the direction of rigorous scientific research. In the process of promoting empirical investigations, however, Hall's own desire to lead the profession provoked some of the quarrels that resulted in unfortunate and unnecessary divisions within the discipline. But despite these problems, he endeavored to promote the good of the profession. In his later work, Hall fostered practical applications of psychology in education particularly in the field of child study. Although no school of Hallians ever developed, his legacy is very much apparent in that both experimental and educational psychology continue to be important sources of information for explaining human behavior and learning.

While Hall was hailing a new dawn for psychology and child-study another contemporary was developing aspects of a new brand of education that would bring him the title of father of progressive education.

Francis W. Parker (1837-1902)

Schooled in a wilderness that failed to distinguish between high and low born, the polyglot nineteenth century Americans were graduating into a self-reliant, independent, and pragmatic people, but their emerging national character was in search of an author who would recast the old customs of Europe into a legitimate new society, with a common identify and destiny. That author was the common school. Francis Wayland Parker grew up with that school, which he considered the greatest manifestation of humankind, but would come to be its greatest critic. Institutionalized as the great national unifier, the common school, he had become a divisive agent during the nation's great industrial transition. He would redeem the institution but cast out its undemocratic and unnatural demons. He would be the prophet of a new education. He would be a protester and a reformer, and his life would bear witness to an effort at democratizing formal education.[5]

YOUTH AND EARLY CAREER

His life and education began on 9 October 1837, in Piscatauquog, New Hampshire, a little town near Manchester which had been founded by his grandfather. His mother was a spinster school teacher until she married widower Robert Parker, and they raised three daughters as well as a son. The son remembered the father only as an invalid, and he died when young Parker was seven. The impoverished widow had to apprentice her son to a farmer, and Francis W. Parker grew to adolescence plowing and snatching a few weeks of schooling between harvests. Five years on the farm turned out to be the best preparation for his theories of education, which he "read" out of the great book of nature. When he was thirteen, he broke bond and ran away to a local academy. He never quite finished his formal education, but began teaching in various country schools, "boarding around," and farming in the summers. Promotion came from the West, and in 1859 he left for Carrollton, Illinois to assume the principalship of the district school there. His teaching was complicated by the breakdown of the Union. Carrollton, lying close to the Mississippi River and the slave culture downstream, was divided on the slavery and secession question. Parker's school directors were definitely pro-Southern, and he had lost their support when he cast a vote for Lincoln. He returned to New Hampshire in the summer of 1861 and helped raise a company of Manchester youths for the Fourth Regiment. He was elected lieutenant and advanced in rank as the war progressed. The problems of a divided people would haunt him the rest of his life and quicken his resolve for social unity. He learned firsthand the horrors of racial division and helped to liberate some of the first slaves at Hilton Head Island. He was at Port Royal when he heard black volunteers raise hosannas at Lincoln's Emancipation Proclamation in 1863. He fought with black regiments in the capture of Fort Wagner, and again during the siege of Petersburg.

Rallying his troops during an engagement along the James River, his neck stopped a minié ball and the war stopped for him long enough to get nursed back to health. (His voice, however, would always be subject to husky and wheezy spells the remainder of his life whenever he engaged in long verbal battles.) During his convalescence, Parker was given leave to participate in the New Hampshire campaign for the reelection of Lincoln. He was then appointed lieutenant colonel of his regiment by the Republican governor of New Hampshire and joined his men as their commanding officer. Just as the last campaign was coming to an end, he was captured by a dashing band of cavalrymen and turned over the "home guards."

Released at the end of the war, he returned to teaching in his hometown in New Hampshire. He saw education, rather than military force, as the great unifier of the people, though he would retain the title of "colonel" as he began to rally forces against traditional education. Known as the "Doughty Colonel" by his enemies, he was a hard campaigner. But in the 1860s there was little vision of what schools might become. Reformers were limited to spreading the gospel of public education but they were bound by the old law of school commandments.

Parker also was slow to disengage himself from the slavish and competitive bonds of the schooling in which he had been reared and for which he served. But he began to dream of something better for the little children who trudged so wearily to school and dropped out as soon as they could, as though they preferred the mines and mills to the daily rounds of bookish lessons and arbitrary rules. Expecting a freer hand to experiment in the West, he abandoned his principalship in Manchester, New Hampshire for a similar position in Dayton, Ohio. It was in 1868 that he encountered racially segregated schools. The Democratic Party which fought the policies of Radical Reconstruction in the South was opposed to the racial integration of schools in Ohio. There was even a movement in Dayton to close the only black schoolhouse. Parker rose quickly to supervising principal of the whole Dayton system, but the schools were not integrated, though black attendance was greatly increased. He was more successful in breaking the traditional segregation of males and females in the classroom. Economy, however, rather than social justice probably broke the ranks of traditionalists.

THEORY INTO PRACTICE

The Germans in Dayton also had their segregated schools. A bane to social unity, such schools nevertheless inspired Parker with their imported "object lessons" and "kindergarten." Parker longed for a theoretical base for his practices that were already turning away from an adult centered classroom and a remote, abstract curriculum. He thought the advanced state of German pedagogy might provide the academic antidote. When his wife died, he left Dayton in 1872 to study pedagogy at the University of Berlin. After two and a half years in Germany, where his massive person was often mistaken for that of Bismark, he brought back the German enthusiasm for national unity as well as their "scientific" approach to child development and lesson planning.

His practices and new theories quickly came into focus in Quincy, Massachusetts where he was hired as superintendent of schools in 1875. Under the powerful sponsorship and national eminence of Charles Francis Adams, Jr., and John Quincy Adams II, his so-called "Quincy System" attracted the attention of the world. Within five years he was even accepted in Boston. Though the walls of traditional ivy were breached, they were hardly overthrown, and Parker had to leave Boston for the burgeoning industrial city of Chicago in 1883. As principal of the Cook County Normal School he began to train the lieutenants who would carry his battle to every corner of the nation. The new education, or what Parker sometimes called progressive education, was on the march. In many quarters the new school movement was simply labeled as Parkerism.

Parkerism, which sprang from the same political climate as Populism, was associated from the beginning with social as well as educational radicalism. It was radical, in the first place, by proposing formal education as the central means of making idealized social progress. Parker recognized other agents of education outside the school, but he would leave as little as possible to the segregated or broken home, to what he often called the licentious press, to boss controlled politics, or even to bigoted sectarianism.

Parkerism was radical, in the second place, by envisioning a world transformed through education. Educating children for the needs of a social democracy, Parker patterned citizenship on Christian as well as democratic and equalitarian principles. These principles fit his religious and political prejudices, but he believed there was self-evident proof for them in the secrets which Darwin had forced out of nature. Parker saw democratic progress as God's design, gradually revealed in natural evolution. People were not fallen but rising angels. Most human beings, he believed, were specimens of arrested development. Humankind could hasten evolutionary progress if the laws of natural development were found and exercised in the classroom. He believed the ultimate law had already been discovered in the Golden Rule. What could be more radical in an age that accepted self-preservation as the first law of nature and society?

Parkerism was radical, in the third place, by opposing the academic absolutism of the educational establishment which he thought trained children to rely on authority rather than themselves. His new education would overthrow the traditional purpose of formal schooling—the transmission of knowledge. Parker was not opposed to knowledge, but held that it should be the means and not the end of education. He aimed instead for the development of human beings—their full physical, mental, and moral powers. All children would have to be educated and developed to their full potentialities. Parkerism, like Jeffersonian democracy, was based on the perfectability of human nature.

HIS WRITINGS

More than twenty years before John Dewey's statement on *Democracy and Education*, Parker chose the same title for the final chapter of his best selling *Talks on Pedagogics*. Somewhat like the "deschoolers" of a century later, Parker criticized the public schools for dividing and isolating the people, providing what he called a "class education," in the manner of the Old World aristocracy which ruled by dividing the many. Parker said there two ways of preventing the lower classes from thinking. Either give them no education at all, or give them the kind of education which makes them believe firmly in absolute authority. He thought the public schools were the expressed demand of the lower classes, wrested from the private educational establishment through the rise of a more popular government, but the curriculum and methodologies of traditional education remained. Borrowed from the Old World these practices were geared to the machinery of oppression. The old methods of pedantry prevented free action of the mind. The old curriculum limited "the mental horizon," and prevented the mind from looking outside a well defined circle of thought. "It was the last ditch," he said, "of the rule of the few—forced by necessity to give the people education, but still acting to keep the people from the highway of freedom." Such education not only drove out the children of the lower classes but made "pauper" minds of those who remained.

Ambivalent on socialism, Parker was not a conscious exponent of Marxian dialectical materialism, but he had his own theory of human action that posited education, not economics, as the mainspring of history. In what might be called "dialectical educationalism," Parker believed education, not economics, divided the classes and caused exploitation and alienation. He divided history between two conflicting ideals—the ideal of limitation, or rule of the few, and the ideal of freedom, or rule of the many. Education was the source of knowledge. Knowledge was power. The ideal of limitation was to keep knowledge and power in the hands of the few and make the many dependent. Traditional education was its method. It used what he called "quantity" methods. Such methods counted words and syllables, broke subjects into parts, prevented an understanding of relations between parts and wholes. It divided life from school, thought from action, mind from body. It did not adjust that which was to be known to the nature of the mind. In short, it prevented what he called "quality" education, the dialectical opposite of "quantity" education, and thereby precluded the ideal of freedom.

"Real progress," he said, "has been along the lines of the lowest state of society. The real history of a people is the history of its humblest homes." Thus, he spoke for the proletariat in its struggle for the ideal of freedom. Unconsciously, perhaps, Parker sought to do away with class education by educating all in the manner of the proletariat. As he often said, the school was to train children into a love of work. In many ways, the school Parker advocated actually resembled the way the lower classes had always learned.

The Parker system was much less rigid and formal than the traditional education of aristocracies. More like a home or shop it bore resemblance to the informal apprenticeship so characteristic of lower class learning. And like the lower classes who responded more to concrete than abstract learning, the Parker school tried to avoid passive selling. Instead it would stress doing more with things than ideas. The lower classes demanded special skills. Only a leisured class could afford knowledge for its ornamental value. Parker thus held to utility and vocation. The lower classes, on the margin of survival, demanded immediate relevance and reward. "Now" was the great word of the new education, according to Parker. He opposed facts learned by rote and "salted down like herring" for some possible future use. But, in the perennial problem of popularizing knowledge without debasing it, Parker would bring education down to the way it was habitually learned by lower classes but not down to what they ordinarily learned. Subject matter was to be held up to the highest human achievements. Parker believed all children began instinctively the study of every subject, and all could be instructed in these subjects at every stage of their development. He said subject matter should be "spiraled" to follow human development in its evolution from the simple to the complex.

In reschooling society for social integration, he used the word "integratism" as the process for bringing people together into a community of common interest and purpose. He would bring the old and the young together as well as the social classes in a common inquiry, in a partnership of learning. He would bring the sexes together in a nonsexist curriculum, which he and his second wife, an ardent feminist, worked to achieve. He would bring the races together. He would not impose racial integration, or anything else. The teacher would supply the conditions so children would discover Christian fellowship for themselves.

HIS INFLUENCE SPREADS

In 1894 Parker addressed the Department of Superintendence (National Educational Association) with a plea for his ideal of freedom at their annual meeting in Richmond. "In the North," he said, "we have the great problem of capital and labor; in the South, the question of what shall be done with the millions of people given liberty through the war, but not given freedom. The only means of freedom is education, and the highest problem on the solution of which we all unite is: How can we take these people and make them useful, important factors in society?" He answered himself with "education into work." He said, "I would have a shop for handwork in every schoolhouse. I would have a small farm or garden surrounding every schoolhouse. I should train these children into a love of work, ability to work, and into the honesty which is developed by honest labor." Booker T. Washington would echo these sentiments the following year at the Atlanta Exposition, but Parker wanted this education into work for white as well as black children. Parker had as much trouble convincing educators that manual training had a place in formal education as Booker T. Washington had in convincing his own people that such education was not slave education. Both Parker and Washington stressed that progress toward social equality required educational rather than political reform.

Parker's "integratism" included the immigrant children of the Old World who must also be "fused, blended, melted into the great army of human progress under the dominance of the new civilization with the Common School for its right hand." The common school, he said, was the "Infant Republic," where children of "all castes, classes, shades of belief meet and learn to love and live for each other." He bitterly berated segregated schools at the National Educational Association meeting in 1891 because "The Common School had for its ideal the common education of all races, classes, sexes and sects in one school." Parker believed there was not much that could be done to improve the present, but the future could be directed toward the ideal of freedom. America could be made more democratic through a revolution from below, rising in one common school.

The problem of reconciling the child to the needs of a greatly expanding body of knowledge was as important to Parker as reconciling the child to the social needs of democracy. The experimental sciences were competing for a place in the already extended curriculum. While Parker supported the claims of science in the curriculum, he deplored the intellectual schism developing between the old and the new subjects. He believed science had to be integrated into the prevailing curricular structures without diminishing the value and moral heritage of the humanities. As the new sciences were gaining piecemeal entrance into the school Parker argued that the problem of separate and isolated subjects so characteristic of the old education was being compounded, and was as divisive as the segregation of separate social classes and races. Self-contained subjects prevented children from seeing beyond a limited "mental horizon." He further argued that there was a lack of economy in stringing separate subjects and skill courses together.

THEORY OF CONCENTRATION

He believed he had the solution to this problem in his theory of concentration which he had been developing at his Chicago normal school. The curriculum should concentrate on the child as its center. The curriculum, like the world, should be of one piece, with all subjects taught as an "organic, inseparable, interdependent unity." Children bring to school a great curiosity about their natural and social environments. "Nature" and "man in nature" were therefore the unifying themes for all subject matter. All disciplines fit into these categories, which he called "integers of life," or "central subjects." All aspects of the child's environment could be used to reveal the interrelatedness of the inorganic and organic sciences upon which the social sciences and the humanities were built. The natural sciences, less complex and less culturally controversial than the social sciences, were to be given more emphasis in the early years. What he called "modes of attention," such as reading and observing, "modes of expression," such as writing, speaking, drawing, modeling, and "modes of judgment" and "modes of form and number" were all developed as the need for them arose in discovering the nature of the world.

Parker was attacked by his enemies as a "materialist," because he stressed science as the foundation of the curriculum and kept defining education as the science of the economy of human effort in the direction of "all-sided human development." His theories were alleged to contain a few islands of thought rising out of a sea of sentimentality. His lack of any earned degree was used by academicians to demean his theories. Parker had to fight them as well as the political bosses who were controlling schools. It was said that the colonel had to "feel for his scalp" each morning at the Cook County Normal School where these bosses and their "hatchet men" were always on the warpath against him.

While Parker kept attacking political corruption and academic snobbishness, he gathered his own supporters—the feminists, women's clubs, and some of the new psychologists. His emphasis on manual training even gained the interest of industrialists who were seeking skilled labor. He formed "mothers' clubs" to reach the parents. Hailed as a "lecturer for the masses," he carried his reforms to the common people. He was known up and down the Chautauqua trails. His lectures were sold out in theaters and opera houses across the country. Like the ubiquitous peddler of patent medicine, to which he was often compared, he went everywhere to sell his brand of cure-all education. His public appearances were often reported as the "event" of the year. His theories were made flesh through the forcefulness of his personality, and when he was not working himself up into a rage he could joke and exaggerate the position of his opponents until audiences were said to double over with laughter.

It was becoming dangerous for politicians to take sides against him, and traditional educators found it difficult to cross swords with him. He was invulnerable to points of logic. He held both absolute and relative values. He advocated social education on one hand and individual education on the other. In spite of the "social nature" of his education, he always argued for individualism. He even opposed utopian socialism, such as that of Edward Bellamy, because he equated it with charity, and even the charity of the teacher was criticized because it was meant to help the child too much. Children should help themselves. He even opposed to collective action of teacher unions, preferring instead that teachers individually, through their merit, make themselves indispensable. He argued for the freedom of teachers as well as of children, and yet this was always couched in God given as well as science given principles.

Parker imputed no sinister motives to traditional educators. They were only what he came to call the "old fogies." "Fogyism," he said, means being stranded in a rut, accepting the "reigning method without question." He called such fogies, "artisan" teachers who produced exact patterns like a good worker. The "artist" teacher, which his normal school was tailoring, did not reproduce after a pattern. The "artist" teacher made new combinations out of old thoughts.

Preeminently a teacher of teachers, he was winning over the next generation. His "normal" education was built around a practice school containing a kindergarten and eight grades. Each grade had its "critic" or regular teacher. The children of all eight grades were divided into a total of about thirty groups, each assigned to a student teacher. As soon as they were ready, the student teachers were moved from group to group and grade to grade. All the while they were impressed with the importance of careful planning in accordance with ideals or principles. Such plans, and their results, were published monthly by the school in order to keep everyone briefed on their progress. Practice and experiment were buttressed with a thorough study of the history and philosophy of education, without which there would be no understanding of the ideals and principles which must motivate methods. Instruction was also provided in the psychological order of learning and the logical order of subject matter.

The rank and file of those he trained in the demonstration classrooms went marching out and took up positions on the front lines of the educational revolution. The public press and many of the professional journals were beginning to headline his struggles and practices, especially after *The Forum* published the Joseph Mayer Rice survey of schools in 1892. Rice muckraked the traditional state of the schools while lauding the work of Parker. By the late 1890s it was recalled that Parker once made "many dry bones to rattle and aroused much indignation while his ideas were denounced as visionary and insane," but it was now difficult to find, the newspapers were reporting, "anyone in the commonwealth who did not acknowledge the greatness of the service he rendered in attacking the old regime."

Some of the "old fogies," as Parker called them, were even coming over to his side. But, Parker feared they were not of the true faith. He once told an audience of laymen, "There are men who feel the new breath that is blowing among the school-rooms of the country. They ask for a few words to label this evident movement; they are told it is the new education, and they hasten to declare they are on that side." He added, with probably a spank on his backside, that they were "old educators with a new education 'lean-to' tacked on, sometimes right in front, sometimes in the extreme *rear*. They are old educators with a 'new education attachment.' "

FINAL YEARS

Parker's own attachment to public teacher education came to an end in 1899 when he reluctantly changed headquarters from his public normal school of

Chicago to the privately endowed Chicago Institute, especially designed for him. The bountiful endowment of Mrs. Emmons Blaine, the McCormick reaper heiress of Chicago, freed the Colonel from political spoilsmen, public apathy, and academic prejudices. Ironically, Parker's new education found more sympathy from the leisured class. The Adamses, children of prestige, sparked his movement in Quincy. Marshall Field and George M. Pullman, symbols of wealth and power in Chicago, advanced the private support he had needed to promote manual training. Mrs. Potter Palmer, acknowledged arbiter of "society" in Chicago, was so much in the Parker camp that the mayor of Chicago once complained that his "social" life was ruined whenever he sided with politicians who sought to depose Parker as principal of the Chicago Normal School.

Now, removed from the political arena, he was nevertheless surrounded with new problems. His dream of a free "slum" school, in connection with Jane Addams, faltered, partly because a suitable site could not be chosen. Other dreams were beginning to awaken his patrons to the high cost of a progressive education. The architectural demands alone were proving prohibitive. It is not certain if financial and administrative desperation finally drove Parker's board of trustees into an alliance with the University of Chicago. President William R. Harper of the University of Chicago, who already had John Dewey on his faculty, had long been interested in Parker. Arrangements were completed in 1901 to team up the Chicago Institute, Parker, staff, and endowment, with the University of Chicago. Dewey would retain his former influence in the department of philosophy, psychology, and pedagogy, and keep his Laboratory School, but Parker was inaugurated as the first director of the university's School of Education.

Ill and depressed over the recent death of his wife, Parker found little to encourage him in the new arrangements at Chicago. Dewey dared not attack "the colonel" openly, but he did harrass Wilbur Jackman, Parker's chief assistant. When Parker died suddenly in 1902, Dewey succeeded him as director of the School of Education and a full-scale war developed with the Parker faculty. Unable to force the Parker staff out, Dewey departed for Columbia University in 1904 to become titular head of the new education.

Dewey had acknowledged Parker as the father of progressive education, but Parker was buried as its practitioner, and Dewey went on to be proclaimed as the movement's major theorist. Parker's published works were neglected after his living force was gone.

John Dewey (1859-1952)

Loved or hated, revered or ignored, John Dewey's life made a difference in the world of thought and education. The first John Dewey died in a scalding accident when he was less then three years old. The guilt stricken mother conceived again and passed the same name, if not the spirit, to the son she bore on 20 October 1859 in the town of Burlington, Vermont. It was as though her suffering child had been reborn, and the second John Dewey must have come to know he was the substitute for the one who came before. He would have to struggle to prove his own identity.[6]

EARLY LIFE AND CAREER

He was descended from English and Flemish origins and four generations of pious Yankee pioneers who had cleared a settlement in the New England wilderness. According to family genealogy there were progenitors of royal blood on his mother's side. Daughter of "Squire" Rich, Lucina married middle-aged Archibald Dewey who was twenty years her senior. Unlike her husband's more practical and plebeian background, she had college educated brothers and brought high expectations to her offspring. Her liberal Universalist religious views, turned Congregational, were strictly passed on, with perhaps an ultimately negative effect on John. The father, from a line of farmers, had broken with the land to become a grocer in Burlington. Yet, he was less ambitious than his wife. He had hoped that at least one of his sons would become a mechanic.

Impressions of poverty and human suffering sprang from John's early experience when his abolitionist mother carried him and his brother into exile to northern Virginia as she followed her husband's cavalry regiment that fought the war to free the slaves and save the Union. He would soon return to his native town on the placid shores of Lake Champlain to begin public schooling and experience the face-to-face democracy of town meetings. He helped his father at the store as it expanded with such imaginative advertising as "Hams and cigars, smoked and unsmoked." He sometimes summered and worked on relatives' farms, and routinely graduated from high school at the age of fifteen. He then went on to the University of Vermont which was conveniently located near his home.

Shy and introspective, he probably had a natural inclination toward the world of ideas, but in his early university days he seemed to have no other goal than to get through his studies and graduate. At one time he was on the demerit list for contributing to a disturbance. In "Record Volume 'A', 1852-1892," his report of grades ranged from 69 in Herodotus (history) and 70 in algebra to 88 in botany and 92 in physiology. Thus science, as he first perceived it through the text of T. H. Huxley, became a greater influence in his thinking than the absolutism of mathematics or the backward glances of history. However, later he would hold that the knowledge of the past was essential to the solving of problems, but it had to be made relevant to the present. His course of study at the University of Vermont, without electives, passed on the general heritage but apparently was not connected to the present. Suddenly, in his senior year, he said there was one course offered to graduating students which was flexibly taught and designed to introduce the maturing student to "the world of ideas." That course, he claimed, stimulated in him a "sense of interdependence and interrelated unity that gave form to intellectual stirrings that had been previously inchoate."

His tardy intellectual awakening did not lead immediately into a professional career of philosophy. In those days most philosophers were members of the clergy. He did not know what to do with his life. Teaching was acceptable for a man as an interlude before a serious career, and he made local inquiries during the summer of 1879 for such a position. He was considered too young looking as well as inexperienced. A cousin, who was the principal of the high school in Oil City, Pennsylvania, wired the unemployed college graduate that he could teach for her at forty dollars a month. He accepted and set off for a booming industrial town where Standard Oil was developing.

Amid oil derricks he drilled students in Latin, algebra, and the natural sciences. Few children, especially from the lower classes, probably survived the academic road blocks to the classical high school studies. His school listed only six graduates in 1880 and thirteen the following year. The young man, under the constant scrutiny of his cousin, apparently had no trouble with the subject matter or the students. He found time to read in philosophy and write "The Metaphysical Assumptions of Materialism," which he submitted to W. T. Harris' *Journal of Speculative Philosophy*. This article and a subsequent one turned up later in the pages of this journal, and the encouragement of its editor led Dewey to consider devoting his life to the study and teaching of philosophy.

After the second year of teaching in Oil City, Dewey returned to Vermont and taught in a local academy while taking private tutoring in philosophy with H. A. P. Torrey. They talked and walked together, and in this informal way Dewey took fire. Perhaps this experience would influence his later criticism of formal educational methods, but at this time he had definitely determined his walk in life would be in the higher realms of education. He sought a fellowship at Johns Hopkins University in Baltimore, the new and pioneering graduate school in America. Even with the recommendation of Torrey, the penniless schoolteacher was denied a fellowship, or even a scholarship. It was through the financial help of an aunt that he was able to pursue his graduate studies at Johns Hopkins in 1882.

He found the logic courses of Charles S. Peirce frustrating because they were so mathematically oriented. (Dewey had not been the best student in algebra and probably did not anticipate the significant contributions Peirce was then making in logic. Later, Dewey would appreciate this pioneering work of Peirce and would expand and nurture the philosophy of pragmatism which Peirce was then articulating.) More to Dewey's liking at that time were the psychology offerings of G. Stanley Hall and the idealistic metaphysics of George Sylvester Morris, the mentor for whom he would later name a son. He completed the doctorate in 1884 with a dissertation on "Kant's Psychology," in which he combined his psychological and philosophical interests and probably developed his lifelong emphasis on the nature of knowledge and the *method* of philosophy.

THE EDUCATIONAL PHILOSOPHER

His preparation was over. Dubbed Doctor of Philosophy by the most prestigious graduate school in the country, he was academically authorized to set out on his mission, which would take him first to teach philosophy at the University of Michigan in 1884. Two years later he married a graduate of that university, Alice Chipman, and settled into domestic as well as academic life. He left Michigan in 1888 for one year at the University of Minnesota before being recalled to Michigan as chair of the philosophy department. During these years the person most influencing him was George Herbert Mead, colleague and friend. In 1894 Dewey was called to the new and dynamic University of Chicago as chair of the department of philosophy, psychology, and pedagogy. It was George Herbert Mead who secured the post for him when President Harper failed to attract any famous professors for $5,000 a year. Mead's lectures on the philosophy of evolution brought to Dewey's attention the importance of biology and the difference betweeen physical and psychological environments.

Chicago brought Dewey under the influence of the social settlement work of Jane Addams and the progressive educational methods of Colonel Francis W. Parker, whose position as principal of the Cook County Normal School was being attacked by political bosses and conservative educators. Dewey sent his children to the controversial but socially prestigious Parker school. Two years after his arrival in Chicago, Dewey established his own "Laboratory School."

Unlike so many others who had followed the same curriculum in philosophy, Dewey came to see philosophy and education as a common endeavor and attempted to implement Harper's dream of making the study of education a legitimate field of paramount importance at the university. Dewey believed that every social experience was essentially educative. In *Democracy and Education* he espoused the view that society can only transmit or reproduce itself through sharing its experience with the young. "What nutrition and reproduction are to physiological life, education is to social life," he wrote.

If Dewey had a special revelation regarding the relation of philosophy and education he would have rejected intuition as its source. His concern for the theory and practice of education appears to have developed partly out his Chicago experience and partly out of his own logic and analysis. If education is the process of forming fundamental intellectual and emotional dispositions, as he argued in *Democracy and Education,* and philosophy is the general theory of forming such dispositions, then philosophy may be defined as the general theory of education. Education was philosophy in action, and people must make themselves an instrument of continuous learning.

In his "Pedagogic Creed," he recapitulated G. Stanley Hall by saying that "all education proceeds by the participation of the individual in the social consciousness of the race." Thus he stressed the psychological and sociological sides of the educational process. School was differentiated from educaton. It was a special social institution which would concentrate on the most effective way of "bringing the child to share in the inherited resources of the race, and to use his own powers for social ends."

Dewey also believed philosophy could not be separated from culture. Culture was a relative and changing human phenomenon, and education was a transmission and transformation of culture. He believed philosophy could best serve its culture by clarifying and criticizing it, by holding up the mirror to ways of behaving that had become habitualized second nature. His critique of the educational establishment, as he found it, was thus more trenchant than the theories he advocated as a substitute.

His quarrel with traditional education was similar to that of Colonel Parker. Traditional education separated the social classes with its academic elitism. It separated leisure and labor, people and nature, mind and body, thought and action. It was itself isolated from society. The separate subjects of its curricula were so isolated from one another that an understanding of the whole of knowledge was precluded. Such subject matter was also oriented to the past and did not connect with the present or lead to a future. Traditional education was "scholiocentric" and tried to fit the child to the school instead of being "pedocentric" and fitting the school to the child. Traditional education was a one way channel of communication—from teacher to student through drill and memorization, fear and competition, with direct and didactic methods and indirect and abstract media.

Quoting Rousseau at length, Dewey advocated reversing the usual methods. He believed the child had intrinsic interest in language, in finding out or inquiring, in making and constructing things, and in artistic expression. While the traditional school taught language for its own sake, with rules preceding use, he would have language follow interest and have its use and practice precede its rules. While it limited inquiry to what others had found out in the past, he would help children find out for themselves. While the traditional school neglected the making and construction of things and artistic expression, he would stress manual training, industrial and domestic arts, as well as free artistic expression into the curriculum. As children followed their interests in making things, they learned language, arithmetic, even history. Capitalizing on these human impulses he made school the place of "occupations" rather than the place of formal study.

Much of the teaching techniques he derived from the practices of Colonel Parker, but it was to his wife and to Ella Flagg Young that he attributed the greatest influence as they tested and implemented his theories in the Laboratory School. It was in the underlying philosophic foundations of the new and progressive educational methods that he made the greatest contribution.

One could not engineer an educational curriculum and prepare youth for participation in society unless one knew the ends toward which the children were to be directed. What was the aim of life? What was the good human being and the good society? As long as education was contolled by the absolute philosophies of Platonic idealism or religious sectarianism, the aim of life, the good life, and the good society were all perfectly known and unchanging. Morals were universal and eternal truths. Teachers could mold children in accordance to an ideal blueprint. But, if the aim of life was growth, as in Dewey's view, there was no absolute and predetermined end for which the youth could be prepared. If the world of life was mutable, as in Darwin's hypothesis, and always changing in terms of its encironment, then educators could have no ultimate model of humanity for which to strive. Schooling was then a matter of natural growth and adjustment, not preparation for a certain future. Children were to be taught how to negotiate continually with the changing world of experience about them.

The experimental nature of education was thus based on Dewey's metaphysics of an unfinished and an experimental world. The discovery method of teaching practiced on the American agricultural frontier for two centuries, Dewey saw as a reflection of the continual problem solving methods of science. Science was also the model for the good, democratic society. Democracy was seen as a continual experiment with laws to test their workability. It was an experimental, shared way of living and working together for common interests. As community is based on communication, the good community must be based on a shared communion between people, a two-way communication between representative rulers and the ruled. So the good school, which he thought should be designed as an "embryonic democracy," must be shared inquiry between teacher and student.

Education, as he found it, was a dead experience. Philosophy as he had found it as a student was a dead exercise, remote from life, suspended in a precarious balance of dualisms from which no action could come. He would struggle to turn it into an instrument for probing the meaning of life, for solving life's continual problems, for reconstructing society and culture on a more scientific, ongoing, self-correcting process.

As he would teach educators to make use of the child's experience, Dewey taught philosophers and psychologists that the primary unit of life was the relative experience of each person as he or she was in transaction with the environment. Thus, individual organisms would not all perceive the environment in the same way. Individuals had to think for themselves. Each individual would have to think her or his way through the problematic situations of life by intelligent reconstruction of the situation as she or he perceived it. Thinking started with a "felt difficulty," or a "forked road" that required a decision. The process of clarifying the problem was refined through stages of hypothesizing, bringing imaginative future possibilities and past experience to bear on the problem. The indeterminate situation could be resolved by a tentative but warranted assertion, tested in the reality of the concrete world and evaluated by the consequences. This method, used by scientists, was the same method of discovery which he advocated for the teaching of children to think for themselves. Only a democracy could tolerate such thinking, and only a democracy could survive in the world that demanded continual adaptations.

COLUMBIA YEARS

Dewey himself was in the process of continual adaptation and readjustment. In 1904 he found his position at the University of Chicago untenable. President Nicholas Murray Butler of Columbia University offered him a professorship of philosophy. From this New York base, he found large numbers of future educators available for his lectures. They were in Columbia's enormously popular Teachers College division. He was also nearer the heart of the country's publishing industry and its intellectual center as well. He also was able to extend his influence to many students from abroad.

At Columbia, Dewey interacted with professors William Heard Kilpatrick and Edward L. Thorndike. Thorndike's work in testing and conditioning through behaviorist theories of stimulus/response/reinforcement was not completely in accord with the problem solving techniques of Dewey, or that of Kilpatrick. This would become an unresolved problem in the development of what was then being called progressive education. Conditioning smacked of authoritarianism, teacher directed control, and might preclude the development of individual thinking and self-growth. It could imply there was no transfer of learning, only a transfer of specific responses.

Furthermore, Dewey, was not completely sold on the rage of student testing. According to his friend and colleague, Professor Horace M. Kallen, "Dewey had no use for measurement. He thought that it was usually a way of stopping growth rather than of facilitating growth." And Herbert W. Schneider reminisced that "Dewey really had a very deep resentment against standardization of all sorts; and I think many people thought that for that reason he was against standards, and every once in a while he spoke that way. I remember once when he was presiding at an educational evening in Teachers College, there was a series of papers on mental testing. And it was all on norms and so on. At the end of the meeting . . . he said, 'Listening to these papers I was reminded of the way we used to weigh hogs on the farm. We would put a plank in between the rails of the fence, put the hog on one end of the plank and then pile the other end of the plank with rocks until the rocks balanced the hog. Then we took the hog off; and then we guessed the weight of the rocks!' '' Nevertheless, both Thorndike and Dewey were on the same side of the educational plank when it came to the use of scientific methods.

In keeping with his philosophy of action, Dewey moved more and more into liberal political circles in New York and worked for social as well as educational reform. He and his wife had long struggled for women's rights, and during one demonstration he drew laughter as he marched down Fifth Avenue with a banner he apparently hadn't read. It bore the words: "Men can vote! Why can't I?"

He worked for racial equality and was one of the original signers of the call to action that resulted in the National Association for the Advancement of Colored People. He supported the American Civil Liberties Union in its early stages. He became a charter member of the New York Teachers Union when it joined the American Federation of Labor. Disenchanted with the two party system, he helped organize a new political party of liberals—the League for Independent Political Action, and he served as its first president.

His concern for academic freedom led him to help organize the American Association of University Professors, which provided a national forum for protecting professors and students in their efforts to teach and learn freely, to pursue truth wherever it might lead. As the initial president, he gave it the power of his name and reputation, thus assuring its subsequent growth and success. The association set national standards so that professors could not be willfully dismissed for unpopular academic pursuits. Such freedom was most prized by those scholars who believed knowledge was continually growing, that there was no certain and absolute truth. Dewey himsef had moved from what he called "absolutism" to "experimentalism" in his intellectual growth. But in one of his rare reminiscences for *Contemporary American Philosophers* in 1930, about the time of his retirement from active teaching at Columbia University, he admitted to absolutism in his early stages of growth and even to the fact that he had always had such inclinations. He recalled the conflict in his early student days between theological intuitionism, rationalism, German idealism, "sensational empiricism," and Scotish common sense. He said he was molded at home and at the University of Vermont in the absolutism of religion and the romantic philosophies which divided reality into the phenomena that could be known by science and the high world of a transcendent God that could be known only by intuition: "I learned the terminology of an intuitional philosophy, but it did not go deep, and in no way did it satisfy what I was dimly reaching for."

He conceded that his later reaction against this unscientific bent in his intellectual formation was probably a reaction against what he said was closest to his "natural tendencies." He confessed that the educational and philosophical controversies for which he had become famous were really battles going on inside himself. The "emphasis upon the concrete, empirical, and 'practical' in my later writings," he wrote, "served as a protest and protection against something in myself which, in the pressure of the weight of actual experiences, I knew to be a weakness."

His early writings were what he called "schematic" or modeled on classical dialectics (contradictory opposites or dualisms), such as materialism versus immaterialism, body versus soul. At that time he said he was unaware of the Hegelian dialectic which synthesized the opposites. He discovered this escape from dualisms from his neo-Hegelian professor of philosophy at Johns Hopkins, and he began to break with the intuition and subjectivity of Kant, the subject of his doctoral dissertation. Hegel's thought "supplied a demand for unification that was doubtless an intense emotional craving." It gave him an "immediate release." (His later books, such as *School and Society, The Child and the Curriculum, Democracy and Education, Experience and Education* represented his opposition to dualisms, his view of interaction between entities that he viewed as part of a continuum, not opposite or unrelated poles.)

Although Dewey believed "Hegel has left a permanent deposit on my thinking," he "drifted away from Hegelianism." Hegel was ultimately too much of an absolutist for the maturing Dewey who would reject the cosmic generalizations that the Hegelians made out of particulars. Dewey said that one great exception to his primary learning from people and situations was the book *Psychology* by Williams James. It helped the slow drift from Hegel and brought his philosophy into the mainstream of psychology, with its emphasis on behavior rather than consciousness. James—who described Dewey as "laboring with a great freight toward the light"—gave Dewey the final push away from Hegel.

In the end, Dewey believed his "intellectual biography" lacked a "unified pattern." He said, "I seem to be unstable, chameleon-like, yielding one after another to many diverse and even incompatible influences; struggling to assimilate something from each and yet striving to carry it forward in a way that is logically consistent with what has been learned from its predecessors." Thus his philosophy and life were a continual struggle, a continual searching. While it was said that he had an aversion for great systems of thought, or any *isms*, he believed otherwise. He longed for an integration of all thought, but none of his books had yet captured it.

His retirement from teaching in 1930 was not the end of his intellectual travels or philosophical quests. His wife had died in 1927, shortly before his visits to the schools in Soviet Russia, but he continued to lecture, to write, to go on growing. He married Roberta (Lowitz) Grant in 1946. They adopted two children. He carried on an extensive philosophical correspondence with Arthur F. Bentley until 6 December 1951, when the aging Bentley wrote, "I haven't heard from you for some time. In much the same figure of speech, however, I might say that I have not heard even from myself."

Dewey kept up with philosophical and psychological developments. On 17 November 1950 he wrote Adelbert Ames, Jr. that "I think your work is by far the most important work done in the psychological-philosophical field during this century—I am tempted to say the *only* really important work."

Within two years he was dead. He died in New York City on 1 June 1952, and accounts of his death were spread in newspapers throughout the world.

HIS THOUGHT EVALUATED

After the flood of eulogies, however, came the wave of criticisms. There were those who claimed he was a weak teacher and writer, and that progressive education for which he stood was all but discredited. (Indeed, the Progressive Education Association survived him only by a few years.) His teachings were crucified as anti-intellectual, anti-religious, radical, and even subversive.

As a teacher, even his friends and apologists were mixed on their assessment of his pedagogic style. Of course, he never had any formal training in teaching, and he was shy by nature. One of his former students recalled that he never looked at his class during the whole semester, but one had the feeling of "actually watching thought going on; it seemed quite laborious." His students found it difficult to take orderly notes. In fact, Dewey often disregarded his own notes when taking to the platform. Horace Kallan had the opinion that Dewey was much more at ease in "communicating with his typewriter than he was face to face, person to person." He said, "There was a kind of withdrawn quality in all his communication, I found." He was said to be somewhat more effective in public speeches, especially when he was carried away by an emotional issue, although it was remembered that he often forgot to bring his speech. Friends would try to get a carbon copy beforehand and thus save the absentminded professor from embarrassment.

It is more difficult to evaluate the charge that his writing was weak, vague, or poorly written. Some critics of his writing had probably not done much reading of the one they criticized, though William James had. He called Dewey's style "damnable." Then he added, "you might say goddamnable." Dewey's style, like his problem-solving techniques of teaching, left much for the reader's discovery. He was not always direct and dogmatic in statement. As in his theory of aesthetics, beauty is in the eye or mind of the beholder. So the meaning of his writing is relative to the experience of his readers, though he never tried to use technical language that would require a trained philosopher to follow all his thoughts. It seems he came to teaching and writing with humility.

While he was associated with progressive education, reaping its praise and blame, he closed his study of *Experience and Education* in 1938 with a "firm belief" that "the fundamental issue is not of new versus old education nor of progressive against traditional education but a question of what anything whatever must be to be worthy of the name *education*. I am not, I hope and believe, in favor of any ends or any methods simply because the name progressive may be applied to them. . . . What we want and need is education pure and simple, and we shall make surer and faster progress when we devote ourselves to finding out just what education is and what conditions have to be satisfied in order that education may be a reality and not a name or a slogan." He also warned his progressive disciples that "It is not too much to say than an educational philosophy which professes to be based on the idea of freedom may become as dogmatic as ever was the traditional education which is reacted against. For any theory and set of practices are dogmatic which are not based upon critical examination of its own underlying principles."

The charge that he was anti-intellectual can be refuted by the wide range of his thinking and writing that touched on every intellectual question of his times. That progressive education was anti-intellectual from the standpoint of subject matter, was even a criticism that Dewey raised in *Experience and Education,* some years after his retirement. He believed the weakest point in progressive schools was the selection and organization of "intellectual subject matter." He said this was inevitable, because progressive schools had scarcely a generation to "break loose from the cut and dried material which formed the staple of the old education." But he insisted that "the underlying ideal is that of progressive organization of knowledge." He argued, "When education is based in theory and practice upon experience, it goes without saying that the organized subject-matter of the adult and specialist cannot provide the starting point. Nevertheless, it represents the goal toward which education should continuously move."

DEWEY'S FAITH

If not anti-intellectual, was John Dewey anti-religious? Were progressive schools promoters of secular humanism because of a godless Dewey? He was born a Christian and attended church regularly until he left the University of Michigan in the 1890s. About that time his psychology began to replace the soul with the body, possibly under the influence of George Herbert Mead. His wife was religious, according to her daughter, but not sectarian. Years before, when teaching high school in Oil City, he had what he called a "mystic experience." He was concerned about the apparent conflict he found in the study of science and his practice of religion. Suddenly, after that experience, the conflict was resolved and it never worried him again. He did make science a kind of religion. In *A Common Faith* he wrote, "The sense of dignity of human nature is as religious as is the sense of awe and reverence [for a supernatural diety] when it rests upon a sense of human nature as a cooperating part of a larger whole. Natural piety is not of necessity either a fatalistic acquiescence in natural happenings or a romantic idealization of the world. It may rest upon a just sense of nature as the whole of which we are parts, while it also recognizes that we are parts that are marked by intelligence and purpose, having the capacity to strive by their aid to bring conditions into greater consonance with what is humanly desirable. Such piety is an inherent constituent of a just perspective in life."

It is in his poems, that he would have had no one read, where the religion of his youth, the intuition and absolutism of his early training, remained throughout his life. When he died, although he had long left organized religion behind, his funeral services were held in the Community Church in New York City. This church had for its purpose a faith in life and the realization on earth of "the beloved community."[7]

It goes without saying that Dewey participated in liberal and even radical causes, but it is hard to believe, as his most violent detractors would have it, that he plotted to undermine the intellectual competence of American youth so that the Soviet Union could overtake American technology. He did favor Roosevelt's New Deal and even stood a little left of that. He favored a form of socialism, but the "socialization" of youth in school was not meant to include any partisan economic or political indoctrination—a word he hated. He was president of the League for Industrial Democracy, and he remained its honorary president until his death. Harry W. Laidler, director of that organization, said, "Dewey thought in terms of democratic socialism, but he was experimental all the way and would have liked to see, say, public ownership of one industry and if that succeeded, go on to other industries. He was pretty near in his thinking to some sort of mixed system, with the retention of a private sector in our economy. With democratic socialists, he insisted upon the strengthening of civil liberties, and contended that public and co-operative ownership was not an end in itself, but a means to enriching the lives of all the people."

While Dewey had approved of the education he had found in the Soviet Union in the days before Stalin's purges, he did not approve of Communism, and he once remarked while in Mexico for the Trotsky trials that it was tragic to see such a brilliant man "locked up in absolutes."

There is no gospel according to John Dewey, if by gospel one means something to be believed implicitly without criticism. He forced people to make their own decisions. Do we believe in the human capacity to create our own destiny, or do we not? Do we believe the school should be organized around the experiences of the student, or do we not? Do we believe in Dewey, or do we not? Dewey would not have posed these either/or questions. He opposed dualisms. He did not want to be followed blindly. His word is not for a progressive education but for the best education possible for the future carriers of a democratic culture.

Though his books are no longer read as a catechism by all educationists in the United States, John Dewey remains the best-known North American educational theorist of the twentieth century. His writing on the interrelationships between education, philosophy, experience, and politics are known around the world, but much of the basis for his mature thought came out of his experiences in Chicago from 1894 to 1904. In addition to Francis W. Parker, two of the most imporant people in the development of his own thought were Margaret Haley and Ella Flagg Young. Both women were in turn influenced by Dewey and by each other. Their careers intertwined significantly for more than a decade and neither can be understood without reference to the other. Haley will be presented first, followed by Ella Flagg Young.

Margaret A. Haley (1861-1939)

One imporant aspect of the progressive movement in education was teacher unionization, and Chicago's Margaret Haley was instrumental in their early formation. Born in Chanahan near Joliet, Illinois on 15 November 1861, "Maggie" was the second oldest of eight children. Her parents, Elizabeth and Michael, were Irish Catholics whose families had emigrated for better working conditions and educational opportunities. From her father Maggie received a heavy dose of liberty in the name of democracy for all. Michael had a strong sense of justice and social reform which he passed on to his eldest daughter. He was largely a self-taught man whose early jobs included bridge building and canal dredging. By the time he had married he owned two stone quarries near the towns of Chanahan and Morrison; he had also become a self-taught expert in geography, economics, and labor politics.

Maggie remembered her early years fondly. Her mother had taught her to read, and by the time she was ten, she was intrigued by school. Her father's quarry was doing well, so she was able to leave the one room town school and enter St. Angela's Academy in Morris. In the beginning the possibility of a college education loomed brightly on her horizon. However, by the time graduation from St. Angela's was imminent the hope of college faded for the sixteen-year-old. It died with the collapse of her father's quarry. Michael Haley owned the quarry in partnership with three other men who wanted to bribe an important contractor in order to get some needed work. Haley refused, and his partners forced the quarry to be temporarily closed. It literally put Haley out of business, because he could not sustain the temporary financial losses the way his wealthier partners could. To make matters worse Margaret found out that the quarry closed during her graduation exercises from the academy. Her father walked into the auditorium and she said: "If I live a hundred years, I'll never forget my father's face and all it conveyed of defeat and the consequences. It meant for me the end of school and I had to prepare to do something else."[8]

EARLY CAREER

That "something else" was teaching, and that summer she began a normal school course of study. By fall she had her first teaching job—a country school near Dresden Heights. It was a few months before her seventeenth birthday and being only five feet tall and weighing less than one hundred pounds the children at first mistook her for a student. She taught in country schools for several years, all the time keeping up with the latest educational methods through normal courses. From there she taught briefly in Joliet and then moved on to the south side of Chicago. Maggie spent the first year or two substitute teaching while she waited for a position vacancy. She also came into contact with the newly arrived progressive educator, Colonel Francis W. Parker of the Cook County Normal School. He was just making a name for himself, and Haley recalled him during his first years there:

> Colonel Parker was by no means pacific in his quest for sweetness and light. He roared, he growled, he stormed, he banged. . . . He scared the wits out of students, and he terrified teachers. He sent for parents and shamed them into aiding their children. He was Reform Rampant—and I watched him with unterrified glee. . . . In him I somehow sensed the fundamental justice of his attitude and saw the need of his method. More surely than anyone else he taught me that a straight line was the shortest distance between two points. I was to remember that twenty years later.[9]

Haley accepted a sixth grade teaching position at the Hendricks school in 1884. The principal there was, by Maggie's standards, incompetent and the pay was meager. These conditions compelled her to join a group of teachers who were organizing on a city wide basis for better working conditions such as a stable salary schedule and tenure protection. The notion that these teachers (mostly women) could have a democratic voice in their professional careers was a new one which had been supported by one of Chicago's district superintendents (and future superintendent) Ella Flagg Young. In such a climate this group had brought a pension plan to passage in 1895, and were working on a salary schedule. However, by 1897 the pension law was being threatened and criticized on actuarial grounds, so at a meeting to address these issues the Chicago Teachers' Federation (CTF) was born. The seeds of democracy and reform which had been planted by Michael Haley began to germinate in his thirty-six year old daughter. She met the author and leader of the pension bill, Catharine Goggin, and together they would lead the CTF through some of their toughest battles.

By the spring of 1899 Goggin and Haley were the CTF's president and vice president respectively. Under their direction the school board had approved a modest salary scale. However, by the fall of 1899 the board said they could not afford all of the 1899 increases or any of those for 1900.

During the Christmas break, while sitting in the reception room of her dentist's office, Margaret overheard a conversation to the effect that certain large corporations had escaped paying taxes on property valued at over $100 million. She contemplated this realizing that if the CTF could bring these tax dodgers under the law, the city's treasury would have the money necessary to pay the increases. Next Haley talked to Goggin who suggested that they get legal counsel from a friend of both of their families—former Governor John P. Altgeld. Altgeld told Haley that she was right in what she wanted to do, but that she would never win against the powerful corporate structure. He himself had tried as governor, but to no avail. Margaret's response to the ex-governor revealed one of the key motivating forces of her personality—a sort of naive determination: "I [do] not see why we should not win if we [are] right." Goggin's response was equally revealing when her cohort told her what Altgeld had said. Catharine responded, "I don't care whether we win or lose if we are right."

THE TAX FIGHT

In January 1900 the CTF voted to pay the salaries of Goggin and Haley so that they could leave their classrooms to devote full time to their tax pursuits.[10] For the next two and one-half years lawyers for the CTF and corporate structure were in and out of the courts. Finally, in 1902, $600,000 worth of back taxes was awarded to the board of education who dealt the teachers another blow: they voted to use the hard won tax money for building and maintenance—not back salaries. This was not the only wound the school board had inflicted upon their employees. They had temporarily weakened the pension plan by making contributions voluntary, and at the direction of Superintendent Edwin G. Cooley, they had instituted a new secret marking system to evaluate teachers for pay increases. Under this system, in order to advance to the top pay levels, teachers had to be: (1) reexamined with another certification test; and (2) secretly evaluated by their principals as to their teaching effectiveness. Finally, the average of both ratings had to equal at least 80 percent. Of the 2,600 teachers eligible for top pay levels, only 61 were receiving it. Instead, most of the teachers were earning $600 a year which was not much even in 1902. Also, this had been the average for twenty years.

At the next meeting of the CTF a very discouraged body of teachers pondered what to do. They listened as a representative from the Chicago Federation of Labor invited them to tell their story to 200,000 voting men. Social reformer Jane Addams spoke next and encouraged them to affiliate with the CF of L. (Later she found herself at a White House luncheon trying to explain to President Roosevelt why she had done this. He did not approve.)[11] The federation voted to affiliate with the labor union, thereby becoming the first teaching group to do so. Slowly but surely the predominantly female CTF was becoming more powerful than anyone had expected a women's group to be—especially when they didn't have the franchise. Their lawyers Isaiah T. Greenacre and his neophyte partner Clarence Darrow secured an injunction against releasing the money to the board, and the board and the teachers went back to court.

In 1904 the courts ruled that the money should be used for back salary increases, but this time the school board attorneys were the ones to secure the injunction against such action. Realizing that this could go on forever, Haley and the CTF entered politics. Along with the CF of L, they campaigned for a reform mayoral candidate, since mayors appointed board members. In 1905 their efforts were rewarded when Edward Dunne was elected. By 1906, two-thirds of the board were Dunne appointees who voted to pay the back salaries. So in June 1906, after six and one-half years of steady fighting, each of 1,653 teachers were paid forty-five dollars in back salary.

From 1906 to 1909 the CTF and board continued to pursue a sort of tug of war battle. Superintendent Edwin G. Cooley tried to keep the schools moving, but in practice his tactics continued to produce a great deal of factionalism throughout the various organs of the school system. At times Haley wondered if the CTF would survive. Finally, in March of 1909, a very tired and battle weary Cooley resigned giving ill health as his reason. It took the school board five months to come to consensus on its new superintendent. That summer they appointed former district superintendent and current normal school principal, Dr. Ella Flagg Young, to the delight of the teachers. Her *Isolation in the Schools* had become the manual for democratizing the schools and giving teachers a voice in their professional lives. From 1909 until she retired in 1915 the school system ran relatively smoothly, and she removed many of Cooley's unpopular practices.

OTHER FIGHTS

Young had barely started her superintendency when Margaret became convinced that the National Educational Association (NEA) could benefit from her pragmatic brand of democracy. For several years Haley had been trying to help teachers gain a voice in the policy-making end of the NEA. Since the 1880s this organization had been controlled by a group of Ivy League presidents and city superintendents called the "old guard." Their autocratic policies had resulted in nonvoting membership status for teachers in general. Maggie's crusade started at the annual 1901 meeting when she challenged Commissioner of Education William Torrey Harris. That June day he had been describing to a hot, tired, convention audience how the educational horizon was without a cloud and how big business was its friend. When he finished the chair threw open discussion to the floor. Haley stood, the first woman to ever address the chair. She refuted what he said by describing certain general revenue facts she had learned from her tax fight. Harris jumped up, pointed his finger at her and said, "Pay no attention to what that teacher has said, for I take it she is a grade school teacher just out of her school room at the end of [the] school year, worn out, tired out and hysterical." Then he continued, "Chicago is no criterion for other parts of the country, but it is morbid, cyclonic and hysterical and you can never tell what is going to happen in Chicago." Haley responded again and when Harris figured out that she was describing the tax fight with the corporate structure he grew quiet. However, the fuse was ignited, and Haley became one of a group of so-called insurgents fighting to democratize the NEA.[12] It is little wonder, therefore, that she thought Young would be a good NEA president, and throughout the 1909-1910 school year, she successfully ran Young's campaign. Amidst the old guard's empty charges of fraud, Young became the organization's first female president. In the following years teachers began voting, and by 1914 the Department of Classroom Teachers held their first set of meetings and programs.

As soon as one battle was over it seemed as if Maggie Haley was embroiled in another. This time it was with the CTF back in Chicago. During the spring of 1915, board president Jacob Loeb announced that, in order to operate in the fiscal black, teachers would have to sustain a seven and one-half percent salary cut for the remainder of the year. Superintendent Young had planned to retire that summer, but with this budget problem she decided to continue on to the end of the fall term. She scrutinized the budget and reduced any deficit, while Maggie lobbied successfully in the state legislature for a larger portion of the tax levy. Consequently, the teachers' pay cut did not go into effect, but President Loeb was not happy. He had never liked the CTF or the two high school teacher organizations which had sprung up since 1902. That summer he got his school board to pass the "Loeb rule" which forbade teachers to belong to: (1) any labor connected group; and (2) any organization whose leaders were not currently teaching. The CTF lawyers secured an injunction against the rule and eventually had it declared illegal in court. But this only made Loeb more furious and more determined. At the end of the 1915-1916 school year the board failed to issue 1916-1917 teaching contracts to sixty-eight teachers. Thirty-eight of these were CTF members. The CTF supported their ousted members, and Goggin and Haley went to work on a tenure bill. By the time this bill became law in spring, however, Haley was left to work alone. Catharine Goggin had been killed by a truck while crossing a street on 4 January 1916. In fall of 1917 the ousted teachers were reinstated, but the battle had its casualties. One occurred when the CF of L recommended official withdrawal of the CTF from their ranks. This was accomplished in 1917, and Haley then joined with other national education figures to found the American Federation of Teachers (AFT) that same year.

Maggie also incurred Loeb's wrath on a more personal level. During the Loeb rule fight he had given a story to the Chicago *Tribune* stating that Haley had been receiving two salaries from 1901-1907: one from the board and the other from the CTF. Although the *Tribune* promised to retract the story, they never seemed to get around to it, so Margaret Haley sued the newspaper for libel to the tune of $50,000. Only then did *Tribune* representatives offer a $10,500 out of court settlement, but the Irish union leader could not be deterred. "What I wanted," she stated, "was not money, but a verdict proving I had been libeled." She won the case, but received only $500 in retribution from the newspaper.[13]

During the 1920s Haley renewed her efforts to get an adequate single salary scale for Chicago teachers. During the decade after World War I, teachers saw no salary raises. The CTF leader found herself lobbying for larger levies, but these never seemed to be enough. Also, property tax assessments and payments were hardly equitable. She continued to crusade against corporate control of public utilities; poor financial use of school lands by the school board; and corporate abuse of the tax system. Toward the end of the twenties she managed to have the city reassessed on a more equitable basis. But tax machinery was slow and big business held the tax assessment up in courtroom litigation. Amid efforts to get these problems resolved and tax revenue flowing again, the stock market crashed and the Great Depression hit. Haley worked tirelessly to alleviate a terrible financial crisis for teachers. In 1934 she helped secure a national loan to bail out the city's schools, but by then teachers had gone through many payless paydays of being issued their salaries in scrip (paper stamped "Insufficient funds").

In 1935 she retired to California where she renewed earlier efforts to complete and publish her autobiography. She died there in 1939 of a heart attack.

The sense of personal commitment to democratic justice and reform without reference to the odds was not only Margaret Haley's banner but it was the slogan of early progressivism. Distrust of big business was also characteristic of Haley and many other progressives. However, her tireless and determined efforts to create/recreate a workable democracy consisting of enlightened men and women from all levels of society have rarely been paralleled. She firmly believed that the public must control utilities and natural resources as well as schools, although her biggest endeavors were directed at the institution in which she began her career. About her work she said:

> The teachers' fight has been a fight in the general cause of liberty. It was a fight for a time-honored American institution, the free public schools, . . . for its integrity and as a means of maintaining democracy in America. The whole idea of the public schools was that democracy had to be based on intelligence of the masses. . . . [It was the] institution through which to obtain and secure and improve in every decade this intelligence. . . . [Unfortunately] it began to run amuck whenever it disturbed a pampered interest.[14]

John Dewey wrote about the philosophical bases of industrial democracy. Margaret Haley—who liked Dewey's work—fought to make democracy real, as did her friend and colleague Ella Flagg Young.

Ella Flagg Young (1845-1918)

Journalist Joseph Mayer Rice had already called attention to the city of Chicago when in 1893 he singled out the educational work of Colonel Francis Wayland Parker at the Cook County Normal. Rice had been positively exuberant in his praise of Parker's progressive (scientific) teaching methods. Cook County was an island in a sea of poorly taught, badly managed, overcrowded, and unhealthy schools throughout the nation. However, it was in this latter category that he placed the city schools of Chicago, so the growing metropolis was both praised and condemned for its educational practices. The city schools were thirteen years away from feeling the effects of progressive reform in the hands of their first female superintendent, Ella Flagg Young.[15]

EARLY LIFE

Ella's parents were of Scottish ancestry and living in Buffalo when their youngest of three children was born. Her father, Theodore, had received little formal education, having been apprenticed to the sheet metal trades at the age of ten. Her mother, Jane, had married at around the age of sixteen or seventeen and had borne a daughter, Cecilia Sarah, then a son, Charles Theodore, and finally Ella.

Although her sister and brother were allowed to go to school at the appropriate ages, Ella was kept at home until the age of ten. It seems to have been her mother's conviction that her youngest was a rather sickly, delicate child who needed the benefits of a mother's protection and lots of sunshine.

At the age of eight or nine, Ella began working to overcome this delicate image. To this point in time, she had not learned to read or write, but at the breakfast table one morning this condition was changed. Her parents were reading an account of a school fire in which young children had to jump from upper story windows in order to escape. Ella asked her mother to read the story to her. Then, crying for the fate of children her age, the little girl took the newspaper and went into another room to try to read it. She remembered how her mother had started the story and matched that up with the words in print. When she got stuck, she asked the maid, until finally, she had worked her way through the whole article.

Ella found other books in the house and began working through those. Most of these were related to Presbyterian doctrines, and one day when her aunt was visiting with some other ladies she expounded on some of her religious knowledge. Her aunt asked her what she had been reading; it was Baxter's *Call to the Unconverted*. While her aunt was amused, her mother was not. Mrs. Flagg calmly but sternly told her young daughter to remove herself to the back yard to garden. Ella obeyed, but in the next couple of days Mother Goose stories replaced Baxter.

By the time she was ten, she had taught herself how to write, and by eleven she was finally allowed to enter the grammar department of the nearby school where her brother and sister attended. Apparently, such accomplishments had convinced her mother to ''let go'' of the baby of the family.

Ella found school a very intriguing place, and she was able to demonstrate her academic skills quickly. She had an aptitude for math—as did her father. This skill was put to use by the teacher who made the young girl a monitor (helper) in math. This meant that her desk was moved up next to the teacher's but this latter circumstance was frowned upon by Mr. Flagg. He thought he noticed a rather "priggish" attitude on the part of his youngest daughter, and he blamed it on the new location of her desk. Ella was told that she could continue to help the teacher after her desk was placed back with the rest of the class.

By the time Ella was thirteen, the Flaggs were on the move to Chicago. Foundry management seemed more lucrative in the new growing town on Lake Michigan than it did in Buffalo. While Mr. Flagg's career in management prospered, his daughter's schooling suffered. Ella had finished the grammar grades in Buffalo; therefore, she was ready for high school. However, she was told that before she could take the entrance exams she would have to complete one year in a Chicago grammar school. The course of study at the Brown school was one Ella had already completed in Buffalo, so the new student was not finding much of a challenge. Also, her parents had never really encouraged her to go to school, and it was not particularly common for girls to continue on into high school anyway. Consequently, after a few months at Brown, Ella dropped out.

Apparently she could not get the idea of schooling out of her mind, and in 1860 when she was fifteen she found a new chance to further her education. One of her friends was going to take a teacher certification test and asked Ella if she would like to go along and take it, too. Ella passed the exam, but was told that she was too young to teach. The superintendent of the city's schools, William H. Wells, asked her if she would like to enroll in the normal department of the Chicago high school. The fifteen-year-old responded with a definite "yes," and she was entered.

Ella Flagg was entering her second year of training when her mother advised her that she thought her daughter would never make a good teacher. Her reasons were as follows: first, Ella was not used to being around young children and knew nothing of their nature and capabilities; second, her daughter was too hard on herself when making mistakes, and she would tend to be this way with children. Determined to test herself under teaching circumstances, Ella looked for and found a classroom where the children were friendly and the teacher was good. She arranged to help the teacher on a weekly basis, thus setting up her own student teaching situation.

EARLY CAREER

After a year's practice teaching experience, her mother removed her objections and had to admit that her daughter seemed to thrive on the experience. In spring of 1862 Miss Flagg graduated from the normal department of the Chicago high school; she was just seventeen years old. The following fall, she began her long teaching career in the primary department of a Chicago ghetto school. Two weeks to the day after she started teaching, her mother died.

By 1863 Miss Flagg was an assistant to the principal of the old Brown school where she had felt rather bored and uncomfortable just five years earlier. From there she went to another grammar school as head of the two practice teaching rooms. In the next seventeen years, Ella Flagg experienced other aspects of public education: she taught math at the high school level; she devised a curriculum based on Pestalozzi's methods of using objects in teaching; and she became principal, first of the Scammon school and next of the largest school in Chicago—the Skinner. She remained at the Skinner as principal until 1887, when she was called to a newly created assistant superintendent's position.

Personally, the years paralleling her climb to the assistant superintendency were mixed with some happiness and much pain. In 1868 her brother Charles was killed in a freak train accident which saw only him lose his life. That same year Ella married a much older friend of the family named William Young. Little is known of the circumstances surrounding her marriage. Mr. Flagg may have encouraged the marriage. He was getting older and with Charles gone, there would be no male to look after his youngest daughter. At any rate, she married Young in December of 1868, but his health was not very good. He went West to recuperate and died there in 1873. That same year her sister and father succumbed to pneumonia. At the age of twenty-eight Ella Flagg Young was widowed and without any living members in her immediate family. She turned her familial affections to the teachers and children of the Chicago schools.

From 1887 to 1899 Young worked as an assistant or district superintendent. This period also witnessed one of the most rapid growth periods for the Chicago schools. Even with the erection of 271 more school buildings between 1884 and 1893, temporary arrangements were still necessary. Total enrollment grew from 630,000 in 1886 to about 1.5 million in 1893, and pupils attending half-day sessions rose from 6,000 to 14,000 over that same period.

Curricular changes accompanied these growth patterns. Many of the progressive reforms were starting to gain some attention. Manual arts, domestic science, music, art, and the kindergarten were some of the innovations that their enemies derogatorily called "fads and frills." And last but not least, many of the elementary school teachers—predominantly women—were holding meetings in order to protest and remedy some of their working conditions. For example, women teachers were not supposed to be married, yet they had no pension system to safeguard their retirement years. Secondly, whenever the city's treasury was found to be lacking, the elementary (women) teachers were the first to receive salary cuts. Finally, they wanted to have some input in preparing and choosing the curriculum—an activity which Assistant Superintendent Young was allowing in her district. The outgrowth of these meetings was the organization called the Chicago Teachers' Federation (CTF) mentioned previously. Their two powerful leaders, Catharine Goggin and Margaret Haley, had been influenced by Young's democratic policies as district superintendent.

In 1895 Ella Flagg Young was feeling the need for more academic preparation and decided to enroll in a course at the University of Chicago's newly opened Department of Philosophy, Psychology and Pedagogy under the headship of a young, ambitious and as yet unknown professor by the name of John Dewey. By 1898 Young was contemplating pursuing a doctorate and giving up the district superintendency. There were several reasons for this: a new superintendent with much more autocratic and conservative policies had been hired; even though she was fifty-four years old, she was not ready to retire and she had gone about as far as she could without an advanced degree; and Dewey was anxious to have her come to Chicago and help him run an experimental school which was quickly falling on its face.

STUDENT, PROFESSOR, PRINCIPAL

In June of 1899 Young submitted her resignation, but the CTF was up in arms. They planned a protest only to discover that Young did not want it. She told them that she could not work in such a harness as the new superintendent had imposed, and she also tried to squelch the rumor that she was going on the faculty at the University of Chicago. (No professorship had been offered her yet, but many rumors circulated to the effect that she had resigned for such a reason.) However, in resigning to pursue a Ph.D., she was sticking to an old motto of hers: "Those who live on the mountain have a longer day than those who live in the valley. Sometimes all we need to brighten our day is to climb a little higher." Ella Flagg Young would climb much higher before she was finished with her career.

On a blistering hot August day in 1900, Young became Dr. Young as she successfully defended her dissertation entitled, "Isolation in School Systems." In essence her dissertation embodied a philosophy of learning by experience and of social freedoms for a school community through a democratically run administration from superintendent to student. Obviously pragmatic in her views, John Dewey was later to say that she "was a practicing pragmatist long before the doctrine was ever in print," and that he got more ideas from her than anyone else when it came to education.

For the next four years Dr. Young served as a professor of education at the University of Chicago. Her mission was generally to bring Chicago teachers to the university for study and specifically to expand Dewey's scope as a leading professor in preparing elementary teachers—something like what Parker was doing. The unfortunate part was that the president of the University of Chicago had just acquired the reknowned Colonel Parker and his faculty for the university's new school of education. Dewey and his lab school were being eclipsed royally. Even after Parker died in 1902, the fighting continued. Dewey refused to acknowledge Parker's influence by trying to rid himself of the Colonel's faculty. Finally, when it did not work, Dewey was forced to resign in order to save his self-esteem. The year was 1904, and Dr. Young, who was tired of the petty politics and playing a middle role of sorts, left too. Rumors had it that the university's president, William Rainey Harper, had offered her a better position if she would stay, but that she turned it down. She had left the city's schools because she did not feel that she could work in another's harness and here she was doing just that. It is little wonder that she did not want to continue.

She left for Europe with her friend and roommate, Laura Brayton. While she was there the principalship of the Chicago Normal School (the old Cook County Normal where Parker had been) came open. Her name was suggested by friends, and in the fall of 1905 she entered upon the duties of principal.

With her demonstrated leadership skills, knowledge of subject matter, familiarity with Chicago's schools, and ability to inspire, she was a good choice. During the four years that she remained head, the normal school became a model of pragmatic and progressive doctrines. Students were interviewed as to their dedication to the teaching profession and their ability to understand children. The new manual arts and domestic sciences were interwoven with traditional subjects in such a manner so as not to lose academic or practical skills. Practice teaching schools were chosen for their ethnicity and not for their Americanism, since the city's population was predominantly foreign-born. But if the normal was running efficiently and effectively, it was one of the few educational institutions in the city that was. By 1909 internal strife and factionalism were tearing the city schools apart; her talents were sorely needed elsewhere—even if she was sixty-four years old.

SUPERINTENDENCY

The series of events which led to such divisiveness had built up over a period of ten years or so (1899-1909) and need a word of explanation here. The biggest single element that produced the most hostility from board of education members was the growth of the teachers' organizations. The CTF, especially, had gained a level of power and independence that transcended classroom routines. The school board and their long arm of control, Superintendent Edwin G. Cooley, had attempted to strike back and squelch this powerful teachers' organization. Through all of this warlike atmosphere, Superintendent Cooley tried to keep the schools moving, but in practice his techniques enhanced a philosophy of divide and conquer. The result was a great degree of tension and hostility throughout the various organs of the school structure. The teachers discovered that their friend on the board, Jane Addams—while a great social reformer—had little stamina for confronting authority. Several times her sentiment lay with the teachers, but her vote was cast with the board. Such was the case with the secret marking system and the voluntary pension bill.

As noted earlier, Cooley resigned in 1909, giving ill health as his reason. It took the board five months to pull itself together enough to agree on a superintendent. They interviewed six candidates in July. Finally on 29 July they unanimously elected Ella Flagg Young on the second ballot. Apparently, the board put its trust in her because they felt that she could best handle the CTF. They had since managed to put back the compulsory clause of their pension fund along with a pension board that was predominantly made up of teachers and a few school board members. (There was also a clause that made the board match pension interest money.) Dr. Young had told the school board that she thought the CTF could be made to equalize that representation if it meant that the school board would match the teachers dollar for dollar. (She had yet to find out how wrong she was.)

The teachers trusted her because most of them had had some personal encounters with her previously. It was said that she knew the names of all six thousand teachers in the system. She began to involve the teachers in decisions that affected their professional lives, and she removed the secret marking system.

From the first she announced that her administration would be characterized by "democratic efficiency. . . . There is to be but one head," she said, "and I am it. Whenever I find that I cannot have complete charge of the educational end of the school system, I will quit. I cannot carry out my ideas unless I am given control of affairs." She was to remain true to her words twice in the next five years.

The first two and a half years of her superintendency were harmonious ones. The schools had courses of study geared to meet individual differences. Grammar schools offered more domestic science and manual arts organized along the lines she had used at the normal school. More vocational work was also offered within the regular high schools and not in separate technical high schools. Sex hygiene—under the name personal purity—was introduced, although many parents were a little concerned at such a topic. Young got salary increases for the elementary teachers as well as the high school teachers in two of her first three years in office.

The various parts of the school system were united enough by 1910 to successfully "boom" her to the NEA presidency. She was the first female to ever head any large school system and her picture had made front pages of most city newspapers including the *New York Times.* Now she was adding another first, for no female had ever been elected to the presidency of the NEA.

The NEA presidency was not without its problems, however, because the old guard was frightened by Young's announced intention of having the organization's permanent fund investigated. Rumors had circulated suggesting that all was not well when one of the fund's trustees—the superintendent of schools in Peoria, Illinois—went to prison for fraud and embezzlement after a bank which he had owned failed. Actually, the fund had not been tampered with, but some of the money was invested in bad stock. The year was stressful because the directors of the permanent fund instituted a campaign of threats and mudslinging. In the end Young emerged, if not victorious, at least as a courageous leader in the eyes of many teachers who appreciated her efforts to make the NEA more democratic.

BOARD WARS

By 1912, with the NEA fight behind, trouble began to loom in Chicago. A new mayor, Carter Henry Harrison, Jr., had appointed a new board under different leadership, and it was changing its relationship to the superintendent, even though it had reelected her and her assistant, John D. Shoop. The new policy was to create special committees to which the superintendent's recommendations were referred before the board considered them. In February 1912 Margaret Haley was campaigning for women's suffrage in the western states when she received a letter from Catharine Goggin. "Mrs. Young feels a little anxious," wrote Goggin and she outlined why: first, because of its new policy on committees, the board had not given the superintendent the same endorsement that she felt it had in the past; second, salaries had been approved without her consultation; and third, three of her recommendations for principalships had recently been turned down. Goggin went on, "I know . . . that the superintendent has been troubled by [these] new developments."

By early summer of 1912, rumors were developing that Mayor Harrison no longer supported her policies. To set the matter straight the mayor wrote to her assuring her that he did support her and asked her to ignore the empty rumors. She acknowledged her appreciation of his support, told him that she had ignored the rumors, and wished his administration well. But her troubles were just beginning.

By the end of July Major Harrison had appointed eight school board members. Four were reappointed and four were new. The fall proceeded much the same as before. Special committees were appointed, and the superintendent's recommendations for a new series of readers was not approved. At the first December 1912 board meeting, however, Mrs. Young and Mr. Shoop were unanimously reelected to their respective positions of superintendent and assistant superintendent. By the second December board meeting the biggest windstorm to date hit: the board took the course of study out of her hands, because there were too many "fads and frills" in the elementary curriculum such as sewing and other handwork. They appointed another special committee to look into a revision that would remove the frills and emphasize the "three R's." Young was visibly upset. "Everytime I start to do anything," she said, "a committee is appointed to take the work out of my hands. It makes one wonder," she continued, "if one can accomplish anything." It must have been quite a blow to her to hear talk of abolishing the very activities that she felt made the academic basics more meaningful to students.

A second important board appointment came in January. A real estate agent named Jacob Loeb was named to fill the vacancy left by death. Also during late winter and early spring two bills concerning the teachers' pension board were written. One came from the school board and provided: (1) that the trustee makeup should be four board members, four teachers, and the superintendent as ex-officio; (2) that the finance committee chairman should be head of the pension board; and (3) that the board should be compelled to match the teachers' contributions dollar for dollar with an option to double it. (At present they were only required to match the interest with an option to match the teachers' contributions as well.) The other bill was a retaliatory effort from the CTF. It maintained provisions in the 1907 bill—membership of six teachers to three board representatives and the compulsory interest matching clause. The superintendent supported the board's bill because it would increase pension revenue. The CTF had wanted a better compulsory revenue clause but not at the expense of the teacher-board ratio. Haley approached Young, asking if the board would ever approve a dollar for dollar clause. The superintendent said she thought so if the representation were more even. She told Haley that she had originally told the board in her July 1909 interview that she would try to do this. Haley looked a little surprised and disappointed, but they both agreed that the teachers would have to decide.

At the next school board meeting, teacher representatives, including Goggin and Haley, were invited to attend. Trustee William Rothmann and President Urion explained the board's pension bill. Rothmann—who as chair of the finance committee would head the pension board under Urion's plan—was strongly in favor of the measure. Urion asked the teacher's representatives what they thought. A couple of them said they approved but most said they would not presume to speak for the teaching corps. Rothmann then said that they would put it to a vote of all the teachers. Upon leaving Haley commended Rothmann and promised not to try to sway the teachers one way or another. Then, he smiled "devilishly" and told her that by not disapproving she had already approved of the bill. Margaret Haley did not understand this. She started asking questions about this Rothmann and discovered that he had absconded with interest money from the police pension fund years earlier. She set about documenting the evidence, and printing it up so that it could be circulated at the next CTF meeting.

When the circulars were distributed at the meeting, there were many questions. The CTF decided to hold a mass meeting where questions could be answered and Rothmann could defend himself if he was so inclined. It was scheduled for a Thursday after school. It opened in chaos. The acting chairman—William B. Owen, Ella's successor at the normal—could hardly get the meeting called to order. Finally, he established order, but both Haley and Young asked for the floor at the same time. Owen did not know whom to recognize, so he asked the pleasure of the convention. "Amidst the cries of 'let her speak' " and " 'no, no, no,' [the superintendent] left the [room] because she thought she had been denied the floor." Owen sent a messenger after her and upon her return she was granted the floor. Young briefly explained that Rothmann would not be able to do anything underhanded with the interest from the pension fund because he would be too closely watched, and also because the laws had been changed to forbid it. Rothmann never arrived. Margaret Haley answered questions and so did Charles Merriam. The meeting was dismissed. When the teachers voted, their preference was against the Urion Bill. Young lost and, what was worse, looked like she had been pitted against the teachers.

RESIGNATIONS

Up until this time her open door policy had seemed to keep her in tune with teachers' sentiment, but now she felt more isolated. She lamented this in her 1913 annual report and called for the adoption of teachers' councils. These would meet on a monthly basis during school hours. Teachers could express their views and make suggestions for her to consider and recommend. It was a natural move for her to make, since she had originated the idea and given it full expression in her Ph.D. dissertation. They were to start in fall 1913, but that spring and summer it looked like they would be starting without her. In June, board members began openly expressing hostility toward her. Rothmann pestered her seeking favors such as wanting her to demote certain CTF teachers, but she always refused. John C. Harding was upset, because she ignored his choice of spellers. In June, Mayor Harrison wrote her another letter of support, to squelch new rumors. It helped, and so did the fact that the new board president, Peter Reinberg, supported her; but hostility from other board members persisted. Loeb was becoming a cohort of Rothmann's in his bullying tactics.

On June 27, under Governor Dunne, a former Chicago mayor, the Illinois women got the franchise. An article in the *Chicago Record Herald* pictured Ella Flagg Young with Jane Addams and Julia Latrhop—a social reformer. The caption read "Three Reasons Why Illinois Women Won the Vote First," but it was little comfort to her in the problems she faced. By the end of July she had made up her mind to resign and submitted her letter to the board president. She told newspaper reporters that she "was the victim of political intrigue among board members." The interview quoted her as saying "that her retention of the superintendency would impair the efficiency of the schools."

Former member of the board Dr. Cornelia DeBey told reporters that it was due to actions "of a lot of cheap politicians and the board. We women won't stand for it." But two other board members said they were sure that the board would accept her resignation. President Reinberg said he would resign if the action was approved. Another board member, William Vincent, alluded to some of her difficulties with three of the board members. One board member, said Vincent, "spoke unpardonably about her." "Someone else," he continued, "whose grammar isn't any good tried to tell Ella Flagg Young how to teach spelling. Another who pretends to be her friend has secretly and publicly antagonized her and her views." "It's too bad," said Vincent, "but it's the only thing she can do to save her self-respect."

Events of the next few days, however, changed things. A delegation of women arrived at the mayor's office to enlist his help in stopping this action; the mayor wrote to the superintendent urging her to reconsider and stay as head of schools; and he apprised her of his three new board appointments— Mrs. Gertrude Britton, Mrs. Florence Vosbrink, and Dr. Peter Clemenson. On 30 July the board met to take action and voted fourteen to one to retain her. (Harding voted against her.) That meant that since both Rothmann and Loeb were there, they had voted to retain her. She was encouraged. "I shall abide by the action of the board of education," she told newspapers. "It will still be my aim to make the Chicago public schools the embodiment of the thought and endeavor of the board and of Chicago herself for the children. The kind words of parents and teachers have touched me deeply." Mayor Harrison announced "her rule should be unopposed in all matters pertaining to the schools."

The fall term went smoothly, but all it meant was that her antagonizers had gone underground. On 10 December the board convened to take up the reelection of superintendent and assistant. In a sudden move, Young's enemies nomiated and elected her subordinate, John D. Shoop, as superintendent. Citywide protests by numerous groups pressured the mayor into making enough new board appointments to bring about Young's reelection. Rothmann was ousted from the board in this process, but Loeb publicly supported Young and waited for a better opportunity.

FINAL YEARS

Both Young and Shoop accepted their old posts, and the school administration began functioning just in time to see the schools open after the holiday break. Through a series of legal appeals, the ousted members were finally reinstated by May 1914. Their original terms, however, expired shortly after they were reseated.

The time from January 1914 to December 1915 moved along without the personal struggles of the previous year but also without the triumphs and unity of the early two years under the first school board that unanimously elected her and then returned her twice. It was a somewhat uneasy alliance even though she was reelected in December 1914 by a fourteen vote majority. Still, she was able to continue her original policies, and she even managed to get a 5 percent salary increase through the board for the teachers. The same board members who had refused to vote for her return smoldered. Her opponents of the board resented the restraint placed upon them by the mayor, and they blamed his long arm of control and the CTF for her reelection. Loeb—by now a dominant force on the board—voted for Young and publicly supported her, but he resented the CTF's power, too. As long as Young remained in office, he was somewhat careful in his overt activities, but when the approach of her retirement became fairly obvious, so did his motives.

Ella had planned to resign by 1 July 1915 to go into retirement. However, she decided to remain until a new budget deficit and threat of salary decrease was cleared. She scrutinized the budget until she found ways to trim it down so that the teachers would not suffer. It worked, and Loeb's threatened salary cut did not go into effect. Toward the end of August 1915, she went on vacation, and while she was gone, the board met. Loeb presented a ruling to be voted on immediately. Known as the Loeb rule, it prohibited teachers from belonging to any labor-connected organization or any group whose executive officers were not teaching at the present time. The board approved it, some because of Loeb's autocratic control and others because business interests compelled it.

When Young returned there was little she could do. Her eminent December retirement made her a lame duck. All teachers had received contracts with clauses containing the new rulings. They had to sign these before the first paycheck was received. Young tried to get some recommendations for promotions approved. Loeb and the board refused approval until the contracts were signed. CTF Attorney Greenacre secured an injunction so that by October the board was prohibited from enforcing such a ruling. Haley went to work for a tenure protection bill in the meantime. So CTF opposition was held at bay until Young retired in December. Before she left town, however, she warned the teachers that the opposiiton was not over—that it was just lying dormant. In spring 1916 under Superintendent Shoop, Board President Loeb refused to issue contracts to sixty-eight teachers for the following year.

Even in her retirement years she kept faith the good will of the teachers. She presented a paper at the NEA meeting in July 1916. Ironically, Jacob Loeb preceded her, defending his stand against teachers' unions. When she heard this she discarded her prepared speech and answered his criticisms. She said "no person should ever be on the board of education who does not send his own children, or did not send them while they were of school age, to the public schools." Loeb's children attended private schools.

By the fall of 1917 the United States was involved in World War I, and Ella Flagg Young, who had rested long enough, was ready to do battle again. She and some friends went to work for the second Liberty Loan Committee. This loan was one of five huge bond issues floated to finance the war and sold to citizens in small denominations.

She continued to attend the NEA's conventions and at Pittsburgh in July 1918, she received a remarkable tribute. When she walked into the meeting hall, everyone spontaneously stood in silent ovation out of reverence. She stepped up to the lectern, and as she began to speak she glanced downward at her well-worn dress and said, "Why, since the war began I haven't even thought of clothes."

In the fall, Young went on another speaking tour for the fourth Liberty Loan. It was a bad time because the Spanish strain of influenza had reached epidemic proportions all over the country. In Wyoming she contracted the flu but refused to go to bed until her trip was finished. She did finish and was able to get to Washington to turn her money in to Secretary of State William McAdoo, but by now she had pneumonia. She died on the 26th of October and her body was broght back to Chicago accompanied by a military regiment. The flags in Chicago were flown at half mast and the board of education offices were draped in black. McAdoo said that she "died in the service of her country, working like a soldier." It was a fitting homage for a great leader of whom Jane Addams had said: "She had more general intelligence and character than any other woman I knew."

Ella Flagg Young had been the archetypical progressive: intelligently altruistic, open to change, always learning, democratic and humane. Even her death typified the progressive notion that everyone should work for the good of the group. Of course, not all educators agreed with the tenets of progressivism— as the next chapter will show.

10

THE CRITICS

The progressives were in the mainstream of educational thought and practice in America until well into the twentieth century. In fact, one could make a good case for the assertion that progressivism still represents the core of theory and procedure. Yet, they were not the only ones concerned about schools. From the turn of the century until World War II, conscientious educators all over the world were struggling with the problems of adapting educational curricula and teaching methodologies to conflicting demands. We have already seen the kinds of social needs that led to the educational proposals of the Progressive Era. The need to handle large numbers of immigrant children as well as special or "subnormal" pupils gave birth to the mental testing movement which arranged society into an intellectual hierarchy closely aligned to social status.

From the 1890s through the 1930s changes took place at all levels of schooling. Some educators saw this as the realization of Plato's desire to sift out the born leaders of society—the philosopher-kings. Psychologists like Carl Brigham of Princeton, H. H. Goddard of the training school at Vineland, New Jersey, and Lewis Terman of Stanford concluded that intelligence was basically hereditary and argued for federal immigration policies that would turn away the intellectually inferior. Social reformers like Jane Addams favored separate schools for the special students, that is, the morally defective, mentally subnormal, and behaviorally deviant. Here again I.Q. tests would sift them out into the appropriate special school, and parents would be told that this procedure was of enormous benefit to their children. In the 1890s, the NEA's Committee of Ten recommended that collegiate education be composed of courses of study that would include choices ranging from the classical liberal arts to modern languages and science.

In 1918, after a three year investigation, the Commission on the Reorganization of Secondary Education (CRSE) advocated a comprehensive high school composed of three tracks: the traditional college prep or general track; a business or commercial track; and the newer technical or industrial track. In addition, the CRSE came up with several recommendations. First of all, they enunciated the Seven Cardinal Principles that should be stressed by comprehensive high schools: (1) health; (2) command of fundamental processes; (3) worthy home membership; (4) vocational training; (5) citizenship; (6) good use of leisure time; and (7) character building. Also, there were to be sports and extra-curricular activities for all students so that the part-time working students could become acquainted with the full-time college bound people. In general the report was seen as an attempt to promote social solidarity among the students whose families came from all social classes and represented all ethnic groups. Finally, in the twenties and thirties elementary reading books like the Sally, Dick, and Jane series sent messages about the standards of American life to newly arrived school-age children.

By the 1920s and continuing to the present, however, many critics offered alternative visions of education. Some developed strains from earlier themes; others offered more novel sounding solutions and ideas. To include all critical contributors would necessitate another volume. Instead, we have chosen the following seven: (1) Maria Montessori for her highly successful application of sensory learning principles; (2) John B. Watson for his advocacy of behaviorism and conditioning; (3) Margaret Naumburg for her insights into the utilization of psychoanalysis for educational settings; (4) Alexander Sutherland Neill for his stress on emotional freedom and creative self-expression; (5) Jacques Maritain for his reassertion of the values of Thomism in modern life and education; (6) W. E. B. DuBois for his critique of the vocational education movement for blacks which had been championed by Coppin and Washington; and (7) George S. Counts for his insistence that progressive educators needed to become political and social reform leaders in order to bring about the world they envisioned. These people did not disagree with each other or with the progressives about everything. Yet their lives and thoughts do illustrate the rich and complex background of the contemporary issues around which debate still swirls in education circles.

Maria Montessori (1870-1952)

In 1914 Professor William Boyd of the University of Glasgow explained the great interest in Maria Montessori's educational views as "no doubt due to the fact that they come before the world at a time when there is widespread discontent with the traditional methods of the schools and an eager desire for some kind of reform that will make popular education more effective than it is at present."[1] The fact that Boyd's remarks are still descriptive of educational ills in the late twentieth century is probably the reason that Montessori's ideas and methods are still prevalent. The perennial nature of her theories will be examined after a look at her life.

EDUCATION

Born at Chiaraville, Italy in 1870 to parents of comfortable social class standing, Maria was no stranger to self-discipline and work. She learned early in life to help with the daily practical chores of the household and to work for those less fortunate than herself. She attended the usual state day school until, at the age of twelve, her parents moved to Rome. There they discovered that Maria had an interest in and aptitude for math. Her career ambitions were anything but common for a young girl to pursue. Her parents suggested that she become a teacher, but she refused to even consider the idea and decided to take up engineering because she liked math. She was one of the few girls of her era to enter the technical curriculum, but by the time she was ready to graduate from the technical institute she had changed her mind. A newly developed interest in biology was largely responsible for her decision to undertake medicine instead of engineering.

Social opposition to such a career was fierce and encompassed even her father, Allessandro, but not her mother, Renilde. Nineteenth century Italy stigmatized both the female student and her family. Despite serious odds Maria convinced herself that she would do it. She entered the University of Rome in 1890. Two years later she entered the four year medical program, but her difficulties were far from over. When attending lectures this singular female medical student had to be accompanied by her father, and while taking her human anatomy labs she had to learn to work alone at night. The reason for this was simple: female students were not allowed to be in the same room with male lab students, because it was regarded as unethical for girls to dissect dead bodies in the presence of men. Nevertheless, in 1896, after exhibiting great stamina and perseverance, she graduated with a double honors degree in medicine and surgery—the first female in Italy to do so.

EARLY CAREER

Shortly after graduation Maria accepted the chair of hygiene at one of the two female colleges in Rome. She also was appointed assistant physician at the University of Rome psychiatric clinic. As part of her duties, she visited the various insane asylums in the city looking for suitable subjects for the clinic. It was a practice of the time to house mentally deficient children in these adult asylums. What she saw on these rounds increased her compassion for the plight of such children. Her contacts with them led her to accept a less popular conclusion of the day: that mental deficiency was more an educational than a medical problem. This premise put her in contact with the works of two French pioneers in the field—Dr. Jean Itard and his student Dr. Edouard Seguin. Itard had gained recognition for his work with the wild boy of Averyon (Chapter 6), and Seguin had been labeled as "the apostle of the idiot" for his success in freeing the deficient mind from the "bondage of its imperfect organs by a physiological education." The written works of these two men held such particular meaning for Montessori that she ended up translating both Itard's book and Seguin's six hundred page volume and writing them out by hand in order to gain "the sense of each word and read in truth the spirit of the authors."[2]

After Maria gave a series of lectures on the education of the feebleminded, the minister of education asked her to direct a newly established state orthophrenic school for deficient children. She remained there from 1899 to 1901. She spent long days—8:00 A.M. to 7:00 P.M.—with the children and then stayed up half of the night assessing her day's work. Ultimately, her endeavors bore fruit. Some of her "mental defectives" passed the public reading and writing examinations taken by normal children. While a chorus of applause greeted their performances, Montessori was pondering its meaning: "Whilst everyone was admiring my idiots, I was searching for the reasons which could keep back the healthy and happy children of the ordinary schools on so low a plane that they could be equalled in tests of intelligence by my unfortunate pupils."[3]

Such reflections led her to resign her directorship in pursuit of the study of philosophy as a student at the University of Rome. In 1904 she was appointed to the chair of anthropology, University of Rome, a position she held until 1908. Throughout these years she also managed to: (1) make a special study of the nervous diseases of children and publish her results; (2) visit and observe children in other European countries; (3) practice medicine in private as well as in the clinics and hospitals of Rome; (4) deliver an address as the Italian representative to a feminist congress at Berlin with such success that her picture appeared in many European newspapers (1896); (5) address a pedagogical congress on moral education at Turin (1899); (6) and write her first major volume, *Pedagogical Anthropology* (English version, 1910). Her manner and style as a lecturer during these years were described by a former pupil and future close associate, Anna Maccheroni:

> The hall was large, and over the lecturer's chair was a canopy. Having taken a place on one of the two benches at the right side of the platform I could see the hall crowded with young people of both sexes. The lecturer herself stood, looking eagerly at them, with her searching look—so penetrating but never disturbing, never making uncomfortable the person at whom she looked. As I found afterwards, she could take in each one, individually, in what was a kind of spiritual contact.
>
> Of course I noticed at once that she was a very goodlooking woman, but what impressed me even more was that she was not following the general custom of the learned women of her time. They were few, and chose to dress in a rather masculine style. Not she! In her attire, however

simple it was, she retained a feminine and elegant touch. And she was smiling.

She spoke—not about anthropology, but about schools. She told us what a school should be like.[4]

THE DIRECTRESS

It was not until 1907, however, that the thirty-seven year old doctor-turned-educator got the chance to practice her approaches on normal children. In that year a building society in Rome decided to take on the project of cleaning up the San Lorenzo quarter, one of the worst slums in the city. It abounded in crime, poverty, and disregard for hygiene. The society resurrected two blocks of new tenement housing which were immediately inhabited by more than one thousand families who promised to observe the rules of decency and hygiene. Most adult members of these households worked, leaving their young children unattended. One member of the society who was familiar with Montessori's work asked her to take up the daily task of caring for these preschoolers. She consented, and her first *Casa dei Bambini* was founded—a barren room in a tenement house filled with sixty tearful, shy, and frightened children. In Montessori's own words:

> I set to work like a peasant woman who, having set aside a good store of seed corn, has found a fertile field in which she may freely sow it. But I was wrong. I had hardly turned over the clods of my field, when I found gold instead of wheat: the clods concealed a precious treasure. I was not the peasant I had thought myself. Rather I was foolish Aladdin, who, without knowing it, had in his hand a key that would open hidden treasures.[5]

Former pupil and colleague E. M. Standing described these treasures, in general, as the "normal characteristics of childhood hitherto concealed under a mask of 'deviations.' Montessori discovered that children possess different and higher qualities than those we usually attribute to them. It was as if a higher form of personality had been liberated, and a new child had come into being." More specifically, she found that: (1) these children had amazing powers of mental concentration regardless of accompanying noise or commotion; (2) they loved to repeat those tasks which held their attention over and over again; (3) when they could understand and grow accustomed to order, they revelled in maintaining it; (4) when given choices they would pick certain activities over others in which to become engrossed; (5) they preferred working with didactic materials to playing with toys; (6) they could exhibit a great deal of motor coordination and control when they themselves were allowed to discover their own clumsiness; (7) they preferred working in silence to working in commotion; and (8) there was no need for reward or punishment. These were traits she first observed in children; they were not arbitrarily imposed. With these revelations, she concluded that a teacher was needed who had a genuine love and respect for the individual child and an ability to observe. Indeed, Montessori's motto was "to wait and to observe while waiting."[6] A prepared environment allowing for the exhibition of the above traits produced a spontaneous degree of self-discipline that amazed even Montessori.

Montessori's casa was different from Froebel's kindergarten (Chapter 6). Both featured developmental growth through self-activity. Froebel called it play and Montessori called it work. While both developed special didactic materials, Froebel's gifts were creations from his own imagination and Montessori's methods came from the endless observations she made while watching children. And finally, while Froebel took a more central and active teaching role, Montessori called herself a directress. She was there to encourage and help when necessary, but mostly she stayed in the background letting the child learn from the materials.

Other casas opened under Montessori's direction, and eventually she resigned her former positions to devote full time to the spread of this type of education. Students from all of the world came to study under her. When they returned to their native countries to open schools, they usually had results similar to those achieved in the original casa. Soon she was being invited to other countries to lecture and conduct her teacher training classes. She visited the United States twice, in 1913 and again in 1915 for a longer stay.

By the time she was making these trips, she was being accompanied by a young teenage boy, Mario, whose biological identity is still shrouded in mystery. In 1913, after he had come to live with her, she identified him as her fifteen-year-old nephew. By the 1920s he was officially her son. Mario himself told a fanciful, fairy tale account of a biological mother who had had a love affair with a certain Dr. Montesano and then given birth to him out of wedlock. He then spent his early years in the country with a wet nurse and her family. At some point a strange unidentified lady (Maria) began visiting him. The little boy became convinced that she was his real mother, and one day as a teenager he asked to go with her to live. She did not refuse. It is difficult to think that Maria was really his biological mother, because prior to and during his birth (spring 1898) she was highly visible addressing conventions and working in her orthophrenic school. What may be more likely is that: (1) this was a fantasy of a young orphaned child which Maria let him keep; (2) Maria knew of his existence, because she knew of her colleague Montesano's affair with someone else; and (3) she decided like many single career women in the late nineteenth and early twentieth centuries to adopt a child. Whatever was the case, the evidence for Mario's being Maria's biological son has not yet surfaced. At any rate, Mario became her closest companion—to him passed her educational legacy. He first became visible to the world on her first trip to the United States.[7]

In the two years between her visits to the States, many Americans such as Dewey and Young praised her efforts. Such notables as Mr. and Mrs. Alexander Graham Bell, Woodrow Wilson's daughter, and S. S. McClure of *McClure's Magazine* became staunch supporters. When McClure offered to set her up in her own school with whatever equipment and facilities she desired, however, she turned down the offer for unexplained reasons. And although Montessori associations sprang up, she was largely forgotten in the United States by World War I. Interest was not rekindled until the late fifties or early sixties. During her lifetime she saw her methods and beliefs spread to virtually all European countries plus India, Ceylon, and Indochina. And she was preparing for a trip to

Africa in 1952 when she died in Holland in one of her adopted homes with her
devoted Mario by her side. She was paid many tributes, but in gratefully acknowledging one of her last, she expressed her lifelong concern. She asked that
they turn their attention from her to what she had been talking about—"the
child."[8] She left the future of her work in the hands of Mario and his family.

THE EPOCHS

What was her legacy and what were these ideas and methods that seem so
controversial yet popular even today? The following description of a casa in
California will serve as an introduction to her theories. This casa was conducted
in 1915 by Montessori's good friend Helen Parkhurst, because Maria did not
speak English. (Parkhurst went on to Columbia University where she developed
her own plan for secondary education, the Dalton Plan):

> We see some thirty to forty children, aged four to seven, scattered over
> a large room, all doing different things. Most are working at little tables,
> but some are on rugs spread out on the floor. It is not in the least like a
> school such as we knew it. . . . Gone are the rows of desks with benches;
> gone is the teacher's high desk and stool; and—most remarkable of
> all—it seems at first glance as if the teacher herself has vanished too. We
> do discover her, eventually, down on her knees at the far end of the room,
> explaining something to a couple of children who are working with num-
> ber materials spread out on a rug. The rest of the children in the room
> (except for two or three who are waiting to speak to her) are all carrying
> on their own business without taking any notice of the directress whatev-
> er. It all fits in with our general impression. This is obviously a kind of
> school in which the adult has retired into the background, whilst the
> children are correspondingly more active; one might almost say have
> taken over the initiative. Even the teacher's blackboard has been trans-
> muted into a long low blackboard built into the wall, at which children are
> writing, not the teacher.
>   Gone too—completely—is the stillness of the old-fashioned school (so
> often a stillness of suppression), and with it that immobility which was the
> immediate cause of it. Instead we are aware of a bustle of activity. In fact
> the scene before us resembles more the busy stir that goes on in a bank
> or store than in a schoolroom as we knew it. We see people coming and
> going, opening and shutting drawers, moving objects here and there,
> conferring together in low tones, working singly or in groups—in fact
> anything except all sitting together listening to one person talking.
>   The most astonishing part about it all is that these persons who are
> doing all this are not grown-ups at all, but children—and quite small
> children at that, the eldest being not more than seven or eight. Yet what
> absorption in their tasks, what seriousness in their expression, what quiet
> purposefulness in their manner, what precision of movement, and what
> astonishing self-discipline! They remind us of "little men and women"; yet
> at the same time they have all the spontaneous charm of childhood.[9]

Through observations of children in her casas and elsewhere Maria discovered that from birth to around the age of eighteen children went through a sort of mental metamorphosis that could be divided into three stages or epochs. The first stage of development spans the ages of birth to six when the mind is like a sponge absorbing impressions from the environment surrounding it. In the first three years the mind operates unconsciously in the child, since it is not self-conscious of what it is doing. In those first months before physical movement, the child takes in the whole of her or his environment with this absorbent but unconscious power. In explaining this mind, Montessori made an analogy between the work of a photographer's camera (child's mind) and the picture drawing of an artist. For instance, the directress had her readers suppose that there was a picture of ten men (or even one hundred). The artist would draw each separately, and it would take much time for ten and longer for one hundred. Now with a camera the photographer could take ten or a hundred instantaneously and have it recorded on film. "It is similar to the absorbent mind," said Montessori. "It works rapidly taking in everything without effort and without will."[10] Continuing with this analogy she went on to explain that just as a photo is taken and developed in darkness before being fixed and then brought to light fixed, so are the impressions in an absorbent mind. They are taken during the unconscious period, developed, fixed, and then finally emerge into consciousness where they remain permanently set.

This brings us to the conscious period of the first stage spanning three to six years. The faculties (such as memory) and processes (such as thinking, writing) are now created to be expanded upon and further developed. As her colleague E. M. Standing said, the child

has forgotten the events and experiences of the preceding [period] (0-3 years); but, using the faculties he created then, he can now will, think, and remember. For memory itself is one of the faculties which has been created. Therefore, *now,* when the things he had acquired unconsciously in the first stage are brought to the surface (through the work of his hands) they are remembered; for memory is now there to receive them.

So too is it with the will. . . . For that, too, has come into being. Before, it was as if a force outside . . . moved [the child]; now it is the child's own ego which guides and directs. . . . Whereas in the first [period] the child absorbed the world through his unconscious intelligence, merely by being moved about in it, now he takes in consciously, using his hands. The hand has now become the instrument of the brain; and it is through the activity of [the] hands that he enriches his experience, and develops [the self] at the same time.[11]

In general this first epoch can be seen as the construction of the human individual through the acquisition and perfection of new functions (faculties). Children do not, according to Montessori, need direct adult help or intervention. Instead, they need to be able to act under their own initiatives. That is why she found it best to place them in environments prepared especially to facilitate these new psychic (but not as yet social) developments. Then, there would be no insurmountable frustrations or obstacles that they could not yet control. Under such conditions children learn writing, reading, and fundamental arithmetic concepts. Montessori called these activities the work of the child. But she thought it happened spontaneously and exhilaratingly without fatigue. By age six, children will have been transformed from rather unconscious, immobile creatures into new psychic individuals. Montessorians described this process as the "revelation of the child."[12]

During the second epoch (six to twelve years), the children show great stability as physical and psychic growth continue along the same lines. Compared to the first and last epochs, little transformation or metamorphosis happens during the second stage. Under rightly prepared conditions, Montessori believed that these second stage children could accomplish much mental work and store a great deal of cultural information. She thought there was a considerable development of the reasoning abilities at this point. Socially, children develop not only individual ego strengths but also a group consciousness—the "gang stage" or the "herd instinct"—with a great interest in fairness and right and wrong. Here again Montessori would prepare a special environment for these developments—one different from stage one.

Finally, the third epoch (ages twelve to eighteen) is another period of transformation and can be subdivided into puberty (twelve to fifteen) and adolescence (fifteen to eighteen), after which growth ceases and the individual simply becomes older. New psychological characteristics emerge, some of which Montessori listed as "doubts, hesitations, violent emotions, discouragement, and an unexpected decrease in intellectual capacity, 'plus' a tendency toward creative work and a need for the strengthening of self-confidence."[13] Whereas during the second epoch the children were extroverted, participating in gangs, now they become more introverted. At the end of this introversion, the adolescent will emerge as a socially conscious adult, not just an individual or a group member but a separate member of the human society. Again, a specially prepared environment is needed so that feelings of dependence, inadequacy, and inferiority do not develop and endure for years.

SENSITIVE PERIODS

Another key in Montessori's theory was the notion of "sensitive periods" in child development. She described a sensitive period as a predisposition "related to certain elements in the environment towards which the organism is directed with an irresistible impulse and a well-defined activity." The periods are transitory, and "serve the purpose of helping the organism to acquire certain functions, or determined characteristics," said her colleague Standing. "This aim accomplished, the special sensibility dies away, often to be replaced by another and quite different one. . . . When a sensitive period is at its height we may compare it to a searchlight—coming from within the mind—illuminating certain parts of the environment, leaving the rest in comparative obscurity."[14]

There are sensitive periods for learning to walk, talk, write, and read; and there are also sensitive periods for such needs as good manners, social developments, and order. This latter sensitivity usually develops in the first epoch, and even very small violations can produce extreme protests, even tantrums, from the child. In her *Secrets of Childhood*, Montessori gave this account:

I found myself one day with a group of people going through Nero's grotto at Naples. With us was a young mother with a child—about one and a half years old—too small to be able to walk the whole length of the way. In fact after a time the child grew tired and his mother picked him up, but she had overestimated her strength. She was hot and stopped to take off her coat to carry it on her arm, and with this impediment once more picked up the child, who began to cry, his screams growing louder and louder.

His mother strove in vain to quiet him; she was plainly tired out and began to grow cross. Indeed the noise was getting on the nerves of all, and naturally others offered to carry him. He passed from arm to arm, struggling and screaming, and everyone talked to him and scolded, but he only grew worse.

I thought of the enigma of infancy, of how reactions must always have a cause: and going up to the mother I said, "Will you allow me to help put on your coat?" She looked at me in amazement, for she was still hot; but in her confusion she consented and allowed me to help her on with it.

At once the baby quieted down, his tears and struggles stopped, and he said, "Mamma, coat on." It was as if he wanted to say, "Yes, Mamma, a coat is meant to be worn"; as though he thought, "At last you have understood me," and stretching out his arms to his mother he came back to her all smiles. The expedition ended in complete tranquillity. A coat is meant to be worn, and not to hang like a rag over one arm; and this disorder in his mother's person had affected the child as a jarring disturbance.

Montessori explained this need for order as being different from adults who might want it but really don't need it. She went on to state that the child who is "constructing himself, out of the elements of the environment" can become ill without it.[15]

What we have described so far are developments that take place in the normal child. But what about the abnormal? Montessori firmly believed that all psychological deviations could be cured, that is, returned to normality, if the casa head (directress) knew what she was doing. In other words, she must treat abnormal children with firmness and respect, being certain to protect the other children from deviates' distorted behaviors. She must also continue to present new occupations to this latter group while still allowing them to roam freely. Then, "one day will come the great event. One day—Heaven knows why—[a deviated child] will choose some occupation . . . and settle down seriously to work at it *with the first spontaneous spell of concentration that he has ever shown.*" The directress would then know that the child is on the road to normality—ready to develop the characteristics listed previously. Now the child is set free from adult intervention in a prepared environment where it "can live its life according to [these] laws of development."[16] This last quotation could be regarded as the summation of Montessori's beliefs, for it was also her definition of school.

The preschool toy market discovered the importance and popularity of many of her materials as they produced stacking toys, wooden puzzles, and post offices with geometric shapes to fit correspondingly shaped slots. And that she greatly influenced the future works of psychologists such as Jean Piaget and Jerome Bruner cannot be denied. Also, it is little wonder that children using Montessori's didactic materials do well on the major or general factor part of I.Q. tests—spatial relations. This of course has not set well with the Arthur Jensens and William Shockley's who would dissociate these mental functions from any environmental factors. Nor, as we shall discover, have they been supported by Margaret Naumburg or A. S. Neill, although Naumburg saw more value in her approach than Neill did. On the other hand, John B. Watson, our next life, would probably have affirmed Montessori's stress on prepared environments, even though he divorced himself from any notions of consciousness.

John B. Watson (1878-1958)

In the early years of the twentieth century, the study of psychology was becoming increasingly scientific and less philosophical. This was true despite the fact that a large segment of the psychological community, including William James and John Dewey, called themselves philosophical psychologists. Yet, even within the growing scientific group, some, like John B. Watson, were becoming annoyed at the fact that psychology was still seen as the study of human consciousness. They were beginning to believe that terms such as consciousness, will, image, perception, and sensation referred to unscientific, philosophical conceptions that only hindered empirical investigations of human behavior, the true subject of psychology. But it took someone like Watson to declare psychology's independence from philosophy and those psychological theories that assumed the existence of consciousness.

EARLY LIFE

This brash young man was born on 9 January 1878 near the town of Greenville, South Carolina. Named for a local popular evangelist, John Broadus Watson was the second of Pickens Butler and Emma Kezia Watson's five children. His father was said to have been a "high tempered" Southerner. As a youth Pickens had fought in the Civil War and for a time thereafter had wandered about the countryside working in sawmills. He apparently never became settled. He was seldom home and thus forced on Watson's mother and older brother, Edward, the tasks of running the farm and rearing the children.

Both Emma and Edward were fanatically devoted to a harsh, literal Baptist doctrine that pervaded the atmosphere of the household. Watson despised this religious fundamentalism, although he did his best to hide it from his mother. Nevertheless, Emma seems to have forgiven his occasional "lapses," since he was her favorite child. He also regretted having permitted himself to be baptized. As an adult he deliberately defied nineteenth century evangelical standards by, among other things, swearing and drinking. This is not to suggest that Watson had been unhappy. He was quite proud of his childhood accomplishments. "At nine years of age," he remarked, "I was handling tools, halfsoling shoes, and milking cows. At twelve I was a pretty fair carpenter."[17] In later life he continued to derive pleasure from these skills. He built a ten room house from blueprints during the summers of 1909 and 1910. Twenty-five years later, he built a stucco garage, and on weekends the following year constructed a thirty-one by sixty-one foot barn of stucco with a copper roof.

Watson began his education in the rural districts of Reedy River, White Horse, and Travelers Rest. He claimed to have walked to one or another of these places from the time he was six years old. When Watson was twelve the family moved to Greenville, a city of twenty thousand people. There he entered the public schools, finishing both elementary and high school. Unfortunately schooling held few pleasant memories for him. As he put it, "I was lazy, somewhat insubordinate, and, so far as I know, I never made above a passing grade."[18] Although not an athlete, he fancied himself a fighter, frequently engaging in boxing matches with a friend when the teacher left the room.

In 1894 Watson entered Furman University at the age of sixteen. His family paid the bulk of his school expenses, while he earned some money in the first two years working as an assistant in the chemistry laboratory. Watson did not enjoy the social life of the campus despite having fallen in love with one of the three women at school and having joined the Kappa Alpha social fraternity. He said that he was unsocial and had few friends. Watson took the classical curriculum. He studied Greek and Latin with some success, but retained little. He passed his senior Greek examination only by cramming all the afternoon and night before the test. In mathematics he did no better. On the other hand, philosophy and psychology aroused his serious interest.[19]

The philosopher/clergyman George B. Moore taught both philosophy and psychology at Furman. Watson took Moore's course in his senior year. He was an honor student that year and obviously enjoyed these subjects, since he later chose to do graduate work in them. Yet, because of a juvenile act he failed Moore's course. Moore had arbitrarily decided that any student who dared hand in a particular paper backwards would fail the course. Watson took the dare and paid the consequences. At that point he vowed to get even someday by having Moore come to him for research. To his surprise and sorrow, Moore did just that when Watson was at Johns Hopkins. He wanted to be Watson's research student, but his eyesight failed before arrangements could be made.

Watson remained at Furman for a fifth year and in 1900 received a master's degree instead of a bachelor's degree. He also spent the year as teacher and principal of Batesburg Institute in South Carolina. During his final year in college, his mother died. This removed the primary source of pressure for him to attend seminary. This event and his genuine interest in philosophy and psychology contributed to Watson's decision to pursue a doctorate. At first he was undecided whether to go to Princeton or the University of Chicago. When he inquired about the language requirement at Princeton, he found that a reading knowledge of Greek and Latin was necessary. He chose Chicago. It is also likely that George Moore had some influence on that decision. Having studied psychology at Chicago during his sabbatical year of 1897-1898, he told Watson about the faculty in John Dewey's department, which perhaps further aroused his interest in philosophy.

UNIVERSITY OF CHICAGO STUDY

In the fall of 1900, John Watson left for Chicago with fifty dollars in his pocket. When he arrived, he met the department chair and philosophy professor John Dewey, the psychologist James R. Angell, and a relative, John Manly. Angell particularly impressed him with his learning, and Watson was at once satisfied with these new acquaintances and his choice of schools. He still had to face the practical problem of financing his education, because his family could no longer afford to help him. Watson earned his way by doing numerous odd jobs. He worked as an assistant janitor, dusted Angell's desk and cleaned his apparatus, delivered books for an instructor's library, and waited tables. In addition, the neurologist Henry H. Donaldson helped him with his expenses by having him tend the white rats in his laboratory.

Angell guided Watson into experimental psychology as his major field, philosophy with Dewey, Addison W. Moore, and James Haydn Tufts as a first minor, and neurology with Donaldson as his second minor. He also took work in biology and physiology with Jacques Loeb. Loeb wanted him to study the physiology of a dog's brain, but neither Donaldson nor Angell thought Loeb would be a good influence on an inexperienced doctoral candidate. Their distrust of Loeb likely stemmed from a disagreement with his strongly mechanistic theories. So they convinced Watson to conduct an experiment to measure the relationship between the increasing complexity in the behavior of young rats and the growth of the myelin sheaths surrounding the nerve fibers in their central nervous systems. In the process of conducting the research, Watson incurred the ire of the local anti-vivisectionists. His combative nature spurred him on, and in 1903 he published his dissertation (entitled *Animal Education: The Psychical Development of the White Rat*) with the aid of $350 lent by Henry Donaldson.

In his graduate work, Watson studied a branch of the new psychology called functionalism. These seeds were planted by William James, and they flourished in the work of Dewey and Angell at Chicago and James McKeen Cattell at Columbia. Functionalism differed from the older structuralism of Edward Titchner. The former was concerned with *why* the individual behaved in a certain way, while the latter focused on *what* happened and *how* it occurred. The rule of functionalism at the time was that you observed the behavior of the animal, used the data to infer the nature of its consciousness, and then indicated how those processes functioned in its behavior. Watson eventually objected to the whole notion of consciousness. But this did not come about until after he graduated.

Compared to his work in psychology, Watson's study of philosophy proved disappointing. He took courses with Dewey, Tufts, Moore, George Herbert Mead, and Edward Scribner Ames. The topics ranged from Greek philosophy to Dewey's instrumentalism, and included Hume, Locke, Hartley, and Kant. He even studied Wilhelm Wundt with Tufts. Out of all of these Dewey became Watson's nemisis. "I got . . . least of all out of Dewey. I never knew what he was talking about then, and, unfortunately for me, I still don't know."[20] He went on to say that Tufts and Moore were patient with him, and bore no burden of blame for his shortcomings in philosophy. As for Mead, Watson's experience with him was paradoxical. In the classroom he did not understand Mead. But in the numerous hours spent together watching Watson's laboratory animals and in Mead's home, he learned to understand, respect, and admire Mead.

During his graduate student years, John Watson faced two personal problems in addition to his constant lack of funds. He pushed himself too hard, working day and night to complete his degree in a little more than three years. As a consequence he suffered from severe insomnia in the fall of 1902. He would awaken at three in the morning and walk eight to ten miles. He finally recovered after a month's vacation, three weeks of which he slept only with a light on. The experience taught him to be more careful with his physical condition and, according to his own account, prepared him to accept a large part of Sigmund Freud's theories.

Watson's second difficulty was a blow to his ego. He graduated in 1903 magna cum laude. But he was deeply disappointed when Dewey and Tufts told him that his examination was much inferior to that of Helen Thompson [Wooley] who had graduated summa cum laude two years earlier. On a happier note, Watson married Mary Ickes in 1903. They later had two children, Polly and John.

Watson remained at the University of Chicago from 1903 to 1907. He had received several job offers, including an assistantship in neurology from Donaldson and an assistantship in psychology from Dewey. Although he was quite proud of the former proposal, he accepted the latter in order to work with Angell. He served in that position until 1905 when he was promoted to the rank of instructor.

An energetic young man, Watson pursued his work with vigor and enthusiasm. He seemed determined to become a first-rate scholar and scientist. He praised Angell both for teaching him psychology and for sharpening his rhetorical skills. He could not say enough about the scientific research techniques he had learned from Donaldson and Loeb. Watson even carried his desire to become a scientist to the point of planning to study medicine following his Ph.D. He had no intention of practicing medicine, but simply wanted to be better able to work with physicians. When it became obvious that he could not afford further schooling, he did not give up. He spent the summer following his first year on the Chicago faculty studying surgical techniques with William Howells at the Johns Hopkins Hospital. While he was in Baltimore he renewed his acquaintance with James Mark Baldwin, an event which began a long friendship and later proved professionally beneficial.

Within a short time after entering the psychological profession, Watson's effort to make a name for himself began to bear fruit. In 1906 he accepted an invitation to prepare the annual summary of comparative psychological literature for the *Psychological Review*. Two years later he became the journal's editor, a position he held until 1915. Also, in 1911 he became editor of the *Journal of Animal Behavior*.

Amid this flurry of activity, Watson's career received a tremendous boost. In 1907 G. M. Stration left Johns Hopkins University and Baldwin offered Watson an associate professorship at the substantial salary of $2,500. Watson hesitated, hoping to receive a better offer from Chicago. Baldwin increased the offer to $3,500 and the rank of professor. At the same time Chicago proposed to make him an assistant professor elect. Although he thought he would be happier remaining at the University of Chicago, he decided that it would be foolish to refuse the Hopkins position.

THE YOUNG PROFESSOR

Watson truly regretted leaving Chicago. In the first place, he was quite busy with several research projects in a laboratory that he had personally wired and that contained equipment which he had constructed. Second, Watson was unhappy about having to leave his comrades, particularly James R. Angell for whom he held great affection and admiration. But Watson found an environment conducive to his professional interests and growth at Johns Hopkins. In 1909 the chair of the psychology department resigned, and Watson inherited the job. At the age of thirty-one, he found himself in a most advantageous position. Not only did he have money and more equipment than he had had at Chicago, he was now able to shape the future of the psychology department at one of America's leading institutions of higher education. He immediately set about convincing the university's president to sever the department's connections with philosophy and strengthen those with biology. As editor of the *Psychological Review*, he was also in a position to present his developing theories to a wide audience.

For some time Watson had been struggling with the idea of building a theory of animal psychology strictly from observed behavior without any inferences about consciousness. Something that James McKeen Cattell had said in a paper in 1904 further stimulated Watson's thinking. Cattell had argued that the goal of psychology was the study of human beings and that psychologists should reject introspective techniques of investigating mental functioning. When he broached this subject with his Chicago colleagues, Watson had found none of them sympathetic to the idea except perhaps Jacques Loeb. At Hopkins he continued this line of research while he taught general psychology along the lines of James' viewpoint and experimental courses using Tichner's manuals.

By 1908 his ideas had begun to jell. In that year he lectured on comparative psychology at three different professional meetings. Having concluded that animal psychology could serve as a basis for human psychology, he attempted to make the point that scientists should not attribute mental content to animals but should stick to objective observations of their behavior. During the next four years, he focused his efforts on producing a more thorough and systematic statement of his position.

THE BEHAVIORIST

Watson achieved that significant milestone in a lecture given at Columbia University in 1912 (published in the *Psychological Review* in 1913). He issued what might be called the behaviorist manifesto, entitled "Psychology as the Behaviorist Views It," in which he boldly declared his independence from traditional psychology. The essence of his argument can be summarized in three important points: 1) Psychology was a natural science relying for its data on objective observations instead of introspection. 2) Unlike traditional psychology which sought to describe and explain consciousness, the goals of psychology were to predict and control behavior. 3) The behaviorist does not recognize any dividing line between humans and animals. The obvious implication was that studies of various laboratory animals were important sources of information for achieving the goals of this brand of psychology.

Watson reiterated and expanded these ideas in *Behavior: An Introduction to Comparative Psychology*. This textbook met with a receptive audience, particularly among American psychologists. In 1915 Watson was elected president of the American Psychological Association. His presidential address dealt with Pavlov's theory of conditioned reflex and suggested that this reaction could become the basis of a theory of human psychology ranging from habit formation to emotional disorders. Even though his behaviorism began as little more than a point of view, it held enormous potential for becoming a serious research program and a systematic theory of human behavior.

World War I interrupted Watson's work in 1917. His eyesight precluded him from becoming a line officer, so he served as a staff officer with the Committee on Personnel in the Army. In that capacity, he was responsible for organizing and conducting the aviation examination boards. He spent his tour in the United States, except for three months with the American Expeditionary Force where he attempted to gather data to aid in the selection of aviators. The Armistice prevented him from having to go overseas a second time. On the whole Watson viewed his military service as a "nightmare." He was particularly disgusted by the incompetence of the career army officers that he encountered. He gladly returned to his work at Hopkins in November 1918.

Beginning where he left off, Watson undertook to develop his behavioristic principles into a human psychology. Clear evidence of the extent of his thinking appeared in 1919 when he published *Psychology from the Standpoint of a Behaviorist*. His first book had been limited to comparative psychology, but this one purported to be a general psychology text. In addition to a description of the field of psychology and its methods, Watson dealt with the psychology of stimulus and response, emotions, instincts, language, and personality development and disturbances. Of particular note in this book was his use of Pavlov's conditioned reflex theory. Watson applied this theory to the discussion of human emotions.

From observations, Watson found that humans had only three kinds of unconditioned reflexes: fear, rage, and love. He also determined that these reflexes were elicited by a narrow range of stimuli. Therefore, he concluded that all other human emotions were the result of conditioning. But Watson had little experimental evidence to support his conclusions. He immediately set about remedying this deficiency by conducting a highly controversial experiment aimed at producing a conditioned fear response in an eleven-month-old child. Though the experiment was successful, today it would raise serious ethical questions.

A BUSINESS CAREER

In the fall of 1920, this apparently brilliant academic career came to a sudden end. John Watson became involved in an affair with his graduate student, Rosalie Rayner. This affair, the divorce from his first wife, and subsequent remarriage to Rayner became a front-page scandal that was too much for Baltimore in 1920. Consequently, the Johns Hopkins University administration decided to ask for Watson's resignation.

Finding his academic career destroyed the resourceful Watson wasted no time in obtaining an opening into the business world. He went to New York and with the help of a friend secured a probationary position with the J. Walter Thompson advertising agency. Following a successful trial assignment to determine the market for rubber boots in the Mississippi River region south of Cairo, Illinois, he sold a well-known brand of coffee to wholesale and retail stores in Pittsburgh, Cleveland, and Erie. With characteristic vigor and enthusiasm, he devoted the next year to learning the advertising business from top to bottom. He later remarked, "I began to learn that it can be just as thrilling to watch the growth of a sales curve of a new product as to watch the learning curve of animals or men."[21] It is not surprising that by 1924 he had become one of four vice presidents in the company.

In the meantime, Watson had not severed all ties to the academic world. Soon after he came to New York, he accepted invitations to lecture at the New School for Social Research and the Cooper Institute. In 1924 he published these lectures in a book entitled *Behaviorism*. This widely acclaimed and very successful book contained discussions of his favorite topics, many of which had appeared in his 1919 textbook but were now expanded and revised.

Watson began his lively discussion by defining behaviorism as a natural science concerned with the entire scope of human adjustment. Like the physical scientist who wanted to control and manipulate natural phenomena, the behaviorist aimed at predicting and controlling human activity. He then presented his most mature theories of human instinct, emotion, and thought. In the latter case, he extended his previous description of thinking to include the psychoanalysts' conception of unconscious thought. Conscious thought was a series of vocal or subvocal responses in a chain where one response served as a stimulus to the next response. But not all responses in the chain had to be verbal; some could be visceral or emotional reactions that he believed were unconscious thoughts.

The most striking feature of this book was Watson's radically environmentalist theory of instinct and emotion. In 1914 he had noted the importance of instinct and habit and the difficulty of finding instincts unaltered by the environment. By 1919 he added that there were only three innate human emotions. Now he carried this line of thinking to its logical conclusion by arguing that virtually all innate factors were obscured by learned responses and could, therefore, be ignored. In addition he accounted for individual differences by suggesting that they were the products of early experiences. He went so far as to argue in a later edition of *Behaviorism* that, given the proper environment and control, he could completely mold an individual's character. Watson admitted that this idea was based on scant evidence, but he had the audacity to expect his readers to accept his "scientific" notion on faith. Since that time, critics of behavioristic theories have asked: "But who will control the controllers?"

FINAL YEARS

In the years following the publication of *Behaviorism*, Watson became further removed from the academy. His work in psychology reflected the shift in his thinking away from scholarly discourse and toward topics of interest to the general public. He wrote several articles for popular magazines. In 1928 Watson and his wife published a book on child rearing entitled *Psychological Care of Infant and Child.* The thrust of their discussion centered around the notion that infants should not be cuddled or spoiled but conditioned to lead independent lives. This enormously successful book became the first in a whole series of child rearing guides to be published in America.

Following the death of his wife in 1935, Watson found his psychological work somewhat circumscribed, and made fewer public appearances. The next year he left the Thompson agency to become vice president of another advertising firm, William Esty and Company. He remained there until his retirement in 1945. John Watson spent the last years of his life farming and working on building projects. He died on 25 September 1958.

John B. Watson was one of the most important and controversial figures in the history of modern psychology. His bold efforts accelerated the growth of the environmentalist viewpoint. He also aided the development of animal studies by emphasizing the analogy between animal and human behavior. Although he had few immediate followers, his extreme positions fostered the work of two generations of behavioristic psychologists. His legacy is apparent in some current theories of educational psychology and classroom management. However, Watson's behaviorism was not without competition in psychology and education. Psychoanalytic theory gave it a good run for its money and it spilled over into the child centered pedagogy of the postwar years. Freudianism, along with a Rousseauan view of children, put pupils in the center of the educational experience. Child centered educators believed that the child was potentially creative and that a school which promoted the free development of those unique abilities was the best assurance of a society truly concerned with the value and achievements of humanity. To this end they promoted psychoanalytic doctrines to develop the creative potentialities of their students. Most prominent among the educators who combined psychoanalysis with the credo of self-expression was Margaret Naumburg, founder of the Children's School— later named the Walden School.

Margaret Naumburg (1890-1983)

Born on 14 May 1890 in New York City, she was the daughter of Max Naumburg, who had come to the United States from Bavaria as a young child, and the former Theresa Kahnweiler of North Carolina. Margaret attended New York Public School 87, the Horace Mann School, and the Sachs School. In 1908 she entered Vassar College for the first year of her undergraduate education. Upon transferring to Barnard College, she took work in economics and in philosophy with John Dewey. In addition to her studies, she served as president of the Socialist Club at Barnard.

SEARCHING FOR A METHOD

Like so many others in the Progressive Era, Naumburg was a determined reformer. She was convinced that society could be improved, but was at first unsure about the most effective means of achieving that end. Upon graduating from college in 1912, she set out for England to continue her study of the "dismal science" at the London School of Economics. There, under the tutelage of the Fabian Socialists Sidney and Beatrice Webb, she observed firsthand the social conditions and labor problems of the British film industry. But within six months she had lost her enthusiasm for socialism. She had apparently concluded that social reform began not with groups and institutions but with individuals.

On her way to London, Naumburg had read *The Montessori Method* and had been immediately impressed by the educational ideas in it. In place of the common method of "stuffing" children's heads with information, she saw that education could become a means of grasping "the fundamental realities of life" by focusing curiosity, interest, and imagination. In January 1913 she departed London for Rome to study with Montessori at the *Casa dei Bambini*. The two women did not get along well, and Naumburg returned to New York the following fall. Despite their personal differences, however, Margaret Naumburg saw sufficient value in Montessori's educational method to accept a position as teacher in Lillian Wald's Henry Street Settlement kindergarten which was organized on Montessorian principles.

Convinced that education was the best means for improving individuals and society, Naumburg was still dissatisfied with the methods she was using to achieve that goal. But the events of 1914 in her professional and personal life would significantly alter her attitude. She had already concluded that Montessori's early introduction of the basic skills was attractive to American parents but that its didactic materials did not lend themselves to the unusual or creative. In an attempt to find a more satisfactory method, she spent the summer of 1914 with Marietta Pierce Johnson at her Organic School in Fairhope, Alabama. Much to her delight, Naumburg found an educational program that viewed children as organisms and aimed at developing them physically, intellectually, and emotionally. Returning to New York in the fall, she took the first steps toward establishing her own school by renting two rooms in the Leet Street schoolhouse where she taught a small group of children ages three to five. At the same time, Margaret Naumburg became associated with a group of people who were intensely interested in the ideas of psychoanalysis.

Sigmund Freud's visit to Clark University in 1909 generated serious interest in his theories. Beginning in 1910, English translations of his works were prepared by psychiatrist A. A. Brill, and some psychiatrists gradually began to see psychotherapy as an effective method for treating neuroses. They recognized, said John Burnham, "the medical value of a constructive intellectual and emotional environment."[22] This led to a concern for their patients' families and the society. It also generated particular interest in the influence of childhood experiences on later life. As a consequence, these psychiatrists soon found themselves committed to social improvement, an effort that Burnham believed had all the characteristics of progressivism.

The excitement over Freudianism was not confined to the medical community. The intelligentsia quickly became familiar with psychoanalysis. Some read the works of Freud, Carl Jung, and Alfred Adler. Others heard interpretations of the doctrines at gatherings in places such as Mabel Dodge's salon in Greenwich Village. Still others encountered psychotherapy on the couches in their analysts' offices. Margaret Naumburg learned about psychoanalysis in all three ways. In 1914, while studying psychoanalytic theory, she began a three year analysis with Jungian psychiatrist Beatrice Hinkle. She presumably hoped that this would alleviate any inhibitions on her own feelings, thereby preventing her from dominating the children in her school. Regardless of its practical value, this was a courageous act at a time when psychotherapy was still in its infancy. Finally, as an active participant in the intellectual life of Greenwich Village, Naumburg absorbed the popular forms of Freudianism. Combined with her knowledge of psychoanalytic theory, this became a fundamental element of her educational ideas.

An equally important thread in the cloth of her educational thought was artistic self-expression. As a proponent of child centered education, Margaret Naumburg was already interested in finding ways of releasing the creative impulses that she believed were within the child. This interest must have been heightened as she moved among people in the Village who depended on their ability to express themselves creatively in a variety of art forms. One such artist was Waldo Frank, a writer and the editor of *The Seven Arts* magazine, whom she married on 20 December 1916. As Frank's wife, she came to know Postimpressionist art and associated with experimenters in writing, painting, and sculpture. Her friends came increasingly from the arts, and she lived in a world pervaded by new forms of expression and technique. The influence of art on her life was apparently sufficient that she later came to see it as a particularly effective medium for psychotheraphy.

HER OWN VIEWS

The war years clearly were a time of intellectual and professional growth for Margaret Naumburg. While she wove the threads of organic education, psychoanalysis, and creative self-expression into whole cloth, she expanded the program of what was at first called the Children's School. In 1915, she added to the school a second group of children and three teachers, including her sister, Florence Cane. Two years later, she moved the school to 34 West 68th Street and changed the name to the Walden School.

The curriculum of the school emphasized the arts, which Naumburg saw as a means of creating socially and emotionally mature children. By building the program on a foundation of psychoanalytic doctrine, she aimed at producing children with integrated personalities. Furthermore, she wanted teachers who were fully prepared to help the students achieve this goal. Thus, she recommended that they undergo analysis. An example of what she intended could be found in the work of Florence Cane. Influenced by Jung and by her analysis under Beatrice Hinkle, Cane focused on painting as a medium of expression. She encouraged the children to paint whatever they felt impelled to as a means of expressing their feelings toward the environment. At other times paintings were to represent dreams or moods. Gradually, art forms that enhanced individuality and self-expression began to replace those of social value in the Walden program. In Naumburg's words, "from our point of view there must be a recognition of the subjective inner life, of feeling as coexistent with and coessential to our life action."[23] Among early twentieth century educators, the excitement over Freud was as intense as that over Rousseau, but not as widespread. Both theorists showed means to natural development. Psychoanalysis in particular served to further the cause of both mental hygiene and artistic self-expression. It complemented the release of the emotional bases for creativity.

In large measure, the writings of Margaret Naumburg reflected these interests. From her earliest essay in 1915 to her detailed description of the Walden School in *The Child and the World*, published in 1928, Rousseau's ideal of natural development recurred often. As she became convinced of the efficacy of psychoanalysis as a means of promoting self-expression, her writings clearly showed the intensity of her belief. It was not, however, the doctrines of Sigmund Freud that influenced her most. Rather, from the time of her analysis with Dr. Hinkle, Naumburg became convinced that Carl Jung's analytic psychology was more compatible with her ideas.

Naumburg's first published statements about education appeared in *Outlook* the summer following the founding of her school at Leet Street. After describing a parade of children from William Wirt's Bronx Public School 45, she indicated her obvious preference for a child centered school.

> To catch the spirit of a Wirt school one ought to be familiar with the atmosphere of the typical public school, with its long hushed corridors, its wriggling classes, and its hordes of silent children shuffling into overcrowded playgrounds. And then step into a Wirt school and see the corridors filled with spontaneous, animated children going and coming about their particular tasks. Everywhere small groups [are] eagerly active in their chosen work in the shops, the studios, the playgrounds, and other special activities.[24]

Naumburg noted with approval that Wirt allowed older children to serve as teaching assistants and younger ones to act as shop helpers. Teachers were in the background—that is, "in their rightful place as sharers and helpers in the children's activities."[25] She undoubtedly was pleased that Wirt had worked against the "intellectualized elementary school" with its prevailing notion that the program was more important than the facilities for the children and the assumption that everyone did the same work, at the same time, and in the same way.

A more significant piece was an essay about the Walden school that Naumburg wrote in 1926 for a yearbook of the National Society for the Study of Education. There she revealed her maturing educational ideas. Without naming other progressive schools, she noted that the Walden School occupied a position between the extreme laissez-faire school and the school that emphasized socialization. Her school did not fully accept either view. The Walden School, she asserted, "believes in the social function of the school towards the creation of a more harmonious and equitable future society, and it believes in the development of individual potentials as the swiftest means of insuring just such a socialization."[26] This statement typified the lack of concern about social reform among many educators and former progressives in the 1920s. It further indicated that Naumburg continued to believe that improving society depended on the proper education of individuals.

Margaret Naumburg saw little good in traditional education. She was outraged at the thought of the "terrible injuries" that occurred to children daily in the name of "orthodox education." In a statement that seemed to blend Rousseau's view of children with Jung's notion of libido as psychic energy, she condemned traditional schools: "The constriction, repression, and misdirection of the original power and spontaneous energy of thousands of school children is something I am prepared to denounce as a menacing evil of orthodox education."[27] To avoid such danger, she opposed the continued use of "outworn methods" and advocated the search for new means of preserving the vitality with which each new group of children entered school. Of course, this was precisely the kind of education the Walden School tried to provide by combining regular school subjects and real life activities and by regarding reading, writing, and arithmetic as necessary means to complete living, not as ends of life. All of this was accomplished in an atmosphere that had the warmth and intimacy of home.

THEORETICAL UNDERPINNINGS

Throughout Naumburg's book, Rousseauan and Jungian themes recurred either separately or together. She believed, as did Rousseau, that the products of nature were good and that people and society corrupted them. She objected to the common belief that equality of opportunity meant giving equal value to all levels of ability because it resulted in an education that ignored the gifted and talented. As she put it: "Nature has always had the sense to cultivate variation in every one of her species. Only man is fool enough to try to improve on nature by a system of education that makes every child as indistinguishable as possible from any other."[28]

At another point, Naumburg described how children learned to distrust adults when they received evasive answers to questions about the sanctity of human values such as private property, social distinctions, or control of human life. The tragic drama that ensued in these instances, she remarked, affected both the child and the adult. By attempting to affirm their innate values with such queries, children brought adults face to face with values that either lay dormant or were denied. When the answers avoided the real questions, the relationship between adults and children often became degraded. A similar result occurred when parents failed to deal with the contradictions between theory and practice on such moral issues as killing. Children were shocked, said Naumburg, when they discovered that adults said one thing and did another. Finally, she complained that society's imposition of time standards on the realities of "joy, sorrow, love, work, and play" in the lives of children made them suspicious of adults. She grudgingly admitted, nevertheless, that a certain amount of routine in the form of habits of order and organization were necessary for adjustment. Then she quickly added that art—which was natural to life and not a specialized function—might help to return values to their proper order. To put it another way, allowing the child's natural creative tendency to develop would ameliorate the harsh effects of society.

Naumburg needed a modern psychological theory to give credibility to her Rousseauan philosophical views. She could have chosen the functionalism of Dewey except for the fact that it was too concerned with the social aspect of psychology. It lacked sufficient concern for the individual in general and human emotion in particular. She turned instead to psychoanalysis. Freud's interest in the neurotic individual and his theory that the source of neurosis lay in human sexuality failed to meet her needs. In contrast Carl Jung's interpretation of the unconscious, the libido, and psychological types supported her beliefs about human nature. Although Naumburg never took the time to define the term unconscious, except to suggest that it contained the major portion of the emotional life, there was a vague connection to Jung's conception that the unconscious held all psychic processes that were not perceptibly related to the ego. Her use of the term libido, however, was much closer to his idea of psychic energy.

For Margaret Naumburg psychoanalysis explained the natural essence of the human being that Rousseau had held would unfold from within, if given the right environment. It gave the emotional life greater importance. At one point, she noted that modern medicine had found that one of its important duties was curing "sick souls." By analogy, modern education ought to pay attention to the spiritual health of the child. In order to accomplish this, teachers had to be aware of their own unconscious life and that of their pupils. Parents, she continued, should also be more concerned about the inward life of their children.

THE WALDEN SCHOOL

From the time of her introduction to psychoanalysis in 1914, Naumburg saw it as a means of helping individuals and groups in school gain a new perspective based on their inner life. At first, because of prejudice against psychoanalysis among physicans and a lack of knowledge of it among educators, she avoided the theoretical jargon. She endeavored to create a correct environment for releasing the unconscious emotional life of children into positive and personal expression. By 1928 the Walden School had a group of teachers and parents who had turned to analysis as a means of understanding their own lives and those of the children. At least one half of the faculty, she claimed, had been psychoanalyzed, and the other half were interested in applying analytic principles to education.

Naumburg believed that the deepest wish in a human being was some form of power and control which manifested itself in various ways depending on psychological type, temperament, and early environment. This power was the motive force of our actions, which psychoanalysis sought to explain. This psychic energy, she contended, may or may not be in harmony with nature. Thus the Walden School was intent on mastering this power for its own purposes. It planned to go beyond intellectual training because external responses were all too often directed by unconscious feelings. Naumburg firmly believed that education provided both the civilization and the individual with a practical means for conveying psychic energy and positive social and personal activities.

Another important Jungian conception that Margaret Naumburg used was that of psychological types—the extrovert and the introvert. She was concerned that educators knew too little about these concepts. "Until we truly comprehend the fundamental difference in psychic mechanisms between the jolly, outgoing, sociable child [extrovert] and the acutely reticent, over-moody one [introvert], we can't help educationally to fulfill their own potentialities or to overcome their psychic difficulties."[29] She and her staff attempted to connect the school's activities with the child's psychological temperament. They also avoided activities that today would be called sexist. The Walden staff refused to educate children according to sexual stereotypes. Rather, they treated them as individuals.

In the early years of the Walden School, various observers found some evidence of creative self-expression among the children in the program. To date, however, no one has attempted to determine if Naumburg's efforts had any enduring effects on the children. Such an investigation would involve examining the school's records and tracing the lives of those who had attended. It might also tell us more about the influence of analytic psychology in education.

LATER YEARS

Margaret Naumburg served as director of the Walden School until 1922, when she relinquished that position to become advisory director. She turned over the responsibility for the daily activities of the school to her longtime associates, Margaret Pollitzer and Elizabeth Goldsmith, who functioned as executive directors. One immediate reason for limiting her professional work was the birth of her son, Thomas, on 12 May 1922. This arrangement also enabled her to maintain contact with the activities of the school and, at the same time, gave her an opportunity to reflect upon its work. In 1926 she ended her official connection with the Walden School. Two years later, she published *The Child and the World* which contained a record of the school's aims and activities and an exposition of her educational thought.

From her early years as a teacher and school director, she was committed to the idea of educating children intellectually, physically, and emotionally. But, because she thought too much emphasis was being given to the first two capacities, especially the first, she tried to shift the weight of educational activities toward emotional growth. As a consequence, Naumburg's educational philosophy and program appeared to be fundamentally anti-intellectual and somewhat opposed to social reform. With regard to the latter, she consistently argued that individual growth had to occur before society would change. This attitude brought her into direct conflict with John Dewey (1928), when she criticized his emphasis on shared concerns and (1930), when she used Jung's doctrine of human types to argue against Dewey's "new individualism."

Despite her disagreements with Dewey, Naumburg's concern for children and their growth never diminished. During the second phase of her career, however, she narrowed the scope of that interest and concentrated on helping children with psychiatric disorders. Combining her belief in the efficacy of analytic psychology and of artistic self-expression, she became a pioneer in the development of analytically oriented art therapy.

In the early 1930s, she began to conduct research and work with children at the New York Psychiatric Institute. Using the techniques which she had perfected at the Walden School, Naumburg attempted to get the children freely to express themselves in their art work. At about the same time, she accepted an appointment as a lecturer at the New School for Social Research. This post, which she held from 1932 to 1952, provided her with a forum in which she could discuss her evolving ideas about art and psychotherapy.

After years of study and research, Naumburg attempted to spread her theories and techniques beyond the confines of the New School. In 1947 she began conducting courses and seminars at leading medical schools and psychiatric clinics in the United States and Europe. She published her ideas in several professional periodicals, including the *Psychiatric Quarterly*, the *Journal of Nervous and Mental Diseases*, *The Nervous Child*, and the *Journal of Aesthetics and Art Criticism*. She also found time to write four books on the subject of art therapy: *Studies of the Free Art Expression of Behavior Problem Children and Adolescents* (1947), *Schizophrenic Art: Its Meaning in Psychotherapy* (1950), *Psychoneurotic Art, Its Use in Psychotherapy* (1953), and *Dynamically Oriented Art Therapy: Its Principles and Practices, Illustrated with Three Case Studies* (1966).

Margaret Naumburg completed her academic career at New York University, where she held two lectureships, beginning in 1959 in the department of art education and a year later in the department of psychology. Naumburg remained in New York City until 1975, when she moved to Needham, Massachusetts. There she lived out the last years of her life near her son, Dr. Thomas Frank of Cambridge, and her five grandchildren. She died at her home on 26 February 1983 at the age of ninety-two.

By 1960 neither Montessori nor Naumburg were prominent among the theorists that American educators read. Indeed, few teachers or administrators would have known anything about either. The psychology that most educationists studied was in the tradition of Watson's behaviorism. Providing for individual differences, a phrase much honored in education texts and superintendents' speeches, meant in practice efficient testing and ability grouping. Perhaps that was one reason for the success of a book that appeared that year under the title of *Summerhill: A Radical Approach to Child Rearing*. Although the book came out in 1960, its contents were written in the twenties and thirties. The theme of the book was freedom — from parental and societal moralizing and coercion. An instant success, it sold hundreds of thousands of copies in several languages over the next few years. Its author was a Scotsman, writing about a school he had been running in England since the 1920s. His name was A. S. Neill.

A. S. Neill (1883-1973)

Alexander ("Allie") Sutherland Neill was one of thirteen children born to Mary Sutherland and George Neill. Several died young. Only those around Allie's age seem to have been particularly significant in his life: Willie, the oldest, a good student who became a minister; (2) Neilie, next oldest, who became a physician; and (3) Cluny, a girl nine months younger than Neill and his closest friend and playmate. The parents had met when they were both teachers in the same village school. From working-class backgrounds, both wanted middle-class respectability. They worked hard themselves and expected their children to do likewise.

EARLY LIFE

Growing up in a family that was trying so hard to better itself produced anxieties. Allie thought he felt these more intensely than did other family members. He did less well in school than his two older brothers and was the only child in the family not sent to nearby Forfar Academy. He assimilated a negative view of his academic talents and performed accordingly. The situation was intensified by his having to go to school — and later teach — under his father, a man who had many self-doubts that he projected onto his third son: "I was obviously the inferior article, the misfit in a tradition of academic success, and automatically I accepted an inferior status," wrote Neill. "If there was a particularly hard and unappetizing heel to a loaf, my father would cut it off with a flourish; with another flourish, he would toss it over the table in my direction, saying 'It'll do for Allie.' "[30]

At fourteen young Neill became a clerk in a manufacturing plant near Edinburgh. Seven months later he returned home to study for the civil service examination, but found that he could not remember what he read. He worked in a drapery shop in his hometown for a time before once more trying to prepare for the civil service exam. When he again failed to make adequate progress, his mother suggested that he become a pupil teacher in his father's school. This was a low paid but official position which lasted four years. "I think I learned my profession well, for I copied my father, and he was a good teacher — good in the sense that he could draw out rather than stuff in," Neill wrote many years later.[31]

The apprentice teaching situation involved two examinations, one at the end of the second and the other after the final year. The best candidates went on scholarship for two years of normal training at Glasgow or Edinburgh and then to good teaching jobs. Neill, however, did badly and had to settle for the designation of ex-Pupil Teacher. This did allow him to become an assistant teacher. At nineteen he began three years in this capacity in two schools near Edinburgh. The Kettle school, where he spent all but two months of this time, · had a strict head. Neill discovered by comparison that his father had run a much more relaxed classroom.

Working as a teacher allowed Neill to develop many of the skills the lack of which had been his nemesis as a child. He saved his money and studied for university admission examinations. In 1908, at the age of twenty-five, he entered the University of Edinburgh. He majored in English literature, had an active social life, edited the school's literary newspaper (*The Student*), and did well enough on his examinations to graduate at the end of the three year course with the equivalent of about a "B" average. His master of arts degree (Edinburgh did not grant bachelor's degrees) gave considerable status in the elitist and class conscious British higher education system. Neill's ambivalent feelings about his academic talents and his lower-class origins kept him from enjoying the experience as much as he might have done or from valuing it highly. Sixty years later he still disparaged his university years:

I held then, and do now, that it is better to write a bad limerick than be able to recite *Paradise Lost*. That is a fundamental thing in education. But the university never asked us to compose even a limerick; it did not ask from us any original opinions about Shakespeare or about anyone else. . . . I was compelled to concentrate on whether a blank-verse line had elision or not, or whether one could trace the rhythm of "Christable" in "The Lotus Eaters." It was all piddling stuff, like taking Milan Cathedral to pieces stone by stone to discover where the beauty lay. I had to read so glorious a thing as *The Tempest* with annotations, painfully looking up the etymological meaning of some phrase that did not matter a scrap.[32]

THE DOMINY

Upon graduation, Neill went to work for an Edinburgh publisher who shortly moved to London. There he took a job as art editor for the *Picadilly Magazine*, a new publication. Before the first issue came out, England was at war with Germany and the periodical went out of business. While waiting for his induction into the Royal Scots Fusiliers, Neill took a temporary position as head of the village school in Gretna Green, Scotland. Law required all school heads (dominies) to keep an official log. Neill also kept an informal diary of his thoughts which he published in 1915 under the title of *A Dominie's Log*: "The 'Three R's' spell futility. . . . My work is hopeless, for education should aim at bringing up a new generation that will be better than the old. The present system is to produce the same kind of man as we see today. And how hopeless he is," Neill wrote. "I am hopeful because I have found a solution. . . . I think I want to make them [the children] realize what life means. . . . Most of the stuff I teach them will be forgotten in a year or two, but an attitude remains with one throughout life. I want these boys and girls to acquire the habit of looking honestly at life." The book is a record of Neill's giving up using the tawse (whip), questioning the value of academic training, and encouraging the children to use their imaginations. It contained the germs of most of what he would later write about education.[33]

Neill's educational views evoked complimentary responses, but a review in *The New Age*, a progressive weekly paper, advised Neill to read Rousseau, Pestalozzi, Froebel, Montessori, and Dewey. The reviewer thought Neill had gone too far in disparaging the regular schools and that he had not devoted enough attention to what should be taught and how to teach it. These criticisms would be repeated many times over the next several decades, but Neill would continue to find most schools, especially state controlled ones, too academic, too dull, too coercive. Even Montessori, who had many of the same criticisms of school that he did, was too structured and authoritarian for Neill's taste. She stressed giving children the liberty to do right! "At every step the little child is patiently and lovingly directed," was a central tenet of hers. Children could choose which didactic equipment or activity to engage in, but having chosen, they were to follow prescribed procedures. Neill thought this inhibited fantasy and play. "The Montessori world is too scientific for me," he wrote. "It is too orderly, too didactic. The name 'didactic apparatus' frightens me."[34]

In 1917 Neill spent a brief period as an officer waiting to go to France, but after a bout with influenza was plagued with insomnia. When he did occasionally fall asleep, he suffered from nightmares. A doctor said he should leave the army. He had recently met a man named Homer Lane, an American running a penal colony called the Little Commonwealth for teenaged offenders. Neill went to see Lane from whom he got two important ideas: (1) the value of Freudian psychology and psychoanalysis, and (2) the absolute necessity of always being on the side of the child. At the Little Commonwealth, this took the form of a weekly meeting at which everyone had one vote. Neill would borrow this procedure later.[35]

SUMMERHILL

Out of the army, Neill worked briefly at a noted "progressive" school (King Alfred) and spent a short stint at editorial work for *The New Era* through which he went to the continent. He joined a few other people in founding an international school near Dresden (a hundred miles south of Berlin). From there, the school moved briefly to Austria. In 1924 Neill and his spouse (he had married the wife of a colleague in the international school) moved with some of the pupils to a rented house in Lyme Regis, Dorset, England. The name of the house was Summerhill. After three years, the school moved to the town of Leiston on the coast about ninety miles northeast of London. He retained the name "Summerhill" for his school.

The school was to offer conventional subjects to boys and girls from preschool through secondary school ages. Primarily a boarding establishment, it had two unusual features. One was that no pupil was ever under any circumstances to be required to attend class. Attendance at lessons was to be entirely voluntary (although teachers had to offer them on a regular schedule). The other was that most rules and adjudication of disputes would take place in a weekly (Saturday evening) meeting of all members of the school community at which each person, whether teacher or five year old pupil was to have one vote. Underlying the whole operation would be a basic respect for individual rights.

Summerhill got more than its share of problem children. At first, Neill welcomed these. "At that stage, I was a proper fool. I thought that psychology could cure everything, barring a broken leg."[36] Many children did benefit, some through P.L.'s—Private Lessons (weekly one-hour psychoanalytic sessions with Neill)—others without these. Neill finally concluded that it was not psychology but freedom that worked the cure.

Neill wrote several books to explain his philosophy of education and life (*The Problem Child, The Problem Parent, The Problem Teacher, Hearts not Heads in the School*). He had wanted to be a writer upon leaving Edinburgh. All were competent and engaging books, but none sold particularly well. A few quotations from a 1937 book, *That Dreadful School*, will illustrate Neill's style and beliefs:

> We set out to make a school in which we should allow children freedom to be themselves. In order to do this we had to renounce all discipline, all direction, all suggestion, all moral training, all religious instruction. We

have been called brave, but it did not require courage: all it required was what we had—a complete belief in the child as a good, not an evil being. And during sixteen years this belief in the goodness of the child has never wavered; rather has it become a final faith. . . .

Today Summerhill pupils are mostly children whose parents want them to be brought up without restrictive discipline from above. That is a most happy circumstance, for in the old days I would have the son of a fire-eating diehard, who sent his lad to me in desperation. Such parents had no interest in freedom for children at all, and secretly must have considered us a crowd of lunatic cranks. It was so very difficult to explain things to those diehards.

I recall the military gentleman who thought of enrolling his nine-year-old son as a pupil.

"The place seems all right," he said, "but I have one fear; . . . my boy may learn to masturbate here."

I asked him why he feared.

"It will do him so much harm," he said.

"It didn't do you or me much harm, did it?" I said pleasantly.

He went off rather hurriedly with his son. . . .

It is necessary even at this late date to explain what is meant by freedom for the child. The usual argument against freedom for children is of this kind: Life is hard, and we must train the children so that they will fit into life later on. We must therefore discipline them. If we allow them to do what they like, how will they ever be able to serve under a boss? How will they compete with others who have known discipline? . . .

Freedom is necessary for the child because only under freedom can he grow in his natural way. I see the results of bondage in new pupils coming from prep schools and convents. They are bundles of insincerity, with an unreal politeness and pseudo manners. Their reaction to freedom is rapid and tiresome. For the first week or two they open doors for the staff, call me "Sir," wash carefully. They glance at me with "respect" which is easily recognized as fear. After a few weeks of freedom they show what they are. They become impudent, unmannerly, unwashed. They do all the things they have been forbidden to do in the past: they swear and smoke and break things. And all the time they have an insincere expression in their eyes and their voices. It takes at least six months for them to lose their insincerity. They lose also their deference to what they think is authority, and in six months they are natural, healthy kids who say what they think without cheek or hate.

When a child comes young enough to freedom he does not go through the stage of insincerity and acting. The most striking thing about Summerhill is this absolute sincerity among the pupils. . . .

No, I won't argue for freedom for children. One half-hour with a free child is more convincing than a book of arguments. Seeing is believing. Yet it is necessary to point out the difference between freedom and license. The other day I sat with Ethel Mannin in Covent Garden. During the first ballet a child in front of us talked loudly to her father. At the end of the ballet Ethel and I found other seats. Said Ethel to me: "What would you do if one of your kids from Summerhill did that?"

"Tell it to shut up," I said.

"You wouldn't need to," said Ethel; "they wouldn't do it."

And I don't think they would. I forget whether in any previous book I told of the woman who brought her girl of seven to see me.

"Mr. Neill," she said, "I have read every line you have written, and even before Daphne was born I had decided to bring her up exactly on your lines."

I glanced at Daphne who was standing on my grand piano with her heavy shoes on. She made a leap for the sofa and nearly went through the springs.

"You see how natural she is," said the mother, "the Neillian child."

I fear that I blushed.

It is the distinction between freedom and license that many parents cannot grasp. In the disciplined home the children have no rights, and in the spoiled home they have all the rights. The proper home is one in which children and adults have equal rights. And the same applies to the school. In Summerhill everyone has equal rights. No one is allowed to walk on my grand piano, and I am not allowed to borrow a boy's cycle without his permission. At a general meeting the vote of a child of six counts for as much as my vote does.[37]

Neill had a playful style of speaking and writing that skated just on the edge of credibility:

Lessons in Summerhill are optional. Children can go to them or stay away from them—for years if they want to. There is a time-table for the staff, and the children have classes according to their age usually, but sometimes according to their interests. Personally I do not know what type of teaching is carried on, for I never visit lessons, and have no interest in how children learn. We have no new methods of teaching because we do not consider that teaching very much matters. Whether a school has an apparatus for teaching long division or not is of no significance, for long division is of no importance whatever.

Children who come as infants attend lessons all the way, but pupils from other schools vow that they will never attend any beastly lessons again. They play and cycle and get in people's way, but they fight shy of any lessons. This sometimes goes on for months, and the recovery time is proportionate to the hatred their last school gave them. Our record case was a girl from a convent. She loafed for three years. The average period of recovery from lesson-aversion is three months.

Strangers to the idea of freedom in the school will be wondering what sort of a madhouse it is where teachers smoke while they teach and children play all day if they want to. Many an adult says: "If I had been sent to a school like that I'd never have done a thing." Others say: "Such children will feel themselves heavily handicapped when they have to compete against children who have been made to learn." I think of Jack who left us at the age of seventeen to go into an engineering factory. One day the managing director sent for him.

"You are the lad from Summerhill," he said. "I'm curious to know how such an education appears to you now that you are mixing with lads from the old schools. Suppose you had to choose again, would you go to Eton or Summerhill?"

"Oh, Summerhill, of course," replied Jack.

"But why? What does it offer that the Public Schools don't offer?"

Jack scratched his head.

"I dunno," he said slowly; "I think it gives you a feeling of complete self-confidence."

"Yes," said the manager dryly, "I noticed it when you came into the room."

"Lord," laughed Jack, "I'm sorry if I gave you that impression."

"I liked it," said the director. "Most men when I call them into the office fidget about and look uncomfortable. You came in as my equal. . . . By the way what department would you like to change into?"

This story shows that learning does not matter, that only character matters. Jack failed in his Matric[ulation examination] because he hated all book learning, but his lack of knowledge about Lamb's *Essays* or the Trigonometrical Solution of Triangles is not going to handicap him in life.

All the same there is a lot of learning in Summerhill. I don't suppose a group of our twelve year olds could compete with a state school class of equal age in—say—neat handwriting or spelling or vulgar fractions. But in an examination requiring originality our lot would beat the others hollow. . . . Parents are slow in realizing how unimportant the learning side of school is. Children, like adults, learn what they want to learn in life, but all the prize-giving and marks and exams sidetrack the personality. Only pedants can claim that learning from books is education. Books are the least important apparatus in a school. All that any child needs is the Three Rs: the rest should be tools and clay and sports and theatres and paint . . . and freedom.[38]

Neill's lively imagination showed in the way he operated Summerhill and in the stories he recounted to illustrate his points.

I had a youth sent to me, a real crook, who stole cleverly. A week after his arrival I had a telephone message from Liverpool. "This is Mr. X speaking (a well-known man in England) and I have a nephew at your school. He has written me asking if he can come to Liverpool for a few days. Do you mind?"

"Not a bit," I answered, "but he has no money. Who will pay his fare? Better get into touch with his parents."

On the following afternoon the boy's mother rang me up saying that they had had a phone message from Uncle Dick, and so far as they were concerned he could go. They had looked up the fare and it was 28s, and would I give Arthur £2 10s?

Arthur had put through both calls from a local call box and his imitation of an old uncle's voice was perfect. It was obvious that he had tricked me, for I had given him the £2 10s before I was conscious of being done. I talked it over with my wife, and we both agreed that the wrong thing to do would be to demand the money back, for that was what had been happening to him for years. My wife suggested rewarding him, and I agreed. I went up to his bedroom late at night.

"You're in luck today," I said cheerfully.

"I jolly well am," he said.

"Yes, but you are in greater luck than you know," I said.

"What do you mean?"

"Oh, your mother has just telephoned again," I said easily. "She says she made a mistake about the fare: it isn't 28*s*, . . . it is 38*s*. So she asked me if I'd give you another ten bob," and I carelessly threw a ten shilling note on his bed and departed before he could say anything.

He went off to Liverpool next morning, leaving a letter to be given to me after the train had gone. It began: "Dear Neill, I have discovered that you are a greater actor than I am." And for weeks he keft asking me why I had given him that ten shilling note. I said to him: "How did you feel when I gave it to you?"

He thought hard for a minute and then he said slowly: "You know, I got the biggest shock of my life. I said to myself: Here is the first man in my life who has been on my side."[39]

A typical week at Summerhill in the 1930s, according to Neill, went as follows (keep in mind that "infants" are children under seven or eight, "juniors" are third through sixth graders, and "seniors" are people of twelve or older):

Breakfast is from 8:15 to 9:00, and the staff and pupils fetch their breakfast from the kitchen hatch which is opposite to the dining room. Beds are supposed to be made by 9:30 when lessons begin. At the beginning of each term a timetable is posted up. Children are divided into classes according to their age and interest, the classes being called by Greek letters. Thus Corkhill in the laboratory may have on Monday the Betas, on Tuesday the Gammas and so on. Max has a similar timetable for English, Cyril for mathematics, Roger for geography, my wife for history. The juniors usually stay with their own teacher most of the morning, but they also go to chemistry or the art room. There is, of course, no compulsion to attend lessons, but if Jimmy comes to English on Monday and does not make an appearance again until the Friday of the following week, the others quite rightly object that he is keeping the work back, and they may throw him out.

Lessons go on until 1:00, but the infants and juniors lunch at 12:30. The school has to be fed in three relays, and the staff and seniors sit down to lunch at 1:45. Afternoons are completely free for everyone. What they all do in the afternoon I do not know. I garden, and seldom see youngsters about. I see the juniors playing gangsters, but some of the seniors busy themselves with motors and radio and drawing and painting. In good weather they play games. Some tinker about in the workshop, mending their cycles or making boats or revolvers.

Tea is at 4:00 and at 5:00 various activities begin. The juniors like to be read to; the middle group likes work in the art room—painting, linoleum cuts, leatherwork, basket making, and there is usually a busy group in the pottery; in fact the pottery seems to be a favorite haunt morning and evening. The Matriculation [university entrance examination] group works from 5:00 onwards. The wood and metal workshop is full every night.

There is no work, that is, no organized work, after 6:00 or 6:30. On Monday nights the pupils go to the local cinema on their parents' bill, and when the program changes on the Thursday those who have the money may go again. Pocket money is given out on Thursday for this reason.

On Tuesday night the staff and seniors have my psychological talk. The juniors have various reading groups then. Wednesday night is lounge night, that is dance night. Dance records are selected from a great pile, . . . and as the lounge is next door to our sitting room I dread Wednesday nights, for the tunes that the children like are to me simply a dreadful noise. Hot rhythm is about the only thing in life that makes me feel murderous. They are all good dancers, and some visitors say that they feel inferior when they dance with them.

Thursday night has nothing special on, for the seniors go to the cinema in Leiston or Aldeburgh, and Friday is left for any special event, such as play rehearsing. Saturday night is our most important one for it is General Meeting night. Dancing usually follows, and Sunday is our theater evening.[40]

HIS VIEWS

"The sex question" in the England of the thirties and forties referred to whether or not boys and girls should be taught together. Most fee charging schools were single sex. Even tax supported schools were not usually coeducational for children past the age of eight. Partly for this reason, and also because of Neill's psychoanalytic orientation, issues related to sex came up often in his writing.

Opponents of coeducation are those who fear that if you have boys and girls educated together they will sleep together. They do not say that this is behind their doubts and fears: they rationalize. . . . Girls have a slower tempo in learning. . . . It makes boys effeminate and girls masculine . . . and so on. But deep down is the moral fear, which is a jealous fear. The old want the young to be moral because the old want to keep the best things in life for themselves. That is the only excuse for morality. All other excuses are evasions. Sex is the greatest pleasure in the world, and it is repressed because it is the greatest pleasure in the world.

So that every now and again an adult comes to the school and says: "But don't they all sleep with each other?" and when I answer that they don't, he or she cries: "But why not? At their age I would have had a hell of a good time."

It is necessary to discuss sex as it appears at various stages. Freud has made us all familiar with the idea that sex is there from the beginning of life, that the baby has a sexual pleasure in sucking, and that gradually the erotic zone of the mouth gives place to that of the genitals. Thus masturbation in a child is a natural discovery, not a very important discovery at first, because the genitals are not so pleasurable as the mouth or even the skin. It is the parental verbot that makes masturbation so great a complex, and the sterner the verbot the deeper the sense of guilt and the greater the compulsion to indulge.

The well-brought-up infant should come to school with no guilty feeling about masturbation at all. There are few, if any, of our cottage children who have any special interest in masturbation, because no verbot has made the interest a guilty, hidden one. Sex to them has not the attraction of something mysterious: from their earliest time with us (if they have not been told at home) they know the facts of birth, not only where babies come from but how they are made. At that early age such information is received without emotion, partly because it is given without emotion. So it comes that at the age of fifteen or seventeen such children can discuss sex without any feeling of wrong or pornography.

It is the removal of the guilt complex about masturbation that makes Summerhill what a doubter would call "safe." It is this freedom from guilt that has given us a record of sixteen years without any signs of homosexuality. Some years ago a public [exclusive prep] school boy tried to introduce sodomy, but he had no success, and was incidentally surprised and alarmed when he discovered that the whole school knew about his efforts. This absence of homosexuality is of the greatest importance. It suggests that homosexuality is masturbation on promotion; ... you masturbate with the other bloke and he shares the guilt with you and thus lightens your burden. When masturbation is not considered a sin the necessity to share guilt does not arise. The root basis of the whole sex question is masturbation. When that is free the child naturally goes on to heterosexuality at the proper time. Many unhappy marriages are due to the fact that both parties are suffering from an unconscious hate of sexuality arising from buried self-hate due to masturbation verbots....

I am often asked if I have any fears that things may happen between the older pupils. I have no fears, because I know that I am not dealing with children who have a repressed and therefore unnatural interest in sex. Some years ago we had two pupils arrive at the same time, a boy of seventeen from a Public School and a girl of sixteen from a girls' school. They fell in love with each other. They were always together. I met them late one night, and I stopped.

"I don't know what you two are doing," I said, "and morally I don't care, for it isn't a moral question at all. But economically I do care. If you, Kate, had a kid my school would be ruined."

I went on to expand the theme.

"You see," I said, "you have just come to Summerhill. To you it means freedom to do what you like. You have, quite naturally, no feeling for the school, and if you had been here from the age of seven I'd never have had to mention it, for you would have had so strong an attachment to the school that you would think of it."

I never spoke to them again on the subject. It was the only possible way of dealing with the problem, for sex is not a moral problem at all.[41]

Neill's approach to language was also practical rather than moralistic.

One persistent criticism of Summerhill is that the children swear. It is true that they swear . . . if saying Old English words is swearing. It is true that any new pupil will swear more than necessary, and at our meetings a girl of thirteen who came from a convent was always being charged with shouting out the word "bugger" when she went bathing [swimming, in this case in a town pool]. It was impressed upon her that she only did it when bathing, and that therefore she was swanking [showing off]. As one boy put it: "You are just a silly little twirp. You want to swank in front of outside people and show that Summerhill is a free school, and you just do the opposite; you make people look down on the school."

In a P.L. I explained to her that she was really trying to do the school harm because she hated it.

"But I don't hate Summerhill," she cried. "It's a topping place."

"Yes," I said, "it is, as you say, a topping place, but you aren't in it. You are still living in your convent, and you have brought all the hate of the convent and the nuns with you. You identify Summerhill with the hated convent, and it isn't really Summerhill you are trying to damage; it is the convent."

But she went on shouting out her buggers until Summerhill became a real place to her and not a symbol. It is the floating population that makes swearing a social difficulty in Summerhill. Not that the old pupils are saintly in mouth, but the old timers swear at the right time, so to speak. They use conscious control.

Children accept swearing as a natural language. Adults condemn it because their obscenity is greater than that of children. Only an obscene person will condemn obscenity. Parents must ask themselves the question:—Shall I allow my children to swear openly, or shall I leave them to be obscene in dark dirty corners like the boys in Huxley's novel? There is no halfway house. The hush-hush way leads to the adulthood of tiresome commercial traveller stories and music hall innuendoes, that is an obscene repressive state. The open way leads to a clear clean interest in all life. At a venture I say that our old boys and girls have the cleanest minds in England.[42]

SIGNIFICANCE

Neill's first wife died in the 1940s and he remarried. His second wife, Ena, became a full partner. Later her son by an earlier marriage taught at the school and a daughter by Neill—his only child—was a riding instructor there. By the late fifties enrollment at Summerhill was low and Neill, well into his seventies, thought of retiring. Harold Hart asked Neill's permission to cut and paste a manuscript about Summerhill from earlier books. Neill apparently did not even read the galley proofs of the "new" book. The result was a best seller and fame for Neill and the school that neither had enjoyed before. England continued to ignore the establishment, but a capacity enrollment—about half of whom were from America—allowed Neill to raise his rates. A stream of international travelers forced the weekly school meeting to pass a rule restricting visitors to

Saturdays. Every weekend brought at least a dozen people taking pictures, and asking the same questions.

Neill's ideas appealed strongly to the "youth movement" of the sixties. For hundreds of thousands of people—especially in America and Germany—who felt their freedom had been abridged by "the establishment," *Summerhill* became a manifesto for individual liberty. A small school that had been known in the thirties (mainly by intellectuals) as one of a small number of "goddam and fornication at five schools," had become an item of substantial curiosity. Then, almost as quickly as interest had sprung up, it disappeared. When Neill died in 1973, Ena continued the school but people were no longer reading the book in large numbers. Twenty years after a majority of undergraduates on American campuses could speak casually about the book, few had even heard of it. Neill would not be surprised: "One day, some history of education will have a footnote about a man called S. A. O'Neill, an Irishman who ran a school called Summerville, and I won't be there to laugh."[43]

Neill grew up a Calvinist, but early on became a freethinker. He remained a religious man, if by that term one means a reverence for life, but he called himself an atheist and felt antipathy toward most churches (and capitalistic and communistic political systems). He particularly disliked Catholicism: "My greatest aversion is the Roman Catholic Church. I hate — as violently as H. G. Wells did — an authority that gives five hundred million a guilt about sex," he wrote in 1972. "To me, this church is anti-life, paternalism writ large. How comic, were it not tragic, that a pope, who has never had a sex life, orders millions of women not to use the Pill. . . . The savage beatings that go on in Catholic schools in Eire must be expressions of bottled-up sex coming out as sadism. . . . Nietzsche was right when he said that the first and last Christian died on the cross."[44] Not everyone who shared Neill's criticism of behaviorism and scientism agreed with his rejection of religion. In the thirties, a political and intellectual movement of substantial proportions developed in Europe. It centered around a revival of Thomas Aquinas' philosophy and theology, but it fostered political liberty of a sort that even A. S. Neill approved. It spread through Europe and Latin America and found a sizeable audience in the United States. Its central author was a French citizen named Jacques Maritain.

Jacques Maritain (1882-1973)

By World War II science had become the principal source of authority for American education. This phenomenon was a result of the radical alteration of American society by science and technology and of the concomitant reorientation of the American mind toward scientific thinking. It was also an outgrowth of the work of educational reformers of the late nineteenth and early twentieth centuries: the Herbartians, the new psychologists, and the progressives. Science had become so important to education that it was surprising to find someone who had the audacity to question its validity. Yet that is exactly what Jacques Maritain did in the 1943 Terry Lectures at Yale University. Not only did he join a growing chorus of voices that were criticizing progressive education, he also harmonized with an ensemble that refused to accept the scientific outlook as the basis of educational theory. Maritain's belief that education could only proceed from a theological and philosophical perspective had its origin in his own intellectual struggle with science and philosophy, and was deeply rooted in the theology of St. Thomas Aquinas.

YOUTH AND EDUCATION

Born in Paris on 18 November 1882, Jacques was the son of Paul Maritain, a Burgundian lawyer, and Geneviève Favre, a vibrant and thoughtful woman. His father had little influence on him. A quiet and philosophical man, Paul Maritain spent his leisure hours studying the poetry of Lamartine. Although he lived to see Jacques enter the Sorbonne, he was said to have been speechless at the thought of his son as a philosopher. Since he was not a practicing Catholic, he was not concerned about the religious education of his children. And following his divorce from Geneviève, he apparently had little contact with them.

Geneviève Favre Maritain, on the other hand, profoundly affected her son's youthful thoughts. The daughter of Jules Favre, an architect of the Third Republic, she passionately believed in republicanism and an intellectual elite as the salvation of France. She was ostensibly a liberal Protestant, but paid little attention to the religious upbringing of her children beyond their baptism by a minister. She was more concerned with gathering a small coterie in her home every Thursday for lunch and conversation about current political and social issues. Undoubtedly young Jacques cut his intellectual teeth amid discussions with such notables as the socialist writer and bookseller Charles Péguy, who later played an important role in his life.

These meetings took place at a time when the French intelligentsia was interested in the ideas of August Comte, Ernest Renan, and Hippolyte Taine. They argued that human progress was inevitable and that empirical science was the only truly positive form of knowledge attainable by the human mind. Many intellectuals held that without science, progress was impossible. This so-called positivism had permeated French secondary and higher education. When Maritain entered the Lycée Henri IV, and later the Sorbonne, he found it at every turn, a condition which proved both satisfying and frustrating. At first, he studied science and positivism with great vigor. He also shared these interests with Ernest Psichari, his best friend, and the grandson of Ernest Renan. Theirs was a deep and abiding friendship that lasted in spirit beyond Psichari's untimely death in World War I. Even their families became close friends. Imagine the lively discussions of science and society that must have occurred between the Renan and Favre-Maritain families.

Despite his interest in science, Maritain became increasingly disatisfied with his teachers' answers to questions about why things were as they described. When he entered the Sorbonne in 1901, he found no more acceptable answers when he questioned the faculty of philosophy, because that ancient discipline also was dominated by positivism. To no avail, he continued to ask "Why?" as he took advanced work in science. His dissatisfaction soon turned to despair, and he began to share his doubts with Raïssa Oumansoff, a science student and the daughter of Russian Jewish immigrants. He had met her while organizing a protest over the treatment of Russian socialist students.

In time, Raïssa and Jacques became inseparable. Their mutual search for answers to the ultimate questions about life led them to vow in 1902 that, unless they found a suitable explanation within one year, they would commit suicide. They took this quest seriously, whether or not they would have actually gone through with their plan. Fortunately, their friend Charles Péguy introduced them to the philosophy of Henri Bergson. Péguy, George Sorel, Psichari, Jacques, and Raïssa joined a growing group of people attending the lectures of Henri Bergson at the Collège de France. Bergson had defied the positivists and developed an intuitionist philosophy grounded in the absolute. He introduced these young pilgrims to metaphysics and to the works of Plotinus and Plato, which seemed to nourish their intellectual appetites. Gradually, they rose from the depths of despair knowing that there were answers to their questions. Yet Bergson's philosophy had its limits, and served principally as the first crucial step of their journey into the world of metaphysics. In the meantime, Jacques and Raïssa decided to marry before he finished his *agrégation* which would entitle him to teach in a state university. Following a delay of some months due to Raïssa's serious illness, they were wed on 26 November 1904. And together they continued their search for philosophic answers.

A RELIGIOUS QUEST

During the next year of their intellectual quest, they rediscovered the religious perspective. The Maritains began reading the works of Léon Bloy, the "thankless beggar," who impressed them with the strength of Christian belief conveyed in his novels. When they finally met Bloy at his home, their lives were permanently altered. A true witness of sainthood, Bloy lived an ascetic life, and devoted his entire effort to religious work. In their conversations with him, Jacques and Raïssa came face to face with the question of God. After several months of discussion and serious thought, they decided to join the Catholic church. On 11 June 1906 the Maritains and Vera Oumansoff, Raïssa's sister, accepted the Roman Catholic faith at the Church of Saint John the Evangelist in Montmartre. Neither the Oumansoffs nor Geneviève Maritain knew of this event at the time. When they found out what had transpired, their reactions were not unexpected. The Oumansoffs took it that their daughters had betrayed their faith and heritage. In time, however, they forgave their children; and in old age both converted to Catholicism. Madame Maritain, on the other hand, was outraged. She did everything possible to get her son to change his mind, including enlisting the aid of Charles Péguy, but to no avail. (She was unaware that Péguy was about to convert to the Catholic faith.) Madame Maritain apparently never forgave her son.

After completing his work at the Sorbonne, Maritain accepted a fellowship from the Michions Fund to study biology at the University of Heidelberg. There he met the biologist Hans Driesch who was working on a theory of dynamic vitalism—that is, life could be explained chemically or mechanically. In the many hours spent with Driesch, their conversations often turned to Bergson's recent book *Creative Evolution*. These discussions revived Maritain's desire for a philosophical career.

From 1906 to 1908 the Maritains enjoyed the peace and quiet of Heidelberg. Raïssa unfortunately was frequently ill which complicated the routine tasks of living. As a consequence, Vera Oumansoff became a permanent member of the Maritain household. She helped to maintain the house and served as Jacques' secretary. When his fellowship ran out, Maritain began looking for work. He could have taken a position in a French state university. But because of the French government's strong anticlerical attitude, he knew that there was no guarantee that he could teach according to his own principles. He chose not to apply for a teaching position. Instead, he accepted an offer from Hachette Publishing Company to compile an orthographic lexicon and a dictionary of practical life. Thus the trio was able to move back to Paris in 1908, where Jacques could work on the books and continue his scientific and philosophical studies.

During the next four years, Maritain worked diligently on the dictionaries. He and Raïssa also spent many hours studying the Catholic faith and the works of the great theologians. Their mentor was Father Humbert Clérissac, a Dominican priest who firmly adhered to the intellectual traditions of his order. He was responsible for introducing the Maritains to the writings of St. Thomas Aquinas. Raïssa found great comfort in *Summa Theologica*, Thomas' great work, and was anxious for Jacques to read it. But it was not until 1910 that he opened the book and found the answers to his questions about life. This proved to be a watershed in his life, from which he emerged as a Thomist. He later described his thoughts about his first encounter with St. Thomas' theology:

> My philosophical reflection leaned upon the indestructible truth of objects presented by faith in order to restore the natural order of the intelligence to being, and to recognize the ontological bearing of the work of the reason. Thenceforth, in affirming to myself, without chicanery or diminution, the authentic value of reality of our human instruments of knowledge, I was already a Thomist without knowing it. When several months later, I was to come to the *Summa Theologica*, I would erect no obstacle to its luminous flood.[45]

For Maritain, Thomism was more than an illuminating theology. He saw it as the foundation of his philosophical vocation when he said, "Woe unto me, should I not Thomize."[46] He began his work by studying the entire range of writings associated with St. Thomas' thought, from its origins in the works of Aristotle to the books of the modern "neo-Scholastics." In 1910 he made his first contribution to the subject in an article entitled "Reason and Modern Science," which appeared in the *Revue de Philosophie*. With great fire and passion, he tried to show the errors and the limitations of modern science, not to turn back the clock, but to put science into perspective. A year later, he published a critique of his philosophical master's ideas in "L'Évolutionnisme de M. Bergson."

These articles brought him the respect of Father Peillaube, editor of the *Revue de Philosophie*, who recommended him for a teaching post at the Collège Stanislas. When the position of instructor was offered in 1912, Maritain did not hesitate to accept it, thinking that he could teach philosophy from a Thomistic standpoint. Much to his dismay, he found many of his colleagues opposed to or skeptical of Thomism. Determined to stand his ground, Maritain persisted and eventually won their approval. And the high academic standing achieved by his students further reinforced his position.

The next year Maritain gave a series of lectures entitled "The Philosophy of Bergson and Christian Philosophy" at the Institut Catholique de Paris. These talks were a part of his continuing critique of Bergson's philosophical system, and marked the beginning of the Catholic renaissance of this century. His provocative and exciting ideas, furthermore, brought him an enthusiastic following particularly among science students who were now reading the works of Paul Claudel, Charles Péguy, Francis Jammes, and Léon Bloy. Maritain rapidly became a leading spokesperson for neo-Thomism, a title which he did not like since he saw himself as a pure Thomist bringing St. Thomas's principles to bear on modern problems. In 1914 he became professor of philosophy at the Institut Catholique de Paris. That same year he published several articles and the 1913 lectures in his book *La Philosophie Bergsonienne: Études Critiques*.

Jacques Maritain continued his work at the Institute during World War I. He also taught at the Collège Stanislas from 1915 to 1916 and at the preparatory seminary in Versailles from 1917 to 1918. Throughout the war he tried in vain to serve in the French army but was rejected for health reasons until August 1918 when he was assigned to an artillery regiment at Versailles. In the meantime, at the request of the French bishops, he began writing a series of seminary textbooks on the various branches of philosophy; only *An Introduction to Philosophy* and *Formal Logic* were ever completed. The war years brought grief to the Maritains. They lost four of their closest friends: Ernest Psichari, Charles Péguy, Father Clérissac, and Léon Bloy.

Toward the end of the war, Maritain became acquainted with Pierre Villard, a French army officer who was experiencing a spiritual crisis. He had developed an interest in Maritain's ideas as well as those of Blaise Pascal and Charles Maurras, the leader of Action Française, a strongly nationalistic organization whose chief goal was restoration of the French monarchy. He apparently found comfort in his correspondence and conversations with Maritain. Two months after Villard died in battle on 28 June 1918, Maritain received the shocking news that Villard had willed a substantial portion of his family's fortune to him and Charles Maurras. The bequest was enough to enable him to give up his salary at the institute in favor of a younger philosopher (although he occasionally lectured at the school) and to devote his time to writing.

The interwar period was a time of important intellectual activity for Maritain. In the fall of 1919, Jacques, Raïssa, and Vera began holding monthly meetings with friends and acquaintances to discuss Thomistic theology and philosophy. By 1923 these gatherings had grown to the point that larger accommodations were needed. They found a house that suited their needs in Meudon, a town located between Paris and Versailles. For the next sixteen years a steady stream of visitors came to the meetings at Meudon: old and young, students and teachers; philosophers, scientists, writers, musicians; members of the clergy including Roman Catholics, Orthodox Christians, Protestants, and Jews; even atheists came to talk with Maritain. There also were annual retreats, at first in Meudon and later in Thomistic centers in England, Switzerland, and Belgium. Among the many participants in these meetings was the Russian author Nicolas Berdyaev with whom Maritain worked to end the rift between the Roman Catholic and Orthodox churches.

THE PHILOSOPHER

Until 1926 Maritain wrote almost exclusively on metaphysics, epistemology, and the philosophy of nature. The thought of writing on political or social issues apparently had not crossed his mind. But he soon changed his thinking, when he unintentionally became embroiled in a controversy involving Action Française. By the middle 1920s a sufficiently large number of Catholics had joined this group so that it appeared to be a semiofficial arm of the church. Although he was not a member Maritain had occasionally written articles for *La Revue Universelle*, a magazine published by the organization. When Action Française began using violence in addition to rhetoric as a means of achieving its goals, Pope Pius XI condemned it.[47] Threatened with the loss of the sacrament of absolution, most Catholics left the organization. But some believed the Pope had overstepped his bounds and refused to resign.

Maritain recognized the seriousness of this affair and the awkwardness of his own implied association with the group. He thus issued a statement in 1927, entitled *The Things that are not Caesar's*, in which he argued that spiritual matters were prior to secular ones. The book won him numerous supporters and secured his position with Catholic officials, but it also cost him several friends and brought a vehement condemnation from Action Française.

This affair marked the beginning of Maritain's career as a political and social philosopher. It did not, however, completely divert his attention from speculative philosophy. He wrote his most important epistemological studies during this time. *The Degrees of Knowledge* came out in 1932. Its sequel, *Science and Wisdom*, appeared in 1935. During the preceding year he had finished his most complete metaphysical work, *A Preface to Metaphysics: Seven Lectures on Being*. In the years not devoted to speculative matters, he turned to the realm of practical philosophy. Beginning in 1933 with the issue of freedom, he published *Freedom in the Modern World*, which was followed in 1936 by a masterpiece of Thomistic philosophy, *True Humanism*. He helped to found the Catholic review *Esprit* and served as an advisor for that periodical and for the Catholic weekly *Sept*. In response to the political extremism of the thirties, Maritain joined Étienne Gilson, Gabriel Marcel, and others in a call for the application of moral principles to all political systems expressed in a pamphlet entitled *For the Common Good*. From this time forward Jacques Maritain focused his attention on political, social, and ethical concerns.

In addition to writing on practical philosophy, Maritain spent much of his time lecturing in both Europe and North America. His European tour took him to Geneva, Salzburg, Louvain, Milan, and Rome. His first trip to North America came in 1931, when he received an invitation to lecture during the coming year at the Pontifical Institute of Medieval Studies, St. Michael's College, an affiliate of the University of Toronto. The following summer he spoke at the University of Chicago, where he met President Robert M. Hutchins and Professor Mortimer Adler both of whom would later join him as critics of progressive education. In 1938 he lectured at the University of Notre Dame and the Catholic University of America.

EDUCATIONAL VIEWS

The Maritain family sailed from Marsailles in January 1940 bound once again for North America, unaware that they would not be able to return home for nearly five years. When they heard the news in June that France had fallen to the Nazis, their distress was tempered by the realization that Jacques could not return home because of his opposition to fascism. The Maritains took up residence in New York, while Jacques continued to lecture at the Pontifical Institute and at Columbia University. In 1942 with the aid of Alvin Johnson, President of the New School for Social Research, Maritain established the Ecole Libre des Hautes Études, a French university in exile. He was a frequent contributor to *Commonweal* and condemned anti-Semitism in *A Christian Looks at the Jewish Question*. He also worked with Professor Carlton J. H. Hayes on the National Conference of Christians and Jews.

In 1943 officials at Yale University invited Maritain to give the Terry Lectures for that year. He took this opportunity to offer the world his thoughts concerning education, which were later published under the title *Education at the Crossroads*. As might be expected Maritain reiterated his fundamental thesis that science, although useful for understanding the physical environment, was insufficient as a source of knowledge about ultimate truth. He began by asserting that the principal task of education was "to shape man, or to guide the evolving dynamism through which man forms himself as man."[48] The bulk of his discussion combined criticisms of American education with suggestions for improving it.

Maritain thought that education was hindered by certain misconceptions held by American, and in particular progressive, educators. First, there was a disregard for ends. Too much emphasis on means or methods for their own sake caused educators to lose sight of the purposes of education. Second, education was too concerned with creating the scientific man. Third, the pragmatic theory of knowledge could do nothing but produce skeptics who distrusted truth. Fourth, education wrongly began by trying to adapt people to society, instead of first making the individual. Fifth, he criticized the demand for specialization then being promoted by traditionalists who believed that essential knowledge was contained in the disciplines. Sixth, he chided those whom he believed wrongly opposed proper intellectual development and tried in the tradition of Rousseau to free natural potentialities, thought to be good, in order to develop the human will. And finally, he pointed out that many educators mistakenly believed everything could be learned. The result was a course to cover every conceivable subject. Maritain thought that as long as educators held to these misconceptions, schools could not produce humane, thoughtful people who could stop the spread of totalitarianism and avoid the tyranny of uncontrolled technology.

A proper education, he argued, began with the Christian conception of humans as animals endowed with reason and intellect who were free in personal relations with God, but who were sinful creatures called to grace through love. With this notion in mind, education was to shape humans by arming them with knowledge, strength of judgment, and moral virtues. It was to convey the heritage of the nation and civilization. And it was to show the utilitarian purpose in these things without allowing that end to supersede the essential aim of molding the human being as a human being. Maritain held that education should endeavor to help humans become intellectually free through the progressive understanding of new truths and socially free through the recognition of their obligations to society.

Like St. Thomas, Maritain saw the art of teaching as analogous to the art of medicine, both aided nature in their respective work. The teacher's intellectual guidance and the student's mental capacity were the active elements in education, but the motive force came from the student's mind. The teacher was to help the student aim at self-perfection by fostering a love of goodness and justice, an acceptance of one's natural limitations, a sense of a job well done, and a sense of cooperation. He also believed that the dynamics of the educational process demanded that certain rules had to be followed in addition to promoting the above dispositions: education must awaken the human spirit; it must unify experience and reason in the mind; and it must liberate intelligence.

Following these rules, according to Maritain, required a curriculum built of that knowledge which would enable the mind to grasp the truth. At the elementary level the child's imagination must be developed by focusing on stories and fables. Adolescent curiosity could only be satisfied if the youth had the intellectual instruments to develop natural reason and to answer those important questions—such tools as languages, grammar, history, natural history, and the art of expression. Finally, the undergraduate curriculum should include a year each of mathematics and poetry, natural sciences and fine arts, philosophy, and ethical and political philosophy. Jacques Maritain fervently hoped that education could foster an integral humanism that would save the world from destruction.

FINAL YEARS

He continued his scholarly activities for most of the next three decades, except for the years 1945 to 1948 when he served as the French ambassador to the Vatican.[49] When his work in Rome was completed, Maritain returned to the United States where he taught philosophy at Princeton University until his retirement in 1953. Although he suffered a heart attack in 1954, he spent most of the next six years writing and lecturing. In 1958 he spoke at the University of Chicago and later published his comments in one of his most popular books, *Reflections on America*. On 31 December 1959 Vera Oumansoff died, and less than a year later Raïssa passed away. For the first time in more than fifty years Jacques Maritain found himself alone.

Soon after Raïssa was buried, he made arrangements to settle in Toulouse, France with a religious order, the Little Brothers of Jesus. In the remaining years of his life he served as a seminar guide for the fraternity, and later took its vows. At the closing session of the Second Vatican Council in 1965, Maritain witnessed the act of reconciliation between the Orthodox and Roman Catholic churches, and heard Pope Paul VI pay tribute to him as a great Christian philosopher. The next year he published what was to have been his final statement, *The Peasant of the Garonne*. But the book caused a storm of controversy when his readers discovered that he did not support many of the recent reforms of the Catholic church. They failed to understand that he had always combined political and social liberalism with religious conservatism. As a consequence he attempted to clarify his position in two more books: *On the Grace and Humanity of Jesus* in 1967 and *On the Church of Christ* in 1970. Maritain died on 28 April 1973 and was buried at Kolbsheim beside his beloved Raïssa.

Jacques Maritain was one of the most important philosophers of the twentieth century. He was instrumental both in the revival of Thomistic thought in philosophy and theology and in the Catholic renaissance in France. He joined his countrymen, Henri Bergson, Étienne Gilson, Gabriel Marcel, and Jean Paul Sartre, in presenting alternative philosophical viewpoints to the positivism and scientism that dominated Western thought at the beginning of this century. His fundamentally liberal political and social philosophy generated some opposition among conservative Catholics in the 1920s, but for the most part won him the admiration of his coreligionists.

However, many failed to understand the paradox of his liberal social and political philosophy combined with traditional and conservative theology. Liberal Catholics were upset at his refusal to endorse all of the positions taken by the Second Vatican Council. Finally, Maritain was an effective and highly respected teacher of philosophy. As a philosopher of education, he strongly criticized progressive education for its overemphasis on means, on society, and, most importantly, on science. Some have viewed this as reactionary; others have said he was dogmatic in his opposition to naturalism. The former criticism ignores Maritain's philosophy as a whole. The latter comment seems more appropriate, but must be qualified. Having found early in his adulthood that science could not answer the ultimate questions of life and that the theology of St. Thomas Aquinas could, Jacques Maritain endeavored to apply the Thomistic standard to a world where scientific truth was necessary, but for him, certainly not sufficient for understanding life.

His religious conservatism was a philosophical element that would have found little support in the views of our next subject, black educator W. E. B. DuBois. On the other hand, Maritain's social and political liberalism might have appealed to DuBois—perhaps as much as the neo-Thomist's native country of France did.

W. E. B. DuBois (1868-1963)

The various biographers of DuBois (pronounced DuBoyce) have been struck by the complex, paradoxical nature of his personality. Meier noted that he skillfully played the roles of "scholar and prophet; mystic and materialist" as well as a "Marxist who was fundamentally a middle class intellectual." In the preface of his biography Moore said that because DuBois' "own being was so paradoxical he could maintain in suspension, like a juggler . . . many sympathies and longings, even while containing intense hostilities and emotional twists."[50] He was shaped by the extreme social conditions of the times. Born only three years after the Civil War he grew up to chafe under the harness of Booker T. Washington's cautious leadership—one that to DuBois could only result in a postponement of civil, political, educational, and social equality for blacks. Picking up Washington's scepter after his death in 1915, DuBois spent the next fifty-five years prodding his race to stand up and be counted. He died in Ghana in 1963, on the hundredth anniversary of the Emancipation Proclamation, without knowing how well his voice had been heard by his black American brothers and sisters.

YOUTH AND SCHOOLING

In his autobiography Will DuBois stated that he was born in Great Barrington, Massachusetts "the day after the birth of George Washington was celebrated, . . . the year that the freedmen of the South were enfranchised," and a week after "Thaddeus Stevens . . . made his last speech, impeaching Andrew Johnson." In other words, he was born on 23 February 1868. He was the product of French Huguenot, Dutch, and African strains. His mother's family, the Burghardts, had been in Great Barrington since the American Revolution. Great-grandfather Burghardt was a slave, emancipated after fighting in the Revolutionary War.[51]

His paternal great-grandfather, Dr. James DuBois of Poughkeepsie, New York, had moved to the Bahamas after having been given several plantations by the governor of New York. In the Bahamas he started a family—Alexander (DuBois's grandfather) and John—with a black woman who was probably his common law wife. Dr. James DuBois brought his sons to Connecticut and to a private school where they stayed until he died in 1820. After his death the seventeen-year-old Alexander left for Haiti, married a Haitian woman, and had a son, Will's father Alfred. Eventually he moved the family to New Haven where Alfred grew up and then fled his own father's strict authoritarianism.[52]

Alfred was known as a barber when he made his way to Great Barrington at the age of forty-two. He met the sad and complacent Mary Burghardt and married her against her family's wishes. Alfred left Great Barrington shortly after his son Will was born. For unknown reasons Mary did not go with her husband—perhaps it was due to her parents' objections. Instead, she suffered a stroke which left her lame in one leg and moved back to her parents' country home with her young son Will.[53]

When Will reached school age Mary moved back to town so that her son could have the best schooling available to him. Great Barrington was a town of five thousand people, fifty of whom were free blacks. The color line did not seem to be evident to Will as a young boy. He was a good student in an integrated school, and his white schoolmates seemed to happily include him in their social activities. However, he never dated while in school and left Great Barrington shortly after graduating first in his twelve member high school class of 1884. He gave the valedictory address, and encouraged by his principal who even raised money for him, made plans to attend college along with two or three other graduates in his class. (He was the only black in his class of twelve.)

He worked at odd jobs for a year to raise money for college. He entered Fisk in the fall of 1885 shortly after his mother's death. (In later years he would credit his mother, Mary and his Harvard professor, William James, with forming the crucial attitudes essential to his successful career.) He was seventeen, slight in build, blue eyed, light skinned, wavy haired, and on his own for the first time in the color conscious state of Tennessee.

At Fisk, DuBois was exposed to students who were five to ten years older than he was and who had experienced lives as southern blacks. They were more worldly and more sophisticated having survived the worst tortures of racial biases. To Will this group of thirty-five students represented the beauty and intellectual power of the race. Although younger than his colleagues, DuBois was not possessed of a modesty about his own accomplishments and capabilities, and he began to envision himself as their leader. He became editor of the Fisk *Herald* and spent three enriching years within the university. During his two summer vacations he worked as a rural school teacher in Wilson County. Here, he learned of the poverty and hardships of the rural black southerner. In the house of his landlady, a lonely and frustrated farm wife, he lost his virginity or as he put it: "I was literally raped by the unhappy wife who was my landlady."[54]

He graduated from Fisk in 1888 after having given the commencement speech. His ambitious future had been fueled by the praise of his teachers, and he looked forward to graduate study at Harvard. Through letters of recommendation his Fisk professors painted a picture of him that included traits such as ambition, manliness, earnestness in study, excellence in scholarship, and a possible conceitedness that would not "prevent faithful work."[55]

He entered Harvard as a junior and took another bachelor of arts degree (this time cum laude in philosophy) in 1890. By now he had assumed for himself a northern white racial bias. He kept his own company at Harvard, never mingling with his white counterparts. As one biographer put it, "He never developed any affection for the university. Glorying in his isolation and eschewing Harvard life . . . he came to think of Harvard as a library and a faculty, nothing more." Through faculty support from George Santayana and William James, DuBois took a master's degree in history in 1891. His thesis became the first volume of the Harvard Historical Studies and was entitled *The Suppression of African Slave-Trade to the United States of America, 1638-1870*.[56]

It was common in the late nineteenth century for young scholars to look to German universities to further their intellectual prowess, and Will DuBois was no exception. In 1892 he applied to the Slater Fund and received a grant (half gift, half loan) to study at the University of Berlin. Originally for one year, the grant was extended to two. He planned to take a Ph.D. there but never did. He spent the time studying at the feet of great German masters, changing his academic thrust from history to political economy/sociology. He traveled in England, France, Italy, Austria, Germany, Poland, and Hungary. These years gave him the chance to think in broader terms about color barriers. He was amazed to find himself being accepted on equal social grounds. He lived with a German family who treated him like a member and he fell in love with their daughter. Although he felt no color barriers, he seemed to become a little anti-Semitic. Returning in steerage class to America in the summer of 1894, he wrote in his diary: "There is in [the Jews] all that slyness that lack of straightforward open-heartedness which goes straight against me."[57]

UNIVERSITY PROFESSOR

Filled with a messianic commitment to black liberation—what he later would call his real life work—DuBois started his scholarly career in Xenia, Ohio at Wilberforce University as the chair of the classics department. Later that summer offers came in from Lincoln Institute in Missouri and Tuskeegee, but Will stuck with his first offer. By 1895 he had his Ph.D. from Harvard and was congratulating Booker T. Washington for his exposition speech at Atlanta. But all was not rosy in Xenia. DuBois found the Afro-Episcopalian dogma stifling. He resented the stress on Sunday school attendance over academic classes and, although he added German to the chair he held in classics, the college authorities refused to allow him to offer sociology. The one bright spot was his association with a pretty young student from Cedar Rapids, Iowa—Nina Gomer—whom he married in 1896. That same year the University of Pennsylvania offered him a fifteen month appointment as assistant instructor to do research on the black community in Philadelphia's seventh ward.

When his work on *The Philadelphia Negro: A Social Study* was completed, DuBois accepted a position as sociologist at Atlanta University where he spent the next thirteen years directing their studies of blacks. He gathered data on the black condition in an effort to affect social policies. Through lectures and publications he tried to present the black plight to the public at large. He taught and trained his students to become cultured intellectuals—the "talented tenth" of the race—capable of leading the masses. Privately he lived the life of a southern black. When he was not in his office, he was on the road lecturing and delivering speeches. In July 1900 he attended the first Pan African Congress in London and was elected as its secretary. He refused to be humiliated, never entering a streetcar, theater, or concert hall. The little social life he had was with a small group of black friends including John Hope and James Weldon Johnson. To this group he showed a side other than the austere, driven, missionary sociologist. Johnson said in 1904 that he was "astonished . . . to find that DuBois's brooding, intransigent, public demeanor could dissolve into joviality, even frivolity." DuBois wrote the *Souls of Black Folk* almost as a eulogy on the death of his infant son, Burghardt, who was denied medical care because he was black. In the book he turned his sense of loss into victory for his son: "Well sped, my boy, before the world has dubbed your ambition insolence, has held your ideals unattainable, and taught you to cringe and bow."[58]

As racial riots broke out in Boston and Altanta, DuBois began to break with Booker T. Washington's conservative message to blacks. He organized the Niagara Movement which held its first conference in 1905. After an Atlanta program the movement held its second conference in 1906, then its third, fourth and last in the succeeding years until 1910 when the movement merged into the National Association for the Advancement of Colored People (NAACP).

NAACP WORK

In 1910 he severed his connections with Atlanta and moved his wife and young daughter, Yolande, to New York where he was to be the director of publications and research for the NAACP. His first issue of *The Crisis* appeared that November, and for the next decade the magazine's subscribers grew from 10,000 in 1911 to 35,000 in 1915, and to 104,000 in 1919. This growth seemed to reflect his claim as the liberal leader of the black cause. DuBois grew farther away from Washington as he became convinced that the latter was "betraying the Negro into permanent servility." He spoke out against the peaceful picture of black conditions that Washington painted to Europe. *The Crisis* became his mouthpiece and, even though the association was becoming more liberal, DuBois, their editor, was becoming radical. His "talented tenth" concept seemed exclusive and aristocratic so that Washington maintained his popularity and leadership position with blacks until his death in 1915.[59]

In the prewar years he grew more aggressive and outspoken, and friction between him and the association grew. He found no friend in any political program including Wilson's brand of progressive democracy, but he did support female suffrage: a vote for white women meant a vote for black women. After a 1916 lynching, *The Crisis* editor sounded a militant tune when he advocated the use of force: "In God's name let us perish like men and not like bales of hay." The period from 1910 to 1920 has been described by one historian as DuBois' great years, and he moved with ease into the leadership position vacated by Washington's death. His influence was felt more in the North than the South. Through his lecture tours he managed to reach most states, and he found particular hope in urban blacks.[60]

During World War I DuBois began to hope again because: (1) Wilsonian policies had produced wartime job opportunities for blacks; and (2) black soldiers had helped to win the war. However, this hope was short-lived when in the "red summer" of 1919 black blood was shed in numerous urban race riots. Also, a study of blacks during the war revealed many discriminatory practices by the army. Hurt, shocked, and angered by such activities, DuBois returned to his earlier threats of violence. His editorials had the tone of an arrogant, self-righteous pedant, and he went so far as to chide a black audience for laughing when Othello strangled Desdemona. These attitudes hardly set well with white liberals, nor were they easing the tensions between himself and the association. Even James Weldon Johnson's appointment as executive secretary to the NAACP staff could not bridge the gap.

Throughout the decade of the twenties and early thirties DuBois became fascinated and preoccupied with Africa. He developed three goals that the association endorsed: (1) the formation of an African state from German possessions; (2) a program for these former colonies to be led by educated, African, American, West Indian and South American blacks; and (3) the spread of science and other modern cultural advantages to existing African institutions. To promote these goals a Pan African conference was organized, first in Paris in 1919, then in London in 1920, and another in Brussels in 1921. Although Europe met them with indifference, DuBois seemed to gain encouragement from the conferences, and he continued to organize them through the twenties. The NAACP withdrew their support after the second one, and his final effort met with collapse in 1929.

In 1926 he took his first trip to Russia and found new hope for his cause in what freedom from color lines and working-class psychology he saw there: The latter promised to replace the millionaire with the worker as the center of power and culture. For DuBois socialism and Russian communism were becoming the voices of the oppressed peoples, both white and black. He was less than enthusiastic about the American Communist Party, however, and after the Scottsboro case he had only contempt for the group. (In 1931 nine black youths were arrested in Scottsboro, Alabama and charged with raping two white girls. The nine turned their case over to a communist labor defense group who, through bribery and sensationalist tactics, lost the case. The NAACP took charge and won, and DuBois denounced the communist tactics in a *Crisis* editorial.)[61]

The onslaught of the depression convinced DuBois that a new direction must be taken in the black cause. By 1934 he believed that full equality would never be gained, and he began calling for nondiscriminatory segregation. What he meant by this was the development of an independent black culture. However, this hit the NAACP executives right between the eyes, since fighting legal and administrative segregation had been the primary reason for the association's existence. The chairperson of the board, Joel Springarn, said that no organ of the NAACP could be allowed to criticize its policies. DuBois said the *Crisis* was never intended to be an organ of the association. Therefore he resigned to accept the chair of sociology back at Atlanta University under the presidency of his old friend John Hope. (Mrs. DuBois remained in Baltimore due to her hatred of the South.)

HIS BLACK LEADERSHIP

From 1934 to 1944 Dr. DuBois was regarded as the stately spokesperson for black politics. Atlanta, Fisk, and Wilberforce bestowed honorary degrees upon him. He gained membership in the National Institute of Arts and Letters. He wrote two more books and started work on a Negro encyclopedia and he was founding editor of *Phylon*. During these years he resumed his efforts to create an intellectual "talented tenth" by transforming black universities into the finest centers for higher learning in the country. Trouble did not really surface until a new and unknown president, Rufus Clement, was elected at Atlanta. Then in 1944, without warning, Atlanta's board of trustees voted to retire Professor DuBois with no pension. Fortunately, Executive Secretary Walter White of the NAACP was once again interested in utilizing his talents but this time as director of special research. Nevertheless, it did not take long for old tensions to surface. DuBois was still out of step with the officers of the association, and when he openly criticized Walter White's appointment as consultant to the United Nation's American delegation in Paris as a political sellout, he was fired. However, this time a pension was included.

He was not destined to close out his final years in peace. After travel to France and Russia in 1949, the eighty-two year old man settled down to head up the Peace Information Center which had been organized to spread sentiment for international peace. He also ran unsuccessfully for the U.S. Senate on the American Labor Party ticket. His wife died in 1950, and by 1951 he was planning a Valentine's Day wedding to Shirley Graham (the daughter of an old friend). Five days earlier he had been indicted for failing to register the Peace Information Center as an agent of a foreign principal. Two days after his marriage he was arraigned, and the trial was set for 2 April. These charges stunned DuBois.

As required by the Foreign Agents Registration Act, DuBois and four others were indicted for "failing to cause the organization" to register. The foreign principal was the World Congress of the Defenders of Peace. DuBois knew that the justice department wanted the center to register. He had not done it because he had conceived it as an American group operated by American citizens. The trial was postponed until November when the case was thrown out by federal judge Matthew F. McGuire. However, it did little to restore DuBois' faith in American policies, nor was it restored by the government's refusal over the next six years to issue him a passport.[62]

Finally, in 1958 he was allowed to travel to China, France, England, Sweden, eastern Europe, and the USSR—where he won the Lenin Peace Prize. He left again in 1961, this time for good, to live in Ghana. It was a hurried departure, since he anticipated that new restrictions would be placed on him now that he had become a communist. President Nkrumah of Ghana had invited him there to do work on an African encyclopedia. In 1963 he finally gave up his American citizenship to become a citizen of Ghana. He died in his adopted country on 27 August 1963.

Poet, novelist, essayist, scholar, teacher, agitator, W. E. B. DuBois became the loudest voice demanding equal rights for blacks, and in so doing he served to bolster the morale of his people. In 1941 when DuBois was attacked as a racial chauvinist, the seventy-three year old responded caustically that "if you want to lose friends and jobs, then oppose wars, defend strikes, and say that even communists have rights." Perhaps Roy Wilkins captured his influence best when on 28 August 1963—the day after his death—he told a crowd of thousands gathered in front of the Lincoln Memorial that DuBois' voice from the beginning of the century has been "calling you here today."[63]

DuBois championed a new social order led by a talented black tenth, but he failed to see this cause realized. After the Great Depression there were other voices added to the call for a new American social order to be led by the teachers and educators of the country. They too were unsuccessful in having their views materialize. Nevertheless, they left a legacy of social reconstructionist thought. Such an advocate was educator/philosopher George S. Counts.

George S. Counts (1889-1974)

For nearly five decades, Counts was a leading but also controversial figure in American education. Through his study of American and Russian civilization, he developed insights into the relationships among social, economic, political, and educational forces. While he enjoyed studying the past, Counts, like his friend Charles A. Beard, saw history as an instrument to shape a plan for a new society. For him education was an important means by which human beings could create a new social order. To some people, Counts, like DuBois, was a dangerous radical bent on bringing a leftist, collectivist, ideology into the schools of America. Others saw him as an educational leader who had a prophetic insight into the course of human events. To friend and foe alike, he was remembered as the man who posed the question, *Dare the School Build a New Social Order?* This was in the depths of the economic depression of the 1930s.

THE MAKING OF AN EDUCATOR

The son of a Kansas farmer, George Sylvester Counts was a true child of America's middle border. Although he was to teach in leading eastern universities and travel through the Orient, South America, and the Soviet Union, Counts' outlook never lost the down-to-earth plainness that came from growing up in America's heartland.

Born in Baldwin, Kansas in 1889, Counts attended local schools and went on to earn his bachelor's degree from Baker University in 1911 and his doctorate from the University of Chicago in 1916. As a graduate student at Chicago, Counts learned the research techniques of scientific education from his mentor, Charles Judd. His work there with Albion W. Small, the pioneer sociologist, gave him skills for the social analysis of education. He taught at the universities of Washington, Chicago, Yale, and Teachers College, Columbia. He also was director of research for the Commission of the American Historical Association on the Social Studies from 1931-1933 and editor of the *Social Frontier* from 1934-1937.

In the decade before the Great Depression, Counts examined education's broader historical, sociological, and philosophical themes. In *The Selective Character of American Secondary Education* (1922), Counts charged that American high schools were not providing students with genuine equality of educational opportunity, and that they served the interests of upper socioeconomic classes. Children of native stock were more likely to attend high school than the offspring of recent immigrants. Also the enrollment of black children in high school was much less than the total proportion of blacks in the population.[64] In *The Senior High School Curriculum* (1926), Counts criticized educators for neglecting the educational implications of social change and for failing to create a curriculum relevant to a technological society.[65] Counts' book, *The Social Composition of Boards of Education* (1927), depicted public education dominated by a powerful socioeconomic elite with boards of education composed primarily of members from the favored occupations of merchants, lawyers, manufacturers, bankers, and physicians.[66] Because of the backgrounds of their members, boards of education were often unresponsive to social change and the needs of lower socioeconomic groups. Increasingly, Counts realized that schools could not function successfully if they remained in isolation from social and economic forces. In *Secondary Education and Industrialism* (1929), he forcefully made the point that the rapid rise of the public high school was a product of America's modernization, industrialization, and urbanization.[67]

Counts could shift easily from the role of sociologist to that of historian. His *The American Road to Culture* (1930) was an historical analysis of public schooling. While he proclaimed the public school to be a major American cultural force, he also chided Americans for their immature faith that schools could be effective social agencies if they remained isolated from social, political, and economic change and controversy.[68]

While Counts enjoyed a reputation as a noted authority on American education, he was also a noted scholar on Soviet culture and education. His *Soviet Challenge to America* was written against the backdrop of the 1930s. For him the absence of social planning was a major cause of social and economic crisis. Like many other liberal intellectuals, Counts saw social planning as a means of solving the economic crisis. In this light, he portrayed the Soviet Union as a nation committed deliberately to the use of thorough social planning to modernize a large but backward nation.

His foreword to *The Soviet Challenge* commented on the American inability to plan its way out of depression:

> The economic depression which . . . continues to hold the entire Western world in its grip, depriving millions of men of employment and bringing misery to vast populations, has revealed weaknesses in the contemporary industrial order and has turned the minds of economists and statesmen everywhere to the question of social planning. Although we in America at least possess a mastery over the forces of production which should enable us to satisfy all of our material wants with ease, multitudes go hungry and experience all the terrors and humiliations of profound physical insecurity. This is tragedy; not because men have not suffered before, but because they now suffer so needlessly. The dreams of mankind through the ages now are at least capable of realization, but our present economic, educational, and political leadership has thus failed to rise to the opportunity created by science and technology. A general condition of uncoordination paralyzes the economic system and dissipates its matchless energies.[69]

DARE THE SCHOOL?

In his writings, Counts dealt with the major social/educational issues that faced American society in the 1930s. He argued that: 1) Because Americans traditionally had viewed schooling as an intrinsically good cultural instrument, they did not comprehend that the school was but one of many educational agencies. Neither did they realize that the school could be used for a variety of social, political, and economic purposes. 2) The American people were facing a catastrophic economic depression that was causing severe social, political, and educational dislocations. 3) Instead of providing strong leadership, American educators were not responding to the problems of the depression. Many progressive educators, devotees of child centered educational theory, scrupulously avoided any attempt to deal consciously with major national issues. Either ignorant of socioeconomic realities or striving for political neutrality, American educators deliberately or unconsciously maintained the status quo.

Counts' *Dare the School Build a New Social Order?* recognized the immediacy of the crisis of the depression.[70] As the nation struggled against massive economic and social dislocation, educators needed to combat retrenchment and restore faith in schooling. Although these were the immediate problems facing the nation and its schools, they were but symptomatic of a larger crisis precipitated by America's feebleness in coming to grips with the great social transformation of the technological revolution. Science and technology had already created an industrialized, urban, and interdependent society. Human material inventiveness, stimulated by the instruments of science and technology, had outdistanced social imagination. Patterned in an age of agricultural and industrial individualism, American political, social, and educational institutions had failed to meet the challenges of human interdependency. In clinging to an obsolete individualism, American society and schools had failed to provide the needed planning and social/educational engineering for the new technological civilization.

Counts challenged educators to transform themselves from schoolmasters into educational leaders. The educator, he argued, needed a stately vision to formulate an educational philosophy and program to meet the immediate problem of the depression and the larger social problems of life in a technological civilization. Such a vision could be attained only as educators critically examined their civilization in terms of its industrial and technological realities. In calling upon educators to make fundamental policy decisions, Counts urged them to cast off a false neutrality: "Any concrete school program will contribute to the struggle for survival that is ever going on among institutions, ideas, and values; it cannot remain neutral in any firm and complete sense."[71]

Dare the School Build a New Social Order? was a dramatic event in the history of American education as well as a daring proposal to educators. While critics condemned his proposal as a dangerous radicalism pernicious to individual and educational freedom, his supporters saw Counts' challenge as a call to revitalize the commitment to democratic and equalitarian education. In retrospect Counts was responding to the problems of a particular decade and also addressing larger issues that would still require answers from future generations of educators.

A CIVILIZATIONAL PHILOSOPHY

Counts also called upon American educators to create an educational philosophy that would sustain and equip them to meet the challenge of a technological society. He accepted his own challenge and sought to formulate a "civilizational philosophy," based on what he viewed as the American heritage. He sought to find vital elements in the American past that lent credence to his educational program and platform. Counts turned to the "new history" of Charles Beard and Carl Becker. As members of the Commission of the American Historical Association on the Social Studies in the Schools, Counts and Beard developed a close personal friendship.[72]

Analyzing the American cultural heritage, Counts found it free of European medieval residues such as feudalism, landed aristocracies, established churches, and social hierarchies. The American heritage did, however, reveal two conflicting historical traditions: Hamiltonianism and Jeffersonianism. Counts defined Hamiltonianism as a political theory which advocated rule by a privileged elite pursuing special interests. In a capitalist economy Hamiltonianism encouraged economic individualism, ruthless environmental exploitation, maximization of profits, and wasteful competition.

In contrast to Hamiltonianism, Counts identified Jeffersonianism as a preferable alternative. He interpreted Jeffersonianism as originating with the independent farmer who, living in basic economic, social, and political equality with his neighbors, believed in a democratic society of equals. During post Civil War industrialization the Jeffersonian tradition was threatened and nearly eclipsed by modern Hamiltonianism. The Jeffersonian tradition—expanded by Jacksonianism, Populism, and Progressivism—had contributed to the American democratic conception of the equality of persons. For Counts the egalitarian, democratic ethic was a viable element in the American heritage that needed to be preserved for the oncoming generations by the nation's schools.

Having identified equalitarian democracy as the ethical component to be transmitted in the schools, Counts developed a theory of social change that predicted the direction of American civilization. Essentially, the United States was experiencing a cultural crisis as it was transformed from an agrarian society into a technological, industrialized, urbanized, and modernized social order. Industrialism had changed American society from a loose aggregation of self-contained rural households and small towns into a mass society of specialization and interdependence. The emergence of an industrialized and technological society not only affected the economic realm but it also had social and cultural repercussions. Science, technology, and invention had advanced far beyond society's reconstruction of ethical, legal, and political systems. The obsolescence of inherited conceptions of human nature, the rejection of traditional theological, philosophical, and political doctrines, and the rise of totalitarianism reflected the anxiety of people caught in profound social crises. Counts continually referred to this "Great Transition," and believed that it was neither possible, nor desirable, to preserve the status quo or "turn back the clock" to simpler but happier times.

Periods of profound social transformation brought not only social turmoil and anxiety but also the promises of greater control over nature, of increased material abundance, and of liberation from the scarcity of a subsistence economy said Counts. Believing in the American progressive or liberal perspective in politics and in education, he thought it possible that the immense social, economic, political, and educational problems of the twentieth century could be solved in a way that would achieve the promise of American life. The time had come, he argued, to replace competitiveness, maldistribution, and exploitation with cooperation, planning, humaneness, and democracy in a technological society. Such a new social order would preserve the democratic ethic by reconstructing it to meet the requirements of the new technology.

THEORY INTO PRACTICE?

Counts developed a "program of action" which called for: (1) affirmation of democratic values and processes; (2) dissemination of the knowledge needed by free people; (3) maintenance of military and police power by legally constituted authorities; (4) guaranteeing of civil liberties; (5) systematic exposure of major campaigns of political propaganda; (6) conservation of the democratic temper; and (7) avoidance of war.[73] But some who were sympathetic to Counts' *Dare the School Build a New Social Order?* claimed that they were inspired by his call but did not know how to implement it. A specific program for social and educational reconstruction was never developed nor was an organization formed to lead the creating of a new society. Nor did Counts associate in any formal sense with those who styled themselves "social reconstructionist" educational philosophers. Although a scholar, Counts was also a political activist. He sought and won the presidency of the American Federation of Teachers in 1939. He was the Liberal Party candidate for the United States Senate in New York in 1952. His programmatic efforts, however, were of limited dimension when compared to the magnitude of his challenge to educators to use schools to improve society.

Counts was operationally and theoretically a cultural relativist in education. When the natural priority moved from the problems of economic depression to the defense of democracy against fascist and Nazi totalitarianism during World War II, Counts' attention also moved in that direction. In the Cold War era, his expert knowledge of Soviet society and education took on a new relevance as he explained Soviet political and educational policies to an American audience.

What were George S. Counts' major contributions to American education? He clearly pointed out that education was related to a given civilization and its problems at a particular time in history. He argued forcefully that schooling could be an instrument of broad and significant national policy. He challenged educators to go beyond daily concerns and formulate policy rather than having the dictates of others imposed on them. He anticipated much of the current research on modernization and its educational consequences. He reasserted that educational philosophy was not a completed product, but rather an instrument for dealing with changing issues in a changing world.

SKETCH OF ELLA FLAGG YOUNG

EPILOGUE

After World War II, educational reform advocated by George S. Counts and others took a back seat. During the fifties and sixties the need to produce scientists who could help win the race to the moon generated interest in science, mathematics and foreign language. The National Defense Education Act (NDEA) of 1958 reflected and supported these concerns. Connected to this were new concerns stemming from old social roots as we learned that the schools continued to be racially and socially biased. The two Brown decisions—that is, *Brown* v. *the Board of Education, Topeka* (1954) and *Brown* v. *the Board of Education, Topeka* (1955) outlawed de facto segregation, and President Lyndon Johnson's War on Poverty was supposed to provide the federal money necessary to equalize educational opportunities for the poor whose ranks were predominantly minority. Programs such as Headstart and

Upward Bound were funded by the Elementary and Secondary Education Act of 1965 (ESEA) and called "compensatory education." They flooded the educational scene until the early seventies when another set of critics explained that most government efforts at compensatory education had failed.

In delineating the reasons for this failure, many people discussed the issues you have already encountered in this volume. Once again the nature/nurture arguments surfaced with new support from contemporary psychologists on both sides of the controversy. Utilizing identical twin studies conducted by Cyril Burt in England, a University of California professor named Arthur Jensen said that intelligence was approximately 80 percent genetic (even though Burt's findings were based on vague measures and poorly controlled research designs). Charges of fraudulent data after Burt's death in 1975 only complicated the issue. Behaviorists such as B. F. Skinner called for modifications in the social/educational environment. In the meantime, Skinner's Harvard colleague, psychologist Robert Rosenthal and his supporters blamed the environment by claiming that both positive and negative self-fulfilling prophesies (Pygmalion effect) were operating in the schools. They said these prophecies were being enforced by school personnel—the significant others in lives of students—and that minority students were fulfilling the negative prophecies that authority figures held for them.[1]

Other voices joined the chorus who blamed the school environment and the political/social system that created and supported it. John Holt, Herb Kohl, and Jonathan Kozol all wrote of their teaching experiences and concluded that it was the educational climate that produced failure. Montessori schools and "free schools" inspired by Summerhill were organized and opened as alternatives to the public institutions. Marva Collins demonstrated in Chicago that "learning disabled" black students could become academic successes. Added to this cadre were many critics and reformers in other countries, for example: Paulo Freire, Ivan Illich, and Albert Memmi. The legacies from these more recent critics have yet to be assessed. It is too soon to tell whose lives will be the material for discussion fifty years hence. But we can be sure that our successors will use the biographies of contemporary figures as their window on the late twentieth century, and that later generations will chronicle the educational activities of those inhabiting a world probably beyond our predicted visions.[2]

Perhaps the most important gain from a collection of educational biographies such as this one is the realization that you and I are part of this venerable process. Whether obscure like Thomas Platter or Johannes Butzbach, or major figures like Plato or Christine de Pisan all of us have a part in the ongoing saga of education. Like Socrates, most readers of this book are or will be teachers: like Emma Willard or W. E. B. DuBois, we hope you will try to help others become better than they think they can be. And so many of your biographies, too, are the stuff of which future educational history will be made. Our hope is that these biographical sketches may further the process by which new "lives in education" emerge to shape the future of generations yet to come.

NOTES

The notes are designed to call attention to the main sources used in preparing this book. Readers who wish to go beyond the notes should consult the appendix in Christopher J. Lucas, *Our Western Educational Heritage* (New York: Macmillan, 1972). This is an excellent book and contains the best note on sources for Western education in print as of this writing.

INTRODUCTION

1. Christopher J. Lucas, "The Scribal Tablet-House in Ancient Mesopotamia," *History of Education Quarterly* 19 (Fall 1979): 305-32.
2. Barbara Tuchman, "Biography as a Prism of History," in *Practicing History* (New York: Alfred A. Knopf, 1981), 80-90.
3. Robinson's book was published London and New York by Harper and Bros. in 1921; Jaynes' book appeared in 1976 from Houghton Mifflin.

CHAPTER 1: THE GREEKS

1. David M. Robinson, *Sappho and Her Influence* (New York: Cooper Square, 1963), 14.
2. Mary Barnard, trans., *Sappho — A New Translation* (Berkeley: University of California Press, 1958), 86.
3. J. P. Mahaffy, *A History of Classical Greek Literature*, 2 vols. (London: Macmillan, 1908), 1: 202; Arthur [Edward Pearse Brome] Weigall, *Sappho of Lesbos — Her Life and Times* (New York: Frederick A. Stokes, 1932), 321.
4. John Addington Symonds, *Studies of the Greek Poets*, 3d ed. (London: A. and C. Black, 1920), 196.
5. Verna Zinserling, *Women in Greece and Rome*, trans. L. A. Jones (New York: Abner Schram, 1973), 8. Spelling Americanized.

6. Beram Salvatvala, *Sappho of Lesbos: Her Works Restored — A Metrical English Version of Her Poems with Conjectural Restorations* (London: Charles Skilton, 1968), 24. Italicized lines are conjectural.

7. Guy Davenport, trans., *Sappho: Poems and Fragments* (Ann Arbor: University of Michigan Press, 1965), 151.

8. Symonds, *Studies of the Greek Poets*, 196.

9. Zinserling, *Women in Greece and Rome*, 8.

10. K. T. Dover, *Greek Homosexuality* (London: Duckworth, 1978), 1.

11. The elaborate code involved is detailed in Thomas Africa, "Homosexuals in Greek History," *Journal of Psychohistory* 9 (Spring 1982): 401-20.

12. Dover, *Greek Homosexuality*, 16.

13. Diogenes Laertius, *The Lives and Opinions of Eminent Philosophers*, trans. C. Duke Younge (London: Henry G. Bohn, 1853). Cf. R. D. Hicks's translation (London: William Heinemann, 1925), 2: 463-69.

14. Plato *Protagoras* (Taylor's translation) 327.

15. Ibid., 319.

16. Diogenes, *The Lives and Opinions of Eminent Philosophers*.

17. Ibid.

18. Taylor, *Socrates: The Man and His Thought* (New York: Doubleday Anchor Books, [1933] 1953). For a recent example of the pedestal view of Socrates, see Henry J. Perkinson, *Since Socrates: Studies in the History of Western Educational Thought* (New York: Longman, 1980).

19. Plato *Protogoras* 315.

20. Alban Dewes Winspear and Tom Silverberg, *Who Was Socrates?*, 2d ed. (New York: Russell and Russell, 1960), 71.

21. Plato *The Republic* (Jowett's translation) 514-517.

22. Plato *Phaedo* (Jowett's translation) 89.

23. Taylor, *Socrates: The Man and His Thought*, 128.

24. Some sources give 429 and some 527 as the date of his birth, but we are following Winspear, *The Genesis of Plato's Thought*, 2d ed. (New York: S. A. Russell, 1956), 161, who argues persuasively for 428. Unless otherwise noted, information about Plato is from this source.

25. Mehdi: Khan Nakosteen, *The History and Philosophy of Education* (New York: Ronald Press, [1965]), 80.

26. Diogenes, *The Lives and Opinions of Eminent Philosophers*, 129.

27. Ibid., 127.

28. Ibid., 128.

29. Ingemar Düring, *Aristotle in the Ancient Biographical Tradition* (Göteburg: Göteburg University, 1957), 249-50.

30. Robert Maynard Hutchins, ed., "Biographical Note — Aristotle," in *Great Books of the Western World*, 53 Vols. (Chicago: Encyclopedia Britannica, 1952), 8: v.

31. John Patrick Lynch, *Aristotle's School: A Study of a Greek Educational Institution* (Berkeley and Los Angeles: University of California Press, 1972), 87.

32. David Ross, "The Development of Aristotle's Thought," in *Aristotle and Plato in the Mid-Fourth Century*, ed. I. Düring and G. E. L. Owen (Göteburg: Elanders Boktryck eri Aktiebolag, 1960), 1-17.

33. H. I. Marrou, *A History of Education in Antiquity*, trans. George Lamb (New York: Sheed and Ward, 1956), 33; Düring rejects the homosexual relationship.

34. Düring, *Aristotle in the Ancient Biographical Tradition*, 263-65.

35. Lynch, *Aristotle's School*, 87-88, 91.

36. Stephen R. L. Clark, *Aristotle's Man: Speculations upon Aristotelian Anthropology* (Oxford: Clarendon Press, 1975), 29, 71 ff.

37. Meyer Reinhold, *A Simplified Approach to Plato and Aristotle* (Great Neck, NY: Barron's Educational Series, [c. 19674]), 57.

38. Ross, "The Development of Aristotle's Thought," 7; Hutchins, *Works of Aristotle*, 8: vi.

39. Ibid.

40. Lynch, *Aristotle's School*, 140, 207.

41. Walter Pater, *Plato and Platonism: A Series of Lectures* (London: Macmillan, 1910), 141.

42. Naphtali Lewis and Meyer Reinhold, eds., *Roman Civilization* 2 (New York: Columbia University Press, 1955): 296-97.

CHAPTER 2: THE ROMANS

1. H. I. Marrou, *A History of Education in Antiquity*, trans., George Lamb (New York: Sheed and Ward, 1956), 229.
2. Titus Livius, *The History of Rome*, trans. Canon Roberts, 6 vols., Everyman Library (New York: E. P. Datton, [1912-1924]).
3. Aubrey Gwynn, *Roman Education from Cicero to Quintilian* (New York: Russell and Russell, 1964).
4. Marrou, *A History of Education in Antiquity*, 268-69.
5. Ibid., 266-67, 274-75, 284-85.
6. Plutarch, *The Lives of the Noble Grecians and Romans*, in *The Great Books of the Western World*, ed. Robert Maynard Hutchins, 53 vols. (Chicago: Encyclopedia Brittanica, 1952), 14: 704; Tranquillus Seutonius, "The Deified Julius," in *Seutonius*, trans. J. C. Rolfe, Loeb Classical Library (New York: G. P. Putnam's Sons, 1930), 73.
7. Gwynn, *Roman Education from Cicero to Quintilian*, 80.
8. William Barclay, *Train Up a Child: Educational Ideas in the Ancient World* (Philadelphia: Westminster Press, 1959).
9. Gwynn, *Roman Education from Cicero to Quintilian*, 105.
10. Plutarch, *The Lives of the Noble Grecians and Romans*, 723.
11. Albert E. Warsley, *501 Tidbits of Roman Antiquity* (Elizabeth, NJ: Auxilian Latinium, 1953), 476.
12. Marcus Fabius Quintilianus, *The Instituto Orcatoria*, trans. H. E. Butler (London: William Heinemann, 1921), bk. 2, ii, 5-7.
13. Timothy Reagan, "The Instituto Oratoria: Quintilian's Contribution to Educational Theory and Practice," *Vitae Scholasticae* 2 (Fall 1983): 405-17.
14. Ernest Cary, trans., *Dios Roman History*, Loeb Classical Library, 8 (London: William Heinemann, 1925), bk. 62, 27.
15. Tacitus, *The Annals*, trans. John Jackson 4 (London: William Heinemann, [1937] 1962): bk. 15, xliv.
16. Kirsopp Lake, trans., "Ignatus to the Romans," in *The Apostolic Fathers* 1 (London: William Heinemann, [1912] 1965): iv, v.
17. Socrates, *The Ancient Ecclesiastical Histories of the First Six Hundred Years After Christ...*, trans., Meridith Hanmer, 3d ed. (London: Richard Field, 1607), bk. 7, xv. Spelling modernized.
18. Ibid.
19. Jacques Chabannes, *Saint Augustine*, trans. Julie Kernan (Garden City, NY: Doubleday, 1962); John J. O'Meara, *The Young Augustine: An Introduction to the Confessions of St. Augustine* (London: Longman, [1954] 1980); Warren Thomas Smith, *Augustine: His Life and Thought* (Atlanta: John Knox Press, 1980).
20. John K. Ryan, trans., *The Confessions of St. Augustine* (Garden City, NY: Image Books, 1960), 55. Much biographical material in the sketch is from books 1-6.
21. Roland H. Bainton, *The Horizon History of Christianity* (New York: American Heritage Publishing, 1964), 131.
22. "A new theory of history [which] ... no longer describe[s] 'the middle ages' by a name which implies a barbaric interlude ... will enable 'medievalists' to produce a truer picture of their period," says Toby Burrows in "Unmaking the 'Middle Ages,' " *Journal of Medieval History* 7 (1981): 127-34.
23. Bainton, *The Horizon History of Christianity*, 37.
24. Helen M. Barrett, *Boethius: Some Aspects of His Times and Work* (Cambridge: University Press, 1940), 33.
25. Charles Henry Costner, *The Indicum Quinquevirale* (Cambridge, MA: Medieval Academy of America, 1935), 62.

26. James J. O'Donnell, *Cassiodorus* (Berkeley and Los Angeles: University of California Press, 1979).

CHAPTER 3: THE MONASTICS

1. David Knowles, *Christian Monasticism* (New York: McGraw Hill, 1969), 12.
2. Ibid., 13.
3. Quoted in Bertrand Russell, *A History of Western Philosophy and its Connection with Political and Social Circumstances from the Earliest Times to the Present Day* (New York: Simon and Schuster, 1956), 379.
4. Clara and Richard Winston, *Daily Life in the Middle Ages* (New York: American Heritage, 1975), 62.
5. Anthony C. Meisel and M. L. del Mastro, trans., *The Rule of St. Benedict* (Garden City, NY: Doubleday, 1975), 10.
6. Augusta Theodosia Drane, *Christian Schools and Scholars — Or Sketches of Education from the Christian Era to the Council of Trent*, ed. Walter Gumbley (London: Burns, Oates, and Washbourne, 1924), 168-69.
7. Meisel and Mastro, *The Rule of St. Benedict*, 9.
8. Drane, *Christian Schools and Scholars*, 292.
9. Ibid., 124; Pierre Riché, *Daily Life in the World of Charlemagne*, trans. JoAnn McNamara ([Philadelphia]: University of Pennsylvania Press, 1978), 225.
10. Drane, *Christian Schools and Scholars*, 119, 123.
11. Ibid.
12. Ibid., 120.
13. Will Durant, *The Age of Faith* (New York: Simon and Schuster, 1950), 732.
14. Cited in John F. Benton, ed., *Self and Society in Medieval France: The Memoirs of Abbot Guibert of Nogent (1064? - c. 1125)* (New York: Harper Torchbooks, 1970).
15. Ibid., 13, 64.
16. Ibid., 12, 95.
17. Ibid., 15, 46.
18. Riché, *Daily Life in the World of Charlemagne*, 225.
19. Ibid., 213.
20. Pierre Riché, *Education and Culture in the Barbarian West: Sixth through Eighth Centuries*, 3d ed., trans. John J. Contreni (Columbia: University of South Carolina Press, 1976), 475.
21. Drane, *Christian Schools and Scholars*, 282-89.
22. Cf. Drane, *Christian Schools and Scholars*, 347, 352; Elizabeth Hamilton, *Heloise* (Garden City, NY: Doubleday, 1967); Gabriel Compayré, *Abelard and the Origins and Early History of Universities* (New York: Greenwood Press, [1893] 1969), 3-23; and Leif Grane, *Peter Abelard: Philosophy and Christianity in the Middle Ages*, trans. Frederick and Christine Crowley (London: Allen and Unwin, 1970).
23. All quotations, except otherwise noted, are from Abelard, *The Story of My Misfortunes: The Autobiography of Peter Abelard*, trans. Henry Adams Bellows (Glencoe, IL: Free Press, [1922] 1958); cf. J. T. Muckle, trans., *The Story of Abelard's Adversities: A Translation with Notes of the Historia Calamitatum* (Toronto: Pontifical Institute of Medieval Studies, 1964).
24. Hastings Rashdall, *The Universities of Europe in the Middle Ages*, ed. F. M. Powicke and A. B. Emden, 3 vols. (Oxford: Clarendon Press, 1936), 1: 279-81.
25. Grane, *Peter Abelard*, 40.
26. Muckle, *The Story of Abelard's Adversities*, 21.
27. Ibid., 23.
28. Rashdall, *The Universities of Europe*, 1: 284.
29. Grane, *Peter Abelard*, 51.
30. Cf. Hamilton, *Heloise*, and Grane, *Peter Abelard*, 63.
31. Ibid., 66.
32. Ibid., 153.
33. Knowles, *Christian Monasticism*, 8.

34. *The Victoria History of the Counties of England, Hampshire, and the Isle of Wright* (Folkestone and London: University of London Institute of Historical Research, [1903] 1973), 2: 132-33.

35. [Guibert], *The Autobiography of Guibert Abbot of Nogent*, trans. C. C. Swinton Bland (London: George Routledge and Sons, 1925), bk. 3, chap. 8.

36. Rashdall, *The Universities of Europe*, 1: 292-401.

37. Iván D. Illich, *Deschooling Society* (New York: Harper and Row, 1971); John Caldwell Holt, *Freedom and Beyond* (New York: E. P. Dutton, 1972).

38. Anthony Kenny, *Aquinas* (New York: Hill and Wang, 1980), 1.

39. Vernon J. Bourke, *Aquinas' Search for Wisdom* (Miiwaukee: Bruce, 1965), 9.

40. Ibid., 43-44.

41. Ibid., 17-18.

42. Ibid., 25.

43. Kenny, *Aquinas*, 2.

44. Robert Maynard Hutchins, ed., *Great Books of the Western World*, 53 vols. (Chicago: Encyclopedia Britannica, 1952), 19: 778.

45. James Mulhern, *A History of Education* (New York: Ronald Press, 1959), 241.

46. Hutchins, *Great Books of the Western World*, 19: vi.

47. James A. Weisheipl, *Friar Thomas D'Aquino: His Life, Thought, and Work* (New York: Doubleday, 1974), 331.

CHAPTER 4: THE HUMANISTS

1. Cf. Denys Hays, *The Italian Renaissance in Its Historical Background* (Cambridge: University Press, 1961), 1; Hans Baron, *The Crisis of the Early Italian Renaissance: Civic Humanism and Republican Liberty in the Age of Classicism and Tyranny* (Princeton: University Press, 1966), xxvii-xxviii.

2. R. R. Bolgar, *The Classical Heritage and Its Beneficiaries* (Cambridge, University Press, 1963), 255.

3. William H. Woodward, *Vittorino da Feltre and Other Humanist Educators: Essays and Versions* (Cambridge: University Press, 1921), 2.

4. James Bowen, *A History of Western Education*, 3 vols. (New York: St. Martin's Press, 1975), 2:225.

5. Woodward, *Vittorino da Feltre*, 16-17.

6. The information on Renaissance classroom practice comes from an unpublished paper by Anthony Grafton of Princeton University, "How the Humanists Learned Greek: A Study in Classroom Practice," presented at the Newberry Library Renaissance Conference, 23 April 1982.

7. Hays, *The Italian Renaissance*, 154.

8. Enid McLeod, *The Order of the Rose: The Life and Ideas of Christine de Pizan* (London: Chatto and Windus, 1976). All biographical details are from this source.

9. For an expanded discussion, see L. Glenn Smith, "From Plato to Jung: Centuries of Inequalities," *Educational Horizons* 60 (Fall 1981): 4-10.

10. Phyllis Stock, *Better than Rubies: A History of Women's Education* (New York: G. P. Putnam's Sons, 1978), 42.

11. McLeod, *The Order of the Rose*, 48.

12. Ibid., 66.

13. Ibid., 70.

14. Ibid., 160.

15. See Clive Wood and Beryl Suitters, *The Fight for Acceptance: A History of Contraception* (Aylesbury, U. K.: Medical and Technical Publishing, 1970). All information on Butzbach is from Johannes Butzbach, *The Autobiography of Johannes Butzbach, A Wandering Scholar of the Fifteenth Century*, trans. Robert Frances Seybolt and Paul Monroe (Ann Arbor: Edwards Brothers, 1933).

16. George Faludy, *Erasmus* (New York: Stein and Day, 1970), 3, 109.

17. Ibid., 91.

18. Raymond Himeluck, trans., *The Enchirdion of Erasmus* (Bloomington: Indiana University Press, 1963), 85.

19. Ibid., 87.

20. Woodward, *Desiderius Erasmus Concerning the Aim and Method of Education,* Classics in Education 19, (New York: Bureau of Publications, Teachers College, Columbia University, [1904] 1964), 36-37, 191.

21. Robert Ulich, ed., *Three Thousand Years of Educational Wisdom* (Cambridge: Harvard University Press, 1961), 257.

22. Woodward, *Desiderius Erasmus*, 48-49, 187, 193-215.

23. T. W. Baldwin, *Small Latine and Lesse Greeke* 1 (Urbana: University of Illinois Press, 1944): 96-97.

24. Craig R. Thompson, trans., *The Colloquies of Erasmus* (Chicago: University of Chicago Press, 1965), 46.

25. Ibid., xxxvi.

26. Donald B. King and H. David Rix, trans., *On Copia of Words and Ideas* (Milwaukee: Marquette University Press, 1963), 9.

27. Ibid., bk. 1, chap. 16.

28. Margaret Mann Phillips, *The "Adages" of Erasmus — A Study with Translations* (Cambridge: University Press, 1964), 171-89.

29. Will Durant, *The Reformation* (New York: Simon and Schuster, 1957), 283.

30. Roberto Ridolfi, *The Life of Niccolò Machiavelli* (London: Routledge and Keegan Paul, 1963), 4-7.

31. Felix Guibert, *Machiavelli and Guicciardini* (Princeton: Princeton University Press, 1965), 20.

32. Ridolfi, *Life of Niccolò Machiavelli*, 6.

33. Ibid., 146.

34. Federico Chabod, *Machiavelli and the Renaissance* (London: Bowes and Bowes, 1958), 42-47.

35. Machiavelli, *The Prince* (New York: W. W. Norton, 1977), 114.

36. Ridolfi, *Life of Niccolò Machiavelli*, 74-75, 207.

37. Chabod, *Machiavelli and the Renaissance*, 88-104, 124, 185-87.

38. Cf. Thomas Babbington Macaulay, "Machiavelli," in *English Essays,* in *The Harvard Classics* 27 (New York: P. F. Collier and Son, 1910): 381-421.

39. John Freddero, "That Notorious Little Book," *The Stanford Magazine* 10, 2 (Summer 1982): 15.

40. Chabod, *Machiavelli and the Renaissance*, 93.

CHAPTER 5: THE REFORMERS

1. Hastings Rashdall, *The Universities of Europe in the Middle Ages*, ed. F. M. Powicke and A. B. Emden, 3 vols. (Oxford: Clarendon Press, 1936), 3: map facing 558.

2. George M. Trevelyan, *England in the Age of Wycliffe, 1368-1520* (London: Longmans, Green, 1925).

3. James E. T. Rogers, *The Economic Interpretation of History* (New York: G. Putnam's, 1888), 75; R. L. Poole, *Wycliffe and Movements for Reform* (New York: AMS Press, [1889] 1978), 88.

4. James W. Thompson, *Economic and Social History of Europe in the Later Middle Ages, 1300-1530* (New York: Century, 1931), 449.

5. J. R. Tanner et al., eds., *The Cambridge Medieval History*, 8 vols. (Cambridge: University Press, 1932), 7: 486-495.

6. F. D. Mathew, ed., *The English Works of Wyclif, Hitherto Unprinted* (London: Truebner, 1880), 96-104.

7. Mandell Creighton, *History of the Papacy During the Reformation*, 5 vols. (London: 1882), 1: 359.

8. Henry Hart Milman, *History of Latin Christianity*, 8 vols. (New York: Sheldon, 1860), 7: 487.

9. A good example of the psychohistorical approach is Erik H. Erikson, *Young Man Luther* (New York: W. W. Norton, 1962).

10. Gordon Rupp, *The Righteousness of God* (London: Hodder and Stoughton, 1953), 105ff.

11. Anders Piltz, *The World of Medieval Learning*, trans. David Jones (Totowa, NJ: Barnes and Noble Books, 1981), 245ff.

12. Cited in John Todd, *Martin Luther* (Westminster, MD: Newman Press, 1964), 36.

13. Ibid., 115.

14. *Resolutio Lutheriana super propositione decima tertia de potestate papae* (Leipzig, 1519), cited in Todd, *Luther*, 162.

15. "Letters to the Mayors and Aldermen of All the Cities of Germany on Behalf of Christian Schools," in *Luther on Education*, ed. F. V. N. Painter (Philadelphia: Lutheran Publication Society, 1889), 186.

16. "Sermon on the Duty of Sending Children to School," in Painter, *Luther on Education*, 264.

17. Clyde L. Manschreck, *Melanchthon: The Quiet Reformer* (Nashville: Abingdon Press, 1958), 140.

18. *Corpus Reformatorum* 11: 298ff., cited in Manschreck, *Melanchthon*, 146.

19. Julia O'Faolain and Laura Martenes, eds., *Not in God's Image: Women in History from the Greeks to the Victorians* (New York: Harper and Row, 1973), 196.

20. Robert Delort, *Life in the Middle Ages*, trans. Robert Allen (New York: Universe Books for Edita Lausanne, 1973).

21. An abbreviated account is Henry Barnard, trans., "School Life in the Fifteenth Century," *American Journal of Education* 5 (1858): 79-90, (based on Karl von Raumer's *Geschichte der Pädagogik vom Wiederaufblühen klassischer Studien bis auf unsere Zeit (History of Pedagogy from the Revival of Classical Learning Down to Our Time)*, 4 vols. (1843-1855). The complete text is in Paul Monroe, trans. and ed., *Thomas Platter and the Educational Renaissance of the Sixteenth Century* (New York: D. Appleton, 1904).

22. See *Felix et Thomas Platter a Montpellier 1552-1559—1595-1599; notes de voyage de deux etudiants balois, publiees d'apres les manuscript originaux appartenant a la bibliotheque de l'Universite de Bale; avec deux portraits* (Montpellier: C. Coulet, 1892) and Thomas Platter, *Journal of a Younger Brother: The Life of Thomas Platter as a Medical Student in Montpellier at the Close of the Sixteenth Century*, trans. by Sean Jennett (London: F. Muller, 1963).

23. A fine recent treatment of the new Reformation historiography is given in John W. O'Malley's "The Jesuits, St. Ignatius, and the Counter Reformation," *Studies in the Spirituality of Jesuits* 14 (January 1982): 1-28.

24. [Loyola], *St. Ignatius' Own Story*, trans. William J. Young (Chicago: Loyola University Press, 1956), 9-11.

25. Cf., Ibid., 17-24, for an account of Ignatius' religious experiences during this time.

26. Paul Dudon, *St. Ignatius of Loyola*, trans. William J. Young (Milwaukee: Bruce, 1949), 148, 204.

27. Cited in George E. Ganss, *Saint Ignatius' Idea of a Jesuit University* (Milwaukee: Marquette University Press, 1954), 24.

28. Allan P. Farrell, *The Jesuit Code of Liberal Education* (Milwaukee: Bruce, 1938), 26.

29. Ganss, *Saint Ignatius' Idea of a Jesuit University*, 24.

30. Cf., for example, Ignatius' letter of 1 June 1551 to Fr. Antonio Brandao, published in [Loyola], *St. Ignatius Own Story*, 99-107.

31. George E. Ganss discusses Ignatius' pragmatic educational philosophy in "Education for Business in the Jesuit University," *Jesuit Educational Quarterly* 23 (January 1961): 137.

32. Loyola, *The Constitutions of the Society of Jesus*, trans. George E. Ganss (St. Louis: Institute of Jesuit Sources, 1970), pt. 4, ch. 6.4, 191; quotation from 12.3, 214.

33. Letter of Ignatius, 1555, cited in Farrell, *The Jesuit Code of Liberal Education*, 136.

34. For a schematic outline of the course of studies, see Ganss, *Saint Ignatius' Idea of a Jesuit University*, 45.

35. Loyola, *The Constitution of the Society of Jesus*, pt. 4, 171-229.
36. Unless otherwise indicated, biographical information is from Mathew Spinka, *John Amos Comenius — That Incomparable Moravian* (Chicago: University of Chicago Press, 1943).
37. "Jesuits, Educational Work of," s.v. *Cyclopedia of Education*, ed. Paul Monroe, 5 vols. (New York: Macmillan, 1911-1913).
38. Raumer, *Geschichte der Pädagogik*.
39. I. L. Kandel and Paul Monroe, "Comenius, John Amos," *Cyclopedia of Education* 2: 135-41.
40. Ibid.
41. Spinka, *John Amos Comenius*, 129-130.
42. John Edward Sadler, *J. A. Comenius and the Concept of Universal Education* (New York: Barnes and Noble, 1966), 225.
43. s. v. all these names in the *Cyclopedia of Education*.
44. Henry Barnard, ed. and comp., "A History of Harvard College, 1636-1684, Primarily from Eliot's History of Harvard College," *American Journal of Education* 9 (1860): 129-38.

CHAPTER 6: THE NEW EDUCATORS

1. Peter Gay, *Age of Enlightenment* (New York: Time-Life Books, 1966), 11. Information for the introduction comes from: M. S. Anderson, *Eighteenth Century Europe, 1713-1789* (London: Oxford University Press, 1966); Max Beloff, *The Age of Absolutism, 1660-1815* (New York: Harper and Row, 1962); Isaiah Berlin, *The Age of Enlightenment* (New York: Mentor Books, 1956); Frank E. Manuel, *The Age of Reason* (Ithaca: Cornell University Press, 1951).
2. Anderson, *Eighteenth Century Europe*, 59.
3. Ibid., 13.
4. Merle Curti, *Probing Our Past* (New York: Harper, 1955), 75.
5. For biographical information see Richard Ithamar Aaron, *John Locke*, 3d ed. (Oxford: Clarendon Press, 1971); Maurice William Cranston, *John Locke, A Biography* (New York: Macmillan, [1957]); John David Mabbott, *John Locke* (London: Macmillan, 1973); Kathleen M. Squadrito, *John Locke* (Boston: Twayne, 1979).
6. John Locke, *Some Thoughts Concerning Education* (New York: 1947), 253-55.
7. Ibid., 256, 272.
8. Locke, *An Essay: Concerning the True Original Extent and End of Civil Government* in Robert Maynard Hutchins, ed., Great Books of the Western World 53 vols. (Chicago: Encyclopedia Brittanica, 1952), 35: 46.
9. Locke, *An Essay Concerning Human Understanding,* ed. Alexander Campbell Fraser, 2 vols. (New York: Dover, 1959), 2: 46.
10. Rousseau, *The Confessions of Jean-Jacques Rousseau, Now for the First Time Translated into English without Expurgation*, 2 vols. (n.p.: privately printed, [c. 1896]), 1: 3; biographical information also comes from Colwyn Edward Vulliamy, *Rousseau* (London: G. Bles, 1931).
11. Rousseau, *Confessions*, 1: 6, 11.
12. Vulliamy, *Rousseau*, 19.
13. Rousseau, *Confessions*, 1: 65.
14. Ibid., 118.
15. Ibid., 197.
16. Vulliamy, *Rousseau*, 78.
17. Rousseau, *Emile, or On Education,* trans. Alan Bloom (New York: Basic Books, 1979).
18. Eleanor Flexner, *Mary Wollstonecraft* (New York: Coward, McCann and Geoghegan, 1972); Ralph Wardle, *Mary Wollstonecraft — A Critical Biography* (Lincoln: University of Nebraska Press, 1951).
19. Juliet Mitchell, *Women's Estate* (New York: Vintage Books, 1975), see chap. 5.

20. Wollstonecraft, *Vindication of the Rights of Woman* (New York: W. W. Norton, 1967), 220, 223, 285.

21. Ibid., 251.

22. Ibid., 122, 226-27.

23. Flexner, *Mary Wollstonecraft*, 181-216; Wardle, *Mary Wollstonecraft*, 185-206, 215-50; C. Keegan Paul, ed., *Letters to Imlay* (New York: Haskell House, 1971).

24. This synopsis is based on Wollstonecraft, *Maria, Or the Wrongs of Woman* (New York: W. W. Norton, 1975).

25. Ibid., 65.

26. Wollstonecraft, *Thoughts on the Education of Daughters* (1786), 81, cited in Mary Anne Warren, *The Nature of Woman: An Encyclopedia and Guide to the Literature* (Inverness, CA: Edgepress, 1980), 497; for the contemporary argument, see Linda McPheron and Joan K. Smith, "Women Administrators in Historical Perspective: Toward an Androgynous Theory of Leadership," *Education Horizons* 60 (Fall 1981): 22-25.

27. Harlan Lane, *The Wild Boy of Aveyron* (New York: Batam Books, 1977).

28. Kate Silber, *Pestalozzi: The Man and His Work* (New York: Schocken Books, 1973), 4. Unless otherwise noted, biographical information is from this source.

29. John Alfred Green, *Life and Work of Pestalozzi* (London: W. B. Clive, 1913), 32.

30. Ibid., 41-42.

31. Silber, *Pestalozzi*, 56, 115.

32. Ibid., 112.

33. Ibid., 114; Green, *Life and Work of Pestalozzi*, 77.

34. Karl von Raumer, "The Life and Educational System of Pestalozzi," in *Pestalozzi and His Educational System*, ed., trans., and comp. Henry Barnard (Syracuse: C. W. Bardeen, [1901]), 84-85. Eva Channing, trans., *Pestalozzi's Leonard and Gertrude*, Heath's Pedagogical Library 6 (Boston: D. C. Heath, 1885): 86.

35. Cf. Hermann Krüsi, *Pestalozzi: His Life, Work, and Influence* (Cincinnati: Wilson, Hinkle, 1875), 13-64, 67-100, and Raumer, "The Life and System of Pestalozzi," 84-86.

36. Silber, *Pestalozzi*, 78.

37. "Pestalozziana," *Blackwood's Magazine* (July 1849), reprinted in the *American Journal of Education* 31 (1881): 35-48.

38. Silber, *Pestalozzi*, 236.

39. Emilie Michaelis and H. Keatley Moore, trans., *Autobiography of Friedrick Froebel* (Syracuse: C. W. Bardeen, 1889), 3. Unless otherwise noted, biographical information is from this source.

40. Ibid., 8.

41. Ibid., 52-60.

42. Ibid.

43. Robert B. Downs, *Friedrick Froebel* (Boston: Twayne, 1978), 28.

44. The gifts are discussed in Downs, *Friedrick Froebel*, 47-54.

CHAPTER 7: THE AMERICANS

1. *Public Records of the Colony of Connecticut, 1678-1689* (Hartford: F. A. Brown, 1882), 8. For a survey of the history of American education, see John Pulliam, *History of Education in America*, 3d ed. (Columbus, OH: Charles E. Merrill, 1980).

2. U.S. Department of the Interior, *Statistics of State School Systems, 1927-28*, Bulletin 1930, 5 (Washington, D.C.: Government Printing Office, 1930), 30.

3. Harry R. Warfel, *Noah Webster: School Master to America* (New York: Macmillan, 1936), 37.

4. Frederick Rudolph, ed., *Essays on Education in the Early Republic* (Cambridge: Harvard University Press, 1965), 59.

5. Warfel, *Noah Webster*, 35-36.

6. Webster, *The American Spelling Book, Containing the Rudiments of the English Language*, last rev. ed. (Wells River, VT.: Ira White, 1843), vi.

7. Warfel, *Noah Webster*, 139.

8. Rudolph, *Essays*, 72-77.

9. Ibid., 45-46, 51.

10. Ibid., 48-55.

11. Ibid., 55-60.

12. Marcus Lee Hansen, *The Atlantic Migration, 1607-1860* (New York: Harper Torchbooks, 1961), 47.

13. Jonathan Messerli, *Horace Mann, A Biography* (New York: Alfred A. Knopf, 1972). Unless otherwise noted all biographical information is from this source.

14. Ibid., 246.

15. Lawrence A. Cremin, ed., *The Republic and the School* (New York: Teachers College, Columbia University, 1957), 8.

16. Ibid., 7.

17. Robert B. Downs, *Horace Mann: Champion of Public Schools* (New York: Twayne, 1974), 151-52.

18. Quoted in Raymond Culver, *Horace Mann and Religion in the Massachusetts Public Schools* (New Haven: Yale University Press, 1929), 231.

19. "Henry Barnard," *American Journal of Education* 1 (May 1856): 663-68.

20. Barnard, "Education in Other States and Countries," *Connecticut Common School Journal* 2 (July 1840): 245.

21. Ibid., 245-48.

22. Barnard, ed., "Mr. Barnard's Labors in Connecticut from 1838-1842," *American Journal of Education* 1 (May 1856): 698.

23. Barnard, *National Education in Europe, Being an Account of the Organization, Administration, Instruction, and Statistics of Public Schools of Different Grades in the Principal States*, 2d ed. (Hartford: Case, Tiffany, 1854), 3-4.

24. Barnard, "History of Common Schools in Connecticut," *American Journal of Education* 15 (June 1865): 330.

25. Ibid., 331.

26. Barnard, *Report of the Commissioner of Education* (Washington, D.C.: Government Printing Office, 1869), xxx.

27. Glenn Smith, "Founding of the U.S. Office of Education," *Educational Forum* 31 (March 1967): 307-22.

28. Robert Owen, *The Life of Robert Owen* 1 (New York: Augustus M. Kelley, !1857! 1967).

29. Robert Owen, "A New View of Society," in John F. C. Harrison, *Utopianism and Education* (New York: Teachers College Press, 1968), 44.

30. Robert Dale Owen, *An Outline of the System of Education at New Lanark* (Cincinnati: Deming and Wood, 1825).

31. Harrison, *Quest for the New Moral World* (New York: Charles Scribner's Sons, 1969), 81.

32. Ibid., 79.

33. Robert Owen, "The Social System," *New Harmony Gazette* 2 (10 January 1827): 113.

34. Gerald Gutek, "New Harmony: An Example of Communitarian Education," *Educational Theory* 22 (Winter 1972): 34-46.

35. Arthur E. Bestor, Jr., *Backwoods Utopias: The Sectarian and Owenite Phases of Communitarian Socialism in America, 1663-1829* (Philadelphia: University of Pennsylvania Pres, 1950), 134-35.

36. George B. Lockwood, *The New Harmony Movement* (New York: D. Appleton, 1905), 84.

37. Ibid., 105-108.

38. Cited in Richard Shaw, *Daggar John* (New York: Paulist Press, 1977), 14.

39. Ibid., 21-22.

40. Ibid., 91.

41. Diane Ravitch, *The Great School Wars* (New York: Basic Books, 1974), 27.

42. Vincent Lannie, *Public Money and Parochial Education* (Cleveland: Case Western Reserve University Press, 1968), 78.

43. Ravitch, *The Great School Wars*, 76.

44. Lannie, *Public Money and Parochial Education*, 256.

CHAPTER 8: THE OUTSIDERS

1. Thomas Woody, *A History of Women's Education in the United States*, 2 vols. (New York: Science Press, 1929); Eleanor Flexner, *Century of Struggle: The Woman's Rights Movement in the United States* (Cambridge: Harvard University Press, 1959); Phyllis Stock, *Better than Rubies: A History of Women's Education* (New York: G. P. Putnam's Sons, 1978).

2. L. T. Guilford, *The Uses of a Life* (New York: American Tract Society, 1885), 32.

3. Henry Fowler, "Educational Services of Mrs. Emman Willard," *American Journal of Education* 6 (1859): 125-68.

4. Ibid.

5. Willystine Goodsell, *Pioneers of Women's Education in the United States* (New York: McGraw Hill, 1931), 20-62.

6. Arthur C. Cole, *A Hundred Years of Mount Holyoke College: The Evolution of an Educational Ideal* (New Haven: Yale University Press, 1940); Elizabeth Alden Green, *Mary Lyon and Mount Holyoke: Opening the Gates* (Hanover, NH: University Press of New England, [1979] 1983).

7. Mary Lyon, *Mount Holyoke Seminary* (Boston: Old South Work Leaflet No. 145, n.d.).

8. Ibid.

9. *Cyclopedia of Education*, s. v. "Lyon, Mary."

10. Elizabeth Blackwell, *Pioneer Work in Opening the Medical Profession to Women: Autobiographical Sketches* (New York: Source Book Press, [1895] 1970); Dorothy Clarke Wilson, *Lone Woman: The Story of Elizabeth Blackwell, The First Woman Doctor* (Boston: Little, Brown, 1970).

11. Estelle Fuchs and Robert J. Havighurst, *To Live on This Earth: American Indian Education* (Garden City, NY: Doubleday, 1970).

12. Catherine S. Fowler, "Sarah Winnemucca, Northern Paiute, 1844-1891," in *American Indian Intellectuals: 1976 Proceedings of the American Ethnological Society*, ed. Margot Liberty (St. Paul: West, 1978); Katherine C. Turner, *Red Men Calling on the Great White Father* (Norman: University of Oklahoma Press, 1951).

13. Meyer Weinberg, *A Chance to Learn: A History of Race and Education in the United States* (Cambridge: Cambridge University Press, 1977).

14. Benjamin Brawley, *Negro Builders and Heroes* (Chapel Hill University of North Carolina Press, 1937); L. J. Coppin, *Unwritten History* (New York: Negro Universities Press, [1919] 1968).

15. Most biographical material is from Washington's two autobiographies: *The Story of My Life and Work* (1900) and *Up From Slavery* (1901).

16. Basil T. Mathews, *Booker T. Washington* (Cambridge: Harvard University Press, 1948), 12-13.

17. Senator "Pitchfork Ben" Tillman to the U.S. Senate, cited in Samuel R. Spencer, Jr., *Booker T. Washington and the Negro's Place in American Life* (Boston: Little, Brown, 1955), 125-26.

18. Louis R. Harlan, *Booker T. Washington* (New York: Oxford University Press, 1972), 113-15.

19. Washington, *The Story of My Life and Work* in *The Booker T. Washington Papers*, ed. Louis R. Harlan, (Urbana: University of Illinois Press,), 1: 47.

20. Spencer, Booker T. Washington, 116.

21. Washington, "Address to the Atlanta Exposition," in Murray Eisenstadt, ed., *The Negro in American Life* (New York: Oxford Books, 1968), 152-53.

22. New York *World*, cited in Spencer, *Booker T. Washington*, 99-100.

23. August Meier, "Toward a Reinterpretation of Booker T. Washington," in August Meier and Elliot Rudwick, eds., *The Making of Black America* (New York: Atheneum, 1969), 126-27.

24. Kelly Miller, Washington's Policy, in Meier and Rudwick, *The Making of Black America*, 123, originally in the Boston *Evening Transcript*, 18, 19 September 1903.

25. Spencer, Booker T. Washington, 105.

26. Meier, "Toward a Reinterpretation of Booker T. Washington," 126-27.

27. Harlan, *Booker T. Washington*, 157-58.

CHAPTER 9: THE PROGRESSIVES

1. Ralph Henry Gabriel, *The Course of American Democratic Thought* (New York: Ronald Press, 1940), 331-40.

2. Samuel Eliot Morison and Henry Steele Commager, *The Growth of the American Republic*, 2 vols. (New York: Oxford University Press, 1961), 2: 443-44.

3. *Clarke University, Worcester, Massachusetts: Opening Exercises, October 2, 1889* (Printed by the University), 18, 24. Quoted in Dorothy Ross, G. Stanley Hall: *The Psychologist as Prophet* (Chicago: University of Chicago Press, 1972), 200.

4. Hall, "Child Study," *Journal of Proceedings and Addresses of the National Education Association, 1894* (St. Paul: Pioneer Press, 1895), 175.

5. Jack K. Campbell, *Colonel Francis W. Parker: The Children's Crusader* (New York: Teachers College Press, 1967). All biographical material and quotations are from this source.

6. Adelbert Ames, Jr., *The Morning Notes of Adelbert Ames, Jr.* (New Brunswick: Rutgers University Press, 1966); Jane M. Dewey, "Biography of John Dewey," in *The Philosophy of John Dewey*, ed. Paul A. Schilpp (Evanston: Northwestern University, 1939); George Dykhuizen, *The Life and Mind of John Dewey* (Carbondale: Southern Illinois University Press, 1973); Sidney Hook, *John Dewey: An Intellectual Portrait* (Westport, CT: Greenwood Press, [1939] 1971); Corliss Lamont, ed., *Dialogues on John Dewey* (New York: Horizon Press, 1959); John J. McDermott, ed., *The Philosophy of John Dewey* (Chicago: University of Chicago Press, 1981); Joseph Ratner, ed., *Intelligence in the Modern World: John Dewey's Philosophy* (New York: Random House, 1039); Sidney Ratner and Jules Altman, eds., *John Dewey and Arthur F. Bentley: A Philosophical Correspondence, 1932-1951* (New Brunswick: Rutgers University Press, 1964).

7. Jo Ann Boydston, ed., *The Poems of John Dewey* (Carbondale: Southern Illinois University Press, 1977). Several love poems hint of a special relationship between Dewey and Anzia Yezierska around the time of World War I.

8. Unpublished Haley autobiography, version 4 (1934-1935), Chicago Teachers Federation Files, Chicago Historical Society, 414; Robert L. Reid, ed., *Battleground: The Autobiography of Margaret A. Haley* (Urbana: University of Illinois Press, 1982).

9. Reid, *Battleground*, 24 for a description of Parker.

10. Ibid., 52-53; unpublished Haley autobiography, version 1 (1910), installment 4, 2-3.

11. Ibid., version 2 (1910-1911), 114-15.

12. Joan K. Smith, "The Changing of the Guard: Margaret A. Haley and the Rise of Democracy in the NEA," *Texas Tech Journal of Education* 8 (Winter 1981): 8-9.

13. Reid, *Battleground*, 167.

14. Unpublished Haley autobiography, version 4 (1934-1935), 145.

15. Joan K. Smith, *Ella Flagg Young: Portrait of a Leader* (Ames, IA: Educational Studies Press/Iowa State University Research Foundation, 1979). All biographical information and quotations on Young are from this source.

CHAPTER 10: THE CRITICS

1. William Boyd, *From Locke to Montessori* (London: George G. Harrap, 1914), 8.
2. Ibid., 88, 91; E. M. Standing, *Marie Montessori: Her Life and Work* (New York: New American Library, 1962), 32.
3. Ibid., 30.
4. Anna M. Maccheroni, *A True Romance: Maria Montessori As I Knew Her* (Edinburgh, Scotland: Darien Press, 1947), 1.
5. Standing, *Maria Montessori*, 39.
6. Maccheroni, *A True Romance*, 42.
7. Rita Kramer, *Maria Montessori: A Biography* (New York: G. P. Putnam's Sons, 1976), citing an interview with Mario. This was approved by the Holland based Association Montessori International. Kramer was probably compelled to interpret it this way, although she provides more conflicting than corroborating evidence. See, for example, 92-94; 184-85; 368-89.
8. Paula Polk Lilliard, *Montessori, A Modern Approach* (New York: Schocken Books, 1972), xiii.
9. Standing, *Maria Montessori*, 184.
10. Ibid., 110.
11. Ibid., 112.
12. Ibid., 113.
13. Ibid., 114.
14. Ibid., 119-20.
15. Ibid., 123-24, 126.
16. Ibid., 173, 118.
17. John Broadus Watson, "Autobiography," in *A History of Psychology in Autobiography*, ed. Carl Murchison (Worschester, MA: New York: Russell and Russell, [1936] 1961), 3: 271.
18. Ibid.
19. Ibid., 271-72.
20. Ibid., 274.
21. Ibid., 280.
22. John Chynoweth Burnham, "Psychiatry, Psychology and the Progressive Movement," *American Quarterly* 12 (Winter 1960): 459-63.
23. Naumburg, *The Child and the World: Dialogues in Modern Education* (New York: Harcourt, Brace, 1928), 115. For a more detailed treatment of Naumburg, see Dalton B. Curtis, Jr., "Psychoanalysis and Progressive Education: Margaret Naumburg at the Walden School," *Vitae Scholasticae* 2 (Fall 1983): 339-61.
24. Naumburg, "A Pageant with a Purpose," *Outlook*, 23 June 1915, 421-22.
25. Ibid., 422.
26. Naumburg, "The Walden School," *The Foundations and Technique of Curriculum-Construction*, in *Twenty-Sixth Yearbook of the National Society for the Study of Education*, pt. 1 (Bloomington, IL: Public School Publishing, 1926), 333.
27. Naumburg, *The Child and the World*, 4.
28. Ibid., 17-18.
29. Ibid., 118.
30. Neill, *Neill! Neill! Orange Peel!—An Autobiography* (New York: Hart Publishing, 1972), 35. Unless otherwise noted, biographical information is from this source.
31. Ibid., 89.
32. Ibid., 119.
33. Published by Herbet Jenkins, London, 1915. Reprinted in *Neill! Neill! Orange Peel!*, 369-468.
34. Ray Hemings, *Fifty Years of Freedom: A Study of the Development of the Ideas of A. S. Neill* (London: George Allen and Unwin, 1972), 41.
35. Homer Lane, *Talks to Parents and Teachers* (New York: Schocken Books, [1928] 1969).
36. Neill, *Neill! Neill! Orange Peel!*, 176.
37. Neill, *That Dreadful School* (London: Herbert Jenkins, 1937), 10-14.

38. Ibid., 24-25, 29.

39. Ibid., 44-45.

40. Ibid., 66-67.

41. Ibid., 75-77.

42. Ibid., 83-84.

43. Neill, *Neill! Neill! Orange Peel!*, 182.

44. Ibid., 252-53.

45. Quoted in Charles A. Fecher, *The Philosophy of Jacques Maritain* (Westminster, MD: Newman Press, 1953), 32-33.

46. Quoted in John M. Dunway, *Jacques Maritain* (Boston: Twayne, 1978), 18.

47. The two previous popes, Pius X and Benedict XV, had been concerned about Action Française. Benedict wrote an unpublished critique of Charles Maurras' works, but neither pontiff acted to separate the church from the organization. See Julie Kernan, *Our Friend, Jacques Maritain: A Personal Memoir* (Garden City, NY: Doubleday, 1975), 70-77.

48. Maritain, *Education at the Crossroads* (New Haven: Yale University Press, 1943), 1.

49. Maritain's counterpart in Paris was Archbishop Angelo Roncalli, the future Pope John XXIII. An associate in Rome was the Vatican Secretary of State, Monsignor Giovanni Battista Montini, the future Pope Paul VI, who later referred to Maritain as his teacher. Kernan, *Our Friend, Jacques Maritain*, 138-46.

50. For accounts of DuBois' character and personality see August Meier, *Negro Thought in America, 1880-1915: Racial Ideologies in the Age of Booker T. Washington* (Ann Arbor: University of Michigan Press, 1963); and Meier, "The Paradox of W. E. B. DuBois," in *W. E. B. DuBois, A Profile*, ed. Rayford W. Logan (New York: Hill and Wang, 1971), 64-85. For biographical accounts see Jack B. Moore, *W. E. B. DuBois* (Boston: Twayne, 1981), quoted from 11; Francis L. Broderick, *W. E. B. DuBois: Negro Leader in a Time of Crisis* (Stanford: Stanford University Press, 1959); and DuBois, *The Autobiography of W. E. B. DuBois* (n. p.: International Publishers, 1968).

51. DuBois, *The Autobiography*, 61.

52. Ibid., 65. James either "took a slave as a concubine, or married a free Negro woman."

53. Ibid., 72-75. Will was Mary's second son. The first was fathered by a cousin out of wedlock. There are discrepancies about how and when Alfred left. DuBois said it was shortly after his birth that Alfred settled in Connecticut, thirty-eight miles from Great Barrington. See also Moore, *W. E. B. DuBois*, chap. 1.

54. Ibid., 280.

55. Broderick, *W. E. B. DuBois*, 10.

56. Ibid., 13, 17. As an undergraduate at Harvard, he got nine A's, three B's, and one C (English Composition). His thesis was published in 1896.

57. DuBois, *The Autobiography*, 161. Will said that Dora wanted to marry him, but that he did not think it would be fair to her to do so. See also Broderick, *W. E. B. DuBois*, 26.

58. Ibid., 54, 46.

59. Ibid., 55.

60. Ibid., chaps. 3, 4.

61. Ibid., 45.

62. Ibid., 216.

63. Ibid., 190; Moore, *W. E. B. DuBois*, 17.

64. Counts, *The Selective Character of American Secondary Education* (Chicago: University of Chicago Press, 1922), 140-43.

65. Counts, *The Senior High School Curriculum* (Chicago: University of Chicago Press, 1926).

66. Counts, *The Social Composition of Boards of Education* (Chicago: University of Chicago Press, 1927), 83.

67. Counts, *Secondary Education and Industrialism* (Cambridge: Harvard University Press, 1929).

68. Counts, *The American Road to Culture: A Social Interpretation of Education in the United States* (New York: John Day, 1930), 184.

69. Counts, *The Soviet Challenge to America* (New York: John Day, 1931), ix.

70. Counts, *Dare the School Build a New Social Order?* (Carbondale: Southern Illinois University Press, 1978).

71. Counts, *The Social Foundations of Education* (New York: Charles Scribner's Sons, 1934), 535.

72. Charles A. Beard, *A Charter for the Social Sciences in the Schools* (New York: Charles Scribner's Sons, 1932).

73. Counts, *The Prospects of American Democracy* (New York: John Day, 1938), 37-38.

EPILOGUE

1. The views of psychologist Cyril Burt, seen in writings such as "The Genetic Determination of Differences in Intelligence: A Study of Monozygotic Twins Reared Together and Apart," *British Journal of Psychology* 57 (1967), 137-53, have been increasingly questioned by other researchers who have carefully studied his notes. His research, however, has profoundly influenced the American Arthur R. Jensen. Perhaps his best known statement is "How Much Can We Boost IQ and Scholastic Achievement?," *Harvard Educational Review* 39 (1969), 1-121.

2. Perhaps the best statement of Paulo Freire's work is found in his book, *Pedagogy of the Oppressed* (New York, Herder and Herder, 1970); For the views of Holt and Kozol see, John C. Holt, *How Children Fail* (New York: Pitman, 1964) and *How Children Learn* (New York: Pitman, 1967); and Jonathan Kozol, *Death at an Early Age* (New York: Bantam Books, 1968); See Ivan Illich, *Deschooling Society* (New York: Harper and Row, 1971) and Samuel Bowles and Herbert Gintis, *Schooling in Capitalist America* (New York: Basic Books, 1976).

SKETCH OF MARIA MONTESSORI

INDEX

Index